A Pentecostal Commentary on
REVELATION

THE PENTECOSTAL OLD AND NEW TESTAMENT COMMENTARIES

Series Preface

Over the last century, the Pentecostal movement has transformed the face of global Christianity. Nevertheless, Pentecostal voices continue to be under-represented in biblical scholarship. Therefore, we would like to introduce *The Pentecostal Old and New Testament Commentaries*. The Pentecostal authors of this series come to the text with a high view of Scripture; however, we desire to say more than has already been said by non-Pentecostals. Thus, the contributors to this series have been charged with the task of articulating a truly Pentecostal perspective on every verse of the Bible.

This grand vision began in the heart of our series founder, Eun Chul Kim. He spent nearly a decade tirelessly advocating for this Pentecostal commentary and recruiting authors. However, like so many of God's servants, it was not given to him to see the fulfillment of the promise. On September 22, 2018, Kim succumbed to cancer, but his vision continues.

The commentaries themselves target the educated layperson, Pentecostal pastor, and student of the Bible and focus their attention on the exegesis and translation of the Greek (NA28) and Hebrew (BHS and BHQ) texts. In keeping with the diversity that characterizes Pentecostals and Charismatics themselves, we have left the authors with a great deal of liberty regarding their approaches. As the editors, we highly value academic freedom. Consequently, although all the authors identify as Pentecostals and greatly esteem the authority of Scripture, we have not required them to espouse any particular theological viewpoints or to take any prescribed theological positions. Accordingly, each author is responsible for what he or she has written and not the editors. Although the approaches of the various authors vary widely, two things have been deemed essential: a rigorously critical approach and a distinctively Pentecostal contribution. This combination will certainly profit Pentecostal believers whether in the pew, the pulpit, or the classroom.

It is our sincere prayer that God will use this commentary series to encourage Pentecostals everywhere to read the Bible *as Pentecostals*.

CHRISTOPHER L. CARTER—New Testament Editor
DAVID C. HYMES—Old Testament Editor

A Pentecostal Commentary on REVELATION

Jon K. Newton

Foreword by John Christopher Thomas

THE PENTECOSTAL OLD AND NEW TESTAMENT COMMENTARIES

Christopher L. Carter—New Testament Editor

WIPF & STOCK · Eugene, Oregon

A PENTECOSTAL COMMENTARY ON REVELATION

Copyright © 2021 Jon K. Newton. All rights reserved. Except for brief quotations in critical publications or reviews, no part of this book may be reproduced in any manner without prior written permission from the publisher. Write: Permissions, Wipf and Stock Publishers, 199 W. 8th Ave., Suite 3, Eugene, OR 97401.

Wipf & Stock
An Imprint of Wipf and Stock Publishers
199 W. 8th Ave., Suite 3
Eugene, OR 97401

www.wipfandstock.com

PAPERBACK ISBN: 978-1-5326-0437-9
HARDCOVER ISBN: 978-1-5326-1070-7
EBOOK ISBN: 978-1-5326-0438-6

01/22/21

To my wife Judy, without whose support nothing of this would be done;
to my colleagues at Alphacrucis College,
whose support has encouraged me all the way;
and to the late Dr. Eun Kim, who invited me to write this commentary.

Contents

Abbreviations	ix
Foreword by John Christopher Thomas	xi
Author's Preface	xv
INTRODUCTION	**1**
COMMENTARY	**55**
Revelation Chapter 1	57
Revelation Chapters 2–3	76
Revelation Chapter 4	119
Revelation Chapter 5	129
Revelation Chapter 6	140
Revelation Chapter 7	157
Revelation Chapter 8	171
Revelation Chapter 9	182
Revelation Chapter 10	192
Revelation Chapter 11	200
Revelation Chapter 12	218
Revelation Chapter 13	236
Revelation Chapter 14	256
Revelation Chapter 15	270
Revelation Chapter 16	277
Revelation Chapter 17	289
Revelation Chapter 18	304
Revelation Chapter 19	320
Revelation Chapter 20	339
Revelation Chapter 21	354
Revelation Chapter 22	373
CONCLUSIONS	**391**
Bibliography	397

Abbreviations

ABR	*Australian Biblical Review*
ACNT	Augsburg Commentaries on the New Testament
ANF	*Ante-Nicene Fathers*
ANZATS	Australia and New Zealand Association of Theological Schools.
Haer.	*Against Heresies* (Irenaeus)
AJPS	*Asian Journal of Pentecostal Studies*
APS	*Australasian Pentecostal Studies*
Bib	*Biblica*
BibInt	*Biblical Interpretation*
BSac	*Bibliotheca Sacra*
BTB	*Biblical Theology Bulletin*
CBR	*Currents in Biblical Research*
CBQ	*Catholic Biblical Quarterly*
EvQ	*Evangelical Quarterly*
ERT	*Evangelical Review of Theology*
ESV	English Standard Version
ExpTim	*Expository Times*
FBS	Fellowship for Biblical Studies
GPH	Gospel Publishing House
HeyJ	*Heythrop Journal*
IBC	Interpretation: A Bible Commentary for Teaching and Preaching
Int	*Interpretation*
ITC	International Theological Commentary
IVP	InterVarsity Press (USA)

Abbreviations

JB	Jerusalem Bible
JBL	*Journal of Biblical Literature*
JEPTA	*Journal of the European Pentecostal Theological Association*
JETS	*Journal of the Evangelical Theological Society*
JPT	*Journal of Pentecostal Theology*
JSNT	*Journal for the Study of the New Testament*
JTS	*Journal of Theological Studies*
KJV	King James Version
LXX	Septuagint (the Greek translation of the Old Testament)
NA28	Nestle-Aland Greek New Testament, 28th revised edition (2012)
NCB	New Century Bible
Neot	*Neotestamentica*
NIBCNT	New International Biblical Commentary on the New Testament
NICNT	New International Commentary on the New Testament
NIGTC	New International Greek Testament Commentary
NIV	New Internaitonal Version (2011)
NKJV	New King James Version
NovT	*Novum Testamentum*
NTS	*New Testament Studies*
NRSV	New Revised Standard Version
NT	New Testament
OT	Old Testament (also known as Hebrew Scriptures)
REB	Revised English Bible
RevExp	*Review and Expositor*
RevQ	*Revue de Qumran*
SBL	Society of Biblical Literature
SR	*Studies in Religion*
TNTC	Tyndale New Testament Commentary
TOTC	Tyndale Old Testament Commentary
TPINTC	TPI New Testament Commentaries
UBS	United Bible Societies Greek New Testament, 3rd edition (1983)
WBC	Word Biblical Commentary
WTJ	*Westminster Theological Journal*

Foreword

There was a time when Pentecostal work on the Book of Revelation was limited to a sub-category of dispensational thought that had proven to be so influential within the tradition. But, to quote Bob Dylan, "The times they are a-changin." For over the last two or three decades, there has been a virtual renaissance in the academic Pentecostal interpretation of the Apocalypse, none of which bear the marks of the dispensational approach that sat so ill at ease with the spirituality of the Pentecostal movement. No less than eight academic monographs have appeared during this time frame and, with the appearance of this commentary, no less than seven commentaries, with others on the way. Indeed, the times have changed so much that there are now several more commentaries written by Pentecostals on the Book of Revelation than commentaries written by Pentecostals on the Book of Acts!

Standing at the forefront of this academic sea change with regard to Apocalypse studies is Dr. Jon Newton, Associate Professor at Alphacrucis College in Australia. Newton is no newcomer to the study of the Apocalypse having previously published two monographs on Revelation entitled, *Revelation Reclaimed: The Use and Misuse of the Apocalypse* and *The Revelation Worldview: Apocalyptic Thinking in a Postmodern World*. These substantial works are joined by numerous academic articles Newton has contributed to a variety of academic journals of international standing.[1] At the same time, as most Pentecostal teachers of Scripture, Newton has also spent considerable time in parish ministry, where the fruit of academic insight is road-tested, discerned, refined, and revised in the light of the experience of the worshipping Pentecostal community.

Dr Newton's commentary is a most welcome volume for a variety of reasons. First, as Apocalypse studies amongst Pentecostal scholars continue to develop, it is essential that voices from a variety of geographical contexts and reading locations be heard. For a tradition like Pentecostalism that is global at its essence, the diversity of voices must be given an opportunity to be heard and to speak in an unmuted fashion, not simply parroting those who have gone before. Newton's commentary, hailing from

---

1. See bibliography for a list of academic articles.

a region of the world whose spirituality has had a global impact on Pentecostal worship, is an important addition to the larger body that might be tempted to function inside an echo chamber of sorts with regard to its understanding of the Apocalypse.

Second, this commentary is a substantive contribution to Apocalypse studies, coming in at just over 200,000 words. Such a hefty offering says something about the magnitude, depth, and painstaking research that has gone into this endeavor. If at one time, Pentecostals were encouraged to "dumb down" their scholarship for potential sales, Newton's work is evidence that publishers are discovering that a growing portion of the Pentecostal reading audience is not content with superficial analyses, but is interested in and ready for serious engagements with the biblical text. In this way, Newton's work joins a growing number of volumes by Pentecostals that are setting a high bar in terms of originality and substantive engagement with the biblical text.

Third, owing to the fact that Pentecostal scholars working on the forefront of Pentecostal hermeneutics have been reluctant to argue for *the* Pentecostal approach, this volume plays an important role in the broader conversation about how to do Pentecostal interpretation. Despite arguments to the contrary, one size does most certainly not fit all, and the interpretive approach that Newton employs adds further breadth and depth to this larger ongoing conversation about how Pentecostals might best approach the text of Scripture in a means befitting this massive movement that we believe God has raised up. Thus, Newton's agreements and disagreements with his Pentecostal counterparts are significant, not only for the way they show his own interpretive similarities and dissimilarities with others in the tradition, but also for the way they provide the readers an opportunity to enter into the discernment process on their own.

Fourth, neither is it insignificant that Newton offers yet another example of how one particular Pentecostal biblical scholar seeks to engage the biblical text in a way that moves beyond the nuts and bolts of interpretation to an integrative engagement that allows for the reader to be interpreted as well as the text. Pentecostal readers are in need of more and better models of how to make this move as we seek to respond more faithfully to the demands of the text before us.

Finally, Newton's commentary is important because it offers the opportunity for decades of research and reflection on the Apocalypse to be brought to the text in a way that bears fruit on every page. This preparation is not simply to be measured in the monographs and articles that have come from the author's pen, but also in the times of prayer, intercession, worship, singing, preaching, teaching, mourning, and celebration with the people of God. Our tradition, like many others perhaps, needs more brothers and sisters who are able to bring such integrated experiences to engage the text. And perhaps it would not be going too far to say that while we may well need more commentaries on the Apocalypse, we also most certainly need more people who have written commentaries on the Apocalypse for the way this kind of sustained and serious engagement with the text forms, shapes, and transforms such readers in the midst of our communities of faith.

While not all readers will agree with every interpretive move that is made in this commentary, I dare say all readers will find a wealth of knowledge, a depth of reflection, and tremendous spiritual insight in its pages. The words of the Apocalypse are perhaps even more timely at the time this commentary appears than before. May God bless it to do its work and may God bless Jon Newton for his contribution to us all.

JOHN CHRISTOPHER THOMAS
Pentecostal Theological Seminary
Bangor University

Author's Preface

My obsession with Revelation started with a vain attempt to "crack the code" and discover the hidden secret that would unveil future history and prove this book of the Bible to be inspired prophecy from God. It would, of course, also enhance my reputation as an inspired interpreter! This attempt was fruitless, not just because my resources were limited, but because I found that Revelation was not really *that* kind of book. I learned that the attempt to read it that way was inevitably infected with various interpretive agendas. Such agendas might include the desire to vindicate one specific form of Christian teaching, the need to identify the enemies of the faith, the obsession with future prediction, and the attempt to prove others wrong.[2]

But as I began to study Revelation seriously towards the end of my master's degree, I found there a never-ending source of fascination, intrigue, mystery, and insights. I discovered that Revelation was relevant in unforeseen ways even as it appeared to be totally foreign, archaic, ethically questionable, and incoherent to many recent commentators. To this day, I find new lines of inquiry prompted by this text, or by other texts that should have nothing to do with it but prompt me with new connections. Some of this I explored in my doctoral study, where I attempted to use Revelation as a means of constructing a Christian worldview for our "postmodern" times.[3] But the journey never seems to stop. Revelation has become the gift that keeps on giving.

My reading of Revelation is provoked by new understanding of the ancient world, by new insights from the Scriptures (especially the Old Testament, but the New Testament too) and other ancient texts, by the arguments of other commentators (sympathetic or hostile), by the works of various theologians, by random comments made by colleagues and other believers, and even by sermons I hear that may even have little or nothing to do with Revelation. I even received a prophetic word once from a visiting speaker who knew nothing of my interest in Revelation. She said that the Lord would give me insight into Revelation and "end times." Such confirmations have helped

---

2. I have spelled these false trails out in my first book on Revelation, *Revelation Reclaimed: The Use and Misuse of the Apocalypse.*

3. This argument has been reworked in my second book, *The Revelation Worldview.*

encourage me to persevere in this study, though my understanding of "end times" now is quite different than what the audience of that prophecy might have expected.

Many Christians have all but given up on Revelation. They tell me they have stopped reading it because it just produces confusion. To some degree, that reaction has been caused by previous futile attempts to read the text as a catalogue containing predictions of specific contemporary events. But I think it also springs from a broader misguided attempt to understand Revelation exclusively with the rational intellect. A fellow New Testament scholar threw his hands up in despair at ever understanding Revelation. Other scholars are sure they do understand it but intensely dislike what they find there. Revelation is not like the letters of Paul or the four Gospels where we find reasoning and fairly straightforward narration, albeit with some tricky material that is hard to understand. As I will explore below, Revelation is apocalyptic literature that speaks to the imagination first, though its images are not unintelligible, and it does teach us as powerfully as the rest of the New Testament.

As I begin this commentary, I want to acknowledge some key people who have helped me on my journey of discovery with Revelation. Research supervisors to begin with: Dr. Greg Forbes of Melbourne School of Theology (my MA supervisor as I first studied this text); Dr. Ian Weeks (my first PhD supervisor), who encouraged me to read widely and especially about the reception history of the book; Prof. Lyn McCredden of Deakin University (my second PhD supervisor), who insisted I justify every assertion I wanted to make; and Prof. Keith Dyer of Whitley College, University of Divinity (a co-supervisor of my PhD), who helped me keep on track exegetically and encouraged me to publish my PhD thesis as a book.

A number of other Pentecostal scholars gave me valuable feedback on the draft manuscript of this commentary, specifically John Christopher Thomas (Clarence J. Abbott, Professor of Biblical Studies at the Pentecostal Theological Seminary), Robby Waddell (Professor of New Testament and Early Christian Literature, Southeastern University), David Ray Johnson (Adjunct Professor Fuller Theological Seminary and Pentecostal Theological Seminary), Melissa Archer (Associate Professor of Biblical Studies, Southeastern University), U-Wen Low (Lecturer and Program Director for MTh, Alphacrucis College), Aaron Robinson (Doctoral candidate, Bangor University, UK), and Rev. Chris Palmer, MTS (Doctoral candidate, Bangor University, UK).

Colleagues at Harvest Bible College and Alphacrucis College (and some students too), and conference delegates to ANZATS and FBS, listened patiently as I presented papers and shared new thoughts and offered critique and support. Congregants at Oasis Church (Hampton, Victoria) put up with me preaching through Revelation over a full year, an exercise that helped me more than it did them. Finally, my wife Judy and my five children (several of whom helped with criticisms of my first book) bore patiently with my withdrawal into "Revelation space."

INTRODUCTION

During his "third missionary journey" (in the mid-50s of the first century), the apostle Paul spent up to three years in Ephesus (Acts 20:31), the largest city in the Roman province of Asia. According to Acts, he began with a small group of disciples, who knew only the baptism of John the Baptist (Acts 19:1–3), building on a short earlier visit and the work of his friends, Priscilla and Aquila (Acts 18:19). From this beginning, Paul not only planted a strong church, but as a result the gospel message spread throughout Asia (Acts 19:10).

This work was marked by confrontation with resistant Jews in the local synagogue (Acts 19:8–9) and "extraordinary miracles" (Acts 19:11). Significantly, there was also a confrontation with demonic power that astounded the residents of the city (Acts 19:13–17) and caused the new Christians to embrace a much deeper work of God in their lives that separated them strongly from their original spiritual culture marked by sorcery (Acts 19:18–19).

As a result, the non-believers in the city, who especially revered the famous goddess of Artemis and her magnificent temple, felt threatened as the economic and spiritual atmosphere of the city was changed (Acts 19:26–27). They responded by instigating a loud and threatening protest in the city's large theater (Acts 19:28–34). But the city leaders in effect took the side of the Christians as many of them had become friends of Paul (Acts 19:31, 35–41).

It seemed like the Christian movement was "taking the world by storm" at this point, but causing inevitable backlashes from time to time as vested interests were threatened. According to C. Kavin Rowe, the threat that the Christian movement posed was real, amounting perhaps to "cultural collapse," bearing in mind the intricate interconnection between religious or spiritual practices (idolatry, sorcery, astrology and the like) and every other aspect of ancient Greco-Roman culture.[1] According to Acts, this is how the churches of Asia (and Europe too) were born, including (most probably) the seven churches to which Revelation is addressed.

About sixty years later in a neighboring Roman province (Bithynia), the Roman governor (Pliny the Younger) wrote a troubled letter to the emperor Trajan. The Christians in his province were multiplying. In fact, "the contagion of this superstition has spread not only through the free cities, but into the villages and the rural districts" (almost repeating Luke's claim in Acts 19:10). As a result, the temples were being deserted, the offerings to the official gods neglected, and meat from offerings made

---

1. Rowe, *World Upside Down*, 46.

to gods was not able to be sold. This was apparently because Christians would not eat meat from sacrificial animals, following the prohibitions of Revelation and Acts 15.

Pliny decided that he had to come down strongly on the Christians, even though he discovered that their practices were rather harmless, such as meeting before daybreak once a week "to recite a hymn among themselves to Christ, as though he were a god" and later to partake of an ordinary meal. However, in response to Pliny's ban of secret societies, they eventually discontinued the meals. Pliny assumed that just being a Christian was illegal,[2] but he could not take accusations at face value. He had to be sure that those accused of being Christians were really guilty, so he devised an effective test: genuine Christians would not make sacrifices to the ancient Greco-Roman gods, nor would they offer incense to the image or statue of Caesar, nor would they curse Christ. Trajan wrote back approving Pliny's actions. As a result of the persecution that ensued, many professing but nominal Christians turned away from the faith, and the pagan temples began attracting worshipers again.[3]

Between these two events, the Roman world had been shaken by a series of crises. In AD 64, a fire ravaged Rome, and Caesar Nero blamed the fire on the Christians in Rome and used the disaster as an excuse to persecute them savagely. This persecution apparently claimed the lives of Peter and Paul and thousands of others, showing, among other things, that the church in Rome had grown to such an extent that it could not escape public and imperial notice, and suspicion.

Soon after this, Nero was overthrown, and when he committed suicide, a series of civil wars soon followed that marked "the year of four emperors" (Galba, Otho, Vitellius and Vespasian, AD 68–69). During this time, the very existence of the Roman Empire hung in the balance, and the violence and unrest of those days did not leave any aspect of the empire untouched. In fact Rome's key spiritual center, the Capitoline temple, was burned down in AD 69.[4] The ripples of unrest reached even to Judea at the edge of the empire. There, in the cradle of Christianity, a Jewish rebellion against Roman rule had erupted in AD 66. It would end with the destruction of Jerusalem and its second temple in AD 70, but some small pockets of resistance would continue to burn until AD 73. In the natural world, earthquakes had devastated parts of Asia in the 60s[5] and in AD 79, the eruption of Mount Vesuvius destroyed several Roman cities and caused much other damage. There were also several famines.

Revelation was written sometime in this period. It shows that the Christian movement was still poised to conquer the world and eliminate pagan worship. Revelation's envisioned conquest would radically reshape the culture of the empire and transfer worship from emperors to God. However, this conquest would not come without a

---

2. Cf. Wilken, *Christians as the Romans Saw Them*, 23.

3. Pliny the Younger, *Letters*, 10:96–97. For a summary of Pliny's correspondence and its historical context, cf. Wilken, *Christians as the Romans Saw Them*, 12–32.

4. MacMullen, *Enemies of the Roman Order*, 142–43.

5. Cf. Boring, *Revelation*, 10.

struggle, and this spiritual war would concern not only ritual but also religious and political allegiance.⁶

Most Jewish synagogues did not recognize Jesus as the promised Messiah, let alone as worthy of worship. Therefore, the Jews opposed the Christians, and accordingly, Revelation speaks of them as a "synagogue of Satan" (Rev 2:9; 3:9). The general populace of the Greco-Roman cities recognized and made sacrifices to the traditional gods whose temples were everywhere. However, the Christians refused to join in, and their growing numbers threatened the viability of those temples and provoked sometimes violent opposition.

It was also hard for Christians to participate in the economic life of their cities which were saturated with observances to the gods (such as the patron gods of trade guilds). Even the meat market products had often been first offered as sacrifices in one of the local temples.⁷ People in the eastern empire also participated with increasing enthusiasm in the "emperor cult." The participants in this cult gave honors to the reigning Caesar somewhat like the honors accorded to the gods (and deceased emperors). In this way, worshippers displayed their loyalty to the empire and curried the favor of the reigning Caesar.⁸ Thus the young Christian churches faced significant dilemmas as they sought to establish themselves as a potent force in their Asian cities. Revelation 2–3 portrays seven typical congregations facing a range of challenges (including internal issues from "false" teachers) and responding to them in varied ways. John calls on them to be "conquerors."

In order to conquer, the Christians of Asia (according to Revelation) needed to take an uncompromising stand against all elements of Greco-Roman religion and also other features of the culture, such as its tolerance of sexual immorality, as well as the imperial cult. Such a pure spiritual "army" would indeed sweep all before it, though in the battle there would be many casualties, that is, martyrs, whose violent deaths would be a witness to unbelievers and overcome the devil (Rev 12:11). In this way, Revelation recasts apparent defeat (11:7; 13:7) into ultimate victory.

Revelation was written to encourage the believers of first-century Asia Minor not to give up but to be the soldiers of Christ (14:1–5) whose testimony against all opposition would draw in more converts and eventually "conquer" the empire (15:4; 20:4). They would do this by bringing the people of the world into allegiance to the one true God and Jesus as Lord.⁹

---

6. I'm assuming that by the second half of the first century, Christianity was already not just a tiny, insignificant, powerless sect as many authors seem to think, but a growing force that posed a real threat to the "powers that be" in the Roman Empire and beyond. I base this conclusion on the evidence of Acts, the Pliny-Trajan correspondence, and the persecution under Nero.

7. Cf. Howard-Brook and Gwyther, *Unveiling Empire*, 100–103. Cities in that day were very crowded and failure to participate in the cults of traditional gods or emperors could not be hidden.

8. Cf. Biguzzi, "Ephesus," 276–90; Friesen, "Myth and Symbolic Resistance," 287–303.

9. Cf. Michaels, *Interpreting the Book of Revelation*, 133–37.

Revelation can thus be seen as having a strong and relevant message for the Pentecostal types of Christianity that are growing rapidly throughout the world today. In Latin America, Africa, and Asia, "Spirit-filled" Christianity is on the march and overcoming the traditional religions and other strongholds of non-Christian cultures. It is "conquering" in spite of often violent resistance, persecution, infiltration by false teachings, sexual scandals, and other challenges. Even in the western world, where traditional Christianity is in decline, the Pentecostal churches are holding their own and growing, even though facing opposition from secular forces. The seven churches of first-century Asia look a lot like the varied Pentecostal churches of the twenty-first century. Revelation's message has never been more needed by Pentecostals.

WHAT IS REVELATION?

Revelation is at once the most perplexing, foreign, engrossing, dangerous, and mysterious book in our Bible. It has been attacked, misused, misinterpreted, and pressed into service in all kinds of strange agendas. It has been viewed as a detailed forecast of events in the distant future (to John) or even of world (or church) history ever since the first century. It has been pressed into service for various modern or postmodern agendas (such as forms of liberation theology) or attacked because it did not easily fit into such agendas (especially by feminist scholars). It has been safely relegated to the struggles of the early Christians in a hostile Roman or Jewish context as a kind of historical artifact, or neatly pigeonholed as an ancient apocalypse.

It has been viewed as a prophetic word from God or attacked as the ravings of a power-drunk church politician. It has been used to attack the Roman Catholic Church, the European Union, the United Nations, the United States, and many other targets. It has been used to defend modern Israel, Fundamentalism, Pentecostalism, and various other Christian sects (and that is just to use recent examples). It has been used to "prove" all kinds of theological, ethical, and political positions. Yet it cannot be ignored. Ian Paul claims, "The book of Revelation is the most remarkable text you will ever read."[10] Because I agree, I hope to share this extraordinary book with you, my reader.

However, I invite you to start reading this commentary with an open mind, realizing that Revelation was presented as a vision related to the times of its original author (John) and audience (the seven churches). Nonetheless, please also keep in mind that we find it in our New Testament canon because Christians through the ages have seen its value for readers in every time and place. So before we read it through, it is important to briefly discuss some key points about this ancient text.

---

10. Paul, *Revelation*, 1.

DATE: WHEN WAS IT WRITTEN?

Revelation is clearly a text from the ancient world, the latter part of the first century, to be precise. But that's where agreement ends. Revelation has been dated anywhere from AD 50 to 110.[11] But the two main theories put it in the late-90s or the mid- to late-60s.

Most scholars accept the later date, towards the end of the reign of the emperor Domitian (AD 81–96). This is based partly on the words of the early church father Irenaeus (ca. AD 130–202), who wrote that John's visions were "seen no very long time since, but almost in our own day, towards the end of Domitian's reign."[12] There are also internal considerations marshalled in support of this dating, such as the nature of the political situation in which the book seems to have been written and the state of the seven churches.[13] For example, could a very early church have developed a tendency to spiritual torpor (Sardis) or lukewarmness and prosperity (Laodicea)? This church claimed to be rich, but Laodicea had been destroyed by an earthquake in AD 60–61. Does not this diagnosis of their condition better fit a church with several decades of history behind it? Christian evidence from the second century says that the church in Smyrna did not even exist until the 60s, and there may also not have been a church in Thyatira until late-first century.[14]

The use of "the Lord's day" (1:10), presumably for Sunday, may reflect a late-first century development.[15] Perhaps Revelation 13 reflects the common rumor that the deposed Nero had not actually died and would return with an army from the East to reclaim his throne. If so, this would require a date for Revelation subsequent to Nero's death in AD 68.[16] Also Domitian was sometimes seen as a "second Nero," and his name on coins may add up to 666.[17] The labelling of Rome as "Babylon" in Revelation 17–18 probably reflects Jewish language from after the destruction of the temple in AD 70, when a parallel was drawn with the destruction of the original Jerusalem temple by the Chaldeans from Babylon.[18] The reference to the "twelve apostles"

---

11. Cf. Court, *Revelation*, 95–103.

12. Irenaesus, *Haer.*, 30.3 (*ANF* 1.559–60). Irenaeus wrote this between AD 182 and 188 (*ANF* 1.312). There is support for this from other early Christian writers (Beale, *Book of Revelation*, 19–20; Aune, *Revelation 1–5*, lix–lx). Mayo argues strongly for the reliability of Irenaeus here (Mayo, *Those Who Call Themselves Jews*, 4–7).

13. See summary in Smalley, *Thunder and Love*, 41–42; for a good argument for this dating, see also Paul, *Revelation*, 11–16.

14. Aune, *Revelation 1–5*, lviii; Beale, *Book of Revelation*, 17; Morris, *Revelation*, 38; Paul, *Revelation*, 16.

15. Gause, *Revelation*, 12.

16. Cf. Koester, *Revelation*, 71, 72, 74; Beale, *Book of Revelation*, 17–18; Thompson, *Book of Revelation*, 14.

17. Cf. Papandrea, *Wedding of the Lamb*, 25, 35.

18. Beale, *Book of Revelation*, 18–19; Aune, *Revelation 1–5*, lxi; Friesen, *Imperial Cults*, 138–39.

(21:14) also suggests a late date since the perspective taken locates the apostles and their era in the past.[19]

This dating assumes that Domitian was a persecutor of the church, of which there is some evidence from early Christian writing.[20] It further assumes that Domitian demanded to be acclaimed as "Lord and God"[21] as the imperial cult rose to new heights. For example, a new "temple of the Sebastoi" was erected in Ephesus in honor of the whole Flavian imperial family in AD 89/90.[22] These arguments are not conclusive, however. Recent scholars have questioned whether Domitian was as bad as painted, or more the victim of his successors' propaganda.[23] Moreover, the decline of some of the churches can also be observed in other early Christian literature, such as Paul's criticisms of the Corinthian church in the late-50s or his even earlier letters to the Galatians and Thessalonians.[24]

A minority of commentators advocate an earlier date for Revelation, during[25] or just after the reign of Nero[26] or sometime close to the fall of Jerusalem and the destruction of the Second Temple in AD 70.[27] These scholars make their argument based on several literary features within the text. These include the interpretation of the mark of the beast (666) as a reference to Nero,[28] Nero's role as the first Roman persecutor of Christians,[29] and the possible allusion to the Jerusalem temple as still functioning (11:1–2).[30] To these one might add the claim of the text to be predicting

---

19. Cf. Aune, *Revelation 1–5*, lxiv; who also builds on this argument in other ways.

20. E.g., 1 Clement 1 (*ANF* 1.5); Tertullian, "Apology," *ANF* 3:22. Cf. Caird, *Revelation*, 20–21; Papandrea, *Wedding of the Lamb*, 23–25.

21. Cf. Morris, *Revelation*, 35–37; Keener, *Revelation*, 35–39; Aune, *Revelation 1–5*, 310–311; Friesen, *Imperial Cults*, 148; Thompson, *Book of Revelation*, 13–17.

22. Friesen, *Imperial Cults*, 45–46.

23. Cf. Koester, *Revelation*, 76–78; Smalley, *Thunder and Love*, 43–44; Aune, *Revelation 1–5*, lxvii–lxix; Thompson, "Ordinary Lives," 29–34; Thompson, *Book of Revelation*, 100–107, 136–37; Moyise, *Old Testament in the Book of Revelation*, 48–50. Beale discusses Domitian at length and concludes that Domitian was probably worse than other emperors and that persecution of Christians did increase in his period as emperor (Beale, *Book of Revelation*, 5–16).

24. Cf. Smalley, *Thunder and Love*, 42–43.

25. For a recent and well-argued case for a very early date, "just before the Roman emperor began to persecute Christians and a few years before conflict broke out in Judea" (maybe about AD 64), see Leithart, *Revelation 1–11*, 36–43.

26. Smalley proposes that Revelation was written well before the other "Johannine" books (*Thunder and Love*, 57, 68–69). See also Gonzalo Rojas-Flores, "The Book of Revelation and the First Years of Nero's Reign."

27. Smalley argues that the revelation of a new Jerusalem would be greatly valuable if the original Jerusalem was about to be destroyed (Smalley, *Revelation to John*, 3). But this would be just as true if it had recently been destroyed, that is, within the memory of the readers of Revelation.

28. But see Beale, *Book of Revelation*, 24.

29. Cf. Aune, *Revelation 1–5*, lxvi.

30. This requires a literal reading of Revelation 11 which may be problematic (cf. Beale, *Book of Revelation*, 21; Aune, *Revelation 1–5*, lx–lxi).

events of the imminent future (1:1, 3; 22:6, 10) and some features of Revelation 17, especially the reference to five past emperors prior to the vision.[31]

Following this line of thought, Smalley puts the date at AD 69, the year when Vespasian became emperor after a turbulent year of civil war following the death of Nero, and shortly before the destruction of the temple.[32] However, he admits that "Vespasian himself did not trouble the church."[33] There are weaknesses in this argument too. Nero's persecution was severe in Rome itself but not apparently widespread.[34] Moreover, the idea advanced by some that the prostitute in Revelation 17 stands for Jerusalem (which is soon to be destroyed) runs up against the allusion to the "seven hills" (Rev 17:9) that seem to refer clearly to Rome and the identification of the woman as "the great city which has dominion over the kings of the earth" (Rev 17:18).[35]

Most of these points will be discussed at the appropriate places in the commentary. I think the "imminence" language points to an earlier date, signaling the great crisis about to hit the church[36] and the world with Neronic persecution, Jewish-Roman war, destruction of the second temple and civil wars across the empire. But the evidence is not definitive for either date. Probably, therefore, no interpretive decision about Revelation should depend on claims regarding its dating.[37] However, it is worth noting that the form of Preterism[38] that makes John's focus the fall of Jerusalem rather depends on the early date.

AUTHORSHIP: WHO WROTE IT?

Revelation simply claims to be written by someone called John. Traditionally this was taken to mean the apostle of that name, the son of Zebedee, who also supposedly wrote the Fourth Gospel and 1–3 John, though this is often disputed today.[39] That the

---

31. Cf. Smalley, *Thunder and Love*, 45–48, on using Rev 17:9–11 to establish the date of Revelation. However, any attempt to definitively identify the kings of Rev 17:9–11 as successive Roman emperors is fraught with difficulty (Beale, *Book of Revelation*, 21–24; cf. Aune, *Revelation 1–5*, lxi–lxiii; Thomas, *Apocalypse*, 31–32). I will discuss this further in the commentary on Revelation 17.

32. Smalley, *Thunder and Love*, 49. Gentry uses the same text to argue for a Neronic date (Gentry, "Preterist View," 69).

33. Smalley, *Thunder and Love*, 49.

34. Domitian was sometimes called a second Nero by Roman writers (Beale, *Book of Revelation*, 18). On using persecution as evidence for dating Revelation, see the clear discussion in Thomas, *Apocalypse*, 34–37.

35. Cf. Koester, *Revelation*, 72–74.

36. In this way, Revelation seems to envisage a similar situation to Second Timothy.

37. Koester concludes that the period AD 80–100 is as close as one can get (Koester, *Revelation*, 79). Thomas argues that perhaps John is deliberately ambiguous, using "the Lord's day" (Rev 1:10) eschatologically to relativize such dating (Thomas, *Apocalypse*, 39–41).

38. See below for an explanation of this term.

39. E.g., Brown, *Community of Beloved Disciple*, 33–34, 94–96, 186.

apostle John wrote Revelation was the unanimous view of the early post-apostolic writers,[40] though in the subsequent centuries of the early church other possibilities were suggested.[41]

However, there are difficulties with interpreting the text this way. First, Revelation seems to see the apostles as a finished and past group (as in 21:14),[42] a point also used to support a later date. Second, John does not make any claim to apostolic authority or position, unlike Paul in his letters. Third, other "Johannine" books do not use the name John anywhere: the Fourth Gospel and 1 John are strictly anonymous, and 2 and 3 John name the enigmatic "elder" as their author. Fourth, though there are many similarities between Revelation and the Fourth Gospel, the Greek style of Revelation is very different.[43]

But what are the alternatives? Could it have been written by another John, maybe "the elder" who may have lived in Ephesus?[44] Could it be the product of a "Johannine community"?[45] Is the text pseudonymous, trying to claim the apostle as its author because the real author has less credibility?[46]

None of these alternatives make much sense to me, nor is the evidence for them strong, so I will assume the author is the apostle John. However, I will try not to base any significant conclusions on this assumption.[47]

However, whoever the (human) author was, we can learn some facts about him from the text itself. First, he was a Christian preacher living in apparent exile on the island of Patmos "on account of the word of God and the testimony of Jesus" (1:9).[48] Second, he had a strong, though sometimes troubled, relationship with seven churches on the mainland of the Roman province of Asia, to which he addressed his

---

40. Justin Martyr and Irenaeus clearly thought this (Smalley, *Thunder and Love*, 35–37). Leithart mounts a strong case for apostolic authorship in Leithart, *Revelation 1–11*, 74–75. Cf. Papandrea, *Wedding of the Lamb*, 16–20.

41. Fiorenza, *Book of Revelation*, 86–87; Morris, *Revelation*, 27–28; Aune, *Revelation 1–5*, l–liii; Thomas, *Apocalypse*, 47–49.

42. Cf. Aune, *Revelation 1–5*, li.

43. Cf. Morris, *Revelation*, 29–30, 32–33; Koester, *Revelation*, 80–83; Smalley, *Thunder and Love*, 64–66; Leithart, *Revelation 1–11*, 22–24, 75–77.

44. Cf. Morris, *Revelation*, 34; Koester, *Revelation*, 68; Smalley, *Thunder and Love*, 38. Smalley makes a strong case against this possibility.

45. Cf. Fiorenza, *Book of Revelation*, 86–101. Fiorenza largely dismisses this hypothesis since the similarities between Revelation and the Fourth Gospel are only those which might be found between any two Christian writers.

46. Koester rightly dismisses this (*Revelation*, 67–68) as do Smalley (*Thunder and Love*, 39–40) and Beale (*Book of Revelation*, 34). Aune takes it seriously, but does not advocate it (*Revelation 1–5*, xlix–l, lx, lxxxiv, lxxxviii).

47. Cf. Smalley, *Revelation to John*, 2–3.

48. See commentary on 1:9 for discussion of this.

manuscript. Whatever the problems in this relationship, however, he seems confident his text would indeed be read aloud in these seven churches (1:3, 11).[49]

Third, he was probably a Jew; certainly he had a mind steeped in the Hebrew Scriptures (the Christian Old Testament) and Judaism, judging by the hundreds of allusions to almost every book of those Scriptures, to the temple ceremonies of Second Temple Judaism,[50] and to other Jewish literature.[51] Fourth, he was familiar with other ancient literature such as the apocalyptic Jewish writings, Greco-Roman mythology, and even Greco-Roman drama and romance literature. Fifth, he was also familiar with the culture and politics of the Roman world of the first century, and the province of Asia in particular, such as astrology and the imperial cult. Sixth, he wrote very unusual, even ungrammatical, Greek, suggesting it was not his first language.[52] Seventh, he regarded himself as a prophet more than an apostle.[53] And finally, he held to an uncompromising form of Christian monotheism that demanded no participation in any form of idolatry or sexual looseness.

AUDIENCE AND SETTING: WHO WAS IT WRITTEN TO?

The short answer to this question, of course, is that it was written to seven churches in the Roman province of Asia (part of modern Turkey). These seven churches were undergoing varying stresses and strains as they tried to live for Jesus Christ in the context of Greco-Roman culture and polytheistic religion, Jewish hostility, and the increasing demands of the Roman imperial cult which was especially strong in this region.[54] They had been born out of a powerful spiritual movement spearheaded by the apostle Paul (as narrated in Acts 19). Several decades later, however, both external pressures and internal problems challenged their spiritual purity and commitment.

But what kind of people were these Asian Christians? If Acts is a reliable guide, they would have been largely Gentiles (that is, mostly Greeks) with a smaller core of

---

49. Cf. Koester, *Revelation*, 137.

50. Second Temple Judaism refers to the period between the rebuilding of the temple around 450 BC and its destruction in AD 70.

51. Cf. Koester, *Revelation*, 68. Aune suggests he was a refugee from Palestine in the wake of the disastrous war of AD 66–73 (*Revelation 1–5*, l). Stramara suggests the original prophecy was given by "a Palestinian Jew devoted to the liturgical purity of temple worship," someone influenced by Qmran, possibly even John the Baptist, but it was added to by a later John, possibly the apostle (Stramara, *God's Timetable*, 102–4, 132–34, 139–40).

52. Cf. Koester, *Revelation*, 69, 83, 139–41. Other possibilities are that his unusual, often ungrammatical, Greek was influenced by Greek translations from Hebrew Scripture or that he deliberately violated the rules of Greek grammar for emphasis (ibid., 140–41). Cf. Smalley, *Thunder and Love*, 64–66; Beale, *Book of Revelation*, 100–7.

53. Cf. Thomas, *Apocalypse*, 41–45.

54. Cf. Koester, *Revelation*, 94–95; Friedrich, "Adapt or Resist?," 188–98. Nearly all the awards of "temple guardian" [*neokoros*] granted by the emperor for temples for the imperial cult went to the province of Asia (Paul, *Revelation*, 20).

Jewish followers of Christ. Their churches may have resembled that of Corinth, for example, with similar problems and issues, such as a tendency to tolerate sexual immorality and compromise with idolatry.[55]

On the other hand, to judge from the nature of the text itself, they must have been strongly familiar with the Hebrew Scriptures. How else would they have recognized John's abundant allusions to those Scriptures, since the author never gives verbal clues to such allusions?[56] Jewish influence in the churches is also reflected by references in Revelation to Passover and Exodus.[57] Perhaps these cities had received an influx of Jewish and Jewish Christian refugees from the Roman-Jewish war of AD 66–70.[58]

It's hard to be sure; probably the best we can say is that, like many early Christian congregations, they included converts from Hellenistic and Palestinian Judaism, former Greek-speaking Jewish proselytes,[59] and "God fearers" who embraced the new faith, and "raw Gentiles" who were swept into the church by massive "people movements" such as that recounted in Acts 19.[60] This implies some influence of Paul as the founding figure of the church in that region. They also seemed to be related to the audiences of the other "Johannine" literature, since Revelation makes frequent references to that.[61] They were probably familiar also with some of the traditions that are embodied in the Synoptic Gospels, which were probably in existence by then.[62]

---

55. See Rev 2:15, 20.

56. Cf. Beale, *Book of Revelation*, 82–83; de Waal, *Aural-Perfomance Analysis*, 34–36; Stramara, *God's Timetable*, 129; Beale, *John's Use of the Old Testament*, 69. Stramara argues that much of Revelation reflects the liturgical readings in the Jewish synagogues, which only those attending synagogues would recognize. Possibly John's "implied audience" is more informed than the actual audience in the seven churches and subsequent audiences (Barr, *Tales of the End*, 25).

57. For example, compare 1 Cor 5:7 with Rev 5:6, 7:14. Cf. Koester, *Revelation*, 83–84.

58. Cf. Aune, *Revelation 1–5*, l, 164; Leithart, *Revelation 1–11*, 41; Bauckham, *Climax of Prophecy*, 233. There doesn't seem to be much evidence of a significant influx of Jews into Roman Asia immediately after the disaster of AD 70, but there were certainly many Jews there by the time Revelation was written, and archaeological evidence supports such a presence in later days.

59. "Proselytes" were Gentile converts to Judaism.

60. Cf. Koester, *Revelation*, 87–88; Smalley, *Revelation to John*, 4–5; Rowe, *World Upside Down*, 41–49.

61. The exact relationship between Revelation and the other Johannine books in the New Testament is debated. Stephen Smalley, Peter Leithart, and John Christopher Thomas detect very strong links between Revelation and the other Johannine literature (Smalley, *Revelation to John*, ix, 4–5, 11–13; Smalley, *Thunder and Love*, 57–73, 122–25, 134–37; Leithart, *Revelation 1–11*, 22–24; Thomas, *Apocalypse*, 22–23, 45–47). Smalley suggests that the churches included followers of John the apostle who moved to Ephesus in the 50s (*Thunder and Love*, 124). Clearly, there are some common themes (e.g., Jesus as the Word of God and the Lamb), but these are not developed in the same way and may simply be themes shared among Christians in general (Koester, *Revelation*, 81–83; cf. Fiorenza, *Book of Revelation*, 85–113).

62. The idea of Jesus "coming like a thief" is shared by Revelation and the Synoptic Gospels (Rev 3:3; 16:15; Matt 24:43–44; Luke 12:39–40). Cf. Koester, *Revelation*, 84–85; Leithart, *Revelation 1–11*, 21.

They certainly had a strained relationship with their Jewish and Gentile neighbors[63] and were apparently sometimes tempted to minimize such tensions by adapting to their neighbors' ways, much to John's disapproval.[64] At times, they faced major hostility from the culture around them, including Jewish synagogues. Jewish attempts to provoke Gentile crowds or Roman authorities to act against Christians are found in several ancient documents. These include the Gospel accounts of Jesus' trial and various places in Acts (e.g., Acts 13:50; 14:2, 5, 19; 17:5–9, 13; 18:12–17). The accounts of Paul's trials in Acts 21–26 also provide another example of Jewish animus against Christians. This may lie behind John calling two groups a "synagogue of Satan" (Rev 2:9; 3:9). The Romans tolerated Judaism, and at first, being viewed as a Jewish sect, Christians enjoyed the same toleration. However, the Jews increasingly disassociated themselves from Christians.[65]

The churches sometimes faced outright persecution and violence. Though, when Revelation was written, such violence was not widespread and mainly localized, the threat of it was not far away.[66] Hence, while some commentators argue that "the crisis is more a matter of perspective than of an objective reality,"[67] implying that John exaggerated the problem for his own ends, I think he had an accurate view of what was coming, which was certainly true when we look at second- and third-century history. However, we need not consider only full-on imperial state persecution as a threat to the early Christians. Just as we read in Acts and hear of in many places today, attacks on believers were often initiated by local officials, religious figures, or mobs responding to rumors of various kinds.[68]

But while some of these congregations were poor, others were prospering under Roman rule, and this affluence was eating away at their Christian commitment and passion, as well as enticing them to compromise for the sake of business.[69] Some of them were faithful to the Christian teaching they had embraced, but others were

---

63. Cf. Koester, *Revelation*, 92–98.

64. Rev 2:14, 20–24; 3:4. Cf. Koester, *Revelation*, 99–101. Membership in trade guilds, for example, required at least nominal recognition of patron deities and the imperial cult (cf. Beale, *Book of Revelation*, 30; Aune, *Revelation 6–16*, 768).

65. Cf. Beale, *Book of Revelation*, 31; Mayo, *Those Who Call Themselves Jews*, 64.

66. Rev 2:9–10, 13; 3:9. Cf. Koester, *Revelation*, 97–98; Beale, *Book of Revelation*, 28–29; Aune, *Revelation 1–5*, lxiv–lxv; Thomas, *Apocalypse*, 25–30; Papandrea, *Wedding of the Lamb*, 21–26; Brown, *Community of Beloved Disciple*, 65. Later (ca. AD 113) there is evidence of accused people being required to prove they were not Christians by offering incense to the emperor's image, invoking the ancient gods and cursing Christ (Pliny the Younger, *Epistles*, 10.96; cf. Boring, *Revelation*, 13–18; Beale, *Book of Revelation*, 31).

67. A. Collins, "Persecution and Vengeance," 729. Thompson sees this as just a part of the apocalyptic genre (Thompson, *Book of Revelation*, 175). Royalty argues that John is trying to "create a crisis in the social world of its audience" (Royalty, *Streets of Heaven*, 13).

68. Cf. Thompson, *Book of Revelation*, 130.

69. Rev 2:4–5, 9; 3:1–3, 15–18; 13:17. Cf. Koester, *Revelation*, 101–103. As many scholars point out, Asia was prospering under Roman rule in the late first century and the local elites at least were vigorously pro-Roman (Koester, *Revelation*, 93–95).

attracted by various forms of false teaching.[70] Finally, they display familiarity with the gift of prophecy and openness to its use (1:3; 22:6), even at times its misuse, as in the case of Jezebel (2:20).[71]

But why did John address his text to these specific churches, given that they were not the only Christian churches in the region? For example, he does not mention the church in Colossae or Hierapolis, referred to in Col. 4:13 along with Laodicea. I'll say more about this later, but the most likely answer is twofold:[72] these are the churches he has a prophetic relationship with, and there are seven because they are representative of the church as a whole. This would include the church today, since the preservation of Revelation in the New Testament implies that it has a message for the church in all times and places.[73]

PURPOSE: WHY WAS IT WRITTEN?

This question has called forth a large range of answers from scholars. The earlier modern answer basically held that John wrote to a persecuted, suffering church (even in danger of being wiped out) to comfort them and encourage them not to give up or compromise. In the end they would be vindicated. After all, the evidence of persecution under Domitian cannot be completely dismissed,[74] and by the early second century, Roman officials were treating Christianity as an illegal religion.[75]

However, in recent years this idea has been criticized on several grounds. First, the text itself does not make such a claim. Second, Roman persecution of Christians at this stage (that is, up to AD 100) was known to be intermittent and localized rather than systematic and widespread. Only Nero had (briefly) systematically attacked the church in Rome.[76] Third, John seemed to be as much upset by internal factors in the seven congregations as by outside threats, judging by the seven prophetic messages of Revelation 2–3.[77]

Recent commentators have tended, therefore, to focus more on those internal issues. Maybe the churches had accommodated too much to the surrounding culture,

---

70. Rev 2:2, 6, 13–15, 20–25; 3:8, 10. Cf. Koester, *Revelation*, 88–89; Smalley, *Revelation to John*, 5–6. See discussion of the nature of this false teaching and its relation to first-century "Gnosticism" and heresies about Jesus in Smalley, *Thunder and Love*, 84–89, 122–37.

71. Cf. Thomas, *Apocalypse*, 42–43; Fiorenza, *Book of Revelation*, 140–146.

72. Keener points to a third possibility, that this selection of cities is close to those where the "leading council of Asiarchs . . . met each year" (Keener, *Revelation*, 67), though with one exception. Cf. Moyise, *Old Testament in the Book of Revelation*, 25–27. This will be discussed further when we reach Rev 2–3.

73. Cf. Thomas, *Apocalypse*, 20–22.

74. Cf. Papandrea, *Wedding of the Lamb*, 23–25.

75. Cf. Wilken, *Christians as the Romans Saw Them*, 23

76. Cf. Thompson, "Ordinary Lives," 29–43.

77. Cf. Smalley, *Revelation to John*, 3–4; Smalley, *Thunder and Love*, 119–121.

eating food offered to idols, compromising with the sexual standards of Greek culture, or displaying too much overt loyalty to the emperor. Hence John was trying to challenge those compromises and push the churches to his own starker stance.[78] Maybe he was concerned that the community "was itself infested with falsehood"[79] (in a similar way to the churches addressed by 1, 2, and 3 John). John thus particularly sought to promote a balanced Christology and good relationships within the churches.[80]

Maybe he was threatened by the rising influence of other Christian groups and individuals in the seven churches. This view suggests John was engaged in a struggle for leadership and influence in which he needed to find grounds to denounce people like "the Nicolaitans" (2:6, 15) and the prophet "Jezebel" (2:20). All these suggestions presuppose that the warnings about persecution were designed to drive a strong wedge between the Christians and other social groups in Asia.[81] However, this strategy could only work if there really *was* a threat of persecution and people like Antipas (2:13) really had been killed for their faith.

Another perspective pursued by some commentators is to see Revelation as protest literature. Bauckham, for example, described Revelation as "the most powerful piece of political resistance literature from the period of the early [Roman] Empire."[82] John is not just protesting about the violent persecution of Christians but making a broader critique of the injustice, violence and oppression of the Roman Empire, not to mention its imperial cult.[83] No doubt there is some truth in this, and it certainly resonates with readers in the twenty-first century. But it may be misleading if one does not define "political" carefully.

John was probably not urging his readers and hearers to engage in a political struggle within the somewhat limited legal space available in his day, still less to start a violent rebellion against Rome, as some of his fellow Jews did in AD 66–70 and again in AD 132–135. On the other hand, his descriptions of Rome in Revelation 13, 17 and 18 were vivid and designed to paint the empire in very negative terms. At least, John is trying to encourage his hearers to "resist" the empire by refusing to submit to its extreme demands for loyalty and even worship, and to give priority in their loyalties to God's kingdom and to Jesus as God's messiah and Lord.[84]

I think the best answer to the question would draw on insights from all sides. As Craig Koester writes, "By portraying opposing forces in vivid terms, the writer seeks to deepen the readers' commitment to God and the Lamb in a society in which other

---

78. Cf. Koester, *Revelation*, 100–101; Beale, *Book of Revelation*, 33; Duff, *Who Rides the Beast?*, 14.
79. Smalley, *Revelation to John*, 6; cf. Smalley, *Thunder and Love*, 121–28.
80. This is argued especially in Smalley, *Thunder and Love*, 121–35.
81. Cf. Royalty, *Streets of Heaven*, 28–30.
82. Bauckham, *Theology*, 38.
83. Bauckham, *Theology*, 38–39.
84. For a full argument along these lines and application to today's capitalist "empire," see Howard-Brook and Gwyther, *Unveiling Empire*.

forces vie for their loyalty."[85] I will argue that John's primary purpose was to stir up his audience to such a vigorous and assertive Christian commitment, one motivated by an ardent love for Jesus (2:4–5; 3:8, 16, 19–20). This commitment would indeed be intolerant of the spiritual and moral weaknesses of the Greco-Roman (and Jewish) culture and the Roman Empire, but its long-term focus would be missional.[86]

Revelation would not be trying to create a dissident sect of Christians but rather empowering them to win many pagans and Jews to loyalty to the One who was claimed as the Messiah of Israel and the Lord of the whole human race. And this is what John confidently expected to happen in the long term. The gospel would indeed conquer the Roman Empire for "a thousand years." But this would only happen if the believers held to a fervent, courageous, prophetic, uncompromising commitment to prosecute the cause of their Savior and Lord in the power of the Holy Spirit in the face of threats and even death itself. Thus, as Harry Maier puts it, "from start to finish the Book of Revelation is a call to Christian discipleship."[87]

GENRE: WHAT KIND OF LITERATURE IS IT?

Revelation is a unique book in the Christian canon of Scripture. However, it has similarities with other literature, both biblical and extra-biblical, and it is not therefore a completely strange genre. It contains narrative like the Gospels and Acts. It is visionary like parts of Daniel and Ezekiel. It is a letter like those of Paul. It contains hymns that resemble some of the Psalms. It has features similar to Hebrew prophetic books like Isaiah, Ezekiel, Daniel, Zechariah, and Joel.

When we read any text, ancient or modern, we form a view of its genre (that is, the kind of writing we are encountering) and shape our expectations and interpretation accordingly.[88] We do not expect accurate science from science fiction, for example, though we may find some stimulating scientific thinking there. In particular, we look for telltale signs of the genre in the beginning of a text. Authors can, of course, play with the readers' minds by not fulfilling their expectations, by combining features of different genres or by springing surprises during or at the end of their text. Hence the readers' initial view of a work's genre can only be tentative. Recent books have helped readers of the Bible also to think generically and not try to derive absolute promises from Proverbs or universal ethics from Joshua, for instance.[89]

---

85. Koester, *Revelation*, 119, cf. 132.

86. This is different than the view of Adela Yarbro Collins, who suggests that John was stirring up feelings of resentment and powerlessness and a desire for vengeance against Greco-Roman society and then bringing a catharsis of such emotions by objectifying the conflict (cf. A. Collins, *Crisis and Catharsis*, 143–53). This interpretation suggests that John's focus was internal and defensive, whereas I am arguing it was more outward-looking, confident, and missional.

87. Maier, *Apocalypse Recalled*, x.

88. Cf. Koester, *Revelation*, 104; Malina, *Genre and Message*, 27.

89. E.g., Fee and Stuart, *How to Read the Bible*.

But what genre is Revelation? What expectations should readers bring to this ancient text? How should they therefore interpret it?

The most obvious answer is that Revelation is **prophecy**. It makes claims to be a prophetic book early on (1:3) and again towards to the end (22:6, 10, 18–19). It also looks like a prophetic book at almost every point. For instance, it represents Jesus as speaking the messages to the seven churches in a manner reminiscent of Old Testament prophets. It also includes "call narratives" like those in Ezekiel and Isaiah and apparently predicts future events (1:1, 3). Mazzaferi therefore claims, "John identifies himself forcefully and unequivocally as a prophet in the noble line of classical OT prophets."[90]

However, fresh questions arise at this point: What is prophecy, anyway? Does it require prediction? After all, much of the message of Isaiah (for instance) was more analysis and criticism of his society than prediction of the future, and the predictions that occur are more short- than long-term. As Daniel Stramara puts it, "There is a marked difference between prophecy and prediction, a theological spin on a current situation, and a divine foretelling of distant future events,"[91] though prediction should not be ruled out of the the territory of prophecy.

And is Revelation more like Old or New Testament prophecy? Is John more a Jeremiah or Ezekiel or more like an Agabus? His reference to the Spirit in each of the seven opening messages to the churches ("Those who have ears, let them hear what the Spirit is saying to the churches") resembles Agabus' "The Holy Spirit says . . ." (Acts 21:11). But his descriptions of his call to prophesy have clear parallels with Ezekiel (compare Rev 10:8–11 with Ezek 3:1–3), Daniel (compare Rev 1:13–17 with Dan 10:5–10), and Isaiah (compare Rev 4:8 with Isa 6:2–3).[92]

The second obvious answer is that Revelation is a **letter**. After introducing his text, John writes: "John to the seven churches that are in Asia: grace and peace to you" (1:4). And he finishes with: "The grace of the Lord Jesus be with all" (22:21). The similarities with the letters of Paul and Peter (but not John!) are obvious. Revelation takes the form of a common Hellenistic letter, though in this case a circular letter addressed to seven different audiences, even as it puts "strange" content between the opening and ending of that letter.[93] Elisabeth Schüssler Fiorenza calls it "a public pastoral letter" also seen as "words of prophecy,"[94] though she concedes it is a very unusual letter.[95] It was not uncommon for ancient letters to incorporate prophetic material, but

---

90. Mazzaferi, *Genre of the Book of Revelation*, 296.

91. Stramara, *God's Timetable*, 8.

92. See the discussion in Koester, *Revelation*, 107–109, which mainly compares Revelation with ancient Hebrew prophecy and Smalley, *Revelation to John*, 7–8, which tries to blend comparisons with Old and New Testament prophesying. Cf. Fekkes, *Isaiah and Prophetic Traditions*, 51–52; Mazzaferi, *Genre of the Book of Revelation*, Chapers 4, 10.

93. Cf. Koester, *Revelation*, 109–12.

94. Fiorenza, "Composition and Structure," 352.

95. Fiorenza, "Composition and Structure," 352–53.

there was no standard genre of prophetic letters. Perhaps John wanted to associate his text with the letters of Paul who had been the founding apostle in that region.[96]

But the third possibility stands out throughout the rest of the book. Revelation opens with these words:

> **A revelation of Jesus Christ, which God gave him to show his slaves what must soon happen, and he made it known by sending (it) through his angel to his slave John, who testified to the word of God and the testimony of Jesus Christ which he saw. (Rev 1:1–2)**

We note here that this is:

- A revelation (an unveiling of what John wouldn't have otherwise seen)
- Given by God
- Mediated by an angel
- Seen by John
- Testified by him

So if this is a prophecy, it is a very specific kind of prophecy. Scholars call this an **apocalypse** (after the Greek word for "revelation"), and this genre has much the same features as those just mentioned.[97]

Many apocalypses were written by Jews (such as 1 Enoch,[98] 4 Ezra, and some literature from the Qumran community)[99] and even later by Christians (such as the *Shepherd of Hermas*). There are also apocalyptic passages in classic Hebrew prophecy (such as Ezekiel 1–3 and Zech 1:7–21). However, the most accessible and obviously relevant example is Daniel 7–12.[100] Here we see Daniel also testifying about being given a revelation by God through an angel in a series of visions. Nonetheless, Revelation doesn't contain all the common features of Jewish apocalypses. (It's harder to be sure about Daniel.)[101] For instance, it isn't obviously pseudonymous (written in the

---

96. Cf. Aune, *Revelation 1–5*, lxxii–lxxv.

97. The standard definition of an apocalypse is "a genre of revelatory literature with a narrative framework, in which a revelation is mediated by an otherworldly being to a human recipient, disclosing a transcendent reality which is both temporal, insofar as it envisages eschatological salvation, and spatial insofar as it involves another, supernatural world" (J. Collins, "Towards the Morphology of a Genre," 9). Cf. Aune, *Revelation 1–5*, lxxvii–lxxxii; Koester, *Revelation*, 64, 104; Newton, *Revelation Worldview*, 98–101; Smalley, *Thunder and Love*, 24; Beale, *Book of Revelation*, 37–42; Thomas, *Apocalypse*, 13–16; Lupieri, *Commentary*, 13–37; Court, *Revelation*, 79–83. See also the theological discussion in Leithart, *Revelation 1–11*, 56–67.

98. Quoted in Jude 14–15. This does not prove it to be Scripture, but shows that New Testament writers read it and saw value in it.

99. This was the community associated with the Dead Sea Scrolls discovered in 1948.

100. See discussion about the contrasting responses to empire in 1 Maccabees and Daniel in Howard-Brook and Gwyther, *Unveiling Empire*, 47–53.

101. Cf. Goldingay, *Daniel*, 320–22; Baldwin, *Daniel*, 46–59.

name of an ancient hero like Enoch or Ezra).[102] It doesn't contain history written in the guise of future prediction, so-called *ex eventu* prophecy. This was commonly used to give a survey of salvation history leading up to and beyond the real authors' time, but ostensibly as prediction of the future by the ancient supposed author.[103]

But it does contain some other generic features of apocalypses, such as travels to heaven (Rev 4) and beyond (17:1), weird animals that clearly stand for human individuals or nations (9:3–11; 13:1–3; compare Daniel 7–8), and interpreting angels (1:1; 10:1–11; 17:1–18; 19:9–10; 21:9–10; 22:6–11, 16; compare Dan 7:16; 8:13–26; 9:21–27; 10:10—12:4). Like Daniel and others, it is written in prose and largely in the first person as a testimony of a vision. Its obsession with numbers also resembles these other apocalypses.[104] It appeals to the audience's imagination more than to their intellect with its imagery and narration.[105] It has something of an apocalyptic worldview; for example, a strong dualistic contrast exists between the visible and invisible world, devils and angels, underworld and heaven, or the present evil age and the coming triumph of God's kingdom. It has a tendency towards determinism (as in Rev.1:1 which speaks of "what *must* soon happen").[106] And it presents itself as a "revelation," something unseen, and unable to be known by ordinary means, that God shows to the author, using angels as mediators.[107]

On the other hand, Revelation should also be read as an ancient *Christian prophecy*[108] or **vision report**[109] as predicted in Acts 2:17–18 and exemplified in Acts

---

102. It has been suggested that John adopts the persona of Ezekiel given the number of references to Ezekiel and the apparent structural influence of that book on Revelation. But John has also been influenced strongly by Daniel and refers to many other OT texts and he never calls himself Ezekiel. Cf. Moyise, *Old Testament in the Book of Revelation*, 78–83.

103. Cf. Koester, *Revelation*, 106–107; Mazzaferi, *Genre of the Book of Revelation*, 250; Stramara, *God's Timetable*, 8–10. The detailed interpretation of the visions found in other apocalypses is also rare in Revelation (Smalley, *Revelation to John*, 7). And John shows relatively little interest in setting out salvation history in neat eras, being more concerned as a prophet with the immediate future of God's judgment (cf. Fiorenza, *Book of Revelation*, 38–50).

104. Cf. Aune, *Revelation 1–5*, lxxxii–lxxxviii; Paul, *Revelation*, 34–39; Papandrea, *Wedding of the Lamb*, 30–42.

105. Cf. Koester, *Revelation*, 138–39; Bauckham, *Climax of Prophecy*, 174–79. One aspect of this is the extensive use of colors in Revelation (Smalley, *Thunder and Love*, 106–107). Pippin suggests that "biblical apocalyptic literature is an early form of what we now call fantasy literature" (Pippin, *Death and Desire*, 89).

106. Cf. Koester, *Revelation*, 105–107; Smalley, *Revelation to John*, 7, 11; Smalley, *Thunder and Love*, 27–29; Newton, *Revelation Worldview*, 101–15.

107. Cf. Beale, *Book of Revelation*, 38. Thompson calls it "deviant knowledge" because of how it was obtained and its attitude to the surrounding society (Thompson, *Book of Revelation*, 181).

108. Cf. Koester, *Revelation*, 90–91, 214; Thomas, *Apocalypse*, 11–13; Mazzaferi, *Genre of the Book of Revelation*, ch. 7. Schüssler Fiorenza claims that Revelation is "a genuine expression of early Christian prophecy whose basic experience and self-understanding is apocalyptic" (Fiorenza, *Book of Revelation*, 140, 133–52).

109. Cf. Paul, *Revelation*, 23. Fekkes appropriately distinguishes between "cultic prophecy" which was manifested in a congregational setting, and visions which were usually received privately, often in

by Agabus (Acts 11:28; 21:10–11), Philip's four daughters (Acts 21:9), the "prophets and teachers" of Antioch (Acts 13:1–2), Ananias (Acts 9:10–16), Peter (Acts 10:9–20; 11:5–12), unnamed Christians (Acts 20:23; 21:4), and Paul (Acts 9:4–6; 13:9–11; 16:9–10; 20:29–30). In other New Testament literature, prophecy is not only found in Paul's letters (1 Thess 4:15–5:3; 2 Thess 2:1–4; 1 Tim 4:1) but also noted among the congregations in Corinth (1 Cor 14), in Thessalonica (1 Thess 5:20–21), and among the audience of 1 John (1 John 4:1). Paul also writes about "a man in Christ who . . . was caught up to the third heaven . . . and heard inexpressible things" (2 Cor 12:2, 4). And as Thompson points out,[110] congregational prophesying in Paul's churches includes "revelations" (apocalypses) received during Christian meetings (1 Cor 14:26, 30). Revelation itself refers to such prophetic activity of others: Jezebel (2:20), two unnamed prophetic witnesses (11:3, 6, 10), "the spirit of prophecy" (19:10), and fellow prophets (22:9). Nearly all the distinctive prophetic and apocalyptic features of Revelation are replicated (if only briefly) in other parts of the New Testament as shown by the examples above. Clearly the early Christians were used to experiences or reports of prophecy, visions, and angelic appearances, so Revelation's claims would not have been strange to them.

However, such a long written prophetic narrative *was* unusual.[111] John clearly expended great effort to create a carefully crafted narrative that shows no signs of being just a spontaneous prophetic word.[112] Moreover, John's claims about his book were much stronger than those appropriate for the usual congregational prophecy (compare Rev 22:18–19 with 1 Cor 14:29–32).[113] Nonetheless, the first-person singular address of most of Revelation would have reminded the audience of other testimonies, such as the two first-person accounts of Paul's encounter with Jesus outside Damascus (Acts 22:3–21; 26:4–18), and Peter's account of his Cornelius adventure to his critics

---

an altered state of consciousness (Paul, *Prophetic Traditions*, 42–49).

110. Thompson, *Book of Revelation*, 72.

111. Cf. Boring, "Apocalypse as Christian Prophecy," 56. Boring attempts to identify some possible features of early Christian prophecy from a kind of form critical study of Revelation (ibid., 43–57).

112. Balancing the claim of John to have seen and heard a vision with the evidence of his own contribution to the shape of the text is one of the key issues for interpreters of Revelation. Pentecostals value spontaneous congregational prophetic words, but clearly a vision report would have to be written after the vision was experienced, thus allowing for the human author to shape it in terms of their own vocabulary and even theology. As Carrell points out, "Dreams and visions do not normally take place within a mind which is a *tabula rasa*," that is, a blank slate (Carrell, *Jesus and the Angels*, 17). An interesting OT parallel is found in Jonah, whose report of his prayer inside the big fish (Jonah 2) is rather literary and was almost certainly not written down while he was there. Also sometimes visions were given in response to prayerful meditation on ancient texts, the language of which was then used in the vision report (e.g., Dan 9:2–23). Cf. Fekkes, *Isaiah and Prophetic Traditions*, 47; Thomas, *Apocalypse*, 44–45; Boring, *Revelation*, 27–28; Smolarz, *Covenant*, 27.

113. Cf. Fekkes, *Isaiah and Prophetic Traditions*, 56–57. I think Fekkes overstates the case when he says, "John has no interest in having his prophecy tested or evaluated by others" even though he praises such testing by others (ibid., 57). In practice, the church *did* test and evaluate Revelation before it was accepted into the emerging New Testament canon.

(Acts 11:4–17). Hence, as Waddell suggests, "John is not using the word ἀποκάλυψις to identify his literary work with a particular genre but rather as a description of his experience."[114]

So the initial readers, or rather hearers (1:3), would have picked up at least three generic clues in the opening section of the book. What would they have expected as a result? First, they would have expected this to be a word from God (prophecy) with some predictive elements for the near future, as it says, "what must soon happen" (1:1) and "the time draws near" (1:3). This would have made them take notice. Provided they believed that John was a credible prophet, they would have heard what God was saying, applied it to their lives, and confidently expected the events to happen soon as predicted.

However, they might also have found this somewhat threatening. Prophecy is controversial, as we can see in the Old Testament. Jeremiah was a prime example; because of his prophetic ministry, he had to withstand opposition from government, priests, and other prophets. Prophecy and other methods of telling the future were also common in the Greco-Roman world and could cause major disruptions, especially if the content related to the Emperor or Rome. The Emperor Augustus took actions against divinations concerning the timing of his coming death when he was seventy four.[115] Earlier he had had over two-thousand books of prophecy burned for similar reasons[116] and during the first century AD, several members of the nobility were put on trial on "charges of inquiring into the destinies of the emperor or his family," mostly through astrology, which was seen as treason.[117]

Second, the hearers would have expected this text to relate to them (as a letter addressed to them).[118] They would have expected to understand it and apply it to their context as Christian congregations. They would not have expected it all to be about a different era of history altogether, even though some long-term prediction might be found there, such as the passages about the coming thousand-year-long era and eras beyond it (20:1–10). They would also have seen it as a personal communication from someone they knew, or at least knew of.

Third, they would have expected it to reveal real truth about heavenly reality, about their own situation, and about the future (as an apocalypse). They would not have been surprised by the weird imagery or angelic mediation, since these were standard features of apocalyptic prophecy. But they would have expected the vision to open up new insights to their minds. They may have expected its message to be

---

114. Waddell, *Spirit of the Book*, 123.
115. MacMullen, *Enemies of the Roman Order*, 129.
116. MacMullen, *Enemies of the Roman Order*, 130.
117. MacMullen, *Enemies of the Roman Order*, 134. His main source is the work of the Roman historian Tacitus.
118. As Koester says, the book thus "speaks 'to' the situations of specific readers" (Koester, *Revelation*, 111). Cf. Smalley, *Thunder and Love*, 101–102; Beale, *Book of Revelation*, 39. Hence, as Boring says, "it was *not* written to *us*" (Boring, *Revelation*, 7; emphasis in the original).

disconcerting, even dangerous, but able to be understood by believers guided by a prophet like John.[119]

But as they listened or read further, they would have been captured by the narrative, the plot that John constructs with his visionary experience, the suspense created by such a powerful story.[120] Their understanding would also have been enriched by other literary features of the text that would have reminded them of other literature and aspects of the surrounding culture. They would have been reminded of ancient myths, such as various "combat myths," when they heard about the dragon, the woman and the male child (Revelation 12).[121] The spectacular features of the narrative would have been reminiscent of the large-scale Roman spectacles they had experienced or heard about.[122]

The narrative structure of Revelation would have suggested it could be read as a kind of novel. The wedding references near the end (19:6–9; 21:2, 9) might have suggested a romantic strand to the story.[123] The strong sense of conflict throughout the narrative suggests it can be read as a war story.[124] It could be read as a drama (even perhaps acted in the theater) or maybe a "visionary drama";[125] in this way, the text, read aloud (1:3), would have held the attention of its audience.

The frequent references to stars and astrologically significant numbers would have reminded them of the contemporary Greco-Roman obsession with astrology.[126] All these allusions would have added extra meaning to the text as the audience experienced it and would have helped to draw them imaginatively into its world. They might even have tried to join in with the worship in heaven, since a number of writers have suggested that Revelation can be read as a liturgical text.[127]

---

119. These points are equally valid if Revelation is read as an "astral prophecy," as proposed by Malina. Such a genre involved a prophetic figure interpreting signs in the sky related to the immediate future of the group with divine guidance or by interaction with celestial beings often in an altered state of consciousness (Malina, *Genre and Message*, 12–46, 51).

120. Cf. Jang, "Narrative Function," 187–89.

121. Cf. Huber, *Like a Bride Adorned*, 15–24; Barr, *Tales of the End*, 27–28.

122. Cf. Frilingos, *Spectacles of Empire*.

123. Cf. Newton, "Reading Revelation Romantically"; Koester, *Revelation*, 118–19; Huber, *Like a Bride Adorned*. The structures of ancient romance novels can be seen as replicated to some degree in Revelation (cf. Newton, *Revelation Worldview*, 261–74).

124. Cf. Longman and Reid, *God Is a Warrior*, 180–92.

125. Thomas and Macchia, *Revelation*, 7–11; Thomas, *Apocalypse*, 8–11. Cf. Smalley, *Thunder and Love*, 103–10; Low, "Postcolonialism," 261–70; Bowman, *Drama of the Book of Revelation*; Bowman, "Revelation to John." As oral enactment would occur during Christian worship, this point connects strongly with Revelation as liturgy (Thomas, *Apocalypse*, 10).

126. Cf. Malina, *Genre and Message*. See critique in Beale, *Book of Revelation*, 42–43.

127. Cf. Koester, *Revelation*, 127–30; Smalley, *Thunder and Love*, 102–3, 160–62. Revelation is the only New Testament book that includes multiple hymns, which in turn draw on Hebrew and Greco-Roman forms, and this becomes a model for the early church as well as making strong theological points. Revelation has inspired a lot of Christian music, most famously Handel's "Hallelujah Chorus" (cf. Koester, *Revelation*, 58–59; Newton, *Revelation Reclaimed*, 47–48). For a Pentecostal discussion of worship in Revelation, see Archer, *Worship in the Apocalypse*.

INTRODUCTION

But we must emphasize that the experience of the original audience was of "hearing" rather than "reading." Most people would have heard the text read aloud (1:3) or even enacted,[128] as there were few copies and many Christians couldn't read.[129] The oral nature of the text must always be "front and center" as the modern interpreter wrestles with interpreting it. And as Schüssler Fiorenza pointed out, "Revelation as a whole makes quite a different impression when it is heard or when it is analyzed."[130] Moreover the oral nature of the reading affects the structure of the text; for example, counting down the sevens (seals, trumpets, and bowls) helps a listening audience keep focused.[131] However, as Sweet points out, "even if the book was in the first instance read aloud as a whole, we can be sure that like Paul's letters it was subsequently pored over in detail."[132]

ANALYSIS: WHAT KIND OF STRUCTURE DOES IT HAVE?

That the book of Revelation is a highly structured text is obvious. Think of the sets of sevens (seals, trumpets, bowls), carefully counted down, for example. As Bauckham observes, "The essential structure of the book, without recognition of which it would be incomprehensible, must have been intended to be perceptible in oral performance."[133] But the structure is complex and subtle, so that new commentators frequently come up with new structural analyses.[134] The story line of the book is far from purely linear, being interrupted frequently by interlocking passages that overlap two sections,[135] reprises, and tangents. It seems that some passages in Revelation repeat the ideas of earlier passages to some extent, such as the bowls repeating aspects of the trumpets, a point made by the oldest commentary on Revelation still surviving.[136] This causes many commentators to suggest that the same basic sequence of events or themes is "recapitulated" in each stage of the narrative.[137] That raises issues about how the narrative of Revelation is meant to represent real events, if it is.[138]

---

128. Cf. de Waal, *Aural-Performance Analysis*, 28–36; Thomas, *Apocalypse*, 8; Seal, "Emotions, Empathy, and Engagement," 3–4. Reading silently was rare in the ancient world, but Revelation is unlike most apocalypses in being "explicitly intended for oral performance" (Aune, *Revelation 1–5*, 20–21; cf. Barr, *Tales of the End*, 10, 46).

129. Pentecostal Pauline scholar Adam White analyzes this dynamic with reference to Paul; similar observations apply to Revelation. See White, "Pentecostal Preaching," 130–32, 146–47.

130. Fiorenza, "Composition and Structure," 345.

131. Cf. Barr, "Apocalypse of John as Oral Enactment," 243–52.

132. Sweet, *Revelation*, 13.

133. Bauckham, *Climax of Prophecy*, 1–2.

134. See good summary in Aune, *Revelation 1–5*, xci and c and the extended discussion in Michaels, *Interpreting the Book of Revelation*, 51–71.

135. The technical word for this is "intercalation." Cf. Beale, *Book of Revelation*, 112–14.

136. Cf. Koester, *Revelation*, 33; Smalley, *Revelation to John*, 19.

137. Cf. Beale, *Book of Revelation*, 121–26.

138. Cf. Aune, *Revelation 1–5*, xcii–xiii.

Nonetheless, as I see it, a narrative structure emerges as one reads the book over and over. The story begins with an introduction (1:1–8) and a prologue (1:9—3:22). Then with the setting comes the problem that launches the plot proper (the struggle to release the sealed document: 4:1—5:14). From here we have the "rising action" where the plot builds, the enemies are introduced, the conflicts intensify,[139] and so on, building to the climax in 19:11–21 with the victory of the rider on the white horse.[140] From there the plot winds down to a satisfying ending in 22:5, followed by a concluding epilogue.[141] Of course, this raises the question that often gets lost in analysis: does John attempt to provide a chronological account of future events in this narrative, or is the structure purely literary?[142]

Other commentators have offered various helpful analyses based on the content of the book. One of the simplest is found in Koester's recent commentary:[143]

1. Introduction (1:1–8)
2. Christ and the Seven Assemblies (1:9—3:22)
3. The Seven Seals (4:1—8:5)
4. The Seven Trumpets (8:6—11:18)
5. The Dragon, the Beasts, and the Faithful (11:19—15:4)
6. The Seven Bowls and the Fall of Babylon (15:5—19:10)
7. From the Beast's Demise to New Jerusalem (19:11—22:5)
8. Conclusion (22:6-21)

This analysis is simple and clear but obscures aspects of the text. For example, why combine the seven bowls and the fall of Babylon into one section when John provides clear markers that chapter 17 starts a new section? All analysis runs into some such issues.[144]

Other structures that try to reflect the signals John gives in the text[145] are built on:

---

139. Thus, the disasters in the seals section are not as bad as the trumpets (with their one-third factor), which in turn are superseded by the greater devastation of the bowls section.

140. Cf. Bauckham, *Climax of Prophecy*, 18–20.

141. Cf. Newton, *Revelation Worldview*, 261–62. David L. Barr sees three separate plots in chs. 1–3, 4–11, and 12–22 (Barr, "Story John Told," 14–19). Resseguie posits a U-shaped plot starting with a stable situation, descending into disaster, and then going up again owing to the rescue work of Christ (Resseguie, *Revelation of John*, 12, 45–46).

142. Cf. Beale, *Book of Revelation*, 116–51. Beale argues that "The primary intention of the numbering is to represent the order of John's visions, not necessarily the order of historical events . . . This is a crucial hermeneutical principle of the book . . . " (ibid., 129; see also 144). Giblin also contends that "The fatal error to be avoided is that of historicizing any aspects of John's vision of the end time" (Giblin, "Recapitulation," 94).

143. Koester, *Revelation*, 112. Compare Bauckham, *Climax of Prophecy*, 21–22.

144. Cf. Koester, *Revelation*, 112–15.

145. Cf. Bauckham, *Climax of Prophecy*, 3. For a more comprehensive and "multi-layered" analysis of the structure of Revelation, see Bandy, "Layers of the Apocalypse."

- The series of explicit sevens (churches, seals, trumpets, bowls). Some commentators find other sevens implied throughout the text.[146]

- The use of the phrase *en pneumati* [in the Spirit], which introduces the visions (1:10; 4:2; 17:3; 21:10).[147]

- The phrase *kai eidon* [and I saw] used to introduce transitions in the narrative, usually of a smaller nature.[148]

- The use of the phrase *ha dei genesthai* [what must happen] in 1:1, 19; 4:1, and 22:6, based on allusion to Daniel 2.[149]

- A chiastic reading which sees parallels between the beginning and ending features and puts the climax in the middle, often in chapters 11, 12, 13, or 14.[150]

- A threefold structure based on the three scrolls mentioned in 1:11, 5:1, and 10:2.[151]

- Parallels between the content of the seven messages of Revelation 2–3 and the rest of the book.[152]

- The nature, content, and relationship between the two scrolls of Revelation 5–6 and Revelation 10.[153]

- Parallels between introductory and concluding language regarding the great prostitute and the bride of the Lamb.[154]

- The repeated references to a heavenly sign in 12:1, 3, and 15:1, which bracket the central struggle of chapters 12–14.[155]

- Use of Old Testament structures, especially that of Ezekiel, but more broadly the lawsuit structure common to Isaiah, Jeremiah, and Ezekiel consisting of oracles

---

146. Such as the seven "beatitudes" (Koester, *Revelation*, 130–32). Cf. Beale, *Book of Revelation*, 115–16, 129; Thomas, *Apocalypse*, 3, 7; Bauckham, *Climax of Prophecy*, 7–18; Aune, *Revelation 1–5*, xciii–xcv. Like Aune and Bauckham, I am skeptical of implied series of sevens that are more subject to individual interpretation. Cf. Bandy, "Layers of the Apocalypse," 475–76.

147. Cf. Herms, *Apocalypse for the Church*, 149–54; Waddell, *Spirit of the Book*, 138–50; Filho, "Apocalypse of John."

148. Cf. Bandy, "Layers of the Apocalypse," 476–77.

149. Cf. Beale, *Book of Revelation*, 111, 160.

150. Cf. Lee, "Call to Martyrdom," 1; Beale, *Book of Revelation*, 130, 143.

151. Barr stresses the similarities between the opening and closing sections and sees Revelation as telling three stories within a common frame (Barr, *Tales of the End*, 15–25).

152. Cf. Beale, *Book of Revelation*, 132–35; Michaels, *Interpreting the Book of Revelation*, 39–40.

153. Cf. Aune, *Revelation 1–5*, xcviii–xcix; Bauckham, *Climax of Prophecy*, 13, 243–57.

154. Cf. Bauckham, *Climax of Prophecy*, 4–5; Thomas, *Apocalypse*, 4; Aune, *Revelation 1–5*, xcv–xcvii

155. Cf. Bauckham, *Climax of Prophecy*, 15–17; Bandy, "Layers of the Apocalypse," 478–79. Bauckham argues that the repetition of this phrasing in Rev 15:1 helps to integrate the preceding chapters into the ongoing narrative begun in chapter 5.

of judgment against God's people, followed by oracles about the nations and then promises of future salvation. Arguably 1:9—3:22, 4:1—16:21, and 21:9—22:5 follow this pattern.[156] Douglas Campbell uses Leviticus 26 to analyze the four sevens—churches, seals, trumpets, and bowls—as expressions of covenant blessings and curses.[157]

Thomas emphasizes the importance of focusing on "literary markers" that would be evident to a "first-time hearer of the Apocalypse,"[158] as opposed to scholars who could pore over the manuscript at leisure. On the other hand, as Michelle Lee has argued, "It seems likely the work was composed in such a way so that the audience would not grasp everything the first time, but would gain a greater understanding or deeper experience with each performance."[159]

COMPOSITION: HOW DID WE GET THE TEXT WE HAVE?

This issue relates to two separate questions: the sources that the author, or a later editor, may have used and the reliability of the Greek manuscripts of Revelation available today. While some commentators argue that Revelation is a composite text, either a combination of several earlier manuscripts or a revised version of an earlier text,[160] often thought to be a Jewish prophecy, the evidence of this seems rather thin to me. As Koester observes, "None of the attempts to reconstruct the stages of composition gained wide acceptance" by scholars.[161] Clearly John drew on many sources for images and ideas, as will be discussed in the next section. However, as Morris comments, "the style of the book is so uniform"[162] that major redaction seems unlikely, although the visions may have been seen over a period of time and the book composed over several years.[163] Thus, in this commentary, I will discuss the text as we have it.

But this leads us to the question of the reliability of the Greek text we have, compared to the original. As with all New Testament books, we do not possess the original document in John's handwriting but only multiple copies of all or part of the text in Greek (papyri, uncials, and minuscules),[164] translations into other ancient

---

156. Cf. Bandy, "Layers of the Apocalypse," 483–87.

157. Campbell, "Findings."

158. Thomas, *Apocalypse*, 2.

159. Lee, "Call to Martyrdom," 193.

160. Most notably among recent commentaries, Aune argues for this. Cf. Aune, *Revelation 1–5*, cv–cxxxiv; Koester, *Revelation*, 70–71; Herms, *Apocalypse for the Church*, 5–19.

161. Koester, *Revelation*, 62. Cf. Fiorenza, "Composition and Structure," 346–50.

162. Morris, *Revelation*, 41.

163. Cf. Smalley, *Revelation to John*, 2; Smalley, *Thunder and Love*, 97–101; Bauckham, *Climax of Prophecy*, x.

164. Papyri refer to material written on papyrus, made from reeds, and often these are the oldest manuscripts, but usually only contain a fraction of the text since this material decays more quickly

languages like Latin, and quotations from Revelation in the writings of early Christian authors. Unlike other New Testament books, there is no lectionary evidence for Revelation, that is no set readings for Christian worship, since it was not regularly set for such readings.[165]

The oldest complete copies are from the fourth or fifth centuries; *the* oldest is from the Codex Sinaiticus, though the fifth-century Codex Alexandrinus may be more reliable. However, copies of parts of Revelation date back as far as the late second or third century. There are many variations among these manuscripts, such as variations on the number of the beast (666 or 616) and either a rainbow [*iris*] or priests around God's throne in Revelation 4:3.[166] However, it can be concluded that such variations do not significantly affect the meaning of the book. Textual critics draw on all available manuscripts to prepare the critical texts on which modern translations are based.

TRANSLATION: WHAT ENGLISH TRANSLATION AM I USING?

In this series of commentaries on the New Testament, we are working from the NA28 critical Greek text. I offer my own translation into English, which will differ from the usual modern translations at times. Where I diverge significantly from such standard translations, I will offer a brief explanation.

All Old Testament Scripture quotations, and quotations from NT books other than Revelation, unless otherwise indicated, are taken from the Holy Bible, New International Version®, NIV®. Copyright ©1973, 1978, 1984, 2011 by Biblica, Inc.™ Used by permission of Zondervan. All rights reserved worldwide. The "NIV" and "New International Version" are trademarks registered in the United States Patent and Trademark Office by Biblica, Inc.™

Sometimes I also use the NRSV (New Revised Standard Version Bible, copyright © 1989 National Council of the Churches of Christ in the United States of America. Used by permission. All rights reserved worldwide).

Generally, my own translation seeks to be gender inclusive unless this leads to a result that is misleading. I translate somewhat literally, which makes the translation somewhat deficient in fluency and English style in places, but I do this to help non-Greek readers get a "feel" for the Greek text. For example, John uses "and" [*kai*] frequently, and this is often obscured in modern translations that give priority to conventional *English* expression. Other features I will discuss during the commentary

---

than others. Uncials and minuscules were documents made of parchment produced from animal skins, which are better preserved. Uncials were written in capital letters only. Minuscules were in a stylized lower case.

165. Beale, *Book of Revelation*, 72, n. 9.

166. This summary is based on Koester, *Revelation*, 144–50. For a more detailed and technical survey of the textual evidence, see Aune, *Revelation 1–5*, cxxxiv–clix; Elliott, "Greek Manuscript Heritage." For a discussion of some major variants, see Michaels, *Interpreting the Book of Revelation*, 75–84.

proper. However, use of brackets needs explanation: words in ordinary brackets (. . .) are words added to make sense of the Greek in translation; words in squre brackets [. . .] indicate words added in some other Greek texts.

I consulted two translator's handbooks in my translation: *Linguistic Key to the Greek New Testament* (Fritz Rienecker and Cleon Rogers) and *Revelation: A Handbook on the Greek Text* (David L. Mathewson).

INTERTEXTUALITY: WHAT CONNECTIONS DOES IT MAKE TO OTHER TEXTS?

Revelation is what many commentators call a highly intertextual text, and this has intrigued me for years. Among other things, this means that Revelation is full of references and allusions to the Hebrew Scriptures (the Christian Old Testament),[167] other Jewish literature (such as apocalypses),[168] Greco-Roman literature and mythology,[169] Persian Zorastrian myths,[170] astrology,[171] and early Christian traditions and writings.[172] It also means that understanding these connections is essential for interpreting Revelation well, not so much because they are formal "sources" for John's ideas but because his thinking is influenced by them and his readings of them in turn influence others.[173] "Reader-response" criticism, which focuses on how readers interpret texts rather than the author's intended meaning, also helps explain how John read and used these earlier texts, and suggests that readers of Revelation themselves create new meanings in dialogue with the text.[174]

167. Revelation may possibly contain as many a three-hundred references or allusions to the OT, but no direct quotes, making it harder for the readers or hearers to notice them (cf. Koester, *Revelation*, 123). Moreover, John is not consistent in using any particular OT text (Hebrew or Greek) that we know of, probably because "he often worked from memory rather than from a written text" (Koester, *Revelation*, 124). Cf. Fekkes, *Isaiah and Prophetic Traditions*, 59–103; Beale, *Book of Revelation*, 76–99; Smalley, *Revelation to John*, 8–10; Leithart, *Revelation 1–11*, 4–11; Smalley, *Thunder and Love*, 83–84.

168. Cf. Howard-Brook and Gwyther, *Unveiling Empire*, 75–81. I have noted some of these allusions in the commentary. For a broad discussion of such Jewish literature in relation to Revelation, see Blackwell et al, *Reading Revelation in Context*.

169. For example, several allusions to the myths of Apollo are identified in Edwards, "Rider," 529–36. John's allusions to Greco-Roman and other Gentile mythology are generally either hostile or involve Christian reinterpretation (Friesen, *Imperial Cults*, 170).

170. Cf. Howard-Brook and Gwyther, *Unveiling Empire*, 73–75.

171. Cf. Malina, *Genre and Message*; Huber, *Like a Bride Adorned*, 22–23.

172. On Revelation's use of NT traditions, especially John, see Leithart, *Revelation 1–11*, 20–24. On its allusions to the Synoptic Gospels, see Bauckham, *Climax of Prophecy*, 94–112. Linton claims that "Revelation appears to draw together in one work all of the various parts of the [OT and NT] canon" (Linton, *Intertextuality*, 106).

173. Cf. Waddell, *Spirit of the Book*, 3. For a survey of the origins and development of intertextuality as a concept, see ibid., 40–66.

174. Cf. Waddell, *Spirit of the Book*, 69–70; Johnson, *Pneumatic Discernment*, 5–7; Moyise, *Old Testament in the Book of Revelation*, 18–20, 23, 108–111, 135; Linton, *Intertextuality*, 61. But see Beale, *John's Use of the Old Testament*, 31–32, 37, 39–41.

The Old Testament allusions are not signaled by the phrases often used in, say, Matthew or Paul's letters, such as "as it is written" (Rom 15:9) or "then what was said through the prophet . . . was fulfilled" (Matt 2:17). Beale suggests instead that many such references are noticeable largely because they cause grammatical issues in the Greek text.[175] Many of the allusions are not so much to isolated verses but to clusters of biblical passages[176] or to stories such as the Exodus, whose plague narratives are recalled in each of Revelation's sevenfold disaster sequences.[177] There are also allusions to non-canonical Jewish texts from the Apocrypha (such as Tobit) and apocalyptic books such as 1 Enoch and 4 Ezra. However, I agree with Moloney that "the Hebrew Bible, and not contemporary Jewish or Jewish-Christian apocalypses, forms the essential literary backbone to the Apocalypse."[178]

In other places, Revelation alludes to the combat myth, the multi-cultural story of heavenly conflict found in Greece, Israel, Egypt, and other cultures in different forms.[179] At times, Revelation follows the chronology of a specific ancient text only to abruptly change direction in bewildering ways.[180] Much of the meaning in Revelation depends on the reader recognizing these references, at least in part, and this is where modern readers are often handicapped.

Calling Revelation "intertextual" means that it makes meaning from all these other texts, but also that it changes the meaning of these texts, sometimes in subtle ways, from what their original authors or audience would have understood.[181] Thus it "creates new possibilities of meaning."[182] For example, Beale argues that "John appears to allude to the OT to show how prophecy has been and is being fulfilled in Christ's coming, Pentecost and the creation of the church."[183] Revelation therefore uses allusions to the Old Testament in a deliberate way, conscious of the context of the passages

---

175. Beale, *Book of Revelation*, 101–3; Beale, *John's Use of the Old Testament*, 62–63, 66.

176. Koester, *Revelation*, 125; Beale, *Book of Revelation*, 79. One example is his choice of references from Daniel (cf. Moyise, *Old Testament in the Book of Revelation*, 45–58).

177. Cf. Fekkes, *Isaiah and Prophetic Traditions*, 81–82. Fekkes suggests that John's audience is so "biblically oriented" that "all that is needed are a few key words of an OT passage to trigger associations and remind the hearers of themes and biblical topoi with which they are probably already familiar" (ibid., 287). Cf. Beale, *John's Use of the Old Testament*, 75–79.

178. Moloney, *Apocalypse of John*, 13.

179. Cf. Koester, *Revelation*, 126; Newton, "Story-lines"; Beale, *Book of Revelation*, 86–88; Huber, *Like a Bride Adorned*, 16–21.

180. Koester, *Revelation*, 125.

181. "John is neither a slave to the Old Testament texts nor can he make them mean whatever he wants them to mean" (Moyise, *Old Testament in the Book of Revelation*, 22). This has been a controversial field for scholars, as Smolarz summarizes in *Divine Marriage*, 5–27. In particular, Moyise and Beale debated the extent to which John respected the original authorial intention and context of the OT passages that he used in Revelation (cf. ibid., 19–22; Newton, *Revelation Worldview*, 56–57; Beale, *John's Use of the Old Testament*, 41–49).

182. Koester, *Revelation*, 124. Cf. Smalley, *Revelation to John*, 14; Smalley, *Thunder and Love*, 63–64; Beale, *Book of Revelation*, 97–99; Waddell, *Spirit of the Book*, 3, 39–40, 69.

183. Beale, *Book of Revelation*, 78;

being alluded to, even where he universalizes passages originally about Israel or inverts their application in an ironic manner.[184]

Jan Fekkes concludes that John's use of the OT would be no different than any "non-Christian Jew with messianic and/or nationalistic concerns."[185] I suggest rather, in agreement with Beale,[186] that his Christian commitment governs his use of the OT and other texts. John believes that Jesus Christ has fulfilled the promises to Israel in the OT, and therefore Israel's restoration is being accomplished as promised in the Hebrew prophetic literature. In this commentary, I will pause frequently to draw out the significance of these literary connections for understanding Revelation.

As already noted, Revelation also has an intertextual relationship with other New Testament literature and traditions found in the Gospels. In particular, a neglected intertext for Revelation until recently was the Acts of the Apostles, as I will show.

Intertextuality also helps readers make sense of the arithmetic in Revelation.[187] Revelation is full of numbers and other arithmetical features. It calls its readers to make arithmetical calculations and to notice arithmetical connections; for example, from the relative size of time periods.[188] But John's interest is not really in mathematics as such, even though he may find spiritual significance in numbers as did the ancient Pythagoreans, for whom mathematics was sacred. Rather, the significance of the numbers derives from their use in earlier texts, especially the Hebrew Scriptures.

For example, the significant number seven would bring to the audience's mind the seven days of creation (Genesis 1), seven days in a week (Exod 20:9–10), the sabbatical years (Lev 25:1–7), the strategies of the battle of Jericho (Josh 6:1–20), and the seven visible planets, among other references. They would remember that the seventh item in a series was often special, such as the Sabbath day. Hence seven would bring a sense of completion and possibly of climax (as in the Jericho story). They would also sense a connection with three and a half, not only because it is half of seven (a kind of broken seven),[189] but also because it would remind them of the drought in Elijah's day (1 Kgs 17:1; Luke 4:25; Jas 5:17) and of the period "time, times and half a time" of oppression in Daniel (Dan 7:25; 12:7). So seven has connotations of climax and completion whereas three and a half is more consistently foreboding. I will comment on other numbers at the appropriate places.

Revelation not only refers constantly to other texts but has its own internal literary cross-references that reinforce the plot structure and help the audience recall and

---

184. Beale, *Book of Revelation*, 79–86, 89–96; Beale, *John's Use of the Old Testament*, 67–71. Cf. Bauckham, *Climax of Prophecy*, x–xi; Leithart, *Revelation 1–11*, 16–20; Fekkes, *Isaiah and Prophetic Traditions*, 102.

185. Fekkes, *Isaiah and Prophetic Traditions*, 285.

186. Cf. Beale, *John's Use of the Old Testament*, 45, 126–28.

187. Cf. Beale, *Book of Revelation*, 58–64; Bauckham, *Climax of Prophecy*, 29–37; Resseguie, *Revelation of John*, 28–32; and Paul, *Revelation*, 34–39.

188. Cf. Newton, "Time Language."

189. Cf. Resseguie, *Revelation of John*, 30.

link significant earlier recurrences of a word or phrase. Some of these repetitions mark structural movements, others simply seem to make narrative or theological points. For example, the messages to the seven churches all contain the phrase, "Those who have ears, let them hear what the Spirit is saying to the churches." This language is then left behind until 13:9, when in the middle of the beast narrative, we find, "If anyone has ears, let them hear." The hearer or reader would likely remember the earlier occurrences of this phrasing and ask why it comes again at this point.[190]

RECEPTION: HOW HAS IT BEEN INTERPRETED? WHAT IS IT ABOUT?

Revelation has been with us for at least 1,900 years and has thus been read, considered, interpreted, applied, misused,[191] and debated many times. It has always been a controversial book and was not easily accepted into the emerging canon of the New Testament.[192] I will not attempt a full survey of the reception history of Revelation; readers interested in this can find good accounts in the recent commentaries of Koester[193] and Thomas,[194] and in the monographs by Kovacs and Rowland[195] and Wainwright.[196] Revelation is traditionally the "last" book in the New Testament; not necessarily because it was the last book written, but because it gives us the end of the big story of the Bible, as the allusions to Genesis 1–3 in Revelation 22 signal,[197] and perhaps also because it was one of the last books to be universally recognized as Scripture.

All readers of Revelation ask themselves the question, "What is this about?" Traditionally, there have developed four main schools of thought giving answers to that question.[198]

---

190. Cf. Bauckham, *Climax of Prophecy*, 22–23, 23–29. Perhaps the most important is the varied phrase about "tribes and languages and nations and peoples" (Rev 5:10; 7:9; 10:11; 11:9; 13:7; 14:6; 17:15).

191. Cf. Newton, *Revelation Reclaimed*, 1–25.

192. Cf. Koester, *Revelation*, 35, 38, 40. There were also debates about Revelation in the Reformation period (ibid., 48–51).

193. Koester, *Revelation*, 29–65.

194. Thomas, *Apocalypse*, 51–86.

195. Kovacs and Rowland, *Revelation*.

196. Wainwright, *Mysterious Apocalypse*.

197. Cf. Thomas, *Apocalypse*, 17–20; Newton, *Revelation Worldview*, 256–60.

198. For an insight into how these four approaches work in practice, see the helpful (though limited) comparative approach in Gregg, *Four Views*, and Pate, *Four Views*. The four views represented in these two books are not identical. Gregg includes the Historicist, Preterist, Futurist, and Spiritual views. Pate includes authors representing Preterist, Idealist, Progressive Dispensationalist, and Classical Dispensationalist.

1. Futurist

This is the reading found in most of the popular books today and is the most common understanding found among Pentecostals. There is some evidence of this view in the early church, but it has become much more popular since the nineteenth century after Protestants became disillusioned with historicist postmillennialism.[199] It assumes that Revelation contains largely long-term prediction of events clustered around the second coming of Jesus and the last judgment. According to Futurists, at least Revelation 4 onwards is speaking of events in the future, not just to John, but to us as well. Revelation 1:19 is often taken to be an outline of the book.

Many Futurists are eagerly looking around them for signs of the end, following the example of J. R. Flower, an early U.S. Assemblies of God leader. As World War I was looming in 1914, he wrote, "We are watching every development of the crisis in Europe with the greatest of interest, with our newspapers in one hand and the Bible in the other, checking off each prophecy as it is being fulfilled, knowing of a surety that the coming of the Lord cannot be long delayed."[200]

Some Futurists read Revelation 2–3 (the messages to the seven churches) as predicting the state of the church in seven successive historical periods leading up to the end. Futurists try to read Revelation's language and symbolism as literally as possible with varying success.[201] It is on this basis that they can argue that certain events described in Revelation must still lie in the future because they haven't happened yet.[202] There are two main variants in the Futurist reading:[203]

a. Pretribulationist

Many Futurists (such as Tim LaHaye with his *Left Behind* novels and movies) take Revelation 4:1 as some kind of reference to the "rapture" (see 1 Thess 4:16–17),[204] which they take to be a sudden "catching away" of true believers in Christ followed by the seven-year Great Tribulation (see Rev 7:14) before the public return of Jesus as told in 19:11–21. Thus, the events of Revelation 4–19 are triggered by the rapture, which could happen any time. Since these events haven't yet happened, Revelation's prophecies are clearly unfulfilled. This reading depends, of course on certain assumptions. Pretribulationists assume that the entire book is predictive, that we should interpret the language as literally as possible, and that the rapture event spoken of by

---

199. Cf. Koester, *Revelation*, 59–61.
200. *The Christian Evangel*, 53, August 8, 1914; as quoted in Johnson, *Pneumatic Discernment*, 184.
201. See comments on literal reading in Beale, *Book of Revelation*, 50–55.
202. Cf. Walvoord, *Revelation*, 101; Beale, *Book of Revelation*, 121.
203. Some modern Futurist commentaries include LaHaye, *Revelation Unveiled*, and Walvoord, *The Revelation* (from a dispensationalist perspective), and Ladd, *Revelation of John* (from a non-dispensationalist perspective which also draws on Preterism).
204. Cf. LaHaye, *Revelation Unveiled*, 99.

Paul is distinct from the second coming as a visible event, as described (probably) in Revelation 1:7.

This third assumption was developed by a school of interpretation known as "dispensationalism," which grew up in the nineteenth century. Dispensationalism teaches that each of seven dispensations (ages) in Scripture ends in human failure, triggering a direct divine intervention; hence the current "church age" will also end in a failed church (perhaps like the church in Laodicea, 3:14–22). Then, subsequent to the rapture of the true church, God will turn his attention particularly to ethnic Israel.[205] Exponents of this reading are looking for the rebuilding of the Jewish temple (based on Rev 11:1–2 and 2 Thess 2:4) and the coming of the antichrist figure (based on Rev 13 and 2 Thess 2:3–12). This person is expected to bring a temporary peace in the Middle East (based on Dan 9:27) before turning on the Jews and building his worldwide empire. The exact chronology differs from author to author, and most of it is constructed from Daniel 7–12 as well as Revelation, Ezekiel, and other biblical books.

Pretribulationists point to the fact that the word "church" doesn't occur in Revelation after chapter 3. Hence, they conclude that the church is not present on the earth, though there are clearly Christian believers around, as in 11:8. They draw on promises of exemption from future trial, such as that made to the Philadelphians in 3:10. However, while there are a number of "catchings away" in Revelation (4:1 is the least impressive; but see 11:12, 12:5, and 14:16), none of them seems to be equivalent to Paul's language in 1 Thessalonians 4. Moreover, Paul clearly teaches that "the dead in Christ will rise first" (1 Thess 4:16), which seems to happen no earlier than the "first resurrection" of Revelation 20:4–6, implying that the "rapture" cannot occur earlier than the start of the millennium.

b. Posttribulationist

Not all Futurists are pretribulationists or dispensationalists. Other Futurists accept the assumption that most of Revelation is as yet unfulfilled, that it mainly describes events around the second coming, and that the language should be taken literally and chronologically as far as possible. So they are also looking for a future antichrist and worldwide Great Tribulation before the second coming. But they don't expect the church to witness it from heaven. Rather, the church will participate in these events and suffer in them, though enjoying some protection from God. So for these readers, it is vital to discern what is represented by the beast, the mark of the beast, and the harlot of Revelation 17 since your life might depend on getting this right, as you won't be safely "raptured" first!

The strengths of a Futurist view are obvious. It emphasizes the second coming, which seems to be anticipated frequently in Revelation (1:7; 16:15; 19:11–21; 22:7,

---

205. Cf. Faupel, *Everlasting Gospel*, 96–98.

20), and which clearly has not yet happened. It helps modern readers to focus and anticipate the unfulfilled predictions, and even count them off as they occur. Many Futurists see the establishment of the modern state of Israel as the first in a series of events leading up to the second coming, for example. Also literalism makes reading Revelation apparently simple.

However, there are serious problems with Futurism. Interpretation of Revelation 2–3 is one difficulty. Futurism seems to require the seven message to the churches to be really directed at seven ages of church history, or to seven future churches at the end, which is hardly a literal reading. However, it is necessary if one is going to draw inferences about the future from promises made to the church in ancient Philadelphia (3:10), which doesn't even exist today.

The second problem is the failure of most recent predictions built on a Futurist reading, especially failed antichrist candidates. Third, this reading violates all the normal principles of biblical exegesis since it virtually ignores what the text could have meant to its original audience (and every audience since).[206] Mounce, among others, insists that John has *both* the immediate crisis *and* the eschatological crisis in mind; both the Roman Empire and "an eschatological beast which will sustain the same relationship with the church of the great tribulation."[207] But once we admit more than one situation as John's focus, what justification is there to limit it to just those two events?

Futurism also tends to lead to some very speculative and politically loaded attempts to equate modern realities with Revelation. For example, successive U.S. presidents get put up as putative antichrists whenever they try to bring peace in the Middle East. The ecumenical movement (and World Council of Churches) get regularly labelled as the beginning of an "apostate church" supposedly on the basis of the harlot in Revelation 17. Other international institutions (European Community, United Nations, and others) are also viewed with suspicion as the beginnings of the beast empire. Most of these institutions are seen by such Futurists as flawed, even Satanic, and therefore they must be the enemies John is visualizing; mostly such identifications don't flow from pure exegesis.[208]

There is also a very sectarian Pentecostal form of Futurism which claims that only "Spirit-filled" believers will take part in a pre-Tribulation rapture. Other Christians will have to suffer through it. Not many Pentecostals now hold this view, but it was common in the early days of modern Pentecostalim, sometimes even mixed with ideas about racial distinctives.[209]

Beasley-Murray, himself inclined to a Futurist reading,[210] put it well nearly fifty years ago, when he wrote, "Whoever maintains that the Revelation was written to

206. Cf. Gonzalez, "Revelation," 49–50.
207. Mounce, *Revelation*, 45.
208. Cf. Newton, *Revelation Reclaimed*, 20–24.
209. Cf. Green, "Spirit that Makes Us (Number) One," 400–401.
210. Beasley-Murray, *Revelation*, 31.

satisfy curiosity has not really pondered the book. And he who seeks to compile from it a history-in-advance will be either disappointed or deceived."[211]

2. Historicist

This interpretation also continues to influence popular eschatology, even though almost no scholars and not many popular authors embrace it these days.[212] However, after emerging in the Medieval Age,[213] partly due to the influence of Joachim of Fiore (AD 1132–1202),[214] it had a few centuries of great popularity, being embraced by no less a genius than Isaac Newton, for example. It became the dominant Protestant interpretation of Revelation for about 250 years.[215] It still survives in the Seventh-day Adventist church, the Jehovah's Witnesses, and a lively Australian Pentecostal church called CRC (originally Christian Revival Crusade).[216]

Historicists read Revelation as a more or less chronological account of (mainly western) church and world history from John's day to the second coming and beyond. Since Revelation begins with the first-century church and ends in the future new Jerusalem, this is a logical deduction. But fitting the descriptions of events in Revelation with known history is more difficult. Historicists take almost the opposite line to Futurists: they interpret nearly everything in Revelation as symbolic code which can only be understood as events unfold.

Nevertheless, they find church history not only in Revelation 2–3 but throughout the book. So, for example, the little scroll in Revelation 10 usually signifies the release of the Scriptures in the vernacular languages of western Europe around the Reformation, in the teeth of resistance from the Roman Catholic church.[217] In this school of interpretation, the Great Tribulation is not a short disastrous period immediately before the second coming, but refers to a much longer era, perhaps 1,260 years as Historicists tend to follow the "day-year" principle of biblical interpretation (see Rev 12:6).[218] This era is seen as equivalent to the period of papal dominance over the western Christian church.

Historicists have been prone to use Revelation and Daniel to predict the dates of significant forthcoming prophetic events, with sometimes disastrous consequences.[219] Other unfortunate results have also flowed out of Historicist interpretation. For

---

211. Beasley-Murray, *Revelation*, 23.

212. One recent expression is found in Taylor, *World History*. Mazzaferi spends some time refuting a recent version in Mazaaferi, *Source-Critical Perspective*, 78–84.

213. Cf. Koester, *Revelation*, 44–48.

214. Cf. Huber, *Like a Bride Adorned*, 8–15.

215. Cf. Koester, *Revelation*, 49–55.

216. Cf. Thomas Foster, *Amazing Book of Revelation Explained!*.

217. Cf. Taylor, *World History*, 59–60.

218. Cf. Taylor, *World History*, 61–63.

219. Seventh-day Adventism emerged from the disappointment that followed when a specific

example, in most versions, the popes and the Roman Catholic church get to play the role of the beast of Revelation 13 as well as the harlot of Revelation 17. This might have been understandable in the upheavals of the sixteenth and seventeenth centuries following the Reformation. But unsurprisingly, this reading is not popular with Catholics. Historicism also violates the rules of exegesis by virtually ignoring what the original audience of Revelation might have understood by it, since mostly they contend that the true meaning of John's predictions will only be clear when their fulfilment is imminent.[220]

Moreover, many conflicting Historicist interpretations have arisen; for example, Seventh-day Adventists are looking for very different tribulation events, focused on enforced Sunday observance, than Pentecostals![221] Finally, Historicism focuses largely on the history of the western church, which is less relevant than ever today when most Christians are from the "east" and "south."

3. Preterist

Modern Preterism emerged as a reaction against Protestant Historicism with its focus on anti-papal interpretation.[222] Contemporary Preterist interpreters are trying to follow the rules of exegesis which most scholars accept for interpreting any ancient text. Interpreters should first look at the historical context and try to work out what the original author could have meant, or at least what the original audience might have understood, by the language of the text. Consequently, Preterists read Revelation primarily as a message to the believers of John's own day; specifically, those seven churches in the province of Asia.

Some Preterist readers would go so far as to claim that the whole book is exclusively about, or fulfilled by, events in the ancient world.[223] Most, however, acknowledge that the events described in Revelation 20–22 have not yet happened, but that Revelation 1–19 make a lot of sense if read against the background of the ancient Greco-Roman (and maybe Jewish) world. In either case, the prophetic messages of Revelation 2–3 are addressed to those seven churches just as 1 Corinthians is addressed to the church in that ancient city, though this need not mean it has nothing to say to us today. Gordon Fee once said, "*a text cannot mean* [today] *what it never meant*

---

prediction of the end failed to materialize. Cf. Koester, *Revelation*, 59–60.

220. E.g., Taylor, *World History*, 14–15.

221. Cf. Newton, *Revelation Reclaimed*, 12, 13, 18.

222. Cf. Koester, *Revelation*, 53, 56, 57. Futurist readings were another reaction.

223. E.g., Gentry, "Preterist View"; cf. Caird, *Revelation*, 12. A different way of understanding this has been proposed by the Italian scholar Eugenio Corsini in *The Apocalypse*. He argues that most of Revelation is about the pre-Christian era, leading up to Christ's atoning work as its climax, grounded in a view of realized eschatology similar to that in John's Gospel. A very recent commentary by Francis Moloney expounds a modified version of Corsini's view (*The Apocalypse of John*). This interpretation contains elements of Preterist, Historicist, Idealist, and allegorical readings.

[to its original readers or hearers],"²²⁴ and Preterists apply this principle somewhat consistently in their reading of Revelation. They often insist that the time markers at the beginning and end of Revelation ("soon," "near") should be taken literally.²²⁵

However, there have been several kinds of Preterists, and many recent commentaries explore new readings that fit only loosely within this category:

a. Jerusalem-focused

Writers like Peter Leithart,²²⁶ David Chilton,²²⁷ and Kenneth Gentry²²⁸ see Revelation's predictions and warnings being fulfilled largely in the events surrounding the destruction of the second temple in AD 70.²²⁹ Adopting a reading method a little like Historicists, these Preterists read the language of Revelation 6–19 as referring to the developments in the Roman-Jewish war of AD 66–70, culminating in the temple's destruction. They especially use the writing of the ancient Jewish historian Josephus, who lived through it all, to interpret these chapters. The harlot in Revelation 17 is seen as Jerusalem and some of Jesus' strong words in Matthew 23–24 are brought into play to interpret this chapter as Rome (the beast) turning on the harlot (Jerusalem) and destroying her. This reading tends to depend on an early date for Revelation, probably in the early the 60s before Nero's persecution and definitely before the Jewish revolt in AD 66.²³⁰

b. Rome-focused

Most recent Preterist writing sees ancient Rome, rather than Jerusalem, as John's main target.²³¹ These commentators are less interested in predictive prophecy than the interpreters so far discussed and tend to read Revelation as a quasi-political tirade. John is writing against the oppressive Roman Empire, and the imperial cult in particular, and exhorting believers not to compromise with Greco-Roman values and ways.²³²

---

224. Fee and Stuart, *How to Read the Bible*, 26.

225. Gentry, "Preterist View," 40–45; Leithart, *Revelation 1–11*, 24–26.

226. Leithart, *Revelation 1–11*, 24–43. Leithart calls his view "typological preterism," which looks first for a specific historical referent in John's day before seeing potential valid applications in later centuries (ibid., 14).

227. Chilton, *Days of Vengeance*.

228. Gentry, "Preterist View."

229. See also Smalley, *Revelation to John*, 3.

230. See critique of this in Beale, *Book of Revelation*, 44–45.

231. An interesting variation can be found in Papandrea, *Wedding of the Lamb*, who sees both Jerusalem and Rome as John's "targets." He refers to the destruction of Jerusalem (AD 70), the great persecutions of the Roman Empire until AD 311, and the "conversion" of Constantine in AD 312 as highly significant reference points for Revelation. See tables in ibid., 243–54.

232. Cf. Koester, *Revelation*, 61; Gonzalez, "Revelation," 55–59.

The only significant prediction they would recognize is the destruction of Rome and its empire (Rev 17–18), a prediction that failed to come true, at least in the short term. Even when the Roman Empire fell in the fifth century, its destruction was not as total as Revelation 18 implies, and the eastern empire continued for another millennium.[233] This approach is the most common scholarly way of reading Revelation today, and many of these scholars see John as simply mistaken.

c. Postmodern and rhetorical

Some recent writers take this kind of reading in a more rhetorical direction, focusing on John's agenda and even his "political" struggles with elements of the seven churches represented by the Nicolaitans and Jezebel. David deSilva, for example, points out that "Revelation clearly has a rhetorical agenda. It seeks to persuade seven different Christian communities to take certain specific actions . . . as well as to engender a firm commitment to certain values . . ."[234] In particular, deSilva sees John as persuading his hearers to dissociate themselves from the values of Greco-Roman culture, expressed in the worship of their gods and the imperial cult.[235]

Others seek to consider the text from a (post) modern framework while maintaining basic Preterist assumptions about its original meaning. Hence they may apply the anti-imperial stance of Revelation to modern struggles for liberation or justice.[236] For example, David Rhoads tells us that, "The Book of Revelation offers a passionate critique of the oppressive political, economic, social, and religious realities of the Roman Empire. It also unveils the vision of a world in the making, a vision of justice and peace embodied in a new heaven, a new earth, and a new Jerusalem."[237]

Such readings of Revelation are self-consciously derived from a particular group's experience, so that we have Black, Feminist, Womanist,[238] Asian, Latino, and other particularist readings.[239] For instance, some Feminist critics find John's attitude to female figures disturbing, androcentric, misogynist, and patriarchal, attributable to ancient attitudes that he hadn't shaken off.[240] Others coming from a postmodern literary perspective reject any decoding approach that seeks to "translate" the text into

---

233. Cf. Beale, *Book of Revelation*, 45.

234. deSilva, "Honor Discourse," 79; cf. Jang, "Narrative Function," 186.

235. deSilva, "Honor Discourse."

236. Cf. Koester, *Revelation*, 63–65; Howard-Brook and Gwyther, *Unveiling Empire*; Rhoads, *Every People*; Fiorenza, *Vision of a Just World*, 5, 10–15.

237. Rhoads, *Every People*, 1.

238. Womanist approaches begin with the experience of African-American women.

239. The collection of articles in Rhoads, *Every People*, is a particularly good sample of such readings.

240. Cf. Huber, *Like a Bride Adorned*, 34, 42–43; Pippin, "Heroine and Whore"; Pippin, *Death and Desire*; Fiorenza, *Vision of a Just World*, 13–14.

propositions or discover a single true meaning.²⁴¹ Rhoads, for example, insists that "*every interpretation is a cultural interpretation.*"²⁴² In practice, however, postmodernist readings, like those of their modernist predecessors, tend to impose a twenty-first century western or non-western worldview onto the text of Revelation.²⁴³

4. Idealist or "Spiritual"

This is the hardest interpretation to "pin down" and defend. It refuses to connect Revelation definitively or exclusively with any historical event, past, present or future. While recognizing the historical context as a major feature in interpretation, Idealist readers see the text as equally applicable to any historical period and conveying spiritual insights behind the evident historical details,²⁴⁴ thus taking "apocalyptic" very broadly as a revelation of unseen forces that affect the Christian church in all times and places.²⁴⁵ So the beast(s) of Revelation 13 do not just refer to Nero or ancient Rome, or to the papacy, or to a future antichrist figure, though all these might be legitimate applications, but to the spiritual principle or force behind them.

Thus, for example, William Hendriksen argues that "the seals, trumpets, bowls, and similar pictures, refer not to specific events or details of history, but to principles that are operating throughout the history of the world, especially throughout the new dispensation."²⁴⁶ The strength of this interpretation is that it makes Revelation always relevant, able to be used as a kind of interpretive "template" for world affairs. As Leithart (not an Idealist himself) says, "Christians *should* use the Scriptures as a lens through which to sort out and evaluate the world around them."²⁴⁷ However, Leithart argues that Idealism "is not . . . consistent with the way biblical poetry works" in that it always has a definite historical referent.²⁴⁸ This is the main weakness of Idealism in its purest form: it plays down the references to ancient Rome and the future of the world and the second coming.²⁴⁹

---

241. Cf. Huber, *Like a Bride Adorned*, 33; Fiorenza, *Vision of a Just World*, 15–20. I have discussed postmodern interpretations in *Revelation Worldview*, 54–61.

242. Rhoads, *Every People*, 4 (emphasis in the original).

243. I argued this in *Revelation Worldview*, 53, 58–61.

244. E.g., Hamstra urges that in the seals section "the symbols represent forces that have been with us all the time" (Hamstra, "Idealist View," 105). Caird argues that it is misleading to say Revelation is about Rome: "because John has couched his message in the language of myth, what he is saying is universal in its application" (Caird, *Revelation*, xii). Cf. Hendriksen, *More Than Conquerors*, 9–10.

245. Cf. Hamstra, "Idealist View," 128–30.

246. Hendriksen, *More Than Conquerors*, 41.

247. Leithart, *Revelation 1–11*, 3; cf. Hendriksen, *More Than Conquerors*, 34–35. Or as Gonzalez suggests, "we read it as depicting a pattern of the way God relates with God's people" (Gonzalez, "Revelation," 51).

248. Leithart, *Revelation 1–11*, 12.

249. Hence Hendriksen is not consistent in his reading, frequently identifying passages in Revelation as more about the very end than principles of all periods (e.g., Hendriksen, *More Than*

However, a modified, historically conscious, less pure, Idealist reading may unpack the message of Revelation best for readers today, as well as the original audience.[250] As Smalley argues, the visions "carry throughout a double reference: their immediate and historical application, indeed, makes possible an interpretation beyond history."[251] Or as Papandrea argues, Revelation " . . . was a book for the here and now in the first century and it remains a book for the here and now in the twenty-first century, as long as we interpret it correctly."[252] This modified Idealist reading would also need to place Revelation within the overall schema of salvation history[253] as befits a book which in its final chapters constantly refers back to themes from the early chapters of Genesis.

A popular variant on the Idealist interpretation during the post-apostolic era was an *allegorical* reading. This reading disconnects Revelation from history much more strongly by making all events in the text "stand for" spiritual realities in the individual believer's life or the new covenant. One example is the oldest commentary on Revelation still extant, by Victorinus of Pettau and written perhaps around AD 260–270.[254] Such readings make Revelation something like Bunyan's famous *Pilgrim's Progress*. For example, the beast(s) represent spiritual struggles that believers face as they move through life towards heaven, represented by the new Jerusalem.[255]

Pentecostals have tended to read Revelation through Futurist "glasses," though sometimes taking Historicist views on board. This is partly due to dispensationalist influence, but it has more to do with the expectation of the first modern Pentecostals of an imminent return of Christ following the "latter rain" of the Holy Spirit. However, dispensationalism has proved difficult to accommodate within a Pentecostal worldview because of its negative expectations regarding the church, its hostility to spiritual gifts today, and its rejection of Pentecostal expectations of restoration of the church to its original purity and power. Hence, many Pentecostal scholars are now trying to de-dispensationalize Pentecostal eschatology and interpretation of Revelation.[256] Nevertheless, some aspects of Futurism (especially the hope of the second coming and a

---

Conquerors, 130–31, 157–59).

250. Cf. Smalley, *Revelation to John*, 14–19. Smalley's interpretation is heavily influenced by his assumptions about the authorship of Revelation and its place in the Johannine collection as the first book by John the apostle. Another version of this reading can be found in Beale, *Book of Revelation*, 48–49, 145–50. A simpler explanation along these lines can be found in Strelan, *Where Earth Meets Heaven*, 8–20.

251. Smalley, *Thunder and Love*, 59. Cf. Hendriksen, *More Than Conquerors*, 44–45.

252. Papandrea, *Wedding of the Lamb*, 213.

253. Cf. Smalley, *Thunder and Love*, 150–52, 180.

254. Victorinus, *Commentary*, ANF 7:344–60.

255. Cf. Koester, *Revelation*, 33–35, 37–38, 231–32; Lupieri, *Commentary*, 2, 3, 13.

256. E.g., Althouse, *Spirit of the Last Days*.

future millennium) remain key features of many Pentecostal readings.[257] It is true that there are clear future elements in Revelation, especially the last judgement (20:11–15) and the final *Parousia*, but in general I don't find Futurism convincing.

So what is Revelation about, then? Putting together the insights provided by the major interpretations just discussed and the intertextual features of Revelation, I see three major answers:

1. Revelation is first *a message for the first-century church, applicable to the church ever since*, encouraging it to committed discipleship and vigorous witness to all nations in the context of impending trouble. The text specifically says it is for seven specific first-century churches, but as part of the canon of the New Testament it is clearly seen as having application in succeeding centuries and wider geographical areas. As William Hendriksen put it, "A sound interpretation of the Apocalypse must take as its starting-point the position that the book was intended for believers living in John's day and age," but "this book was intended *not only* for those who first read it, but for all believers throughout this entire dispensation."[258]

2. Revelation is about the *fulfillment of prophecy* from the Old Testament in the new era released by the life, death, resurrection, and ascension of Jesus Christ. Or more specifically, it is about the fulfillment of the promises made concerning *the restoration of Israel*, sometimes referred to as the "new exodus" by commentators on Isaiah and a major concern of Daniel (see Dan 9, particularly). This is seen especially in Revelation's use of Daniel, Isaiah, Ezekiel, Zechariah, and other Old Testament prophetic literature, but specifically in references to the Exodus story. Revelation contains clear allusions to the blood of the (Passover) Lamb, the plagues on Egypt, persecution of God's people, incidents from Israel's journey to the promised land (e.g., Balaam), and the call to come out from Babylon. Especially, the last chapters draw on hopes in the prophets of a restored and glorious Jerusalem as a kind of world capital. Resseguie calls all this a "masterplot."[259]

3. Revelation is about *the completion of God's redemptive project for the whole world* released by the atoning work of Christ, carried forward by the mission of the church in the power of the Holy Spirit, and climaxing in Jesus' second coming and the restoration of all things (Acts 3:21). This is especially clear from the sealed scroll crisis and the scope of Christ's redemption (5:9), subsequent universalist statements (7:9; 15:4), and, of course, the ending of the story (21:1–22:5). Revelation unifies these two hopes.[260] This does not mean that Revelation expects total

---

257. Cf. Horton, *Ultimate Victory*, 18–21. Like most Futurists, Horton places a lot of emphasis on literal interpretation.

258. Hendriksen, *More Than Conquerors*, 10 (emphasis in the original).

259. Resseguie, *Narrative Commentary*, 17; cf. Howard-Brook and Gwyther, *Unveiling Empire*, xxiii.

260. Pattemore, *People of God*, 199.

universalism in terms of salvation, but it does expect a future world in which everyone serves and worships the one true God and his Messiah.[261]

PERSPECTIVE: WHAT MIGHT A PENTECOSTAL READING CONTRIBUTE?

Pentecostals have been preaching and writing about Revelation for years. However, this discussion has become a whole lot more sophisticated in recent years as a new generation of Pentecostal scholars has emerged. These scholars are able to tackle the hard exegetical and hermeneutical issues and engage confidently with the best scholarship on this important text. In this section, I will survey some recent scholarly Pentecostal writing on Revelation and then propose what I believe are distinctive features of an authentic Pentecostal reading of Revelation.

Clearly a lot of this discussion will depend on the definition of "Pentecostal." This has been debated quite a lot recently[262] and perhaps there will never be a consensus. Here I operate with a twofold definition. First, Pentecostals are all those Christians who actively seek to experience the Holy Spirit's work released on the day of Pentecost and described especially in Acts, even though their specific positions on Spirit baptism, tongues, and eschatology may vary. Second, a Pentecostal *perspective* is one informed primarily by the release of the Spirit at Pentecost and its results as seen in Acts and the rest of the New Testament.[263]

I begin with a survey of recent scholarly Pentecostal works on Revelation, (largely) in chronological order of publication. I will limit this survey to book length treatments of a scholarly nature published since 2000.[264]

---

261. I am following a position between those who play up the universalist language to imply complete universalism (e.g., Bauckham) and those who play it down (e.g., Beale). For example, Herms argues that "universal language does not necessarily presuppose universal salvation; rather, it serves to vindicate the faithful community, and validate their present circumstances in light of a future reversal" (Herms, *Apocalypse for the Church*, 260). This seems to play the language down too much.

262. Some of the authors I am considering offer these definitions or descriptions: a movement born "at the beginning of the twentieth century" consisting largely of marginalized, non-white members with a theology focused on "the major tents of the so-called 'full gospel'" (Waddell, *Spirit of the Book*, 103, 107); a movement whose "theological heart" is the "fivefold gospel" (Thomas and Macchia, *Revelation*, xv); "a global movement whose adherents now number in the hundreds of millions" and which is so diverse that "Pentecostal*isms*" is a better label (Archer, *Worship in the Apocalypse*, 39, 45). Cf. Anderson, *Introduction to Pentecostalism*, 1, 9–14; Althouse, *Spirit of the Last Days*, 12.

263. Cf. Keener, *Spirit Hermeneutics*, 3–4.

264. This excludes two influential commentaries published before 2000, those by Stanley M. Horton (1991) and Hollis Gause (1983). Horton follows a modified dispensational view of Revelation whereas Gause's exposition "was written from the perspective of historic premillennialism . . . and against a dispensational view" (K. Alexander, "Under the Authority of the Word," 8). I also omit Ronald Herms' impressive monograph, *An Apocalypse for the Church and for the World: The Narrative Function of Universal Language in the Book of Revelation,* and Philip Mayo's impressive monograph, *"Those Who Call Themselves Jews": The Church and Judaism in the Apocalypse of John,* because they

INTRODUCTION

Craig S. Keener's contribution to the NIV Application Commentary on Revelation[265] explores the original meaning of the text before discussing "bridging contexts" and "contemporary significance" at length. He signals early on that he is breaking out from populist readings of Revelation common among Pentecostals (especially those based on dispensationalism).[266] Instead, he moves towards a broad-based scholarly reading[267] that involves "focusing on the ancient rather than modern background for understanding the book,"[268] a less than "literal" interpretation of Revelation's language,[269] and avoidance of predictions based on Revelation and other parts of the Bible.[270] He rarely refers to Pentecostalism, and infrequently to the Holy Spirit,[271] but presents a strong affirmation of healings, miracles, and prophetic gifts for the whole Christian era.[272] On the issue of the millennium, he argues for a broad premillennial (but posttribulationist) view.[273]

From an explicitly Pentecostal series comes *Rebecca Skaggs* and *Priscilla Benham's* commentary.[274] The editor's Preface sets out the "distinctively Pentecostal perspective"[275] of this series, which the editor[276] defines largely in theological terms of the "fivefold Gospel: Jesus as Savior, Sanctifier, Holy Spirit Baptizer, Healer, and Coming King."[277] However, the Pentecostal perspective in this commentary lies more in a broad attachment to common classical Pentecostal approaches to Revelation: the imminence of the second coming,[278] a futurist reading,[279] including a future Tribula-

---

are not overtly Pentecostal. However, both books are cited, and their arguments discussed at several points below. I also omit Kevin J. Conner's mammoth *Book of Revelation (An Exposition)* because, although it contributes to a (somewhat idiosyncratic) Pentecostal reading, it doesn't engage with contemporary scholarship. I omit several shorter (but serious) books by Pentecostal authors for similar reasons. For a broader survey of Australian and New Zealand Pentecostal readings of Revelation, see Newton, "Patmos and Southland."

265. Keener, *Revelation*.
266. Keener, *Revelation*, 166–67, 388–89.
267. Keener, *Revelation*, 15, 21.
268. Keener, *Revelation*, 21.
269. Keener, *Revelation*, 22–23, 30.
270. Keener, *Revelation*, 23–27.
271. Keener, *Revelation*, 84, 460, 507, 517, and no mention in the index.
272. E.g., Keener, *Revelation*, 57, 301–302, 357, 519. This is an ongoing focus for Keener. Cf. Keener, *Spirit Hermeneutics*, 5.
273. Keener, *Revelation*, 463–82 (on premillennialism), and 153–54, 177–79, 327, 359–60, 388–89 (on the Tribulation).
274. Skaggs and Benham, *Revelation*. The authors are twins. The commentary was begun by Benham and completed by Skaggs after Benham's death.
275. Skaggs and Benham, *Revelation*, vii.
276. John Christopher Thomas.
277. Skaggs and Benham, *Revelation*, viii.
278. Skaggs and Benham, *Revelation*, 20, 104, 231–32.
279. Skaggs and Benham, *Revelation*, 59, 66, 11, 113, 116, 128, 137–39.

tion (and perhaps a pretribulation rapture), a quasi-dispensationalist differentiation between Israel and the church, and premillennialism.[280] The authors also toy with a "literal" interpretation.[281] Pentecostalism is also reflected in attention to the Holy Spirit[282] and especially a focus on worship in Revelation.[283] Importantly, the commentary asserts that "the Spirit will continue working through his prophets and bond-servants to bring about God's plan for the future of the world."[284]

Robby Waddell's monograph[285] concentrates largely on the role of the Holy Spirit in Revelation, obviously a key concern for Pentecostals. Perhaps his most important contribution to a Pentecostal reading of Revelation, however, is his development of a "Pentecostal hermeneutic" for this text.[286] He argues that such a reading must be Spirit-led[287] and must acknowledge "the context of the community"[288] and "what God is presently saying through the scriptures."[289] He proposes "an explicit theological hermeneutic" in order to "produce a Pentecostal reading of a text."[290] Such a reading will approach the text using a Pentecostal eschatology that includes "an apocalyptic expectation that the *Parousia* is imminent"[291] and the fivefold "full gospel," which includes "the pre-millennial return of Christ."[292] It will seek to engage the imagination and to encounter the living God by the Spirit;[293] this in turn requires "an open heart" instead of a "hermeneutic of suspicion."[294]

Such a reading of Revelation will use experience as a guide to interpretation, especially when considering John's "description of his experience."[295] Finally, Waddell advocates intertextuality as a theory that helps construct a coherent Pentecostal reading.[296] This particularly helps him wrestle with Revelation 10–11, during which discus-

---

280. Skaggs and Benham, *Revelation*, 49–50, 90–93, 113, 121, 129, 131–33, 158, 205–9. However, the commentary is sceptical about such dispensationalist details as the reinstatement of the OT sacrificial system (ibid., 208).

281. E.g., Skaggs and Benham, *Revelation*, 111–13, 213.

282. Skaggs and Benham, *Revelation*, 18, 21, 22, 27, 63, 227, 230, 235.

283. Skaggs and Benham, *Revelation*, 15–16, 60–66, 73–74.

284. Skaggs and Benham, *Revelation*, 230.

285. Waddell, *Spirit of the Book*.

286. Waddell, *Spirit of the Book*, 97–118, 122–31.

287. Waddell, *Spirit of the Book*, 88–90, where he unpacks five key features of such interpretation.

288. Waddell, *Spirit of the Book*, 58, 86, 98.

289. Waddell, *Spirit of the Book*, 98, 118, 127.

290. Waddell, *Spirit of the Book*, 101. See also 102, 109–12, 122.

291. Waddell, *Spirit of the Book*, 106.

292. Waddell, *Spirit of the Book*, 107.

293. Waddell, *Spirit of the Book*, 111, 117, 128.

294. Waddell, *Spirit of the Book*, 118.

295. Waddell, *Spirit of the Book*, 89, 123, 128. Waddell stresses the reality of this vision (ibid., 77, 85–86).

296. Waddell, *Spirit of the Book*, 131.

sion he claims that the mighty angel of Revelation 10 represents the Holy Spirit[297] and that the episode of the two witnesses (Revelation 11) represents the Spirit-empowered prophetic witness of the church.[298]

One of the most famous scholars in modern Pentecostalism, *Gordon D. Fee*, issued a commentary on Revelation in 2011.[299] This commentary makes no claim to be Pentecostal; rather, in the Preface, Fee tells readers that his concerns are exegetical, theological, and doxological.[300] Nonetheless, his conviction that in John's mind, the Spirit has "come to be with God's people until the End"[301] is central to his reading. Fee follows the scholarly consensus view of Revelation on most points, disavows any focus on the second coming,[302] and contends that John is not interested in time periods like a literal tribulation period[303] or a literal millennium.[304]

John Christopher Thomas has recently authored two commentaries on Revelation, one by himself[305] and the other in collaboration with Frank D. Macchia.[306] The co-authored commentary begins by affirming the five-fold gospel and acknowledging the problems with a lot of popular Pentecostal eschatology of the later twentieth century.[307] The commentary is not overtly Pentecostal; rather, the discussion sticks closely to the text as original readers would have heard it, especially if they were familiar with the Johannine texts of the New Testament.[308] Nevertheless, the commentary contains references to modern Pentecostal experience as a factor in interpreting what John is experiencing,[309] a repeated emphasis on "pneumatic interpretation" or "discernment" of the text,[310] and a focus on Revelation as early Christian prophecy for a prophetic community.[311]

The authors advocate an acceptance of John's visionary experience(s) (as opposed to seeing him as a skillful exegete of the Old Testament, for example)[312] and make frequent references to the Holy Spirit. For example, they speak of a "more

297. Waddell, *Spirit of the Book*, 156–60.
298. Waddell, *Spirit of the Book*, 162–91.
299. Fee, *Revelation*.
300. Fee, *Revelation*, ix–x.
301. Fee, *Revelation*, xiii.
302. Fee, *Revelation*, 65
303. Fee, *Revelation*, 113–14.
304. Fee, *Revelation*, 270, 282–85.
305. Thomas, *Apocalypse*. I reviewed this commentary in *Australian Biblical Review* 62 (2014) 94–96.
306. Thomas and Macchia, *Revelation*.
307. Thomas and Macchia, *Revelation*, xv.
308. Cf. Thomas and Macchia, *Revelation*, 16, 39–40, 75.
309. E.g., Thomas and Macchia, *Revelation*, 39.
310. E.g., Thomas and Macchia, *Revelation*, 37, 84, 92, 135, 205, 487, and many other places.
311. Thomas and Macchia, *Revelation*, 8–10, 20–21, 36–38.
312. Thomas and Macchia, *Revelation*, 38–39.

full-blown prophetic pneumatology in Revelation" than is found in the Fourth Gospel and 1 John,[313] argue for the Holy Spirit as the referent of "the seven spirits" in Revelation 1:4, 3:1, 4:5, and 5:6,[314] and emphasize the Spirit as the origin of the vision.[315]

A Pentecostal emphasis on the Spirit empowering the church as a prophetic community to bear a convincing witness to the world is found, or implied, in many places in the commentary.[316] Thomas and Macchia's interpretation of the eschatological teaching of Revelation follows classic Pentecostal lines to some degree, affirming the future hope of the imminent second coming[317] and arguing for a premillennial position without explicitly discussing alternative views,[318] but rejecting a preoccupation with "future 'end-time events.'"[319] In the second part of the book, Macchia asserts that "In Revelation, God has made the vindication and fulfillment of the divine claim to creation dependent on the missions of the Son and the Spirit."[320]

Melissa Archer wrote a groundbreaking contribution to the study of Revelation and Pentecostal worship published in 2015.[321] Archer sets up a Pentecostal reading strategy for examining worship in Revelation[322] and surveys references to the Apocalypse in early North American Pentecostal literature on worship.[323] This is followed by a lengthy narrative exploration of worship in Revelation[324] on the basis of which she discusses a Pentecostal theology and practice of worship.[325]

Archer includes a discussion of Pentecostal hermeneutics—emphasizing issues such as the role of the community and the Spirit in interpretation.[326] Her hermeneutical apprach also draws on narrative criticism, since Pentecostals tend to read the Bible mainly as story and "the Apocalypse is a narrative,"[327] as well as a liturgical text in which "worship becomes a proleptic experience where the future breaks into the

---

313. Thomas and Macchia, *Revelation*, 16.

314. Thomas and Macchia, *Revelation*, 76, 139, 148–49.

315. Thomas and Macchia, *Revelation*, 38, 80, 92–93, 374

316. E.g., Thomas and Macchia, *Revelation*, 336–37 (discussing Rev 19:10), 392, 400. See also the theological discussion in pages 494–96.

317. Thomas and Macchia, *Revelation*, 78, 91, 123, 286, 338, 392, 395, 402, 586. The question of delay in the second coming is discussed by Macchia on pages 618–20.

318. Thomas and Macchia, *Revelation*, 354–56, 591, 618, 619.

319. Thomas and Macchia, *Revelation*, 590.

320. Thomas and Macchia, *Revelation*, 585.

321. Archer, *Worship in the Apocalypse*

322. Archer, *Worship in the Apocalypse*, 38–67.

323. Archer, *Worship in the Apocalypse*, 68–118.

324. Archer, *Worship in the Apocalypse*, 119–294.

325. Archer, *Worship in the Apocalypse*, 295–332.

326. "Pentecostals read their Bible with an eye towards the whole; that is, the Old and New Testaments are viewed as a single story" (Archer, *Worship in the Apocalypse*, 46; see also ibid., 47–54).

327. Archer, *Worship in the Apocalypse*, 61.

present."³²⁸ The worship scenes in heaven are seen as a model for earthly liturgy: "What the heavenly hosts sing, the churches are to sing."³²⁹ Much of modern Pentecostalism is vindicated and supported in her analysis and her conclusion is that a Pentecostal reading of Revelation will of necessity focus on its worship.³³⁰

Another monograph that is strongly informed by early Pentecostal literature is David R. Johnson's *Pneumatic Discernment in the Apocalypse*. Johnson's work, as the title implies, concentrates on examining one particular theme in Revelation which, following Thomas, he calls "pneumatic discernment." Johnson seeks to define a Pentecostal hermeneutic grounded in *Wirkungsgeschichte*, a kind of reception history³³¹ that focuses primarily on early modern Pentecostalism, especially in North America,³³² and governed by "the hermeneutical triad: Spirit, Scripture, and community" first postulated by J. C. Thomas (but now common among many Pentecostal thinkers).³³³

Johnson reviews scholarly work on pneumatology and pneumatic discernment in the Apocalypse³³⁴ before surveying in detail these themes in the literature of early North American "Wesleyan-Holiness"³³⁵ and "Finished Work"³³⁶ Pentecostalism. He then examines the relevant passages in Revelation itself³³⁷ before drawing significant conclusions about "Pneumatic Discernment, the Apocalypse, and Pentecostal Theology."³³⁸

In summary, what we learn from this survey is that there is indeed a move towards a distinctively Pentecostal reading of Revelation,³³⁹ characterized by these features:

- Concentration on the final form of the text (Waddell, Archer).

- Sympathetic approach. John's claims are accepted, and his authority as an apostle or true prophet is respected (Keener, Waddell).

- Acceptance of John's visionary experience as a literal event rather than as an authorial construction (Waddell, Thomas and Macchia).

- A place for experience in interpretation (Archer, Waddell, Thomas and Macchia).

---

328. Archer, *Worship in the Apocalypse*, 141

329. Archer, *Worship in the Apocalypse*, 181.

330. Archer, *Worship in the Apocalypse*, 37.

331. Johnson, *Pneumatic Discernment*, 24–27.

332. Johnson, *Pneumatic Discernment*, 9, 23. However, he explains that not only early Pentecostalism but the "church catholic" and recent scholarship must also be listened to (ibid., 27–34).

333. Johnson, *Pneumatic Discernment*, 19–22.

334. Johnson, *Pneumatic Discernment*, 50–100.

335. Johnson, *Pneumatic Discernment*, 101–56.

336. Johnson, *Pneumatic Discernment*, 157–92.

337. Johnson, *Pneumatic Discernment*, 193–346.

338. Johnson, *Pneumatic Discernment*, 347–90.

339. Cf. McQueen, *Toward a Pentecostal Eschatology*.

- A strong role for the Pentecostal community, including early Pentecostalism, in interpretation (Waddell, Archer, and Johnson).
- The fivefold gospel as a prism for interpretation (Skaggs and Benham, Waddell, Thomas and Macchia).
- Search for vindication of Pentecostal practices and experiences, including Pentecostal worship (Keener, Skaggs and Benham, Archer).
- Stress on the role of the Holy Spirit in Revelation and in the interpretation of Revelation (Skaggs and Benham, Waddell, Thomas, Johnson, and Macchia).
- Emphasis on Spirit-empowered prophetic witness and mission (Waddell, Thomas and Macchia).
- Immediate application (Waddell and Archer).
- Futurist reading (Skaggs and Benham and Thomas).
- Premillennial position (Keener, Skaggs and Benham, Waddell, Thomas and Macchia, but not Fee).
- Embrace of intertextuality in relation to the use of the Old Testament in Revelation (Waddell and Johnson).

However, there has been little or no discussion of the relevance of concepts like the fivefold gospel,[340] restorationism, and the "latter rain."[341] More importantly, the significance of Pentecost itself as an eschatological event has not been explored much, though Larry McQueen comments, "In the light of the Spirit's role in the book of Revelation, the outpouring of the Spirit on the day of Pentecost (Acts 2.33) marks the beginning of the Spirit's special mission as the seven horns and seven eyes of the Lamb, 'sent forth into all the earth (Rev.5.6)."[342]

Moreover, I think common Pentecostal assumptions about the future fulfillment of Revelation and premillennialism deserve to be examined more critically by Pentecostal scholars. Nearly all classical Pentecostal denominations are officially premillennial and nearly all the scholarly works surveyed here support that view.[343] But I would argue that there is no theological necessity for this connection: the hope for the "latter rain" may sit equally well, if not better, with an amillennial or even postmillennial reading of Revelation.[344]

---

340. McQueen attempts to bring the fivefold gospel into dialogue with Pentecostal *eschatology* (McQueen, *Pentecostal Eschatology*, 214–84). This includes substantial discussion of Revelation, especially Revelation 21–22. See also Newton, "Full Gospel and Apocalypse."

341. Cf. Althouse, *Spirit of the Last Days*, 16–21.

342. McQueen, *Pentecostal Eschatology*, 245.

343. Cf. Faupel, *Everlasting Gospel*; Waddell, *Spirit of the Book*, 106; Althouse, *Spirit of the Last Days*, 1, 11, 16–17.

344. See discussion in Althouse, *Spirit of the Last Days*, 59–60. A recent article (Isgrigg, "The Latter Rain Revisited") explores the origins of the "latter rain" metaphor in the developing premillennial

Bringing together the useful work done by the scholars I have surveyed and focusing on some points that need more emphasis, I want to propose the following as distinctive features of a Pentecostal reading of Revelation.

First, a Pentecostal reading will be *sympathetic and literal* in the sense that Pentecostals believe that John is telling the truth. In other words, he really did have the visionary experiences he recounts in the text,[345] and he was inspired by the Holy Spirit as he constructed his narrative. It will largely avoid the suspicious readings found in some recent critical work that sees John as shaping his vision narrative in order to win an internal political battle in the seven churches or as motivated by intense envy of Rome and the pagan world generally.[346]

Pentecostal readers will assume that John, whoever he was,[347] was a true prophet of God with an authentic message for the church then and now. Pentecostal experience also allows Pentecostals to read Revelation in the light of recent stories of supernatural dreams, visions, and prophetic words.[348] A literal reading, however, is not literalistic:[349] it does not try to interpret the imagery as representing literal historical events (either current or imminent), as found in the worst populist interpretations of the text. And a sympathetic reading will still acknowledge the human element of the text and give attention to the rhetorical strategies of Revelation in relation to its historical context.[350]

Second, a Pentecostal reading will give *strong attention to the role and work of the Holy Spirit*, as all the Pentecostal scholars discussed earlier do. It will especially highlight the work of the Spirit in empowering the church for mission and witness and supernatural manifestations. In this way, Pentecostal readers will read Revelation in the light of Acts (and *vice versa*). Pentecostals will give strong attention to the role of the Spirit in creating *and interpreting* the text of Revelation. They will tend to see Revelation as a paradigmatic example of early Christian prophecy and perhaps in some respects as a model for contemporary Christian prophesying.[351]

---

context of the nineteenth century.

345. Cf. Beale, *Book of Revelation*, 80–81.

346. Some examples of this suspicious approach to Revelation include Royalty, *Streets of Heaven*; Pippin, *Death and Desire*; Fiorenza, "Reading the Apocalypse Theologically," 1–20; Carey, "Ambiguous Ethos," 163–80.

347. The authors I have been examining are not strongly committed to a particular view on this.

348. Cf. Keener, *Spirit Hermeneutics*, 6; Johnson, *Pneumatic Discernment*, 171–72.

349. The concept of "literal" interpretation is quite slippery and has been misused frequently by dispensationalists and others. Pentecostals sometimes speak of interpreting Scripture literally when what they really mean is that they apply passages directly to themselves with no consciousness of different horizons. With respect to Revelation, I would affirm that what John says he saw faithfully reflects what he actually saw, but what it means, to what it refers, and how it can be applied, are different issues. Cf. Beale, *Book of Revelation*, 50–57.

350. On the rhetorical aspects of Revelation, see deSilva, *Seeing Things John's Way*.

351. I argued for this previously in "The Scope of Christian Prophecy" and in the section on genre in this Introduction.

Third, a Pentecostal reading will also be shaped with *reference to the fivefold (or fourfold) "full" gospel*.[352] While Pentecostals should not try to force the text into some kind of Pentecostal doctrinal mold, they should look for genuine references to Jesus as Savior, Sanctifier, Healer, Baptizer in the Spirit, and Coming King. Pentecostal readers should allow such passages in Revelation also to shape and modify their understanding of these full gospel emphases.[353] In spite of my reservations about the pride of place given by some of the authors surveyed above to the literature of early North American Pentecostalism based on the theory of *Wirkungsgeschichte*, these five points remain a significant "touchstone" of Pentecostal thinking.

Fourth, a Pentecostal reading will focus on *Pentecost itself and its implications* for the program of God in the world, including the church's Spirit-empowered mission.[354] As Amos Yong suggests, we are looking for a "Post-Pentecost-al" hermeneutic based not so much on modern classical Pentecostalism as on the Day of Pentecost and its outworking ever since in Christian history.[355] Hence, as McQueen argues, a narrative-canonical reading of the Johannine literature invites the reader to view the book of Revelation as a kind of Johannine "Book of Acts," according to which the age of the Spirit is an age of missional enablement and accomplishment that is characterized by the faithful witness of Jesus in the context of severe conflict with principalities and powers.[356]

A Pentecostal reading will therefore be optimistic about the triumph of God's plan based on the Spirit's powerful work today and reject a dispensationalist pessimism about the church and an escapist rapture doctrine.[357] It will be influenced by the restorationism found in early modern Pentecostalism, which looked for a powerful and lively renewed Christianity as part of the "latter rain" of the Spirit. While some of the exegesis of this idea by the early Pentecostals may have been faulty,[358] we are now seeing much of what they hoped for, especially in the "global south."[359] As Macchia puts it,

> The goal of the church is not to escape the earth in a flight to heaven but to prepare for the coming of heaven to earth, or to provide a witness in the here and now to God's coming reign. The liberating reign of God is already foreshadowed in the church but will one day be brought to earth to a significant degree *through the church's prophetic witness*.[360]

---

352. Whether it is "fourfold" or "fivefold" depends on whether or not sanctification is included.
353. I have put forward some suggestions on these issues in Newton, "Full Gospel and Apocalypse."
354. Cf. Keener, *Spirit Hermeneutics*, 39, 43.
355. Yong, "Science, Sighs, and Signs."
356. McQueen, *Pentecostal Eschatology*, 245. Something similar is said in Leithart, *Revelation 1–11*, 20.
357. Cf. Althouse, *Spirit of the Last Days*, xii, 23–25.
358. Cf. Keener, *Spirit Hermeneutics*, 49–54.
359. Cf. Keener, *Spirit Hermeneutics*, 27–28.
360. Thomas and Macchia, *Revelation*, 509. Emphasis added.

This insight will tend to modify the premillennialism of most Pentecostal readers.

Fifth, a Pentecostal reading of Revelation will be *pragmatic* in the sense of being oriented to practical application in the here and now. Pentecostal readers should, of course, read the text responsibly in the light of its historical context. But they will not be satisfied that a historical-critical reading is sufficient to explain what Revelation is about. Revelation is inspired Scripture that must be allowed to speak to the church today. Pentecostal readers will insist on seeing themselves in almost every part of the text *in this life*, without looking for literal fulfillments based on some kind of "newspaper exegesis." They will read devotionally, prayerfully, and experientially,[361] as worshippers, not just academically or speculatively, as Christians should do with all of Scripture.

Sixth, a Pentecostal reading will highlight the *praise and worship* (liturgical) features and message in Revelation. Archer's book shows the way here.

Seventh, a Pentecostal reading for these days will engage in a *fruitful dialogue with other kinds of readings* rather than taking an isolationist tack. Fee and Waddell have modeled this in their interaction with evangelical and postmodernist commentators, respectively. For example, Pentecostal readers are naturally intertextual and tend naturally to interpret the Bible as narrative since their founding beliefs were drawn from the narrative of Acts. A narrative approach to Revelation can thus easily be appropriated by Pentecostal interpreters.[362] Pentecostal scholarship is also increasingly ecumenical in the sense of interacting with thinking in the wider Christian and academic community.

And eighth, a Pentecostal reading will be *eschatological* in nature. Not necessarily Futurist or premillennialist, but with an eye to the future and the second coming of Jesus. This was often expressed in early Pentecostalism with the confession of the "imminent" or "soon" return of Jesus after the final "latter rain." While events did not work out quite as they hoped or expected, their focus on the second coming was not faulty in itself. Whatever reading of Revelation Pentecostals adopt and whatever eschatology they affirm, the hope of the return of Jesus as King and the "new heavens and new earth" must never be lost.

WHAT GUIDING PRINCIPLES DOES THIS COMMENTARY FOLLOW?

In this commentary, then, I will follow five principles that I believe are fundamental to understanding what John (or the Holy Spirit) is trying to say to us through this book.

---

361. Cf. Keener, *Spirit Hermeneutics*, 5, 24–27. An example of reading Revelation this way, especially in relation to devotion to Jesus, is seen in Newton, "Reading Revelation Romantically."

362. Cf. Archer, *Worship in the Apocalypse*, 46–48, 61–65; Resseguie, *Narrative Commentary*; Newton, *Revelation Worldview*, 253–55.

1. Historical context. Revelation was not written to us in the twenty-first century but to seven churches in the Roman province of Asia in the first century. Hence it cannot be understood without some knowledge of that time—including prevalent social, economic, and religious factors along with some of the specific events that changed people's lives in sometimes dramatic ways. Recent research is shedding increasing light on what life was like in the Greco-Roman world, and thus helping us get a feel for how its original hearers and readers would have understood Revelation. We also need to read Revelation in terms of the genres of its day. But the historical context also includes the development of early Christianity as traced to some degree in Acts[363] and events in the first to fourth centuries AD.[364]

2. Narrative. As David Barr points out, "it is easy to miss the most important thing for understanding the Apocalypse: it is a narrative."[365] As I said earlier, Revelation is most profitably read as a story, a story of conflict and war, but also a romance leading up to a divine wedding.[366] This does not imply that Revelation is fiction. But it does imply that it takes on fictional literary shape at times, which helps us not to take the imagery in the story too literally. The narrative drama draws the reader or hearer into its world and appeals to the imagination more than the intellect. We experience Revelation rather than decipher it. A narrative reading also demands that we interpret the book in the light of its ending. As Stephen Pattemore insists, "any study of the people of God in Revelation must include consideration of the final visions or risk serious distortion of John's message."[367]

3. Audience focus. Revelation was originally read aloud or performed in the local churches rather than read in silence as we might do today. Most people didn't read, few had access to books anyway (which had to be copied by hand, making them very expensive), and people mostly didn't read silently at that stage of history. When we read Revelation, we need to be aware that it was first of all an oral text. John Christopher Thomas' commentary has broken new ground by taking this aspect of Revelation seriously throughout. This aspect of the text also underlines the need to focus first on the original audience and be aware of the rhetorical aspects of the text: John is trying to get his audience to respond in certain specific ways by narrating his vision.[368]

4. Intertextuality. As we just noted, Revelation refers to a wide range of oral and written literature of its day and earlier. In particular, it picks up some famous stories and reinterprets them as a way of getting its message across. I will draw

---

363. Cf. Leithart, *Revelation 1–11*, 360.
364. This is argued especially in Papandrea, *Wedding of the Lamb*.
365. Barr, *Tales of the End*, 1.
366. Cf. Koester, *Revelation*, 115–22; Newton, "Reading Revelation Romantically."
367. Pattemore, *People of God*, 197.
368. Cf. Koester, *Revelation*, 132–36.

attention to this during the commentary proper, but it is appropriate to mention a few at the start: the Exodus Story of the Old Testament (and its "new exodus" theme in Isaiah), the stories and prophecies of men like Ezekiel and Daniel, the ubiquitous "combat myth," and the events of the early chapters of Genesis. There are allusions in Revelation to almost every book of the Old Testament and to features found in the New Testament too.

5. Pentecostal and Missional Theology. Everyone reads Revelation through the lens of their own theology, whether it is the Fundamentalist looking for a description of events after the "rapture" or the historical-critical scholar trying to explain the text in terms of its sources or the liberation theologian looking for a message of freedom and justice in John's vision. In this commentary, I will read largely through the lens of modern Pentecostalism, though not without some critical analysis as I explain below. This will allow me to take John's claims seriously, if not literally, even when they clash with a modern or postmodern worldview. It will also help me focus on the centrality of Jesus; Pentecostals' fourfold or fivefold gospel slogans all center on the work of Jesus as Savior, Healer, (Sanctifier), Spirit Baptizer, and coming King. A Pentecost-al lens, however, equally refers to the historic outpouring of the Spirit on the day of Pentecost[369] and its effects in the mission of the church to the world, which I increasingly see as *the* major idea behind Revelation.

DIALOGUE PARTNERS: WHAT OTHER COMMENTARIES AND OTHER BOOKS HAVE I USED MOST FREQUENTLY AND RECOMMEND TO THE READER?

Obviously, I have read many books, commentaries, journal articles, and other literature during my journey with Revelation and while preparing this commentary. A complete list is found in the bibliography and the footnotes will show whom I have mainly interacted with or drawn from. I have cited over two-hundred items at least once.

However, my major dialogue partners for the whole book were five diverse commentaries:

- John Christopher Thomas, *The Apocalypse: A literary and Theological Commentary* (2012), a recent scholarly commentary on Revelation by a Pentecostal scholar.
- Craig R. Koester, *Revelation: A New Translation with Introduction and Commentary* (2014), a recent general scholarly commentary with illuminating insights from the Greco-Roman context of Revelation.

---

369. Interestingly, many Jewish authors shortly before or around the time of Christ saw the feast of Pentecost as central to God's program (Stramara, *God's Timetable*, 10–21).

- David E. Aune, *Revelation*. 3 vols. (1997–1998), the most comprehensive source, especially for relevant ancient texts and detailed examination of textual and translation issues.
- G. K. Beale, *The Book of Revelation* (1999), perhaps the best guide to OT and Jewish intertextual references and their significance for interpreting Revelation.
- Peter Leithart's two volume commentary (2018) argues frequently (and sometimes persuasively) for minority scholarly positions especially on the dating, authorship, and interpretation of the text, and he surprisingly confirmed some of my own discoveries in Revelation.

In addition, I have benefited greatly from some key monographs, especially:

- Richard Bauckham's two monographs of 1993, *The Climax of Prophecy* and *The Theology of the Book of Revelation*.
- Robby Waddell's *The Spirit of the Book of Revelation* due to its conscious Pentecostal perspective, and its interaction with modern thinking on intertextuality.

Of course, my decisions on interpretive questions were my own and cannot be blamed on any of these fine authors.

COMMENTARY

Revelation Chapter 1

Revelation has three beginnings in chapter 1. The story-cum-testimony proper begins in 1:9, but there are two prefaces beginning in 1:1 (a kind of title) and 1:4 (a letter opening) which were probably added after John wrote his testimony proper. These three beginnings have certain features in common:

- The author's name (John) (1:1, 4, 9)
- The audience: seven churches of Asia (1:1, where they are simply "his slaves,"[1] 1:4, 11)
- References to heavenly beings (1:1, 4, 10)
- Focus on Jesus Christ (1:1, 2, 5, 7, 9)

1:1–3 The First Beginning

> **A revelation of Jesus Christ, which God gave him to show his slaves what must soon happen, and he made it known[2] by sending (it) through his angel to his slave[3] John, who testified to the word of God and the testimony of Jesus Christ which he saw. (Rev 1:1–2)**

---

1. Thomas suggests this might be a reference to prophets (Thomas, *Apocalypse*, 88), but I think it is more likely referring to Christians in general, the audience of Revelation. Cf. Aune, *Revelation 1–5*, 13.
2. Or "signified" (Greek ἐσήμανεν [*esēmanen*]).
3. Greek δοῦλος [*doulos*]; many translators translate this as "servant," but "slave" is more literal, so I translate it this way throughout.

This is an *apokalypsis*, that is, a revelation of something otherwise unknown that comes from God[4] via an angelic mediator (as in 22:6, 16)[5] to a human prophetic messenger called simply John (v. 1), who testifies to what he *saw* and heard (v. 2).[6] The whole book may be called a testimony, a category familiar to modern Pentecostals. The original audience might be familiar with "revelation" as a form of spiritual gift known to happen in congregational gatherings (1 Cor 14:6, 26; 2 Cor 12:1, 7; Gal 2:2).[7] They would also know that revelation is a central feature of God's relationship with human beings, a key perspective of the Old Testament and particularly of Daniel (see Dan 2:28–30, 45, 47).[8]

This revelation is "of Jesus Christ" (v. 1), either "from Jesus Christ" as its origin or "about Jesus Christ" as its subject, depending on how the genitive is understood.[9] Perhaps the origin alternative fits the immediate context better, but the subject alternative might have appealed to those in the audience who knew of Paul's more theological use of "revelation" to describe the gospel (Rom 16:25–26; Gal 1:12; Eph 3:3–5).[10] This objective alternative also sums up much of what readers encounter throughout the text and helps interpret it. Revelation is very much a revelation of who Jesus is and what he has accomplished.[11]

The English phrase "made it known" (v. 1) translates the aorist (past)[12] tense of *sēmainō*, which can mean "show by a sign," as in the Greek translation of Daniel 2:45. So the implication may be that the revelation is communicated in a symbolic way, which of course is what we see in the rest of the book. As Beale argues, this militates

---

4. The audience might recall Daniel 2:28, 47, part of the famous statue passage about the four successive kingdoms leading up to God's kingdom, where God's unique ability to reveal mysteries is emphasized. Leithart argues that in the Septuagint (Greek) OT, *apokalypsis* "refers to a literal uncovering, the sexual uncovering of nakedness" and that family systems "often revolve around a secret" which has to be exposed in order to bring healing (Leithart, *Revelation 1–11*, 69). Thus, Revelation can be seen as unveiling the dirty secrets of the ancient world: "the hidden truth of *everything* is disclosed" (ibid., 70). However, it is primarily a revelation "of Jesus Christ."

5. Angelic mediators were a ubiquitous feature of ancient Jewish apocalypses but not restricted to them. Consider Zech 1:9–19; Judg 13:3–21; Acts 5:19–20; 8:26; 27:23. Here the author points to a single angelic mediator, though the text presents a more complex picture.

6. For a comparison with the openings of OT prophetic books, see Fekkes, *Isaiah and Prophetic Traditions*, 106–7.

7. Thomas, *Apocalypse*, 87.

8. Cf. Beale, *Book of Revelation*, 181, where Beale shows parallels between v. 1 and these verses in Daniel.

9. Cf. Koester, *Revelation*, 211; Keener, *Revelation*, 53–54. The genitive phrase in Koine Greek can be either subjective (like an English possessive or a source, equivalent to "from") or objective (more like "about").

10. The phrase "revelation of Jesus Christ" occurs only in Revelation and Pauline (or post-Pauline) literature (Fiorenza, *Book of Revelation*, 150–51).

11. Cf. Barr, *Tales of the End*, 3–5.

12. The Greek aorist is not exactly equivalent to the English past tense but that is the best translation.

against literalism in interpreting Revelation.[13] However, the same language is used in Acts 11:28 of Agabus' prophecy, which was not symbolic.[14]

Next we note that the content of this revelation is about "what must soon happen" (v. 1). The language emphasizes the guaranteed fulfilment ("must"; Greek, *dei genesthai*, emphasizing its necessity)[15] and its imminence ("soon"; Greek *en tachei*, meaning "speedily, quickly, without delay").[16] The audience must have expected that the events to be predicted would be imminent *to them*, not just to readers centuries later.[17] This somewhat undermines a Futurist reading of Revelation.[18]

John is testifying to "the word of God and the testimony of Jesus Christ"[19] (v. 2), phrases that will arise again during the narrative to distinguish the focus of faithful Christians (starting with John at 1:9). This phrase acts almost as an alternative title describing what the author saw or what the book is about and is loaded with Christological significance to those familiar with the Gospel of John (see John 1:1 and 18:37).[20] The emphasis on what John saw (v. 2) might also remind listeners of the opening words of 1 John, "That . . . which we have seen with our eyes" (1 John 1:1), though the kind of seeing referred to there was different from what Revelation is about to describe. As Ian Paul points out, "John breaks down the distinction between seeing and hearing, since he 'sees' a 'word.'"[21]

> **Blessed is the one who reads (it aloud) and those who hear the words of the prophecy, and keep what is written in it, for the time (draws) near. (Rev 1:3)**

The message is also a prophecy, not the usual long-term prediction claimed in apocalyptic messages (as in Dan 2:28, 29, 45 and 12:4–13),[22] but one that is soon to be fulfilled (vv. 1, 3). Look at the parallel construction between the Greek of verse 1 ("to *show* . . . what things *must soon* happen") and Daniel 2:28 LXX[23] ("he *showed* . . . . what things *must* take place *in the latter days*"). This suggests that Revelation is about to show that Daniel's prophecies are in the process of being fulfilled. In other words, Daniel's "latter days" have arrived with the death and resurrection of Jesus![24]

---

13. Beale, *Book of Revelation*, 50–52.
14. Cf. Aune, *Revelation 1–5*, 15.
15. Cf. Koester, *Revelation*, 222, on the use of *dei* in Revelation.
16. The same phrase occurs in Acts 12:7 (translated "quick" in NIV) and 1 Tim 3:14. Cf. Koester, *Revelation*, 222–23; Beale, *Book of Revelation*, 181–82, 185.
17. Cf. Leithart, *Revelation 1–11*, 70–71.
18. Cf. Keener, *Revelation*, 60–65.
19. The "and" here may be "epexegetical," i.e., "the word of God" is *equated with* "the witness of Jesus Christ" (Aune, *Revelation 1–5*, 6).
20. Cf. Thomas, *Apocalypse*, 89; Leithart, *Revelation 1–11*, 76–77.
21. Paul, *Revelation*, 60.
22. Cf. Beale, *Book of Revelation*, 137.
23. LXX denotes the Septuagint, the Greek translation of the OT.
24. Beale, *Book of Revelation*, 153–54; Beale, *John's Use of the Old Testament*, 115; Leithart,

However, "the time [*kairos*] draws near" may also imply more than simple fulfillment of old or new predictions. See Mark 1:15, where Jesus says, "The time has come . . . The kingdom of God has come near. Repent and believe the good news." The language of v. 3 may imply that a great event or opportunity (or threat) is soon coming which will require a strong response from John's audience.[25]

Hence the prophecy demands a response: it must be read aloud in a meeting, and the audience must "hear" and "keep" the written text (v. 3). The scenario envisaged by John is of a gathered group (church or *ekklesia*) listening to a dramatic reading (a kind of performance)[26] with rapt attention, because this is a message from God.[27] Though John is separated from the seven churches, his prophetic revelation is intended for a liturgical setting.[28] The passage also offers a reward of unspecified blessing or happiness [*makarios*][29] for those who make that response (v. 3), a promise to all readers in all ages, not just John's contemporaries or those living at the very end of history.[30] This is the first of seven blessings offered to the hearer or reader who qualifies (the others are found in 14:13; 16:15; 19:9; 20:6; 22:7, 14).

Summing up, this first beginning tells the reader to expect a word from God through Christ in the form of a revelation of unknown imminent events, communicated symbolically and visually to John and relayed in the form of a testimony. This is to be read aloud in the churches and demands a response from the hearers.

1:4–8 The Second Beginning

John to the seven churches that (are) in Asia: grace and peace to you from the one who is and who was and who is coming and from the seven spirits which are before his throne and from Jesus Christ, the faithful witness, the firstborn of the dead and the ruler of the kings of the earth. (Rev 1:4–5a)

Before John commences his testimony proper, he addresses his audience in a style much like what we read at the beginning of Paul's letters.[31] Here John follows Hellenistic letter

---

Revelation 1–11, 71, 82. Cf. Moyise, *Old Testament in the Book of Revelation*, 46–47, 58. It is parallel to such texts as Acts 2:17; 1 Cor 10:11, and Heb 1:2.

25. Cf. Paul, *Revelation*, 60. I think we must take seriously this language of imminence in relation to John's original audience and not try to avoid it, as Beasley-Murray seems to be doing with his "foreshortening—one might call it telescopic—view of history" (Beasley-Murray, *Revelation*, 52).

26. On Revelation as performance, see deWaal, *Aural-Performance Analysis*.

27. Cf. Koester, *Revelation*, 213, 222.

28. Cf. Thompson, *Book of Revelation*, 72.

29. On such beatitudes or "makarisms" in ancient Jewish and Christtian literature, cf. Aune, *Revelation 1–5*, 10–11. Aune argues that John "refers here to a traditional saying of Jesus preserved in Luke 11:28" (ibid., 20). deSilva argues that these "makarisms" instead represent how people gain honor before God (deSilva, "Honor Discourse," 103–7).

30. Cf. Hendriksen, *More Than Conquerors*, 10.

31. On common elements in Revelation and Paul, cf. Fiorenza, *Book of Revelation*, 148–50.

conventions, starting with his own name (without any explanation, unlike many other NT letters) and then identifying his addressees (v. 4a). This text is not just addressed to God's servants generally (as in v. 1) but to seven very specific gathered churches in a specific time (the first century) and place (the Roman province of Asia). Asia was a region where Christianity had quickly taken hold in a massive and powerful move of the Spirit (as related in Acts 19). It was infused with Hellenistic culture and traditions and had become strongly pro-Roman after its Greek kingdoms had been absorbed into the Roman Empire. It also had a significant Jewish presence. As many as one-million Jews and over fifty Jewish communities lived in this region; they had some special privileges, paid a special tax, and were somewhat enmeshed in Hellenistic culture.[32] These features of Asia will become very relevant as we read the text.

Again like Paul, John then invokes a special blessing of "grace and peace" on his audience (vv. 4b–5a) from a threefold source. First, it comes from "the one who is, and who was, and who is coming," obviously God, with an allusion to Exodus 3:14 where God names himself, "I am who I am." Second, it is from "the seven spirits which are before his throne," a phrase which will come up later, such as in 4:5.[33] Finally, it is from "Jesus Christ." While this is not explicitly Trinitarian, it appears that John thinks in Trinitarian categories.[34] The blessing in most other New Testament letters is from "God the Father and from the Lord Jesus Christ" (Rom 1:7) or similar language, but John distinctively uses a more "prophetic" title for God[35] and adds "the seven spirits which are before his throne."[36]

The focus is then very much on the (human and messianic) figure of Jesus. He is described first as "the faithful witness," later (in 3:14) expanded to "the faithful and true witness," much like John himself and Antipas (2:13), and with a possible allusion to John 18:37.[37] He is also "the firstborn of the dead," referring to his resurrection, implying that he is the first of many to be raised, and using the same Greek phrase as in Colossians 1:18.[38]

---

32. Aune, *Revelation 1–5*, 29, 168–72.

33. See the discussion of Rev 4:5 below.

34. Cf. Leithart, *Revelation 1–11*, 85–89. Taushev instead sees the Trinity in the threefold name of God as "him who is, and who was, and who is to come" based on the ancient commentary of Andrew of Caesarea (Taushev, *Apocalypse in the Teachings of Ancient Christianity*, 62).

35. Aune, *Revelation 1–5*, 31.

36. Thomas, *Apocalypse*, 91, links this greeting with Jesus' words in the Gospel of John, but similar blessings are found in every Pauline letter (Rom 1:7; 1 Cor 1:3; 2 Cor 1:2; Gal 1:3; Eph 1:2; Phil 1:2; Col 1:2; 1 Thess 1:1; 2 Thess 1:2; 1 Tim 1:2; 2 Tim 1:2; Tit 1:4; Phlm 3), and those of other apostles (1 Pet 1:2; 2 Pet 1:2; 2 John 3 and Jude 3).

37. See also 1 Tim 6:13. However, Aune argues that the testimony of the earthly Jesus is not in view here, but rather "the exalted Jesus who guarantees the truth of the revelation transmitted through John" (Aune, *Revelation 1–5*, 37). Cf. Rev 22:20.

38. Colossians was addressed to a church in the same region as the audiences of Revelation. See Aune, *Revelation 1–5*, 38–39.

Third, he is described as "the ruler of the kings of the earth," using strongly messianic language alluding to Psalm 89:27. This is the first clear intertextual reference to the Hebrew Scriptures or Old Testament (the first of many). Psalm 89 is a strong affirmation of God's covenant with King David, emphasizing the promise of an everlasting dynasty (vv. 3–4, 28–29, 34–37) grounded in God's own throne (v. 14). David is chosen and anointed (v. 20), given victory (vv. 21–24), and dominion (vv. 25–27). In verse 27, God says, "And I will appoint him to be my firstborn, the most exalted of the kings of the earth," language very similar to Revelation 1:5. However, the rest of Psalm 89 bemoans the fact that David's throne has been cast down and asks, "where is your former great love, which in your faithfulness you swore to David?" (v. 49). Now John is affirming that Jesus is the Messiah, the restored Davidic ruler,[39] ruling not only Israel but "the kings of the earth."[40]

He is called "King of kings" and "Lord of lords" in Revelation 17:14 and 19:16. Hence, he fulfills the messianic expectations of the Old Testament generally, but in a special way and based on a unique event, signaled by the phrase "the firstborn of the dead." Jesus is not a world ruler as in the common image of an emperor, nor is his rule based on military or economic might.[41] Nonetheless, this is a bold claim, not only in conflict with the thinking of most first-century Jews but also with the claims of the Roman Empire, a "clash of myths."[42] It offers the "kings of the earth" two alternatives: serve Babylon and be destroyed (17:14; 18:9; 19:19–21) or submit to God and the Lamb and be part of the new Jerusalem (21:24).[43]

> **To the one who loves us and released us from our sins by his blood and made us a kingdom, priests to his God and Father, to him be the glory and the strength forever [and ever], Amen. (Rev 1:5b–6)**

John now moves from the titles of Christ to a doxology that emphasizes Jesus' saving acts for his people ("us"). First, he "loves us," speaking of his motivation.[44] Second, he "released us[45] from our sins by his blood," describing his atoning achievement through

---

39. Cf. Leithart, *Revelation 1–11*, 90.

40. Cf. Herms, *Apocalypse for the Church*, 213–15.

41. Cf. Caird, *Revelation*, 16–17; Moyise, *Old Testament in the Book of Revelation*, 117–18.

42. "Myths" does not mean fairy tales; a clash of myths means a context between rival stories that explain the world. Later we hear that the prostitute is "the great city that has dominion over the kings of the earth" (17:18) which contradicts what is said here in 1:5. Cf. Howard-Brook and Gwyther, *Unveiling Empire*, 224–25.

43. Cf. Blount, "Active Resistance," 39. See also Psalm 2 and Koester, *Revelation*, 227. Daniel also tells how God shows an interest in Gentile kings such as Nebuchadnezzar (Dan 2–4), Belshazzar (Dan 5), and Darius (Dan 6) and calls them to submission to God.

44. Cf. Gal 2:20; Eph 5:2, 25.

45. Literally "having released us" (Greek *lusanti*, an aorist participle). Some ancient manuscripts have λούσαντι (*lousanti*, "washed") instead of λύσαντι (*lusanti*, "released" or "freed" or "loosed"). This alternative text was followed by the KJV. Either way, the thought of salvation through Jesus' blood is clear and the washing imagery is found in 7:14 and 22:14, though using different Greek verbs. Cf.

his violent death. Third, John mentions the results of this salvation, stated in terms reminiscent of God's promise to Israel in Exodus 19:6 at Sinai. There God promised Moses' generation, "you will be for me a kingdom of priests and a holy nation." Clearly John is saying the church (that is, "us")[46] will now play this role of mediating God's rule and presence to the world, both in this age and after the resurrection.[47]

The linking of "kingdom" and "priests" reflects the connection of "the bearers of political power and sacral authority" in ancient societies, including the Roman Empire.[48] The doxology ascribes "the glory and the strength forever and ever" to Jesus, anticipating the worship offered to him in Revelation 5. The oral reading of this passage, or indeed its singing,[49] may well climax in a crescendo leading to the "Amen," with the audience breaking out in applause as in a Pentecostal (or African-American) sermon.[50]

> **Behold, he is coming with the clouds,**
> **and every eye will see him,**
> **and those who pierced him;**
> **and all the tribes of the earth will mourn over him.**
> **Yes, Amen. (Rev 1:7)**

So far John has told the hearers of what Jesus has already done and its present application. The focus now perhaps moves to the future: Jesus has won our salvation by his death, he now bears witness and rules kings on earth, and he will come again.[51] However, the Greek *erchetai*, the ordinary word for "come," is in the present tense, and is also used of God's "coming" in verses 4 and 8.[52] He is coming "with the clouds" in such a powerful and public way that "every eye will see him." John emphasizes this with the word "Behold" [*idou*].[53] The language of "clouds" [*nephelōn*] is often associated with Jesus "coming" in passages the audience of Revelation may have known (Acts 1:9–11;

Smolarz, *Covenant,* 309–16.

46. I.e., the church is those saved by Jesus' blood, not an institution.

47. Contra Koester, *Revelation,* 217, 228, and Fiorenza, *Book of Revelation,* 68, 75, who restrict at least the reigning aspect to the future age. Cf. Beale, *Book of Revelation,* 192–95.

48. Fiorenza, *Book of Revelation,* 68.

49. Cf. Archer, *Worship in the Apocalypse,* 127.

50. de Waal, *Aural-Performance Analysis,* 91.

51. Victorinus, in the oldest existing commentary on Revelation (written in the late third century) understands this as Jesus coming again "to judgment manifest in majesty and glory" (Victorinus, *Commentary,* ANF 7:344).

52. See also similar phrases in Rev 3:11; 16:15; 22:7; 22:12. Jesus' "coming" seems to mean different things in different places in Revelation, e.g., local comings in the Spirit (as in John 14:18; Rev 1:7?; 3:11?, 20; 22:7?, 20?), local comings of a disciplinary nature (2:5, 16, 25; 3:3; 16:15?), Jesus' heavenly exaltation (1:7?), and Jesus' return in glory for judgment (22:7?, 12?, 20?).

53. I find this hard to translate well. Modern English translations opt for "Look" (NIV, NRSV) or retain the older "Behold" (ESV). Aune has "Indeed" (Aune, *Revelation 1–5,* 53–54). Neither translation completely captures the sense of "listen here" or "pay attention" implied by this word that John uses frequently (twenty-six times).

Matt 24:30; Mark 13:26; Luke 21:27; 1 Thess 4:17; but see Matt 26:64). However, this is perhaps a threatening idea rather than a comforting one because "those who pierced him" will be among those who see him (see also John 19:37). Indeed "all the tribes of the earth will mourn over him."

John draws from Daniel 7 and Zechariah 12[54] here. Daniel in a night vision sees "one like a son of man, coming with the clouds of heaven," but not from heaven to earth; rather "He approached the Ancient of Days [i.e., God] and was led into his presence." There "He was given authority, glory, and sovereign power; all nations and peoples of every language worshiped him. His dominion is an everlasting dominion that will not pass away, and his kingdom is one that will never be destroyed" (Dan 7:13–14). This seems to describe Jesus' ascension and glorification (which will be portrayed again in Revelation 5) rather than his second coming. Luke's description of the ascension in Acts 1:9 mentions Jesus being hidden by a cloud, suggesting he was fulfilling Daniel's prophecy. That prophecy also echoes the thought in 1:5 of Jesus' rule over the earth's kings. Perhaps this explains why "the tribes of the earth" are mourning: they have rejected his rule and now face the consequences. Perhaps this is the imminent event referred to in v. 3.

However, there is also another thought in Daniel 7 that connects with Revelation 1:6. The interpretation of Daniel's vision predicts that the Son of Man's rule is shared with "the holy people of the Most High" (Dan 7:27; see also v. 22).[55] Also, as Daniel sees it, this sovereignty of Christ and his people is only accomplished after a strictly limited period ("a time, times and half a time" [Dan 7:25]) of suffering by the holy people at the hands of a "fourth beast" and a "little horn" (Dan 7:7–8, 11, 19–27). Leithart calls this the "birth pangs" of a new order.[56] This theme will be taken up strongly in Revelation.

Meanwhile, Zechariah prophesies of a time when Jerusalem is besieged by the nations and ultimately vindicated (Zech 12:1–9). As part of that process, he says, "I will pour out on the house of David and the inhabitants of Jerusalem a spirit of grace and supplication. They will look on me, the one they have pierced, and they will mourn for him as one mourns for an only child, and grieve for him as one grieves for a firstborn son" (Zech 12:10). The ensuing verses specifically make the Israelites the subjects and this mourning sounds like a mourning of repentance, or at least yearning, but in Revelation 1:7 this is not clear. Moreover, in John's prophecy it is "all the tribes of the earth" who mourn, not just Jerusalem. So what is John doing with his sources?

Verse 7 is often taken as the first reference to the second coming in Revelation, and this seems entirely plausible. But some commentators see it rather as his coming

---

54. Matt 24:30 draws from the same OT Scriptures.

55. Leithart maintains, "That exaltation of the Son of Man *in the exaltation of the saints* is the theme of Revelation" (Leithart, *Revelation 1–11*, 95, emphasis in the original). Cf. Pattemore, *People of God*, 118–24.

56. Leithart, *Revelation 1–11*, 130.

in judgement on Jerusalem in AD 70. This view is justified by the earlier references to imminent events and the possible alternative translation of verse 7b as "all the tribes of the land [*pasai hai phulai tēs gēs*] will mourn over him," in keeping with the meaning in Zechariah 12.[57]

However, the intertextual dialogue with Daniel and Zechariah opens up a third possibility. Perhaps John is speaking of the victory following a desperate (though short) struggle that leads to a worldwide (or Israel-wide) repentance and embrace of Jesus Christ.[58] Or at least Jesus' "coming" makes such an outcome possible. If this is what he means, the "seeing" in verse 7 could be figurative or spiritual rather than literal. The response of the audience to Peter's Pentecost speech may be illustrative of this. We read, "When the people heard this [of their guilt in the crucifixion of Jesus and God's glorification of him], they were cut to the heart and said to Peter and the other apostles, 'Brothers, what shall we do?'" (Acts 2:37 NIV; compare Matt 24:30; 26:64; Mark 13:26; 14:62; Luke 21:27; Gal 3:1).[59] The clear connotation of the link between the grieving and the crucifixion of Jesus makes this a likely interpretation.[60] For example, John 19:34–37 also alludes to Zechariah 12 and mourning over Jesus' death is highlighted in Luke 23:27–28, 48. Whatever John means, he underlines its certainty: "Yes, Amen," a common liturgical response to ancient Christian prayers (1 Cor 14:16).

"I am the Alpha and the Omega," says the Lord God, "who is and who was, and who is coming, the Almighty." (Rev 1:8)

The second beginning finishes with something rare in Revelation: God himself speaks.[61] He makes a divine self-declaration in prophetic language. This underlines God's sovereignty and eternity with "the Alpha and the Omega," using the first and last letters of the Greek alphabet[62] and recalling Isaiah 44:6 and 48:12. Then it emphasizes God's power as "the Almighty" [*pantokratōr*], a title also used in 4:8; 11:17; 15:3; 16:7, 14; 19:6, 15, and 21:22.[63] The language of verse 8 parallels verse 4 so as to mark off this section.

---

57. Cf. Leithart, *Revelation 1–11*, 83, 97. But see Bauckham, *Climax of Prophecy*, 320–21.

58. Cf. Beale, *Book of Revelation*, 196–98; Beale, *John's Use of the Old Testament*, 100–104. Beale sees this prophecy as fulfilled by the repentance of Gentiles throughout the church era.

59. Cf. Koester, *Revelation*, 219, 229; Leithart, *Revelation 1–11*, 97; Bauckham, *Climax of Prophecy*, 322.

60. Cf. Corsini, *Apocalypse*, 70–71, 78–79. Bauckham also points to a link with the original promise to Abraham of all nations being blessed through him (Gen 12:3; Bauckham, *Climax of Prophecy*, 321). Malina argues that "the purpose of Revelation is to get all the tribes of the land . . . to acknowledge publicly the wickedness of Jesus' execution" (Malina, *Genre and Message*, 71).

61. The only other occasion is at Rev 21:5–8.

62. This also implies that the other letters in between are included, that is, God is the origin and destiny of history and supervises everything in between (cf. Mathewson, *Handbook*, 8).

63. Malina sees this as an assertion of God's control over all other cosmic forces (Malina, *Genre and Message*, 261). The term is only used in 2 Cor 6:18 elsewhere in the New Testament (Keener, *Revelation*, 73–74).

Two features of this passage deserve further note:

1. Its personal nature, like a letter from John to his friends, including them in his circle with first person plural phrases.
2. Its high Christology. As we will see later, this Christology would be a threat to at least three kinds of people in this region: those loyal to the Roman emperor (who was the literal "ruler of the kings of the earth"), those loyal to Greco-Roman religion (which featured a panoply of competing deities), and those loyal to the teaching of the local synagogues and Jerusalem temple (who would reject the claims for Jesus to messianic rule and even deity here).

1:9–20 The Beginning of the Testimony

Now the story itself begins as John recounts the visionary experience he had. I describe this as testimony rather than apocalypse (both terms are valid), partly because that is the language John uses. It also draws a parallel with modern Pentecostal testifying, which I think helps Pentecostal readers enter sympathetically into John's narrative, even though their own testimonies are not on this level.

This passage is sometimes viewed as a prophetic call narrative like that of Isaiah 6:1–8, Jeremiah 1:4–12, or Ezekiel 1–3, and it certainly contains some similar elements. For instance, it is a first-person account of a supernatural encounter (compare Jer 1). It records a fearful response from the prophet (as opposed to guilty in the case of Isaiah), followed by a reassurance from God (not so much in Ezekiel), and a commission to bring a message from God to his people. But as Aune points out, this is not portrayed as "John's *inaugural* vision,"[64] by which I take him to mean it does not portray John's call to minister. It is rather a commission to a specific prophetic task to be undertaken by an experienced prophet. There is also a second commissioning scene in Revelation 10.

> **I, John, your brother and partner in the tribulation[65] and kingdom and perseverance in Jesus, came to be[66] on the island called Patmos on account of the word of God and the testimony of Jesus. (Rev 1:9)**

---

64. Aune, *Revelation 1–5*, 70. Emphasis in the original. Aune suggests the passage is most like an ancient "symbolic vision" like Rev 7:1–17 and Rev 17:1–18, containing the vision itself followed by an interpretation (ibid., 71–73). However, its importance as the inaugural commissioning vision of *Revelation* cannot be ignored.

65. Greek θλίψις [*thlipsis*], afflictions, trouble, or tribulation. I am translating this as "tribulation" so as to identify this specific term that has doctrinal implications later.

66. John often uses forms of the Greek γίνομαι [*ginomai*], become, happen, take place. Often this can best be translated by forms of "to be." But where possible, I try to translate this is a way that shows an event, a happening, or a shift of some kind.

This is a first-person account from John[67] who has already been identified in verse 1 as the final recipient of the "revelation" and in verse 4 as the author of this letter to the seven churches. He is now further described as "your brother and partner in the tribulation and kingdom and perseverance in Jesus." Clearly, he is one of them, he is experiencing similar things to his audience and is known to them; both are undergoing tribulation (the same word used later in 7:14)[68] requiring "perseverance."[69] John does not offer any other identification; he assumes they know who he is.

However, he does tell them about his location[70] and why he was there, that is, "on account of the word of God and the testimony of Jesus." While this could mean he was visiting the island to preach, it is more likely that he had been exiled there as a form of punishment because of his Christian witness, that is, because of opposition to the Christian message, or possibly that he had fled there because of such opposition.

This raises its own questions, however, as most Christian leaders suffered much worse punishments.[71] Perhaps John's status was high enough among the Roman authorities to warrant such a privileged punishment, a kind of exile mainly used for noble offenders or priests.[72] After all, Paul used his Roman citizenship to avoid arbitrary treatment (Acts 22:23–29; 25:9–12), and he had powerful friends in Ephesus who protected him from the mob (Acts 19:31). It is not, then, impossible to imagine that John also got a softer exile than the penalty inflicted on other Christians or those in other places. The later stories that John was suffering severe treatment on Patmos (for example, working in mines or being boiled in oil) do not appear to have a solid historical foundation.[73] The past tense may imply that John was no longer on Patmos when he wrote Revelation.[74]

> **I became "in the Spirit" on the Lord's day, and I heard behind me a loud voice like a trumpet saying, "What you are seeing[75] write in a scroll and send to the**

---

67. "I, John" is a phrase unique to Revelation in the NT (Rev 22:8) and is parallel to "I, Daniel" in the apocalyptic sections of *Daniel* and similar phrases in other apocalypses (Aune, *Revelation 1–5*, 75).

68. See also Acts 14:22; 2 Cor 4:17; 1 Thess 1:6.

69. Cf. Koester, *Revelation*, 250.

70. For information on Patmos itself, see Koester, *Revelation*, 239–42. Revelation does not appear to allude to any of the geographical or social features of the island.

71. Thompson argues that a peaceful visit to Patmos fits the evidence better (Thompson, "Ordinary Lives," 32–34).

72. Thomas, *Apocalypse*, 99; Aune, *Revelation 1–5*, 78–82, 116; Howard-Brook and Gwyther, *Unveiling Empire*, xxvii, 117; Caird, *Revelation*, 21; A. Collins, "Persecution and Vengeance," 742–44.

73. Cf. Koester, *Revelation*, 242–43. However, Victorinus does support the idea that John was "condemned to the labor of the mines by Caesar Domitian" and then released after Domitian's death (Victorinus, *Commentary*, ANF 7:353).

74. Cf. Aune, *Revelation 1–5*, 77–78.

75. Generally I am translating present tense verbs as continuous, in this case "are seeing" as opposed to "see," to emphasize the present reality.

> **seven churches: to Ephesus, and to Smyrna, and to Pergamum, and to Thyatira, and to Sardis, and to Philadelphia, and to Laodicea." (Rev 1:10–11)**

He says that "on the Lord's day" (probably Sunday, the first day of the week, when Jesus rose again,[76] though we can't be sure)[77] he was or became "in the Spirit" (v. 10). The Greek reads literally "became in spirit" (*egenomēn en pneumati*),[78] a phrase used at several significant points in the text (4:2; 17:3; 21:10). It indicates a strong encounter with the Spirit leading to a revelatory experience, possibly comparable to Ezekiel's experience (Ezek 2:2; 3:12, 14, 24; 11:1, 24; 37:1; 43:5). This could simply indicate a sense of the Spirit's leading or empowerment, the likely sense of this phrase in 1 Corinthians 14:2, 15, 16 (where it refers to speaking in tongues); Luke 2:27; Romans 8:9; Ephesians 3:5, 6:18; and John 4:23–24.[79]

But it could mean falling into a trance. John does not describe his experience psychologically.[80] "Out of body" revelatory experiences are not part of the modern (western) world's worldview but are common in many, perhaps most, other cultures, ancient and contemporary.[81] Acts gives us several such accounts, the most famous being Peter's experience on the rooftop in Joppa (Acts 10:9–16; 11:5–10), but also experiences of Paul (Acts 9:3–9; 16:9; 18:9–10; 22:6–11, 17–18; 23:11; 26:12–19; 27:23–24) and Ananias (Acts 9:10–16). Pentecostals sometimes report similar experiences of the Spirit; at least, they find them credible, unlike some other Christians, though the issue of discerning between valid and spurious claims to visionary experiences is still perplexing.

So being "in the Spirit," John first hears something strange "behind" him: "a loud voice like a trumpet" (v. 10). It reads somewhat like Ezekiel's experience when "the Spirit lifted me up, and I heard behind me a loud rumbling sound as the glory of the LORD rose from the place where it was standing" (Ezek 3:12). Ezekiel interprets this as "the sound

---

76. From early on, this was the day Christians gathered (see 1 Cor 16:2; Acts 20:7). Calling it "the Lord's day" was a challenge to the Roman order; the province of Asia decided to make Augustus Caesar's birthday the New Year's Day in 9 BC (Price, *Rituals and Power*, 54–56; Friesen, *Imperial Cults*, 32–36).

77. Thomas, among others, argues for seeing this as referring to an eschatological "day of the Lord" (Thomas, *Apocalypse*, 101), which may be a secondary reference; John's language here seems more mundane. For discussion of all possibilities, see Aune, *Revelation 1–5*, 83–84; de Waal, *Aural-Performance Analysis*, 94–96.

78. I put this phrase in quotation marks to accentuate it as a specific state of consciousness.

79. Many of these cases have a congregational setting, which Leithart proposes for this case (Leithart, *Revelation 1–11*, 108).

80. Aune translates verse 10 as "I fell into a prophetic trance" (Aune, *Revelation 1–5*, 62, 82–83). The parallels with use of "in the Spirit" later in the book suggest that it implies a visionary journey, probably to the heavenly throne room as in 4:1–2 (ibid., 71). Thompson suggests that John was "possessed" by the Spirit in way analogous to many non-western cultures (Thompson, "Spirit Possession," 137–50). See aso Bauckham, *Climax of Prophecy*, 150–59.

81. Cf. Aune, *Revelation 1–5*, 82–83; Howard-Brook and Gwyther, *Unveiling Empire*, 138; Craffert, "Altered States of Consciousness"; de Smidt, "Spirit in Revelation," 29–30.

of the wings of the living creatures brushing against each other and the sound of the wheels beside them" (Ezek 3:13).[82] The difference here is that John hears a "voice" that speaks to him from behind (possibly alluding to Isa 30:21).[83] Loud voices are common in Revelation, which is probably the noisiest book in the New Testament (see 4:1; 5:12; 6:1, 10; 7:2, 10; 10:3; 11; 12, 15; 12:10; 14:2, 7, 15, 18; 16:1, 17; 18:2; 19:1, 3, 6; 21:3).[84]

In this case, the loud voice commissions John to write a scroll about what he is seeing and to send it to seven specified churches (v. 11), already alluded to in verse 4. This section, starting in verse 4 (the greeting to the seven churches) and verse 9, introduces the messages to the seven churches in chapters 2–3. This then is a discrete section (1:9—3:22)[85] since the *seven* churches of Asia are never mentioned again as a group (Rev 22:16 only speaks of "the churches").

> **And I turned around to see the voice which was speaking to me, and having turned around, I saw seven golden lampstands . . . (Rev 1:12)**

Who is speaking? John turns around to see and has the first true vision in the text. This hearing-then-seeing pattern becomes a feature of Revelation: the seeing interprets (or reinterprets) what is heard (compare 5:5–6; 7:4 and 9; 8:13 and 9:1). John gives a detailed description of what he saw (vv. 12–16), his response (v. 17), and the interpretation of the imagery in the vision (vv. 18–20), following "the typical pattern of visions in the OT and Jewish apocalyptic literature."[86]

The vision begins with "seven golden lampstands" (v. 12), a variant on the seven-branched lampstand (menorah) of the old tabernacle and the second temple (Exod 25:31–39; Zech 4:2). If indeed Revelation was written *after* the fall of Jerusalem in AD 70, this would have special significance since the literal lampstand had been taken by the Romans, as pictured on the triumphal arch of Titus, still there in Rome. These seven lampstands may be viewed as a replacement for the sacred lampstand now lost.[87] It may be significant that John saw the lampstands (churches) *before* he noticed "one like a son of man" (vv. 12, 13). While Christ is obviously superior, the focus of Revelation is the church which reveals him.[88]

> **. . . and in the midst of the lampstands (was one) like a son of man[89] clothed in a long robe and wrapped about his breasts with a golden belt. (Rev 1:13)**

82. But there is also an allusion to the trumpet sounds at Sinai (Exod 19:16, 19), a comparison that identifies the voice as divine (see Beale, *Book of Revelation*, 203, 205).

83. Isa 30:21 ("your ears will hear a voice behind you, saying, 'This is the way; walk in it'") is in context of the promised experience of restoration for Israel.

84. Cf. Thomas, *Apocalypse*, 101; Aune, *Revelation 1–5*, 85.

85. Cf. Herms, *Apocalypse for the Church*, 155.

86. Beale, *Book of Revelation*, 205.

87. See Aune's sceptical comments in *Revelation 1–5*, 65, 88–90.

88. Cf. Leithart, *Revelation 1–11*, 109, 111–12.

89. Greek ὅμοιον υἱὸν ἀνθρώπου [*homoion huion anthrōpou*], meaning "like a human being," but the more literal "son of man" captures better the reference to Daniel and possibly the Gospels.

Among the lampstands is "one like a son of man"[90] (see also 14:14). This would be seen by informed listeners as another reference to Daniel 7:13.[91] However, the "son of man" here resembles the "man dressed in linen" in Daniel 10:5, 16,[92] who comes to give Daniel a revelation (Dan 10:1; see also Dan 8:15–16) and the "figure like that of a man" who appears to Ezekiel, whose upper body "looked like glowing metal, as if full of fire" (Ezek 1:26–27). He is "dressed in a long robe" ("reaching down to his feet" in the NIV), which may suggest he is a priest.[93] He has a golden belt "wrapped about his breasts," similar to the man in Daniel 10:5, also implying priestly status, though this feature will be replicated in the seven angels in Revelation 15:6. The reference to his breasts [*mastois*] is a feminine image, as in Luke 11:27.[94]

> And[95] his head and hair were white as wool, (white) as snow, and his eyes (were) like flaming fire, and his feet (were) like burnished bronze as burning in an oven, and his voice (was) like the sound of many waters . . . (Rev 1:14–15)

Here there is a resemblance to the Ancient of Days in Daniel 7:9, about whom we read, "His clothing was as white as snow; the hair of his head was white like wool. His throne was flaming with fire, and its wheels were all ablaze." But the sound is similar to the "man dressed in linen" whose voice was "like the sound of a multitude" (Dan 10:6) or to Ezekiel 43:2, where the voice of "the God of Israel" is "like the roar of rushing waters"[96] as he comes to restore Israel. John's reference to Daniel and Ezekiel here is not accidental, as these are the two books which refer to a "son of man," here identified as Jesus as in verse 7. However, this is a ghostly, even divine, figure,[97] somewhat like God in the visions of Ezekiel and Daniel, and it is no wonder John is scared (v. 17), just like Daniel had been (Dan 10:7–8).[98]

---

90. John uses this kind of language of "something/someone like . . . " twenty-one times in all (Paul, *Revelation*, 72).

91. It could possibly allude to Ezek 2:1, 3, 6, 8; 3:1, 3, 4, 10, 17, etc., though this is less likely, as in Ezekiel the son of man is the prophet receiving the vision, whereas in Daniel, he is seen by the prophet, as here in Rev 1.

92. Cf. Moyise, *Old Testament in the Book of Revelation*, 37–38.

93. Beale, *Book of Revelation*, 209; Victorinus, *Commentary*, ANF 7:344. However, Koester and Aune disagree (Koester, *Revelation*, 245–46; Aune, *Revelation 1–5*, 93–94).

94. Cf. Leithart, *Revelation 1–11*, 111; Paul, *Revelation*, 72–73.

95. Or "but" (Greek δε [*de*]), a mild adversative contrasting with the string of uses of "and" (Greek και [*kai*]) found throughout Revelation.

96. Cf. Rev 14:2 and 19:6.

97. Cf. Aune, *Revelation 1–5*, 91. Identification of "the son of man" with "the Ancient of Days" in Daniel is a tradition that may be much older than Revelation.

98. Cf. Corsini, *Apocalypse*, 88–91.

> **. . . and he had in his right hand seven stars and from his mouth came out a sharp, two-edged sword and his appearance[99] (was) like the sun shining in its full strength. (Rev 1:16)**

Before we read of John's response, we note three other features of this son of man. First, "he had in his right hand seven stars." This is about to be explained, but the audience might first think of the seven visible planets of the ancient world: the sun, moon, and planets Mercury, Venus, Mars, Jupiter, and Saturn.[100] This adds to the cosmic and even astrological nature of the vision, since many people in the ancient world "thought that the stars shaped a person's destiny."[101] Malina argues that "the cumulative effect of these designations is to mark off Jesus the Messiah as supremely eminent because of his power."[102]

However, it may also have had political overtones. For example, Koester writes of a coin from Domitian's reign that displays the emperor's son as a young Jupiter "extending his hands to seven stars in a display of divinity and power."[103] Or the hearers may be reminded of Daniel 12:3 which states that "those who lead many to righteousness" will shine "like the stars for ever and ever."[104]

Next, "from his mouth came out a sharp, two-edged sword" (see also 2:12, 16, and 19:15, 21, where the sword strikes down the nations). The audience may not know of Hebrews 4:12, but they would be reminded of Isaiah 11:4, where the branch from the roots of Jesse (most likely the Messiah) "will strike the earth with the rod of his mouth."[105] Or they might think of Isaiah 49:2, in which the servant of God[106] has his mouth made "like a sharpened sword" by the LORD, while still unborn.[107] Clearly this is a reference to the prophet's or Messiah's speech, which is highly relevant in John's context since this glorious figure (fulfilling Isaiah's prophecies) is about to speak to *him*. The total picture is partly visual, partly symbolic (try drawing it!), and it's the symbolism that will be interpreted.

Finally, "His appearance (or face) was like the sun shining in its full strength." One simply can't look such a being in the face any more than one can look at the sun directly for long.[108] It's important also to note that John is here experiencing the

---

99. Literally "face" (Greek ὄψις [*opsis*]).

100. Cf. Aune, *Revelation 1–5*, 97–98. Alternatively, ancients might think of the constellation of Ursa Major or that of Pleiades. Cf. Leithart, *Revelation 1–11*, 127–28.

101. Koester, *Revelation*, 246.

102. Malina, *Genre and Message*, 263,

103. Koester, *Revelation*, 253; cf. Barr, *Tales of the End*, 74.

104. Beale, *Book of Revelation*, 211.

105. See also 2 Thess 2:8. Victorinus sees the "two-edged" sword as standing for Christ speaking to people in both the Old and New Testaments and bringing a message of judgment (Victorinus, *Commentary*, ANF 7:345).

106. The servant is seen as Israel or the servant to Israel (Isa 49:3, 5).

107. Fekkes, *Isaiah and Prophetic Traditions*, 117–22.

108. Cf. Thomas, *Apocalypse*, 103. Leithart also sees parallels with the woman's description of her

"son of man" in the present, not looking forward to the future, as in Daniel 7:13.[109] This confirms what I said earlier about verse 7 being about this age, not (just) the eschatological future.

Further, if Revelation is "a revelation of [about, not from] Jesus Christ" (v. 1), this experience and description is a vital part of that. John is seeing Jesus *as he really is* since his death, resurrection, and ascension. He has already confessed Jesus as messiah (vv. 1–2, 5), faithful witness (vv. 2, 5), "firstborn from the dead," "ruler of the kings of the earth" (v. 5), and Savior by his blood (vv. 5, 7). This revelation will be deepened as Revelation goes on, but is founded on this encounter.

> **And when I saw him, I fell down at his feet as (if) dead, and he placed his right hand on me, saying, "Do not fear. I am the First and the Last and the Living One, and I became dead and behold, I am alive forever and ever and I have the keys of Death and of Hades." (Rev 1:17–18)**

John's immediate response is not curiosity but fear. This is quite appropriate as a response to a heavenly apparition. In Daniel 8:15–18, Daniel "was terrified and fell prostrate" and "was in a deep sleep with my face to the ground." In Daniel 10:8–9, he says, "I had no strength left, my face turned deathly pale and I was helpless" and then "I fell into a deep sleep, my face to the ground." In Ezekiel 1:28, the prophet "fell face down." In Isaiah 6:5, Isaiah cries out "Woe to me! I am ruined!"[110] To see the glorified Christ as John did can only provoke incredible fear and helplessness, stripping away our usual sense of earthly security.[111] John may have actually fainted or slipped into "the cataleptic state associated with trance experiences."[112]

Jesus' response (because this "son of man" can only be the glorified Jesus)[113] is also typical of such an encounter. As in the case of Daniel (Dan 8:18; 10:10) and Ezekiel (Ezek 2:2), where the human figure lifts them back on their feet,[114] here the son of man brings a comforting touch and words of encouragement[115] (compare Isa 43:1; Dan 10:12; Luke 1:13; 5:10). As Thomas points out, however, this placing of the hand is more than just an act of comfort, especially as this hand also holds the seven stars.[116]

---

lover in Song 5:10–16, a passage referred to in other parts of Revelation (*Revelation 1–11*, 103–5, 111).

109. Aune, *Revelation 1–5*, 93.

110. Leithart suggests that such an action "is also the act of a defeated enemy" (as in Ps 18:38), not that John was Jesus' enemy, but he surrenders to him voluntarily (Leithart, *Revelation 1–11*, 119). Some of the audience might also have heard the story found in Luke 5:8, where Simon Peter, awe-struck by the miraculous catch of fish he has just had, "fell at Jesus' knees and said, 'Go away from me, Lord; I am a sinful man.'"

111. Though the responses of the three inner circle apostles to Jesus' transfiguration belie this generalization (see Luke 9:32–33).

112. Aune, *Revelation 1–5*, 100.

113. Aune, *Revelation 1–5*, 116.

114. He lifts Daniel at least to his "hands and knees" in Dan 10:10.

115. Possibly "stop being afraid" (Aune, *Revelation 1–5*, 66), but see Mathewson, *Handbook*, 15.

116. Thomas, *Apocalypse*, 104.

Nearly everywhere in the Bible, such an action conveys or signifies an impartation of authority, power, blessing, healing, or honor.[117] In this case, John is being authorized to write his vision, in what Aune calls "an act of investiture."[118]

Jesus then makes several significant *ego-eimi* ["I am"] statements[119] about his identity and achievements. "I am the First and the Last" (v. 17) implies deity, which was already implied by his appearance,[120] although it is only used of Christ (not God) in Revelation.[121] The implication of deity is confirmed when we compare verse 8 and Isaiah 41:4; 44:6; and 48:12; in each of these cases, the prophet is contrasting the true God with idols. "I am the Living One" by itself is a claim of deity, but what follows turns this on its head: "I became dead and behold, I am alive forever and ever" (v. 18; compare 2:8). This son of man is both divine and human, and he has passed through death to eternal life. This is, of course, a clear reference to the death and resurrection of Jesus, which even makes the appearance of this person more meaningful (is he white like death?).

But perhaps even more significant is his claim, "I have the keys of Death and of Hades" (v. 18). This is not just a resuscitated corpse: his experience of death and resurrection has given him a unique position of power and authority. John has already claimed that Jesus is the "ruler of the kings of the earth" (v. 5). Now he affirms him as Lord even over death and the underworld (Hades).[122] These are the terrible enemies of all humanity who will be unleashed in the fourth seal (6:8), who hold many of the dead (20:13), and who will ultimately be consigned to the "lake of fire" (20:14).[123] Death and Hades are temporary jailers; it is the second death that people should fear. But if Jesus has the keys of Death and Hades,[124] he clearly has the power to release their prisoners. This short passage thus adds to the "high Christology" we find in Revelation and feeds the hope of John's hearers.

> **"Write therefore what you are seeing and what is and what is about to happen after these (things)." (Rev 1:19)**

---

117. E.g., Gen 48:12–20; Num 27:18–20; Deut 34:9; Acts 6:6; 9:17; 1 Tim 4:14; 2 Tim 1:6.

118. Aune, *Revelation 1–5*, 100.

119. *Ego eimi* statements are notably present in the Gospel of John (twenty-four times) but also in the other Gospels (Aune, *Revelation 1–5*, 100). Cf. John 6:20; 8:24, 28, 58; 13:19; 18:5, 6, 8 (where the phrase has no predicate; i.e., Jesus just says, "I am"); John 6:35, 48, 51; 8:12; 10:7, 9, 11, 14; 11:25; 14:6; 15:1, 5 (where the phrase has a predicate; e.g., "I am the bread of life" in John 6:35) and Rev 1:8, 17; 2:23; 21:6; 22:16. All these amount to a claim to deity (see also 21:6; 22:16).

120. Cf. Koester, *Revelation*, 254; Thomas, *Apocalypse*, 104; Carrell, *Jesus and the Angels*, 171–72.

121. Fekkes, *Isaiah and Prophetic Traditions*, 126.

122. This includes the Greek goddess of the underworld, Hekate (Paul, *Revelation*, 74).

123. Cf. Koester, *Revelation*, 248.

124. In ancient Greek thought, the keys to Hades were held by various gods and heroes; the Jews thought that "an angel had power over Hades" (Koester, *Revelation*, 247).

Jesus returns to his original agenda, the mission John is called to carry out. John is to *write*, like Daniel and *unlike* most classical Old Testament prophets who *spoke* the word they were given.[125] Writing is very important in Revelation: this command is repeated several times (1:11, 19; 2:1, 8, 12, 18; 3:1, 7, 14; 14:13), and once John is restrained from *writing* (10:4). The words *written* in John's scroll have special power (22:7, 9, 18–19) and are to be read aloud (1:3); similarly, the sacred scroll *written* on both sides and unveiled by Jesus has special significance (5:1–7), as does the "little scroll" of 10:2, 8–10. Moreover, people need to have their names *written* in the Lamb's book of life (3:5; 13:8; 20:12, 15; 21:27). People can also have special *written* names like Jesus himself (3:12). Clearly, written words have power, most likely because they are more permanent than speech. Here John draws on common assumptions held by his hearers and readers.[126]

John is to write about three things in particular:[127] "what you are seeing" (meaning the vision he was then having of the risen, glorified Christ), "what is" (interpreting the situation of the churches in the first century), and "what is about to happen after these things." This implies that the predictive aspects of the text are only one of three foci and that they relate (mostly) to the near future for John and his hearers, as verses 1 and 3 have already implied. The common dispensationalist interpretation of verse 19, in which what is seen, what is, and what will be become the structural guideposts of the book, rests on slender foundations. Moreover, adopting such an approach forces the bulk of Revelation (chs. 4 onwards) into the mold of prediction, including the long-range variety.[128]

The distinction between these three elements is not nearly as clear or defined as some readers have imagined, since John moves back and forth among all three with a fair degree of freedom.[129] For example, as we will see, chapter 13 is at least partly an analysis of the Roman Empire as it was then, rather than a prediction of a future version of it. Revelation 2–3, which may be matched to "what is," also includes elements of "what you are seeing" and "what is about to happen after these things." And later passages also speak of what John is seeing (such as 6:1), "what is" (17:10, explicitly), and "what is about to happen after these things" (such as 21:1–5). The dispensationalist reading tends to assume, rather than prove, a Futurist approach to the text. Verse 19 can best be read as a rough summary of the contents of Revelation rather than a precise structural guide.[130]

---

125. But see Exod 17:14; Isa 30:8; Jer 30:2.

126. Cf. Aune, *Revelation 1–5*, 85–87.

127. Aune reads this as just two things; "what you see" involves "what is" and "what will take place later" (Aune, *Revelation 1–5*, 105).

128. E.g., Walvoord, *Revelation*, 47–49.

129. Cf. Beale, *Book of Revelation*, 161–62.

130. Cf. Aune, *Revelation 1–5*, 105–6. Verse 19 would also have reminded the original hearers of the similar wording of Dan 2:28, 29, and 45, supporting the idea of fulfilment here (cf. Beale, *Book of Revelation*, 139, 155–57).

J. Ramsey Michaels, however, draws attention to an alternative translation of the second phrase "what is"; it could be translated "what they are" [*ha eisin*], implying that the text will explain or interpret what John sees. He points out that there is indeed "a pattern of things 'seen' followed by an explanation of what they 'are'" throughout the book.[131] We'll notice this at appropriate times in this commentary, but the first example follows immediately.

> **"The secret of the seven stars which you see in my right hand and the seven golden lampstands: the seven stars are the angels of the seven churches and the lampstands are (the) seven churches." (Rev 1:20)**

Finally, the first authoritative interpretation of John's vision; there will be similar explanations in 7:13–14 and 17:7–18. The seven stars in the initial vision are explained allegorically as references to "the angels of the seven churches"[132] and the seven lampstands represent the seven churches themselves (v. 20).[133] Thus, as Koester puts it, "Readers find that *they* are the lampstands. They are communities in which the risen Christ is *already present*."[134] And Leithart adds, "If the angels of the churches are stars, then the church is set in the sky, joined with Christ in heavenly places."[135] This leads us into the next section of the text, Revelation 2–3, which consists of seven prophetic words to these seven specific congregations.

---

131. Michaels, *Interpreting the Book of Revelation*, 98–99.

132. We will consider the meaning of that phrase in the next chapter.

133. This structure resembles the pesher interpretations favored in the Dead Sea Scrolls, where prophecies from the Hebrew Scriptures were interpreted as applying to the situation of the Qumran community (Aune, *Revelation 1–5*, 106). However, in this case, the risen Jesus is interpreting the "mystery" or "secret" of the symbolic features John was seeing in the vision, a common feature in Jewish apocalypses. I translate μυστήριον [*mustērion*] as "secret" rather than "mystery" as the point is not its mysterious character but that it stands for something that needs explaining. Aune translates "secret meaning" (cf. Aune, *Revelation 1–5*, 67–68).

134. Koester, *Revelation*, 249; the emphasis is in the original. See also Beale, *Book of Revelation*, 206–7.

135. Leithart, *Revelation 1–11*, 117; alluding to Eph 1:3; 2:20–23; 3:10.

Revelation Chapters 2–3

John has addressed his text to "the seven churches in Asia" (Rev 1:4), to which he has been ordered to send a written version of his experiences and prophecies (1:11, 19). These churches have appeared in the vision in symbolic form, represented by seven golden lampstands (1:12, 20), showing that they operate in their cities as channels of light, even as Jesus said, "you are the light of the world" (Matt 5:14). The local churches function in some way parallel to the sacred seven-branched lampstand of the original tabernacle, an image that begs further questions, some of which will come up in chapter 11.

The initial vision also showed John a picture of seven stars in the right hand of the son of man, which were explained as representing the "angels" of the seven churches, which is also somewhat enigmatic. Certainly, these images establish the extreme importance of the churches in the mind of the seer, and indeed in the mind of Christ. These messages also provide rich ideas for considering today's churches and evaluating them by the standards set by the risen Jesus. We also noted above that chapter 2 does not start a new section; rather, the risen Jesus who appears in 1:10 continues to speak until 3:22.

So as we begin to explore the seven specific messages to these seven churches, we need to address some broad questions:

1. Why seven churches, when there were more than that number in the Asia region, and why choose Asia?
2. What are the "angels" of the seven churches, and why are the messages addressed to them rather than directly to the congregations?
3. How do we understand the seven churches themselves in the light of our reading strategy for Revelation?
4. What kind of messages are these, and how are we meant to read them?

1. Why seven churches? And why Asia?

We know that there were more than seven churches in the province of Asia in the late first century. There was Colossae, to which Paul[1] wrote a letter. There was Hierapolis (Col 4:13). According to Acts 19:10, "all the Jews and Greeks who lived in the province of Asia heard the word of the Lord," so there must have been others besides. So why does John write to seven only? As I said earlier, there are two most likely reasons, other than the possibility that these were the most prominent churches in the province of Asia (which we can't assume).[2] The first is that these are the churches he has a prophetic or pastoral relationship with, and the second is that they are in some sense representative.

The number seven is common in Revelation (specifically mentioned fifty-four times)[3] and one of its common connotations is completeness (as in the seven days of creation), so these seven stand for the church at large, perhaps.[4] As the ancient commentator Victorinus argued, "Not that they are themselves the only, or even the principal churches; but what he says to one, he says to all."[5] Leithart adds what he calls "two incontestable contextual features" relevant to the choice of these cities: "most of the cities of Asia had sizable Jewish populations" and "many were centers of the imperial cult."[6] But these features are not unique to these specific seven churches, or indeed to Asia.

So why send this prophecy to Asia in particular? After all, the problems and issues mentioned in Revelation 2–3 were found in many other Christian churches, as a reading of the New Testament letters shows. Commentators like Leithart must also face the question, "Why not Jerusalem?" or specifically Jewish groups if the key prediction of Revelation is the fall of Jerusalem, and Jerusalem is the harlot of Revelation 17. Leithart offers an explanation that has to do with "the theological geography of the Mediterranean world." According to him, "Asia is liminal space between Israel and Rome, therefore the space where Jews and Gentiles are knit together into one humanity."[7]

2. What are the "angels" of the seven churches?

Determining what John means by the "angels" of the seven churches is harder, since every possibility has its negative sides. The Greek word *angelos* literally means "messenger" and need not refer to a heavenly being, but it seems to have this sense in the many other

---

1. Many scholars argue that Colossians was not written by Paul but by one of his followers.
2. Some commentators speculate about an ancient postal route following the route through these seven cities, but the evidence seems thin. John would not have had access to any public postal service (cf. Leithart, *Revelation 1–11*, 141; Aune, *Revelation 1–5*, 131; Moyise, *Old Testament in the Book of Revelation*, 25–26).
3. Aune, *Revelation 1–5*, 115.
4. Cf. Koester, *Revelation*, 244; Aune, *Revelation 1–5*, 130–31; Beale, *Book of Revelation*, 186–87, 204.
5. Victorinus, *Commentary*, ANF 7:345.
6. Leithart, *Revelation 1–11*, 142.
7. Leithart, *Revelation 1–11*, 141; see also 41, 83–84.

references to angels in the Book of Revelation. The idea of churches having angels is unique to Revelation. Paul speaks of angels as potential spectators of local church behavior (1 Cor 11:10)[8] and Hebrews calls the angels "ministering spirits sent to serve those who will inherit salvation" (Heb 1:14), but neither of these are as specific as Revelation.

John may have derived the idea of supervising or protecting angels from the Jewish apocalyptic literature, especially Daniel. Daniel presents the angel Michael as the "prince" and protector of the Jewish people in conflict with the princes of the empires ruling over or threatening them (Dan 10:13, 20–21; 12:1).[9] This thought is also perhaps behind Revelation 12:7, where "Michael and his angels" fight against "the dragon and his angels." Guardian angels of individuals are implied by Matthew 18:10 ("their angels in heaven always see the face of my Father in heaven") and perhaps Acts 12:15.[10] But the heavenly figure identified with the church in Acts is Jesus himself, as shown by the accounts where Jesus calls Saul from heaven, "why do you persecute me?" (Acts 9:4–5; 22:7–8; 26:14–15). None of these comparisons is much help, so it is necesary to consider the alternative possibilities for the church angels here.

a. They could be human messengers: the "bishops" of the churches, since they seem to represent each church in all its failures as well as successes,[11] or prophets of each church.[12] Papandrea argues for this view on the basis that stars represent kings in the Bible.[13] However, Revelation never uses *angelos* of human leaders elsewhere.[14] Moreover, it is not clear that local churches had "monarchical" (single) bishops as early as this.[15] However, if the stars in Revelation 1:20 allude to the wise people in Daniel 12:3, as Beale suggests,[16] perhaps the "angels" are the founders of the churches now in heaven, a conclusion not drawn by Beale himself, and implausible if John is addressing the *current* state of these churches.

b. They could represent the *ethos* or "spirit" of the churches since the words of Jesus seem to address this. However, Jesus addresses specific people and

---

8. Here Paul argues that "a woman ought to have authority over her own head, because of the angels."

9. Cf. Aune, *Revelation 1–5*, 110.

10. Cf. Koester, *Revelation*, 248.

11. Leithart makes a strong argument for this interpretation and attempts to carry it through his analysis of the seven prophecies, but it doesn't quite work to my mind, as the message in each case slips into describing the congregation or its individual members. At the most, the "bishop" is seen as somehow responsible for the health of the congregation. Cf. Leithart, *Revelation 1–11*, 123–26; Taushev, *Ancient Christianity*, 70.

12. Cf. Bucur, "Hierarchy, Prophecy, and Angelomorphic Spirit," 193.

13. Papandrea, *Wedding of the Lamb*, 70.

14. Other NT books do use *angelos* of humans; e.g., Luke 7:24; 9:52; Mark 1:2; Jas 2:25.

15. The early Christian writer Ignatius, writing perhaps just after Revelation, urges churches in that geographical area to submit to their bishops, which may suggest that "monarchical" bishops are being accepted, or perhaps rather that Ignatius was advocating this (cf. Fiorenza, *Book of Revelation*, 142–45).

16. Beale, *Book of Revelation*, 211; cf. Johnson, *Pneumatic Discernment*, 204–5.

groups as well, so it makes for an awkward reading. Perhaps a better word is "culture"; we all know how a church develops a culture over time that is either healthy or unhealthy, depending on decisions made by its leaders and others in specific situations and contexts. The church culture then takes on a life of its own and becomes almost a kind of stronghold.

c. They could be simply a literary device, not to be taken literally. The messages are mostly in the second person singular, but it soon becomes clear that the messages are not *really* addressed to the "angels" but to the humans in each church.[17] Koester argues, "writing to an angel rather than directly to the congregation allows readers to picture themselves maintaining a respectful distance from the overwhelming majesty of Christ while an intermediary receives the message they are to hear."[18] But what would be the point of doing this, especially since no other Christian writing of that time does anything similar?

d. They are literal "guardian" angels and they are held responsible for the failings of each church as well as its successes. The idea of angels being "grey" figures (as opposed to purely of God or the devil) is certainly unique, if that is what John intends.[19] However, he does appear to want to break down the distinctions between angels and humans to some extent, as in the two places where John tries to worship angels (19:10 and 22:8–9).[20]

Whatever John's intention here, the seven messages clearly address the churches themselves and particular (human) individuals and groups in them, rather than angels as such.

3. How do we understand the seven churches themselves in the light of our reading strategy for Revelation?

Most commentators agree that John is addressing seven literal first-century congregations with their individual histories and problems. The attempts to match features of each message with aspects of the known history, culture, or geography of each city

---

17. Aune, *Revelation 1–5*, 109, 120. However, Aune later argues that these are meant to be literal angels (ibid., 131).

18. Koester, *Revelation*, 235.

19. Wink pursues this possibility more consistently than anyone else I know but ends up adopting something like the second view: angels as the *ethos* of each church (Wink, *Unmasking the Powers*, 69–81). Beale argues that they are "heavenly beings who also represent the church" using a concept of "corporate representation" and thus "there is some sense in which the angels are *accountable* . . . for the churches" (Beale, *Book of Revelation*, 217; see also 218–19). See also Caird, *Revelation*, 24–25, who also points to the conflict in heaven as a parallel.

20. Cf. Stuckenbruck, *Angel Veneration*, 234–38. Gause sees the "angels" as messengers of Jesus whom he places in each church; they are essential to each church's identity (Gause, *Revelation*, 48).

clearly implies this.[21] The situations described in each message also correspond with what we know of the early church from the New Testament and other sources. But is there a secondary or prophetic sense of what the churches stand for?

> a. Do they represent seven eras in the history of the church?[22] This historical interpretation is common among Futurist readers, especially dispensationalists, though its origins are much older.[23] In this view, commonly Ephesus stands for the early (post-apostolic) church with its clear doctrines but supposedly declining spiritual fervor. Smyrna stands for the early church standing up under severe Roman persecution. Pergamum stands for the papal church compromising with pagan customs. Thyatira stands for the state-supported church after Constantine, infested with false teaching. Sardis stands for the church in the Reformation (divided into two distinct groups). Philadelphia stands for the church in the post-Reformation revivals. Finally, Laodicea is the church now, just before the "rapture."[24]
>
> The problem here is that one has to force the words about each church into this kind of grid and radically oversimplify what was happening in each of these historical periods, as well as limiting consideration to the *western* church, to make this plausible. For dispensationalists, Laodicea is a good place to end because they have a pessimistic view of the church derived from J. N. Darby's "church in ruins."[25] It also helps fashion a rhetorical weapon to attack the main-line, Pentecostal, or other churches they don't agree with. However, if this is the last church, what about all those good dispensationalists? Are they also Laodicea? This line of thought frequently leads to a modification of the interpretation, making Philadelphia also an end-time church, especially as it seems to be escaping the future tribulation (3:10). And who knows if today is really the last stage of the church?
>
> b. Do they represent seven kinds of churches in the last days, immediately before the "rapture"? This is also favored by many Futurists. Like all

---

21. The two most important attempts to do this are Ramsay (1904) and Hemer (2000). Cf. Koester, *Revelation*, 233. As Koester points out, however, in such attempts, the facts have to be "molded to fit the distinctive imagery in Revelation" (ibid.) and "the seven cities had more similarities than differences" (ibid., 266); cf. Thomas, *Apocalypse*, 109–10.

22. Another possibility proposed by Moloney is that they represent stages in the history of Israel in the OT (Moloney, *Apocalypse of John*, 27, 61–85). While the parallels he draws are intriguing, and clearly John *is* referring back to that history, this interpretation is also somewhat forced and pays too little attention to the situation of those first century congregations, which Moloney says we don't have enough independent information about.

23. This idea goes back to the Medieval Age or earlier (Koester, *Revelation*, 232). Joachim of Fiore (12th cent.) was a major advocate (Corsini, *Apocalypse*, 103–4).

24. Cf. Koester, *Revelation*, 233.

25. Darby was the pioneer of modern dispensationalism in the nineteenth century. An Anglican minister in Ireland originally, he despaired of renewal or restoration of the church to anything like its NT vigor, which makes his views very different to those of Pentecostals.

predictions of Futurist readings, it is impossible to falsify this view. However, it inevitably leads to speculation, especially to oversimplified judgments of today's churches. It also makes the identifications of specific groups as equivalent to, say, Thyatira, much more serious, especially if the interpreter is also looking for clues to the imminence of the *Parousia*.

c. Do they simply represent typical churches (or church conditions) of all periods throughout church history? As Hendriksen puts it, "The sevenfold condition of these churches actually existed at that time. It exists today. It has existed during the entire intervening period."[26] This view allows us to read John literally, meaning that he is thinking of real first-century churches he knows, and still apply the messages to our own time, much as we would do with the other New Testament literature. There is still the danger of speculation and judgment, as in option (b) above, but the resulting critique of any specific church is less "loaded" than in that option. This seems the wisest course to me.

4. What kind of messages are these and how are we meant to understand them?

Frequently they are called "the letters to the churches." This idea is supported by the fact that they are written to each church and are "from" the risen Christ. On the other hand, they don't have the features of letters as seen in 1:4–5, for example.[27]

Some commentators read them as edicts, parallel to edicts of Caesar to his subjects in each city of the empire.[28] This is supported by the authoritative tone of each message: there is no reasoning or discussion such as we find in the Pauline letters, for example. But the parallels with imperial edicts are not uniform, and I'm not sure the churches would recognize them. Others have drawn parallels with the Ancient Near Eastern covenant form used in Deuteronomy, which is helpful since the content of these messages depends on a covenant relationship between Christ and his churches similar to that between God and Israel in the Old Testament.[29] Leithart suggests "priestly pronouncements to the church,"[30] based partly on the temple language of Revelation 1:12–16.

But on the whole, I think they should be read as prophetic messages comparable to the oral messages or sermons of the Hebrew prophets of old. These, of course, often

---

26. Hendriksen, *More Than Conquerors*, 79. Similar thoughts are found in Gause, *Revelation*, 45.

27. Cf. Leithart, *Revelation 1–11*, 131. Prophetic letters did exist in the ancient world and the Hebrew Scriptures but did not follow the form used here (Aune, *Revelation 1–5*, 125–26).

28. The strongest case is in Aune, *Revelation 1–5*, 126–29. Aune argues that Revelation is setting up Jesus as a superior authority to the Roman emperor. Cf. Leithart, *Revelation 1–11*, 114.

29. Cf. Beale, *Book of Revelation*, 227; cf. Campbell, "Findings," 73–81.

30. Leithart, *Revelation 1–11*, 131–32.

contained "covenant lawsuits,"[31] criticizing Israelites for their disloyalty to the Mosaic covenant. This is the part of Revelation that most resembles classical prophecy. Each message has a clear audience of God's people, begins with a prophetic introductory phrase claiming that the source is Christ (not John), passes judgment on the congregation concerned, and offers warnings and promises depending on the response of the audience.[32] This is quite different than the text as a whole with its more universal and deterministic flavor.

We should also note that these messages, as well as the rest of Revelation, would be read aloud during a worship service in each of these seven congregations.[33] Modern readers from more traditional churches would envisage something like the Scripture readings that form a regular part of their liturgy. But Pentecostals would envisage something like a congregational word of prophecy that might be given spontaneously during a Pentecostal worship service.

Before exploring the details of each message, we should notice some common structural features of each of the seven messages.[34]

- Apart from the first message, they begin with "and" (*kai*) in the Greek text.
- They each then begin with an address "to the angel of the church in . . ." and a command to "write," recalling the commands of 1:11 and 19.
- Consistent with that address, most of the messages are written in the second-person singular (that is, to the "angel"), though sometimes this breaks down and the message transitions to second-person plural.
- This is followed by the prophetic formula, "thus says" (*tade legei*), reminiscent of Hebrew prophets' "thus says the LORD."[35]
- They then identify the author as the risen Christ, picking out one of the features of the vision from chapter 1 to focus on.[36] This fulfills the command to John to write "what you are seeing" (1:11, 19).

---

31. Campbell calls them "mini covenant lawsuits" with a structure parallel to the ancient covenant treaties explored by Meredith Kline (Campbell, "Findings," 75–80).

32. See discussion in Koester, *Revelation*, 234–35 and Aune, *Revelation 1–5*, 126.

33. Cf. Archer, *Worship in the Apocalypse*, 135–36.

34. Beale also posits a chiastic structure for this section, that is, a structure where the first and last items (a) are parallel, likewise the second and second last (b), etc. Usually the emphasis then falls on the middle item(s). Here he sees an abcccba structure based on the condition of each church with the congregations most seriously in danger at the beginning and end, the most obedient churches second and second last, and the "mixed" churches in the middle, with the implication being that "the Christian church as a whole is perceived as being in poor condition" (Beale, *Book of Revelation*, 226; cf. Leithart, *Revelation 1–11*, 130, 136–37). This may be oversimplifying the message of the arrangement.

35. But similar language is used in Persian royal diplomatic letters and edicts (Aune, *Revelation 1–5*, 121, 141–42).

36. Cf. Koester, *Revelation*, 234–36. The phrases seem to be designed to heighten the respect for the speaker and hence for John's prophetic message, or, as Leithart suggests, to provide a full view of Christ as part of the process of becoming like him (Liethart, *Revelation 1–11*, 133–35).

- Next comes the introductory phrase "I know" [*oida*] followed by (1) commendations and (2) reproofs. Some of the messages don't have both, which makes them stand out, as we will see.[37] Here John is writing "what is" (1:19).

- There are various promises, calls to repent, and warnings based on the commendations and reproofs.[38] Some of the promises anticipate later aspects of John's vision.[39] Some aspects of the messages refer to various Old Testament passages as identified below,[40] implying a certain continuity between the story of Israel and the church (compare 1 Cor 10:1–11). The promises and warnings are "what is about to happen after these things" (1:19), depending on the church's response to the prophecy.

- Finally, there are two common statements (which switch their order after the first three messages): a promise to "the conquerors" and a general exhortation, "those who have ears, let them hear what the Spirit is saying to the churches."[41] So each message begins with Christ and finishes with the Spirit as the author, which suggests an identification between Christ and the Spirit.[42]

2:1–7 The Church in Ephesus

To the angel of the church in Ephesus write:
Thus says the one who holds the seven stars in his right hand, who walks in the midst of the seven golden lampstands. (Rev 2:1)

Remembering that chapter and verse divisions were not part of the original text, we read 2:1 as leading straight on from 1:20. This is how the original hearers would have heard it and it implies that this is a continuation of the vision of 1:9–20. After addressing this message to "the angel of the church in Ephesus," John describes the speaker in language from the initial vision. He stresses Jesus' close relationship with the churches and their angels, a relationship of protection (holding them) and inspection (walking among them).[43] Certainly these messages read like an inspection report to some degree.

---

37. Cf. Koester, *Revelation*, 236–37.
38. Cf. Leithart, *Revelation 1–11*, 137–40.
39. Leithart argues that the letters "lay out the plotline of Revelation" (Leithart, *Revelation 1–11*, 143).
40. Cf. Beale, *Book of Revelation*, 224. Leithart argues that each church reflects a stage in Israel's history (Leithart, *Revelation 1–11*, 130–31; cf. Corsini, *Apocalypse*, 105–7).
41. Cf. Koester, *Revelation*, 237. Koester points out that these promises and exhortations are in the singular; i.e., "each individual is called to respond."
42. Cf. Bucur, "Hierarchy, Prophecy, and Angelomorphic Spirit," 185–88. Bucur sees an identification of Christ and the Spirit here, but tends to view the Spirit as a kind of angelic being inspiring the prophet.
43. Cf. Thomas, *Apocalypse*, 111.

> **I know your works and your labor and your perseverance and that you cannot bear bad (people), and you tested those who say they are apostles and are not, and have found them false . . . (Rev 2:2)**

As in most of the other messages, the report starts with the positives. This must have been a very strong church in the biggest city of the province of Asia,[44] in a sense perhaps the "mother church" for this region.

We read in Acts 19 of the powerful move of God involved with the founding of the church in Ephesus by Paul, including the spread of the gospel throughout the province of Asia (v. 10), extraordinary miracles (vv. 11–12), a deep reformation of people's lives exemplified by the burning of valuable magic books (vv. 17–20), and changes to the economy that provoked violent opposition (vv. 23–41). Interestingly, in this incident, Paul was protected by powerful civic leaders in a unique way (vv. 31–41). Ephesus thus became, and remained for centuries, a strong center of Christianity. However, according to Acts and 1 Timothy, the church was infected with false teaching before long (Acts 20:29–30; 1 Tim 1:3; 5:20–21). These included struggles about law (1 Tim 1:7–11), leadership (1 Tim 2:11—3:13; 5:17–22), food laws (1 Tim 4:1–8), rules about widows (1 Tim 5:3–16), and money (1 Tim 6:5–10).[45]

Apparently though, according to Revelation, and assuming it was written later than Acts and 1 Timothy, the church had come through these challenges stronger and purer. In Revelation 2, Jesus testifies that they had demonstrated intolerance of "bad people" (v. 2), tested and rejected false apostles (v. 2), and rejected the "works of the Nicolaitans" (v. 6).[46]

They had specifically rejected false claims to apostolic authority.[47] This is particularly relevant to Pentecostal movements today. Because of their restorationist theology (expecting the church to be restored to first-century purity and power), Pentecostals are open to the possibility of modern apostles and prophets. In fact, there are many claims to apostleship among Pentecostals, some more credible than others, but all carrying a measure of spiritual danger if they are accepted uncritically. However, the existence of "false apostles" here also suggests that true apostles were around, or at least that the church was open to such a possibility,[48] supporting such a Pentecostal view.

---

44. For information on ancient Ephesus, see Koester, *Revelation*, 256–60; Aune, *Revelation 1–5*, 136–41. The city was a mixture of prosperity and evil forces such as the slave trade, imperial cult, Artemis cult (Acts 19:23–34), other pagan cults, and emphasis on magic or sorcery (Acts 19:19).

45. Similar issues with false teaching are found in the letter of Ignatius, a famous early Christian leader and martyr, to the Ephesians in about AD 110. Cf. Beale, *Book of Revelation*, 229.

46. Probably a different group since they are a present danger whereas the false apostles were in the past (Aune, *Revelation 1–5*, 143, 147).

47. Cf. Thomas, *Apocalypse*, 113–14. The testing process involved is not spelled out (cf. Koester, *Revelation*, 262). This was not an unprecedented problem, as 2 Cor 11:13 makes clear. The later Didache contains a testing process for itinerants like this. Cf. Aune, *Revelation 1–5*, 144–45.

48. Cf. Keener, *Revelation*, 109.

> ... and you have perseverance and have borne up on account of my name and have not grown weary. (Rev 2:3)

So we have a picture of a church that works hard, perseveres under pressure, shows great spiritual discernment (since things are not always what they seem, a strong theme in Revelation), and refuses all forms of false teaching.[49] Today such a congregation as this one in ancient Ephesus would be greatly admired and respected by the wider church, especially the more "respectable" Pentecostal churches.

> But[50] I have against you that you have left your first love. Therefore, remember from where you have fallen, and repent, and do the first works. And if not, I am coming to you and I will move your lampstand out of its place, if you do not repent. (Rev 2:4–5)

This church had one serious flaw, apparently unknown to them and yet serious enough that their very existence as a legitimate church was under threat as a result (v. 5). In the midst of their becoming a strong, orthodox congregation, Jesus says, "You have forsaken the love you had at first" (v. 4 NIV). Clearly, this is a very serious accusation and would have come as a shock to the audience after the positive commendation in verses 2–3. It was a culpable sin; the prophecy uses the word "left" or "forsaken" or "abandoned."[51] Clearly, the church had made some deliberate decisions that caused it to move away from this "first love," even while enduring hardships for Jesus' name, maybe as part of their suppression of false teaching.

It reminds me of the response of many orthodox evangelical churches to the Charismatic movement in the 1960s and 1970s. By suppressing or resisting what they saw as a deviant teaching and experience, they lost their enthusiasm and vigor in the interest of maintaining orthodox teaching. Something similar happened in many Pentecostal churches after they were strongly established, for similar reasons, and it may be seen as a common danger.[52] Any church launched in revival faces invasions of false teachings and general waning of their first fervor.

Second, it was a flaw not so much in teaching as in practice. Was it their love for Jesus or their love for one another that they had abandoned? First John, perhaps written by the same person as Revelation, stresses the tight connection between both kinds of

---

49. Cf. Leithart, *Revelation 1–11*, 146–47. Contrary to current postmodern thinking, in Revelation "intolerance is invariably a *virtue*," says Leithart. I think *discernment* is more the virtue John has in mind. The text is not advocating intolerance in general, only intolerance of evil and falsehood. As Leithart says, what is going on here is spiritual warfare (ibid., 148).

50. Greek had two main contrasting words which may be translated "but": a stronger word ἀλλα [*alla*], used here, and a weaker contrast *de* which sometimes would be translated "and" or "now." Both words are used more often in Revelation 2–3 than elsewhere in Revelation (Aune, *Revelation 1–5*, 146).

51. This is the Greek, ἀφῆκες [*aphēkes*] from ἀφιημι [*aphiēmi*], usually meaning "cancel" or "forgive a debt."

52. Some early Pentecostals were alive to this danger; e.g., Johnson, *Pneumatic Discernment*, 179.

love (1 John 4:7–21). But Revelation focuses more on passionate devotion to Jesus,[53] so I am inclined to think that is what the main focus is here. However, G. K. Beale makes an interesting related suggestion: he interprets this fall from "first love" as the church being slack in witnessing to Christ among unbelievers and thus failing to shine the light from their lampstand. This would explain the precise punishment threatened in their case. He then adds that "suppression of the spiritual gifts" may be a factor because they "were necessary for the Christian community's witness to be effective."[54]

Third, the church's issue involved a decline in their spiritual condition, as indicated by "left your first love" and the language of the next verse: "Consider from where you have fallen" and "do again the first works." The church used to be "on fire" for Jesus; now it had become cold in spite of its diligence. Likely, their focus had gone from Jesus himself to being correct or orthodox; maybe they were even proud of their discernment and adherence to good teaching. But Jesus stresses their fallen condition, with its potential allusion to Satan, Babylon, or other enemies of God (compare Rev 9:1; 12:9, 13; 14:8; 18:2, 21; and Isa 14:12) or ancient Israel (see Jer 2:2–5),[55] or even the original fall of humankind in the Garden.[56] This church had perhaps become almost an enemy of God in spite of its good qualities.

This serious language is followed by an equally serious threat if they don't repent: "I am coming to you, and I will move your lampstand out of its place" (v. 5). Since the lampstand is an image of the church itself, Jesus here is threatening to remove this church altogether, perhaps "to disperse the congregation," as Victorinus wrote.[57] Either the congregation ceases to exist, or it is no longer recognized by Jesus as a true church. As Koester points out, John cannot take such action; only Jesus can do so. Therefore, the warning is only powerful to the extent that the hearers recognize this as a true prophetic word from God.[58]

This warning calls to mind the emphasis by Pentecostals on the need for the true church to be full of the Holy Spirit and passionately devoted to Jesus. In their judgment, many church institutions lack such power and devotion. But of course, such a fate could just as easily befall a Pentecostal church, and has done.[59]

---

53. Cf. Newton, "Reading Revelation Romantically."

54. Beale, *Book of Revelation*, 231; see also 230–32. Leithart, following his contention that the "angels" are the bishops of the churches, suggests that "An angel who leaves his first love is one who proves himself a hireling, who abandons the church when wolves attack" (Leithart, *Revelation 1–11*, 149). This would fit Acts 20:29, which was addressed to the elders of Ephesus, and John 10:12. But it doesn't seem to fit Rev 2:1–6; the "angel" is commended as a good shepherd in his resistance to wolves like the Nicolaitans.

55. Cf. Smolarz, *Covenant*, 286–87.

56. Cf. Moloney, *Apocalypse of John*, 68. This is supported by the promise to the conquerore of access to the tree of life (v. 7).

57. Victorinus, *Commentary*, ANF 7:346.

58. Koester, *Revelation*, 268.

59. The Australian Christian Churches (Assemblies of God), Australia's largest Pentecostal movement, has been known to close down assemblies when they become moribund. This has been done

The threat is predicated on a condition: "if you do not repent" (v. 5). This suggests, first, that the ultimate fate of the church was in its own hands and, second, that Christians are often in need of repentance. Repentance (Greek *metanoia*, literally "a change of mind, heart, ways") is more than a formal confession of sin or acts of penance or contrition. In this case, the Ephesian church is being called to take a hard look at itself and make some serious decisions about restoring its passion for Jesus. To put it another way, orthodoxy (right belief) and orthopraxis (right actions) are not sufficient; we need also orthopathy (right affections or emotions).[60]

Another point is worth making here. Jesus' threat begins with "I am coming to you" (v. 5), using the Greek word *erchomai*, the ordinary word for "come," in the present tense (as in 1:7). Such a coming is not necessarily desirable (compare 22:17, 20), and neither is it to be identified with the *Parousia*.[61] The church would not see Jesus coming with their physical eyes; they would only know he had come by the consequences. Ironically, a church renowned for discernment might fail to discern Jesus' coming to sort them out. "As long as the congregation at Ephesus continues to gather, the readers will find it difficult to conclude that their lampstand has been moved."[62] This is a challenge to the modern church: if Jesus withdraws his presence from us, would it make a difference or would we go on as usual?

> **But this you have, that you hate the works of the Nicolaitans, which I also hate. (Rev 2:6)**

The hard words of verses 4–5 are modified slightly by the concession in verse 6, though it also uses strong language. We don't know precisely who the Nicolaitans were[63] but clearly they were professing Christians, infiltrators into the Asian churches (see also 2:15), and apparently advocates of compromise with the pagan culture, as we will discuss later. Russian Orthodox commentator Averky Taushev, drawing on the fifth-century commentary of Andrew of Caesarea, identifies them as a group of proto-Gnostics, those denounced in 2 Peter 2:1 and Jude 4,[64] which would make sense. Victorinus, writing in the late third century, said that they were "false and troublesome men, who, as ministers under the name of Nicolaus, had made for themselves a heresy, to the effect that what had been offered to idols might be exorcised and eaten, and that

---

even when the churches still adhere to the denominational policies and doctrines.

60. Cf. Land, *Pentecostal Spirituality*.

61. However, as Thomas argues, "Jesus' ongoing activity would be seen as eschatological activity," so the distinction between such "comings" and the final *Parousia* should not be exaggerated (Thomas, *Apocalypse*, 119; cf. Beale, *Book of Revelation*, 232–33).

62. Koester, *Revelation*, 270.

63. Cf. Koester, *Revelation*, 263–64; Aune, *Revelation 1–5*, 148–49; Paul, *Revelation*, 81.

64. Taushev, *Ancient Christianity*, 79. Full-blown Gnosticism, a heresy that posed a very serious threat to the early church in the second century, probably had not emerged at this stage, but the trends that led to this might well have been present here. For more on Gnosticism, cf. Evans and Porter, *Dictionary of NT Background*, 414–18.

whoever should have committed fornication might receive peace on the eighth day."[65] At least the church in Ephesus was on the right side in this point. There is a need for balance here: love for Jesus and one another, but hatred for sin and idolatry, is always a hard balance to maintain.

> **Those who have ears, let them hear what the Spirit is saying to the churches. To those who conquer I will give them to eat from the tree of life, which is in the paradise of God. (Rev 2:7)**

The message to Ephesus concludes with a further call to decision. Individual Christians are called to stand up against the majority, if necessary, a process requiring a pneumatological discernment[66] and immense courage. The phrase about having ears to hear also recalls the language of the Gospels concerning Jesus' teaching and parables (Matt 11:15; 13:43; Mark 4:23), with which the audience of Revelation may have been familiar. Perhaps not all will hear the message, but some will.[67] And these hearers may become conquerors.

The prophecy says, "To those who conquer [*tō nikōnti*][68] I will give to them to eat from the tree of life, which is in the paradise of God" (v. 7). Perhaps not all the hearers will conquer; some may instead be conquered! There is a real struggle implied here. In this case, the church had won one battle (for right teaching and resistance to pagan culture) but lost another (for passionate allegiance and witness). The Christian life is a constant battle and victory cannot be taken for granted. Moreover, the consequences are very serious: being disowned by Jesus on the one hand (v. 5) or being rewarded with final salvation on the other. The tree of life and the paradise of God (v. 7) are both images reflecting the original Garden (Gen 2:8–9; 3:24) and associated with the new Jerusalem (Rev 22:2), though the term "paradise" is not repeated (but see 2 Cor 12:4; Luke 23:43).[69] In other words, we have here a strong binary mindset, as is reflected throughout Revelation: people are either saved or lost, conquerors or defeated (fallen), and apparently even professing Christians may be lost.[70]

2:8–11 The Church in Smyrna

> **And to the angel of the church in Smyrna write:**

---

65. Victorinus, *Commentary*, ANF 7:346.
66. Thomas, *Apocalypse*, 121–22.
67. Cf. Beale, *Book of Revelation*, 236–39. John occasionally addresses the hearers or readers directly as in 13:9 (similar to here), 13:18 (a call to "calculate the number of the beast"), and 22:18–19 (a warning against tampering with the prophetic text).
68. I.e., "to the one conquering or overcoming." For background to this language, see Koester, *Revelation*, 265. English translations use different phrases here, e.g., "the one who is victorious" (NIV), "the one who conquers" (ESV), "whoever conquers" (NRSV).
69. Cf. Thomas, *Apocalypse*, 124; Aune, *Revelation 1–5*, 150–52.
70. Cf. Beale, *Book of Revelation*, 272.

> **Thus says the First and the Last, who became dead and lived (again). (Rev 2:8)**

The message to the church in Smyrna[71] starts with a different emphasis derived from the original vision (compare 1:17–18).[72] This suggests an image of Jesus as the model victor out of suffering and death. Again, there is a balance between emphasizing his deity ("First and Last") and his humanity and history, including his death and resurrection ("became dead and lived again").

> **I know your tribulation and poverty, but you are rich, and the slander from those who say they are Jews and are not, but a synagogue of Satan. Do not fear what you are about to suffer. Behold the devil is about to throw (some) of you into prison so that you may be tried, and you will have tribulation for ten days. Become faithful until death, and I will give you the crown of life. (Rev 2:9–10)**

Jesus' victory in suffering is highly relevant to the situation in which this church finds itself: one of afflictions, poverty, slander, suffering, prison, persecution, and even death (vv. 9–10). Whereas the problem with the church in Ephesus largely related to their internal situation and false teaching, this church faces massive external pressures from Jewish (v. 9) and perhaps Roman (or Roman-authorized) sources (v. 10). Their poverty may result from this opposition; as Gause suggests, "it is likely that the economic depression was imposed by their enemies in a refusal to employ them or to trade with them."[73] This is similar to the economic pressure mentioned in 13:17.

On the face of it, this church was doing it tough! There is little evidence of any external support from influential people, such as Paul had enjoyed in Ephesus (Acts 19:31–41). Moreover, the problems they faced had a diabolical origin: the slander[74] from the false Jews and the impending time in prison are both attributed to Satan or the devil.[75] The spiritual warfare implied in the message to Ephesus (and Ephesians 6) is here very overt and physical.

The figure of Satan or the devil looms large in Revelation and forms part of its dualistic worldview. By this I mean dualistic in an ethical or spiritual sense, not ontological. God is always still dominant and all-powerful relative to the devil. Satan can do significant harm, especially in persecution of the saints (v. 10; also 2:13; 12:11; 13:2, 7, 10). However, his work is limited: "you will have tribulation for ten days" (v. 10).

---

71. For information on the city, see Thomas, *Apocalypse,* 125; Koester, *Revelation,* 271–73; Aune, *Revelation 1–5,* 159–60. Smyrna was strongly pro-Roman, and this had helped it gain permission to build the second temple for the imperial cult in AD 23 (cf. Friesen, *Imperial Cults,* 36–38). Leithart adds a different slant with his comment that Smyrna means "myrrh," with implications for the love relationship between Jesus and the church (Leithart, *Revelation 1–11,* 154).

72. There may be reference here to the history of the city of Smyrna, which was refounded in 290 BC, three centuries after being destroyed (Aune, *Revelation 1–5,* 161).

73. Gause, *Revelation,* 52.

74. Or denunciation (Koester, *Revelation,* 274–75); Greek βλασφημίαν [*blasphēmian*].

75. Cf. Koester, *Revelation,* 281.

Satan's periods of apparent dominance are always brief (ten[76] days; 1,260 days; one hour) relative to the victory of God (a thousand years; forever and ever). Moreover, God is operating even through Satan's worst actions and this impending suffering is described as a test (v. 10). Perhaps the devil is trying to test the Christians in the hope of seeing them defect from Jesus, but God is also testing them to prove their faithfulness (as in 1 Pet 1:6–7 or the book of Job).[77]

Jesus "knows" everything these Christians are going through (v. 9), and his knowledge here has a note of sympathy as opposed to the more objective note of similar words in the message to Ephesus. Also Jesus' words to this church are entirely positive: it is one of only two of the seven (the other is Philadelphia in 3:7–13) which are not condemned in any way.[78] In the midst of intense pressure, the church in Smyrna, seemingly poor,[79] is actually rich (v. 9), the opposite of Laodicea (3:17).

This is a common theme throughout Revelation, and particularly in the seven messages: things are not what they seem, often the very opposite. As Johnson suggests, John wants these believers "to see through Christ's fiery eyes and discern a reality that is contrary to appearances."[80] Clearly, the riches of the church in Smyrna are spiritual or eschatological,[81] like the poverty of the church in Laodicea, though the message doesn't explain.

In a similar way, this church is slandered by self-claimed Jews, "a synagogue of Satan" (v. 9), another example of things being the opposite of what is seen or claimed and parallel to the false apostles of 2:2.[82] Either this is a rogue group of Jews (unlikely)[83] or Jesus is referring to the main synagogue at Smyrna that resisted and opposed the new Christian movement and even perhaps took them to Roman tribunals for punishment. This reflects accounts in Acts 17:5–9; 18:12–17, and perhaps 13:50; 14:2, 19; 17:13; 20:19 (see also 1 Thess 2:14–16).[84]

---

76. This number has consistent negative connotations in Revelation (cf. Thomas, *Apocalypse*, 130).

77. Cf. Beale, *Book of Revelation*, 242. Beale argues that there is a reference here to the testing of Daniel and his friends for ten days in Dan.1:12, 14, but that was instigated by the conscience of the Jews, though the common issue may be food offered to idols; cf. Leithart, *Revelation 1–11*, 162.

78. In parallel, two churches receive no praise: Sardis (3:1–3) and Laodicea (3:14–22).

79. It was, however, part of a prosperous city (Thomas, *Apocalypse*, 126). For possible reasons behind this poverty, see Koester, *Revelation*, 274, 279; Aune, *Revelation 1–5*, 161. Cf. Jas 2:5.

80. Johnson, *Pneumatic Discernment*, 212.

81. Thomas, *Apocalypse*, 126–27.

82. Cf. Thomas, *Apocalypse*, 127–28. As Thomas points out, the issues between the church and synagogue are focused on the identity of God's people.

83. Another possibility is that they were Gentile or Christian Judaizers like those Paul attacks in Gal 1. Cf. Mayo, *Those Who Call Themselves Jews*, 54–59.

84. Cf. Koester, *Revelation*, 275–76, 279–80; Aune, *Revelation 1–5*, 162–64; Beale, *Book of Revelation*, 240. Bredin, in "Synagogue of Satan," argues that the problems were related to economic stress (Jewish business success), Christian proselytizing of Jews, relation to Rome (Jews seen as too friendly to the Empire), and especially the tax on Jews used for the Capitoline temple in Rome which was extended to Christians by Domitian. The tax gave Christians licence to practice their religion, but the

By rejecting the message of the Messiah and denouncing Christ's followers to the pagans, a form of blasphemy or slander, the synagogue lost its validity, just as the church in Ephesus was in danger of doing. It became "a synagogue of Satan,"[85] the archetypical accuser (Job 1:6–12; 2:1–6; Zech 3:1–5). Something similar seems to have happened in this exact city in the second century involving Jewish pressure and leading to the martyrdom of the Christian bishop Polycarp.[86] John is implying that the Christians in Smyrna are the true Jews because of their allegiance to the Messiah, Jesus.[87]

Jesus' words to this church are encouraging. They are rich, and they should not be afraid of an impending serious struggle, even though potentially some of them will be killed and most will be imprisoned briefly.[88] Provided they remain faithful, even until death, and thus pass the test, they are promised "the crown of life" (v. 10). As Leithart states, "The saints overcome Satan by spilling their blood in and with Jesus. It looks as if they are being judged and defeated by Satanic assault. In fact, they are, like Jesus, judges of their judges, witnesses against their accusers."[89]

As in all these seven prophetic messages, the ultimate end of the believers is conditional on their response to the message, a theme familiar to readers of Hebrew prophetic literature (such as Jer 18:7–10). A victor's crown or wreath [*stephanos*] was different to a king's crown [*diadēmata*] in that it was usually a prize for an athletic (or other) achievement.[90] In this case, the achievement is staying faithful even if martyred.

> **Those who have ears, let them hear what the Spirit is saying to the churches. Those who conquer will not be hurt by the second death. (Rev 2:11)**

The message finishes in the same way as the previous one, with a call to hear the Spirit's message and a promise to conquerors (v. 11). The promise is in contrast to the one in the message to Ephesus: protection from "the second death." The implications are similar, however: professing believers may actually fall foul of the second death (later revealed as the "lake of fire" in 20:14). This is the ultimate eschatological

---

money was being used for a pagan temple!

85. Paul was perhaps expressing similar thoughts in Rom 2:28–29; 9:6–13 and 11:17. See also John 8:44. Similarly the Qumran sect, whose documents comprise the Dead Sea Scrolls, referred to other Jews as an "assembly of Belial" (Koester, *Revelation*, 276); cf. Aune, *Revelation 1–5*, 165; Beale, *Book of Revelation*, 241; Leithart, *Revelation 1–11*, 158–62.

86. Cf. Paul, *Revelation*, 85; Aune, *Revelation 1–5*, 162–63; Leithart, *Revelation 1–11*, 159; Hendriksen, *More Than Conquerors*, 64; Mayo, *Those Who Call Themselves Jews*, 34–37.

87. Cf. Mayo, *Those Who Call Themselves Jews*, 61–62.

88. In ancient times, prison was rarely a long-term experience. People were in prison awaiting either interrogation, trial, or execution. At this stage, Christians were only liable to prison or punishment if denounced to the civic authorities, as seems to be the case here, and the actual punishments meted out varied widely (cf. Koester, *Revelation*, 276–77; Aune, *Revelation 1–5*, 166).

89. Leithart, *Revelation 1–11*, 158.

90. Cf. Koester, *Revelation*, 277–78; Mathewson, *Handbook*, 25–26; Aune, *Revelation 1–5*, 172–75. I am tempted to translate this as "medal." But this word often translates a word for a royal crown in the Greek OT (Smolarz, *Covenant*, 289).

dualism: paradise or the second death, heaven or hell, loyalty to God or the devil. The issues here are extremely serious; this is a real war. Many modern Pentecostal (and other) churches face similar challenges to the church of Smyrna, especially in countries where Christians are a minority. One of the insights common to both Pentecostalism and Revelation is in understanding that behind their trials lies real spiritual warfare between the forces of God and Satan.

2:12–17 The Church in Pergamum

> **And to the angel of the church in Pergamum write:**
> **Thus says the one who has the sharp, two-edged sword. I know where you dwell, where the throne of Satan is, and you hold fast my name and did not deny my faith even in the days of Antipas my faithful witness, who was put to death among you, where Satan dwells. (Rev 2:12–13)**

This church lived in just as threatening an environment as Smyrna. Indeed, Satan's throne is there (v. 13), implying that this city is the center of the devil's activity in the province of Asia. As Leithart says, "The most important fact about the church in Pergamum is *where* it is."[91] As in Smyrna, the main source of the problems was Satan himself. Pergamum was a central point for the worship of Zeus (the chief god of the Greeks, equivalent to the Roman Jupiter), with an enormous altar dedicated to him.[92] The city also had temples to Athena (the city's patron deity), Asclepios (the god of healing), and the Roman emperor. Pergamum was the capital of the original province of Asia after its king bequeathed the territory to the Romans in 133 BC[93] and the first city in Asia licensed in AD 29 to build a temple "dedicated . . . to 'divine Augustus and the goddess Roma.'"[94]

Koester understands the reference to the location of Satan's throne as referring to the fact that only here has a Christian been executed, rejecting explanations built on altars and temples.[95] But this sounds like confusing symptoms with causes. The implication seems to me that Antipas was killed because Satan no longer felt safe on his throne of pagan worship due to the progress of the gospel (compare Acts 19:25–27). So perhaps it was appropriate that Jesus is introduced as "the one who has the sharp, two-edged sword" (vv. 12; see 1:16; Isa 49:2). This suggests his ability to "cut through" and separate truth from lies (compare Heb 4:12) and his final victory over resistant nations (19:15, 21). He will show the believers what is really going on in the city, and

---

91. Liethart, *Revelation 1–11*, 165, emphasis in the original.
92. This has been reconstructed in a museum in Berlin (Aune, *Revelation 1–5*, 194).
93. Cf. Aune, *Revelation 1–5*, 180, which also gives more details of the city's history.
94. Thomas, *Apocalypse*, 133, drawing on the Roman author Tacitus. See Koester, *Revelation*, 284–85.
95. Koester, *Revelation*, 286–87; cf. Aune, *Revelation 1–5*, 182–84; Beale, *Book of Revelation*, 246; Friesen, "Satan's Throne," 356–67.

he will ultimately dethrone Satan on behalf of the true God who "sits on the throne" (4:2; 5:1, 7, 13).[96]

In a similar way to the previous message, this one starts positively. Jesus knows where they live and the difficulties asssociated with their particular locale (v. 13). They have withstood the intense pressure, probably referring to the pressure to join in the Greek and Roman cults of the city. He says that they "hold fast my name" (the Greek word *krateis* is the same as that in 2:1 of Jesus "holding" the stars of the churches) and "did not deny my faith" (v. 13).[97] They did this even when one of their leaders was actually killed, the first mention of an actual martyrdom in the book and the only specific case.[98] Opponents of Christianity would often attack the leaders of the church particularly in order to warn off the others and leave the infant churches without proper leadership (see Acts 4:1–3, 18–21; 5:17–18, 27, 40; 6:12–14; 7:54–60; 12:1–4). While Antipas is not called a leader, he is described as "my faithful witness" (v. 13), just like Jesus (1:5), so at the least, he is a model hero for the believers in Pergamum and all those who hear this prophecy.[99] Remaining true to the name of Jesus is a core value of Revelation (v. 13; see 2:3).

> **But I have a little against you, that you have there those who hold to the teaching of Balaam, who taught Balak to throw down a stumbling block before the sons of Israel, to eat idols' food and commit sexual immorality. So also, in the same way, you have those who hold fast the teaching of the Nicolaitans. (Rev 2:14–15)**

The tone of this prophetic report changes ominously, if at first subtly, with the words "I have a little against you" (v. 14). While these Christians have withstood the pressure to worship Satanic forces, they have apparently compromised at the edges of the conflict. In parallel with the Old Testament story of Balaam and Balak, some of them have apparently been seduced by the Nicolaitans (vv. 14–15).[100]

The story in Numbers 25 would be familiar to many of Revelation's listeners and has a clear application to their situation. Balak, king of Moab, was terrified of the Israelites who were invading the region *en route* to their promised land, especially as they easily defeated his neighboring kings in battle (Num 22:2–3). Armed resistance seemed futile, but Balak thought of a different, spiritual strategy; he would hire a spiritually powerful person, a prophet or shaman, to place a curse on the Israelites. Balaam (the eminent shaman chosen by the king) resisted the king's entreaties and offers of money at first, but finally was persuaded to come on board. However, Balaam knew enough about spiritual things and had enough connection to God, not to mention a funny experience with an angel and his own donkey, to be careful only to say what

---

96. Cf. Koester, *Revelation*, 292.
97. Cf. Thomas, *Apocalypse*, 134–35.
98. On the possible implications of the name "Antipas," see Leithart, *Revelation 1–11*, 166–67.
99. Cf. Thomas, *Apocalypse*, 136.
100. Cf. Thomas, *Apocalypse*, 137–38.

God gave him. Hence, the result was disastrous for Balak; in fact, the prophet ended up blessing his enemies instead of cursing them (Num 22–24).

But the wily prophet-shaman had his own spiritual strategy. Instead of opposing the Israelites by force or sorcery, why not seduce them into paganism and then God would perhaps destroy them? The plan devised by Balaam (Num 31:16) involved the Moabite women inviting the Israelite men to the sacrificial meals of their gods with the inclusion of sex (Num 25:1–2). As planned, this defection from exclusive allegiance to the Lord caused God's anger to come against the men, and as a result, 24,000 people died by plague. Others were executed by Israel's judges, and especially the hero Phinehas (grandson of Aaron), whose intervention caused the plague from God to stop (Num 25:3–13). The Balaam plan was thus very successful for a time and showed that God's people could most effectively be defeated by seduction as opposed to persecution or force.[101]

The parallels with the later history of Israel and Judah are obvious, especially in the case of events leading to the Babylonian captivity. But this strategy could also work with the Christians who were "advancing" all over Asia (see 2 Pet 2:17; Jude 11). Persecution had limited effect, as here, but some Christians were open to compromise and seduction in the form of sexual immorality and eating food offered to idols. These behaviors were strictly forbidden to all believers, Gentiles as well as Jews, by the Jerusalem "council" (Acts 15:20, 28–29).[102] But these prohibitions were almost impossible for many to adhere to, such as slaves and members of trade guilds,[103] membership of which required at least nominal worship of patron deities. They also left open lots of practical questions.[104]

Paul in 1 Corinthians confronts both issues. He is unbending in condemnation of all sexual sin (1 Cor 5; 6:9–20), though he allows room for sexual drives to be satisfied in marriage, including nuanced divorce and remarriage provisions (1 Cor 7). In the case of food offered to idols, Paul balances condemnation of all idolatry with practical advice for Christians having to operate in a society where food offered to idols was ubiquitous and sometimes the only meat available (1 Cor 8–10). When he alludes to the Balaam story, he places the stress on the sexual sin (1 Cor 10:8). However Paul's argument is interpreted, and I think ultimately he supports the ruling of Acts 15, it shows that Christians (especially those from a Gentile background) were struggling to live up to such a high standard.

---

101. Cf. Aune, *Revelation 1–5*, 187–88; Beale, *Book of Revelation*, 249. Balaam's financial motivations are regularly alluded to in OT and NT references; e.g., Jude 11; 2 Pet 2:15; Num 22:7, 17, 18, 37; 24:11, 13.

102. Aune, *Revelation 1–5*, 187.

103. Aune contends that no such "guilds" with "regulatory or protective functions" existed then; the *collegia* were more like associations (Aune, *Revelation 1–5*, 186). Nonetheless they would be a vehicle for a kind of "peer pressure" on people of a certain trade.

104. Cf. Thomas, *Apocalypse*, 138; Koester, *Revelation*, 292–93; Aune, *Revelation 1–5*, 186, 192–94; Beale, *Book of Revelation*, 249.

It would appear that the Nicolaitans[105] were a Christian or quasi-Christian group who tried to soften the demands of the Jerusalem ruling by proposing some degree of compromise. Perhaps, like Paul's interlocutors in 1 Corinthians, they argued that Christians could eat meat offered to idols and even take part in pagan ceremonies. They backed this with the argument that idols have no real existence (1 Cor 8:4–7; 10:19), and Christians are free from food laws (1 Cor 8:8; 6:12–13), and the Law in general (1 Cor 9:20; 10:23). Their suggestions would have added force in that Roman religious demands were focused on ritual practices rather than beliefs, so it was plausible that a Christian could maintain their Christian beliefs while compromising in the area of religious and moral practice—a view rejected by the apostles, however.[106] Somewhat similar arguments seemed to have appeared in Corinth regarding sex (1 Cor 6:12–13).[107] John, however, calls the church in Pergamum to take a strong stand.

Therefore repent, and if not, I am coming to you quickly and will fight against them with the sword of my mouth. (Rev 2:16)

Such teaching can provoke God's judgment, according to Paul (1 Cor 10:7–10, 22). So here Jesus threatens that, if the Christians involved do not repent, he will fight them. This implies, first, that not all the believers in Pergamum had been following the Nicolaitans, only "some" (v. 14), and Jesus would only fight against "them" (v. 16). Second, the warning implies that the church itself is a scene of spiritual warfare. The struggle is not only against the surrounding enemies (unbelieving Jews and Gentiles) but within the congregation itself,[108] a point often forgotten. Third, all the believers are called on to repent, which implies that they all are in some measure responsible to withstand such seduction and accountable if they tolerate the inroads of the Nicolaitans.

The impending coming of Jesus was a real threat to the peace of this congregation, whatever form it might take, and John doesn't specify what that might look like. Would Jesus raise up a strong prophetic voice that would have the power ascribed to someone like Jeremiah (see Jer 20:9)? Would he use outside enemies to destroy the Nicolaitans and their supporters, as God used Nebuchadnezzar in the days of Jeremiah? Would John himself come in and purge the church?

---

105. Possibly named after Nicolas of Antioch (Acts 6:5), though he was not necessarily the source of their ideas. Some commentators have exploited the literal sense of the word "conquerors of the people (laity)," usually to promote the idea of the Nicolaitans as pre-papists of the third era of church history, but this is anachronistic and out of context. Cf. Aune, *Revelation 1–5*, 148–49.

106. Cf. Fiorenza, *Book of Revelation*, 117; "Followers of the Lamb," 138–39.

107. I take the language of sexual immorality seriously, even literally, here, unlike many commentators who see it only as metaphorical language denoting idolatry, which it can sometimes be. Both Paul's language in 1 Corinthians and external evidence confirm that sexual immorality was rife in the Greco-Roman world of the first century, that it was frequently associated with pagan temples, and that Christians were known to fall into such temptations. Cf. Thomas, *Apocalypse*, 138–39; Koester, *Revelation*, 288–89, 293; Beale, *Book of Revelation*, 250; Leithart, *Revelation 1–11*, 169–70.

108. Cf. Thomas, *Apocalypse*, 139–40.

Would the Nicolaitans and their supporters get sick and die prematurely, as is predicted of Jezebel's group in 2:22–23 and as happened to Ananias and Sapphira in Acts 5:3–11? This seems a likely scenario; the sword in Jesus's mouth has a similar devastating effect in the battle with the beast armies in 19:21. I agree with Koester that this is "a limited disciplinary visitation before the end."[109] Thomas sees this as an eschatological coming but concedes that "an immediate visit by Jesus in judgment is not ruled out altogether."[110]

Once again Jesus presents the believers with a clear choice. They can follow the Nicolaitans and find themselves fighting against Jesus (v. 16). Or they can repent and be victorious in this challenge, defeating the devil's strategies; while Satan is not named at this point, he is clearly here in his capital city.

> **Those who have ears, let them hear what the Spirit is saying to the churches. Those who conquer, I will give (some) of the hidden manna, and I will give them a white stone, and on the stone a new name written which no one knows except the one who receives it. (Rev 2:17)**

Once again, the Christians are called to hear the Spirit's message (that is, the prophetic word John has sent them), not the propaganda of the opponents. Once again, they are promised good things associated with ultimate salvation if they do this. The "hidden manna" (see Exod 16:32–34)[111] is relevant in view of the allusion to Israel's wilderness journeys, during which they were sustained by the manna from the sky.[112] The implication here is that the conquerors are the true Israelites, even if this does not appear to be so. Jesus acknowledges them and feeds them secret manna, even his own body, if John 6:31–35, 48–58 is any guide.[113] So there may be an allusion to the Lord's supper here.

The white stone with a secret new name on it (v. 17) is harder to understand,[114] but new secret names are not uncommon in Revelation (see 3:12; 14:1; 19:12; 22:4; and in contrast, 13:17). They have significant precedent in patriarchal times where Abraham and Jacob both received new names from God, reflecting a new identity or status (Gen 17:5; 32:28).[115] The secrecy may have a background in sorcery: to know someone's name was to gain power over them and certain divine names were seen as having magical powers.[116] An example of this belief is found in Acts 19:13–17, refer-

---

109. Koester, *Revelation*, 289; see also 294.

110. Thomas, *Apocalypse*, 140.

111. Some manna was preserved in the original most holy place as a memorial of the wilderness journey (cf. Gause, *Revelation*, 57).

112. Cf. Aune, *Revelation 1–5*, 189; Leithart, *Revelation 1–11*, 164.

113. Cf. Thomas, *Apocalypse*, 141.

114. See extended discussion in Koester, *Revelation*, 290; Aune, *Revelation 1–5*, 190.

115. This also happened to Simon Peter and perhaps Paul (John 1:42; Acts 13:9). Beale shows it also has a prophetic basis in Isa 56:5; 62:2; 65:15 (Beale, *Book of Revelation*, 255).

116. Cf. Beale, *Book of Revelation*, 257–58.

ring to an incident during the spiritual movement that started the churches in Asia.[117] In this case, the conquerors will be safe because no one else will know their new name. The newness here may also refer to the new covenant and the new name may actually be Christ's name[118] or simply the name of Christian.[119] Also white is a significant color in Revelation, as we will discuss later.[120]

The ethical-spiritual dualism continues; everyone must take sides in this great struggle. Pentecostal churches today face the kinds of divisions that disturbed the church in Pergamum, especially when surrounded by non-Christian religions with their prominent buildings and ceremonies, including sacrifices. The Pentecostal believers are themselves often converts from those religions and face strong pressure to continue some level of adherence to local and family traditions, often combined with fear of spiritual forces associated with these. This may draw them into a measure of syncretism, combining essentials of Christianity with other religions in a way that deprives their Christian faith of power. John would urge them to be uncompromising in their exclusive loyalty to Jesus, but that isn't always easy to do, especially at important times like family weddings and funerals.

2:18–29 The Church in Thyatira[121]

> **And to the angel of the church in Thyatira write:**
> **Thus says the Son of God, whose eyes are like flaming fire and whose feet are like burnished bronze. I know your works and love and faithfulness and your service and perseverance, and your last works are greater than the first. (Rev 2:18–19)**

This message begins and ends with somewhat violent imagery which is in keeping with much of the contents of the whole message. Jesus is seen as a fiery being, with eyes "like flaming fire" and feet "like burnished bronze," which also has connotations of fire (see 1:15). This is a person you wouldn't want to cross, a man of passion, a man who'd been through the fires of testing, an awesome, even frightening picture. But also "the Son of God" (v. 18), the only time this phrase occurs in Revelation, with connotations of messianic kingship and deity, and challenging the claims of the Roman Emperor.[122] This is the central and longest of these messages, an indicator perhaps of its importance.[123]

---

117. Cf. Aune, *Revelation 1–5*, 190–91.
118. Cf. Hendriksen, *More Than Conquerors*, 68–71.
119. Cf. Victorinus, *Commentary*, ANF 7:347.
120. Cf. Thomas, *Apocalypse*, 141; Murphy, *Fallen*, 133; Beale, *Book of Revelation*, 253.
121. For information on the city, see Koester, *Revelation*, 295–97.
122. Koester, *Revelation*, 297–98, 304–5. There is a reference to Ps 2:7, a psalm alluded to later in this message, and perhaps to Dan 3:25 (Beale, *Book of Revelation*, 259). Certainly the phrase is used with "polemical intention" (ibid., 260).
123. Thomas, *Apocalypse*, 143.

The first note of his report is positive. This church is seemingly doing well, indeed even better than at first (unlike the Ephesians). Full of love, faith, service, and perseverance (v. 19).[124] This is an excellent church, indeed!

> **But I have against you, that you tolerate the woman Jezebel, who says she is a prophet and teaches and deceives my slaves to commit sexual immorality and eat idols' food. (Rev 2:20)**

The reproof, however, is much longer. This church has a serious problem even though not all are involved (v. 24). There is a group within the congregation who are followers of a female prophet whose false teachings seem rather like those attributed to the Nicolaitans in the previous message. She "teaches and deceives my servants to commit sexual immorality and eat idols' food" (compare v. 14).[125] John calls her Jezebel, probably not because it was her actual name, but to draw a kind of parallel to Queen Jezebel of Israel, the consort of King Ahab, under whose reign Israel was captivated by the worship of Baal, the god introduced by Jezebel and her "prophets" from her original land of Sidon (1 Kgs 16:31–33; 18:19; 2 Kgs 9:22).[126]

This was a dark period in Israel's history, and Elijah was commissioned by God to stand against the tide. He began by calling down a drought of three-and-a-half years (1 Kgs 17:1; 18:1; Jas 5:17), a very significant time period in Revelation. Then he challenged the prophets of Baal to a contest that showed who indeed was God, that is, Yahweh (1 Kgs 18). However, Jezebel continued to influence Israel and Judah for evil, even after her own violent death (2 Kgs 9:30–37), until the downfall of her grand-daughter Athaliah in Jerusalem (2 Kgs 11:1–16). Jezebel drew the Israelites away from God and into a syncretistic combination of Yahweh and Baal worship, which may have involved sacred prostitution[127] and instigated a persecution of the true prophets of God (1 Kgs 18:13; 19:10, 14). Hence the name used of the Thyatira prophet is a warning against the seriousness of her false teaching and its consequences.[128]

> **And I gave her time so that she might repent, but she is not willing to repent of her immorality. Behold I will throw her into a sickbed, and those who commit adultery with her into great tribulation, unless they repent of her works, and**

---

124. Cf. Thomas, *Apocalypse*, 144–45; McIlraith, "For the Fine Linen," 515–18.

125. Note that this time the immorality is mentioned before the idolatry, the reverse of verse 14. To me this implies that actual sexual activity is in mind, which would not be surprising given, say, the situation Paul confronts in 1 Corinthians (contra Aune, *Revelation 1–5*, 204, 205).

126. Cf. Thomas, *Apocalypse*, 146–47; Koester, *Revelation*, 298, 306; Thimmes, "Women Reading Women," 134–35.

127. The exact phenomenon often referred to as "sacred prostitution" has been called into question. The evidence of women (or men) having sex in a temple for which payment is made is open to challenge. However, having sex in certain pagan temples was common enough.

128. Some commentators accuse John of using naming as a means of control. Certainly, some readers have done so. There is no justification here for labelling other Christians with "the spirit of Jezebel" or similar phrases where the issues are not as serious as here. Cf. Thimmes, "Women Reading Women," 135–36.

> her children I will put to death. And all the churches will know that I am the one who searches minds and hearts, and I will give to each of you according to your works. But I say to the rest of you in Thyatira, those who do not have this teaching, who have not known the "depths of Satan" as they say, I will not put on you any other burden; just hold fast what you have until I come. (Rev 2:21–25)

John makes several accusations against Jezebel. She is a self-appointed prophet (v. 20),[129] not one sent by the Spirit like John. Her teaching is dangerous, potentially disastrous and originates in Satan (vv. 20, 24).[130] Third, she is influencing large numbers of believers in Thyatira to follow her (vv. 20–23). These John describes as adulterers (v. 22) because they are not being faithful to Jesus alone; he is not suggesting a literal sexual relationship with Jezebel herself. It would appear that her attraction was strong: her teaching offered believers an honorable compromise with the surrounding pagan culture.[131]

Such might be especially appealing in a city with a large number of trade guilds that would demand participation in activities such as banquets honoring their patron gods.[132] It could also be rationalized by appeal to some special insights or secrets: "the 'depths of Satan,' as they say" (v. 24). This phrase carried overtones of mystery religions or proto-Gnosticism but is otherwise hard to understand, though it shows that Satan is at work here as much as in Smyrna (v. 10) and Pergamum (v. 13). It may be a warning against too much interest in the work of the devil even for the sake of fighting him, in which case it would apply to some modern Pentecostals who study spiritual warfare too much.[133]

Jezebel is stubborn and refuses to listen to Jesus or repent of her ways (v. 21). Interestingly, Jesus has given her time to repent (v. 21), a common feature of God's judgments (Gen 15:16; 18:20–32; Ps 103:8; Amos 4:6–12; Rom 2:4; 2 Pet 3:9). This may imply that she had started well as a Christian, even as a prophet, before going astray; there have been similar cases in the contemporary Charismatic or Pentecostal movements. Perhaps she had already been confronted by a true prophet, maybe John himself, but had not responded.[134]

---

129. This is a similar case of false claims to those in 2:2 (false apostles) and 2:9 (false Jews). "Questions of true and false prophecy underlie the dispute" (Koester, *Revelation*, 305), reflecting the situation in Elijah's day with the contest between Jezebel's prophets and Elijah. For detailed discussion of how the early church tested prophets, see Newton, "Holding Prophets Accountable."

130. There are clear parallels with "Babylon" later in the book (Beale, *Book of Revelation*, 262).

131. Cf. Koester, *Revelation*, 305; Beale, *Book of Revelation*, 265–66; Friedrich, "Adapt or Resist?," 198–207.

132. Aune, *Revelation 1–5*, 201; Beale, *Book of Revelation*, 261; Thimmes, "Women Reading Women," 139.

133. Cf. Thomas, *Apocalypse*, 153–54; Koester, *Revelation*, 300–301; Aune, *Revelation 1–5*, 207–8.

134. Thomas, *Apocalypse*, 148–49.

Significantly, the accusation is not based on her gender, although it is mentioned (v. 20).[135] There is no suggestion that women as such could not be genuine prophets, as was common not only in that culture but also in the Scriptures, including the prophecy of Joel 2:28, and in the early church (Acts 2:17–18; 21:9; 1 Cor 11:5).[136] Clearly, she is well known (v. 20).

The church, on the other hand, is condemned because they "tolerate" her.[137] Unlike the Ephesian church (2:2), they appear to have been weak in discernment and testing of false prophets. They are too much like the Israelites in Elijah's day who tolerated the original Jezebel (1 Kgs 18:21). But Jesus will show no such tolerance. He has given her time to rethink her ways. Now, both Jezebel and her followers in Thyatira will undergo "great tribulation"[138] and even die, though the door to repentance is still open. This death will not come from Satan but from Jesus himself (vv. 22–23).[139] The language of a bed or sickbed (v. 22; *klinēn*) conveys multiple images of immorality, feasting, and sickness.

Jesus is a warrior in these scenes: he threatens to remove a church (2:5), fight against compromising believers (2:16), and cause sickness and death for some Christians here (vv. 22–23; compare Acts 5:5–10; 1 Cor 11:30), a shocking thought to many Pentecostals who confess Jesus as their healer. As a result, his nature as "he who searches minds and hearts" (v. 23), the truth behind the image of the blazing eyes, will be revealed to "all the churches" who will also acknowledge the strict justice of his actions (v. 23). The message to Thyatira is thus of wider application even more specifically than the others.[140]

This is a Jesus quite unlike the Victorian "gentle Jesus, meek and mild." Rather, he is a prophet like Elijah who had the prophets of Baal lynched (1 Kgs 18:40), like the one who violently overturned the tables of the money changers in the temple (Matt 21:12–13; Mark 11:15–17), a Jesus to be feared as well as loved. But he is a just Jesus who repays people according to their deeds (vv. 23–24). Thus he brings disasters on the Jezebel group but exempts those in Thyatira who have disassociated themselves from Jezebel's teaching.[141] Those who withstood the pressure and seduction of the

---

135. Many feminist interpreters suggest that gender and power are big issues in this message and that John is somehow afraid of a woman prophet. Cf. Thimmes, "Women Reading Women," 132–37.

136. Cf. Thomas, *Apocalypse*, 147–48; Koester, *Revelation*, 298–29, 303.

137. Cf. Leithart, *Revelation 1–11*, 175. Leithart argues that the main culprit is the church's leader or "angel."

138. This uses the same language as Rev 7:14.

139. For discussion of the details, see Thomas, *Apocalypse*, 149–51; Koester, *Revelation*, 299–300, 307. Death by a plague is one possibility (ibid., 300). See also Aune, *Revelation 1–5*, 198.

140. Cf. Thomas, *Apocalypse*, 152. There is an allusion to Jer 17:10, where God searches hearts and minds and rewards people "according to their conduct, according to what their deeds deserve." Cf. Koester, *Revelation*, 300; Aune, *Revelation 1–5*, 206–7.

141. This might look like a "church split" in today's context. Christians are sometimes justified in withdrawing from a church that is seriously compromised.

false prophet are commended and given just one command: "I will not put on you any other burden;[142] just hold fast what you have until I come" (v. 25). This coming is presumably in judgment, implying that the disasters threatened for Jezebel and her followers won't come just yet.

There appear to have been three groups in the church in Thyatira therefore. First, the Jezebel party (her "children" or devoted followers, vv. 22–23),[143] then those who will have no truck with her teaching ("the rest" of v. 24), and third, the many who "tolerate" her without necessarily endorsing her views completely (v. 20). This resembles situations that sometimes occur in modern Pentecostal churches, when a strong prophetic figure arises or comes in, and people are forced to take sides for or against them. In too many cases, the result is division, and frequently the divisive prophet is found to be false, or at least flawed. Sexual sin is frequently exposed.

Therefore, many in these churches are wounded and reject the whole idea of contemporary prophecy. I remember specifically speaking with a group of rural pastors in Myanmar (Burma) who had suppressed all prophesying in their congregations because certain female prophets were trying to usurp their authority, or so they thought. I tried to convince them that the answer to false prophecy is good teaching and true prophecy. Of course, this is not a new problem, as passages like 1 John 4:1–6 and 2 Peter 2:1–3 illustrate. Thomas explains that the message is that "there is to be no toleration of even 'prophetic' figures who advocate a theology of accommodation by means of the deep things of Satan."[144]

> **And those who conquer, and keep my works until completion, I will give them authority over the nations, and they will shepherd them with a rod of iron as pottery vessels are crushed, as I also have received from my Father, and I will give them the morning star. Those who have ears, let them hear what the Spirit is saying to the churches. (Rev 2:26–29)**

At the end of this message, the good Christians in Thyatira, the victorious ones, are given a much stronger promise than the previous churches, whose reward was basically salvation. These conquerors will be people of authority, sharing in Christ's own authority over the nations (vv. 26–27).

Here there is the first of several clear allusions to Psalm 2,[145] which according to Leithart, "sets the terms of the Apocalypse."[146] In this psalm, the nations (or

---

142. Possibly a reference to Acts 15:28–29 since this ruling covered the two areas where Jezebel was promoting sin (Thomas, *Apocalypse*, 154–55; but cf. Aune, *Revelation 1–5*, 208). If this is so, it implies that Jesus/John is not trying to make life too difficult for believers living in such unholy cultures, but there must be clear boundaries.

143. In a case of seriously mixed metaphors, her followers are described as her partners in adultery (v. 22) and then as her children (v. 23).

144. Thomas, *Apocalypse*, 158.

145. See the layout of Psalm 2:8–9 and Rev 2:26–27 in Aune, *Revelation 1–5*, 209.

146. Leithart, *Revelation 1–11*, 71; cf. Fekkes, *Isaiah and Prophetic Traditions*, 67–68; Herms,

Gentiles) rise up against Yahweh and his "anointed" (the root of the term Messiah) who have conquered them, and try to break off the chains and shackles that bind them (Ps 2:1–3). But they cannot succeed, because God declares, "I have installed my king on Zion, my holy mountain" (v. 6). The messiah is described as God's anointed (v. 2), God's king (v. 6), God's son (vv. 7, 12), and his appointed heir of the nations (v. 8). As a result, "You will break them with a rod of iron; you will dash them to pieces like pottery" (v. 9). The whole psalm constitutes a warning to the nations and peoples to submit to the rule of the Messiah or face the consequences: anger, destruction, and wrath (v. 12).

In Acts 4, this passage is appealed to by the infant church in prayer, in view of the opposition of the Jerusalem authorities. They apply the opposition of the nations in Psalm 2 to the sufferings of Jesus under Herod, Pilate, the Gentiles, and the Jerusalem Jewish authorities (Acts 4:23–27), and by extension to the threats they were facing. However, they were confident of more boldness and miracles flowing from Jesus' exaltation as Messiah (Acts 4:29–30). In a similar way, here in Revelation 2, Jesus declares that he has already received authority over the nations from God (v. 27)[147] and will share that with the victors in Thyatira who will also "shepherd them with an iron rod as pottery vessels are crushed" (v. 27; see also 19:15).[148] If John's thinking is anything like Luke's in Acts 4, this promise is not just for the *eschaton* but for now also, if these believers follow the example of those in the infant church of Jerusalem.[149]

The language of verse 27 has strong, even violent, elements ("iron rod," "crushed"), but the shepherding image may suggest something less authoritarian, as in 7:17.[150] There is a strong sense of warfare, of struggle, but John is not advocating "armed struggle or the practice of violence,"[151] as we will see throughout the book.

More ambiguously, Jesus also promises them "the morning star" (v. 28), perhaps referring to a new day dawning when they will indeed rule the nations in some way. This idea alludes to Numbers 24:17 and is picked up in Revelation 22:16, where Jesus himself is called the morning star.[152] For the first time, the last two parts of these

---

Apocalypse for the Church, 178.

147. See also Rev 1:5; John 17:2; Matt 28:18.

148. Thomas, *Apocalypse*, 157; Leithart, *Revelation 1–11*, 179.

149. Beale argues that the conquerors exercise this authority by bearing witness "through suffering to Christ's death and resurrection" (Beale, *Book of Revelation*, 268). Modern Pentecostals would be more inclined to "claim" this promise in a missionary context based directly on Psalm 2, judging from the number of songs based on Psalm 2:8 ("Ask of me, and I will make the nations your inheritance, the ends of the earth your possession"). Pentecostals may be guilty of triumphalism at such times, taking such promises out of context and not embracing the obedience and suffering that such victories require, but their instincts are not wrong, as the thrust of this commentary argues.

150. Jon Morales makes a strong case for a positive reading of shepherding language here and throughout Revelation in Morales, *Christ, Shepherd of the Nations*. But see Aune, *Revelation 1–5*, 210–11; Beale, *Book of Revelation*, 267.

151. Friedrich, "Adapt or Resist?," 209.

152. Cf. Aune, *Revelation 1–5*, 212–13. There is a similar thought in Luke 1:78, based on Mal 4:2.

messages swap places and the exhortation to "those who have ears" is at the very end of the message (v. 29).

3:1–6 The Church in Sardis[153]

And to the angel of the church in Sardis write:
Thus says the one who has the seven spirits of God and the seven stars. I know your works, that you have a name that you are alive, and you are dead. (Rev 3:1)

This is the first church in the series that has no positive report; in fact, Thomas calls this "the most severe judgment among the seven messages."[154] This message begins with a reference to "the seven spirits of God" and "the seven stars" (the angels of the churches) both being held by the risen Christ.[155] Jesus is Lord of the church and the source of the Holy Spirit for the church, if indeed the "seven spirits of God" is a reference to the Holy Spirit, viewed as the sevenfold spirit on the promised Messiah in Isaiah 11:2.[156] He ultimately has both the Holy Spirit and the angels of the churches, which reminds the hearers that his criticisms of each church's angel have "teeth" since they are ultimately accountable to him and under his final control. Even the Spirit is in a sense subservient to Christ.

The first direct words to the Sardis church are then very stark: "you have a name [contrasting with the name that the conquerors in Pergamum are promised, 2:17] that you are alive, and you are dead" (v. 1). For a Pentecostal church this would be almost the ultimate insult, but it has been true of many modern Pentecostal congregations and even whole movements as a result of "quenching the Spirit" (1 Thess 5:19), division, authoritarian leadership, bureaucracy, and neglect of spiritual gifts. For example, Pastor David Cartledge wrote of the Assemblies of God in Australia in the post-war period, that it "resembled an old wineskin more than a real revival movement."[157] In many places, most of the "Pentecostals" have not been baptized with the Spirit or do not speak in tongues.[158] But the name "Pentecostal" implies to others and themselves that they are spiritually alive.

---

153. For information on the ancient city, see Thomas, *Apocalypse*, 159; Koester, *Revelation*, 309–12; Aune, *Revelation 1–5*, 218–19. One significant feature was the presence of a large and influential Jewish community.

154. Thomas, *Apocalypse*, 161.

155. Aune suggests the "and" can be read "epexegetically"; i.e., as "even" or "namely," which would mean the seven spirits and the seven stars are the same, i.e., both angels (*Revelation 1–5*, 215, 219). See comment below on Rev 4:5.

156. See discussion on 4:5 below.

157. Cartledge, *Apostolic Revolution*, 11.

158. Cf. Cartledge, *Apostolic Revolution*, 51; Poloma, *Assemblies of God*; Cettolin, *Spirit Freedom*, 51, 61–63, 70.

The human reputation of this church belies its true state. This is a common theme in Revelation where frequently nothing is quite what it seems or claims. We read of "those who say they are apostles and are not" (2:2), those who are poor but really rich (2:9), "those who say they are Jews and are not" (2:9; 3:9), Jezebel "who calls herself a prophet" (2:20) and the self-proclaimed rich church, which is really "wretched, pitiful, poor, blind and naked" (3:17). Victorinus held that these people were "Christians only in name."[159]

> **Become watchful, and strengthen the rest which is about to die, for I have not found your works completed before my God. Remember therefore what you have received and heard and keep (it) and repent. (Rev 3:2–3a)**

In the case of the church in Sardis, all is not yet lost: the church is not literally dead but more like asleep and can still "wake up" (NIV), "strengthen the rest[160] which is about to die" and repent (vv. 2–3).[161] As Beale points out, if the "seven spirits" refers to the Holy Spirit, this is reminding the church of the "supernatural source empowering the church's witness,"[162] and therefore available to revive them. Apparently, this church has a great heritage and has benefited from great teaching (v. 3a), but its spiritual growth has seemingly been stunted. The prophecy says, "I have found not your works completed [or "fulfilled"; *peplērōmena*] before my God" (v. 2).[163] At some point, it would seem that this church stopped moving on with God, started relying too much on its human reputation and never fulfilled its great potential.

There are many such cases today of churches (and other Christian organizations) living on a reputation they once deserved but no longer live up to. There is no mention of significant external pressure or internal issues here; maybe things were just too easy for this congregation! Maybe they had avoided a public profile and aggressive witness that might provoke opposition.[164] Their spiritual muscles became flabby from lack of use, and thus, they are called to "strengthen" what remains of their original spiritual energy and enthusiasm and reclaim the teaching they had formerly accepted (v. 3a).

Like the church in Ephesus, this begins with remembering: in this case, "remember what [or possibly "how"][165] you received and heard" (v. 3a).[166] There are several

---

159. Victorinus, *Commentary*, ANF 7:347.

160. Either "what is about to die" (NIV) or "who," referring to people who are spiritually sick and near death but not actually dead yet (compare Gal 6:1; Aune, *Revelation 1–5*, 216, 219). Either way, the phrase is a bit ambiguous, but implies that there is some life left, maybe referring to their worship, prayer life, or witness to the world.

161. Cf. Koester, *Revelation*, 317.

162. Beale, *Book of Revelation*, 274.

163. Hence Hendriksen suggests that this church had the forms of godliness but they were empty (Hendriksen, *More Than Conquerors*, 74).

164. Cf. Beale, *Book of Revelation*, 273–74.

165. Koester, *Revelation*, 313.

166. Cf. Thomas, *Apocalypse*, 163.

parallels between this message and the one directed to Ephesus.[167] In both cases, Jesus mentions having the seven stars (v. 1; 2:1); both have fallen from a previously vibrant condition (vv. 2–3; 2:4–5); both are called to "remember" that (v. 3; 2:5); in both cases the reward for conquering is "life" (v. 5; 2:7). This is a word that would fit some Pentecostal churches today.

But lest this exhortation be seen as trivial, we should note the strong language used. They are dead (v. 1). They need to repent (v. 3). They have "defiled their garments" (v. 4), which implies perhaps a moral fall, and they are threatened with an unexpected visitation by Jesus that would apparently be very unpleasant (v. 3)!

> **Therefore, if you do not wake up,[168] I will come as a thief, and you will not know at what hour[169] I come to you. (Rev 3:3b)**

The language here invites further investigation. Sometimes this is seen as an allusion to the city of Sardis being conquered (twice) in the past, in spite of its impregnable location, because of lack of watchfulness. Koester thinks this is improbable.[170] However, it is possible that the church had become acculturated and infected with the complacency of the city.[171]

The thief imagery, and the unexpected timing, are often associated with prophecies of the second coming of Jesus, as in Rev 16:15; Matt 24:36, 42–44; 2 Pet 3:10; and 1 Thess 5:2–4. This may also be implied by the acknowledgment promised in v. 5. But there are reasons to believe that this is not what Jesus is speaking of here, since the warning is conditional ("if you do not wake up") and directed at a specific first-century congregation. Seemingly this and similar warnings to these churches indicate that Jesus will come to them suddenly, unexpectedly, and in a form that they may not recognize, but with very definite consequences (compare 2:5, 16, 25; 3:11).[172] Perhaps the prophet expected the *Parousia* imminently. Certainly a "coming" of Jesus to the churches was expected in the near future, whatever form it might take. And such an expectation is valid for churches today. Whether or not the final, public second advent comes in our lifetime, Jesus continues to come in salvation and judgment (correction) to his churches.[173] We dare not be complacent as if nothing will happen to interrupt our cozy church games!

167. Cf. Beale, *Book of Revelation*, 275.
168. Following NIV; literally "become watchful" (γρηγορηήσης [*grēgorēsēs*]).
169. Cf. Leithart, *Revelation 1–11*, 184.
170. Koester, *Revelation*, 313.
171. Cf. Gause, *Revelation*, 63.
172. Cf. Koester, *Revelation*, 318. Koester points out that the church is not told "*what* Christ might do if he comes." See also Aune, *Revelation 1–5*, 221–22; Beale, *Book of Revelation*, 275–76; Gause, *Revelation*, 83, n. 32.
173. Thomas writes of "the tension between Jesus' ongoing juridical activity in the life of the churches and his eschatological advent" (Thomas, *Apocalypse*, 164) since he interprets the language here as referring to the *Parousia* (ibid., 164–65).

> **But you have a few names in Sardis who have not defiled their garments, and they will walk with me in white, for they are worthy. (Rev 3:4)**

The report is not all bad. Apparently, there was a minority ("a few names," contrasting with the "name" of the church in verse 1) who were not as sleepy as the rest. These ones had not "defiled their garments" and are promised that they "will walk with me in white, for they are worthy." Possibly this recalls Zechariah 3, where Joshua the high priest was "dressed in filthy robes" (v. 3), but these were replaced by clean and fine garments (vv. 4–5), representing a removal of his sin and the accusation of Satan (v. 1).[174]

Jesus again discriminates between the faithful and flawed believers here as he did with Thyatira. Judgment is finally individual. The faithful minority will be rewarded in this life with fellowship with Christ and in the end with salvation. Their white clothing indicates their righteous acts (compare 19:8), their salvation (22:14), and their perseverance through suffering (6:9–11; 7:9, 14).[175]

> **Those who conquer, likewise will be clothed in white garments, and I will never wipe out their name from the book of life, and I will confess their names before my Father and before his angels. Those who have ears, let them hear what the Spirit is saying to the churches. (Rev 3:5–6)**

The reward for the conquerors is salvation. Their names will not be wiped out from the book of life (compare 13:8; 17:8; 20:12, 15; 21:27; recalling Exod 32:31–33; Dan 12:1).[176] They will be acknowledged by name "before my Father and before his angels" (v. 5; compare Matt 10:32; Mark 8:38; Luke 12:8). Naming is central to this prophetic message: there are four mentions of names in verses 1, 4, and 5.[177]

The theological implications are astonishing. Members of the same congregation who have taken part in fellowship, worship, evangelism, and other activities together may finally end up with different eternal futures. The warning "one shall be taken and the other left" (Matt 24:40–41) perhaps refers to two believers. However, for those who are alert, this is a strong assurance of salvation: "I will *never* wipe their name from the book of life," using a double negative for emphasis.

Some Pentecostal interpreters have divided up Christians into three groups: nominal believers (finally lost), victorious believers (safely "raptured"), and a mass of sleepy but otherwise faithful Christians who are purged by the Tribulation. The language of this passage, however, is too dualistic for this interpretation. The sleepy believers had better wake up or their names might well be wiped out of the book of

---

174. Cf. Thomas, *Apocalypse*, 166. For a different discussion, see Koester, *Revelation*, 314, 319. The language of walking with Jesus may recall what is said of Enoch and Noah who "walked faithfully with God" (Gen 5:24; 6:9).

175. Cf. Beale, *Book of Revelation*, 277–79.

176. There are allusions also to other Jewish texts (Aune, *Revelation 1–5*, 223–25); and the practice of Greco-Roman cities keeping rolls of their citizens; peoples' names were removed if they were convicted of a capital crime (Koester, *Revelation*, 315).

177. Cf. Thomas, *Apocalypse*, 165, 169–70.

life![178] Only those whose robes are washed, and thus are dressed in white, "have the right to the tree of life" (22:14).

3:7–13 The Church in Philadelphia[179]

> **And to the angel of the church in Philadelphia write:**
> **Thus says the Holy One, The True One, who has the key of David, who opens and no one shuts, and shuts and no one opens. (Rev 3:7)**

A church with few redeeming elements is followed by one with virtually no flaws. The message to the church in Philadelphia begins with a description different than the initial vision: "Thus says the Holy One, the True One,[180] who has the key of David" (v. 7), as opposed to the "keys of death and Hades" (1:18). This key of David refers to his authority to open and shut at will, irreversibly. This represents an application of Isaiah 22 to Christ using typology.[181] Isaiah rebukes the palace administrator in Jerusalem who is cutting out his own grave in a time of crisis for the nation (the ultimate corrupt official). He will be hurled away and deposed from his office of authority (vv. 15–19). Instead God will raise up his own servant into this trusted position and will "place on his shoulder the key to the house of David; what he opens no one can shut, and what he shuts no one can open" (v. 22).[182]

The prophet Isaiah asserts God's ultimate control and authority over the Davidic kingdom, and the prophet John clearly places that authority in the hands of the risen Jesus. He is the rightful heir of David, the legitimate ruler of the Jews, the one who can open the "palace" to whomever he chooses. As this is the messianic kingdom, rule over the Gentile nations is also implied (see 1:5; 2:26–27),[183] as well as their access to the kingdom of God, spelled out in 21:24–26. Jesus is thus seen as the door-keeper to salvation, similar to John 10:7–10 and 14:6.[184] There may also be an allusion to Isaiah 45:1, which speaks of the Persian king Cyrus as the LORD's "anointed," whose "right

---

178. Beale resists this conclusion, arguing that "If they are genuine believers, then their names, indeed, have already been written down in 'the book of life,' they are destined for a salvific inheritance, and nothing will prevent them from possessing it" (Beale, *Book of Revelation*, 280), though he qualifies this in his subsequent discussion (ibid., 280–82). Whatever exact theological conclusions are warranted, the message to Sardis is warning the professing believers of the spiritual danger they are in and affirming the salvation only of the conquerors. Cf. Leithart, *Revelation 1–11*, 186–87.

179. For information on this city, see Koester, *Revelation*, 321–23; Aune, *Revelation 1–5*, 234–35. It was completely destroyed in a major earthquake in AD 17 (Caird, *Revelation*, 51).

180. Cf. Thomas, *Apocalypse*, 171–72. This is clearly a claim to divinity which will be implicit in this message (see also Isa 60:14) and a likely point of contention with the Jews. Cf. Koester, *Revelation*, 323; Beale, *Book of Revelation*, 283.

181. Cf. Beale, *John's Use of the Old Testament*, 118–21.

182. Cf. Aune, *Revelation 1–5*, 235; Fekkes, *Isaiah and Prophetic Traditions*, 68.

183. Cf. Koester, *Revelation*, 329; Beale, *Book of Revelation*, 284–85.

184. Cf. Beale, *John's Use of the Old Testament*, 117.

hand" God takes hold of "to open doors before him so that gates will not be shut," as part of God's mission to release and restore Israel. The point there is that nothing can stop Cyrus on this mission. Thus, the application would be that nothing can stop Jesus and his church here.[185]

> **I know your works, behold I have set before you an opened door, which no one is able to shut, because you have a little power and kept my word and not denied my name. (Rev 3:8)**

Just like Jesus promised the victors in Thyatira, now he promises the whole church in Philadelphia a share in his authority: "I have set before you an opened door that no one is able to shut." This may imply an open door of fruitful ministry (as in 1 Cor 16:9 and possibly Col 4:3; 2 Cor 2:12).[186] But the context suggests it is access that is in view: access to the house of David, access to the messianic kingdom, access to the coming wedding of the Lamb (19:9; compare Matt 25:10),[187] access perhaps to God's throne (see v. 21; 4:1), access to the new temple (v. 12), implying honor and authority and privilege and answered prayer.[188] Only Jesus can grant such access, he who claims in John 14:6, "I am the way and the truth and the life; no one comes to the Father except through me."

This promise is significant for several reasons. First, this congregation doesn't seem to have the outward reputation of others ("you have a little power" [*mikran dunamin*], perhaps an implied contrast to Acts 1:8) but "you . . . kept my word and not denied my name" (v. 8). Pentecostal churches highly value (spiritual) power, so such a church might not be highly reputed in modern Pentecostal circles, though the power which the church lacked was maybe social or political rather than spiritual, somewhat like some Pentecostal churches who are marginalized.[189] Apparently the pressure was on them, maybe from the synagogue, to deny Jesus, and without much strength, they might have been expected to buckle under it, but they didn't![190] Jesus is clearly proud of this seemingly insignificant church. As Leithart comments, comparing this situation with John 9, "That closed synagogue door is in fact an open door."[191]

> **Behold I give (you some from) the synagogue of Satan, those who say they are Jews and are not, but lie. Behold I will make them that they will come and bow down before your feet and know that I have loved you. (Rev 3:9)**

---

185. Cf. Beale, *Book of Revelation*, 289; Leithart, *Revelation 1–11*, 188, 192.

186. Cf. Beale, *Book of Revelation*, 286, 287.

187. Cf. Smolarz, *Covenant*, 291.

188. Cf. Koester, *Revelation*, 324, 329; Fekkes, *Isaiah and Prophetic Traditions*, 132; Paul, *Revelation*, 106; Aune, *Revelation 1–5*, 236.

189. Koester, *Revelation*, 329; cf. Aune, *Revelation 1–5*, 229.

190. Early Christian leader Ignatius, in a letter to this church around 107, warns them against Judaism (Ignatius, *Letter to the Philadelphians* 6; in Staniforth, *Early Christian Writings*, 112–13).

191. Leithart, *Revelation 1–11*, 193.

Jesus' promise of the open door is part of another "reversal of fortune" that frequently happens in Revelation. Jesus promises that they will be vindicated with the unbelieving Jews, the false Jews who constitute a "synagogue of Satan" (v. 9; compare 2:9).[192] In an apparent reference to Isa 49:23 and 60:14, where the restored Jews are promised that the Gentile nations will bow down before them, the false Jews of Philadelphia will instead be caused to "bow down (or worship [*proskunēsousin*]) before your feet and know that I have loved you" (v. 9).[193] This is a potentially scandalous promise. Revelation has very strict boundaries about who may be worshiped (compare 19:10 and 22:8–9), so it is better to translate "bow down" or even "grovel," or understand that John means they will worship the Jesus of the church, not the church itself.[194] In fact, John is in such a position of falling down before Jesus as he receives these prophetic messages (1:17).

Moreover, the Isaianic promise is fulfilled in the faithful Messianic congregation and the false Jews play the part of the Gentiles. Even their entry to the new Jerusalem is apparently usurped by the church (v. 12)! This message uses a lot of Old Testament or Jewish phrases and images (David, synagogue, Jews, temple, Jerusalem), implying that disputes with the synagogue over Old Testament concepts and Jewish identity must have been severe in Philadelphia.[195]

On the other hand, this promise may imply that some of these Jews will come to faith in Christ, since Jesus says he will give some of them to the church.[196] Perhaps the thought here is similar to Paul's in Rom 11:11–14, where he hopes to make his fellow Jews envious and thus motivate them to embrace Christ. Note also the "romantic" element here; in contrast to the Ephesians, who are attacked for having left their first love (2:4), here the Philadelphians are singled out as those he loves (v. 9), which is language of election.[197]

---

192. Such language is suspect today, but John is presumably only saying what he hears from the Spirit and, as Koester points out, he doesn't refer to the Jews in other cities this way, only here and Smyrna where the Jews are attacking the local church (the only two churches described as poor or powerless but commended unreservedly); cf. Koester, *Revelation*, 330.

193. Cf. Beale, *John's Use of the Old Testament*, 122–23; Fekkes, *Isaiah and Prophetic Traditions*, 133–35.

194. Cf. Thomas, *Apocalypse*, 177–78; Koester, *Revelation*, 324–25; Aune, *Revelation 1–5*, 238; Leithart, *Revelation 1–11*, 194–95. Stuckenbruck points out that such language is used in the Greek OT and other Jewish works of bowing down to human or angelics beings, without apparently challenging God's unique right to be worshipped (*Angel Veneration*, 83, n. 96). However, Revelation appears to reject such actions emphatically, as happens in Acts 10:25–26 (cf. ibid., 98).

195. Cf. Koester, *Revelation*, 328, 330–31.

196. Beale, *Book of Revelation*, 288–89; Caird, *Revelation*, 51–53; Mayo, *Those Who Call Themselves Jews*, 68. There may be an allusion here to Isa 43:4 where God promises, "I will give people in exchange for you," though in context that promise has a different implication; the people are not given to Israel but either destroyed instead of Israel or given to Cyrus in return for him liberating the Jews (see Isa 43:3–7; 44:28—45:7; Motyer, *Isaiah*, 331–32).

197. Aune, *Revelation 1–5*, 238; Fekkes, *Prophetic Traditons*, 137.

> **Because you have kept my word of perseverance, I will also keep you from the hour of testing which is about to come on the whole world to test those who dwell on the earth. (Rev 3:10)**

This relatively, or apparently, powerless church is also given another significant promise here. Note the poetic symmetry here, not uncommon in Revelation: they *kept* the command to endure, so Jesus will *keep* them—using two variations on the Greek [*tēreō*].[198] This is justice: they endured pressure from their opponents and their reward is protection from much greater opposition.

This is the first mention of an imminent worldwide time of trial, probably referring to the "great tribulation" of 7:14 and the pressure of the beasts in 13:7–10, 15–17. Both of these would test the saints and all the world's inhabitants, as predicted in Dan 12:1 (with very similar wording to 3:10). These may be the imminent events referred to in 1:1, 3. Contrary to Dispensationalist thinking, there is no suggestion of a "rapture" here; the believers in Philadelphia are simply promised protection during an impending worldwide trial,[199] a theme taken up in several places in the vision (7:3; 9:4; 11:5–6; 12:13–16; 18:4).

This may well refer initially to the Neronic persecutions of the 60s. This was also followed by the Roman-Jewish and Roman civil wars of AD 66–70, which led to "the destruction of the temple and the collapse of the Julio-Claudian dynasty in Rome."[200] This was a particularly critical time in the fortunes of God's people. There were repeated seasons of strong, even empire-wide persecution between then and AD 312. But in any such troubles, there will always be pockets of peace.

However, the worldwide church is not given such a promise as made to the Philadelphians, and today we see severe trials besetting the church in many nations. The rest of John's prophecy will spell out what testing they must endure, without necessarily blaming other churches for what they will go through, any more than the church in Smyrna is blamed for the test of suffering they are about to face (2:10). Clearly, John expects that, not only the church, but "the whole world,"[201] will face a short period of intense trial [*peirasmos*].[202] The implication is that this will affect and "test" all "the inhabitants of the earth,"[203] and later passages such as 9:20–21 show that unbelievers largely fail the test.

---

198. Also translated keep, observe, keep under guard, keep back. See also John 17:15, where Jesus asks for his followers to be "protected from the evil one"; cf. Thomas, *Apocalypse*, 179; Aune, *Revelation 1–5*, 231.

199. Cf. Koester, *Revelation*, 325–26; Aune, *Revelation 1–5*, 239–40; Beale, *Book of Revelation*, 290–92.

200. Leithart, *Revelation 1–11*, 195.

201. Greek οἰκουμένης [*oikoumenēs*] normally referring to the unbelieving world; cf. Thomas, *Apocalypse*, 180.

202. A period or process of testing; a related verb "to test" is used in the same verse.

203. Cf. Beale, *Book of Revelation*, 290.

> **I am coming quickly. Hold onto what you have, so that no one takes your crown. (Rev 3:11)**

This is warning language (see 2:5, 16, 25; 3:3) even for those who are doing well. The believers who are so strongly praised are urged to be alert and hold onto what they have, lest it be stolen from them. There is no room at all for complacency; the Philadelphians could lose their crown even at this stage if they failed to hold on.

> **Those who conquer, I will make a pillar in the temple of my God and they will never go out again, and I will write on them the name of my God and the name of the city of my God, the new Jerusalem, which is coming down out of heaven from my God, and my new name. Those who have ears, let them hear what the Spirit is saying to the churches. (Rev 3:12–13)**

The promises to the conquerors return to images from the end of the book, particularly "the city of my God, the new Jerusalem" (v. 12). But this is not just Futurist language. The first promise is to be made "a pillar in the temple of my God" forever (v. 12). There is no temple in the new Jerusalem (21:22), since God and the Lamb constitute its temple, and the promise here in 3:12 hardly refers to the troubled second temple in Jerusalem, perhaps mentioned in 11:1. The most likely temple being referred to is that in heaven (11:19 and 15:5), which again suggests that access is the main issue, and specifically "a permanent place in God's presence,"[204] unless John is referring to the church as God's temple (as Paul does in 1 Cor 3:16–17).[205]

The second promise here has to do with naming, a big theme throughout Revelation (and particularly in the previous message to Sardis), and hence with identity. Jesus promises to "write on them the *name* of my God and the *name* of the city of my God . . . and . . . my new *name*" (v. 12; compare 14:1; 22:4). This implies that they are identified with God, his city and his messiah, quite a reward![206] Most likely, there are allusions to Isaiah 56:5, 62:2, and 65:15, all of which promise new names to the faithful restored Israelites, and to foreigners and eunuchs previously excluded.[207] Beale comments, "to know someone's name, especially that of God, often meant to enter

---

204. Thomas, *Apocalypse*, 183.

205. Cf. Koester, *Revelation*, 332. In this case, John may be using pillars metaphorically to refer to prominent and foundational leaders as Paul does in Gal 2:9 and 1 Tim 3:15, which is common usage in the Greco-Roman world (Aune, *Revelation 1–5*, 241). Another reading (in Beale, *Book of Revelation*, 294–95) sees a kind of transition here, with Jesus opening the temple door (vv. 7–8) to the church as opposed to the synagogue (v. 9) so that the conquering believers end up as pillars in the end-time temple envisaged by Ezek 40–48, which is equivalent with the new Jerusalem (v. 12) with its open gates (Rev 21:25).

206. Cf. Thomas, *Apocalypse*, 183–84. Beale also argues that "among all the passages in the New Testament, this one comes closest to equating Christ with true Jerusalem or Israel" (Beale, *John's Use of the Old Testament*, 113).

207. Cf. Beale, *Book of Revelation*, 293–94; *John's Use of the Old Testament*, 112–14.

into an intimate relationship with that person or to share in that person's character or power."[208] They will constitute a privileged elite.

But again, it's not just in the ultimate future: the new Jerusalem "is coming down from heaven from my God" (v. 12; present active participle in the Greek).[209] In other words, this reality is not just something to hope for, but even to enjoy now! Revelation constantly balances the "already" and the "not yet." Certainly, the victorious believers in Philadelphia can enjoy being part of the new Jerusalem and the true temple and having access to God through the Davidic messiah, even while also being protected from the hour of trial.

3:14–22. The Church in Laodicea[210]

> **And to the angel of the church in Laodicea write:**
> **Thus says the Amen, the faithful and true witness, the ruler[211] of the creation of God. (Rev 3:14)**

The original hearers of John's text being read aloud in each of the seven churches must have experienced an emotional "roller coaster" as they listened. Not only would they have felt tense about the report their church would receive, but the order of the seven messages certainly doesn't correspond to increasing or decreasing grades. They would be buoyed up or challenged by the praise given to the church of Philadelphia only to be brought "down to earth" with the final message. Indeed, Leithart calls this message "a fall story" parallel to Genesis 3.[212] No wonder that Dispensationalists and others thought the church would not end well; no wonder that they and others saw signs of Laodicean Christianity all around them. Today, too we can easily see this condition especially in the western churches. But thank God for the churches that look more like Philadelphia or Smyrna, especially Pentecostal-like churches in the "global south."

This message also departs from the initial vision of Christ. Both phrases in the opening sentence allude to 1:5–6: Jesus is "the Amen,[213] the faithful and true witness," just as there, and "the ruler of the creation of God" (v. 14), not just of earth's kings as 1:5 declared.[214] This is a very high Christology because only God could be described as the ruler of creation, although claims are made about Jesus in this area elsewhere in the New Testament (John 1:3; Col 1:15–17).[215] Jesus is both human and divine, it

---

208. Beale, *Book of Revelation*, 254.
209. But see Beale, *Book of Revelation*, 296.
210. For information on this city, see Koester, *Revelation*, 333–35.
211. Greek ἀρχὴ [*archē*], "beginning, origin, ruler."
212. Leithart, *Revelation 1–11*, 198.
213. Cf. Thomas, *Apocalypse*, 186; Leithart, *Revelation 1–11*, 199–200.
214. Cf. Koester, *Revelation*, 336.
215. Beale argues strongly that this is a reference, not to the original creation, but to the risen

would appear. As the "faithful and true witness," he represents true Israel fulfilling its call to bear witness to the true God as against idols (see Isa 43:8–13).[216]

> **I know your works, that you are neither cold nor hot. I wish you were cold or hot. So because you are lukewarm, and neither hot nor cold, I am about to vomit you out of my mouth. (Rev 3:15–16)**

As in many of the messages, Jesus begins, "I know your works" (v. 15; compare 2:2, 19; 3:1, 6). This can imply praise or castigation; here it is the latter. In fact, Jesus's words here are very strong. Three times he states that the church is "neither cold nor hot," both preferable to "lukewarm"[217] or vacillating.[218] Colloquially he is saying, "I am heartily sick of you"; the language of vomiting recalls an ancient dining scene, where diners deliberately vomited up some of their food to make room for more.[219] It also recalls the prophetic threat to a defiled Israel of being vomited out of the promised land (Lev 18:24–28; 20:22).[220] This church is characterized by lukewarm faith (vv. 15–16), self-satisfaction, complacency, and self-deception (v. 17). Thomas suggests its "lukewarmness" implies adaptation to the surrounding culture, like food or drink at "room temperature."[221] Beale suggests the Laodiceans were "ineffective in their faith" with "an innocuous witness" due to nonexistent or compromised faith.[222] Many modern commentators see parallels with contemporary Christianity here.[223]

> **Because you say, "I am rich and have become wealthy, and have no need of anything," and do not know that you are wretched and pitiful and poor and blind and naked. (Rev 3:17)**

Unlike the poor church of Smyrna that was really rich, or the weak church of Philadelphia that was surprisingly strong, this church is the reverse.[224] Outward prosperity masked inward spiritual poverty and shame.

Christ as inaugurating a new creation (Beale, *Book of Revelation*, 297–98).

216. Cf. Beale, *Book of Revelation*, 300, 302.

217. Either the prophecy is saying that both hot and cold are good qualities, and lukewarm is bad, or Jesus prefers hot above all, but even cold is better than lukewarm, or even the reverse, hot is bad (representing lack of self-control) and cold is good. Cf. Koester, *Revelation*, 336–37; Aune, *Revelation 1–5*, 257.

218. Aune, *Revelation 1–5*, 258.

219. Cf. Koester, *Revelation*, 342–44. This is probably not a reference to the local water supply as is sometimes suggested (ibid., 337). As Koester points out, it might be difficult for the church to know when they had actually been "vomited out" (ibid., 344).

220. Cf. Leithart, *Revelation 1–11*, 202.

221. Thomas, *Apocalypse*, 188–89; cf. Koester, *Revelation*, 344; Gause, *Revelation*, 74.

222. Beale, *Book of Revelation*, 303.

223. Cf. Johnson, *Pneumatic Discernment*, 179.

224. Cf. Thomas, *Apocalypse*, 190–191; Beale, *Book of Revelation*, 305.

This prosperity language may recall Hosea's words about the northern kingdom of Israel (Hos 12:8).[225] If so, the context suggests the wealth was obtained by dishonest trade (Hos 12:7; compare 1 Enoch 97:8–9), which may be applicable to the Laodiceans. At the very least, they seem to have been complicit with the idolatrous and oppressive economy of the Roman empire.[226] How revealing for this church to say, "I don't need anything (even from Jesus)!" How often has the organized church of Christendom fallen into the same trap!

All the cities mentioned in Revelation 2–3 were quite prosperous, but not all the churches. However, the city of Laodicea must have been particularly rich because it could afford to rebuild after a damaging earthquake in AD 60 without the usual Roman assistance offered in such cases.[227] Perhaps the church in Laodicea also had a greater proportion of wealthy and high-status people than other churches, particularly compared to the church in Smyrna. Many commentators have noticed that increasing affluence in a church can be a trap, but is almost inevitable over time. This is often called "redemption and lift."[228] New believers adopt frugal habits, stop wasting money on drink and gambling, and thus become increasingly wealthy, which in turn makes them comfortable and less spiritually passionate.[229]

I'm reminded of the (probably apocryphal) story of Thomas Aquinas who entered the presence of Pope Innocent II, before whom a large sum of money was spread out. The Pope observed, "You see, Thomas, the Church can no longer say, 'Silver and gold have I none.'" "True, holy father," replied Aquinas; "neither can she any longer say, 'Arise and walk.'"[230]

However, the problem may have been deeper. The riches this church boasted of may have been spiritual in nature. The ancient commentator Victorinus saw them as people highly knowledgeable in the Scriptures, capable of sophisticated theological discussions, and very proud of this, but not living the life of Christ.[231]

> **I counsel you to purchase from me gold purified by fire so that you may be (truly) rich, and white garments, so that you may be clothed, and the shame of**

---

225. Cf. Thomas, *Apocalypse*, 190; Beale, *Book of Revelation*, 304.

226. The fabulous wealth of Rome was also its downfall as seen in Rev 18; cf. Koester, *Revelation*, 346; Beale, *Book of Revelation*, 304–5; Mathews, "Imputed Speech," 331–35.

227. Aune, *Revelation 1–5*, 249; Koester, *Revelation*, 334.

228. A phrase attributed to Donald McGavran. Cf. McGavran, *Understanding Church Growth*, 209–20. However, the idea goes back to John Wesley whose Methodist movement lifted thousands of British people out of poverty. See Butler, "John Wesley's Church Planting Movement."

229. Wesley said, "For wherever true Christianity spreads, it must cause diligence and frugality, which in the natural course of things, must beget riches!" (quoted in Butler, "John Wesley's Church Planting Movement.")

230. Bruce, *Acts*, 84. This story is attributed to Cornelius a Lapide. However, it is historically doubtful as the dates of Innocent II's reign and Aquinas' life don't match.

231. Victorinus, *Commentary*, ANF 7:347. This was perhaps similar to the church in Corinth (1 Cor 4:8; cf. Aune, *Revelation 1–5*, 259).

your nakedness may not be apparent, and eye-salve to rub on your eyes, so that you may see. (Rev 3:18)

This church, which thought it needed nothing, is instead advised to "purchase" the true spiritual qualities it urgently needed, symbolized by gold, white clothes, and eye-salve (v. 18). This was presumably not with money, but as in Isaiah 55:1–3, such buying is associated with serious listening to God's word.[232] These qualities don't come cheaply, it is implied: the gold must be "purified by fire," suggesting a purging experience for the lukewarm believers. Or perhaps it means a testing of their faith, if John's thinking is like Peter's in 1 Peter 1:7,[233] similar to what their Lord had experienced (1:15, 19; 2:8, 18).

The "white clothing" is to cover "the shame of your nakedness," as in 16:15. Clothing is frequently mentioned in Revelation and stands for spiritual condition or standing. White clothes usually symbolize righteous deeds (19:8), purity (3:4–5), or having been cleansed by Jesus' blood (7:13–14; 22:14).[234] The eye-salve addresses their self-deception; they are blind and need to see again. The exact nature of these remedies is not spelled out, but they have to be "purchased" from Jesus. This means at least that the need of them must be acknowledged and Jesus must be approached as the source for meeting these needs, an attitude of humble dependence quite unlike the arrogant self-sufficiency this church is displaying.

Those who are my friends[235] I rebuke and chasten. Therefore, be zealous and repent. Behold, I am standing[236] at the door and knocking. If anyone hears my voice[237] and opens the door, I will come in to them and dine with them and they with me. (Rev 3:19–20)

All is not lost. Jesus apparently still loves these wayward people, enough to "rebuke and chasten" them (v. 19; compare Prov 3:12; 1 Cor 11:32). Like others, they are called on "to be zealous"[238] (the opposite of lukewarmness) and repent. There follows a famous piece of imagery immortalized in preaching, paintings, and songs. Jesus stands outside the door of the church (metaphorically since churches didn't own buildings then) and knocks, promising to enter the lives of those who respond (v. 20). This promise has been used by many evangelists in their "altar calls" and was part of my own conversion.

---

232. Isa 55, like Rev 3:14–21, uses imagery of eating to make a point; cf. Thomas, *Apocalypse*, 191.

233. Cf. Thomas, *Apocalypse*, 192–93.

234. Cf. Koester, *Revelation*, 347–48.

235. Or "those whom I love as friends" (Greek ὅσους ἐὰν φιλῶ [hosous ean philō]).

236. Literally "I have been standing," in the Greek perfect tense, emphasizing that this situation has been going on for a while; cf. Mathewson, *Handbook*, 56.

237. Or it could be "the sound (of my knocking)." The Greek φωνῆς [phonēs] can indicate a voice or just a sound.

238. Greek ζήλθυε [zēleue].

However, in its original context, it is more radical. The Savior himself is forced to knock for entry into his own congregation, perhaps while they are feasting, in light of the eating imagery in this message. What does this say about the state of that church?[239] He hopes that some at least will hear him (as in John 10:3–5, 16), open the door, and invite him in. There is here an appeal to hospitality obligations[240] and a contrast to the prohibition on eating banquets in honor of idols.[241] It is an ironic contrast to the promise of access made to the Christians of Philadelphia (v. 8).

It seems that in this image, there is also an allusion to the Song of Solomon, the dramatic poem of the growing love between a young man and woman. In one episode (Song 5:2–7), the girl is in bed in her room when her lover knocks at the door. But she has washed and retired and hesitates to respond. By the time she eventually opens the door, the lover has disappeared, and she can't find him. The city watchmen beat her and take away her cloak and she is distraught. This too is a case of lukewarm affection; he is passionate, she is reticent at first, vacillating. If John or the Spirit intends the passage in Revelation 3:19–20 to refer to Song 5, the message is clear. Jesus loves these people passionately and they need to respond with like passion, and those who do will experience that love intimately, whereas those who don't face "rebuke and chastening." This romantic imagery is one of the themes that can be traced through the narrative of Revelation, climaxing in the wedding of the Lamb to his devoted bride (19:7–9).[242]

Another allusion to the parable now found in Luke 12:35–40 also makes sense. In that case, the servants are waiting for their master and need to open the door (to his own house) when he knocks. If they are watching when he returns, he will wait on them in a meal. This parable teaches that "You also must be ready, because the Son of Man will come at an hour when you do not expect him" (Luke 12:40).[243] This plausible allusion gives 3:20 a much stronger eschatological flavor.

> Those who conquer, I will grant to sit with me on my throne, as I also conquered and sat down with my Father on his throne. Those who have ears, let them hear what the Spirit is saying to the churches. (Rev 3:21–22)

The promise to the conqueror in this case perhaps trumps all the preceding examples. Just as Jesus has promised the victors in Thyatira "authority over the nations" (2:26), so now he promises the victors in Laodicea a place on the very throne of God and

---

239. There is perhaps a parallel to the situation described in 3 John where Diotrophes excludes the writer and others from the church.

240. Cf. Thomas, *Apocalypse*, 197; Koester, *Revelation*, 348–49.

241. Cf. Aune, *Revelation 1–5*, 251. Eating is a prominent metaphor in Revelation, as in the rest of the Bible, as reflected in the picture of the "tree of life" and its fruit (22:2), referring back to significant eating events in Genesis 3. In this case, a reference to the Eucharist is probable; cf. Archer, *Worship in the Apocalypse*, 169–70.

242. Cf. Beale, *Book of Revelation*, 308; Leithart, *Revelation 1–11*, 206. For other possible readings of this verse, see Koester, *Revelation*, 340–41; Aune, *Revelation 1–5*, 250–54.

243. Cf. Bauckham, *Climax of Prophecy*, 105–9.

Christ (v. 21). Possibly the audience would think of Psalm 110:1, a common passage quoted in the New Testament, which says,

> The LORD says to my lord:
> "Sit at my right hand
> Until I make your enemies
> A footstool for your feet."

That's mind-blowing! But perhaps the biggest prizes are promised to those with the hardest fight on their hands *within* the Christian churches. The mixture of images of doors and thrones (vv. 7, 8, 20, 21) also sets the hearers up for chapter 4.

Some Final Thoughts

These seven messages are confronting and unsettling. First, they help disabuse the reader of any idealization of the early church. These seven congregations were highly varied in spiritual faithfulness and strength, often compromised, divided, and deceived,[244] though with commendable elements of courage and holiness.[245] Their problems and victories reflect what we find in the rest of the New Testament and later history.

Second, these messages warn the reader against complacency in any form. In fact, the promise of Jesus to come to these churches is more like a warning, and they all face the prospect of rejection in some form if they don't respond as Jesus calls them to. His coming is the imminent crisis they all face, and if we are living near the final coming again of Jesus, these seven messages are especially pertinent for us. This clashes wildly with the idea of "once saved, always saved," although there are many positive assurances to the faithful believers.

Third, Jesus' persistent love for each church stands out; he hasn't given up on any of them; he stands ready to forgive and restore.

Fourth, these messages place the responsibility on the individual. No matter how bad the church is, individual believers can still respond with repentance to the message of the Spirit. This is emphasized in the messages that differentiate between different groups in the church (as in 3:4), but is also implied by the promises to the conquerors and the exhortation to "those who have ears."

Fifth, the kind of believer that Jesus is looking for is clear. It is not so much someone who is doctrinally correct or successful (not that these are unimportant), but one who is faithful, persevering, willing to suffer, uncompromising with the world, and passionately devoted to Christ. As Thomas puts it, one who gives "faithful witness" to

---

244. Johnson rightly points out that "discernment is the central theme" of these messages (*Pneumatic Discernment*, 229).

245. See diagrams in Friesen, "Satan's Throne," 354–55, on the asessments of the seven churches.

Christ.[246] These are the ones who will be the heroes of John's narrative. So, "Those who have ears, let them hear what the Spirit is [still] saying to the churches."

Sixth, if the "angel" of each church represents the culture of the church in some way, this is a powerful lens through which to assess local churches today. Culture is one of the most powerful forces in any church and very hard to shift if it proves unhealthy in some way. And it is shaped by the church's relationship with the surrounding society's culture, just as was the case with many of the seven churches in Revelation. Deep repentance is often needed, based on prophetic revelation of the problem.[247]

Finally, these messages are highly relevant to Pentecostal or Charismatic churches today, which is not surprising if the early church was full of the Pentecostal Spirit. Pentecostal churches today often face the same issues identified in these messages. They abandon their fervent love for Jesus, as a result of concentration on orthodoxy or successful growth and affluence. They face persecution instigated by rival religions or the state. They are challenged by the infiltration of false prophets, especially as Pentecostals are open to contemporary Christian prophecy. They are pressured to soften their radical stance and compromise with surrounding culture,[248] or just tempted to "settle down" and go to sleep. Pentecostals need to keep listening to the words of the Spirit via his true prophetic voices, including John! But thankfully, there are many Pentecostal churches today, especially in Asia, Africa, and Latin America, who resemble Smyrna and Philadelphia: marginalized, persecuted, poor, in a sense powerless, but faithful and effective as witnesses to Jesus.

---

246. Thomas, *Apocalypse*, 200.

247. For some modern analyses of church culture, see Blandino, *Creating Your Church's Culture* and Chand, *Cracking Your Church's Culture Code*.

248. The move by classical Pentecostals in many western countries away from their earlier pacifism is perhaps a case in point; cf. P. Alexander, *Pentecostals and Nonviolence*.

Revelation Chapter 4

If we read Revelation as a narrative or drama, chapter 1 functions as a kind of prologue. Chapters 2–3 set the scene on earth. They anticipate the story to come, and they help the readers or hearers to anticipate that story and look for its relevance to their lives.

Chapter 4, however, represents the beginning of the main vision which continues to the end of chapter 16, at least. The structural marker *en pneumati* next occurs in 17:3 just after the completion of the seven bowl judgements. Chapter 4 sets the scene in heaven for the events that will begin in chapter 5. However, we should not read everything here as meant to be *chronologically* after chapters 1–3. For example, Jesus has already been victorious (1:18) and received supreme authority from God (2:27; 3:21). In chapter 5, this enthronement is narrated apocalyptically.[1] Also a number of commentators have observed the liturgical aspect of the main vision: there is a worship service going on in heaven (and possibly to be copied by the churches on earth) all through this section of Revelation.[2] This underlines a truth often forgotten in Protestant Christianity: the cosmic significance of worship.

4:1–2a A New Stage in the Vision

> **After these (things), I saw, and behold a door opened in heaven,[3] and the first voice which I heard like a trumpet spoke to me saying, "Come up here, and I will show you what must take place after these (things)." Immediately I became "in the Spirit" . . . (Rev 4:1–2a)**

There is an abrupt shift from the outset here. We've been listening to the message of Christ by the Spirit to those seven churches. Now John says he saw a door literally "having been opened," perhaps by Jesus using the key of David mentioned in 3:7 (see

---

1. Cf. Beale, *Book of Revelation*, 311–12.
2. Cf. Leithart, *Revelation 1–11*, 209.
3. Or the sky (Greek οὐρανος [*ouranos*]). Mostly I am translating this as "heaven" but often "sky" is a better translation.

also Ezek 1:1).[4] This is literal visioning, reminding hearers of the initial appearance of the risen and glorified Jesus in chapter 1. And John is about to be transported through a special door into a different realm. It may remind us of a star gate in science fiction, perhaps, or the magic wardrobe in C. S. Lewis' *The Lion, the Witch and the Wardrobe*.

Ancient hearers would understand this as a literal door in the sky envisioned as a vaulted roof.[5] However, the hearers might also be reminded of other stories, such as that of Jacob's dream of the ladder into heaven (Gen 28:10–17; see also John 1:51), or even the design of some local temples.[6] Doors have been significant in the seven messages: the church in Philadelphia has been promised "an opened door" (3:8). Jesus speaks as one knocking on the door to the church in Laodicea from the outside (3:20), and keys imply doors (3:7; 1:18). Doors speak of access or denied, access to God, access to society, and access to the church or the individual believer. Maybe John's journey is the same as that promised to the Philadelphian believers. Visionary travel such as he now experiences was also a feature of apocalyptic literature, particularly 1 Enoch. But Victorinus points out that an opened door implies one that had previously been shut; access to the throne of God is now open through the work of Christ[7] (compare Heb 4:16; 10:19–20).

John hears a trumpet-like voice,[8] the same one he'd heard in chapter 1 (that of Jesus), inviting him to "come up here" (v. 1). This immediately triggers a fresh experience of the Spirit (v. 2), using the phrase that marks new stages in John's visionary journey.[9] This suggests that John is having a new visionary experience, maybe a little time after that of chapters 1–3, a vision of heaven itself. But before we explore that, let's notice that his being "caught up" like this is for the purpose of being shown "what must take place after these things" (v. 1; compare 1:19). Note, it says, "what *must* take place" (as in 1:1). Unlike the warnings and promises of chapters 2–3, this revelation is about developments that are apparently unconditional and unable to be averted (compare Dan 2:28), though he isn't told *why* they must happen.

And it's what must take place "after these things," that is, after the responses of the seven churches (Rev 2–3) and their immediate outcome, or after John's current experiences. As noted previously, it is not necessarily *chronologically* after everything in the previous chapters, still less after the history of the seven churches.[10] There is

---

4. Thomas, *Apocalypse*, 202; cf. Leithart, *Revelation 1–11*, 218–19. Ezekiel 1 was a liturgical reading for the feast of Pentecost (Stramara, *God's Timetable*, 37).

5. Cf. Malina, *Genre and Message*, 80–84.

6. Cf. Aune, *Revelation 1–5*, 281.

7. Victorinus, *Commentary*, ANF 7:347.

8. Cf. Leithart, *Revelation 1–11*, 219.

9. Cf. Thomas, *Apocalypse*, 201, 204. Aune dismisses any reference to the Holy Spirit in the phrase *en pneumati* (literally "in spirit") and translates "a prophetic trance" (Aune, *Revelation 1–5*, 283).

10. Cf. Beale, *Book of Revelation*, 316–19. Beale's attempts to equate "after these things" with the more general "days to come" of Dan 2:28 may be overstating things, but I think his instincts are right in seeing the vision as "including the eschatological past and present as well as the future" (Beale, *Book*

no suggestion that we are entering a completely new era, as some dispensationalist commentators have asserted, nor that this event represents a pretribulation rapture of the church.[11] In fact, there is no explicit *physical* ascension of John here: his coming up is in the Spirit, a visionary experience, not a literal or bodily "catching up" (compare 2 Cor 12:1–4) and by the end of the vision, John is still very much on earth.[12] And "heaven" is not necessarily a physical place, but more the control center of the whole universe for those with eyes to see as God sees.[13]

4:2b–8a A Vision of God and His Throne

> ... and behold a throne there in heaven, and on the throne (someone) sitting ... (Rev 4:2b)

Having gone up "in the Spirit," what he sees is a throne in heaven and one seated on it. This is the first revelation of God as such, God the Father, and he is revealed as enthroned,[14] a focus that will be repeated many times in the book. There is a probable allusion to Isaiah's vision (Isa 6:1), which begins, "I saw the LORD seated on the throne ... " Ezekiel's opening vision also includes God's throne (Ezek 1:26). In both cases, God seated on his throne implied judgment to come,[15] an ominous thought for John's audience. However, the fundamental truth about God is divine sovereignty: he is truly and uniquely God, in other words. This sovereignty is not obvious to earth dwellers. John has to be taken up in the Spirit to see it as a revelation. But it underlies everything in the book. This is why the things coming "after these things" *will* take place as planned. The world often seems "out of control" to us, but that is an illusion. God is still on his throne.[16] This also implies that sovereignty is a personal reality: there is a Person on the throne, not impersonal Fate or karma. This truth encourages prayer, faith, and hope in the Christian.

> ... and the one sitting (there) (was like) in appearance to jasper stone and carnelian, and a rainbow surrounded the throne in appearance like emerald. (Rev 4:3)

---

of Revelation, 318).

11. Cf. Walvoord, *Revelation*, 101–3. Walvoord, a dispensationalist author, concedes that 4:1 does not describe the rapture, but sees it as having already happened since the "church" is not mentioned in chapters 4–19.

12. Cf. Koester, *Revelation*, 351.

13. Cf. Corsini, *Apocalypse*, 126–27.

14. For a discussion of various kinds of throne visions in Scripture and other ancient Jewish literature, see Aune, *Revelation 1–5*, 277–78. Leithart translates "on the throne an Enthronement" to capture the Greek construction here (Leithart, *Revelation 1–11*, 215, 219). Resseguie points to the passivity of this posture, implying sovereignty (Resseguie, *Narrative Commentary*, 39).

15. Cf. Taushev, *Ancient Christianity*, 108.

16. Cf. Beale, *Book of Revelation*, 320.

What does God look like in such a vision? John compares him to jasper and carnelian:[17] words break down in the effort to describe such an awesome reality, though Ezekiel is bolder (Ezek 1:26) with his description of a human-like figure.[18] John quickly moves on to the objects around that throne, beginning with a rainbow resembling emerald (v. 3).[19] This also calls to mind Ezekiel's vision (Ezek 1:28). But also rainbows bring to mind the Noahic flood story and God's promise never to send such a disastrous flood again (Gen 9:13), though equally destructive events are about to happen in John's vision.[20] At least, this rainbow is a symbol of God's mercy and faithfulness to his promises, and a hint of a new creation to come, employing some of the same precious stones just mentioned (21:11, 18–20).[21]

> **And around the throne (were) twenty-four thrones, and on those thrones twenty-four elders sitting clothed in white garments and on their heads golden crowns. (Rev 4:4)**

God is not alone in his throne room: John begins to describe concentric circles around the throne,[22] making a statement about fundamental cosmological reality. After the rainbow, there are twenty-four elders who also sit on thrones[23] clothed in white with golden crowns. Are these elders angels[24] or human beings, maybe exalted leaders of God's people taken up into heaven, people like Enoch and Elijah, who were taken up without dying, or martyrs?

They seem to have delegated authority suggested by their thrones and crowns. In several places in the OT, it appears that God has a heavenly council of advisers (see 1 Kgs 22:19–22; Jer 23:18), whose deliberations some prophets get to witness.[25] Perhaps Satan himself was part of this body if they are the "sons of God" mentioned in

---

17. Cf. Leithart, *Revelation 1–11*, 226. NIV has "ruby"; cf. Mathewson, *Handbook*, 58.

18. Cf. Whitaker, *Ekphrasis*, 108–110.

19. Other translations have "an iris" or "a halo." These precious stones resemble those on the high priests' sacred breast piece, suggesting that they are "tied to the identity of God" (Thomas, *Apocalypse*, 205).

20. Cf. Leithart, *Revelation 1–11*, 227–28.

21. Cf. Thomas, *Apocalypse*, 205–6; Beale, *Book of Revelation*, 321.

22. Cf. Aune, *Revelation 1–5*, 286; Beale, *Book of Revelation*, 320; Leithart, *Revelation 1–11*, 216–17. Leithart suggests that this is a "heavenly sanctuary, fitted out like every sanctuary in Scripture" (ibid., 220), though there are significant differences to the OT tabernacle/temple (ibid., 221).

23. As well as God's and the elders' thrones, the audience hears of Satan's throne (2:13), and the conquering believers will share in Christ's throne (3:21) (Thomas, *Apocalypse*, 204).

24. Leithart thinks that these are angels whose thrones will eventually be vacated and occupied by redeemed humans (20:4) (Leithart, *Revelation 1–11*, 229–32). Malina links them to be ancient "astral deities known as decans" who may also be referred to as "rulers," "authorities," and "powers" in Ephesians (cf. Eph 1:21; 3:10; 6:12; Malina, *Genre and Message*, 94–97), but Ephesians sees these as evil forces whereas Revelation sees the elders as God's servants.

25. Caird, *Revelation*, 60–61; Grabiner, *Revelation's Hymns*, 49–52.

Job 1–2.[26] God is sovereign, but he is not an arbitrary ruler: he rules by his own constitution or laws derived from his nature and character as God. This answers the old conundrum: Does God do right because it is right (conforming to a standard outside himself), or is what God does automatically right by definition (seemingly arbitrary)? The answer is that God does right by conforming to his own holy nature. And this "constitution" gives his creatures (and especially those council members) grounds to stand on when they approach him in prayer. Satan does this aggressively in Job 1 and 2, and Abraham does the same submissively in Genesis 18:20–32.

The fact that there are twenty-four elders may be a reference to the roster of priests in 1 Chronicles 24:1–19 or Levitical singers in 1 Chronicles 25:1–31, suggesting that David's organization of temple worship mirrored heavenly reality, or it may be a mathematical suggestion, since 24 = 2 x 12. Twelve is a significant number in Revelation, and the new Jerusalem is built on the foundation of the twelve tribes of Israel and the twelve apostles of the Lamb (21:12–14). Numbers and arithmetic have great significance in Revelation, as we shall see, and multiples of twelve seem to stand for God's people.[27]

The clothing of the elders is also significant. Clothing is always meaningful in Revelation. John uses clothing language fifteen times: *periballein* twelve times, and *enduein* three times, both meaning "to wear."[28] The elders are clothed in white (v. 4; see also 3:4–5, 18; 7:9, 14; 19:14; 22:14) suggesting purity or perhaps purification (see 7:14).[29] All of these details together (the number, their white clothing, their thrones, and the promise of thrones in 3:21 and even their crowns) lead me to think of these elders as glorified human leaders rather than angels. This is what the word "elders" might imply, given its historical background; for example, the elders of Israel in Exodus 24:9, Numbers 11:16, and eschatologically in Isaiah 24:23, even perhaps the conquerors of Revelation 2–3.[30] Thus, they would be motivating figures for the audience; as Robyn Whitaker puts it, "hearers are asked to identify with the elders as their deceased brethren and potential future selves."[31]

---

26. Cf. Aune, *Revelation 1–5*, 277; Leithart, *Revelation 1–11*, 224; Grabiner, *Revelation's Hymns*, 53–60. Grabiner's interpretation of Isaiah 14 and Ezekiel 28 as related to the primordial fall of Satan is controversial as he is not named in either passage.

27. Koester, *Revelation*, 368.

28. Aune, *Revelation 1–5*, 292–93.

29. However, pagan worshipers and celebrants of the emperor also wore white robes (Koester, *Revelation*, 369).

30. Cf. Thomas, *Apocalypse*, 206–8; Beale, *Book of Revelation*, 322–24; Whitaker, *Ekphrasis*, 110–14; Paul, *Revelation*, 122–24; Archer, *Worship in the Apocalypse*, 178. Ian Paul notes that twenty four was also the number of attendants or bodyguards for Roman consuls and emperors from the time of Domitian. For other interpretations, cf. Koester, *Revelation*, 360–63; Aune, *Revelation 1–5*, 287–92; Beale, *Book of Revelation*, 323–26; Leithart, *Revelation 1–11*, 235–43.

31. Whitaker, *Ekphrasis*, 127.

> **And from the throne went out lightning and noise and thunder, and seven lamps of fire were burning in front of the throne, which are the seven spirits of God ... (Rev 4:5)**

This is a theophany like the description of God's descent on Mount Sinai (Exod 19), an awesome scene in the original meaning of that word, including the element of being overpowered, even afraid. Similar features will reappear at other significant places in Revelation, usually at the end of one of the series of disasters (8:5; 11:19; 16:18; the others also add earthquakes).[32] God's presence and activity are marked by such signs of power, which show that "God is not some distant passive deity, but . . . active in creation and human history."[33]

Next, John tells his readers or hearers of seven lamps or torches of fire burning before the throne, which he interprets as "the seven spirits of God," previously mentioned in 1:4 and 3:1. The torches probably recall the seven-branched "menorah" in the tabernacle (Zech 4:2).[34]

What are these seven spirits? Commentators mainly suggest two possibilities: they are archangels (as in some of the Jewish apocryphal books and apocalypses) or they refer to the "sevenfold" Spirit of God (as in Isa 11:2) that would rest upon the Messiah.[35] I think the latter interpretation makes the most sense, first, because this is how Zechariah interprets his vision of the gold lampstand (Zech 4:6), when he hears, "Not by might nor by power but by my Spirit, says the LORD Almighty."[36] This was originally a promise to the Jewish leader Zerubbabel that he would be empowered to complete the second temple against all odds. This would be relevant to John's audience because the church in John's time was similarly threatened and could only be guaranteed by the work of the Spirit.[37]

Second, the Holy Spirit is plural because of his multitudinous and varied works, seven because seven suggests completeness (see discussion later in this commentary),[38] and "in front of the throne" because of his proximity to God. It is true that the Spirit is not *on* the throne, unlike Christ and the Father,[39] but this does not negate his de-

---

32. Thomas, *Apocalypse*, 209; Aune, *Revelation 1–5*, 294–95.
33. Thomas, *Apocalypse*, 208.
34. Aune, *Revelation 1–5*, 295.
35. For the former view, see Aune, *Revelation 1–5*, 33–35; Koester, *Revelation*, 216. For an extended discussion of both views, see Waddell, *Spirit of the Book*, 9–21, 176. For the latter view, see Thomas, *Apocalypse*, 92, 209, 223; Skaggs and Benham, *Revelation*, 21–22; Osborne, *Revelation*, 61; Beale, *Revelation*, 189–90; Bauckham, *Theology*, 110; Smalley, *Revelation to John*, 33–34. The oldest extant commentary on Revelation by Victorinus supports this view (Victorinus, *Commentary*, ANF 7:344). For a creative mediating position, cf. Bucur, "Angelomorphic Spirit." Fekkes sees Zech 4 as more significant than Isa 11:2 here (Fekkes, *Prophetic Traditions*, 107–10; cf. Johnson, *Pneumatic Discernment*, 85).
36. This is, of course, a famous verse among Pentecostals, for good reason.
37. Cf. Bauckham, *Climax of Prophecy*, 163.
38. Cf. Leithart, *Revelation 1–11*, 233.
39. Cf. Bucur, "Hierarchy, Prophecy, and Angelomorphic Spirit," 184.

ity since the Spirit's role is more immanent and intermediary, that is, to represent and convey Christ to us. Ian Paul sees the fire here as a reference to Pentecost when "tongues of fire" rested on the disciples as they were about to be filled with the Spirit.[40]

> . . . and in front of the throne (something) like a sea of glass like crystal. (Rev 4:6a)

The next thing John notices is a sea of glass like crystal before the throne, mentioned again in 15:2. This adds to the sense of awe, and may have a secondary reference to the Red Sea story of Exod 13–14, the appearance of God to the elders of Israel in Exod 24:10, and the bronze sea in the temple of Solomon (1 Kgs 7:23–26; 2 Chr 4:2–6).[41] John is drawing on language from the Old Testament that describes such theophanic visions, particularly the description of Ezekiel's initial vision (Ezek 1–3; see Ezek 1:22, especially).[42] Of course, the sea often has negative connotations in both the Old Testament and Revelation, but John may see "the chaotic powers of the sea as calmed by divine sovereignty."[43]

> **And in the midst of the throne and around the throne (were) four living beings covered with eyes in front and behind. And the first living being (was) like a lion, and the second living being (was) like an ox, and the third living being had a human face, and the fourth living being (was) like a flying eagle. And the four living beings, each of whom had six wings, (are) covered with eyes around and within . . . (Rev 4:6b–8a)**

Then John describes four living beings;[44] this "throne room" scene is getting crowded! They are similar in some ways to the creatures in Ezekiel's initial vision (Ezek 1:5–24) though not identical in detail.[45] Four is another significant number in Revelation, usually associated with creation, perhaps because of the four directions (see 7:1). These beings are also similar to the seraphim in Isaiah 6.[46] They are not exactly angels, nor are they human, but some kind of hybrid (the first of many in Revelation) and in some way seem to represent creation[47] in heaven. They are around and on each side of the

---

40. Paul, *Revelation*, 124.
41. Cf. Leithart, *Revelation 1–11*, 233.
42. Cf. Beale, *Book of Revelation*, 327. To Leithart, "the crystal sea corresponds to the waters above the firmament" of the second day of creation, the firmament described in Ezek 1:22 ("vault" in NIV) (Leithart, *Revelation 1–11*, 233).
43. Beale, *Book of Revelation*, 328; Leithart, *Revelation 1–11*, 234.
44. Cf. Thomas, *Apocalypse*, 211. Aune translates "cherubim" because of the influence of Ezek 1 and 10:20 (Aune, *Revelation 1–5*, 272) and also suggests references to passages where God is said to "ride" on the cherubim (2 Sam 22:11; Ps 18:10) or is enthroned above them (Pss 80:1; 99:1) (Aune, *Revelation 1–5*, 297; cf. Leithart, *Revelation 1–11*, 220, 236).
45. Cf. Moyise, *Old Testament in the Book of Revelation*, 68–70.
46. Cf. Leithart, *Revelation 1–11*, 241–43.
47. Cf. Thomas, *Apocalypse*, 212. For their possible relation to the zodiac, see Leithart, *Revelation 1–11*, 239–41.

throne (v. 6 NRSV)[48] and "covered with eyes around and within," which suggests they are either bodyguards or an honor guard, either protecting the throne or adding to its glory (or both).

The description of the four beings resembles Ezekiel's vision. The four living beings are distinctive: the first like a lion (notice: like a lion, not an actual lion; these are symbolic images), the second like an ox, the third with a human face, and the fourth like an eagle in flight (v. 7).[49] Thomas concludes that this shows that humans are not central but only one part of God's creation,[50] discouraging an anthropocentric view of reality. They have six wings, like Isaiah's seraphim (whose words are almost the same as here), and unlike Ezekiel's living creatures who have four wings (compare Isa 6:2 and Ezek 1:6). They are full of eyes and perform endless praise to God (v. 8), though they later act as agents of judgment (6:1, 3, 5, 7; 15:7).[51] So the overall impression of all these details is that God and His throne are glorious beyond measure, but his heavenly throne room is also populated with active creatures.[52]

We have been noticing frequent references to Ezekiel 1 in this passage. John and Ezekiel see almost the same things but in a different order,[53] as shown in this table:

Item	Ezekiel 1	Revelation 4
Heaven opened	v. 1	v. 2
Lightning	vv. 4, 13	v. 5
Four living creatures	vv. 5–21	vv. 6–8
A crystal vault	v. 22	v. 6
A throne	v. 26	v. 2
A human-like figure	vv. 26–28	1:13–16

48. Cf. Aune, *Revelation 1–5*, 271–72; Beale, *Book of Revelation*, 328–29, 331.

49. They are counted off, a numerical pattern found frequently in Revelation (cf. Thomas, *Apocalypse*, 211–12). The early church, beginning with Irenaeus (2nd cent.), came to see them as symbolic of the four Gospels (Koester, *Revelation*, 351–53; Aune, *Revelation 1–5*, 300; Leithart, *Revelation 1–11*, 236–37) and thus of Christ's nature (Victorinus, *Commentary*, ANF 7:348–49). Some modern interpreters see them as astrological symbols representing constellations (Koester, *Revelation*, 353; Malina, *Genre and Message*, 52–53, 97–100).

50. Thomas, *Apocalypse*, 212.

51. Beale speculates that these "beings" are not "literal heavenly creatures" but "only a symbolic depiction" due to discrepancies in how they are described in different biblical passages (Beale, *Book of Revelation*, 330–31). But if this is so, what are they symbolic of?

52. Unlike modern ideas, space is not seen as empty here. God and humans are not the only entities in existence. We live in what philosopher James K. A. Smith calls an "enchanted universe" (Smith, *Thinking in Tongues*, 12).

53. Beale argues strongly that Daniel 7 is the dominant reference of Revelation 4–5 (Beale, *Book of Revelation*, 314–16). However, it seems to me that Daniel 7 comes into play more in Revelation 19–20. For example, Beale argues that Ezekiel fades out in Revelation 5, not mentioning books for example (Rev 5:1; Dan 7:10); but neither does Daniel 7 mention the single significant scroll focused on in Revelation 5; it only comes up in Dan 12:7. The books (plural) of Dan 7:10 are more parallel to Rev 20:12.

4:8b–11 Heavenly Worship

> ... and they have no rest day and night, saying:
> "Holy, holy, holy, Lord God Almighty,
> who was and who is and who is coming."
> And when the living beings give glory and honor and thanks to the one sitting on the throne, who lives forever and ever, the twenty-four elders fall down before the one sitting on the throne and worship the one who lives forever and ever, and throw their crowns before the throne, saying:
> "Worthy are you, our Lord and God,
> to receive the glory and the honor and the power,
> for you created all things,
> and because of your will they were and were created." (Rev 4:8b–11)

Heaven is a place of thrones (especially the throne of God) and of special beings. Readers/hearers now see it also as a place of continual worship. The four living beings never stop acclaiming God (v. 8), and the elders (by implication) never stop falling down, worshipping and throwing down their crowns (vv. 9–10),[54] crowns they had earned by living victorious lives (3:11).[55] This worship is described in terms that are both physical (such as falling down and throwing down crowns)[56] and verbal or confessional (making true statements to and about God),[57] though not yet musical.[58]

The fact that that the living beings take the lead in this liturgy may be significant; Beale suggests that as representations of creation, "they are performing the function that all creation is meant to fulfill."[59] This theme of all creation (not just humans and angels) praising God is strong in Psalms (e.g., Pss 96:1, 11–13; 98:7–9) and Revelation (5:13). The focus here is first on who God is. The living beings confess God as holy, sovereign (Greek *kyrios*, "Lord"), divine, almighty (Greek *pantokrator*, literally "all-powerful"), and eternal (v. 8; compare Isa 6:3). Then the confession of the twenty-four elders focuses on God as Creator: "you created all things, and because of your will they were and were created" (v. 11).

---

54. But see Aune, *Revelation 1–5*, 307; Beale, *Book of Revelation*, 334; Moloney, *Apocalypse of John*, 94–95. These commentators challenge the idea of constant falling down in worship here based on the use of the Greek ὅταν [*hotan*]—meaning "whenever"—elsewhere, and the future tense of the verbs in the main clause. Beale suggest it refers rather to "a once occurring event." Leithart likewise says "it is an event, not a continuous ceremony" and will happen in Rev 5:8 (Leithart, *Revelation 1–11*, 230–31; compare Mathewson, *Handbook*, 66). Moloney makes a similar case. However, the link with verse 8, "they have no rest day or night," overturns this argument to my mind, a nexus which Beale has to deny.

55. Victorinus, *Commentary*, ANF 7:349.

56. Both falling down and throwing crowns are signs of submission to a Higher Power or conqueror; cf. Aune, *Revelation 1–5*, 308–9. Ian Paul sees a reference to the practice of city elders casting down thir crowns before approaching rulers, beginning with Alexnder the Great (Paul, *Revelation*, 124).

57. Cf. Thomas, *Apocalypse*, 216.

58. Leithart, *Revelation 1–11*, 246.

59. Beale, *Book of Revelation*, 332.

This liturgy is described as giving "glory and honor and thanks" (v. 9) and worship (v. 10). God is worthy of such praise and worship (v. 11), uniquely worthy, and this will be a vital point throughout the book as we see at least three different implications.[60] First, angels are not worthy of worship—only God (19:10; 22:8–9). Second, the devil covets such worship, directly and through his agents (13:4, 8, 14–15). And third, the Lamb is worthy of worship and thus divine (5:8, 12–14). The struggle over worship is central to the plot of Revelation, and indeed of the whole Bible, which is why the struggle against idolatry is so vital in the seven churches (2:14, 20), and why there can never be any toleration of rival gods.

More positively, hearing of this worship in heaven would motivate and encourage the churches to worship likewise;[61] as Melissa Archer suggests, "the hymn has a pedagogic function."[62] In particular, the audience in the seven churches are inspired to join with the heavenly worship with confident access (especially in Philadelphia, 3:8, 12).[63] But we must also note the subversive aspect of this worship in a context of Greco-Roman worship of gods and even emperors.[64] In fact, the whole scene in chapter 4 parodies the courts of Roman and Hellenistic rulers.[65] Specifically, the phrase "our Lord and God" (v. 11), which parodies the titles perhaps demanded by the emperor Domitian and commonly used of Caesar,[66] signifies a personal relationship between the worshipers and God.[67]

---

60. Cf. Thompson, *Book of Revelation*, 58–59.

61. Koester, *Revelation*, 367; Aune, *Revelation 1–5*, 305.

62. Archer, *Worship in the Apocalypse*, 181.

63. Cf. Nogueira, "Celestial Worship." Nogueira discusses similar ideas in Jewish literature of the same period.

64. Cf. Aune, *Revelation 1–5*, 316–17; Beale, *Book of Revelation*, 334–35; Leithart, *Revelation 1–11*, 225; Howard-Brook and Gyther, *Unveiling Empire*, 198, 202–5, 221.

65. Leithart, *Revelation 1–11*, 222–24.

66. Koester, *Revelation*, 365–66; Aune, *Revelation 1–5*, 310–11.

67. Cf. Thomas, *Apocalypse*, 217.

Revelation Chapter 5

At this point, the first tension emerges in the narrative proper. To put it in dramatic terms, there is a problem which kicks off the plot![1] Heaven is not only a place of rule, a place of strange beings, and a place of ongoing worship; it is also a place of decision and struggle. In fact, Revelation 12 will also tell of war in heaven!

5:1–4 The Problem Posed

> **And I saw in the right (hand) of the one sitting on the throne a scroll written inside and outside, sealed up with seven seals. (Rev 5:1)**

God's worthiness has been loudly proclaimed (4:11). But a different kind of worthiness is now sought for. John begins by noticing a sealed scroll in the right hand of God. This is a new development; it was not noticed in the previous chapter. This scroll is obviously of great importance: it is in God's right hand, the place of royal decrees, or perhaps at God's right side, since the word "hand" is not in the Greek text. This suggests we are looking at a messianic issue, since the messiah sits at God's right hand (Pss 110:1; 80:17). Leithart suggests, "David's throne is unoccupied, and the scroll is waiting for a worthy candidate."[2]

But what exactly is it, why is it written on both sides,[3] and why is it sealed with seven seals? Sealed documents like this could represent decrees, wills, or land titles. Such seals were often put there by witnesses ready to vouch for the document's authenticity.[4] The fact that it was sealed suggests that "the document is complete in all

---

1. See analysis of the dramatic structure in Aune, *Revelation 1–5*, 329.
2. Leithart, *Revelation 1–11*, 249; see also 254. Thus, John may be seeing the situation prior to Jesus' ascension (ibid., 250).
3. Cf. Koester, *Revelation*, 373–74; Aune, *Revelation 1–5*, 341–43.
4. Thomas, *Apocalypse*, 219; Koester, *Revelation*, 383; Aune, *Revelation 1–5*, 342; Beale, *Book of Revelation*, 344–45; Paul, *Revelation*, 129–30. There was even a bill of divorce (Deut 24:1, 3; cf. Leithart, *Revelation 1–11*, 254).

legal details and requirements for execution."[5] In Ezekiel 2:9–10, a scroll was unrolled with "words of lament and mourning and woe" on both sides,[6] apparently representing God's impending judgments on Israel (see also Zech 5:1–4).

The scroll might be sealed because the true owner or heir had not appeared to claim the property or because there was an impediment to them doing so, as in the story in Jeremiah 32.[7] Or it might be that this is the scroll "rolled up and sealed until the time of the end" in Daniel 12:9 (and also Dan 8:26; 12:4), predicting the final destiny of Israel. Perhaps at last "the time of the end" has arrived when this prophecy can be fulfilled.[8] A similar idea is implied in Isaiah 29:11–12, where "this whole vision is nothing but words sealed in a scroll," though whether this is a vision of hope or judgment is unclear.[9] Or perhaps it represents the Old Testament as whole, awaiting its final fulfilment and the opening of its true meaning (compare Luke 24:45–46).[10] More simply, perhaps it represents the contents of the rest of the book of Revelation.[11] Or it contains "God's plan of judgement and redemption," his "covenantal promise of inheritance."[12]

These are not exclusive possibilities; the scroll probably has several lines of significance, but the events of this chapter suggest these are overwhelmingly positive. Beasley-Murray, for example, suggested, "it must signify a deed which conveys the promise of the kingdom of God to mankind."[13] The fact that the scroll is in God's hand implies that the situation is not out of his control. Its sealing may rather imply that the dilemma arises from God's nature and plan. God wants to save his world, but he must adhere to his own constitution of justice and righteousness. Moreover, the world deserves disaster, not grace, as the "prosecuting" accuser (Satan) keeps arguing (see 12:10).

> **And I saw a strong angel proclaiming in a loud voice, "Who (is) worthy to open the scroll and release its seals?" And no one was able, in heaven or on earth or under the earth, to open the scroll or to see (inside) it. And I cried a lot, since no one was found worthy to open the scroll nor to see (inside) it. (Rev 5:2–4)**

The problem now arises: a mighty angel proclaims "in a loud voice" (common in Revelation) a huge question, "Who is worthy to open the scroll and release its seals?" (v. 2), and

---

5. Gause, *Revelation*, 94.

6. Cf. Aune, *Revelation 1–5*, 339–40, 343–44.

7. In this case, the prophet buys a field shortly before the whole country of Judah is taken over by the Chaldeans (Jer 32:10–21) as a sign of future restoration (Jer 32:15, 43–44).

8. Cf. Aune, *Revelation 1–5*, 346; Beale, *Book of Revelation*, 347; Leithart, *Revelation 1–11*, 254.

9. Cf. Smolarz, *Covenant*, 330.

10. This was Victorinus' view; see Victorinus, *Commentary*, ANF 7:349–50.

11. See the narrative explanation in Koester, *Revelation*, 373 and 384, which equates this sealed scroll with the open scroll in chapter 10. Cf. discussion in Aune, *Revelation 1–5*, 344–46, 374 and Beale, *Book of Revelation*, 339–48.

12. Beale, *Book of Revelation*, 340, 528.

13. Beasley-Murray, *Revelation*, 123.

by implication put its contents into effect.[14] The hearers might be reminded of Isaiah 6:8 ("Whom shall I send? And who will go for us?"), but the issue is bigger here. Apparently, God is not going to break the seals, which implies that the rightful heir (if this is what we are looking for) is a created being, an angel or a human being, perhaps: someone worthy of the original dominion conferred on humanity in Genesis 1:26–28, someone of very great moral stature. As Caird comments, "The divine decree waits, sealed with seven seals, for the emergence of a human agent, willing and worthy to put it into effect, one who will place himself unreservedly at the disposal of God's sovereign will."[15]

But no one "in heaven [so not the four living beings or the twenty-four elders] or on earth [so no human being] or under the earth [so no demons]" could open the scroll or even look inside it (v. 3). The theological implications are strong: none was worthy to open the scroll, which implies that no prophet or religious leader was worthy, not Moses or Elijah, not Buddha or any other religious hero.[16]

The narrative is at an impasse; even God is seemingly frustrated, which shows again how important this scroll must be and what kind of hero is being sought. Does the scroll represent the title deeds to the earth, or to the land of Israel (since Israel was under Gentile control and had been virtually since the Babylonian captivity), or a document prescribing the destiny of Israel or of all humanity? Whatever the true meaning, John gets involved himself and weeps uncontrollably, again underlining the importance of all this.

5:5–7 A Solution Found

> **And one of the elders said to me, "Don't cry, behold the Lion of the tribe of Judah, the Root of David, has conquered (so as) to open the scroll and its seven seals." (Rev 5:5)**

John (and his readers/hearers) are not kept in suspense for long: one of the heavenly elders announces the solution. A worthy person has been found, "the Lion of the tribe of Judah, the Root of David," who "has conquered" and is therefore able "to open the scroll and its seven seals." This is clearly messianic language: the hoped-for messianic savior has appeared, and the destiny of Israel (and all humanity, as we will see) is assured. John's Christian hearers would not only remember the promises in Revelation 2–3 to those who "conquer," but Jesus' prophetic claim to have already conquered (3:21).[17] They already associate worthiness with conquest, a common theme in the Roman Empire.[18]

---

14. Beale, *Book of Revelation*, 345–46.
15. Caird, *Revelation*, 73.
16. Cf. Thomas, *Apocalypse*, 221–22; Koester, *Revelation*, 384; Aune, *Revelation 1–5*, 348.
17. There are also similar statements in the Fourth Gospel (Thomas, *Apocalypse*, 223); cf. Koester, *Revelation*, 376.
18. Koester, *Revelation*, 384–85.

There are also clear allusions in verse 5 to several messianic prophecies, beginning with Jacob's prophetic blessing on Judah (Gen 49:8–12). This blessing includes promises of dominion (v. 8), imagery of lions (v. 9), imagery of wine and blood (v. 11). Moreover, verse 10 contains specific royal and messianic language.

> The scepter will not depart from Judah,
>
> Nor the ruler's staff from between his feet,
>
> Until he to whom it belongs shall come
>
> And the obedience of the nations shall be his. (Gen 49:10)[19]

David and his line are descendants of Judah (1 Chr 2:3–17); he and his descendants receive a covenant promise of everlasting dominion from God through the prophet Nathan (2 Sam 7:11–16; compare Ps 89:19–37). Several later prophets indicate that this will be fulfilled by a new ruler from David's line. Isaiah speaks of a special child who will permanently "reign on David's throne and over his kingdom" (Isa 9:6–7) and of a "shoot" that "will come up from the stump of Jesse [David's father]" (Isa 11:1).[20] This one will be endowed with the sevenfold Spirit of the Lord (Isa 11:2; compare Rev 5:6) and "with righteousness . . . will judge the needy" and "strike the earth with the rod of his mouth" (Isa 11:4; compare Rev 1:16; 19:21). This will result in a peaceable world (Isa 11:6–8).[21]

Isaiah later invokes the covenant of David in predicting that he will be "a witness to the peoples, a ruler and commander of the peoples" (Isa 55:3–4; compare Ps 89:27; Rev 1:5). Jeremiah says, "I will raise up for David a righteous Branch, a King who will reign wisely and do what is just and right in the land. In his days Judah will be saved and Israel will live in safety," and his name is "The LORD Our Righteous Savior" (Jer 23:5–6). Ezekiel prophesies, "I will place over them [the sheep of Israel] one shepherd, my servant David" who will be "prince among them" (Ezek 34:23–24).[22] So clearly the soon-to-be-revealed conqueror is the promised Messiah.

> **And I saw in the midst of the throne and of the four living beings, and in the midst of the elders, a lamb standing as if slaughtered, having seven horns and seven eyes which are the [seven] spirits of God sent out into all the earth. (Rev 5:6)**

What John has *heard* (about the triumph of the lion of the tribe of Judah) and what he now *sees* are incongruent. Clearly, this messiah is different than the Davidic picture suggested by the Lion of Judah and the various Davidic prophecies we have just reviewed. Now the readers' or hearers' minds are directed to other Old Testament pictures. They would

---

19. Cf. Koester, *Revelation*, 375.

20. Cf. Fekkes, *Isaiah and Prophetic Traditions*, 150–53.

21. Cf. Thomas, *Apocalypse*, 223–24.

22. Hence the Messiah "must be a descendant of the royal house of David" (Aune, *Revelation 1–5*, 351), which explains the emphasis on Jesus' genealogy in the New Testament (especially Matt 1:1–17 and Luke 3:23–38).

recall the Passover Lamb (Exod 12), which redeems Israel from death and bondage to Egypt, so as to serve God as priests.[23] They would think of the whole Levitical sacrificial system and the phrase describing the Lord's servant as being "led like a lamb to the slaughter" (Isa 53:7),[24] as he suffers vicariously for Israel (Isa 53:8, 11).[25]

John's vision brings together these two contrasting prophetic threads—the conquering messianic king and the slaughtered servant of God—as only the Christian gospel could do. As Koester puts it, "the promise of the Lion is *kept* through the slaughter of the Lamb."[26] The Lamb is seen "standing[27] in the midst of the throne," that is, right at the heart of God's rule, and among the four living beings and the elders. I get the idea of a kind of "team hug" here; the Lamb has just scored! The heavenly vision is transformed by having the Lamb suddenly appearing in the middle.[28]

Next we see that the Lamb had "seven horns and seven eyes, which are the seven spirits of God sent out [*apestalmenoi*][29] into all the earth." The horns speak of authority and power (compare 12:3; 13:1, 11; 17:3, 7, 12, 16 with Pss 89:17, 24; 92:10; 132:17). The fact that there are seven speaks of completeness, as I will discuss below. The "seven spirits" refer to the sevenfold Holy Spirit on the Messiah (a point confirmed by the declaration that the seven spirits are the seven eyes of the Lamb), and they are sent out into all the earth, a missional image.[30]

Previously the seven spirits were before the throne as fiery torches (4:5); now they are the eyes of the Lamb and sent out into all the earth. This implies that something significant has happened, perhaps the same claim as Peter made on the

---

23. Cf. Koester, *Revelation*, 377; Bauckham, *Climax of Prophecy*, 184.

24. Cf. Jer 11:19. Like Isa 53, this speaks of a servant of God being "like a gentle lamb led the slaughter" but the result is not atonement but punishment of those threatening to kill the prophet (Jer 11:21–23). Cf. Smolarz, *Covenant*, 332.

25. Cf. Aune, *Revelation 1–5*, 353; Beale, *Book of Revelation*, 351; Koester, *Revelation*, 386. Koester emphasizes Jesus' death as a faithful witness, but while this is highlighted elsewhere in Revelation, it is not the focus here. Aune relates this language to the "classic" theory of the atonement (Aune, *Revelation 1–5*, 349); Beale relates it to penal substitution (Beale, *Book of Revelation*, 353). Leithart says that the language here "does not necessarily imply sacrifice . . . but in the LXX it frequently does" (Leithart, *Revelation 1–11*, 260). For a summary of different allusions found by scholars, see Fekkes, *Isaiah and Prophetic Traditions*, 155–56.

26. Koester, *Revelation*, 385 (emphasis in the original); cf. Caird, *Revelation*, 73–75; Beale, *Book of Revelation*, 353; Bauckham, *Climax of Prophecy*, 179–83, 213–215; Friesen, *Imperial Cults*, 176. Some recent scholars contest this traditional reading, either arguing that lambs stand for rulers in apocalyptic literature or that *arnion* is better translated "ram" (since rams have horns and lambs don't) or that the Lamb acts more like a lion or ram in the rest of Revelation (cf. Koester, *Revelation*, 387–88; Leithart, *Revelation 1–11*, 258; Skaggs and Doyle, "Lion/Lamb"; Malina, *Genre and Message*, 101–2; Aune, *Revelation 1–5*, 323, 352, 368–73).

27. Perhaps this is "an oblique reference to the *resurrection* of Jesus" (Aune, *Revelation 1–5*, 352), which is implied by the fact that the slaughtered Lamb was alive.

28. Cf. Thomas, *Apocalypse*, 224–25. The scene is difficult to visualize but the point is clear (cf. Mathewson, *Handbook*, 73).

29. From the same Greek root as "apostle."

30. Cf. Beale, *Book of Revelation*, 355.

day of Pentecost (Acts 2:33). Zechariah 4:10 also speaks of "the seven eyes of the Lord that range throughout the earth,"[31] in the context of anointed servants and the word, "'Not by might nor by power but by my Spirit,' says the Lord Almighty" (Zech 4:6).

Putting this together, we get the picture of the Lamb sending the Spirit on the Lord's mission throughout the earth. This may remind readers of Acts 1:8 where Jesus promises the power of the Spirit to enable his apostles (that is, sent ones) to bear witness to him "in Jerusalem and in all Judea and Samaria, and to the ends of the earth."[32] In other words, this imagery suggests a reference to the Pentecost event, which for Pentecostals signifies prophetic empowerment for worldwide witness. The idea of the "seven spirits" as the "seven eyes" of the Lamb also implies that "the Lamb perceives everything precisely as it is."[33]

> **And he came and took (the scroll) from the right hand of the one sitting on the throne. (Rev 5:7)**

He is the one person declared worthy, able and confident to do this, whether we understand the Greek in verses 7–8 in a more active way ("took") or something more passive ("received"; Greek *lambanō* can be rendered either way). This is therefore an apocalyptic way of describing the results of the enthronement[34] of Jesus Christ as King. This fulfills Psalm 110:1 ("The Lord says to my lord: Sit at my right hand until I make your enemies a footstool for your feet") and Dan 7:13–14, which envisages "one like a son of man" being led to the "Ancient of Days" and invested with supreme authority over every people and language.[35] And note that in verse 8, this is in the past (Greek aorist) tense.[36] While Greek tenses have a variable relation to actual time and here John uses a variety of verb forms, it implies that Jesus has already done all this. Clearly, as Thomas observes, we have here "a remarkable turning point within the plot" of Revelation.[37]

5:8–10 The Lamb's Victory

> **And when he took the scroll, the four living beings and the twenty-four elders fell down before the Lamb, each one having a harp and golden bowls full of incense, which are the prayers of the saints . . . (Rev 5:8)**

The elders fall down before the Lamb, just as they did before God's throne in 4:10. Such expression of worship is forbidden to be done towards angels in 19:10 and 22:8–9;

---

31. See also 2 Chr 16:9.
32. Cf. Thomas, *Apocalypse*, 226–27.
33. de Smidt, "Spirit in Revelation," 43.
34. Or "investiture," if one accepts Aune's interpretation (Aune, *Revelation 1–5*, 332–38).
35. Cf. Beale, *Book of Revelation*, 356.
36. Verse 7 uses the Greek perfect tense, but it translates best as a past tense in English.
37. Cf. Thomas, *Apocalypse*, 228.

therefore, John is making a profound statement about the Lamb.[38] Leithart calls it "a monstrously high Christology."[39] Moreover, it is followed by verbal and musical expressions of praise and even the use of incense. This is a highly liturgical scene[40] with connotations of the temple where incense was burned twice every day (Exod 30:7–8). Incense was also part of the annual day of atonement (Lev 16:12–13), and its use in the temple was strictly confined to priests (Num 16:6–10, 17–18, 35–40; 2 Chronicles 26:16–19). Each elder had a harp (a musical instrument; as in 15:2), and they were holding "golden bowls[41] full of incense (compare 8:3–5), which are the prayers of the saints" (or "holy ones," Greek *hagiōn*); compare 8:3 and Daniel 7:21–22, 25; 8:24; 12:7.

The mention of the saints seems to be a clear allusion to the troubled scenes of oppression and final victory in Daniel 7–12.[42] Especially it reminds readers of the victory of the "son of man" in Daniel 7 on behalf of the saints who had been oppressed by the fourth beast and its little horn. Daniel 7:21–22 says, "this horn was waging war against the holy people and defeating them, until the Ancient of Days came and pronounced judgment in favor of the holy people of the Most High, and the time came when they possessed the kingdom." This event is associated with the coming of "one like a son of man, coming with the clouds of heaven" and receiving authority over all nations (Dan 7:13–14).[43]

If Revelation 5 intends such a parallel, the hearers are being assured that the Lamb is indeed already vindicated and enthroned[44] (see also 1:5), no matter what their circumstances might suggest. Moreover, the prayers of the saints stand out here, represented by the incense (compare Ps 142:2), suggesting that they are an integral part of the Lamb's work or that the Lamb is the answer to their prayers.[45] We will meet this emphasis again.

38. Thomas, *Apocalypse*, 229.

39. Leithart, *Revelation 1–11*, 263.

40. The whole chapter may be read as a liturgical scene following on from the worship in chapter 4. The problem raised in verse 2 perhaps follows a formula in Greek hymns to their gods (Aune, *Revelation 1–5*, 331), but the problem here is unlike those raised in such hymns. Early Christian worship, however, did not involve incense (Paul, *Revelation*, 135).

41. Greek φιαλας [*phialas*], an offering bowl used in the Jerusalem temple and other cults (Aune, *Revelation 1–5*, 356–58). Aune claims that the fact that the elders "have harps and incense pans suggest their angelic status" (ibid., 358), but I see no reason why a glorified Christian should not function as a priest since those purchased by the Lamb are to be priests.

42. See also Acts 9:13 and many other places in the NT.

43. Cf. Aune, *Revelation 1–5*, 337–38. Beale argues that Rev 4–5 is largely modelled on Dan 7, showing that John saw Daniel's prophecy as being fulfilled in Christ and thus the reign of Christ being inaugurated over the whole world, issuing in judgement and then redemption (Beale, *Book of Revelation*, 366–69).

44. Whitaker argues that Revelation 5 is not an enthronement scene but more an "epiphany" (Whitaker, *Ekphrasis*, 142–43), that is, Jesus' ascension and exaltation is presupposed by this scene but now revealed.

45. Beale suggests that the prayers here are "especially requests that God defend the honor of his reputation for justice by judging the persecutors of his people"; see Ps 141:5–10 (Beale, *Book of Revelation*,

> . . . and they sang[46] a new song, saying.
> "You are worthy to take the scroll and to open its seals,
> for you were slaughtered,
> and with your blood you purchased for God
> (people) from every tribe and language and people and nation
> and made them to be a kingdom and priests to our God,
> and they will reign on the earth." (Rev 5:9–10)[47]

The "new song" alludes perhaps to Psalm 98:1, a psalm which speaks of God's salvation for Israel and the nations, as well as to other psalms,[48] Daniel 7, Exodus 12:3–7 (the slaughtered Passover lamb), and Isaiah 53 with its affirmation of the triumph of the suffering servant. It is a new song also because it celebrates the new covenant made by Jesus' blood (compare Luke 22:20; Heb 8:6–13; 10:11–18). As Victorinus said, "It is a new thing to give remission of sins to men. It is a new thing for men to be sealed with the Holy Spirit."[49] The triumph of the declaration is unmistakable, even if at this stage the nature of the enemy triumphed over is not fully revealed, though the members of the seven churches know.

In narrative terms, we now see clearly where the story is heading, even though the final description of that destination is delayed until chapter 21:

1. The slaughter of the Lamb is his triumph,[50] and it has both sacrificial[51] and redemptive significance: "you purchased for God (people) . . . " (v. 9). The Greek verb here is *agorazō*, meaning "buy, redeem, ransom." It is sometimes used in a Christian soteriological sense (1 Cor 6:20; 7:23; 2 Pet 2:1).[52] But originally it had other connotations for people with an experience of the slave trade and thus used to people being bought and sold as part of everyday life.[53] Both "purchased" and "worthy" are economic terms.[54]

2. Those purchased are "from every tribe[55] and language and people and nation" (v. 9), a universal note that signals the final outcome of the struggle narrated in

---

357).

46. Or "chanted" (Aune, *Revelation 1–5*, 325).

47. Some ancient manuscripts have this in the first-person plural, i.e., *we* were purchased for God and became a kingdom and will reign, etc. Cf. Beale, *Book of Revelation*, 360, 364.

48. See also Pss 33:3; 40:3; 96:1; 144:9; 149:1; Isa 42:10.

49. Cf. Victorinus, *Commentary*, ANF 7:350. Hence this is "a Christian song, known and comprehended only by Christians" (Thompson, *Book of Revelation*, 59).

50. "[T]he symbol of conquest is the symbol of sacrificial death" (Thomas, *Apocalypse*, 227).

51. Cf. Koester, *Revelation*, 379.

52. See also 1 Pet 1:18–19, which uses a different Greek word.

53. Schüssler Fiorenza argues that John mainly has the liberation of prisoners of war in mind here (Fiorenza, *Book of Revelation*, 74).

54. Cf. Leithart, *Revelation 1–11*, 263–64.

55. Tribes are not necessarily a reference to Israel. As Koester explains, there were kinship tribes

Revelation.⁵⁶ It also undermines the imperial claims of Rome,⁵⁷ being derived perhaps from the imperial language in Daniel 3:4, 4:1, and 6:25.⁵⁸ It also recalls the original promise of blessing "all peoples on earth" made to Abraham in Genesis 12:3, after the dispersal of the peoples in Genesis 11 and the "table of nations" in Genesis 10.⁵⁹ This phrase will be used both of the redeemed (7:9; 14:6, perhaps; 15:4, in abbreviated form) and of those opposed to Christ (11:9; 13:7; 17:15), signifying the universality of the coming struggle.

3. Those purchased will be promoted to positions of power: "You have made them to be a kingdom and priests⁶⁰ . . . and they will reign⁶¹ on the earth" (v. 10; compare 20:4, 6; 22:5; Dan 7:18, 27; Exod 19:6).

The triumph of the Lamb clearly will lead to the universal triumph of his followers from every people group on earth as Daniel 7:18 had promised. This final outcome interprets the scroll, and is therefore a key to understanding what is coming, especially the turmoil scenes in Revelation 6–19. God's goal is clear: universal salvation in his kingdom based on the redeeming work of Jesus in his bloody death. This work of redemption has released God's gracious intention for humanity and uniquely made him the only Savior of human beings. The cross of Christ is thus seen as the turning point in history, ending the old order of sin and the old covenant of the Law and releasing salvation and restoration for all humanity in the new realm of God's Kingdom.⁶²

5:11–14 Praise to God and the Lamb

And I saw and I heard (the) sound of many angels surrounding the throne and the living beings and the elders, and the number of them was myriads of myriads and thousands of thousands . . . (Rev 5:11)

The multitudes in heaven are in no doubt about the Lamb and what he has done. Following the lead of the living creatures and the elders, a huge cast of angels appears (see Dan 7:10). John makes his hearers work hard at their mathematics (such as "myriads

---

in Asia and civic tribes (such as those in the same kind of work) in Greco-Roman cities (Koester, *Revelation*, 380).

56. Cf. Thomas, *Apocalypse*, 232.
57. Cf. Koester, *Revelation*, 388–89.
58. Cf. Aune, *Revelation 1–5*, 361–62; Bauckham, *Climax of Prophecy*, 328–29.
59. Cf. Leithart, *Revelation 1–11*, 265; Bauckham, *Climax of Prophecy*, 327–28.
60. This alludes not only to Israel's priests but to the priesthoods of the gods of the various regions and of the empire (Koester, *Revelation*, 389–90).
61. Or possibly "they reign," as found in some manuscripts (Koester, *Revelation*, 380–81; see also 389; Beale, *Book of Revelation*, 362–64; Howard-Brook and Gwyther, *Unveiling Empire*, 208).
62. Cf. Corsini, *Apocalypse*, 130–31; Moloney, *Apocalypse of John*, 8. O'Donovan concludes that "the sacrificial death of God's Messiah is the event to interpret all events" (O'Donovan, "History and Politics," 30).

or myriads" which equates to 10,000 x 10,000 x whatever) or perhaps just wants them to get an overall impression of the bigness of the scene. They encircle the throne, the living creatures, and the elders.

> ... saying in a loud voice,
> "Worthy is the Lamb (that was) slaughtered, to receive
> the power and wealth and wisdom and strength and honor and glory and blessing."
> (Rev 5:12)

Compare this with 4:11. The Lamb receives extra things beyond what is ascribed to God there: wealth, wisdom, and strength are his, perhaps, as a human being, as gifts from God.[63] There are seven attributes received by the Lamb, which is also significant, based perhaps on David's prayer in advance of the building of the first temple in 1 Chronicles 29:11–12;[64] see also Revelation 7:12.[65] And there is an implicit political statement being made when all of creation worships not a great military victor but a person crucified, by order of the official representative of the Roman Empire, for sedition.[66]

> And all creation that is in heaven and on the earth and under the earth
> and in the sea, and everything that is in them, I heard saying,
> "To the one sitting on the throne and to the Lamb
> be the blessing and the honor and the glory and the might,
> forever and ever."
> And the four living beings said, "Amen." And the elders fell down and worshiped.
> (Rev 5:13–14)

The scene climaxes in one enormous paean of praise from "all creation that is in heaven and on the earth and under the earth and in the sea, and everything that is in them." This represents John's complete cosmology (compare v. 3 and 20:11–13)[67] and portrays all creation, acclaiming both "the one sitting on the throne and ... the Lamb." The four living creatures affirm this with an "Amen" and the elders fall down again in worship (v. 14). The high Christology again stands out as Jesus is acclaimed by all of God's creation in every place, even perhaps by the fallen angels.[68] This also implies God's concern for the whole creation, not just human beings.

These two chapters have offered us a stunning picture of heaven and an equally powerful lesson in praise and worship. Revelation does not mirror existing worship practices in the church or synagogue (though it does draw extensively on the Hebrew

---

63. Cf. Aune, *Revelation 1–5*, 365.
64. Cf. Thomas, *Apocalypse*, 234–35.
65. Leithart sees these gifts as passed on to his followers (Leithart, *Revelation 1–11*, 266) as "the sevenfold graces of the sevenfold Spirit" (ibid., 271).
66. Koester, *Revelation*, 391–92.
67. Cf. Aune, *Revelation 1–5*, 318–19, 366; Leithart, *Revelation 1–11*, 266–69.
68. Cf. Gause, *Revelation*, 101.

Scriptures). Rather, it draws God's people to new heights of worship to God and Christ.[69] As Archer puts it, "the hymns heard in heaven are to be the liturgy of the churches on earth."[70] This was successful: the worship scenes in Revelation have inspired the church throughout its history, including some musical masterpieces like Handel's *Messiah*,[71] and more recently, Pentecostal worship in particular.[72]

These scenes show us at least these aspects of heavenly worship that the church could follow or learn from:

1. Worship is due to God and Christ (the Lamb) on the basis of who they are and what they have done in creation (4:11) and redemption (5:9).[73]

2. Worship and praise include verbal affirmations of truth about God and Christ (4:8, 11; 5:9, 10.12).[74]

3. Worship in heaven never ceases (4:8).

4. Worship includes, as well as verbal praise, such actions as falling down (4:10; 5:8, 14), singing with musical accompaniment (5:8–9), burning incense (5:8), and shouting (5:12).

5. Worship sometimes uses liturgical formulas such as "Holy, holy, holy" (4:8) and "Amen" (5:14) from the Old Testament Scriptures.

Later scenes in Revelation will add more to this picture. But Leithart makes an observation consistent with some Pentecostal teaching on "the tabernacle of David" (based on Acts 15:16 KJV). He points out that heavenly worship here follows a progression from saying (4:8, 10) to singing, then to singing with music and incense (5:8–9). Moreover, this progression matches the new forms of worship that King David introduced in the OT. Thus, the worship itself declares that the Davidic king Jesus has come![75]

---

69. Cf. Aune, *Revelation 1–5*, 315–17; Beale, *Book of Revelation*, 312–13.

70. Archer, *Worship in the Apocalypse*, 191.

71. Cf. Newton, *Revelation Reclaimed*, 47–48.

72. As discussed in Archer, *Worship in the Apocalypse*, esp. 69–118, 179–83.

73. Cf. Archer, *Worship in the Apocalypse*, 191.

74. Friesen points out that "at least 17 examples of spoken worship appear in Revelation" (Friesen, *Imperial Cults*, 197).

75. Leithart, *Revelation 1–11*, 262–63.

Revelation Chapter 6

Chapters 4 and 5 have opened up heaven to John and his readers/hearers. They have been "blown away," we imagine, by the description of heaven and the revelation of the triumph of the Lamb. This triumph would include them, and this would give them strong hope during their struggles with false Jews, Greco-Roman society, false apostles and prophets infiltrating their assemblies, and the Roman Empire itself. The final outcome that God has in mind has been revealed to them in chapter 5. And it is vital to keep this in mind as they, and we today, experience the extreme turmoil of chapters 6–19.

This is the hard part of Revelation. Chapters 1–5 and 20–22 are fairly clear in their message and relate strongly to the teaching of the New Testament as a whole. Chapters 6–19 are another story. However, if we keep chapters 1–5 in mind, we may be able to see that Chapters 6–19 reveal the tortuous pathway from the church of today to the final ending in the New Jerusalem. Keep the end in view!

It is, then, appropriate to begin with some discussion about how one reads chapters 6–19.

Futurist readers see this as "the great Tribulation," the final events before the second coming, which will be truly "apocalyptic" in scope if we take John's language literally.[1] They envisage that the church will either sit this out, having been "raptured" immediately prior to these events, or will have to go through them (wholly or in part). Such readers are always looking for signs that this period is about to start. Many early Pentecostals used this section of Revelation to comment on their experience during World War I, seeing this as resembling the four horseman (Rev 6) or the oppression of the beast (Rev 13).[2]

Historicist readers see here a coded and symbolic detailed description of world and (mainly western) church history until the second coming, beginning in John's own day.[3]

---

1. Cf. Walvoord, *Revelation*, 122–23.
2. E.g., Johnson, *Pneumatic Discernment*, 166
3. Cf. Koester, *Revelation*, 354.

Preterist readers see chapters 6–19 as predicting the woes of the Jews, especially the war of AD 66–70, or as graphically denouncing the Roman Empire and Greco-Roman culture generally, promising vengeance on the persecutors of the church.

Idealist readers see these chapters as describing common turmoils and themes in Christian history before the second coming, including persecution of Christians, general shakings and the advance of the gospel in the face of opposition.

I think a mixture of Preterist and Idealist readings does the most justice to the text in view of its original readers' situation and its application to subsequent Christian readers. Revelation 5 has spoken of the ascension of Jesus and therefore, as Leithart says, "Whatever follows as the seals are opened are events that followed the ascension of Jesus,"[4] the event described in Acts 1:9–11 (see also Luke 24:51; Mark 16:19; Acts 3:21).

Acts can help us here. Acts is, of course, the unfinished story of the Christian church from its birth in Jerusalem and its earliest struggles within Judaism to its spilling out of the Jewish context and expansion as far even as Rome itself. It tells us about the preaching, the miracles, the struggles, the opposition, and the breakthroughs. But on the day of Pentecost, often seen as the "birthday" of the church, we see Peter stand up and interpret what was beginning through the prophecy of Joel (Acts 2:17–21; Joel 2:28–32).

This prophecy speaks of a mighty and universal outpouring of the Holy Spirit in "the last days" (Acts 2:17) with supernatural outcomes in visions, dreams, and prophecies (Acts 2:17–18) and with salvation for "everyone who calls on the name of the Lord" (Acts 2:21). Peter goes on to explain how this works in terms of Jesus' life, death, resurrection, ascension, and outpouring of the Spirit (Acts 2:22–36). He then calls the people to respond with repentance and "be baptized in the name of Jesus Christ" (Acts 2:38). The rest of Acts shows how the Joel prophecy is worked out in the early days of Christianity.

However, two verses are all but ignored in the subsequent Acts narrative:

> I will show wonders in the heavens above
> and signs on the earth below,
> blood and fire and billows of smoke.
> The sun will be turned to darkness
> and the moon to blood
> before the coming of the great and glorious day of the Lord. (Acts 2:19–20)

These dramatic wonders aren't mentioned in Acts; the signs and wonders related there seem to be mainly in the area of healing and people being set free from demons. However, we do read such things in Revelation 6–19. Many Futurist readers take this to mean that these events have been delayed until the very end, perhaps after the "rapture." But another possibility is that they do happen all the way through the Christian

---

4. Leithart, *Revelation 1–11*, 271.

era, just as the earthly miracles do.[5] In other words, maybe Revelation and Acts are like two sides of a coin, both revealing the full picture of our era.[6] Or to put it another way, Revelation shows the back-story of Acts, giving us a spiritual or prophetic-apocalyptic interpretation of the expansion of Christianity as a kind of spiritual warfare. As Acts is *the* key text for Pentecostals, a Pentecostal reading drawing on such parallels is important. I will explore this possibility as we read chapters 6–19 together.[7]

The other important perspective for my reading of this section is narrative. We have seen that Revelation is a story, and the plot really opens up in chapter 5 with the problem in the form of the sealed scroll. While this problem is "solved" in a way with the appearance and declarations of the Lamb, this is in fact only the opening scene in a long saga that will climax in chapter 19. So in terms from the theory of drama, what we see here is the "rising action" where the plot heats up, the conflict intensifies, and the opposing characters act out their roles.[8]

We also need to be aware of the structural and mathematical factors in this section. We have three sets of seven disasters (seals, trumpets, and bowls) all meticulously counted off. As in the seven messages of Revelation 2–3, the sevens are often broken into two sections, a 4–3 or 3–4 split.[9] And frequently John asks us to do various mathematical calculations, most famously with the 666 number, but not only there; for example, there are the various formulas equivalent to three-and-a-half years.

And the other perspective I am using all through this commentary is an intertextual one. I draw on the references to the Old Testament and other ancient literature that John uses to make his point in Revelation. As the theory of intertextuality affirms, John (or the Spirit) uses these references and adapts their original meaning to the new context. However, the original context and meaning is not totally ignored, and often it shows the reader more about Revelation's intended meaning.

6:1–4 The Four Horsemen of the Apocalypse

This section of the seven seals begins with the four horses and their riders, so the seven seals contain a 4–3 structure.[10] Each horse has a different color and the first three riders have something symbolic in their hand: a bow (v. 2), a sword (v. 4), and a pair of scales (v. 5).

---

5. Cf. Beale, *Book of Revelation*, 385.
6. Cf. Leithart, *Revelation 1–11*, 271–75, for a similar interpretation.
7. For an ancient view on this, see Victorinus, *Commentary*, ANF 7:352.
8. Cf. Newton, *Revelation Worldview*, 261–62.
9. Cf. Bauckham, *Climax of Prophecy*, 10–11.
10. For a more detailed analysis, see Leithart, *Revelation 1–11*, 275–85. Corsini suggests that there is an allusion here to the traditional "four empires" that lie behind Daniel 2 (Corsini, *Apocalypse*, 143).

The Lamb has the right to open the scroll (a truly apocalyptic action revealing unseen truth)[11] on the basis of his violent death, which purchases people for God from every group on earth and makes them a kingdom and priests to God (5:9–10). He is worthy to receive praise and worship alongside God (5:12–13). And he, Jesus, has been previously revealed as "the ruler of the kings of the earth" (1:5), "the First and the Last" and risen one who even holds "the keys of death and Hades" (1:18). It's as the triumphant Lamb that he now exercises his sovereign power over history.[12]

> And I saw[13] when the Lamb opened one of the seven seals, and I heard[14] one of the four living beings say in a voice like thunder, "Come." And I saw, and behold a white horse, and the one who (was) sitting on it had a bow, and a crown[15] was given to him, and he went out conquering and so that he might conquer. (Rev 6:1–2)

What was John expecting to see? Will he be reading the contents of the scroll, or are these events leading up to that reading once all the seals are broken?[16] Since the Lamb was declared worthy to open the seals on the basis of his redemptive death, maybe he will release the power of the Spirit on the earth, as declared in Acts 2:33. But if so, what happens next might have been shocking by contrast.

In a reminder of 1:10–12 and 5:5–6, he first *hears* and then *sees*. He hears "one of the four living beings say in a voice like thunder,[17] 'Come.'"[18] Clearly, this process is being driven from heaven;[19] this is where John is "in the Spirit" and the living creatures seem to be primed to act as soon as the Lamb starts opening the seals. He then sees "a white horse" whose rider had a bow,[20] was given a crown, and rode out as a conqueror bent on conquest (v. 2). Visually this is happening in heaven but clearly it relates to earth. What does it all mean?

There have been many interpretations of this first horseman. Perhaps it refers to the conquest of the world by the Roman Empire. Alternatively, it might refer to the Parthians, whose empire was east of Rome's in what we now call Iraq and Iran. The Parthians were famous for their mounted archers who often rode sacred white

---

11. Cf. Leithart, *Revelation 1–11*, 285.
12. Cf. Thomas, *Apocalypse*, 238–39; Caird, *Revelation*, 79.
13. Greek καὶ εἶδον [*kai eidon*], "I saw," which is used repeatedly as John describes events in his vision.
14. Greek ἤκουσα [*ēkousa*], "I heard," often used after *kai eidon*.
15. Greek στέφανος [*stephanos*], a wreath given as a prize in athletics or a similar honor.
16. Cf. Koester, *Revelation*, 405; Leithart, *Revelation 1–11*, 273.
17. Cf. Leithart, *Revelation 1–11*, 286, on the significance of thunder.
18. Parallel to the final chapter, 22:17, 20, where the call to "come" is addressed to Jesus (Leithart, *Revelation 1–11*, 283).
19. Cf. Thomas, *Apocalypse*, 239; Leithart, *Revelation 1–11*, 288.
20. This recalls Genesis 9's rainbow again, thus perhaps signifying the end of God's patience with the earth (Leithart, *Revelation 1–11*, 286–87).

horses.[21] Or maybe it refers to warfare in general, or to the antichrist.[22] John Court suggests it is about the spread of a mystery religion such as Mithraism very popular with the Parthian and Roman armies.[23] But perhaps it refers to the conquest of the earth by Christ and the gospel (among other possibilities), fulfilling Acts 1:8.[24]

Parallels with the next three horsemen suggest one of the first four interpretations as they portray the results of literal conquest and warfare.[25] However, the language of the first horseman itself suggests the fifth interpretation.[26] It is a white horse and white is used only of Christ and his followers (1:14; 3:4–5; 6:11; 7:14).[27] Indeed, a white horse occurs in 19:11, where its rider is clearly Christ himself, "bookending" the narrative, implying that Christ starts and finishes this saga. Moreover, the language of conquest has just been used of the Lamb (5:5) and previously of the conquering believers (2:7, 11, 17, 26; 3:5, 12, 21),[28] making it likely that the original hearers would interpret the language this way.[29] Also this rider is given a bow (see Zech 10:4, where we find that "the battle bow" comes from Judah)[30] and a crown (Greek *stephanos*).[31] Crowns are also associated with Christ and the Christian conquerors in Revelation (2:10; 3:11; 4:4, 10).

---

21. Cf. Koester, *Revelation*, 394–95, 406; Keener, *Revelation*, 201–2. The Parthians defeated Rome three times and remained a threat (Dyer, "Four Horsemen," 143).

22. Beale comes close to this view, partly because of the "false Christs" predicted by Jesus in the Olivet Discourse and partly because he sees the four horsemen as a literary unit representing Daniel's four kingdoms (Beale, *Book of Revelation*, 376–77, 388–389). Moloney suggests that "the four horses and the four riders are the empires that are given authority over a quarter of the earth as a result of sin" (Moloney, *Apocalypse of John*, 110). Cf. Walvoord, *Revelation*, 126–28.

23. Court, *Revelation*, 31.

24. Cf. Aune, *Revelation 6–16*, 393–94; Beale, *Book of Revelation*, 375–78; Leithart, *Revelation 1–11*, 281. Moloney sees it as a kind of allegory of original humanity before the fall (Moloney, *Apocalypse of John*, 104–106).

25. Cf. Koester, *Revelation*, 394; Aune, *Revelation 6–16*, 395; Dyer, "Four Horsemen."

26. Cf. Thomas, *Apocalypse*, 240–41; Taushev, *Ancient Christianity*, 125; Papandrea, *Wedding of the Lamb*, 114.

27. Cf. Thomas, *Apocalypse*, 167. However, Koester points out that "victorious military leaders . . . sometimes appeared with white horses" (Koester, *Revelation*, 393). Leithart sees all four horses as referring to the apostolic church being "ridden" by Christ (Leithart, *Revelation 1–11*, 281–84).

28. As Thomas points out, nearly all uses of conquering language in Revelation refer to believers or Christ (Thomas, *Apocalypse*, 123). Cf. Hendriksen, *More Than Conquerors*, 94–96. Hendriksen also sees an allusion to Ps 45:3–5.

29. There is strong evidence of this interpretation in the early church. For example, Irenaeus seems to suggest this (*Haer.* 4.21.3 in *ANF* 1, 493) and Victorinus's commentary (the earliest commentary on Revelation still preserved) specifically says, "the white horse is the word of preaching with the Holy Spirit sent into the world" (*Commentary*, *ANF* 7:350). Cf. Hendriksen, *More Than Conquerors*, 26–27.

30. The bow is also "the common symbol associated with Apollo," a Greek god who is often a target in John's rhetoric (Paul, *Revelation*, 144).

31. Cf. Thomas, *Apocalypse*, 240.

The message seems to be that[32] the world has been invaded by the incarnate and ascended Christ. This invasion unsettles and challenges the world's religious and political authorities (as is graphically evident in the trial scenes in the Gospels), and it provokes violent reactions, including the slaughter of the Lamb (5:6, 9). The resultant struggle will be visually portrayed with apocalyptic language in the rest of Revelation. Though Jesus is portrayed in Isaiah as the "prince of peace" (Isa 9:6), there can be no peace until the resistance to his rule has been destroyed. This is a similar thought to what we read in Psalm 2, one of Revelation's most popular intertextual references. And the same notion lies behind Acts 17:6–7 NRSV ("these people who have been turning the world upside down . . . saying that there is another king named Jesus").

This approach to the four horsemen is consistent with its probable intertextual referent in Zechariah 1. Zechariah has a night vision where he sees "a man mounted on a red horse" with "red, brown and white horses" behind him (Zech 1:8; see also 6:1–6).[33] These mounted horses are interpreted as a kind of reconnaissance patrol, and they report back that they found "the whole earth at rest and in peace" (Zech 1:11). This might seem good news to us, but in the historical context it is tragic, since their peace is built on the destruction of Jerusalem and Judah (Zech 1:12–14). In fact, God says, "I am very angry with the nations that feel secure. I was only a little angry, but they went too far with the punishment" (Zech 1:15). The implication is that God will shake the nations' peace in order to restore Jerusalem and the temple there (Zech 1:16).

Something similar is going on in Revelation, I believe.[34] God is shaking the nations (see also Hag 2:6–9 and Heb 12:26–28) in order to build a "new Jerusalem" (Rev 21) on the basis of a "new exodus," like the original exodus which followed the shaking of Egypt. New exodus is a concept we will refer to in several places, as it is suggested by regular references to the original exodus in Revelation, based on the slaughtered Lamb of chapter 5.[35]

There is a similar thought in Habakkuk 3. Habakkuk has been protesting with God about the injustice in Israel (Hab 1:2–4), only to be told that God will punish Israel through the Babylonians (Hab 1:5–11) with their amazing cavalry (Hab 1:8; compare Rev 9:16). Habakkuk accepts the word that God's purpose is to punish (Hab 1:12), but he still finds it hard to accept that God will use a nation much more wicked than Israel to punish his people, a nation that will give the glory to their own idols (Hab 1:13–17). God replies that the prophecy is for a future time (Hab 2:3), and the

---

32. Cf. Leithart, *Revelation 1–11*, 282–83.

33. Beale reads Zech 6 as the four groups of horses executing divine judgement (Beale, *Book of Revelation*, 378), but there is no mention in the text of what their role is, except an enigmatic suggestion at the end that "those going towards the north country have given my Spirit rest in the land of the north" (Zech 6:8).

34. Cf. Leithart, *Revelation 1–11*, 278–79.

35. For a different "take" on the four horsemen based on ancient astrology, see Malina, *Genre and Message*, 121–28. See also Aune, *Revelation 6–16*, 390; Leithart, *Revelation 1–11*, 280–281.

Babylonians themselves will fall (Hab 2:4–20) in the time of "the end" (Hab 2:3). Then "the righteous person will live by his faithfulness" (Hab 2:4, quoted in Rom 1:17) and "the earth will be filled with the knowledge of the glory of the LORD as the waters cover the sea" (Hab 2:14). Finally, Habakkuk responds with an extended prayer song, asking God to repeat his deeds in his day and "in wrath remember mercy" (Hab 3:2). He rehearses those ancient deeds of the Exodus period,[36] using military language like "you rode your horses and your chariots to victory" (Hab 3:8) and cosmic language such as "the mountains saw you and writhed" (Hab 3:10) and "sun and moon stood still" (Hab 3:11). Habakkuk finally accepts God's plan with patience and even joy (Hab 3:16–18). From this, we see that God's dealings are often likened to military invasion (with horses, chariots, bows, and arrows) and cosmic upheavals just like what happens as the seals unfold, but the end result is the dispersion of the knowledge of God worldwide. In this case, "The Spirit's conquest is the conquest of the gospel, the victorious announcement of the kingdom by the apostles after Pentecost."[37]

> **And when he opened the second seal, I heard the second living being say, "Come." And another horse, fiery red, came out, and to the one sitting on it was given (power) to take peace from the earth and so that they should slaughter each other, and a large sword was given to him. (Rev 6:3–4)**

This image differs from the first. The second horse is "fiery red," and its rider was given power to release violence across the earth (v. 4), as symbolized by his "large sword." There is a tension in this description. The people involved will slaughter each other; the reason for this is that the rider on this horse makes this happen by taking peace from them. The power to do this is "given" to him, apparently by God or the Lamb. This is what scholars call the divine passive in Revelation, in which God specifically permits evil actions by human or Satanic forces.[38] In other words, the second rider is somehow "licensed" by God to take away peace and bring in war, which may be a reference to the famous *Pax Romana*. Roman peace was based on conquest and brutal force but was also brittle and likely to be interrupted by civil wars, struggles for power, and frequent local conflicts.[39]

This idea of God "licensing" war cuts against how we imagine God and Jesus, especially in view of the Sermon on the Mount. But Jesus is not just a peace-lover in the Gospels. We see this in his violent actions in the temple (Matt 21:12; Mark 11:15–16; Luke 19:45; and graphically in John 2:14–16) and his predictions of the violent

---

36. Cf. Leithart, *Revelation 1–11*, 287.
37. Leithart, *Revelation 1–11*, 288.
38. Cf. Thomas, *Apocalypse*, 242; Aune, *Revelation 6–16*, 395; Thompson, *Book of Revelation*, 91. Beale and Hendriksen maintains that John has the persecution of Christians in mind here (Hendriksen, *More Than Conquerors*, 99–101; cf. Beale, *Book of Revelation*, 379–80), but if so, it is not specific until the fifth seal.
39. Cf. Koester, *Revelation*, 395–96, 407; Aune, *Revelation 6–16*, 395; Paul, *Revelation*, 145, 148.

destruction of the temple (Matt 24:2; Mark 13:2; Luke 19:41–44; 21:6).[40] Certainly the original hearers of Revelation would find this pericope believable, having lived through warfare themselves. This would have included the civil wars in the Roman Empire (AD 68–69), various wars on the borders of the empire, and in the case of Jews, the infamous and tragic Roman-Jewish war of AD 66–70, which ended with the destruction of Jerusalem and its temple just as Jesus had predicted.

The idea that God could use war as a judgment on the world or on his people has a long history in the Old Testament. For instance, Jeremiah speaks of the invading Chaldeans wreaking havoc on Judah and Jerusalem as God's judgment, calling the Babylonian king Nebuchadnezzar God's servant (Jer 27:8), and then predicting Babylon's own violent downfall (Jer 50–51).

A similar idea is present in at least several statements from Jesus in the Gospels (such as Luke 19:41–44). The predictions in this section of Revelation have significant parallels with Jesus' "Olivet Discourse" (Matt 24; Mark 13; Luke 21). In each version, Jesus warns his audience of increased warfare (Matt 24:6–7; Mark 13:7–8; Luke 21:9–10) and the following details have parallels with other events in Revelation 6, as we will see. Maybe the seven seals should be read as John's apocalyptic version of this "Olivet Discourse."

This implies that "Rev. 6:1–8 describe the operation of the destructive forces that were unleashed immediately on the world as a result of Christ's victorious suffering at the cross, his resurrection, and his ascent to a position of rule at his Father's right hand" and "not reserved exclusively for a period of severe trial immediately preceding Christ's final coming."[41] Better still, the division and violence here result directly from the gospel invasion of the first horse and rider. Leithart speaks of "a horse of fire, the church burning with the fire of the Spirit . . . that divides and consumes families."[42] Acts, of course, is full of this strife resulting from gospel preaching, but the language of Revelation 6:4 doesn't seem to directly reflect this.

> **And when he opened the third seal, I heard the third living being say, "Come." And I looked, and behold a black horse, and the one sitting on it had scales in his hand. And I heard like a voice in the midst of the four living beings that said, "A quart[43] of wheat for a denarius[44] and three quarts of barley for a denarius, and do not harm the oil and the wine." (Rev 6:5–6)**

The third seal begins much like the first two, but this time we see a black horse whose rider "had scales in his hand" (v. 5). The interpretation speaks of shortages and

---

40. Cf. Beale, *Book of Revelation*, 388.
41. Beale, *Book of Revelation*, 371.
42. Leithart, *Revelation 1–11*, 289; cf. Matt 10:34–36; Luke 12:49–53. See also Taushev, *Ancient Christianity*, 126.
43. A quart (Greek χοῖνιξ [*choinix*]) was a dry measure equal to about a liter or nearly two pints.
44. This was the usual daily wages for a laborer.

inflation: "A quart of wheat for a denarius and three quarts of barley for a denarius" (v. 6).[45] This is probably the result of the warfare depicted in the previous horse: warfare (especially if sieges are involved) tends to produce food shortages, especially affecting the basics of life and the poorer people who depend on them. But such shortages could also be caused by droughts, ships being lost at sea, or disease. Koester states that, "Food crises occurred in Rome during the reign of virtually every emperor in the first century CE."[46] In fact, in this case the shortage is very much limited to basics, for the voice adds "do not harm the oil and the wine" (v. 6).

The Roman Empire depended on large-scale cultivation of wheat, especially in Egypt and northern Africa, and some of it was compulsorily acquired for the poorer (free) people in Rome itself, lest they rebel against the Empire. However, landowners (especially in the province of Asia to which Revelation was sent) could make much better profits growing olives (the source of oil) and grapes for wine, to be purchased by the more affluent members of society. Hence the emperor Domitian placed strict limitations on cultivation of grapes (between AD 90 and 93) at around the time Revelation may have been written, perhaps to encourage more grain growing, perhaps in response to a particularly severe famine in AD 91.[47] His edict "was exceedingly unpopular in Asia Minor."[48] However, Thomas points out that oil and wine were necessities for all people and maybe the point here is that such crops would survive longer in a drought.[49] Interestingly, in this case there is no language of God explicitly permitting all this.[50]

> **And when he opened the fourth seal, I heard the voice of the fourth living being say, "Come." And I saw, and behold a pale green horse, and the one sitting on it was named Death, and Hades followed after him, and authority[51] was given to them over a fourth of the earth to kill by sword and by famine and by death and by the wild beasts of the earth. (Rev 6:7–8)**

The fourth seal unveils a sickly looking horse. The color here is *chlōros*, green or pale, possibly "the greenish-grey pallor of a person who is sick, dying, or terrified."[52] The rider has a name this time, Death, followed by Hades, presumably on another horse (v.

---

45. This would be ten to twelve times the normal prices according to Thomas, *Apocalypse*, 244; sixteen times according to Koester, *Revelation*, 396; cf. Aune, *Revelation 6–16*, 397; Beale, *Book of Revelation*, 381; Howard-Brook and Gwyther, *Unveiling Empire*, 99.

46. Koester, *Revelation*, 408; see also Fox, *Classical World*, 389; Aune, *Revelation 6–16*, 399. Extreme inflation ravaged Germany in the 1920s and, more recently, Zimbabwe and Venezuela. Gause suggests that the problem was not shortage but greed (Gause, *Revelation*, 106).

47. Cf. Aune, *Revelation 6–16*, 399–400.

48. Aune, *Revelation 6–16*, 399.

49. Thomas, *Apocalypse*, 244–45. For other possibilities, see Koester, *Revelation*, 397.

50. Leithart, however, argues that it speaks of a spiritual impoverishment of the resistant synagogues (Leithart, *Revelation 1–11*, 291–296).

51. Greek ἐξουσία [*exousia*], "authority" or perhaps "control, power, licence."

52. Koester, *Revelation*, 397; see also Aune, *Revelation 6–16*, 382, 400–401.

8). Thomas comments, "it generates a scene where all the victims of Death are quickly captured by Hades."[53] Hades in Greek thought was the place of dead souls, originally the name of the god of the underworld,[54] roughly similar to Sheol in Hebrew. Jesus claims to have "the keys of death and Hades" in 1:18, and these two are finally thrown into the lake of fire after being forced to release their captives (20:13–14). That suggests they are enemies of humanity and servants of the evil one;[55] however, here they act like servants of the ascended Christ.[56]

Christians have nothing to be afraid of when they face death, but for everyone else, these ancient enemies are frightening. Using the divine passive (as in v. 4), we hear that they were given authority (or power) over a fourth of the earth to kill by sword, famine, death (probably plague), and wild beasts (v. 8). This sounds like a breakdown of order that might come as a result of an invasion, with probable allusions to Jeremiah 15:2–3; 43:11 and Ezekiel 5:12, 17; 6:12.[57] Ancient people prized order and feared chaos, but chaos is exactly what they get in this scenario. And chaos comes from well-known causes: violence, famine (a fairly frequent problem then and even now in places; compare Acts 11:28), plague, and wild beasts. These beasts would roam out of control in depopulated eras as a result of large-scale war or plague.[58]

But there are boundaries: just as the third horseman could not touch the oil and wine, so here the destruction comes only on a fourth of the earth. Later it will increase to one-third; fractions are an important feature of apocalyptic arithmetic. God is still in control. Again, Christian hearers would think of phrases from Jesus' "Olivet Discourse." He says, "there will be famines and earthquakes in various places" (Matt 24:7; compare Mark 13:8). The version in Luke 21:11 adds "pestilences" and "fearful events."

> **And when he opened the fifth seal, I saw under the altar the souls of those slaughtered on account of the word of God, and on account of the testimony which they had. (Rev 6:9)**

---

53. Thomas, *Apocalypse*, 246.

54. Koester, *Revelation*, 397; Aune, *Revelation 6–16*, 401. An intriguing context here is the under-earth shrine of Hades recently uncovered by archaeologists at Hierapolis, part of the province of Asia and near to Laodicea (cf. Dyer, "Four Horsemen," 138–40).

55. Cf. Beale, *Book of Revelation*, 382–83.

56. Beale, *Book of Revelation*, 385; cf. Leithart, *Revelation 1–11*, 299.

57. See also Deut 32:24–25; Lev 26:18–28 and Ezek 14:12–23. These references would suggest some kind of covenant curse is being released here, or in the seven seals as a whole. Cf. Pattemore, *People of God*, 71; Beale, *Book of Revelation*, 372–74, 384; Stramara, *God's Timetable*, 49–50. Similar language is used in an account of the second Roman-Jewish war of AD 132–35 (Aune, *Revelation 6–16*, 402). Beale sees a satanic element as dominant here, though subject to divine sovereignty (Beale, *Book of Revelation*, 383).

58. Beale argues for a reference to the beast of Revelation 13 and his persecution of believers here (Beale, *Book of Revelation*, 386–88). However, I think a broader meaning makes good sense in the context of Revelation 6; cf. Leithart, *Revelation 1–11*, 297.

With the fifth seal, the structure changes. No horse or rider this time; instead, John sees the souls of martyrs. The description of the basis of their death recalls 1:2 (where the whole vision is described as "the word of God and the testimony of Jesus Christ") and 1:9 (where John's exile to Patmos is "on account of the word of God and the testimony of Jesus"). This phrase seems to sum up the core message of the Christian faith for John. The death of these believers was violent: they were "slaughtered" (using the same verb as in 5:6, 9, and 12) just like their Lord, anticipating the two witnesses in 11:7–9, and showing a strong identification between Jesus and his folllowers.[59] These martyrs were primarily Christians, but may have included Jewish martyrs going all the way back to Abel, whose blood cried out to God from the ground (Gen 4:10; compare 2 Macc 7; Matt 23:30–38).[60]

But here specifically, it is their "souls" [*psuchas*] that are in view and which are about to speak, perhaps implying a kind of dualism of body and soul.[61] And these souls are "under the altar." So far, no altar has been mentioned in Revelation, though incense (5:8), the temple of God (3:12), and lampstands similar to those found in the temple (1:12, 20; 2:1) have all appeared. Hence the full furniture of the Jerusalem temple might be expected to have its counterparts in heaven. Certainly, altars will be mentioned several times in later passages (8:3, 5; 9:13; 11:1; 14:18; 16:7), as will the heavenly temple (11:19; 14:15, 17; 15:5, 6, 8; 16:1).[62] The temple imagery is balanced by the throne room imagery which dominated Revelation 4–5.

So what does it mean to say that the martyrs' souls are "under the altar"? It seems to be a place of sacrifice: their blood is added to that of the Lamb (compare 12:11)[63] and accomplishes some kind of justice or atonement.[64] It may simply indicate that their blood is in the earth like Abel's, not in heaven since "the life of a creature is in the blood" (Lev 17:11).[65] The altar may also be a place of reward or refreshing for what they have suffered (compare 7:14–17); there is an implied contrast with the people captured by Death and Hades under the previous seal. These souls are in heaven, not Hades.[66]

> **And they cried out in a loud voice, saying, "Until when, holy and true master, will you not judge and avenge our blood from those who dwell on the earth?"**

---

59. Cf. Pattemore, *People of God*, 77–78, 86.

60. Cf. Beale, *Book of Revelation*, 390–91; Moloney, *Apocalypse of John*, 114. Beale interprets this as including all faithful believers, not just literal martyrs. Pattemore argues the reverse: Pattemore, *People of God*, 79–80.

61. Cf. Koester, *Revelation*, 399.

62. This assumes John is referring to the altar of God in heaven. But David M. May makes a strong case, partly based on Roman coins, that the reference is to a Roman altar on which the martyrs are figuratively sacrificed. Their deaths thus undermined the ideology of Rome (May, "Interpreting Revelation").

63. Cf. Thomas, *Apocalypse*, 248–49; Koester, *Revelation*, 398; Beale, *Book of Revelation*, 391.

64. Cf. Leithart, *Revelation 1–11*, 303–5.

65. So Leithart, *Revelation 1–11*, 302–3.

66. Cf. Aune, *Revelation 6–16*, 403–4.

Revelation Chapter 6

And to each of them was given a white robe, and they were told that they must wait a little longer, until their fellow slaves and their brothers were fulfilled who are about to be killed as they were. (Rev 6:10–11)

These souls are not satisfied. A second dramatic problem is raised with their loud voices[67] asking God, "How long . . . until you judge the inhabitants of the earth and avenge our blood?" (v. 10 NIV). The reply to this question dominates the rest of the narrative at least to chapter 19.[68] But the initial reply comes from an unspecified source, after they have each been given "a white robe" (v. 11), a significant reward (compare 3:4–5; 7:9, 13, 14).[69] It tells them that they must "wait[70] a little longer," until the full number of their fellow slaves has been killed (v. 11). As Leithart comments, "The martyrs will not be vindicated until there are more martyrs."[71]

Time periods are very important in Revelation. Some of them are very specific, such as a thousand years (20:2–3), one day (18:8), or forty-two months (13:5); others are more general such as "the time is near" (1:3) or "the hour of trial" (3:10). It seems that it is their relative length rather than absolute literal time that is in view. The "forty-two months" may actually extend until Jesus' second advent, but that is still short compared to a "thousand years." Or, as Koester puts it, "visionary time does not correspond to ordinary time."[72] So here "a little longer" may be a fairly long time by human standards; it is, however, a set time determined by a set number: somehow the final judgment cannot occur until this full number of martyrs have been killed.

However, the word "number" is not in the Greek text, so the sense may rather be that they wait until the work of the martyrs is fulfilled.[73] Either way, this shows that the lives of these martyrs are of great value to God. They are counted, a scenario that resembles Jesus' words in a similar context about disciples' hairs being numbered (Matt 10:30; compare Luke 21:18). It also implies that the future is more "open" than the language in other parts of Revelation might suggest; John has spoken of what "must soon happen" (1:1), but how and when it must happen is not clear and perhaps not even fixed.[74]

---

67. The emotional nature of this prayer is emphasized in the sound of the Greek words here (Seal, "Emotions, Empathy, and Engagement," 7–8).

68. Cf. Heil, "Fifth Seal," 242.

69. Cf. Thomas, *Apocalypse*, 252; Beale, *Book of Revelation*, 394; Caird, *Revelation*, 86.

70. Or "rest" (Greek ἀναπαύσονται [*anapausovtai*], "rest, relax"), a mark of God's reward (Rev 14:13; Koester, *Revelation*, 400) or a temporary stage towards their final enthronement (Leithart, *Revelation 1–11*, 308).

71. Leithart, *Revelation 1–11*, 353.

72. Koester, *Revelation*, 400.

73. Cf. Koester, *Revelation*, 400–401; but see discussion in Aune, *Revelation 6–16*, 385, 391, 412; cf. Bauckham, *Climax of Prophecy*, 51–53; Leithart, *Revelation 1–11*, 308–9.

74. Contra Beale who argues that "Christ rules over such an apparently chaotic world and that suffering does not occur indiscriminately or by chance . . . It is Christ sitting on his throne who controls all the trials and persecutions of the church" (Beale, *Book of Revelation*, 370). In a sense, this

The main intertextual reference here may be to Zechariah 1:12, also following a revelation of four horses, where the "angel of the LORD" asks "how long will you withhold mercy from Jerusalem and from the towns of Judah, which you have been angry with these seventy years?" If so, it's the sufferings of the Jews or Jewish believers that would come to the minds of John's audience in the fifth seal, and maybe the whole passage reflects the Roman-Jewish war of AD 66–70.

Or more broadly, the reference is to Psalm 90, where the question, "How long?" also arises (v. 13)[75] in the context of human suffering and mortality. There the human perspective is relativized by the statement that, "A thousand years in your sight are like a day that has just gone by" (v. 4), a thought picked up in 2 Peter 3:8 where it is used to explain the delay in Christ's return, a delay caused by God's patience "not wanting anyone to perish, but everyone to come to repentance" (2 Pet 3:9). Human decisions and events have a big effect on the unfolding of God's plans. Certainly, the Book of Revelation places great emphasis on the value and victory of martyrdom. And here again the text parallels the "Olivet Discourse," where warnings of great hostility to the disciples come after the language of wars and famines (Matt 24:9–10; Mark 13:9–13; Luke 21:12–19).

But why do the souls of the martyrs cry out for vengeance? Why don't they pray for forgiveness of their persecutors as did Jesus (Luke 23:34) and Stephen (Acts 7:60)? The answer of Revelation is that it is a question of justice: innocent suffering ought to be avenged.[76] A New Testament example of this might be the untimely death of Herod after he executed James, though the two events are not explicitly connected by the author of Acts 12.

Here the intertextual connection is more likely Genesis 4:10, which speaks of the first martyr's blood crying out to God from the ground, or 2 Kings 9:7, where a prophet tells Jehu to "destroy the house of Ahab your master, and I will avenge the blood of my servants the prophets and the blood of all the LORD's servants shed by Jezebel." And Deuteronomy 32:43 says, "Rejoice, you nations, with his people, for he will avenge the blood of his servants . . ." This is seen as happening later in Revelation (16:6, 18:20, 19:2).[77]

More deeply, the prayer of the martyrs is for the full accomplishment of God's great plan, the plan written in the scroll now being opened, the plan for which they have given their lives. This plan is fully unveiled at the end of Revelation but forecast in 5:9–10. It is God's plan for the salvation of "persons from every tribe and language

---

is unremarkable, but it can imply that Jesus inflicts persecutions on his own church (see Acts 9:4–5).

75. Compare Pss 13:1–2; 74:10; 79:5; 89:46; 94:3; Jer 12:4; Hab 1:2. This cry expresses what God's people feel under oppression while their enemies triumph. Cf. Bauckham, *Climax of Prophecy*, 51; Thomas, *Apocalypse*, 250–51; Beale, *Book of Revelation*, 392–93.

76. Cf. Thomas, *Apocalypse*, 251–52; Koester, *Revelation*, 410; Beale, *Book of Revelation*, 392; Leithart, *Revelation 1–11*, 306–7.

77. Cf. Aune, *Revelation 6–16*, 409–10.

and people and nation" and for them to "reign on the earth." The souls here are told that this can't happen until many more martyrs die,[78] but eventually their deaths will be vindicated. To put it another way, these souls are praying, "your kingdom come, your will be done, on earth as it is in heaven" (Matt 6:10), a prayer whose answer must include judgment and even violence, as the rest of Revelation shows.[79] And this prayer is obviously effective, since the rest of the book shows how God answers it.[80] Thus, John's audience is called to join in and pray for God's plan to be completed, even at the cost of their lives (see 7:14; 11:7–11; 12:11; 13:15; 17:6; 20:4).

> **And I saw when he opened the sixth seal, and a great earthquake happened, and the sun became black like sackcloth of hair, and the whole moon became like blood and the stars of heaven fell to earth, as a fig tree throws off its unripe figs when shaken by a strong wind, and the sky[81] was torn apart as a scroll is rolled up, and every mountain and island was moved from its place. (Rev 6:12–14)**

The opening of the sixth seal begins the answer to the prayer of the souls under the altar as it unveils a highly climactic scene. It begins with cosmic language of "a great earthquake"[82] and disruptions to the sun, moon, and stars (vv. 12–14). As Thomas observes, this language would suggest "cosmic collapse."[83] However, it is impossible to take this description as referring to a literal scenario. If the stars fell to the earth, nothing would survive; even if these "stars" were asteroids, powerful enough to move all the mountains and islands, the earth would become uninhabitable.

The interpreter might view this as phenomenological language: this is what it would look like; we all occasionally see red moons, eclipses of the sun and even "falling stars," and ancient people saw these as portents of disaster.[84] Alternatively, it is prophetic language referring to political or social upheavals,[85] "the end of a political

---

78. I'm reminded of Jesus' conversation with the apostles in Acts 1:1–8. When they asked, "are you at this going to restore the kingdom to Israel?" (v. 6), he told them "it is not for you to know" (v. 7) but "you will receive power when the Holy Spirit comes on you; and you will be my witnesses . . . " (v. 8). The end does not come until their witness is completed. Cf. Pattemore, *People of God*, 88–89.

79. As David Seal paraphrases it, "The prayer is more than a request for the justice of God to be enacted—it is a longing for the eschatological consummation" (Seal, "Emotions, Empathy and Engagement," 9).

80. For a fuller argument along these lines, see Heil, "Fifth Seal"; cf. Pattemore, *People of God*, 90–116.

81. Greek οὐρανὸς [*ouranos*], "heaven, sky."

82. This region was prone to earthquakes; twelve cities were destroyed in one in AD 17 (Aune, *Revelation 6–16*, 424; Bauckham, *Climax of Prophecy*, 206).

83. Thomas, *Apocalypse*, 254; cf. Koester, *Revelation*, 401–2.

84. Aune, *Revelation 6–16*, 413–18. There were many such portents during the civil strife of AD 68–70 in Rome and Jerusalem (ibid., 417–18).

85. Cf. Beale, *Book of Revelation*, 397–98. John might also be undermining astrology here; the heavenly bodies are totally under God's control (Gause, *Revelation*, 111).

universe"[86] or a great religious shaking.[87] Intertextual references will help here.[88] For example, Isaiah 34:2–4 says:

> The LORD is angry with all nations;
> his wrath is on all their armies.
> He will totally destroy them,
> he will give them over to slaughter.
> their slain will be thrown out,
> their dead bodies will stink;
> the mountains will be soaked with their blood.
> All the stars in the sky will be dissolved
> and the heavens rolled up like a scroll;
> all the starry host will fall
> like withered leaves from the vine,
> like shriveled figs from the fig tree.

In context, this is referring to judgment on the land of Edom (Isa 34:5–15). The language is full of imagery and hyperbole to make a strong point about the cataclysmic nature of what will happen.[89]

Similarly, in a prophecy against Babylon (Isa 13), the prophet speaks of a great army that will destroy that country (Isa 13:2–5) and uses language of "the day of the LORD" for the event (Isa 13:6, 9).

> The stars of the heaven and their constellations will not show their light. The rising sun will be darkened and the moon will not give its light. (Isa 13:10)

But clearly this is all about the Medes invading Babylon (Isa 13:17). Jesus alludes to this language in the same "Olivet Discourse" that runs parallel to the seals in Revelation 6 (Matt 24:29; Mark 13:24–25; compare Luke 21:25–26).[90] However, the hearers and readers of Revelation 6 would have been impressed with the scenario as John saw it.

John's hearers might also be reminded of Joel 2:10, which speaks of the results of the locust plague, and more significantly, Joel 2:30–31:

> I will show wonders in the heavens and on the earth, blood and fire and billows of smoke. The sun will be turned to darkness and the moon to blood before the coming of the great and dreadful day of the LORD.

---

86. Leithart, *Revelation 1–11*, 312. What Leithart means is that the old order of things in the old covenant is collapsing, as seen in the fall of the temple and Jerusalem in AD 70. That is not *exactly* the interpretation I am offering, but it has some similarities.

87. Victorinus saw it as the last great persecution of the church (*Commentary*, ANF 7:351).

88. Beale lists twelve possible OT references here (Beale, *Book of Revelation*, 396).

89. Cf. Beale, *Book of Revelation*, 396–97.

90. Cf. Koester, *Revelation*, 357–58.

This passage comes, of course, just after the promise of the outpoured Holy Spirit (vv. 28–29) referred to in Acts 2:17–20. This suggests that cataclysmic events like this will characterize the age of the Spirit rather than just the final judgment.[91]

> And the kings of the earth and the great ones and the commanders and the rich and the strong and every slave and free person hid themselves in the caves and in the rocks of the mountains and said to the mountains and to the rocks, "Fall on us and hide us from the face of the one sitting on the throne and from the wrath of the Lamb, for the great day of their wrath has come, and who is able to stand?" (Rev 6:15–17)

The world order that everyone relied on is falling apart, as the previous cosmic language accentuates, and this leaves everyone exposed to the wrath of God, and the wrath of the Lamb![92] Here Revelation virtually quotes Hosea 10:8,[93] in which the high people of Israel face destruction:

> Then they will say to the mountains, "Cover us!"
> and to the hills, "Fall on us!"

This verse is also quoted by Jesus in Luke 23:30, in reference to the coming destruction of Jerusalem by the Romans in AD 70. Clearly, the world faces extreme judgment.

But two points stand out. First, this is the wrath of the Lamb, not just God. Why is the Lamb so full of wrath? Is it just because the Jewish leaders rejected him? Perhaps, but Jesus prayed, "Father, forgive them for they do not know what they are doing" (Luke 23:34). In context, what arouses his wrath is their treatment of his representatives,[94] those viewed in the fifth seal episode, who have also cried out for vengeance (v. 10). The final punishment of the world city specifically mentions this as a grounds for punishment (Rev 16:5–6; 18:24).[95]

Second, a specific time is at hand: "the great day of their wrath" (v. 17; compare Zeph 1:14), the time for the vengeance for the lives of the martyrs and general judgment on human sin.[96] Some commentators see this as a specific reference to the de-

---

91. Contra Beale who argues that "the scene depicts figuratively the inauguration of the last judgment" (Beale, *Book of Revelation*, 398, see 398–401 for the full argument). If Beale is right, we need a recapitulation interpretation of the narrative, one that keeps reiterating the progress to final judgement. Leithart in *Revelation 1–11*, 314–19, reads this as a specific judgment upon unrepentant Israel and its temple in AD 70. This rightly locates these events in a first-century context but narrows the focus to Judea and just the first century.

92. Cf. Thomas, *Apocalypse*, 256–57. Beale sees this as judgment especially on idolatry; "creation itself . . . has become an idol that must be removed" (Beale, *Book of Revelation*, 402).

93. But see also Isa 2:10, 19–21.

94. Cf. Leithart, *Revelation 1–11*, 308–9.

95. Caird argues that the wrath of the Lamb is simply the "paranoiac delusion" of the frightened people in verses 15–17 (Caird, *Revelation*, 92). I find that difficult to accept in view of the whole storyline of Revelation.

96. Cf. Koester, *Revelation*, 404; Aune, *Revelation 6–16*, 421–23.

struction of Jerusalem and its temple in AD 70, which Matthew 23–24 might support, and possibly Luke 21:20—24 and 23:30. Matthew reports Jesus saying to the high priest at his trial, "From now on you will see the Son of Man sitting at the right hand of the Mighty One and coming on the clouds of heaven" (Matt 26:64), in fulfilment of Daniel 7:13. But perhaps this is too narrow an interpretation. The wrath of God will descend on more than the Jewish nation; it will affect the whole ancient world and perhaps the modern world too.[97]

In conclusion, in Revelation 5–6 the readers/hearers have heard three big questions that dominate the narrative of the book:

1. Who is worthy to open the seals (5:2)? Answer: the Slain Lamb is worthy and proceeds to open them.

2. How long, Lord, till you judge the earth and avenge the martyrs' blood (6:10)? Answer: not until the full quota of martyrs have died or their work is completed.

3. Who can withstand the day of the wrath of God and the Lamb (6:17; see also Nah 1:6; Mal 3:2; 1 Sam 6:20)? Answer: to be decided, though there may be a hint in Nahum 1:7, which says, "The LORD is good, a refuge in times of trouble." Clearly, those speaking in 6:16–17 cannot withstand this wrath, but two other groups will be described in chapter 7.

Chapter 6 then ends with a note of suspense as the third question is not yet answered, and how the first two answers will work out is not clear either. But we have one more seal to be broken from the scroll.

---

97. Cf. Beale, *Book of Revelation*, 374, 385; Leithart, *Revelation 1–11*, 313–19.

Revelation Chapter 7

As I keep saying, there were no chapters or verses in the original manuscripts of the books of the Bible. It is therefore a good practice to read over the chapter divisions and look for the original textual structures and pauses.

Chapter 6 is clearly unfinished. It has begun to count off the opening of the seven seals by the Lamb, a saga that began in chapter 5, but only got to seal six. The dramatic events portrayed under the sixth seal could have been the end of the world. If the original readers were conscious of the connections with Jesus' "Olivet Discourse" (recorded in Matt 24, Mark 13, and Luke 21), they might now be expecting the second coming as the seventh seal is opened. But this is delayed. In fact as we move into chapter 7, we get a pause in the whole forward thrust of the story, though as Leithart observes, this is still part of the sixth seal[1] and continues the cosmic collapse scenario of that seal. It also begins to answer the two questions in chapter 6: "Until when, holy and true master, will you not judge and avenge our blood from those who dwell on the earth?" (6:10) and "who is able to stand" (6:17) in the day of wrath?[2] This pause makes way for two important scenes, first on earth and then in heaven.

7:1–8 The Sealing of the Twelve Tribes

> **After this I saw four angels standing at the four corners of the earth, who were holding back[3] the four winds of the earth so that no wind might blow on the earth nor on the sea nor on any tree. (Rev 7:1)[4]**

Hearers/readers of Revelation have been counting down the seals as the Lamb has been opening them, but instead of hearing, "I watched as he opened the seventh seal,"

---

1. Leithart, *Revelation 1–11*, 310.
2. Leithart, *Revelation 1–11*, 320.
3. Is there any connection to the restraint on the "man of lawlessness" in 2 Thess 2:6–7? That, of course, is Paul, not John.
4. Aune analyses parallels between this passage and other "angelophonies" in Revelation, showing that there is a common literary form at work (Aune, *Revelation 6–16*, 435).

they hear/read something different. The number four is always associated in Revelation with directions and the earth at large, which is probably why there are four living creatures, and in this case the "four corners" speak of "God's complete control over the earth."[5] So the whole earth is being prepared for something here, but first, there is a delay. And the events about to unfold seem threatening since the hearers have just been hearing about the imminent wrath of God and the Lamb (6:16–17), preceded by the four horsemen of the first four seals (6:1–8). Moreover, the four winds is "a traditional sign of God's destructive power in the OT."[6]

> **And I saw another angel coming up from the east who had a seal of the living God, and he cried out in a loud voice to the four angels to whom it was given to harm the earth and the sea, saying, "Do not harm the earth nor the sea nor the trees, until we have sealed the slaves of our God on their foreheads." (Rev 7:2–3)**

This impending threat (v. 1) is now confirmed since the four angels are going to "harm the earth and the sea." There is also an allusion here to Daniel 7, where the "four winds of heaven" were seen "churning up the great sea" before "four great beasts . . . came up out of the sea" (Dan 7:2–3), representing the four great empires.[7] The fact that the four winds are held back in 7:1–3 suggests that the rise of the coming beast (coming up in Rev 13) is being delayed until the church (portrayed in the rest of this chapter) is well established and able to stand.[8]

The other angel "coming up from the east" (v. 2), who apparently has authority over the four destructive angels, gives us God's reason for this delay, which is that the slaves of God must be sealed. This is partly an answer to the "how long?" of 6:10; the delay in God's judgment allows for the sealing and gathering of people from every nation,[9] referring back to 5:9 and perhaps similar to 2 Peter 3:9. So who are these slaves of God and what is the sealing about? We aren't given a direct answer to the second question until chapter 9, but the intertextual reference here is likely to be first, Genesis 4:15 (the mark placed on Cain by God to protect him) and more importantly, Ezekiel 9.[10]

---

5. Thomas, *Apocalypse*, 258; Beale, *Book of Revelation*, 406. Or it's showing God's control of the land of Israel if one accepts Leithart's reading (Leithart, *Revelation 1–11*, 320). On the mention of trees in vv. 1 and 3, see Leithart, *Revelation 1–11*, 321.

6. Thomas, *Apocalypse*, 258; cf. Jer 49:36; Dan 7:2; Zech 6:5; but see Ezek 37:9 where the winds play a more positive role. Cf. Koester, *Revelation*, 414–15; Beale, *Book of Revelation*, 406–8. Beale sees the four winds as referring back to the four horsemen of ch. 6 whose work is being held back in ch. 7. There could also be an allusion to a prophecy reported by Josephus from about AD 62 and repeated for over seven years, which said "A voice from the east, a voice from the west, a voice from the four winds, a voice against Jerusalem and the holy house, a voice against the bridegrooms and the brides, and a voice against this whole people" (Josephus, "War of the Jews" 6:301). Leithart argues that the winds are "the saints, the Spirit-blown people of God" (Leithart, *Revelation 1–11*, 321).

7. In a similar way, Zechariah's four chariots are "the four spirits (or winds) of heaven" going out in all four directions (Zech 6:5–6). Cf. Pattemore, *People of God*, 125–27.

8. Cf. Perry, "Political Authority," 56–60.

9. Koester, *Revelation*, 424.

10. Pattemore, however, argues that the differences with Ezekiel 9 are too great and proposes that

Ezekiel 9 portrays God about to release slaughter in Jerusalem and the temple (Ezek 9:5–7), but first calling a "man clothed in linen who had a writing kit at his side" (v. 3) to "Go throughout the city of Jerusalem and put a mark on the foreheads of those who grieve and lament over all the detestable things that are done in it" (v. 4). This is so that they would be exempted from the slaughter (v. 6).[11] Here too, in Revelation 7, the angelic beings are to put a seal on the foreheads of "the slaves of our God" (v. 3). Presumably they will be exempt from coming harm,[12] either physically or in terms of their spiritual life and faith,[13] in partial answer to the question at the end of chapter 6: Who can stand in the great day of wrath?[14]

A similar promise has been given to the church in Philadelphia: "I will keep you from the hour of testing that is about to come on the whole world" (3:10). So we must infer that the people to be sealed are victorious Christians who were faithful like the Philadelphians and who did not compromise with the surrounding culture as some of the other churches did, in a similar way to the sealed people in Ezekiel 9.[15] Protection of the Israelites from some of the plagues on Egypt in Exodus is also in view (Exod 8:22; 9:4–7, 26; 10:23; 12:12–13), especially as the sealed ones are described as belonging to the tribes of Israel.

This is the first forehead sealing in Revelation, though also anticipated by the promise to the Philadelphian church of names written on them (3:12; compare 14:1). Many people puzzle over the name of the beast written on people's foreheads (13:16–18), but this forehead marking is more significant.[16]

Early Pentecostals often interpreted this sealing as referring to Spirit baptism, in line with Ephesians 1:13–14 ("When you believed, you were marked in him with a seal, the promised Holy Spirit, who is a deposit guaranteeing our inheritance until the redemption of those who are God's possession . . . ").[17] While this is Paul's language, not John's, and perhaps confuses an initial experience of new believers with a reward

---

the three main allusions are to the sealed scroll of ch. 5, the common understanding of sealing as a mark of ownership and "the early Christian concept of being sealed by the Spirit as God's possession" (Pattemore, *People of God*, 132–33; for the full discussion see 128–33).

11. Cf. Thomas, *Apocalypse*, 261; Koester, *Revelation*, 416; Beale, *Book of Revelation*, 409–10; Leithart, *Revelation 1–11*, 323. Similar wording is found in Psalms of Solomon 15:6, 9.

12. This reflects a common idea in ancient Jewish and Greco-Roman magic, representing protection against, or control over, demons (Aune, *Revelation 6–16*, 453–54). There may be a parallel with the lamb's blood on the doorposts in Exodus 12 (ibid., 456).

13. Cf. Beale, *Book of Revelation*, 409–10; Pattemore, *People of God*, 134.

14. Cf. Beale, *Book of Revelation*, 405. Beale sees the "standing" in Revelation 7 as referring to resurrection.

15. Cf. Thomas, *Apocalypse*, 262–63.

16. Cf. Koester, *Revelation*, 425. Some commentators (e.g., Beale, *Book of Revelation*, 411) see a reference to tattooing of slaves as a mark of ownership since the verse talks of the "slaves of our God" (v. 3), but Koester points out this practice was more a punishment for slaves who "ran away or committed an offence" (Koester, *Revelation*, 416–17). Cf. Aune, *Revelation 6–16*, 457–58.

17. Cf. Johnson, *Pneumatic Discernment*, 107–8, 119.

for ongoing perseverance, it is as good a suggestion as any. The location of the seal on the forehead (v. 3) would correspond to the laying on of hands often associated in Acts with reception of the Spirit (Acts 8:17–18; 9:17; 19:6).[18]

> **And I heard the number of those being sealed:**
> **144,000 being sealed from every tribe of the sons of Israel:**
> **From the tribe of Judah 12,000 were sealed,**
> **from the tribe of Reuben 12,000,**
> **from the tribe of Gad 12,000,**
> **from the tribe of Asher 12,000,**
> **from the tribe of Naphtali 12,000,**
> **from the tribe of Manasseh 12,000,**
> **from the tribe of Simeon 12,000,**
> **from the tribe of Levi 12,000,**
> **from the tribe of Issachar 12,000,**
> **from the tribe of Zebulun 12,000,**
> **from the tribe of Joseph 12,000,**
> **from the tribe of Benjamin 12,000 were sealed. (Rev 7:4–8)**

What is this about? The audience of the Apocalypse may be reminded of the army of 12,000 chosen for battle in Numbers 31:4–6; however, this group is twelve times the size.

This is one of most controversial passages in Revelation. Many modern readers would remember the big play Jehovah's Witnesses made on this number as the elite or pioneers of their group. But there are five main interpretations of the 144,000. First, commentators influenced by Dispensationalism contend that they could represent a literal number of "Jewish evangelists" who operate powerfully in the (future) tribulation after the church has been raptured,[19] or more broadly Jews saved during this time.[20] Second, they might represent the original Jewish Christians, the initial core of the infant church.[21] Third, they might represent the faithful "remnant" of Israel, but not necessarily Christians.[22] Fourth, they could represent the whole

---

18. Cf. Aune, *Revelation 6–16*, 458–59, 479; Leithart, *Revelation 1–11*, 322; Pattemore, *People of God*, 132–33. This would refer to receiving the Spirit after water baptism (Acts 19:6; 8:17–19), but later this was taken simply as baptism, which included marking the new believer with a sign of the Name of Christ. Cf. Koester, *Revelation*, 425; Paul, *Revelation*, 157. Beale comments that "the seal empowers the 144,000 to perform the witnessing role intended for true Israel" and functions as a mark of "genuine membership in the community of the redeemed" (Beale, *Book of Revelation*, 411). It may indeed be "identified with the Holy Spirit" (ibid.).

19. Cf. La Haye, *Revelation Unveiled*, 149–57.

20. Cf. Walvoord, *Revelation*, 139.

21. Or they represent OT Israel, the faithful believers from the twelve tribes (cf. Corsini, *Apocalypse*, 158–59).

22. This is the view that Mayo contends against (Mayo, *Those Who Call Themselves Jews*, 89–102).

church symbolically as a new Israel.[23] Or fifth, they might also represent Christian martyrs in particular.[24]

Leaving aside arguments based on Paul (especially Rom 9–11),[25] the first interpretation is unsustainable because the number seems too "rounded" and "ideal" to be taken literally and there has been no indication of a "rapture" so far in Revelation. John does not appear to use numbers literally but more as either relative indications of size or to make a theological point, or both, as I think he does here. Moreover, the tribes of Israel listed in verses 5–8 do not correspond exactly to the historic tribes, which in any literal sense came to thirteen anyway, with two tribes of Joseph (Ephraim and Manasseh) being included, but the Levites not counted in Israelite censuses to make it twelve again. But here Levi is *included* and Dan *omitted*. Whatever the reason for this (see below), it again appears to make the list "ideal" rather than empirical. The arithmetic is symbolic: 144,000 = 1,000 x 12 x 12, where the twelves stand for the Israelite tribes and/or the twelve apostles (see 21:12–14) and the thousand for a relatively large number or a complete entity (as in Rev 20).

The second interpretation (the 144,000 stand for early Jewish Christians), and perhaps the third, may also be weakened by the same factors. However, in their case, this weakness is not decisive since it could be said that an incomplete listing of tribes symbolically identifies the faithful remnant (compare Isa 10:22 and Rom 11:5) among the Israelites. Thus, the omission of Dan would not be a major drawback, and it is a historic fact that the Jewish believers were the core of the infant church. This is perhaps why the 144,000 are referred to as the "first fruits" in 14:4 (see also Eph 1:12; Rom 11:16).

Certainly Revelation takes pains to emphasize the Israelite nature of the 144,000; imagine the initial hearers listening as the reader has to read each statement about each tribe and its 12,000 in verses 4–8.[26] This view also makes good sense of the fact that those sealed are taken out of the twelve tribes rather than being the whole number of the tribes; they would be seen as the faithful remnant of Israel.[27] In fact, though, the early Jewish believers in Christ did not represent all twelve tribes, but mainly Judah, Benjamin, and Levi, since the old northern kingdom of Israel was taken captive by Assyria and never returned to the promised land, unlike the southern tribes.

The main difficulty with this view is that later references to the sealed ones (ch. 9) and the 144,000 (ch. 14) make more sense if all the faithful conquering Christians are included. As Charles and Beasley-Murray have pointed out, "the sealing must

---

23. Cf. Koester, *Revelation*, 355, 427.

24. Cf. Aune, *Revelation 6–16*, 443–45; Koester, *Revelation*, 427; Beale, *Book of Revelation*, 413; Leithart, *Revelation 1–11*, 322–24, 332–33.

25. Taushev applies Romans 11 to his interpretation, seeing the 144,000 as Jews converted to Christ in the last days (Taushev, *Ancient Christianity*, 137).

26. Cf. Aune, *Revelation 6–16*, 440–42; Leithart, *Revelation 1–11*, 324.

27. Cf. Aune, *Revelation 6–16*, 460. Walvoord emphasizes that the term "Israel" only refers to literal descendants of Jacob in the NT (Walvoord, *Revelation*, 142–43).

be coextensive with the peril, and must therefore embrace the entire Christian community,"[28] or at least those who withstand the pressures from their enemies.[29]

These first three interpretations differentiate strongly between the 144,000 and the much large number of people mentioned next (v. 9). But the fourth interpretation identifies them. This interpretation argues that the 144,000 and the "large crowd which no one was able to number" (v. 9) are two different ways of describing the church as a whole as both a new Israel and a universal international company.[30] As Mayo puts it, "the 144,000 represent the spiritually faithful, both Jews and Gentiles, who follow the Lamb as the true Messiah and are sealed as protection from the wrath of God coming upon those who dwell on the earth."[31]

This is partly based on the heard/saw structure used to interpret theologically events earlier (such as in 1:10, 12; and 5:5–6).[32] A strong case can be made for this interpretation, especially if the Jewish context of the original reading and audience is played down, in the light of the 144,000 in Revelation 14 and the way that the sealing of God operates to protect people in Revelation 9.[33]

But I'm not sure the original audience (Jewish and Gentile believers) would have heard it exactly that way. Jewish prophetic and apocalyptic traditions expected the regathering of all twelve tribes,[34] for example, and while John is not endorsing this, he is probably evoking that hope in the Jewish members of the churches.[35]

Moreover, the fourth interpretation plays down the significant differences between the two companies. They have a very different size. 144,000 is a large number, perhaps comparable to the number of Jewish Christians in existence at the time (compare Acts 21:20), but insignificant compared to an innumerable multitude. Moreover, their ethnic identity is different: "from every tribe of the sons of Israel" (v. 4) compared to "from every nation and tribe and people and language" (v. 9).[36]

Can we somehow retrieve the strengths of both the Jewish and church views of the 144,000? Can we hold onto God's plan for Israel *and* for the international church,

---

28. Cf. Beasley-Murray, *Revelation*, 140.

29. Cf. Mayo, *Those Who Call Themselves Jews*, 90–97.

30. Cf. Aune, *Revelation 6–16*, 447; Paul, *Revelation*, 166; Pattemore, *People of God*, 141–42; Beasley-Murray, *Revelation*, 140; Keener, *Revelation*, 230–32, 237–38; Beale, *Book of Revelation*, 412–13, 416–26. However, Beale more precisely sees the 144,000 as a remnant of the professing church (ibid., 423).

31. Mayo, *Those Who Call Themselves Jews*, 77; cf. 106–8.

32. Cf. Thomas, *Apocalypse*, 267–68, 277; Koester, *Revelation*, 424; Beale, *Book of Revelation*, 425.

33. Cf. Aune, *Revelation 6–16*, 442; Pattemore, *People of God*, 135–136; Mayo, *Those Who Call Themselves Jews*, 89–102.

34. Koester, *Revelation*, 426–427; Aune, *Revelation 6–16*, 436, 441–42, 460–61; Beale, *Book of Revelation*, 419; Leithart, *Revelation 1–11*, 328; Bauckham, *Climax of Prophecy*, 219–20.

35. Walvoord points to other NT evidence of the ongoing existence of all twelve tribes in James 1:1 (Walvoord, *Revelation*, 143).

36. Cf. Thomas, *Apocalypse*, 268; Aune, *Revelation 6–16*, 440; Leithart, *Revelation 1–11*, 333.

avoiding a crass "replacement" theology?[37] In view of the historical context when Revelation was written and the likelihood that there were many Jews in the original audience, these two pictures (one "heard," one "seen") probably describe the actual church as it has been developing. There was a smaller (though sizeable) pioneering Jewish core rapidly being outnumbered by the massive number of Gentile converts,[38] a trend destined to accelerate to the point where the Jewishness of the early Christians would virtually disappear. I think there is a similar contrast in Revelation 11.

To put this another way, the uncountable multitude may include the 144,000 but would not be exactly identical to it.[39] Smolarz argues, "This remnant of Jews, toether with a countless multitude of every ethnic group and family, constitute in Revelation the Bride of Christ, a restored Zion of God."[40] I'd qualify this; the *original* 144,000 were perhaps Jewish (people like John and the twelve), but subsequently they represent the "conquerors" who blaze the trail in every generation, leading to the salvation of the uncountable multitude. Or perhaps, as Mayo suggests, the church is "not Israel's replacement but its fulfillment"[41] or "an extension of the covenant promises of Israel to the nations through the Lamb."[42]

What then of the list of the tribes itself? First, we note that it does not correspond in number or order with any Old Testament list of the tribes (see Gen 29:31–30:24; 35:16–21; 46:8–25; 49:1–28; Exod 1:1–5; Num 1:5–53; 2:3–33; 13:4–15; 34:18–28; Deut 33:1–25; 1 Chr 2:1–2; 12:23–37; Ezek 48:1–7, 13, 23–34, 30–34).[43] It certainly bears no relation to the birth order of Jacob's sons. Perhaps logically, it begins with Judah, the tribe of David and the tribe of the main expected messianic figure (compare Rev 5:5), the dominant tribe by the first century AD, and the tribe into which Jesus was born.[44] The firstborn son of Jacob, Reuben, comes next but is followed by three of the tribes whose mothers were Jacob's servants (vv. 5–6), often listed last. It contains both Manasseh (v. 6) and Joseph (as opposed to Ephraim, Joseph's other son,

---

37. Replacement theology asserts that the church has replaced ethnic Israel and inherits all the promises to Israel in the OT prophets. There is some truth here, but it negates important perspectives in the OT and NT. Dispensationalism goes to the opposite extreme by sharply differentiating between Israel and church. I think the NT steers somewhere between these extremes, as seen especially in Romans 9–11, and I will try to keep this balance throughout this commentary.

38. Cf. Thomas, *Apocalypse*, 270. This reality may lie behind Romans 9–11 and especially Paul's olive tree analogy in Rom.11:17–24.

39. Cf. Aune, *Revelation 6–16*, 466.

40. Smolarz, *Covenant*, 372.

41. Mayo, *Those Who Call Themselves Jews*, 202.

42. Mayo, *Those Who Call Themselves Jews*, 204. See his careful discussion of these categories in ibid., 24–26.

43. Cf. Koester, *Revelation*, 417–41; Aune, *Revelation 6–16*, 462, 464–65; Beale, *Book of Revelation*, 421, n. 134; Leithart, *Revelation 1–11*, 325–31; Paul, *Revelation*, 159–60; Mayo, *Those Who Call Themselves Jews*, 79–87.

44. Cf. Thomas, *Apocalypse*, 264; Koester, *Revelation*, 418; Beale, *Book of Revelation*, 417–18; Pattemore, *People of God*, 137; Mayo, *Those Who Call Themselves Jews*, 83–84.

v. 8).⁴⁵ It includes Levi (v. 7) who was counted separately in Israelite censuses.⁴⁶ And notoriously, it omits Dan, unlike every single tribal list in the Old Testament.⁴⁷ There are many theories as to why Dan is left out, but none of them are conclusive to my mind.⁴⁸ Aune urges that it has "no particular theological significance."⁴⁹

A final point: Why number the people at all? Censuses in Israel were inherently dangerous: David received a strong reprimand and a plague on Israel when he called such as census in 2 Samuel 24:1–17 and 1 Chronicles 21:1–17. Mostly this was because of their association with warfare (2 Sam 24:2–3; 1 Chr 21:3, 5; Num 1:3, 45; 26:2); as Bauckham observes, "In the Old Testament a census is always a counting up of the *military* strength of the nation,"⁵⁰ and a ransom tax had to be paid for every soldier counted (Exod 30:12–16). So the intertextual associations here suggest that this group of 144,000 is an army of some kind, which will be confirmed in Revelation 14.⁵¹ Having Judah first would also reflect the fact that Judah was the leading tribe in battle order (Num 2:3; 10:14).⁵² The fact that they are numbered implies that God is engaged in a holy war, though not by normal military means, as the text will make clear.⁵³ The sealing would protect God's "soldiers" as they engage in (spiritual) warfare.

7:9–17 The International Multitude

> **After these (things) I saw, and behold a large crowd, which no one was able to number, from every nation and tribe and people and language, standing before the throne and before the Lamb clothed in white robes with palm branches in their hands . . . (Rev 7:9)**

John uses numbers frequently for their relative (as opposed to absolute) size. So here a large number (144,000) is contrasted with a much larger (literally infinite) one (v. 9).

---

45. Cf. Mayo, *Those Who Call Themselves Jews*, 86–87.

46. Levi is, however, included in the list of gates in Ezek 48:30–34. Cf. Mayo, *Those Who Call Themselves Jews*, 81–82.

47. Cf. Thomas, *Apocalypse*, 264–67. Caird states that Chronicles omits Dan (Caird, *Revelation*, 99); while it is true that Dan's descendants are omitted in 1 Chronicles 2–7, he is included in the list of Israel's sons in 1 Chronicles 2:1—2.

48. Cf. Koester, *Revelation*, 418; Aune, *Revelation 6–16*, 462–63; Beale, *Book of Revelation*, 420–21; Leithart, *Revelation 1–11*, 329; Caird, *Revelation*, 99; Gause, *Revelation*, 116; Pattemore, *People of God*, 138; Stramara, *God's Timetable*, 121; Mayo, *Those Who Call Themselves Jews*, 84–85.

49. Aune, *Revelation 6–16*, 479.

50. Bauckham, *Climax of Prophecy*, 217. In fact the "thousand"s here may be a kind of "technical term for a military unit in Israel" (Longman and Reid, *God Is a Warrior*, 185, n. 9).

51. Cf. Bauckham, *Climax of Prophecy*, 215–29; Koester, *Revelation*, 426; Aune, *Revelation 6–16*, 436, 443; Beale, *Book of Revelation*, 422–23. However, the inclusion of Levi is puzzling, since that tribe was explicitly exempt from warfare (Aune, *Revelation 6–16*, 463).

52. Cf. Pattemore, *People of God*, 138–39.

53. Cf. Bauckham, *Climax of Prophecy*, 210–13, 225–26.

This enormous crowd must have been overwhelming to John even though he'd heard the song about the Lamb purchasing just such an international company in 5:9.[54] Among other things, it was much bigger than the number of Christians in his day.[55]

He notices several features of the crowd apart from its enormous size and multi-ethnic nature. First, they are "standing before the throne and before the Lamb" (v. 9), possibly answering the question earlier, "who is able to stand?" (6:16). They are in heaven in the intimate presence of God and Christ without fear.

Second, they are "clothed in white robes" (v. 9), which would remind the audience of the promise to the faithful minority in Sardis (3:4–5) and the clothing of the martyrs in 6:11;[56] white robes are a reward for faithfulness there and in 19:8.[57] However, here the explanation is a little different (v. 14): these people have white robes because of the operation of the Lamb's blood (compare 22:14).[58]

Third, this large number had "palm branches in their hands" (v. 9), a feature never repeated in this text. However, it may recall Jesus' triumphant entry into Jerusalem (Matt 21:8; Mark 11:8; John 12:13; see also Ps 118:27).[59] This in turn recalled the celebration of the victory of the Jews in the Maccabean war against the Syrian Greeks (2 Macc 10:7; 1 Macc 13:51)[60] or the Feast of Tabernacles (Lev 23:40; Neh 8:15).[61] Or the audience may think of victory in general in the Greco-Roman world or early Judaism.[62] If Jesus' triumph is what the hearers/readers are meant to infer, the palm branches may signify their loyalty to Jesus as Messiah and their participation in his victory which is celebrated here.

> ... and they cried out in a loud voice, saying, "Salvation (belongs) to our God who sits on the throne and to the Lamb." (Rev 7:10)

---

54. This might also be seen as fulfilling God's promise to Abraham in Gen 12:3 that "all peoples on earth will be blessed through you," with the subsequent statement of a huge number of descendants (Gen 15:5). Cf. Pattemore, *People of God*, 142.

55. Thomas, *Apocalypse*, 268. See discussion of alternative identities for this group in Aune, *Revelation 6–16*, 445–47. For estimations of the number of Christians at the time, see Aune, *Revelation 6–16*, 467.

56. Leithart deduces from this that they are also martyrs (Leithart, *Revelation 1–11*, 333). I find this unlikely given the huge numbers here.

57. Cf. Thomas, *Apocalypse*, 269.

58. On whiteness in Revelation, see Thompson, *Book of Revelation*, 79.

59. Cf. Aune, *Revelation 6–16*, 469; Leithart, *Revelation 1–11*, 334. Leithart urges that "it spells doom for the temple" as well as coming harvest (ibid.).

60. Koester, *Revelation*, 420; Aune, *Revelation 6–16*, 468–69.

61. Koester, *Revelation*, 428; Aune, *Revelation 6–16*, 469–70; Beale, *Book of Revelation*, 428; Pattemore, *People of God*, 144–46. Some Pentecostal streams see the Feast of Tabernacles as typifying a great ingathering of people into the kingdom of God before the second coming (e.g., Conner, *Book of Revelation*, 242, 258–60).

62. Aune, *Revelation 6–16*, 468–69.

Loud voices are not an uncommon feature in Revelation, which must rate as the loudest book in the Bible. Their loud declaration is all about salvation or victory.[63] These people have experienced salvation and their declaration is bold and controversial in the Roman context where salvation (Greek *sōtēria*, "salvation, deliverance, release") is mostly attributed to Caesar.[64] Such a declaration would land you in big trouble if made in public at that time: not only was it monotheistic in a polytheistic culture, but it exalted the Lamb (Jesus) as Savior. Clearly, the theology of this statement clashes with the surrounding worldview; at the very least, it implies a view of salvation much deeper than Roman religion or ideology could understand. And this is a contrast that continues to this day, especially where people are again looking to the state as their provider and savior and Christians are being persecuted for refusing to give such strong allegiance to the state.

> And all the angels stood around the throne and the elders and the four living beings and fell down before the throne on their faces and worshiped God, saying, "Amen. Blessing and glory and wisdom and thanks and honor and power and strength (be) to our God for ever and ever. Amen." (Rev 7:11–12)

This is all happening in heaven. The declaration of the international multitude is being heard by all those in heaven and it has a powerful effect on them, so that "they fell down before the throne on their faces and worshiped God" (v. 11), as they had done with reference to the revelation of the Lamb's atoning death (5:8–9). They endorse the monotheistic declaration of the multitude in defiance of all other pretenders to divinity. No wonder that many commentators have seen the Book of Revelation as itself a service of worship![65] As in previous cases (chs. 4–5), the worship here has content: the worshipers are saying something definite about God, ascribing a list of positive features to him.

> And one of the elders replied, saying to me, "Those who are clothed in white robes, who are they, and where did they come from?" And I said to him, "My lord, you know." (Rev 7:13–14a)

The heavenly conversation continues and for the second time (compare 5:4), John is drawn into it by a question: Who are these people and "where did they come from?" (v. 13).[66] In a sense we already know the answer: these are people saved by God and the Lamb out of "every nation and tribe and people and language" (v. 9). They are the Gentile and Jewish believers in Christ. But clearly there is more to learn; the elder

---

63. Aune translates the Greek *sōtēria* [σοτηρια] as "victory" in v. 10 (Aune, *Revelation 6–16*, 470). Cf. Beale, *Book of Revelation*, 431.

64. Cf. Kraybill, *Apocalypse and Allegiance*, 117.

65. E.g., Leithart, *Revelation 1–11*, 345.

66. As Aune points out, John never asks for an interpretation of his vision, unlike what happens in most Jewish apocalypses; compare Dan 7:16. But the explanation is introduced in a way common to such literature (Aune, *Revelation 6–16*, 472–73).

wants to enlighten John further. And he dutifully replies, "my lord, you know" (Greek *Kurie*[67] *mou, su oidas*) (v. 14).

This reply might remind some of the listeners of Ezekiel 37:3, where the LORD asks Ezekiel, "Son of man, can these bones live?" and Ezekiel replies "Sovereign LORD, you alone know." This discussion was about the state of Israel in captivity and was followed by a declaration to the four winds to breathe life into Israel (Ezek 37:9–10) and form them into "a vast army" (Ezek 37:10). This signified the restoration of Israel as a sanctified people under the messiah (Ezek 37:18–28). The parallels with Revelation 7 are significant.[68] So was the elder implying that this vast crowd was Israel restored in fulfilment of Ezekiel's prophecy?

This would also be a fulfilment of the original promise to Abraham of offspring as numerous as the stars or the sand on the seashore (Gen 15:5; 22:17; 32:12), though this was also seen as fulfilled by Solomon's time in the growth of national Israel (1 Kgs 3:8; 4:20; 2 Sam 17:11).[69] It appears that these two groups symbolize the goal of John's narrative—the restoration of Israel *and* the salvation of the whole world—which is ultimately a single goal. This is possibly alluding to Isaiah 49:6. Here the Servant's mission is to "restore the tribes of Jacob" *and* become "a light to the Gentiles, so that my salvation may reach to the ends of the earth."[70] Paul uses this verse to summarize his mission to the Gentiles (Acts 13:47).

> **And he said to me, "These are those coming out of the great tribulation and they have washed their robes and made them white in the blood of the Lamb." (Rev 7:14)**

This statement has also been subjected to many interpretations. What is this "great tribulation" (Greek *tēs thlipseōs tēs megalēs*)? The Greek word *thlipseōs* means "trouble, distress, hard circumstances or suffering," and we know that this is something Christians in the ancient world faced repeatedly (see John 16:33). But the phrase seems to designate a specific time or experience of severe suffering which these people had to undergo, since they came "out of" (Greek *ek*) it, and their experience in heaven seems to be one of comfort after suffering (vv. 16–17).

It may be the same as "the hour of trial that is going to come on the whole world" (3:10), which the Philadelphian church was being kept from. It alludes to the unprecedented "time of distress" predicted by Daniel (Dan 12:1), when the faithful ("everyone whose name is found written in the book") will be delivered, a time which will coincide with the general resurrection of the dead (Dan 12:2; see also Jer 30:7).[71]

---

67. This word is usually, but not always, used in Revelation for deity or for Caesar.

68. Leithart comments, "They form the liturgical army that Ezekiel envisioned, the new Israel born of the Spirit of which Jesus spoke" in John 3 (Leithart, *Revelation 1–11*, 339).

69. See also Exod 1:7; Deut 1:10; 10:22; cf. Aune, *Revelation 6–16*, 466; Beale, *Book of Revelation*, 426–31.

70. Cf. Fekkes, *Isaiah and Prophetic Traditions*, 173.

71. Cf. Beale, *Book of Revelation*, 433.

This language is picked up by Jesus in his "Olivet discourse" (Matt 24:21–22; Mark 13:19–20; Luke 21:23).[72] So what is this great tribulation? When does it occur? And who endures it?[73]

Many Pentecostals, influenced by Dispensationalism, have seen the great tribulation as a short period (seven years in most versions) immediately before the public appearance of Christ in glory. The Jews experience it, but not the true church, since it has been raptured before it begins. It is supposedly described in the remaining chapters of Revelation. This is consistent with the two different groups in chapter 7, a Jewish group apparently on earth and being sealed to protect them before the tribulation begins and an international group apparently in heaven having been caught up there, though many Dispensationalists actually see the international group as Gentiles converted and martyred during the great tribulation after the rapture.[74]

However, this theory has at least three problems. First, John has not heard of or seen a church rapture up to now in his vision. Second, the multitude here seems to have come out from the tribulation, not avoided it completely. And third, most importantly, there seem to be quite a few Christians on earth and suffering in the subsequent narrative. In fact, the martyrs are the real heroes of Revelation, which tends to conflict with the idea of unbelievers or nominal Christians being "left behind" to face tribulation as a kind of punishment.[75] Another Futurist view sees the church experiencing the great tribulation and only being caught up to heaven (as Paul describes in 1 Thess 4:16–17) at the time Jesus publicly returns to earth, most likely in Revelation 19.

One Preterist view identifies the great tribulation with the Roman-Jewish war of AD 66–70, matching some of John's language in Revelation 6–19 with Josephus' description of the horrors of that struggle, preceded perhaps by the persecution of the church by the Jews and by the emperor Nero. This reading draws on Jesus' language in Matt 24:9–35, Mark 13:9–31, and Luke 21:12–33; in each of these passages, Jesus speaks of great trouble in Judea and insists it will happen in "this generation."[76]

However, if we take the size of the crowd in 7:9 seriously, it may be more appropriate to see the great tribulation as extending throughout the Christian era as the gospel goes forth and causes powerful and violent reactions from people in every ethnic group while many of them are also coming to faith in Christ. The present participle ("coming out") may imply that this period had already begun when John saw the vision.[77] It would have begun at Pentecost, it would have been intensified in the

---

72. Cf. Thomas, *Apocalypse*, 273.

73. Cf. Koester, *Revelation*, 421–22; Pattemore, *People of God*, 147–49.

74. Cf. Walvoord, *Revelation*, 144–49.

75. Many Dispensational interpreters like Walvoord accept that many people will come to Christ during the tribulation but classify them as not belonging to the "church" (cf. Walvoord, *Revelation*, 139, 144). This argument seems incoherent to me as Walvoord insists they are saved in the same way as Christians now.

76. Cf. Beale, *Book of Revelation*, 435; Leithart, *Revelation 1–11*, 26–32, 340

77. Cf. Thomas, *Apocalypse*, 272. But see Aune, *Revelation 6–16*, 430, 473.

events of the 60s, it would get worse during the struggle with the Roman Empire (2nd and 3rd cent.), but continue throughout the age.[78] In this interpretation, John is seeing these believers (basically all believers starting from Pentecost) standing before God and Christ in the future and receiving their reward for their endurance.

Whoever they are exactly, they are said to "have washed their robes and made them white in the blood of the Lamb" (v. 14), a phrase that has elicited much scorn from many thinkers,[79] but it is one of John's favorite metaphors of salvation.[80] The white robes signify purity which can only be achieved by the atoning death of Jesus (see also 22:14, though there the blood is not mentioned). This is, of course, a very common Christian theological idea; in fact, John has already alluded to it in 1:5 and 5:9.

It perhaps suggests that Jesus' blood is the unspoken means of purification in the trial referred to in Daniel 11:35 and 12:10[81] and the cleansing of the high priest Joshua in Zechariah 3:3–5. There may be a strong Exodus allusion, as in the succeeding verses; for example, the Israelites had to wash their clothes before encountering God at Sinai (Exod 19:10, 14).[82] The audience would also probably think of God's promise in Isaiah 1:18, "Though your sins are like scarlet, they shall be white as snow."[83] They might also recall Genesis 49:11, which predicts that Judah "will wash his garments in wine; his robes in the blood of grapes."[84] This passage may even imply that Jesus' death is itself the archetypical "great tribulation" that brings salvation to this international crowd.[85] Certainly, this statement shows that having white robes is not just an achievement of conquerors (as in 3:4–5, 18), but results from Jesus' redemptive death (the two ideas are combined in 12:11).[86]

> "Because of this, they are before the throne of God, and they serve him day and night in his temple, and the one who sits on the throne will shelter them. They will not hunger any more, nor will they thirst any more, nor will the sun beat down on them nor any heat, for the Lamb that is in the midst of the throne will shepherd them and guide them to springs of living water, and God will wipe away every tear from their eyes." (Rev 7:15–17)

---

78. Koester, *Revelation*, 429.

79. For example, novelist D. H. Lawrence was critical of the imagery, which he saw as "... really ugly, like all the wadings in blood ... and people washed in the blood of the Lamb" (*Apocalypse*, 6).

80. Leithart argues that "A company with robes washed in blood is a royal company, true Jews" and priests since "blood is sprinkled on Aaron's garments" during the priests' consecration ceremony in Exod 29:19–25 (Leithart, *Revelation 1–11*, 342).

81. Cf. Aune, *Revelation 6–16*, 474–75; Beale, *Book of Revelation*, 437.

82. Fekkes, *Isaiah and Prophetic Traditions*, 167.

83. Cf. Fekkes, *Isaiah and Prophetic Traditions*, 168.

84. Pattemore argues strongly for this allusion (Pattemore, *People of God*, 151–52).

85. Cf. Corsini, *Apocalypse*, 160; Moloney, *Apocalypse of John*, 121.

86. Cf. Pattemore, *People of God*, 152–53.

They are now viewed in heaven enjoying blessing and reward: a privileged place before God's throne, where they "serve him day and night in his temple" (v. 15)[87] in a priestly role (recalling 1:6; 5:10),[88] while being sheltered by his presence (v. 15).[89] They experience relief from all the disadvantages and shortages of earthly life (v. 16; see also Isa 4:6). They enjoy the shepherding of the Lamb who will "guide them to springs of living water" (v. 17), imagery derived partly from Psalm 23 and Ezekiel 34:23, but more fully vv. 16–17 almost quote directly from Isaiah 49:10, part of Isaiah's "new exodus."[90] There is an end to all sorrow since "God will wipe away every tear from their eyes" (v. 17; see Isa 25:8).

The "springs of living water" might recall language from John's Gospel, referring to eternal life (John 4:14) and the gift of the Holy Spirit as "rivers of living water" (John 7:38–39).[91] This suggests that Christians can experience some of these blessings even in this life.[92] As this passage in John 7 includes Jesus interpreting the Feast of Tabernacles, this might also connect with the palm branches in v. 9. The language of verses 15–17 anticipates 21:4, 6 and contrasts with what is to come on the earth; for instance, the protection from the sun's heat (v. 16) contrasts with the bowl plague, where "the sun was allowed to scorch people with fire" (16:8). In other words, these believers experience in heaven what all believers will enjoy in the new heavens and new earth.[93] The portrayal of the Lamb also contrasts with the previous chapter, which spoke of his "wrath" (6:16). To these believers, the Lamb is their savior (v. 10) redeemer (v. 14) and shepherd (v. 17; see also Ezek 37:24).

---

87. Compare Luke 2:37, which uses almost identical language of the prophet Anna, and Acts 26:7. Cf. Pattemore, *People of God*, 155.

88. Cf. Beale, *Book of Revelation*, 439–40.

89. This would recall Isa 4:5–6, and may also be another allusion to the Feast of Tabernacles or Booths (Aune, *Revelation 6–16*, 476–77; Beale, *Book of Revelation*, 441), though Stramara argues it refers to Pentecost (Stramara, *God's Timetable*, 54–59). The Greek here reads ὁ καθήμενος ἐπὶ τοῦ θρόνου σκηνώσει ἐπ'αὐτούς [*ho kathēmenos epi tou thronou skēnōsei epʾautous*], "the one who sits on the throne will *dwell with* them," or "will *pitch his tent over* them," which is very similar wording to 21:3. The NIV tries to use both ideas when it translates, "he who sits on the throne will shelter them with his presence."

90. Fekkes, *Isaiah and Prophetic Traditions*, 68–69, 170; Thomas, *Apocalypse*, 275; Aune, *Revelation 6–16*, 477–78; Beale, *Book of Revelation*, 442–43; Pattemore, *People of God*, 157–58. Pattemore also suggests Ezek 37:24–28 as an intertext (ibid., 157). Exodus language may be in the background here (cf. Beale, *Book of Revelation*, 438–39). Morales also points to the link with Ps 2:9 which uses shepherding language, as picked up in Rev 2:27 (Morales, *Shepherd of the Nations*, 146–47).

91. Cf. Thomas, *Apocalypse*, 276–77; Aune, *Revelation 6–16*, 478–79.

92. Cf. Pattemore, *People of God*, 154, 158.

93. Cf. Koester, *Revelation*, 430; Beale, *Book of Revelation*, 443–45.

Revelation Chapter 8

Finally, after a long digression and delay, the seventh seal is about to be opened. The narrative has come to a kind of climax with the sixth seal and its cosmic events (6:12–17). There is a sense of foreboding with the language about the imminent "great day of their wrath" (6:17), and the temporary restraint on the angels who will shortly "harm the land or the sea or the trees" (7:3). Meanwhile, there has been a break in the action while two significant and related groups of God's people are set in place: representatives of the twelve tribes of Israel (7:4) and "a large crowd that no one was able to number, from every nation and tribe and people and language" (7:9). The first group is being sealed to protect them in the coming troubles; the second group is described as if they had already been through them and they are now in heaven (at least in the vision).

Everything is ready to move forward. So it's important to recapitulate at this point. As I see it, the goal to which God is working is the salvation of the world, which includes the restoration of Israel. This is what we see at the end of the book, it has been celebrated in 7:10 and is expanded with the vision of the massive multitude in 7:9, which has been anticipated in the vision of the Lamb in 5:9. As part of his divine strategy, God is in effect invading the earth, as symbolized by the first horse of 6:2, which is causing immense upheavals in the earth (6:3–8) and violent resistance to the witnesses of Jesus (6:9). God will win this war, but first the struggle is about to get more severe.

8:1–5 The Seventh Seal

And when he opened the seventh seal, it became silent in heaven for about half an hour. (Rev 8:1)

I can imagine the first hearers of Revelation "on the edge of their seats" as the seventh seal is opened. But they would be surprised, because when it happens, everything goes quiet. Half an hour may not seem long, but to keep silence that long is a real effort; even the minute's silence we sometimes are asked to observe can seem very stretching.

Pentecostals, in particular, don't really like long silences. And Revelation is known for its loud noises, starting with the "loud voice like a trumpet" (1:10) that starts the whole vision. So why a period of silence?

John Christopher Thomas offers three possible effects on the audience. It is a time of contemplation after the loud noises of celebration and praise; it functions as a reminder of prophetic calls for silence before God when he is about to act, usually in judgement (Hab 2:20; Zech 2:13; Zeph 1:7; Isa 41:1); and it anticipates a fresh vision following the pattern of things heard/seen earlier in Revelation.[1]

Koester adds another possibility: silence was a common custom (among Jews and pagans alike) when prayers and offerings were being made, as in the celebrations in Rome over the victory over the Jews in AD 70.[2] In this case, as Beale argues, the silence is so that the saints' prayers for judgment can be heard and "an indication that God has heard the saints' prayers."[3] Leithart calls it "an act of faith" in God's sovereignty.[4]

There are two other possibilities that I have read. Perhaps it represents a de-creation, an "eschatological return to primordial silence."[5] Or it represents the death of Christ, or the period between his death and resurrection, since this silence means a pause in the worship of God going on always in heaven, which is in itself a striking event.[6] This idea has real possibilities. The duration of the silence as "about half an hour" may recall similar uses of "halves" to denote crisis or judgement (11:9; 12:14; Dan 7:25; 9:27; 12:7).[7]

> **And I saw the seven angels who stand before God, and seven trumpets were given to them. (Rev 8:2)**

This is the first mention of seven angels, and it may draw on Jewish literature where there were often seven archangels (Tob 12:15; 1 En 20:1–7 Greek version).[8] Certainly, seven is a key number in Revelation, and it is very much in focus here: the seventh seal, seven angels, and then seven trumpets (v. 2). There is a contrast with the four angels mentioned in the previous chapter.[9] Seven in the Old Testament is a number

---

1. Thomas, *Apocalypse*, 278–79; cf. Bauckham, *Climax of Prophecy*, 70; Koester, *Revelation*, 431; Beale, *Book of Revelation*, 445–54. Beale sees this as "the calm either preceding or following the final judgment" (ibid., 448).

2. Koester, *Revelation*, 434; Aune, *Revelation 6–16*, 508. Contra Leithart, *Revelation 1–11*, 346, who sees the silence as representing the Christians' refusal to participate in Greco-Roman idolatry.

3. Beale, *Book of Revelation*, 451; Bauckham, *Climax of Prophecy*, 71.

4. Leithart, *Revelation 1–11*, 346.

5. See 4 Ezra 6:39; 7:30; Aune, *Revelation 6–16*, 507; Beale, *Book of Revelation*, 448–49.

6. Cf. Corsini, *Apocalypse*, 161–63; Moloney, *Apocalypse of John*, 125.

7. Beale, *Book of Revelation*, 453; Leithart, *Revelation 1–11*, 347–48.

8. Cf. Aune, *Revelation 6–16*, 509; Beale, *Book of Revelation*, 454. Beale comments, "it is tempting to identify them with the seven guardian angels of the seven churches" (ibid.).

9. Thomas, *Apocalypse*, 280.

of completion, as in the seven days of creation, or climax, as in the story of Elijah's servant looking out for a sign of rain which appears the seventh time, as a sign of the drought in Israel being broken (1 Kgs 18:43–45).

Sometimes the seventh item breaks the pattern, as does the seventh day of creation: the creation is finished in six days, and then there is rest on the seventh. Something similar can be seen here with the half hour of silence. But the mention of seven trumpets in verse 2 suggests the silence will soon be broken. Also the seven trumpets emerging from the seventh seal suggests 7 x 7, which for Jewish hearers would remind them of Pentecost and the year of Jubilee.[10] So the ensuing events perhaps have justice as one of their goals.

Trumpet sounds have hitherto been associated with the voice of the risen Christ (1:10; 4:1), but the audience would have many associations in their minds as they wait for these trumpets to be blown.[11] In the Pentateuch, trumpets marked "the first day of the seventh month" (Lev 23:23), later seen as a kind of "New Year's Day" or as signaling Judgement Day.[12] Trumpets were to be used to summon the congregation together (Num 10:1–3), to order a forward march in the journey (Num 10:5–7), to ask God for help in battle (Num 10:9), and to draw God's attention to festive sacrifices (Num 10:10).

Elsewhere, trumpets were used as part of worship of God as victor (Pss 47:5; 98:6) and to proclaim the accession of a king (1 Kgs 1:34, 39; 2 Kgs 9:13). Only priests were to blow them (Num 10:8). In Nehemiah 12:35, priests with trumpets took part in the dedication service for the rebuilt walls of Jerusalem. Joel 2:1 calls for trumpets to "sound the alarm on my holy hill" to warn of the imminent "day of the LORD" in the form of a locust plague and thus to call for repentance (Joel 2:12–17).[13] This reference is quite relevant since the trumpet plagues signally fail to produce repentance (9:20–21). Perhaps, as Henriksen argues, "trumpets warn," and these disasters call "the ungodly to repentance."[14]

But in the light of what is happening here, including the numbering of God's army (7:4–8), it is the military use of trumpets that is likely to be prominent.[15] In fact, the period of silence (v. 1) and the seven trumpets (v. 2) are likely to recall the battle of Jericho. The purpose of this battle was to destroy a powerful stronghold of the

---

10. Cf. Stramara, *God's Timetable*, 52–53.

11. Cf. Koester, *Revelation*, 432; Beale, *Book of Revelation*, 468; Leithart, *Revelation 1–11*, 355–56; Aune, *Revelation 6–16*, 510. In some other NT books, trumpets signal the second coming (Matt 24:31; 1 Thess 4:16; 1 Cor 15:52), but apparently not here (ibid.).

12. Caird, *Revelation*, 109–110.

13. Caird, *Revelation*, 107–111. For other warnings accompanied by trumpets, see Jer 4:5; 6:1, 17; Ezek 33:3–6; Isa 58:1. Eschatological uses of trumpets can be seen in Isa 27:13; Zech 9:14; and Zeph 1:16.

14. Hendriksen, *More Than Conquerors*, 116.

15. Koester, *Revelation*, 432, 435; Aune, *Revelation 6–16*, 497. *Apocalypse of Zephaniah*, a Jewish apocalypse dated to the first century BC or AD, uses a golden trumpet to signal significant events.

Canaanites so that the Israelites could mount a successful invasion of the "promised land." It was the climax of the story that begins in Exodus.

This story includes the release of Israel from bondage in Egypt (including the ten plagues and the Passover Lamb; Exod 1–12), the crossing of the Red Sea (Exod 13–15),[16] the journey through the wilderness, and the encounter with God at Mount Sinai (Exod 19–20). Next came the establishment of the tabernacle, priesthood, and sacrificial system (Exod 25–31, 35–40; Leviticus), the abortive attempt to enter the land (Num 13–14), the forty years of wandering (Num 15–20), the conquest of the east side of the Jordan (Num 21–36), and the miraculous crossing of the Jordan from east to west (Josh 1–4). There are many allusions to this story in Revelation.

Obviously, the slain Lamb alludes to the Passover story and earlier there is a reference to the incident of Balaam and Balak (2:14), suggesting that the early church faced similar temptations to compromise as those faced by the Israelites as they approached the Jordan as a mighty, invincible, army (see Num 22:2–4). In chapter 7, we have a census that brings army language to mind.

God gave Joshua (the Old Testament Jesus) an unusual strategy for conquering Jericho:

> March around the city once with all the armed men. Do this for six days. Have seven priests carry trumpets of rams' horns in front of the ark. On the seventh day, march around the city seven times, with the priests blowing the trumpets. When you hear them sound a long blast on the trumpets, have the whole army give a long shout; then the wall of the city will collapse and the army will go up, everyone straight in. (Josh 6:3–5)

The army was to march in silence, however, until that final moment (Josh 6:10), partly because this was God's battle and God's divine sovereignty needed to be respected. In this victory, God left no place for human effort. Clearly, there are significant connections here in Revelation 8, i.e., the silence, the army, the sevens, and the trumpets. This is warfare language and we are to expect a mighty victory when the seventh trumpet sounds.[17] But first there is another important scene in heaven.

And another angel[18] came and stood at the altar, having a golden incense container, and much incense was given to him, so that he might add (it) to the prayers of all the saints on the golden altar before the throne. (Rev 8:3)

The golden incense altar was a key item in the tabernacle and temple (Exod 30:1–10; 37:25–28). It was placed in front of the curtain hiding the Most Holy Place, and incense was to be burned there every morning and at twilight; nothing else was to be offered at this altar (Exod 30:7–9). Incense was also part of the Day of Atonement

---

16. In this case, silence is implied by Exod 14:14–15; cf. Beale, *Book of Revelation*, 450.
17. Cf. Beale, *Book of Revelation*, 468–70; Leithart, *Revelation 1–11*, 348–50.
18. Cf. Beale, *Book of Revelation*, 454.

ceremony (Lev 16:12–13), where its smoke protected the high priest during his annual visit inside the Most Holy Place.

Only the priests would see this daily ritual as this golden altar was inside the tabernacle. But it seemed to be a ceremony of worship and prayer, as opposed to sacrifice.[19] Thus, Psalm 141:2 says, "May my prayer be set before you like incense; may the lifting up of my hands be like the evening sacrifice." Similarly, in Luke 1:10, while the priests was burning the incense, "all the assembled worshipers were praying outside."[20] This connection between incense and prayer is remembered here in 8:3–4 and previously in 5:8. It suggests that the prayers of God's people are valued in heaven and are offered as incense before the throne of God.[21]

Such attention to the prayers of the saints precedes both the seven seals and now the seven trumpets.[22] It implies that the coming battle is waged preeminently through prayer, perhaps like the Exodus plagues which were controlled through Moses' prayers (Exod 8:12–13, 29–31; 9:28–29, 33; 10:17–19).[23] Leithart says therefore, "The trumpets announce and enact a series of plagues on a new Egypt, identified in 11:8 as the city where the Lord was crucified," that is, Jerusalem.[24]

> **And the smoke of the incense went up with the prayers of the saints from the hand of the angel before God. And the angel took the incense container and filled it from the fire of the altar and threw it onto the earth, and there was thunder and noise and lightning and an earthquake. (Rev 8:4–5)**

As Thomas points out, the same angel offers the prayers and incense with the same censer on the same altar and then pours it out with fire, underlining the connection between prayer and the resulting fire from heaven: "it appears that the fire that is cast

---

19. A longer discussion of incense offerings may be found in Aune, *Revelation 6–16*, 513–14, and Beale, *Book of Revelation*, 456.

20. Cf. Bauckham, *Climax of Prophecy*, 80–81.

21. Cf. Archer, *Worship in the Apocalypse*, 202. I'm assuming that the prayers referred to here are not just prayers for judgement or those of the martyrs in 6:10. But if instead the prayers are mainly those of the martyrs or mainly for retribution, then it might be fair to conclude that 6:12–17 and 8:1 "must be understood as depicting the last great judgment" (Beale, *Book of Revelation*, 455, 463; Leithart, *Revelation 1–11*, 351).

22. Thomas, *Apocalypse*, 281–82. On the likely content of these prayers, see Koester, *Revelation*, 435; Beale, *Book of Revelation*, 455–57; Aune, *Revelation 6–16*, 494–95, 512–13.

23. For a discussion of the Exodus plagues in relation to Revelation, see Koester, *Revelation*, 445–47, 452; Aune, *Revelation 6–16*, 499–506; Beale, *Book of Revelation*, 465–67, 487. Pss 78:43–51 and 105:27–36 may reflect an ancient tradition that there were seven plagues, not ten, in Egypt; see also Amos 4:6–11 (Aune, *Revelation 6–16*, 502).

24. Leithart, *Revelation 1–11*, 359. In Leithart's reading, "the trumpets describe the period between the early ministry of the apostles and the beginning of Roman persecution of Christians in the 60s AD," including "the corruption of Judaism in its opposition to the church" (ibid., 360, 354). There is a lot of merit in this reading, but in spite of Leithart's qualification that "the trumpets do not correspond in simple one-to-one fashion with historical events or persons" (ibid., 360), it seems too narrow to me.

down from the altar is fueled by the prayers of the saints."[25] Many Pentecostals would intensely (and rightly) desire such results, crying out, "Let the fire fall!" (thinking of a baptism of fire as in Matt 3:11–12 and Luke 3:16–17, and the "tongues of fire" at Pentecost, Acts 2:3), though perhaps not looking for quite what happens next. As O'Donovan points out, the saints' prayers are powerful, but the results are not always what they expected or wanted, at least in the short term.[26]

The falling of fire from heaven is usually a matter of destruction such as on Sodom (Gen 19:24), on those wanting to arrest Elijah (2 Kgs 1:10–14), on Job's sheep and servants (Job 1:16), on Jerusalem (Ezek 10:2, 6, 7)[27] and on the wicked generally (Ps 11:6). This suggests that the restraint on the destroying angels (Rev 7:2–3) has now been removed. On the other hand, fire from heaven was what vindicated Elijah, and showed Israel who was God, in 1 Kings 18; this will be contested in 13:13 when the second beast does it.

Some of John's audience might also have heard of the words of Jesus in Luke 12:49—"I have come to bring fire on the earth, and how I wish it were already kindled! But I have a baptism to undergo, and what constraint I am under until it is completed!" As Leithart points out, "Fire from heaven can be good or bad, transforming or destructive."[28] Meanwhile the immediate effects of the fire—"peals of thunder, rumblings, flashes of lightning and an earthquake" (v. 5 NIV)—underline the significance of what is happening. Such features were part of the original revelation of heaven in 4:5 and would reappear at key moments in the narrative with increasing and frightening intensity (11:19; 16:18; see Exod 19:16–18).[29]

8:6–13 The First Four Trumpets

And the seven angels who had the seven trumpets prepared so that they might sound them. (Rev 8:6)

Now that the silence has been observed and the fire has been hurled to earth, signifying what might be about to happen, the seven angels get ready to blow their trumpets. And we have a similar pattern to the previous seven, where the first four events are

---

25. Thomas, *Apocalypse*, 283; Taushev, *Ancient Christianity*, 144.
26. O'Donovan, "History and Politics," 33, 35.
27. Cf. Beale, *Book of Revelation*, 459–60.
28. Leithart, *Revelation 1–11*, 377.
29. Thomas, *Apocalypse*, 284; cf. Aune, *Revelation 6–16*, 517–18; Beale, *Book of Revelation*, 457–61. Beale argues that "when the Sinai or exodus earthquake is explicitly alluded to as an eschatological event, it is always a sign of the climactic destruction of the world" (ibid., 458). However, this does not mean that such destruction is happening yet; in fact, Beale later argues that the trumpet woes cover the "period of the entire church age" (ibid., 463) in parallel with the seals. Certainly, this is not the final end of John's narrative even if we interpret this section as recapitulation of the seals section (cf. ibid., 472).

different than the last three. In particular, in this series we have a one-third factor in terms of the extent of the disasters portrayed. And whereas the first four seals were associated with human actions (warfare) and their results, the first four trumpets seem to call forth natural calamities.[30]

> **And the first (angel) sounded (his trumpet), and there came hail and fire mixed with blood, and it was thrown onto the earth, and a third of the earth was burned up and a third of the trees were burned up, and all the green vegetation was burned up. (Rev 8:7)**

This disaster has overtones of the Exodus plagues in Egypt, while not being exactly the same. For instance, there was a plague where the Nile turned to blood (Exod 7:17–21) and one involving a huge hailstorm with thunder and lightning that caused devastation to fields (Exod 9:22–25), like the third seal affecting food supplies in Revelation 6:5–6.[31] This calamity increases the devastation from the seals events from one-quarter (6:8) to one-third. While some commentators see the trumpet disasters as recapitulating the seals, this suggests that the plot is intensifying,[32] but God is still restricting the extent of the disasters.[33]

Could this disaster literally happen on a planet-wide scale? The eruption of a large volcano has at times affected temperatures and life across the whole planet, and if the earth was struck by a sizeable asteroid, something like this might be possible. But it's likely that the vision would recall a more local event, possibly like a large volcanic eruption; depending on the dating of Revelation, the original hearers would have known of the famous eruption of Mount Vesuvius in AD 79 that destroyed the cities Pompeii and Herculaneum in Italy.[34]

However, fire here need not be literal, any more than it would be in verse 5. For example, in Joel 1:19–20 a locust plague is likened to a wildfire destroying the fields. But the mention of blood suggests that we may be dealing with a warfare situation,[35] and this language has some similarity with what Josephus tells us about the Roman invasion of Judea in response to the Jewish rebellion in AD 66. The fractions here also recall the siege predicted by Ezekiel (Ezek 5:2, 12) and the salvation of just one-third of the Jews in Zechariah 3:8–9. At this stage, only one-third of the world (or

---

30. For a discussion of how this section of Revelation has been interpreted over the centuries, see Koester, *Revelation*, 437–38.

31. Cf. Beale, *Book of Revelation*, 474; Leithart, *Revelation 1–11*, 362–63.

32. Cf. Thomas, *Apocalypse*, 287; Koester, *Revelation*, 443–45.

33. Cf. Beale, *Book of Revelation*, 486.

34. Cf. Aune, *Revelation 6–16*, 519–20.

35. Koester points out that "blood raining from heaven . . . was often considered to be a portent of war in Greco-Roman sources . . . and Jewish writings" (Koester, *Revelation*, 448). Thomas and Koester see it more as recalling the cry for vengeance for the blood of the martyrs in Rev 6:10 (Thomas, *Apocalypse*, 286; Koester, *Revelation*, 453); cf. Aune, *Revelation 6–16*, 519; Leithart, *Revelation 1–11*, 363; Beale, *Book of Revelation*, 475. Beale suggests there may be an allusion to the judgment on the army of Gog in Ezek 38:22.

land) is affected.[36] Whatever the details are, this disaster would shake the nations that experienced it.

> **And the second angel sounded (his trumpet), and (something) like a great mountain burning with fire was thrown into the sea, and a third of the sea became blood, and a third of the living creatures that were in the sea died, and a third of the ships were destroyed. (Rev 8:8–9)**

This recalls the first plague on Egypt where the Nile and other waterways were turned into blood (Exod 7:19–24), perhaps as a judgment because of the Israelite children thrown into the river (Exod 1:22).[37] But it may also have caused listeners to think of a volcanic eruption, with lava and rocks being thrown into the nearby sea causing massive devastation.[38] Or the mountain may be an image of an evil kingdom, such as "the great city" thrown down like a large boulder in 18:21 (see also Jer 51:25, 63–64).[39] In either case, a disruption of maritime trade is implied.[40]

> **And the third angel sounded (his trumpet), and a large star burning as a lamp fell from the sky, and (it) fell on a third of the rivers and on the springs of water, and the name of the star was called Wormwood,[41] and a third of the waters were turned bitter, and many people died from the waters that became bitter. (Rev 8:10–11)**

Literally, this could be a result of a volcanic eruption, a meteor,[42] or, in modern thinking, perhaps nuclear warfare.[43] However, if we are talking of planet-wide events, it would be difficult for the effects to be restricted like this. The audience might recall

---

36. Cf. Aune, *Revelation 6–16*, 500; Beale, *Book of Revelation*, 474; Leithart, *Revelation 1–11*, 364.

37. Cf. Leithart, *Revelation 1–11*, 366.

38. Cf. Aune, *Revelation 6–16*, 519–20. But see Koester, *Revelation*, 449. Leithart prefers to give the emphasis to biblical allusions and hence to Mount Sinai (Leithart, *Revelation 1–11*, 365–66). Thus "the second trumpet vision shows Sinai or the temple mount or the people of Israel thrown into the sea of Gentiles" (ibid., 366). This interpretation requires several interpretive steps to become persuasive, though the references to Jesus' words (Matt 21:21; Mark 11:23) may support it. Leithart offers a second possibility: the burning mountain refers to the church (see Dan 2:35) under persecution from the Gentiles (Leithart, *Revelation 1–11*, 367).

39. Cf. Beale, *Book of Revelation*, 475–76.

40. Leithart interprets sea references as standing for the Gentile nations (Leithart, *Revelation 1–11*, 365).

41. On the absinthe plant translated "Wormwood," see Aune, *Revelation 6–16*, 521–22.

42. This was seen as another portent of disaster in ancient times (Koester, *Revelation*, 449; Aune, *Revelation 6–16*, 520).

43. Some recent commentators saw a parallel with the effects of the nuclear accident at Chernobyl in 1986 (e.g., Baxter, "Chernobyl—Third Trumpet of Revelation?"). This was part of a train of events that led to the fall of the USSR and the communist regimes of eastern Europe, a modern "fall of Babylon." This is one of a number of possible applications of Revelation to recent situations, but there is no way John or his audience could have seen this as *the* meaning of his prophecy.

Jeremiah's warnings to his contemporaries (Jer 8:14; 9:15; 23:15)[44] and not interpret this as literal bitter water but as a metaphor for bitter suffering more broadly.[45]

Moreover, this is the second time Revelation has spoken of stars falling from heaven: "the stars in the sky fell to the earth" at the opening of the sixth seal (6:13), and soon the hearers will learn of another "star that had fallen from the sky to the earth" (9:1). Given the fact that ancient people saw stars as living beings, the text is signifying more than a natural disaster here. Beale suggests the star may represent a sinful nation, that is, Babylon (see Isa 14:12–15).[46] In view of the star fallings of 9:1 and 12:9, 13, it is possible that this star also refers to Satan or a related being. Revelation rarely uses star language literally (think back to 1:20). Leithart may well be right when he introduces Luke 10:18 and claims, "Satan falls because of the Lamb and the success of the mission of the apostles,"[47] and he then pollutes the temple so that it must be destroyed.[48]

> **And the fourth angel sounded (his trumpet), and a third of the sun was struck and a third of the moon and a third of the stars so that a third of them were darkened, and they did not shine for a third of the day and the night likewise. (Rev 8:12)**

This could also be the effect of an eclipse or a volcanic eruption, as the smoke from such an eruption can travel long distances and obscure the sun's light for long periods.[49] The audience would also recall the cosmic disturbances at the sixth seal (6:12–14), the plagues of darkness in Egypt (Exod 10:21–23), Ezekiel's predicted judgment on Egypt (Ezek 32:7–8), and the darkness in Joel's locust plague (Joel 2:2,10). This last passage is about to become prominent in Revelation 9. Or they might be reminded of the prophecy of Amos 8:9 of darkness at noon, the day of the LORD in Isaiah 13:10, Joel 3:15, and Zephaniah 1:15, and perhaps the darkness reported during the crucifixion of Jesus in the Synoptic Gospels (Matt 27:45; Mark 15:33; Luke 23:44–45).

Beale argues, "the darkness is probably not literal" but represents "those divinely ordained events intended to remind the idolatrous persecutors that their idolatry is folly and that they are separated from the living God."[50] It may also signify judgment for a breach of God's covenant by Israel (see Jer 33:20–26) or the

---

44. Cf. Thomas, *Apocalypse*, 289; Koester, *Revelation*, 450, 454.
45. Cf. Beale, *Book of Revelation*, 480. Beale sees the first three trumpets as signifying famine in particular. This was a common occurrence in the ancient world and since. Or as Leithart says, wormwood and bitterness are the results of idolatry in the OT (Leithart, *Revelation 1–11*, 370).
46. Beale, *Book of Revelation*, 478–79.
47. Leithart, *Revelation 1–11*, 369.
48. Leithart, *Revelation 1–11*, 370–71.
49. Cf. Aune, *Revelation 6–16*, 523.
50. Beale, *Book of Revelation*, 482.

nations.⁵¹ Or, as Leithart suggests, it is about God's judgment on Israel's leaders such as Herod (Acts 12:21–23).⁵²

In whatever way we are meant to understand the vision here, it is certainly speaking of earth-shattering events that cause massive problems for the civilization affected and hamper its ability to survive independent of God.⁵³ Such shakings are meant to remove "created things" to make way for God's kingdom (Heb 12:26–28); "the basic content of creation is being systematically undone."⁵⁴ Even now, the gospel is growing fastest where things are being shaken by wars, famines, and other natural disasters, whereas it's struggling to get a hearing in places where life is comfortable. However, the "one-third" language is meant to assure the hearers that, whatever may happen, God is in control and able to restrict the disaster.

> **And I saw, and I heard an eagle flying in mid-heaven saying in a loud voice, "Woe, woe, woe to those who dwell on the earth from the rest of the sounds of the trumpets of the three angels who are about to sound." (Rev 8:13)**⁵⁵

The trumpets series is not over yet. It is about to get more intense. The three "woes" function to some extent as literary markers helping the audience to count them off as they did the seven seals and were now doing with trumpet blasts.⁵⁶ This is the first time we hear of a message that does not come from one of the heavenly beings, though the fourth living creature in heaven "was like a flying eagle" (4:7).⁵⁷ Koester suggests that eagles were commonly viewed as divine messengers,⁵⁸ as in Hosea 8:1, but in the Jewish apocalypse 4 Ezra 11, there is a dream of an eagle coming up from the sea with "twelve feathered wings and three heads," and this represents a dominant anti-God empire.

Similarly, Deuteronomy 28:49, 52 warns recalcitrant Israel, "The LORD will bring a nation against you from far away, from the ends of the earth, like an eagle swooping down, a nation whose language you will not understand" who "will lay siege to all the cities throughout your land." The passage gives graphic details of the sufferings involved (Deut 28:49–57; see also Ezek 17:3, 7, 12–15; Hab 1:6–8). So in this case, the eagle may represent the Roman army whose standards included images of eagles;⁵⁹ the victorious Roman soldiers in Jerusalem in AD 70 offered sacrifices to

---

51. Beale, *Book of Revelation*, 483–84.
52. Leithart, *Revelation 1–11*, 372.
53. Cf. Beale, *Book of Revelation*, 488.
54. Beale, *Book of Revelation*, 486.
55. On the three woes, see Koester, *Revelation*, 442–43; Leithart, *Revelation 1–11*, 373–74.
56. Cf. Bauckham, *Climax of Prophecy*, 11–12.
57. Cf. Thomas, *Apocalypse*, 291.
58. Koester, *Revelation*, 450–51; cf. Aune, *Revelation 6–16*, 523–24.
59. Evans and Porter, *Dictionary of New Testament Background*, 992.

these standards.⁶⁰ If these disasters represent the Roman invasion of Judea, this would amount to a Roman threat to the remaining resistant Jews.

There are many "woe" statements in the Old Testament. The scroll revealed to Ezekiel had on both sides "words of lament and mourning and woe" (Ezek 2:10). Isaiah has a series of discourses that commence with "Woe to . . . " In chapter 5, he pronounces woes on "those who add house to house" (v. 8), "those who rise early in the morning to run after their drinks" (v. 11), "those who draw sin along with cords of deceit" (v. 18), "those who call evil good and good evil" (v. 20), "those who are wise in their own eyes" (v. 21), and "those who are heroes at drinking wine" (v. 22). Later woe discourses are addressed consecutively to unjust rulers (Isa 10:1), "the pride of Ephraim's drunkards" (Isa 28:1), "Ariel, Ariel, the city where David settled!" (Isa 29:1), "the obstinate children" (Isa 30:1), "those who go down to Egypt for help" (Isa 31:1), and "destroyer, you who have not been destroyed!" (Isa 33:1).

Some of John's audience might also have witnessed, or heard about, the mad prophet Jesus, son of Ananias, in Jerusalem in the AD 60s who proclaimed the imminent demise of the city including repeatedly saying, "Woe, woe to Jerusalem."⁶¹ The purpose of such woe discourses seems to be to shake the audience up, disturbing their comfort in order to turn them from their wicked ways back to God.

No doubt this message in Revelation has a similar purpose. While those who experience the trumpet disasters are hardened and do not repent (9:20–21), the audience of the vision may be awakened from their lethargy as they hear all this because they themselves could experience these plagues (22:18).⁶² Koester argues that "the warning signs are given in forms that people throughout the ancient world could be expected to understand,"⁶³ but John's main audience is the Christians in the seven churches.

---

60. Josephus, "War of the Jews" 6:6:316. Josephus also tells of a large golden eagle being erected by Herod the Great over the great gate of the Jerusalem temple, a great offence to those who saw this as contrary to the law prohibiting images (Exod 20:4) (Josephus, "Antiquities" 17:6:151).

61. As reported by Josephus, "War of the Jews" 6:5:300–309. Stramara believes parts of Revelation were originally referring to this Jesus (Stramara, *God's Timetable*, 96–99). This is very doubtful.

62. Cf. Beale, *Book of Revelation*, 486.

63. Koester, *Revelation*, 454.

Revelation Chapter 9

As with the seven seals, the latter trumpets are given more space, and in fact the seventh trumpet is delayed, just like the seventh seal, and doesn't sound until chapter 11. Huge heavenly disasters have shaken civilization to its core with the sounding of the first four trumpets. An eagle has warned that things will get worse and introduced a different structure of "woes" into the vision (Rev 8:13). What will this look like?

9:1–12 The Fifth Trumpet and First Woe

> **And the fifth angel sounded (his trumpet), and I saw a star having fallen from heaven[1] to the earth, and the key of the shaft of the abyss was given to it . . . (Rev 9:1)**

The fifth trumpet blast introduces a different, more specific, element into the narrative. This is the third mention of falling stars (see 6:13 and 8:10–11, and perhaps 2:5), but this one is different. We note here John's cosmological structure: sky-earth-abyss,[2] in descending order, not that the passage intends to teach us a scientific truth.[3] Rather, the comparative "height" of these three states is moral or spiritual or ontological. Heaven is "up" because it is the abode of God and his attendants (4:1–2); the earth is "down" in the sense that it is the dwelling place of God's physical creation; the abyss is "below" earth (we could translate "underworld") because it is the place of uncontrolled destructive forces (see also v. 11). Both heaven and the abyss have doors that humans cannot access freely.

The Greek *abussos* is sometimes translated as "bottomless pit," and in Romans 10:7, it seems to be the place of the dead, whereas in Luke 8:31, it may be the prison

---

1. The Greek οὐρανος [*ouranos*] can also be translated as "sky."
2. The Greek ἀβύσσος [*abussos*] can also be understood as referring to the sea because the abyss is equivalent to the depths of the sea in the Septuagint (Leithart, *Revelation 1–11*, 377–78); the beast rises out of the abyss in 11:7 and 17:8 and out of the sea in 13:1. Smoke out of the sea is hard to imagine, though sometimes an undersea volcano emerges in an eruption and becomes a permanent island.
3. Cf. Aune, *Revelation 6–16*, 526.

of demons.[4] Later the beast comes up from the abyss (11:7; 17:8), and it becomes the prison of the devil for a thousand years (20:1–3). It seems to be a prison because it has to be opened with a key (v. 1; 20:1–3), otherwise it is locked. It may be roughly equivalent to Hades whose keys are now held by the risen Christ (1:18).[5] On the other hand, the unlocking of the abyss here and its locking again in 20:1–3 seem to have special significance in the plot: something chaotic or demonic is being released into the earth for a specific period of time.

The "star" mentioned here straddles all three levels since it falls from heaven to earth and then opens the shaft of the abyss. What kind of "fall" is envisaged here? Clearly, not just an accident: the "star" has personal features such as the ability to handle a key (even though this language is metaphorical),[6] and the fall is probably spiritual or moral. In other words, we are probably looking at a fallen angel (compare the language of 2 Pet 2:4; Luke 10:18; and Rev 12:7–9) or a political leader perhaps (as in Isa 14:12).[7] The alternative is one of God's angels who "descends" rather than "falls," but the Greek suggests a fall (unlike a similar scene in 20:1, which uses a different Greek verb).[8] The divine passive is used again here: "the key of the shaft of the abyss was given to it" (Rev 9:1). God is permitting or releasing this process.

> . . . and he opened the shaft of the abyss, and smoke came up out of the shaft like the smoke of a great furnace, and the sun and the air were darkened from the smoke of the shaft. And out of the smoke, locusts came onto the earth, and power[9] was given to them like the scorpions of the earth have power. (Rev 9:2–3; cf. 8:12)[10]

Colloquially, we might say that all hell is about to break loose! In fact, a demonic army comes out from the abyss to wreak havoc (v. 11).[11] Locusts are agents of destruction arousing great fear in the hearts of farmers whose crops are at great risk of destruction,

---

4. Cf. Pippin, "Peering into the Abyss," 254.

5. Cf. Koester, *Revelation*, 456–457; Paul, *Revelation*, 176. Taushev thinks it may be Gehenna (Taushev, *Ancient Christianity*, 151).

6. Thomas, *Apocalypse*, 293.

7. Cf. Leithart, *Revelation 1–11*, 376.

8. Contra Koester, *Revelation*, 455–56; Gause, *Revelation*, 137; cf. Aune, *Revelation 6-16*, 525; Beale, *Book of Revelation*, 491–93.

9. The Greek ἐξουσία [exousia] is normally translated "authority." This points to their being authorized by God. Aune argues that this power or authority signifies the way such scorpions intimidate humans (Aune, *Revelation 6-16*, 527).

10. This may be another allusion to volcanic activity (Aune, *Revelation 6-16*, 527) or to the temple being filled with smoke, as in Isa 6:4, showing that the temple is a place of demons and "a stairway to hell" (Leithart, *Revelation 1–11*, 377). It also recalls the plague of darkness over Egypt (Exod 10:21–29; cf. ibid., 378).

11. This demonic attack is provoked by the coming of the Spirit at Pentecost, according to Leithart, *Revelation 1–11*, 377.

and seen as "as sign of God's judgment" (Deut 28:42),[12] and scorpions are agents of pain to all who are bitten by them.[13]

While this passage would remind the hearers again of the Exodus plagues (Exod 10:4–6, 12–15, 19),[14] the main intertextual reference is probably Joel 1–2. This passage tells of a massive invasion of Israel by a series of locust plagues (Joel 1:4), like a military invasion (Joel 1:6; 2:2–9), devastating the vines, olive trees, fruit trees, grain crops, and pastures for animals (Joel 1:7–12, 16–19). Joel calls for organized national repentance (Joel 1:13–14; 2:1, 12–17), describing the coming disaster as "the day of the LORD" (Joel 1:15; 2:1, 11) and using cosmological imagery similar to Revelation 6:12–14:[15]

> Before them the earth shakes,
>
> the heavens tremble,
>
> the sun and moon are darkened,
>
> and the stars no longer shine. (Joel 2:10)

But this is the LORD's army (Joel 2:11), and hence desperate repentance and prayer may avert the plagues since God is "gracious and compassionate, slow to anger and abounding in love, and he relents from sending calamity" (Joel 2:13), and God promises to respond to such actions (Joel 2:18–27). Apocalyptic language has a more deterministic edge than the Old Testament prophets. However, the principles are surely the same, and therefore, the possibility of this plague being averted is there if people repent (compare Jer 18:7–10; Jonah 3:4—4:11). Revelation 9:20–21 tells us they don't, but that implies that if they had repented, things might have changed. Certainly, this plague is highly targeted.

> **And they were told that they may not damage the vegetation of the earth nor any green (plant) nor every tree, but only the people who did not have the seal of God on their foreheads. (Rev 9:4)**

This is a very unnatural command since devouring vegetation is what locusts usually do,[16] which suggests these are not literal locusts; after all, they come out of the abyss. Also, they could only hurt "people who did not have the seal of God on their foreheads" (v. 4; see 7:3).[17] God's army is protected from this disaster. God is able to protect his people even without removing them from the scene, as he did with the

---

12. Thomas, *Apocalypse*, 294.

13. Cf. Thomas, *Apocalypse*, 294.

14. Cf. Beale, *Book of Revelation*, 495. Moloney suggests it's more referring to primeval history, "the origins of the suffering and disorder that have marked the human story from all time" (Moloney, *Apocalypse of John*, 141).

15. Cf. Leithart, *Revelation 1–11*, 379.

16. Cf. Aune, *Revelation 6–16*, 529–30.

17. There is a clear parallel or contrast involved here: the angels in 7:2–3 are not to harm the earth, sea, or trees *until* the servants of God are sealed; in 9:4, the "locusts" are not to harm the vegetation or trees *but only* those who have not been sealed (Aune, *Revelation 6–16*, 528–29).

plagues on Egypt (see Exod 8:22–23; 9:4–7, 26; 10:23; 11:7), including a locust plague (Exod 10:3–20).[18]

> **And they were restrained from killing[19] those people, but they may torment (them) for five months,[20] and their torment (was) like the torment of a scorpion when it stings a person. And in those days people will seek death but never find it, and they will long to die, and death will flee from them. (Rev 9:5–6)**

This limitation is taken up again in verse 10 and reflects Luke 10:18–19, where demons are portrayed as "snakes and scorpions."[21] The actions of these locusts are targeted exclusively at unbelieving humans. The divine control over all this is indicated by the limitations God has placed on their activity.[22] Moreover, the divine passive reflected in the phrase "was/were given" (Greek *edothē*; vv. 1, 3, and 5 in the Greek text) suggests that God stands behind their activity as the one permitting it to take place. God's permissive will in all this finds further support in the appearance of the Greek word *exousia* ("power," literally "authority" in vv. 3 and 10).

The language of torture (or "torment," Greek *basanismos*) dominates this passage and heightens the pain (compare 12:2; 14:10). People cannot even find relief in death![23] This language conjures up the torture chamber of old; the victim must be preserved alive until the torturer has done his work.[24] According to Glancy, "In the Roman world, torture, conceived as a mechanism to extract truth from flesh, was used in judicial interrogation, most commonly in interrogation of slaves and other low-status persons."[25] This raises the question here, what truth are the torturers trying to "extract"? Thomas suggests "one of the implications of the fact that no lives are

---

18. Cf. Beale, *Book of Revelation*, 496.

19. A more literal translation might read: "And it was given to them they might not kill . . ."

20. These five months might refer to the normal life span of a locust (Thomas, *Apocalypse*, 296), or to the dry season when locusts were active (Beale, *Book of Revelation*, 497). Alternatively, five might just be a round number meaning "a few" (cf. Koester, *Revelation*, 458–59; Aune, *Revelation 6–16*, 530), the time between Pentecost and the Day of Atonement (Leithart, *Revelation 1–11*, 383), or the approximate length of the siege of Jerusalem in AD 70 (Papandrea, *Wedding of the Lamb*, 117).

21. Cf. Aune, *Revelation 6–16*, 531. For ancient descriptions of the pain from a scorpion's bite, see Koester, *Revelation*, 459.

22. Thomas, *Apocalypse*, 295; Beale, *Book of Revelation*, 494–95, 497. In fact, Leithart argues that Jesus gave the key to the abyss to this fallen being since he has the keys (1:18; 3:7) (Leithart, *Revelation 1–11*, 377).

23. Pliny the Younger reports a similar experience uring the eruption of Vesuvius in AD 79 (cf. Aune, *Revelation 6–16*, 531). Osborne comments that this language "could refer to attempting suicide," which for Stoics "was not just honorable but exemplary since by it the individual was taking control over fate." For noble Romans, suicide was "preferable to political disgrace," and in some circumstances for Jews suicide was preferable to "surrender to pagan armies" as at Masada in AD 73 (Osborne, *Revelation*, 368).

24. Under Roman law, testimony of slaves was only accepted under torture, since a slave would otherwise only say what their master desired (Lowell, "Judicial Use," 220).

25. Glancy, "Torture," 107.

lost during this judgment might be that humanity is being given a specific period of time in which to repent."[26]

> **And the likeness of the locusts was like horses prepared for battle, and on their heads (was something) like golden crowns,[27] and their faces (were) like human faces, and they had hair like the hair of women, and their teeth were like those of lions, and they had breastplates like iron breastplates, and the sound of their wings was like the sound of many horse-drawn chariots rushing into battle . . . (Rev 9:7–9)**

These are not literal locusts.[28] But language breaks down here: John can only say they are "like" this or that. Some recent writers have tried to identify what he saw with some modern phenomena like helicopter gunships![29] This is, of course, highly speculative. What we can see is that the "locusts" were like horses or soldiers in an army. They looked "like horses prepared for battle" (v. 7), they had "breastplates like iron breastplates" (v. 9), and their wings made a sound "like the sound of many horse-drawn chariots rushing into battle" (v. 9). In these respects, they were like Joel's locust army (Joel 2:4–5).[30] But they also had human features: heads and faces and hair.[31] And "their teeth were like those of lions" (v. 8), like one of the four living beings in 4:7 (see also Joel 1:6). So, we have now two armies on earth: God's human army counted in 7:4–8 and a demonic army here. Spiritual warfare is imminent, but what form will it take?

> **. . . and they have tails like scorpions and stings, and in their tails is their power[32] to harm the people for five months. They have as their king the angel of the abyss, whose name in Hebrew is Abaddon, and in Greek, he has the name Apollyon. (Rev 9:10–11)**

The overall effect of this image is threatening. These "locusts" are "hybrid monsters,"[33] powerful, ugly, destructive, capable of inflicting severe pain, highly intelligent, and effective. And they are highly organized by their king, "the angel of the abyss, whose name in Hebrew is Abaddon,[34] and in Greek, he has the name Apollyon" (or Destroy-

---

26. Thomas, *Apocalypse*, 297.

27. The Greek στέφανοι [*stephanoi*] could also be translated "wreaths," but this is hard to visualize.

28. Cf. Koester, *Revelation*, 463. John frequently describes hybrid creatures that combine features of various species.

29. Ian Paul helpfully suggests a reference to a mythical being referred to in Greco-Roman sources called a "manticore" (Paul, *Revelation*, 179).

30. Invading armies are compared to locust plagues in Jer 51:14, 27 (cf. Beale, *Book of Revelation*, 501–2).

31. Cf. Koester, *Revelation*, 459–60; Aune, *Revelation 6–16*, 532; Leithart, *Revelation 1–11*, 381–82.

32. The Greek ἐξουσία [*exousia*] is normally translated "authority."

33. Koester, *Revelation*, 464; Leithart, *Revelation 1–11*, 382; for astrological references here, 381.

34. This is normally the name of the place of the dead (see the Hebrew text of Prov 15:11 and Ps 88:11).

er) (v. 11).³⁵ The Greek name is similar to Apollo, a god often claimed to be identified with Roman emperors, especially Nero, so there may be an allusion to Nero here.³⁶ This angel might be a fallen angel who dwells in the abyss, or he might even be Satan himself.³⁷ A less likely alternative would be to identify him with a godly angel who unlocks the door to the abyss and who leads and controls the "locust" army under the permissive decree of God.³⁸

Most likely, John's audience would interpret this as "demonic powers being turned loose on their own devotees,"³⁹ possibly causing "fear and despair."⁴⁰ Or as Aune puts it, "The 'authority' scorpions have, then, is the inherent ability to *intimidate* and *tyrannize* and, in the case of the demonic locusts, to *terrorize*."⁴¹ Or as Leithart suggests, these composite beasts represent the fanatical Jews and Judaizers attacking the gospel,⁴² though they can only sting those not sealed in chapter 7. Leithart's suggestion at least takes the implied spiritual warfare here seriously.

> **The first woe has gone. Behold two more woes are coming after these (things). (Rev 9:12)**

Two more woes are coming next, either chronologically or in the narrative sequence without reference to real time.⁴³ John and his audience are counting down the trumpet sounds and the woes.

9:13–21 The Sixth Trumpet and a Huge Army

> **And the sixth angel sounded (his trumpet), and I heard a voice (from) the [four] corners of the golden altar before God, which said to the sixth angel, who had the trumpet, "Release the four angels who are bound at the great river Euphrates." And the four angels who had been prepared for the hour and day and month and year, so that they might kill a third of mankind, were released. And the number of the cavalry was twice ten thousand times ten thousand. I heard their number. (Rev 9:13–16)**

---

35. Cf. Thomas, *Apocalypse*, 299.

36. Cf. Aune, *Revelation 6–16*, 535; Beale, *Book of Revelation*, 503–4; Leithart, *Revelation 1–11*, 383; Paul, *Revelation*, 179–80.

37. Cf. Koester, *Revelation*, 461; Beale, *Book of Revelation*, 503. In the Greek version of Amos 7:1, an army like a swarm of locusts is led by king Gog, alluding to Ezek 38–39 and picked up in Rev 20:8 (cf. Beale, *Book of Revelation*, 503).

38. Cf. Aune, *Revelation 6–16*, 534–35; Beale, *Book of Revelation*, 504.

39. Koester, *Revelation*, 462.

40. Beale, *Book of Revelation*, 496, 498; Deut 28:20–48.

41. Aune, *Revelation 6–16*, 527; emphasis in the original. Beale emphasizes the *deception* wrought by this demonic locust army (Beale, *Book of Revelation*, 503), but the text focuses more on the *terror*.

42. Leithart, *Revelation 1–11*, 381–84.

43. Cf. Beale, *Book of Revelation*, 505.

An army of locusts is followed by an apparently human army. Once again there is an allusion to Joel, which tells of a locust plague (Joel 1:1—2:27) followed by a new age of God's Spirit (Joel 2:28–32) and then a new war in which God will exact vengeance on behalf of his people against the Gentile nations (Joel 3:1–21). There are many references to Joel 3 in Revelation, as we will see. However, the army here seems to be serving a different purpose.

The sounding of the sixth trumpet leads to the sound of a voice coming from the incense altar where the incense and prayers went up to God (8:3). The voice instructed the sixth angel to "release the four angels who are bound at the great river Euphrates" (v. 14). This may be a reference back to 7:2–3, where four angels were restrained from harming the earth until God's servants were sealed.[44] This sealing has been proven to work in the locust plague (v. 4), and now it is time for the four angels to do their harmful work of killing "a third of mankind" (v. 15).

The timing is precise, as is the geography; the Euphrates is significant as a kind of boundary for armies invading Israel or the Roman Empire[45] (see also 16:12), and the emphasis on God's sovereign control of events is very clear.[46] The "one-third" factor is repeated from the first four trumpets. However, this time it is one-third of human beings who are killed. And we immediately learn how this will happen: through the invasion of a huge cavalry force ("twice ten thousand times ten thousand" in size, that is, 200 million).[47] John reports, "I heard their number," recalling the hearing of the number sealed in 7:4, but this army is much larger.

> **And thus I saw the horses and those who sat on them in the vision. They had fiery red and hyacinth and sulfur-yellow colored breastplates, and the horses' heads (were) like the heads of lions, and out of their mouths came forth fire and smoke and sulfur. By these three plagues, they killed a third of mankind, by the fire and the smoke and the sulfur that came out from their mouths. For the power[48] of the horses is in their mouths and in their tails, for their tails are like snakes, which have heads and by them do harm. (Rev 9:17–19)**

This is the only time John explicitly states he is having a "vision" (Greek *orasei*).[49] Once again, we get the familiar hear-see pattern: immediately after John hears the number

---

44. Cf. Thomas, *Apocalypse*, 301. But see Koester, *Revelation*, 466. Koester claims that these "angels" are demonic since they have been "bound." (ibid., 471); cf. Aune, *Revelation 6–16*, 536–37; Beale, *Book of Revelation*, 506–7.

45. Cf. Koester, *Revelation*, 471–72; Beale, *Book of Revelation*, 506–7; Caird, *Revelation*, 122.

46. Thomas, *Apocalypse*, 302; Koester, *Revelation*, 472; Beale, *Book of Revelation*, 508.

47. Or simply an incalculably huge number (cf. Koester, *Revelation*, 466–67, 472; Beale, *Book of Revelation*, 509–510). Paul estimates that this would be approximately the population of the world in John's day (Paul, *Revelation*, 181). Koester, Aune and Beale interpret this as a demonic army (Aune, *Revelation 6–16*, 538, 539; Beale, *Book of Revelation*, 513); cf. Ps 68:17; Jer 46:23; Dan 7:10. In 1 Enoch 56:5–6, angels are said to incite the Parthians and Medes to attack the holy land (Aune, *Revelation 6–16*, 538).

48. Greek ἐξουσία [*exousia*], normally translated "authority."

49. Thomas, *Apocalypse*, 303; cf. Aune, *Revelation 6–16*, 539.

of the army, he sees the horses and "those who sat on them" and attempts to describe them (v. 17). He mainly focuses on the horses, not the riders,[50] as he describes the color of the breastplates and the "the horses' heads" which resembled the heads of lions (a frightening thought recalling the locusts in v. 8). "Out of their mouths came forth fire and smoke and sulfur" (v. 17),[51] matching the colors just mentioned. By these three plagues "a third of mankind was killed" (v. 18).[52]

Such plagues recall the judgment on Sodom and Gomorrah (Gen 19:24; Deut 29:23) and the disaster to be visited on the army of Gog (Rev 20:9; Ezek 38:22), which will later be visited on those who take the beast's mark (Rev 14:10–11) and the devil himself (20:10). John notes that "the power of the horses is in their mouths" (v. 19), suggesting perhaps some kind of verbal assault,[53] though the emphasis till now has been on the "fire, smoke and sulfur" coming from the mouths. But the tails of these awful horses are also dangerous (v. 19).[54] Beale maintains that "spiritual torment" is involved.[55]

These are not natural horses. Leithart regards this army as "agents of God's justice and vengeance, by which he avenges the blood of the martyrs," parallel to the two prophetic witnesses of chapter 11 and opposed to the locust army of verses 3–11.[56] This is partly based on the size of this army: compare Psalm 68:17 ("The chariots of God are tens of thousands and thousands of thousands"), which refers both to the exodus and the ascension, and Numbers 10:36 ("Return, Lord, to the countless thousands of Israel"). Certainly, this army may well be opposed to the army of locusts, but it is still a judgment on people, just as that army was. After all, this army kills a third of mankind (v. 18); even if they do it by prayer and the word of God,[57] this is still a plague (v. 20).

What do all these trumpet plagues represent?

Some of them resemble disasters known to the original hearers. This would include massive destructive earthquakes that had devastated several of the cities in which they lived, the huge eruption of Mount Vesuvius (AD 79) which obliterated the cities of

---

50. Thomas, *Apocalypse*, 304. Thus he ties this sight to the earlier description of the locusts in vv. 7–10. For a layout of the parallels, see Leithart, *Revelation 1–11*, 386–87.

51. These creatures resembled some mythical beings in Greco-Roman traditions (Koester, *Revelation*, 467; Aune, *Revelation 6–16*, 539–40), perhaps ancient mythical chimaeras (Paul, *Revelation*, 182).

52. This perhaps refers to both physical and spiritual death (Beale, *Book of Revelation*, 512).

53. This may have the purpose of deception, as Beale argues (Beale, *Book of Revelation*, 513–14).

54. Cf. Thomas, *Apocalypse*, 305; Beale, *Book of Revelation*, 514. Beale points out the parallel with Luke 10:19, where snakes and scorpions are part of the devil's power which Jesus' followers can trample on and not be harmed by (Beale, *Book of Revelation*, 515).

55. Beale, *Book of Revelation*, 512.

56. Leithart, *Revelation 1–11*, 388.

57. Leithart, *Revelation 1–11*, 391–92.

Pompeii and Herculaneum, the fire of Rome (AD 64), the horrible war between the Romans and Jews (AD 66–70), and so on.

Others would be meaningful to later readers, such as the black plagues that killed around one-third of Europe in the fourteenth century or the Thirty Years' War that killed one-third of the population of Germany in the seventeenth century. More recent examples would be the terrible devastation of two world wars, the Spanish influenza epidemic of 1918–1920, the Shoah (Holocaust) of 1939–1945, the massive famines in the USSR, and China under Communist rule in the twentieth century, or more recently the AIDS epidemic worldwide. As I write (2020), the world is undergoing a fresh coronavirus pandemic. In other words, these descriptions do not demand a futurist interpretation though they are compatible with one. They certainly provide us with a framework for interpreting current disasters.

Selected Deadliest Natural Disasters in History

I have constructed this table from information in Wikipedia. It is selective, as the number of deaths from pandemics and famines far exceeed other causes. China is disproportionately represented due to its huge population. I haven't included deaths from warfare.

Date	Location	Event	Death Toll
1331–1820	worldwide	Black Death	100,000,000
1918–1920	worldwide	Spanish influenza	50,00,000–100,000,000
1958–1961	China	Great Chinese Famine	15,000,000–43,000,000
1907	China	Famine	25,000,000
1876–1879	China	Famine	9,000,000–13,000,000
1783–1784	India	Chalisa and Doji Bara famines	11,000,000[58]
1315–1317	Europe	European famine	7,500,000
1931	China	Floods	4,000,000
1887	China	Yellow River floods	Over 900,000
1556	China	Shaanxi earthquake	830,000
1970	Bangladesh	Bhola cyclone	Over 500,000
2010	Haiti	Earthquake	316,000

> And the rest of humankind, those not killed by these plagues, did not repent of the works of their hands, so that they might not worship demons and idols of gold and silver and bronze and stone and wood, which cannot either see or hear or walk, and they did not repent of their murders, nor of their sorcery, nor of their sexual immorality nor of their thefts. (Rev 9:20–21)

---

58. There are many other famines and pandemics that could be included, but I chose to incorporate other kinds of disasters.

It's a disappointing end. It suggests that the trumpet plagues had to some degree failed in their purpose. They should have produced fear and repentance. This didn't happen. Either the people refused to repent or their hearts were sovereignly "hardened," as happened to Pharaoh in the plagues in Exodus (see Exod 7:13, 22; 8:15, 19, 32; 9:7, 12, 34–35; 10:20, 27; 10).[59] Commentators disagree about whether or not the trumpet plagues were *intended* to provoke repentance since this has to be inferred from the narrative.[60] Koester and Thomas say "Yes,"[61] Beale and Aune say "No."[62] The emphasis here is on the people's responses, though the overall emphasis in the passage is on God's work.

John seemingly indicts the ancient world as whole, as opposed to the Jewish world.[63] The sins he accuses them of are the standard ones of the Greco-Roman world, seen from a Jewish perspective. These include, first, idolatry and worship of demons, what we might call "polytheism," the basic religious outlook of all the Gentiles in the first-century world.[64] Second, there are "murders," that is, violence; all cultures of the day glorified violence and Rome even made it a form of mass entertainment; the Colosseum had been built shortly before Revelation was written. Third, there are magic arts; sorcery, spells, and astrology were rife, and Ephesus led the world in magic.[65] Finally, John mentions sexual immorality, particularly rife in Greek culture and often associated with certain temples as in Ephesus, and thefts.

The list might remind the hearers of Paul's attack on ancient society in Romans 1:18–32 and by implication in 1 Corinthians 6 (see also Eph 4:17–19) and similar lists are repeated in Revelation 21:8 and 22:15. Fekkes notes that John stresses five areas of sin in such lists: immorality, falsehood, murder, idolatry, and sorcery.[66] Whatever the intention of the trumpet plagues, the effect on the *hearers* of these words must surely be to call *them* to repentance, as John has repeatedly done in his initial messages to the seven churches (2:5, 16, 22; 3:3, 19).[67]

But there is still one more trumpet blast and one more woe to come, after another delay in the narrative.

---

59. Cf. Thomas, *Apocalypse*, 305–6.

60. Cf. Aune, *Revelation 6–16*, 541.

61. Koester, *Revelation*, 468; Thomas, *Apocalypse*, 305. Gause asserts that "All judgments which in their results come short of eternal damnation are intended to call people to repentance" (Gause, *Revelation*, 131).

62. Aune, *Revelation 6–16*, 545; Beale, *Book of Revelation*, 517.

63. But see Leithart, *Revelation 1–11*, 393–95.

64. Koester, *Revelation*, 473–74; Aune, *Revelation 6–16*, 543–44. John here asserts that demonic influence lies behind worship of idols, as Paul also teaches in 1 Cor 10:19–21 (cf. Thomas, *Apocalypse*, 306–7; Koester, *Revelation*, 468; Aune, *Revelation 6–16*, 542; Beale, *Book of Revelation*, 518–19). For examples of idols in the seven cities, see Koester, *Revelation*, 469.

65. Cf. Koester, *Revelation*, 470. Sorcery was often condemned in Greco-Roman society but widely practiced nevertheless. John accuses Babylon of this in Rev 18:23.

66. Fekkes, *Prophetic Traditions*, 147–48.

67. Cf. Thomas, *Apocalypse*, 306; Beale, *Book of Revelation*, 520.

Revelation Chapter 10

Let's review the narrative so far. The Lamb has been revealed as the only person worthy to open a sealed scroll since he has redeemed people from all nations and tribes by his violent death (ch. 5). As he opens the first six seals, the gospel invades and destabilizes the Greco-Roman world, which is shaken by wars, famines, and other disasters. The martyrs cry out "How long?" and the shaking comes to a cosmic climax (ch. 6). Two related (and perhaps identical) groups of God's people are described: 144,000 from the twelve tribes of Israel and an uncountable multitude from all nations and tribes (ch. 7). After the seventh seal is opened and after a short silence, a new series of disasters are heralded by prayer and trumpet blasts of angels. Four of these result in the destruction of one-third of their respective targets; the last three are called "woes" (ch. 8). The fifth and sixth trumpets lead to targeted plagues by weird locusts and an army of 200 million cavalry; in spite of all this, the survivors refuse to repent (ch. 9).

From all this, it appears that God is working to bring out from the nations the persons from "every tribe and language and people and nation" purchased by the Lamb with his blood (5:9). In fact, these people are envisaged in heaven in Revelation 7:9. He is shaking the nations of the world in order to release these people, much like the Exodus plagues were aimed at setting Israel freed from Egyptian oppression; in this case, Egypt is perhaps replaced by the Roman Empire. However, although there are many martyrdoms (6:9–11), there must be many more before God's purpose is completed. So far, the program has not been outwardly successful. The nations are resistant, just like the ancient Egyptians under Pharaoh, which might cause the audience to ask, "What will it take to release the saints or to force the ungodly empire to submit?" The possibilities could be frightening in view of what happened in Exodus. The seventh trumpet has not yet been sounded; in fact, the second woe is not yet completed (see 11:14). There is another interlude first.[1]

This chapter is therefore very significant. It appears to mark a new beginning in the narrative, a fresh commissioning of John as a prophet, perhaps a fresh strategy of God to save the world in view of the resistance described at the end of chapter 9.

---

1. On the purpose of this interlude, see Beale, *Book of Revelation*, 520–22.

In fact, as Ian Paul points out, the language itself seems to change (at least until ch. 14) from a vision report (in the past tense) to a predictive prophecy (in the future tense).[2] We shouldn't read too much into the Greek tenses used by John, but this change should be taken into account. As Aune points out, the prophecy language in chapters 10–11 (e.g., 10:7, 11; 11:3, 6, 10, 18) certainly does intensify and multiply. Moreover, two distinctly prophetic actions augment the language: eating a scroll and measuring a temple.[3]

10:1–11 The Mighty Angel and the Little Scroll

> **And I saw another strong angel coming down out of heaven clothed in a cloud, with a rainbow on his head and his face was like the sun, and his legs like fiery pillars. And he had in his hand a little scroll opened. And he placed his right foot on the sea and the left on the land, and cried out in a loud voice like a lion's roar. (Rev 10:1–3a)**

Yet another "strong angel" takes center stage in John's vision (v. 1). The audience might remember 5:2, where such a mighty angel posed the challenge about the original sealed scroll.[4] But this angel is enormous, indeed unique.[5] He comes down from heaven, "clothed in a cloud, with a rainbow on his head, and his face was like the sun, and his legs[6] like fiery pillars." Once again there are many intertextual references as well as references to an earlier part of the narrative. The cloud perhaps reminds the hearers of 1:7 (and Dan 7:13) with its connection to the "son of man" in heaven. The rainbow would take them back to the vision of God in 4:3, with further references to Genesis 9:12–16, where the rainbow stood for God's promise not to flood the earth again.[7] The face like the sun would remind them of the appearance of Christ in 1:16. The "fiery pillars" might remind them of the "pillars of fire" leading out the Israelites across the wilderness (Exod 13:21; see also Dan 10:6).[8]

---

2. Paul, *Revelation*, 186.
3. Aune, *Revelation 6–16*, 555.
4. Cf. Bauckham, *Climax of Prophecy*, 245.
5. Cf. Thomas, *Apocalypse*, 309. Bauckham argues that this is the key angel intermediary referred to in Rev 1:1 and 22:16, the angel that John tries to worship in 22:8 (Bauckham, *Climax of Prophecy*, 254–55).
6. Literally "feet," but that makes no sense (cf. Aune, *Revelation 6–16*, 548–49; Beale, *Book of Revelation*, 524).
7. Or it could signify a halo such as was attributed to angels, gods and the emperor Augustus (Koester, *Revelation*, 475; Aune, *Revelation 6–16*, 548).
8. Beale, *Book of Revelation*, 524–25.

This is some angel! In fact, many commentators see this as another image of Christ himself[9] (or in the view of one Pentecostal author, the Holy Spirit),[10] perhaps connected to the enigmatic "angel of the LORD" in the Old Testament (see 1 Chr 21:16).[11] John is usually careful to distinguish between angels and either Christ or God (see 19:9–10; 22:8–9), so I think we have to see this super-angel as just that, an archangel perhaps.[12] But the boundaries are blurred, just as the boundaries between angels and humans in chapters 2–3 and 19:10.[13]

Now significantly, this super-angel was holding a little scroll, "opened" (a perfect passive participle, literally "having been opened"), in his hand (v. 2; compare Ezek 2:9–10). Compared to the scroll which the Lamb has just finished opening, this one is described as small. The Greek word is *biblaridion*, a little book or scroll in verses 2, 9, and 10, as opposed to *biblion*, a book or scroll, the word used of the sealed scroll in Revelation 5–6 and of this scroll in verse 8. So it is probably not that original scroll.[14] It is also somewhat ironic that such a huge super-angel is holding just a little scroll.

But it is significant, as we will see, and signals a new development in John's narrative. The shouting of the super-angel "like a lion's roar" (v. 3) might remind some in the audience of Hosea 11:10, where God's lion-like roar calls the exiles home, or Amos 3:8, where it is compared with a prophecy of judgment.

> **And when he cried out, the seven thunders spoke in their own voices.[15] And when the seven thunders spoke, I was about to write, and I heard a voice from heaven that said, "Seal up what the seven thunders said and do not write it." (Rev 10:3b–4)**

---

9. Victorinus, the oldest commentator we have access to, adopted this vew (Victorinus, *Commentary ANF*, 7:353).

10. Waddell, *Spirit of the Book*, 157–63; cf. Leithart, *Revelation 1–11*, 402.

11. Cf. Beale, *Book of Revelation*, 522–26; Leithart, *Revelation 1–11*, 398–402.

12. Cf. Carrell, *Jesus and the Angels*, 139–40, 170; Thomas, *Apocalypse*, 309–10; Koester, *Revelation*, 476.

13. Cf. Thompson, *Book of Revelation*, 78.

14. Also it is "*a* little scroll," not "*the* little scroll," which implies that it is a new entity. However, many commentators see this as the original scroll, now finally open and able to be read since all seven of its seals have been broken. Cf. Bauckham, *Climax of Prophecy*, 243–57; Thomas, *Apocalypse*, 310–12; Koester, *Revelation*, 476–77; Leithart, *Revelation 1–11*, 397–98; Waddell, *Spirit of the Book*, 150–55; Aune, *Revelation 6–16*, 571. While this cannot be ruled out, the seventh seal was broken in Rev 8:1, and we are now almost through the resulting trumpets. Cf. Herms, *Apocalypse for the Church*, 142; Beale, *Book of Revelation*, 527–32. I agree that this "does not radically alter the overall interpretation" (Beale, *Book of Revelation*, 531). Howard-Brook and Gwyther mount a similar case to Bauckham without identifying the two scrolls (Howard-Brook and Gwyther, *Unveiling Empire*, 148–51). Moloney argues instead that it is a little scroll because it represents "God's saving intervention in Israel, mediated by an angel" (Moloney, *Apocalypse of John*, 152).

15. Perhaps they were interrupting the angel or interpreting what the angel had said (Aune, *Revelation 6–16*, 559) or responding to the angel's voice as a command (Beale, *Book of Revelation*, 533).

The hearers have not heard of seven thunders before, so they might well have anticipated a new series of seven disastrous events.[16] John could apparently understand what they said, because he was about to write it down, implying that he was writing down the visions as they came to him,[17] but he was ordered not to this time. So here, shortly after the opening of the original sealed scroll, we have an open scroll and a command to "seal up" another message. It seems that God is very specific about what is opened for reading and what is still hidden (see also 22:10 compared with Dan 12:4, 9). Either there is a timing issue here or the secret part of the revelation is only for a special group of the wise, like John.[18] Koester suggests, "The command to seal up what they said interrupts the movement toward increasingly devastating judgments, showing that they represent threats that are not to be carried out";[19] this might be consistent with the shift in emphasis from devastation to gospel in this interlude.[20]

> And the angel which I saw standing on the sea and on the land[21] raised his right hand to heaven and swore by the one who lives for ever and ever, who created heaven and what is in it, and the earth and what is in it, and the sea and what is in it, that, "there will be no more delay . . . (Rev 10:5–6)

The language here reminds hearers of the worship of God in 4:8–11 and 5:13 and expresses again John's ancient cosmology. Here he divides the cosmos into heavens/earth/sea, as opposed to 9:1 where the parts were heaven/earth/abyss.[22] Such strong oath language is reminiscent of Daniel 12:7, where a "man clothed in linen" makes an oath about the breaking of the holy people's power and the completion of the events prophesied after "a time, times and half a time." That man and the super-angel here may well be the same being, as the language in Daniel 10:5–6 is quite strong, though it is closer to the language used of the appearance of Jesus in Revelation 1:13–15.

The audience might also recall Deuteronomy 32:40 where God says, "I lift my hand to heaven and solemnly swear," especially as the things God swears to do are replicated in Revelation: vengeance on his enemies with much blood, avenging "the blood of his servants" (v. 43) and making atonement for his people.[23]

---

16. Thomas, *Apocalypse*, 313. The phrase "the seven thunders" would imply that the audience had heard of them before, maybe in Psalm 29's descriptions of "the voice of the LORD" (Thomas, *Apocalypse*, 313). See also Koester, *Revelation*, 477–78; Aune, *Revelation 6–16*, 559–61; Beale, *Book of Revelation*, 535.

17. Beale, *Book of Revelation*, 533.

18. Cf. Thomas, *Apocalypse*, 313–15; Koester, *Revelation*, 478–79; Aune, *Revelation 6–16*, 562–63; Beale, *Book of Revelation*, 534–36.

19. Koester, *Revelation*, 478; see especially, 489.

20. Cf. Bauckham, *Climax of Prophecy*, 259–60. But see Beale, *Book of Revelation*, 534.

21. This image may evoke memories of the Colossus of Rhodes (Thomas, *Apocalypse*, 315; Aune, *Revelation 6–16*, 556–57) or representations of the Roman emperor (Koester, *Revelation*, 490–91).

22. Cf. Aune, *Revelation 6–16*, 565–67. This phrasing reflects Exod 20:11, part of the Sabbath commandment (cf. Lichtenwalter, "Creation and Apocalypse," 131, n. 42.)

23. Cf. Beale, *Book of Revelation*, 537–38. The context also speaks of God's judgments being sealed

This oath suggests a very significant announcement or declaration is about to follow,[24] and sure enough the super-angel swears "There will be no more delay"; literally "time will no longer be" (Greek *chronos ouketi estai*) (v. 6b).[25] This is significant since the hearers have experienced delay after delay to this point since the scroll was first being opened. There was delay for the full number of martyrs to be killed (6:10–11); delay for the day of wrath (6:17); delay in harming the land and sea (7:3); half an hour of silence after the seventh seal was opened (8:1); and delay in sounding the seventh trumpet until now. Time language is very significant in Revelation. Beale comments, "there will be no delay to God's bringing an end to history (11:11–13, 18), when the full number of suffering believers has reached the predetermined number (6:10; 11:7a) and impenitence has reached its intractable height (9:21; 11:7–10)."[26]

> "... but in the days of the sound of the seventh angel, when he is about to sound his trumpet, the secret plan of God will be fulfilled, which he preached as good news to his own slaves the prophets." (Rev 10:7)

There are four things to note here. First, this is just *before* the seventh trumpet sounds.[27] Second, the "secret plan" or "mystery"[28] of God will be "fulfilled" (or completed or perfected, Greek *etelesthē*).[29] Third, it is a fulfilment of prophecy, presumably from the Old Testament.[30] And fourth, this mystery was "preached as good news to . . . the prophets" (Greek *euēngelisen*),[31] referring perhaps to Isaiah's "good news" of restoration in Isaiah 40:8, 52:7, and 61:1. Thus, this "good news" brings to mind the restoration of Israel and sharply contrasts with imperial Roman propaganda.[32] This suggests a more positive goal for the end, not just judgments. As the first mention of gospel in Revelation,

---

up until the appropriate time (Deut 32:34).

24. On oaths and their significance, see Koester, *Revelation*, 479. In Ezek 20:5–6, God says, "I swore with uplifted hand . . . " about the exodus and conquest of Canaan. Cf. Leithart, *Revelation 1–11*, 405–6.

25. Cf. Thomas, *Apocalypse*, 315–16; Koester, *Revelation*, 479–80; Aune, *Revelation 6–16*, 568; Beale, *Book of Revelation*, 539. But see the extended discussion with a philosophical bent in Leithart, *Revelation 1–11*, 406–10.

26. Beale, *Book of Revelation*, 522. Cf. Leithart, *Revelation 1–11*, 397; Bauckham, *Climax of Prophecy*, 262–63.

27. But cf. Beale, *Book of Revelation*, 539–41.

28. Cf. Koester, *Revelation*, 480–81. Another possibility here is a reference to the final resurrection (see 1 Cor 15:51–52 and Beale, *Book of Revelation*, 547).

29. Cf. John 19:30, where Jesus on the cross declares, "It is finished." See also Thomas, *Apocalypse*, 317.

30. Cf. Amos 3:7. A reference to the work of New Testament prophets may be included too (Thomas, *Apocalypse*, 318; Koester, *Revelation*, 481).

31. Only here and 14:6 in the NT is this verb in the active voice (Aune, *Revelation 6–16*, 570). Aune denies any Pauline-type gospel reference here, seeing this as "the message of the coming of God to judge and to save" as in the synoptic Gospels (ibid.). I'm not convinced this is a strong distinction. Cf. Beale, *Book of Revelation*, 546.

32. Cf. Koester, *Revelation*, 481.

this brings at least a hint of a new stage in God's plan, the first judgment stage having failed to bring repentance. Possibly the "little scroll" refers to the Christian gospel itself.

The oath language would tend to send the first-century reader to Daniel 12, where we see many parallels with Revelation. Daniel mentions a great time of distress (v. 1; see Rev 7:14), the deliverance of those whose names are in the book (v. 1; see Rev 3:5; 13:8; 20:15), the resurrection of the good and the bad (v. 2; see Rev 20:4–6, 12–13), and the shining of the righteous like stars (v. 3). Daniel 12 also contains the sealing up of a scroll (vv. 4, 9; see also Rev 5:1–5), a "How long?" question (v. 6; see Rev 6:10; 10:6), a period of "a time, times and half a time" (v. 7; see Dan 7:25; Rev 12:14), and the breaking of the saints' power (v. 7; see Rev 13:7). Are these the prophecies that are about to be fulfilled?

The parallels between Daniel 7 and 12 and the succeeding events in Revelation are quite close, and both appear to describe a period of intense struggle and persecution of the saints, during which the saints appear to be abandoned to the destructive power of empire for a time. Caird comments, "The persecution of the church is thus the secret weapon by which God intends to win his victory over the church's persecutors and to achieve his purpose of redemption."[33]

The concept of a "secret plan" or *mystery* is harder to interpret. This word is used sparingly in Revelation. First, in 1:20, it is used when Jesus is explaining the seven stars and lampstands. Later, in 17:5 and 17:7, it refers to the woman Babylon. In all these cases, the "mystery" is an image standing for an historical entity, and its meaning is immediately explained. The word seems to have an eschatological significance here, perhaps related to the opening of the seven seals. The seals themselves express concretely the concept of something hidden becoming revealed, with more connections to Daniel 12:4, 9. I followed Aune in translating it as "the secret plan of God."[34]

However, this language is common enough in Paul's undisputed letters and others attributed to him, where it often refers to the gospel secret of the church as the union of Jews and Gentiles in Christ (Rom 11:25; 16:25–26; 1 Cor 2:7; Eph 1:9–10; 3:3–6, 9; 5:32; 6:19; Col 1:26–27; 2:2; 4:3; 1 Tim 3:16), a truth which has been on display in Revelation 7. It is impossible to know if the "mystery of God" here has the same significance as in Paul (or as the "mysteries of the kingdom" in the Synoptic Gospels), but it would be consistent with the overall goal that God seems to be working towards, based on 5:9 and 7:9, which had suffered a serious setback in 9:20–21. Perhaps it's the work of the gospel itself that is about to bring a breakthrough.[35] But if so, both Revelation 7:14 and Daniel 12 warn us that there will be a mighty struggle first.[36]

---

33. Caird, *Revelation*, 128. Cf. Beale, *Book of Revelation*, 541–46.

34. Aune, *Revelation 6–16*, 568–69; Bauckham, *Climax of Prophecy*, 261. Beale calls it "God's overt decree that the saints suffer" (Beale, *Book of Revelation*, 545). Leithart describes it as "the Top Secret Story, sealed since the time of Daniel, now being released" (*Revelation 1–11*, 398; see also 405).

35. Cf. Howard-Brook and Gwyther, *Unveiling Empire*, 150.

36. Cf. Beale, *Book of Revelation*, 543.

> And the voice which I heard from heaven spoke to me again and said, "Go and take the opened scroll in the hand of the angel who stands on the sea and the land." (Rev 10:8)

Meanwhile the audience's attention is taken from Daniel to Ezekiel. A different voice identified as "the voice which I heard from heaven" (v. 8, referring back apparently to v. 4) now gives John an assignment. John is sometimes just a spectator in the story, but sometimes he has a part to play. He weeps over the lack of a worthy person to open the seven-sealed scroll (5:4). He is questioned about the identity of the uncountable multitude (7:13–14). He almost gets to write down the message of the seven thunders (10:4). But this is the first time he is asked to physically move.[37] The voice says, "Go and take [Greek *labe*, the same words used of the Lamb taking the original scroll in Rev 5:7–8][38] the opened scroll in the hand of the angel who stands on the sea and on the land" (v. 8).[39]

Taken literally, this is faintly ridiculous: the super-angel is huge, John is just human-size, and the scroll is little.[40] The scroll *is* open, so it would appear possible for its contents to be revealed. However, John is not actually told to read it or study it.

> And I went off to the angel, saying to him to give me the little scroll. And he said to me, "Take it and eat it,[41] and it will make your stomach bitter, but in your mouth, it will be as sweet as honey." And I took the little scroll from the hand of the angel and ate it, and in my mouth, it was sweet like honey, but when I had eaten it, my stomach became bitter. (Rev 10:9–10)

This is a very clear allusion to Ezekiel 2–3.[42] As part of the call narrative that opens that book, Ezekiel is told not to be intimidated by the rebellious Israelites and not to join their rebellion but "open your mouth and eat what I give you" (Ezek 2:8). It isn't clear who is speaking, but Ezekiel looks and sees "a hand stretched out to me. In it was a scroll, which he unrolled before me. On both sides of it were written words of lament and mourning and woe" (Ezek 2:10). This represents the judgement on Israel, and this section of Revelation is integrated into the three "woes," so this is not coincidental. Ezekiel is told to eat the scroll and then "go and speak to the people of Israel" (Ezek 3:1), which he does. "So I ate it, and it tasted as sweet as honey in my mouth" (Ezek 3:3), though clearly the message was far from sweet. Does this reference imply that John's

---

37. "Nowhere in the Apocalypse does John more fully enter into this visionary drama than here" (Thomas, *Apocalypse*, 321).

38. Beale, *Book of Revelation*, 548–49. Beale argues that John's action signifies his sharing in the reign of Christ through suffering.

39. Thomas, *Apocalypse*, 319, 321.

40. Thomas, *Apocalypse*, 319; Leithart, *Revelation 1–11*, 413.

41. The language here might also remind the audience of the institution of the Lord's supper. Matt 26:26 says, "Take and eat; this is my body."

42. Aune, *Revelation 6–16*, 570–71.

scroll message is specifically for Israel? If members of the audience think so, they are immediately corrected.

> **And they said to me,**[43] **"You must again prophesy to many peoples and nations and languages and kings." (Rev 10:11)**

What does it all mean? In both Ezekiel and Revelation, this is a call narrative. Ezekiel is called to confront the rebellious Israelites and *not* the potentially responsive Gentiles (Ezek 3:5–6). John, however, is called to prophesy to, or about, or even against,[44] many nations.[45] Perhaps the audience would be reminded of the two groups in Revelation 7, the first from Israel's tribes and the second from all nations. Ezekiel's message is about laments and woes, and John is in the midst of three woes. Both are called to somehow digest and embody their message,[46] which is "sweet" in itself (being God's word) but sickening in that the message is unsettling,[47] one of trouble, which will also bring great trouble to the messenger.[48]

In this case, this amounts to a second commissioning,[49] perhaps in contrast to the first in that the original prophecies were to be sent to the seven churches, and the forthcoming ones are to the nations.[50] Bauckham sees something more significant here; after the failure of the nations to repent in response to the shakings of Revelation 6–9, as signified in 9:20–21, "the scroll is to reveal a more effective strategy."[51] This is in keeping wih my argument that God's plan is to bring the nations to himself.

---

43. This expression is probably equivalent to a passive, "I was told" (as NIV) (Koester, *Revelation*, 483; Aune, *Revelation 6–16*, 573). Leithart, however, suggests it is the seven thunders of vv. 3–4 who articulate this commission as John will prophesy their message (Leithart, *Revelation 1–11*, 415, 417). Waddell suggests the super-angel (i.e., the Spirit) and voice from heaven are the speakers (Waddell, *Spirit of the Book*, 164, n. 103).

44. Cf. Aune, *Revelation 6–16*, 573–74, 575; Beale, *Book of Revelation*, 554–55. This suggests that the prophecy has a largely negative purpose. But cf. Bauckham, *Climax of Prophecy*, 265–66; Morales, *Shepherd of the Nations*, 75–77.

45. Cf. Koester, *Revelation*, 493.

46. Cf. Thomas, *Apocalypse*, 320; Koester, *Revelation*, 492–93. Jeremiah has a similar experience in Jer 1:9 and 15:16. See also Aune, *Revelation 6–16*, 572–73.

47. This would remind the audience perhaps of Daniel's reaction in Dan 10:8–17.

48. Cf. Koester, *Revelation*, 482–83; Beale, *Book of Revelation*, 550–53

49. Cf. Koester, *Revelation*, 488; Beale, *Book of Revelation*, 550, 553. Leithart argues that John is moving from his earlier role as "a secretary taking dictation" to a prophet who "speaks God's words in his own voice" (*Revelation 1–11*, 404). However, John has already been more than a secretary, and he continues to record what he sees; moreover, he is told to "prophesy *again*" (v. 11), implying that he has already been doing that.

50. Cf. Beale, *Book of Revelation*, 553–54.

51. Bauckham, *Climax of Prophecy*, 258. I don't agree with Bauckham that the redemption of "persons from every tribe and language and people and nation" (5:9) is for the purpose of making them a witness that will cause all the nations (every Gentile?) to repent; rather, I see 5:9 as announcing the outcome of the church's witness. 5:9 does not just describe an "initial effect" (ibid.) but the ultimate goal. It's a small difference but may help guard against the full universalism to which Bauckham's overall argument in "The Conversion of the Nations" is vulnerable.

Revelation Chapter 11

11:1–14 The Two Witnesses

> **And a measuring rod like a staff was given to me,[1] saying, "Rise up and measure the temple of God and the altar and those who are worshiping in it." (Rev 11:1)[2]**

This verse is awkward and ambiguous as it does not say who gave John the staff and told him to "rise up and measure the temple." The NRSV translates, "Then I was given a measuring rod like a staff, and I was told, 'Come and measure the temple . . . '" Possibly this action was initiated by one of the angels in chapter 10, or "the voice" of 10:8, since there were no chapter breaks in the original Greek. Chapter 11 is really a continuation of chapter 10, but by verse 3, it is clearly God or Christ speaking, so either of them might be giving John his orders here.[3]

The hearers would perhaps be reminded of Ezekiel 40:3, in which passage Ezekiel, having been taken in visions back to the land of Israel, "saw a man whose appearance was like bronze; he was standing in the gateway with a linen cord and a measuring rod in his hand."[4] The man measures what seems to be a new temple, into which the glory of God would return after departing from the first temple (Ezek 43:2–5). This is thus a vision of restoration following on from repentance by the Israelites (Ezek 43:7–11). However, Ezekiel's vision is more like what John sees in Revelation 21 than here in chapter 11.[5]

---

1. Probably 2–3 meters long (Koester, *Revelation*, 483).

2. Aune translates "count its worshippers," as people are counted more than measured in such a context (Aune, *Revelation 6–16*, 578, 605). John is never actually said to do the measuring (cf. ibid., 585).

3. Cf. Waddell, *Spirit of the Book*, 162–63. As Waddell points out, the identities of the speakers in this chapter are ambiguous, but if the super-angel of chapter 10 refers to the Spirit, the Spirit could be the speaker in chapter 11 without difficulty.

4. Cf. Aune, *Revelation 6–16*, 603.

5. Cf. Beale, *Book of Revelation*, 559; Mayo, *Those Who Call Themselves Jews*, 119–20.

Another possible intertextual reference is from Zechariah,[6] a series of prophetic oracles also referring to the restoration of Israel after the Babylonian captivity. Zechariah opens with a call to repentance (Zech 1:2–6), followed by a vision report featuring multi-colored horses (Zech 1:8–10), and an announcement of the restoration and rebuilding of Jerusalem and Judah (Zech 1:12–17). In this setting, the prophet hears of a "measuring line . . . stretched out over Jerusalem" (Zech 1:16) and sees "a man with a measuring line in his hand" (Zech 2:1). He is about to measure Jerusalem (Zech 2:2), which is destined to be a much greater size so that it can accommodate the huge number of returning refugees from Babylon (Zech 2:4–7).

This passage is referred to in the measuring of the new Jerusalem in Revelation 21:15–16, subsequent to a new call for God's people to "come out of" Babylon (Rev 18:4). In these four passages (Ezek 40:3; Zech 1:16; 2:1; Rev 21:15–16), the measuring is for a positive purpose: the rebuilding of God's temple after the end of the Babylonian captivity.

This also recalls Daniel 9:25, which states that Jerusalem would be "rebuilt with streets and a trench, but in times of trouble." And indeed, this is what Ezra and Nehemiah tell us: the temple and the city are rebuilt under much stress during the rule of the Persian Empire. These passages, taken together, might imply that the measuring that John is told to carry out is also for the purpose of rebuilding the temple, even in a time of opposition and stress. The hearer might think that John is predicting the literal rebuilding of the Jerusalem temple again after its destruction by the Romans in AD 70.[7] Other measuring line incidents in the Old Testament, however, are not so positive. Indeed, they are often associated with judgment and destruction (2 Sam 8:2; 2 Kgs 21:13; Isa 28:17; 34:11; Lam 2:8; Amos 7:7–9). So here too, the measuring could be associated perhaps with the destruction of Jerusalem in AD 70.[8]

A third possibility is that the measuring here is for protection or preservation, since in the ancient world temples were seen as places of asylum or refuge.[9] Aune draws a parallel with the sealing of the 144,000 in Revelation 7, which serves to protect them from the strange locusts in 9:4.[10] And a fourth possibility, suggested by Leithart, is that measuring is associated with holiness: "measured things . . . are *holy* things" as are counted people (7:3–4), set apart to God. Hence, "measuring distinguishes holy and profane"[11] as the passage goes on to portray (v. 2). But the significant difference in this case is that the prophet himself is told to do the measuring.

6. Cf. Waddell, *Spirit of the Book*, 165–66.

7. This is a line taken by Dispensationalists, who expect a literal third temple. Cf. Walvoord, *Revelation*, 175–83. But see Mayo, *Those Who Call Themselves Jews*, 120–21.

8. This is the contention of Den Dulk in "Measuring the Temple." Some commentators think John has taken over, and perhaps Christianized, an original Jewish prophecy of God's protection of the temple during the war of AD 66–70 (cf. Beasley-Murray, *Revelation*, 176–83).

9. Cf. Koester, *Revelation*, 484; Aune, *Revelation 6–16*, 604–5, 630.

10. Aune, *Revelation 6–16*, 605; Beale, *Book of Revelation*, 560.

11. Leithart, *Revelation 1–11*, 418.

> "And the court that is outside the temple exclude[12] and do not measure it, because it is given to the Gentiles, and they will trample the holy city (for) forty-two months." (Rev 11:2)

The story John tells is more complex than those previous measurings. First, he is commanded to measure only part of the temple. This may recall Dan 8:10–14, which tells of a small horn that "threw some of the starry host down to the earth and trampled on them" (v. 10) and "took away the daily sacrifice from the Lord, and his sanctuary was thrown down" (v. 11). This is also described as "the surrender of the sanctuary and the trampling underfoot of the Lord's people" (v. 13) over a period of "2,300 evenings and mornings" before the re-consecration of the sanctuary (v. 14).[13] Also Daniel 9:27 speaks of a coming ruler who will "put an end to sacrifice and offering" and "at the temple . . . will set up an abomination that causes desolation . . . " for a short period, perhaps half a week or three-and-a-half years (compare Dan 12:7, 11; 7:25).[14]

All this was literally fulfilled by the actions of the Greek king Antiochus IV Epiphanes, who defiled the temple by offering a pig to Zeus and caused its sacrificial system to be closed down for about three-and-a-half years.[15] This may also be what Isaiah 63:18 refers to when it says that "our enemies have trampled down your sanctuary."

In the memory of the hearers of Revelation, the Jewish war with Rome had lasted a similar length, marked from the ceasing of the daily temple sacrifice on behalf of Caesar until the destruction of the temple by Caesar's armies in AD 70.[16] The trampling of the outer court of the temple is therefore ambiguous. Is it a temporary obstruction to the rebuilding of the temple, or perhaps something more ominous, a warning of greater destruction to come or a more permanent prevention of the temple's reconstruction? Perhaps this recalls Luke's version of Jesus' prophecy that "Jerusalem will be trampled on by the Gentiles until the times of the Gentiles are fulfilled" (Luke 21:24).[17]

All these alternatives, however, assume that we are talking about a literal building. And the temple in Revelation 11 may indeed refer to the second temple (the one destroyed in AD 70),[18] or to a future third temple (maybe that envisioned by Ezekiel). But in every other temple or altar reference in Revelation, the temple is in heaven (3:12;

---

12. Literally "thow outside" (Greek ἔβαλε ἔξωθεν [ekbale exōthen]). Most translations have "exclude" (NIV) or "leave out" (NRSV) or a similar phrase, as it makes no sense to "throw outside" a court. Cf. Den Dulk, "Measuring the Temple," 442–44.

13. Cf. Bauckham, *Climax of Prophecy*, 270–71; Waddell, *Spirit of the Book*, 168–69; Mayo, *Those Who Call Themselves Jews*, 119–20.

14. Cf. Koester, *Revelation*, 494.

15. Cf. Corsini, *Apocalypse*, 193–94.

16. Cf. Aune, *Revelation 6–16*, 609; Beale, *Book of Revelation*, 566; Mayo, *Those Who Call Themselves Jews*, 127–128.

17. Cf. Aune, *Revelation 6–16*, 608. For a full discussion of the temple area and the scenario of vv. 1–2, see ibid., 604–8; cf. Bauckham, *Climax of Prophecy*, 268–73.

18. For the main arguments in favor of this interpretation, see Aune, *Revelation 6–16*, 596.

6:9; 7:15; 8:3–5; 11:19; 14:15, 17; 15:5–8; 16:1, 17).[19] At the end of the story, the holy city comes down out of heaven to earth (21:2, 10), but there is no literal temple, "because the Lord God Almighty and the Lamb are its temple" (21:22; compare John 2:21).

I can only see one exception to this, and that is the seven churches that are pictured as lampstands, perhaps signifying that they are like mini-temples in their cities, in contrast to the many pagan temples in the region (1:20). Since John is specifically measuring the worshipers, not just the building, in verse 1, Thomas's conclusion that the three components refer to "the believing community in the very presence of God"[20] makes sense, confirmed by Daniel 8:13, where it is the people who are trampled on and in keeping with some other early Christian texts that portray the church as a temple (1 Cor 3:16; 2 Cor 6:16; Eph 2:20; 1 Pet 2:5).[21] Beale puts this well when he asserts, "Rev 11:1–2 depicts the temple of the age to come as having broken into the present age."[22]

This also seems to be consistent with what comes next in John's vision. If the temple is to be understood as the church, then the outer court given over to the Gentiles would represent either the vulnerable aspect of the church,[23] the compromising Christians (as identified in Rev 2–3), the unbelieving Jews, the second temple as a whole (destroyed by the Romans), or the unbelieving world in general.[24] The measured temple itself would signify perhaps the spiritual preservation of the faithful Christians or the building up of the true church as promised by Jesus in Mattew 16:18. As Beale puts it, "the measuring connotes God's presence, which is guaranteed to be with the temple community living on earth before the consummation. The faith of his people will be upheld by his presence . . . "[25]

However, we need to note more precisely what John says here: the outer court is not just excluded, but "thrown out," as we saw, and the "holy city" is trampled on by the Gentiles. This would appear to mean that the unbelieving Jews or compromising Christians are not measured. In other words, they are evicted from the church (perhaps like 1 Cor 5:13 and Acts 5:1–11), but the faithful believers are measured as part of the building of the church, and then trampled on, that is, persecuted, just like the two witnesses whose story is about to be told.[26] This might remind the audience

---

19. Cf. Aune, *Revelation 6–16*, 596–97; Mayo, *Those Who Call Themselves Jews*, 122–23.

20. Thomas, *Apocalypse*, 325. See the full discussion in ibid., 323–27; cf. Beale, *Book of Revelation*, 571; Waddell, *Spirit of the Book*, 166; de Smidt, "Spirit in Revelation," 41.

21. Cf. Koester, *Revelation*, 484–86, 494–95. Koester argues out that "the use of temple imagery for the Christian community fostered a sense of distinctive identity in the face of competing religious claims" and "also gives the followers of Jesus a place in Israel's tradition" (ibid., 495). See also Beale, *Book of Revelation*, 562–65; Aune, *Revelation 17–22*, 1191; Mayo, *Those Who Call Themselves Jews*, 123–24.

22. Beale, *Book of Revelation*, 562; Beale, *John's Use of the Old Testament*, 106–7.

23. This means its exposure to persecution (cf. Beale, *Book of Revelation*, 561, 568–69).

24. Cf. Koester, *Revelation*, 438–39, 485–86; Aune, *Revelation 6–16*, 597–98. For a summary of five interpretations of the scenario here, see Beale, *Book of Revelation*, 557–59.

25. Beale, *Book of Revelation*, 559.

26. Cf. Leithart, *Revelation 1–11*, 422–25; Hendriksen, *More Than Conquerors*, 127–28.

of Jesus' words, warning the compromising or sleepy Christians in 2:5, 16, 22, 23; 3:3, 16 and encouraging the faithful ones even in the midst of opposition in 2:10, 13, 24, 25; 3:4, 5, 8–10, 20.

All these ideas assume that the trampling of the outer court or city is negative, but Gentiles had the right to be in the "outer court" of the Jerusalem temple,[27] which was to be "a house of prayer for all the nations" (Isa 56:7). So another possibility is that John's image refers to Gentile believers, who are "thrown out" by the unbelieving Jews and cannot be measured because they are too numerous, unlike the Jewish believers. This would be similar to the two contrasting images of Revelation 7 and might be an implication of Luke 21:24. However, this interpretation might stretch the imagery too far.

What I am trying to do here is expand our understanding in a positive direction. Mayo, for example, says, "What is made clear for the Asian Christians is that their suffering will continue but is only temporary."[28] The implication here, and by some other authors, is on the "poor suffering church" that needs comfort and hope, but while there is definitely struggle and persecution here, Christ is building his church, and the conquerors are not looking for comfort, but power to be witnesses (as in Acts 1:8; 4:29–30; Matt 16:18).

> "And I will appoint[29] my two witnesses, and they will prophesy one thousand two hundred and sixty days clothed in sackcloth." These are the two olive trees and the two lampstands that stand before the Lord of the earth. (Rev 11:3–4)[30]

Witnesses are central to Revelation, as has been clear (1:2, 5; 2:13), and there are two of them, the minimum number needed in the Torah to establish a claim,[31] perhaps reflecting a Jewish expectation of two messianic figures (compare Jer 6:26; Jonah 3:5–8; Isa 20:2; Dan 9:3),[32] and reminding some hearers of Jesus sending out his disciples in pairs (Mark 6:7; Luke 10:1).[33] The sackcloth stands for repentance or mourning, as might befit a time of crisis, as in Joel 1:8, 13, where there is a specific crisis affecting the temple (a passage alluded to in ch. 9).[34] This is the only indication of the witnesses'

---

27. Cf. Beale, *Book of Revelation*, 560–61; Corsini, *Apocalypse*, 191. Corsini does not make the same deduction I am suggesting here.

28. Mayo, *Those Who Call Themselves Jews*, 126.

29. Literally "give to" (Greek δώσω [*dōsō*])

30. The direct speech is concluded by the NIV at the end of verse 3, then resumed briefly in verse 4, implying that the rest of the passage is a direct prophecy by John; cf. Aune, *Revelation 6–16*, 585, 586.

31. Num 35:30; Deut 17:6; 19:15; cf. Thomas, *Apocalypse*, 328; Beale, *Book of Revelation*, 575. The fact that there are two witnesses may also allude to the fact that only two of the seven churches are pure and effective (Beale, *Book of Revelation*, 575) or to the two tablets of the Law (ibid., 582–83).

32. Aune, *Revelation 6–16*, 611.

33. Cf. Beasley-Murray, *Revelation*, 184.

34. Cf. Koester, *Revelation*, 498, 508; Beale, *Book of Revelation*, 576.

message,[35] though the fact that they are witnesses who prophesy may also suggest they are witnesses to Jesus, like Antipas (2:13).[36]

Moreover, as Thomas points out, their prophetic witness is for the same period as the trampling of the holy city, suggesting a prophetic resistance to those trampling it.[37] And the hearers of Revelation would, of course, remember that lampstands stand for local churches in the initial vision (1:20).

There is also a clear intertextual reference to Zechariah 4.[38] In this chapter, Zechariah sees "a solid gold lampstand with a bowl at the top and seven lamps on it, with seven channels to the lamps. Also there are two olive trees by it" (vv. 2–3). When he asks the meaning of this, he is told, "This is the word of the LORD to Zerubbabel: 'Not by might nor by power but by my Spirit, says the LORD Almighty . . .'" (v. 6). The prophecy goes on to encourage Zerubbabel that, having laid the temple's foundation, he will also complete its rebuilding (vv. 7–10). He is also told that the "two olive branches" are "the two who are anointed to serve the Lord of all the earth" (vv. 12–14), probably referring to the civil ruler Zerubbabel and the high priest Joshua.[39]

Clearly, there is a connection between Zechariah's message about the rebuilding of the second temple and John's revelation about temple and witnesses.[40] As Bauckham observes, behind John's vision here is the story of "Joshua and Zerubbabel, standing for the hope of a new Jerusalem amid the ruins of the city which the Gentiles had trampled."[41] But before we speculate on what that connection is, let's read on in Revelation 11.

> **And if anyone wants to harm them, fire comes out from their mouth and devours their enemies; and if anyone wants to harm them, thus they must be killed. (Rev 11:5)**

This scene ironically recalls the cavalry of 9:17–18, where there was fire coming out of the mouth of the horses.[42] The two prophetic witnesses first sound like Zerubbabel

---

35. Aune, *Revelation 6–16*, 611.

36. Cf. Waddell, *Spirit of the Book*, 171–72.

37. Thomas, *Apocalypse*, 328–29; Beale, *Book of Revelation*, 572. Revelation makes several references to equivalent periods using three different descriptions, all in chapters 11–13. Koester comments here that "the specific time indicates that the nations' power to dominate is real and yet is limited by God" (Koester, *Revelation*, 486; see also ibid., 438–39, 487, 495–96; Aune, *Revelation 6–16*, 609–10; Beale, *Book of Revelation*, 565–67; Leithart, *Revelation 1–11*, 426–27). Another way of looking at this is in terms of comparative lengths of time. Three-and-a-half years is very short compared to a thousand years, for example.

38. Cf. Thomas, *Apocalypse*, 330; cf. Koester, *Revelation*, 498; Aune, *Revelation 6–16*, 579, 612; Waddell, *Spirit of the Book*, 172–73.

39. Cf. Aune, *Revelation 6–16*, 631; Leithart, *Revelation 1–11*, 431.

40. Cf. Beale, *Book of Revelation*, 577–79.

41. Bauckham, *Climax of Prophecy*, 169.

42. See extended parallels in Beale, *Book of Revelation*, 585–86.

and Joshua, but now they start to look more like Elijah and Moses.[43] This would especially remind the hearers of two incidents in the life of Elijah: his calling down fire onto the sacrifice on his altar after challenging the prophets of Baal to do this (1 Kgs 18:38) and his calling down fire on a group of soldiers sent to bring him to King Ahaziah of Israel (2 Kgs 1:10, 12). However, verbally Jeremiah 5:14 is closer, where God says to Jeremiah, "I will make my words in your mouth a fire and these people the wood it consumes." Koester comments, "Revelation sees a war of words, using metaphors to depict the speech of Christ, his witnesses and their adversaries."[44]

In both cases, Elijah and Jeremiah, the prophet is standing up for God against false prophets and the unfaithful Israelites. The audience would also likely recall that among the opponents of Moses and Elijah were Balaam and Jezebel, respectively—both of whom have been mentioned in the messages to the seven churches (2:14, 20).[45] This might imply that the struggle here is within the church, which would be appropriate if the context is the building of the church-as-temple. In this case, the people who want to harm the witnesses, and suffer death as a result, might be at least nominal Christians (see 2:23)!

More likely, this is a worldwide struggle that affects the churches, as in the struggles in the succeeding chapters. Satan is both persecuting, and trying to infiltrate, the church while Jesus builds it (Matt 16:18). As Pattemore argues, "this interpenetration of church and world is the reality within which John's audience live."[46]

Moses and Elijah are also focused on in the closing words of Malachi (Mal 4:4–6). Here Elijah is coming to bring reconciliation between parents and children in order to prevent a situation of "total destruction" (Mal 4:6), a situation also envisaged in Micah (Mic 7:6; compare Matt 10:21–22). In a crisis like this, even normal family relationships are threatened. Moses and Elijah, of course, appear with Jesus on the mount of transfiguration (Matt 17:2–4; Mark 9:4–5; Luke 9:30–33). They discuss Jesus' imminent "departure" (or "exodus," Greek *exodon*) (Luke 9:31), and Jesus identifies John the Baptist as Elijah who has already come and been rejected (Matt 17:10–13), implying that Malachi's threat of "total destruction" is imminent. So two figures like Moses and Elijah signify a rather threatening situation.

Note too the use of "must" (Greek *dei*), as in 1:1 and 4:1. This reads as a kind of conditional determinism: if certain actions are taken, a certain result is determined.

They have authority to shut up heaven so that no rain falls (during) the days of their prophesying ... (Rev 11:6a)

---

43. Cf. Beale, *Book of Revelation*, 582–85; Leithart, *Revelation 1–11*, 430; Bauckham, *Climax of Prophecy*, 275–77.

44. Koester, *Revelation*, 499. See also Isa 11:4; cf. Waddell, *Spirit of the Book*, 179; Aune, *Revelation 6–16*, 613–14; Beale, *Book of Revelation*, 580–581; Caird, *Revelation*, 136–37.

45. Cf. Pattemore, *People of God*, 162–63.

46. Pattemore, *People of God*, 163.

This also reminds hearers of Elijah because this was exactly what he did (1 Kgs 17:1; 18:1). Moreover, Luke 4:25 and James 5:17 tell us that this drought lasted for three-and-a-half years, the same period mentioned in verses 2–3.[47] Clearly, the audience of Revelation is meant to make the connections: the same prophetic ministry of Elijah is being released again, and in a Jewish context (temple, witnesses, prophecy). Nonetheless, some questions remain. Is John calling the Jews to repentance like Elijah? Or is this addressed to the churches? But the focus changes again immediately:

> . . . and they have authority over the waters to turn them into blood and strike the earth with every plague whenever they want. (Rev 11:6b)

Now the hearers are reminded of Moses and the plagues on Egypt (see Exod 7:17–21), which were already alluded to in the earlier trumpet disasters. This has the effect of focusing their minds on the Gentiles, already mentioned in verse 2. So the target of the two prophets seems to be both Jews and Gentiles.[48]

> And when they have finished their testimony, the beast that comes up[49] from the abyss will make war against them and conquer them and kill them. (Rev 11:7)

The two witnesses are supernaturally enabled and protected for a set period of time (1,260 days in v. 3, equivalent to the "forty-two months" of v. 2),[50] but not forever. The protection only lasts until their work is completed,[51] even as the church must complete its witness before the end of the era (compare Rev 6:11; 2 Pet 3:9).[52] But now the audience hears the first mention of the beast, who emerges from the abyss (first opened in 9:1–2), what we might colloquially call "the pit of hell."[53]

Seemingly, this is allowed in the providence of God, just like the other plague from the abyss in Revelation 9. Nonetheless, the audience of Revelation may well be shocked that this enemy is able to conquer God's prophets, as until now conquest was

---

47. Cf. Koester, *Revelation*, 499; Aune, *Revelation 6–16*, 615; Beale, *Book of Revelation*, 565, 584. For other nearly literal three-and-a-half year periods, see Leithart, *Revelation 1–11*, 426–27, though he omits the Elijah drought and the Antiochus Epiphanes shut down of the temple and focuses mainly on the persecution under Nero and the siege of Jerusalem.

48. Cf. Thomas, *Apocalypse*, 332–33.

49. The phrase is "temporally vague enough to include the idea that the beast has been characterized as rising from the abyss throughout the period of the church's witness . . . the beast's spirit has stood behind the earthly persecutors throughout history, and at the end he will manifest himself openly to defeat the church finally" only to be "destroyed by Christ at the *Parousia* (so 17:8–14)" (Beale, *Book of Revelation*, 589).

50. Possibly referring to "the number of 'stations' or places where God's people camped during the journey through the wilderness according to . . . Numbers 33" (Paul, *Revelation*, 197; see also 206–7). This would fit the Exodus background to this section of Revelation.

51. Thomas points to a parallel with Jesus in John's Gospel, suggested by the Greek τελεϲῶϲιν [*telesōsin*] (Thomas, *Apocalypse*, 333).

52. Cf. Beale, *Book of Revelation*, 587; Hendriksen, *More Than Conquerors*, 130–31.

53. Cf. Aune, *Revelation 6–16*, 616–17.

the mission of the churches.⁵⁴ They would perhaps remember Daniel 7:21, where the little horn from the fourth beast " . . . was waging war against the holy people and defeating them."⁵⁵ There is also a justice issue, since the witnesses are killed in spite of their service of God. The injustice of their deaths and those of the other witnesses, including Jesus himself, is an essential part of their power, because it demands reversal by God.⁵⁶

> **And their corpses (will lie) on the square of the great city which is spiritually called Sodom and Egypt, where also their Lord was crucified. And (those) from the peoples and tribes and languages and nations will look at their corpses for three and a half days and will not allow their corpses to be placed in a tomb. And those who dwell on the earth will rejoice over them and celebrate and send gifts to one another, for these two prophets tormented those who dwell on the earth. (Rev 11:8–10)**

The two witnesses are martyrs for Jesus (v. 8) and their deaths are patterned on his. The beast and his international allies (v. 9) celebrate and underline this victory with an act of dishonor, indecency, and humiliation by publicly exposing the bodies and refusing burial⁵⁷ and celebrating their demise (v. 10).⁵⁸ The beast has seemingly won a significant victory over God's servants, a victory which is hugely popular with most people (v. 10) who had been "tormented" (Greek *ebasanisan*, the same language as used of the locusts in 9:5) by their prophetic words. Even more, they would celebrate because of the plagues these prophets had called down on the earth (vv. 3–6).⁵⁹ Perhaps if a recapitulation reading is valid, these two witnesses may have actually been responsible for the trumpet plagues.⁶⁰

This episode seems to take place in Jerusalem. The passage begins in the temple (v. 1) and the "holy city" (v. 2), the prophets resemble Israelite prophets (vv. 5–6) who were traditionally killed in Jerusalem (Matt 23:37; Luke 13:33–34), and "the great

---

54. Cf. Thomas, *Apocalypse*, 334; Koester, *Revelation*, 500; Waddell, *Spirit of the Book*, 181.

55. Cf. Beale, *Book of Revelation*, 588.

56. Koester, *Revelation*, 509, 510–11.

57. Cf. Koester, *Revelation*, 500, 509–10; Aune, *Revelation 6–16*, 622. The definite articles suggest that the audience would know the identity of the square and city referred to (Aune, *Revelation 6–16*, 580, 618). There is probably a reference to Ps 79:2, although in that case the exposure of the bodies reads more like the ordinary result of warfare, as in Rev 19:21, than a specific act of dishonor (cf. Beale, *Book of Revelation*, 595).

58. Cf. Thomas, *Apocalypse*, 337–38. As Koester reports, such dishonoring of martyrs was common in later Christian accounts (Koester, *Revelation*, 501–2). The description of the festivities would remind the audience of the Roman festival of Saturnalia (ibid., 502; cf. Aune, *Revelation 6–16*, 623) or possibly the celebations after the downfall of Haman and the deliverance of the Jews leading to the festival of Purim in Esth 9:22 (cf. Bauckham, *Climax of Prophecy*, 281–82). Beale interprets this figuratively as referring to persecution driving the church underground (Beale, *Book of Revelation*, 590–91).

59. Cf. Beale, *Book of Revelation*, 596.

60. Cf. Waddell, *Spirit of the Book*, 180.

city" where their bodies lie "is spiritually⁶¹ called Sodom and Egypt" (calling to mind Isa 1:10 in context) and then described as the place "where also their Lord was crucified" (v. 8).⁶² The "spiritual" language suggests that it takes spiritual discernment to see this reality.

However, the phrase "the great city," while once used of Jerusalem by Jeremiah (Jer 22:8), was originally used prophetically of Nineveh (Jonah 1:2; 3:2; 4:11),⁶³ is later applied to Babylon, traditionally Jerusalem's enemy and conqueror,⁶⁴ and even here seems to be an international city (v. 9).⁶⁵ And while Jesus' crucifixion took place outside Jerusalem and was instigated by the Jewish temple authorities, Jerusalem remained part of the Roman Empire, and it was ultimately the Roman authorities who killed Jesus.⁶⁶ The allusion to Sodom underlines the inhospitable nature of the city's refusal to let the witnesses be properly buried as Sodom's sin was in part a refusal of hospitality to Lot's two angelic visitors (Gen 19:5–8).⁶⁷

> **And after the three and a half days a spirit of life from God entered into them, and they stood up on their feet, and great fear fell on those watching this. (Rev 11:11)**

The celebration by the beast and his popular following (parallel to the three-and-a-half years of oppression of the holy city) turns sour when the two prophets are resurrected. The listeners may well be reminded of Ezekiel's prophecy of the resurrection of Israel (Ezek 37:1–14). Here Ezekiel sees Israel as a field of dry bones but prophetically speaks to them such that they come to life because "breath" enters them and they "stood up on their feet—a vast army" (Ezek 37:10). This is interpreted as signifying the life of the Spirit indwelling the resurrected Israelites (Ezek 37:13–14).⁶⁸ The two prophets in some way stand for Israel, dead and risen again to life (see also Ps 79:1–3).

> **And they heard a loud voice from heaven that said to them, "Come up here." And they went up to heaven in the cloud, and their enemies watched them. (Rev 11:12)**

---

61. Greek πνευματικῶς [*pneumatikōs*]. Cf. Thomas, *Apocalypse*, 336; Waddell, *Spirit of the Book*, 182–83; Aune, *Revelation 6–16*, 581, 620 (Aune refers to "charismatic exegesis of the OT").

62. Cf. Leithart, *Revelation 1–11*, 433; Mayo, *Those Who Call Themselves Jews*, 137–41. Mayo argues that John is attacking Jews for persecuting Christians here as in 2:9 and 3:9, but as a Jewish prophet (ibid., 141).

63. Cf. Leithart, *Revelation 12–22*, 210–11.

64. Cf. Thomas, *Apocalypse*, 336.

65. Thomas, *Apocalypse*, 336–37; cf. Koester, *Revelation*, 500; Aune, *Revelation 6–16*, 587, 619–621; Beale, *Book of Revelation*, 568–70, 591–94; Bauckham, *Climax of Prophecy*, 172; Waddell, *Spirit of the Book*, 181–83.

66. Cf. Koester, *Revelation*, 506.

67. Cf. Koester, *Revelation*, 500–1.

68. Cf. Koester, *Revelation*, 502; Beale, *Book of Revelation*, 597; Waddell, *Spirit of the Book*, 184–85. Perhaps Jesus' breathing into his disciples after the resurrection (John 20:22) may be seen as fulfilling this promise and reviving a core of a new Israel (cf. Dumbrell, *End of the Beginning*, 155).

These events also clearly remind John's audience of Jesus' crucifixion, his resurrection after three days and his ascension in a cloud (Acts 1:11)[69] and perhaps the future events of their own bodily resurrection and ascension (1 Thess 4:14–17). In fact, this could be John's "apocalyptic" way of describing the *Parousia*; if so, we must note that it is a public event, not some kind of "secret rapture."[70]

They might also think of the Roman mythology of the deification of the emperor on death, which involved his ascent to heaven, often symbolized by an eagle at his funeral and sometimes testified to by witnesses.[71] Ironically, here it is Rome's *victims* who ascend to heaven.[72] The public nature of this ascension is hard to imagine, but it recalls the ascension of Elijah (2 Kgs 2), as well as that of Jesus, before eyewitnesses. John may be thinking of the public executions of Christian martyrs whose demeanour in dying demonstrated their spiritual ascension to Jesus and thus helped turn others to Christ. As Mayo points out, John is also combining "two traditions" from the Hebrew prophets and Jesus, as part of his overall theology of the people of God as a new spiritual Israel.[73]

> **And in that hour there was a large earthquake and a tenth of the city fell and seven thousand named people were killed and the rest became afraid and gave glory to the God of heaven.[74] (Rev 11:13)**

If this is the same city as mentioned in verse 2 ("the holy city") and verse 8 ("the great city"), the statistics here are credible for first-century Jerusalem, that is a population of 70,000.[75] But something remarkable is happening here. Until now, in spite of the huge disasters inflicted on the world by God under the trumpets, the people have resisted God's judgment and refused to repent (9:20–21). But now their resistance starts to crack; the survivors this time "became afraid and gave glory to the God of heaven" (v. 13), the response later called for in 14:7.

Whether this means they truly repented, as Bauckham argues convincingly, based on the similarity of this language with its use elsewhere in the text,[76] or represents only

---

69. Cf. Beale, *Book of Revelation*, 594–95, 599–600; Bauckham, *Climax of Prophecy*, 280; Pattemore, *People of God*, 164.

70. Cf. Aune, *Revelation 6–16*, 624; Waddell, *Spirit of the Book*, 186; Hendriksen, *More Than Conquerors*, 131. Aune calls this "a *rapture* story" because the witnesses ascend bodily to heaven (Aune, *Revelation 6–16*, 625, emphasis in the original). But Beale disagrees (Beale, *Book of Revelation*, 598–99, 601).

71. Aune, *Revelation 6–16*, 627.

72. Cf. Koester, *Revelation*, 511.

73. Mayo, *Those Who Call Themselves Jews*, 136–37.

74. On the phrase "the God of heaven," see Aune, *Revelation 6–16*, 629.

75. Cf. Koester, *Revelation*, 504; Aune, *Revelation 6–16*, 628; Beale, *Book of Revelation*, 602–3. Ezek 38:19 also predicts a great earthquake in Israel associated with the invasion by Gog.

76. Bauckham, *Climax of Prophecy*, 278–79.

a reaction of fear, it stands in contrast to that earlier failure.[77] It seems that the witness of the two prophets, the supernatural power they exhibited, their humiliating death, and triumphant resurrection has achieved something that an earthquake alone could not.

There is another significant detail here. We have noticed repeated references to the Elijah story in this episode. Hearers who knew this story well would remember that after Elijah's triumph over the prophets of Baal, he fled in fear from Jezebel, and complained to God that "I am the only one left, and now they are trying to kill me too" (1 Kgs 19:14). But God corrected the despondent prophet, saying, "I will reserve seven thousand in Israel—all whose knees have not bowed down to Baal and whose mouths have not kissed him" (1 Kgs 19:18). Seven thousand were faithful to God in spite of Queen Jezebel's promotion of Baal worship; the rest of Israel fell into line with the false prophets. Now in Revelation 11, seven thousand are killed and the rest respond to God. It's a kind of reversal. The two prophets (Elijah-like figures) have achieved a breakthrough greater than Elijah, against the same forces that Jezebel represented (as in 2:20), the same forces that had triumphed in 9:20–21 and apparently in 11:7–10 with the killing of the prophets of God.[78]

> **The second woe has gone. Behold the third woe is coming soon. (Rev 11:14)**

John's audience are still called to count down the events. The second woe had begun in 9:13. Now they are awaiting the third.

Interpreting the Two Witnesses

So what are we to make of this episode so far? What events in history, if any, is it telling us about? As far as I can see, there are three main possibilities. The first possibility is that John is retelling or speaking of an event (or series of events) in his own time, whether in the immediate past or immediate future. For example, it might refer to the period of the Roman-Jewish war when Jerusalem and its temple were under

---

77. Cf. Koester, *Revelation*, 504, 511–12; Aune, *Revelation 6–16*, 628–29; Leithart, *Revelation 1–11*, 434; Waddell, *Spirit of the Book*, 187–88; Beale, *Book of Revelation*, 597–98, 603–8, 751–54. Beale argues for an unbelieving fear in this case, partly because "a conversion at the time of historical consummation is an idea found nowhere else in the Apocalypse, one that contradicts the basic thought that those to be redeemed are a 'limited group' or remnant . . . " (ibid., 607). He bases this partly on a comparison with other events, such as the experience of Nebuchadnezzar in Daniel 4, which led to him saying, "I . . . praise and exalt and glorify the King of heaven" (Dan 4:37), and yet there is no evidence of him undergoing "true conversion to the faith of Israel" (Beale, *Book of Revelation*, 603). Rather, he is forced to acknowledge God's sovereignty but does not give up his idols. But all these points could be challenged. For instance, is this passage really about "the time of historical consummation" as Beale asserts? Second, in many places, Revelation does expect masses of Gentiles to be redeemed (5:9; 7:9; 15:4; 21:16–17, 24; 22:2). And third, while Nebuchadnezzar (and parallel cases such as the sailors and Ninevites in Jonah) probably were not fully "converted" in the NT sense, something significant apparently happened to them (e.g., Dan 5:21–22).

78. Cf. Thomas, *Apocalypse*, 341–42; Bauckham, *Climax of Prophecy*, 282–83; Waddell, *Spirit of the Book*, 187.

attack and "trampled on." The two prophetic witnesses were perhaps Peter and Paul (who were martyred under Roman Emperor Nero in AD 64)[79] or the two Jameses. James, the brother of John and son of Zebedee, was killed under the orders of one of the Herods (Acts 12:1–2). James, the brother of Jesus, who became the leader of the church in Jerusalem (Acts 12:17; 15:13; 21:18), was murdered by the anti-Christian Jews during a period between two Roman governors (AD 63). His murder was apparently a major factor leading to the rebellion against Rome, which in turn led to the destruction of the second temple.

However, there is no evidence that anything quite like the events described in Revelation 11 happened during this time, either in Jerusalem or Rome. Perhaps the nearest event is the slaying of the priests Ananus and Joshua in Jerusalem by the Idumeans, during the revolt against Rome, since their bodies were left unburied[80] Another suggestion is that they are John the Baptist and Jesus.[81]

The second possibility is that John is foretelling events that will literally happen in the future, his future and ours, since nothing like this has happened since. The two prophets are two future Christian prophets, or even Elijah and Moses[82] literally returning from heaven, since Elijah ascended there without dying, Moses' body was never found, and both conversed with Jesus on the mount of transfiguration.[83] Sometimes it is suggested that the ministry and subsequent death of the witnesses will be seen by an international audience via satellite television.[84]

This view implies a literal third temple, which is not envisaged anywhere else in Revelation and seems contradictory to the new covenant.[85] But it's impossible to disprove. Both of these readings envisage a literal temple building (vv. 1–2). A variation sees the two witnesses as Moses and Elijah in their original context as witnesses to the Messianic promise, representing the Law and the Prophets (as in John 5:39, 46). This is argued by Italian commentator Eugenio Corsini,[86] who sees Revelation as building up towards the first coming of Jesus and the Cross, rather than his second coming.

---

79. Cf. Beale, *Book of Revelation*, 583.

80. Cf. Josephus, "War of the Jews" 4.5.314–325. However, they were not Christians and were not physically resurrected as Revelation 11 narrates. Some commentators see this passage as derived from an earlier prophecy from the time of the Jewish revolt, based partly on Josephus' description of many false prophets being active then (cf. Koester, *Revelation*, 441; Aune, *Revelation 6–16*, 593–96, 598; cf. Beale, *Book of Revelation*, 556).

81. All these views are summarized in Aune, *Revelation 6–16*, 601–2. See also Leithart, *Revelation 1–11*, 429.

82. The prophets might also be Elijah and Enoch since neither of them died and some Jewish literature expected them to return in the end; this was the most common view in Christian exegesis from the late second century (cf. Aune, *Revelation 6–16*, 588–89, 599, 610). Victorinus, however, takes them to be Elijah and Jeremiah (Victorinus, *Commentary*, ANF 7:354).

83. Cf. Aune, *Revelation 6–16*, 600.

84. E.g., Walvoord, *Revelation*, 181.

85. Cf. Beale, *Book of Revelation*, 560.

86. *Apocalypse*, 28–31, 194–98; compare Moloney, *Apocalypse of John*, 158.

The third possibility is more spiritual in nature. It understands the temple language as referring to the church, in line with the imagery of Revelation 1–3, and the trampling as referring to persecution. The "holy city" thus refers to the church which is being built by Christ (as promised in Matt 16:18) and the "great city" is the "city" of this world which is always hostile to God.[87] The language is seen as apocalyptic, not literal,[88] showing the martyrdom of the believers and their ultimate triumph,[89] even leading to the conversion of their persecutors.[90] As the ancient Christian leader Tertullian remarked, "the blood of the martyrs is seed."[91] The witnesses stand for the whole faithful anointed church, which is called to be a prophetic anointed witness,[92] fulfilling Ezekiel's famous "dry bones" prophecy of Israel as noted earlier, or perhaps the combined witness of Jewish and Gentile Christians.[93]

This may sound unlikely at first, but is supported by the parallels with Zechariah 4, the reference to lampstands as local churches in 1:20, and the image of believers as anointed witnesses to Christ (see Acts 1:8), so it is a natural reading for Pentecostals.[94] If this reading is accepted, the "three-and-a-half years" perhaps stands for the complete church age, during which believers undergo persecution, bear faithful witness, and ultimately "conquer."[95] Whatever approach one takes to this passage, it certainly represents a significant development in the narrative of Revelation.

---

87. Augustine developed these concepts in his classic, *City of God*.

88. Bauckham calls it "a kind of parable" (Bauckham, *Climax of Prophecy*, 273).

89. Cf. Beale, *Book of Revelation*, 561, 566.

90. This conclusion suggests that Beale is mistaken in suggesting that "the main ministry of the witnesses is to pronounce judgment" (Beale, *Book of Revelation*, 600). They do pronounce, even execute, judgment, but like all witnesses of Jesus, their main purpose is redemptive or evangelistic.

91. More specifically, "The oftener we are mown down by you; the more in number we grow; *the blood of Christians is seed*" (Tertullian, "Apology," *ANF* 3:55). There may also be an ironic reference to the day of Pentecost in the reference to "(those) from the peoples and tribes and languages and nations" (see Acts 2:5–11).

92. Cf. Acts 1:8 and 2:17–18, important Pentecostal passages. Cf. Beale, *Book of Revelation*, 574–75; Bauckham, *Climax of Prophecy*, 170–71. As Waddell comments, "as the primary location in which the Spirit operates, the church plays a vital role in the accomplishment of the Lamb's victory" (Waddell, *Spirit of the Book*, 177).

93. Cf. Leithart, *Revelation 1–11*, 432.

94. Cf. Thomas, *Apocalypse*, 331; Waddell, *Spirit of the Book*, 174–77; Koester, *Revelation*, 439–40, 497–98, 505–6; Aune, *Revelation 6–16*, 602–3, 631; Mayo, *Those Who Call Themselves Jews*, 133–35. There are obvious parallels between this story and the story of Jesus' earthly witness, showing how Jesus' followers must follow in his pathway (Bauckham, *Climax of Prophecy*, 171–72)

95. Cf. Beale, *Book of Revelation*, 567, 572–73; Hendriksen, *More Than Conquerors*, 143.

11:15–19 The Triumph of the Kingdom

> **And the seventh angel sounded (his trumpet), and there were loud voices in heaven, saying, "The kingdom of the world has become (the kingdom) of our Lord and of his Messiah, and he will reign forever and ever." (Rev 11:15)**

We now come to a major climactic event in the story.[96] Hearers of the text are anticipating a "third woe" (v. 14) and the seventh trumpet when "the secret plan of God will be accomplished" (10:7). Finally, we hear a major announcement of the triumph of God's kingdom, a major breakthrough in the struggle that has been underway since chapter 6.

The hearers may well be reminded of the seventh day of the campaign against Jericho, when the Israelites marched around the city seven times after six days of marching and trumpet blowing with no discernible impact. However, the seventh time was climaxed with a trumpet blast, and a great shout that led to the collapse of the wall and the successful taking of the city (Josh 6:1–20).[97] Here in Revelation 11, we also hear of a seventh trumpet and a loud shout, and the downfall of the hostile kingdom of this world,[98] leading to its capture by God and the Messiah, with echoes of Psalm 2:2.

The audience might also recall Daniel 2:44, where, in the climax to the prophecy of successive kingdoms, "the God of heaven will set up a kingdom that will never be destroyed, nor will it be left to another people. It will crush all those kingdoms and bring them to an end, but it will itself endure forever" (see also Dan 7:14; 2 Sam 7:13; Isa 9:7). As Beale argues, "the consummated fulfillment of the long-awaited messianic kingdom prophesied in the OT finally has come to pass."[99]

> **And the twenty-four elders sitting on their thrones before God fell on their faces and worshiped God, saying, "We give you thanks, Lord God Almighty, the One who is and who was, because you have taken your great power and reigned." (Rev 11:16–17)**

The elders give thanks to God (in a way that functions as model for the churches' worship)[100] for this great victory. Archer notes that this is the only place where language of thanksgiving (Greek *eucharistoumen*, "we give thanks") is explicitly

---

96. Aune calls it "an apparently anticlimactic continuation of 8:1–9:21" (Aune, *Revelation 6–16*, 635). It could be anticlimactic if the hearers are expecting a massive disaster, but not if one keeps an eye on the goal of the narrative.

97. Cf. Beale, *Book of Revelation*, 619. The seventh trumpet could also suggest "the end of the week of history" (ibid., 620). For other allusions here, see ibid., 620.

98. Cf. John 12:31; Col 1:13; Dan 2:44; see also Koester, *Revelation*, 513–14.

99. Beale, *Book of Revelation*, 611.

100. Cf. Koester, *Revelation*, 517; Aune, *Revelation 6–16*, 640–42; Archer, *Worship in the Apocalypse*, 213–15.

used in Revelation.[101] The prayer of thanksgiving is spelled out in several stanzas. First, "you have taken your great power and reigned" (v. 17); that is the advent of God's kingdom.[102] This is the reason for thanksgiving to the eternal God. The earlier description of God as "the One who is and who was, and who is coming" (1:4, 8; 4:8) is modified to "the One who is and who was, because you have taken your great power and reigned."[103] The phrasing indicates a decisive advance in God's kingdom,[104] as anticipated in the Psalms (see Pss 93:1; 96:10–13; 98:11–9). I emphasize this by translating *eilēphas* as "taken," not "received."[105]

The expression of praise parodies Greco-Roman worship of their deities and deified emperors.[106] The fact that this worship is initiated by the twenty-four elders is signficiant too, if one accepts my earlier assertion that they are glorified human forerunners of the believers in the first-century churches. They would be especially grateful for this outcome, for which they had personally given their lives.

And the nations were enraged and your rage came . . . (Rev 11:18a)

The second stanza of the elders' hymn fulfills the threat of 6:16, "the great day of their wrath has come." The language also recalls Psalm 2, a psalm often referred to in Revelation. In this psalm, "the nations conspire and the peoples plot in vain . . . against the Lord and against his anointed . . . " as they try to break free from their rule (vv. 1–3), but "the one enthroned in heaven laughs . . . He rebukes them in his anger and terrifies them in his wrath" (vv. 4–5).[107] The psalm goes on to promise the Messiah as God's Son, "Ask me, and I will make the nations your inheritance, the ends of the earth your possession" (v. 8) and "you will break them with a rod of iron" (v. 9). These are themes central to the plot of Revelation; as we have noted before, the redemption of the nations is God's core goal in Revelation.[108]

. . . and the time for the dead to be judged and to give reward to your slaves the prophets, and to the saints, and those who fear your name,[109] the small and the great, and to destroy those who are destroying the earth. (Rev 11:18b)

---

101. Archer, *Worship in the Apocalypse*, 214.
102. Cf. Aune, *Revelation 6–16*, 646–47.
103. Cf. Beale, *Book of Revelation*, 613.
104. Cf. Beale, *Book of Revelation*, 613–14.
105. Following the NIV; cf. Aune, *Revelation 6–16*, 643.
106. Cf. Koester, *Revelation*, 518, 520.
107. Cf. Koester, *Revelation*, 514; Leithart, *Revelation 12–22*, 7.
108. Cf. Koester, *Revelation*, 519.
109. Potentially three groups though in all likelihood only two or even just one; that is, we have here three ways of describing God's people; cf. Thomas, *Apocalypse*, 348–49; Beale, *Book of Revelation*, 616–17.

This actual event seems to be later in the story (20:12–15),[110] unless John is recapitulating his climax repeatedly in his narrative.[111] Otherwise the struggle is not over yet, but certainly the outcome is not in doubt. The hearers are warned of the risk they take, if they reject the vision and the gospel message. They are stirred to be among the class of those who "fear your name" and are rewarded.[112] Otherwise this will indeed be a "woe" to them.[113]

Today's readers may be particularly challenged by the fate of "those who are destroying the earth," in view of today's stronger ecological consciousness, and they can appeal to the conservation elements in the Torah, such as the sabbath year,[114] though the original meaning here may refer more to moral destruction of *people*.[115] As Dunham argues, John is pointing to a distinction between lives that are destructive to the earth and those that "treat the earth with love and respect."[116]

> **And the temple of God in heaven was opened, and the ark of his covenant was visible in his temple ... (Rev 11:19a)**[117]

This climactic victory of God's kingdom is now visualized in a special way. The temple being "opened" would itself be seen as a significant sign by John's audience, though not necessarily a positive one.[118] But the ark of the covenant was a very special symbol of God's presence and favor under the old covenant. It was literally carried from place to place in the journey from Mount Sinai to the promised land. It went before Israel as they journeyed (Num 10:33–36), and as they crossed the flooded Jordan river. The priests carrying the ark literally stood in the middle of the dammed-up river, while the Israelites crossed over (Josh 3–4).

The ark had an interesting and varied history after that. It was hidden behind the heavy curtain in the Most Holy Place in the sacred tent (Exod 40:3). It was temporarily captured by the Philistines after the people of Israel tried to use it as a kind of magical weapon (1 Sam 4–6). It was eventually brought to Jerusalem by King David, after one of his men was killed for touching it on the first attempt (2 Sam 6), and it was finally parked in the Solomonic temple (1 Kgs 8:1–21). But during the Babylonian invasion

---

110. Cf. Koester, *Revelation*, 521.

111. Beale writes, "The seventh trumpet, like the seventh seal and the seventh bowl, narrates the very end of history" (Beale, *Book of Revelation*, 611).

112. Cf. Thomas, *Apocalypse*, 348; Koester, *Revelation*, 521; Aune, *Revelation 6–16*, 644–45; Beale, *Book of Revelation*, 615; Leithart, *Revelation 1–11*, 436.

113. Cf. Beale, *Book of Revelation*, 610.

114. Cf. Howard-Brook and Gwyther, *Unveiling Empire*, 212–13.

115. Cf. Aune, *Revelation 6–16*, 645–46; Koester, *Revelation*, 516–17; Beale, *Book of Revelation*, 615–16.

116. Dunham, "Ecological Violence," 105.

117. As Aune argues, this verse also serves to introduce the events of ch. 12 (Aune, *Revelation 6–16*, 661–62). There were no chapter or verse divisions in the original manuscript.

118. Cf. Aune, *Revelation 6–16*, 676–77.

and destruction of that first temple, the ark was presumably captured[119] and never found again. The second temple had no ark, a potentially fatal flaw,[120] though there were legends promising its eventual return (2 Macc 2:7).[121] So the vision of the ark in heaven would bring great encouragement to John's audience, signifying perhaps the final return from exile and restoration of God's people, and reminding them of the tearing of the temple curtain when Jesus died.[122]

> ... **and there was lightning and noise and thunder and an earthquake and large hail. (Rev 11:19b)**

These are signs of a great theophany reminiscent of Mount Sinai (Exod 19:16–19) and other parts of John's vision (Rev 4:5; 8:5). Victory is at hand! The kingdom of God has arrived effectively, as a result of the empowered witness of his prophetic people.

---

119. This is not specifically mentioned, but it seems that everyone drew this conclusion (Aune, *Revelation 6–16*, 678).

120. For example, when the Roman general Pompey breached Jewish law by entering the "holy of holies" in 63 BC, he saw "in that temple the golden table, the holy candlestick, and the pouring vessels, and a great quantity of spices" but no statue of a god nor the ark of the covenant (Josephus, "Antiquities" 4:72).

121. Cf. Koester, *Revelation*, 541; Aune, *Revelation 6–16*, 678; Stramara, *God's Timetable*, 64.

122. Cf. Beale, *Book of Revelation*, 619; Leithart, *Revelation 1–11*, 437; Corsini, *Apocalypse*, 203–5.

Revelation Chapter 12

Let's review again. The seven seals have been opened. The seven angels have blown their trumpets. The earth has been devastated by disasters of all kinds. After stubborn resistance by the ungodly world, the testimony and martyrdom of the witnesses has finally achieved "a crack in the devil's armor." Then, with the final trumpet, the ungodly kingdom has fallen, and God's kingdom has triumphed. Is this the end of the story? Apparently not, because we are only half-way through in terms of numbers of chapters. Either John is constantly retelling the same sequence of events leading up to the final judgment, recapitulating the story, or he is about to show us more of how this victory is worked out in time. Let's consider these possibilities.

Recapitulation? This reading notes parallels between the events narrated in the vision, all apparently climaxing in the final judgment, and concludes that they are parallel accounts; that is, John takes us to the final judgment and then retells the same story from another perspective. The oldest existing commentary on Revelation, by Victorinus, for example, says, "frequently the Holy Spirit, when He has traversed even to the end of the last times, returns again to the same times, and fills up what He had *before* failed to say."[1] The best way to make this clear is by a table of events.

---

1. Victorinus, *Commentary*, ANF 7:352 (emphasis in the original).

Seals	Trumpets	Beast sequence	Bowls	Rev 20 events
1. Conquest	1. Disaster to earth	Fall of dragon	1. Plague of sores	Imprisonment of dragon
2. War	2. Disaster to seas	Emergence of sea beast	2. Sea to blood	First resurrection
3. Famine	3. Disaster to waters	Emergence of land beast	3. Rivers and springs to blood (because of martyrdoms)	Millennial reign of martyrs
4. Plagues	4. Disaster to heavens	Martyrdoms	4. Sun scorching	Release of Satan
5. Martyrdoms	5. Locust plague	Kingdom fightback	5. Darkness	Final battle and defeat of the devil
6. Cosmic Shaking	6. Invasion	Three angels	6. Gathering for battle	*Final judgement*
Imminent wrath	Martyrdoms	*Threat of final wrath*	7. Massive collapse of cities	*Lake of fire for the ungodly*
7. Pause	7. Kingdom victory		Fall of Babylon	
	Imminent wrath		Defeat of the beasts and *thrown into lake of fire*	

Each of these series of events contains a significant shaking and downfall of ungodly empires, finishes with the wrath and judgment of God, and contains a significant reference to martyrdom.[2] Many of them finish with a big earthquake (often accompanied by other big turbulence), either in heaven or on earth, especially the three sevens: 6:12 in the sixth seal; 8:5 after the seventh seal; 11:29 after the seventh trumpet; 16:18 in the seventh bowl.[3]

However, while the parallels here are clear, there is also a sense of intensification, such as the move from the one-third destructions in the trumpet sequence to the total destruction in the bowls sequence. Also some of the later sequences clearly depend on the earlier ones; for example, the millennial sequence depends on the martyrs having been put to death earlier, as they are now raised again to reign (20:4). Similarly, the judgement in the bowls is predicated on the previous murder of God's saints and prophets (16:6). Hence, I read this narrative more like a good thriller today: the events come close to resolution, but then, the story-teller surprises the readers with further delays and more potential climaxes.[4] So then, wrath is anticipated and to some degree experienced, but the end is not yet.[5]

---

2. Cf. Hendriksen, *More Than Conquerors*, 16–22. For a helpful discussion and setting out of the parallels between the trumpets, bowls, and Exodus plagues, see Beale, *Book of Revelation*, 808–12.

3. Cf. Filho, "Apocalypse of John," 218–19.

4. Cf. Herms, *Apocalypse for the Church*, 158.

5. See Thomas' reading of this section of Revelation in Thomas, *Apocalypse*, 352.

Koester provides another structural analysis, suggesting that Revelation 12 (or more precisely the opening of the ark in 11:19) literally introduces the second part of Revelation, in which "the conflict between the Creator and the destroyers of the earth will be the dominant theme . . . The author successively introduces Satan, the beast and false prophet, and finally the whore. Then he describes the defeat of each one in reverse order."[6]

Beale proposes a sevenfold structure for 12:1—15:4 based on what is "seen"[7] and suggests that the vision of chapters 12 and following "goes into the deeper dimension of the spiritual conflict between the church and the world." Chapter 12 specifically "reveals that the devil himself is the deeper source of evil."[8]

12:1–17 The Fall of the Dragon

Chapter 11 finishes with the opening of the temple in heaven and the sight of the ark of the covenant there. Chapter 12 opens with two visual signs in heaven, opposite in imagery and spiritual significance.[9] As I have said before, these chapter divisions were not found in the original Greek text, so we need to read over them as much as possible, while using them as a convenient way of managing the story.[10] In this case, it is appropriate to visualize these signs as related to the ark just made visible in heaven.[11]

> **And a great sign was seen in heaven, a woman clothed with the sun, and the moon under her feet, and a crown of twelve stars on her head . . . (Rev 12:1)**

This is the first mention of a heavenly sign in the text, though the language of signification is found at the outset (1:1) and various signs or images are interpreted from the early part of the narrative (e.g., 1:20). If this is a sign, readers must ask, what is it a sign of?[12] Is it is portent of a coming event or a symbol of an important reality? It is also only the second time a female character has appeared in the book. The first female, Jezebel (2:20), was a negative human character, but this (unnamed) woman is a cosmic figure, even a "queen of the cosmos"[13] with cosmic dominion, "the moon under her feet."[14]

---

6. Koester, *Revelation*, 523; the full discussion continues to page 525; cf. Beale, *Book of Revelation*, 623.

7. Beale, *Book of Revelation*, 621–22.

8. Beale, *Book of Revelation*, 622; cf. Hendriksen, *More Than Conquerors*, 134. For an alternative structural analysis of chapters 1–15/16, see Leithart, *Revelation 12–22*, 7–10.

9. On the parallels here, see Thomas, *Apocalypse*, 352–53.

10. According to Aune, for example, "a careful analysis of both internal structural features and analogous external literary forms . . . strongly suggests that 11:19 functions both as an introduction to 12:1–7 and as a conclusion to 11:15–18" (Aune, *Revelation 6–16*, 661). He considers that the introductory function is primary (ibid., 661–62). Cf. Beale, *Book of Revelation*, 621.

11. Cf. Leithart, *Revelation 12–22*, 3–4. The opened temple and visible ark refers hearers to the annual Day of Atonement in Israel, the only time when the high priest entered the Most Holy Place where the ark was located.

12. Cf. Koester, *Revelation*, 541–52.

13. Aune, *Revelation 6–16*, 680.

14. As Thomas comments, she dwarfs the super-angel of chapter 10 (Thomas, *Apocalypse*, 353).

But who or what is she? Astute listeners to the text would remember the dreams of the young Joseph in Genesis 37, especially the one where "the sun and moon and eleven stars were bowing down to me" (Gen 37:9), understood as meaning that his parents and brothers would bow down to him (Gen 37:10). So clearly this woman in some way represents Israel with its twelve tribes, as has been mentioned in 7:4–8.[15] However, the twelve stars may also remind the audience of the initial vision of Christ holding the seven stars, representing the "angels" of the seven Asian churches,[16] in which case she also represents the church somehow.

> ... and she was pregnant, and cried out in birthpains and the agony of gving birth ... (Rev 12:2)

Both Jezebel and this woman have children (2:23; 12:2, 4–5, 17). This probably alludes to Genesis 3:15–16, which foretells conflict between the seed of the woman and the seed of the serpent, and painful childbirth on Eve's part. The crying out would also remind the audience of other positive figures who also "cry out" (Greek *krazei*) in Revelation: the martyrs (6:10), an angel (7:2), the multitude before the throne (7:10), and the super-angel of 10:3.[17] The language used of her "birthpains" (Greek *basanizomenē tekein*, literally "being tormented to give birth") might remind the audience of similar language used of the pain inflicted by the locusts-cum-scorpions in 9:5.[18]

Coming straight after the opening of heaven and the appearance of the ark of the covenant, this is potentially an exciting development, especially if hearers anticipate the fulfillment of the ancient promise about the seed of the woman in Genesis 3:15, which I will discuss below.

Many hearers would also recall the words of Isaiah 66:7–11:[19]

> Before she goes into labor, she gives birth;
>
> before the pains come upon her, she delivers a son ...
>
> No sooner is Zion in labor
>
> than she gives birth to her children ...
>
> Rejoice with Jerusalem and be glad for her,
>
> all you who love her ...
>
> For you will nurse and be satisfied at her comforting breasts

Then there is Isaiah 54:1:

---

15. Cf. Thomas, *Apocalypse*, 354; Beale, *Book of Revelation*, 625–28. However, there may be a secondary contrasting reference to the cult of the goddess Roma associated with the emperor cult (Caird, *Revelation*, 148).

16. Cf. Johnson, *Pneumatic Discernment*, 275.

17. Thomas, *Apocalypse*, 355.

18. Beale argues therefore that the pain here is not that of childbirth as such, but that of persecution of the faithful people of God represented by the woman (Beale, *Book of Revelation*, 629).

19. Cf. Beale, *Book of Revelation*, 641.

> Sing, barren woman,
>
> you who never bore a child;
>
> burst into song, shout for joy,
>
> you who never were in labor;
>
> because more are the children of the desolate woman
>
> than of her who has a husband . . .

These are both great promises of restored Israel, particularly Jerusalem, and hearers of Revelation would have great expectations as they hear this language.[20] But first comes another struggle.

> . . . and another sign was seen in heaven, and behold a great fiery red[21] dragon, which had seven heads and ten horns, and on his heads seven diadems, and his tail dragged a third of the stars of heaven down, and threw them onto the earth. (Rev 12:3–4a)

Both of these amazing signs have clear astrological references in keeping with the aforementioned sun, moon, stars (including twelve stars, suggesting the zodiac), and sky.[22] This is a key feature of Revelation and certainly gives the whole story a cosmic edge. The dragon is described in huge terms, somewhat like the woman, and also the super-angel of chapter 10. This suggests that big issues are in play. It would be somewhat threatening but also awesome to the audience. The dragon's seven heads perhaps have an ambiguous connotation: the Lamb has seven horns, so is the dragon's seven-ness an implicit challenge to the Lamb?[23]

Its ten horns would remind them of the fourth beast in Daniel's vision (Dan 7:7, 20), whose ten horns are explained as representing "ten kings who will come from this kingdom" (Dan 7:24).[24] That beast was clearly violent, dominating, and hostile to God (Dan 7:7, 19), and from it emerged a "little horn" that would oppress the "holy people" for a set period: "a time, times and half a time." (Dan 7:25). But in Daniel's vision, this

---

20. Cf. Leithart, *Revelation 12–22*, 26. For a similar passage from the Dead Sea Scrolls, see Aune, *Revelation 6–16*, 682.

21. The dragon's red color would remind the listeners of the red horse whose rider took peace from the earth (6:4). The Greek πυρρὸς [*purros*] is based on *pur*, "fire." Later we hear of "a woman sitting on a scarlet beast" (17:3; using a different Greek word).

22. Cf. Aune, *Revelation 6–16*, 681, 683; Leithart, *Revelation 12–22*, 15–16. Ancient astrology was almost universally recognized in the first century. John is not endorsing horoscopes, but he sees cosmic significance in the movements of heavenly bodies. Cf. Ps 19:1–6; Matt 2:1–2.

23. Cf. Thomas, *Apocalypse*, 356–57; Beale, *Book of Revelation*, 634–35. Thomas interprets the seven as "suggesting . . . the complete and universal nature of the dragon's rule." See also Koester, *Revelation*, 544–45; Aune, *Revelation 6–16*, 683–84. Both the heads and the horns would suggest rulers. Some ancient myths include multi-headed monsters (Aune, *Revelation 6–16*, 685). Leithart reminds us that the total number of heads on Daniel 7's beasts is seven (Leithart, *Revelation 12–22*, 24).

24. Some in the audience might also recall the story in *Bel and the Dragon*, part of the Greek text of Daniel, in which Daniel kills a dragon that the Babylonians had worshiped (Bel and the Dragon, i.e., Dan 14:23–27; cf. Stramara, *God's Timetable*, 39).

horn and the beast would be destroyed when the holy people "possessed the kingdom" (Dan 7:22), apparently because of the coming of "one like a son of man" who was given "authority, glory and sovereign power" (Dan 7:13–14). John has already referred to this in 1:7; his hearers would probably expect that Daniel's beast would be destroyed by Jesus.

But the majesty and power of the dragon are enormous. Its ability to fling a third of the stars to the earth cannot be taken literally, but the imagery is mind-blowing. The audience would recall the powerful destructive tails of the locusts and horses in 9:10, 19, and the fraction (a third) would recall the earlier trumpet plagues (8:7–12). But they would also think again of Daniel and the small horn that "grew until it reached the host of the heavens, and it threw some of the starry host down to the earth and trampled on them" (Dan 8:10).

Are these stars that are dragged out of heaven fallen angels? This could be a reference to the ancient story of such a fall among God's angels in some Jewish apocalyptic literature (see 2 Pet 2:4; 1 Enoch 6–11),[25] but why would the dragon sweep his own followers out of heaven? On the other hand, how could the dragon have power to sweep God's angels down? The third possibility is that the stars stand for the saints, drawing on Daniel 12:3,[26] but this is not how Revelation normally interprets stars, and also has unacceptable theological implications if taken too literally: Can the devil cast down saints out of heaven? Perhaps he could, if God permitted it; the audience in Ephesus might recall the fall Jesus accused them of (2:5). There is no easy answer to this, but certainly this dragon is a match for the woman in terms of the imagery of the text.

> **And the dragon stood in front of the woman who was about to give birth, so that when her child was born he might devour (it). (Rev 12:4b)**

This dragon is indeed threatening to God's plans as embodied in the coming child. The vision of Isaiah (see above) is being challenged, perhaps parallel to the devouring of Zion by Nebuchadnezzar "like a serpent" (Jer 51:34). There is an apparent allusion to the struggle between the serpent and the woman and her childbearing in Genesis 3:15–16.[27] Maybe too, the dragon is trying to shut down God's attack on its kingdom, as predicted in Daniel 7. But the audience would probably also think of the Exodus narrative, especially in the light of references like Ezekiel 29:3 which label Pharaoh as a "great monster" since Pharaoh sought to devour all the male children of Israel (Exod 1:15–22).[28] Interestingly, this story focuses especially on the women in the deliverance of Moses (Exod 2:1–10).

---

25. Cf. Victorinus, *Commentary*, ANF 7:255; Leithart, *Revelation 12–22*, 25. Leithart suggests that John is describing an infestation of second temple Judaism with demonic forces, as implied by Jesus' many demonic encounters in the Synoptic Gospels.

26. Cf. Beale, *Book of Revelation*, 635–37. Beale sees this as a reference to persecution, mainly before Christ's time, and targeting Israel since the stars in verse 1 point to Israel.

27. Cf. Thomas, *Apocalypse*, 358. There is also an allusion to Isa 26:17–27:1 in the Septuagint (cf. Beale, *Book of Revelation*, 632).

28. Cf. Stramara, *God's Timetable*, 68–69; Leithart, *Revelation 12–22*, 23.

Indeed, reading back through the Old Testament in the light of Gen 3:15–16, we can see the serpent constantly trying to destroy the seed of the woman (the ancestors of Christ) in order to prevent his coming.[29]

> **And she gave birth to a male son,[30] who is about to shepherd[31] all the nations with a rod of iron. And her child was forcefully taken up to God and to his throne. (Rev 12:5)[32]**

John now gives us a broad hint of the identity of the child. This is messianic language with a clear reference to Psalm 2 (one of John's favorite intertextual sources); there God declares, "I have installed my king on Zion, my holy mountain" and promises that king, "I will make the nations your inheritance, the ends of the earth your possession. You will break them with a rod of iron" (Ps 2:6, 8, 9). John follows the Septuagint here, using *poimainein* ("shepherd") rather than the Hebrew *tērōēm* ("break"); the "iron rod" still implies a somewhat authoritarian treatment, but the shepherding language modifies it,[33] as has already been mentioned in 2:27 (and see 7:17).[34]

Clearly, then, the dragon has every reason to feel threatened by this birth, if it represents a mighty kingdom that the messiah will rule over, covering "all the nations" (Greek *panta ta ethnē*).[35] Behind this apocalyptic language may be a reference to real events such as that narrated in Matthew 2: the attempt of Herod the Great to eliminate the messiah by destroying all the newborn male infants in and around Bethlehem. Or, as Caird suggests, this is a reference to the Cross as the major struggle that gave birth to the new era of salvation.[36] Probably the whole of Jesus' life is in view, not just his infancy.[37] The text is apparently encapsulating Jesus' earthly life by its beginning and end events;[38] but whatever references to real history or myth may be intended, the dragon is unsuccessful.

---

29. See the detailed survey of OT history in Hendriksen, *More Than Conquerors*, 137–40.

30. Possibly another reference to the "seed" in Gen 3:15 (cf. Thomas, *Apocalypse*, 358–59), but also to Isa 7:14, where Isaiah prophesies, "the Lord himself will give you a sign: The virgin will conceive and give birth to a son, and will call him Immanuel" (cf. Beale, *Book of Revelation*, 631). There are significant verbal parallels to Rev 12 here, with the language of a sign and the birth of a divine son.

31. Greek ποιμαίνειν [*poimainein*], from *poimainō*, "tend like a shepherd, rule." Most translations translate "rule" (NIV, NRSV).

32. Perhaps the male child actually takes his mother's place in heaven (cf. Leithart, *Revelation 12–22*, 13).

33. Cf. Aune, *Revelation 6–16*, 652–53; Beale, *Book of Revelation*, 639–40; Morales, *Shepherd of the Nations*, 87–92.

34. Cf. Thomas, *Apocalypse*, 359; Koester, *Revelation*, 547.

35. A fixed phrase used in Revelation and frequently elsewhere in NT (Aune, *Revelation 6–16*, 688).

36. Caird, *Revelation*, 149–50; cf. Gause, *Revelation*, 167. The Cross is not mentioned here but it is central to the interpretation in verse 11. Cf. Pataki, "Non-combat Myth," 258–63, 267–72.

37. Cf. Thomas, *Apocalypse*, 361; Beale, *Book of Revelation*, 639. But Koester sees the birth of Jesus as the main focus (Koester, *Revelation*, 546).

38. Cf. Koester, *Revelation*, 547; Aune, *Revelation 6–16*, 689.

The fact that Christ was forcefully taken up into heaven might remind the audience of the ascension of the two prophetic witnesses in 11:12. However, the forceful language of the aorist passive of *harpazō* ("caught up" or "taken up") is not like the language used there, or that used of Christ's ascension elsewhere. The only other places in the NT where this occurs are 1 Thessalonians 4:17, in relation to the catching up of the saints at Christ's return, Acts 8:39, where the Spirit "suddenly took Philip away" from the road to Gaza, and 2 Corinthians 12:2, 4, of a man caught up to the third heaven.[39] Here it seems to imply a forceful rescue of Christ from the danger of the dragon's scheme.[40]

> **And the woman fled into the desert, where she had a place prepared by God, so that there they might nourish her one thousand, two hundred and sixty days. (Rev 12:6)**[41]

How can readers make sense of this story? Who is the woman? Who or what is the dragon? What events, if any, is John referring to? How would his audience have understood it?[42]

The woman may be Mary (many Roman Catholic writers assume this)[43] or the church or Zion or Israel or even Eve.[44] The story may be about the Virgin Mary's ongoing struggle with the devil or the restoration of Israel. Most likely the audience would have seen the woman as representing Zion, as in the Isaiah prophecies identified above, understood as the faithful people of God (Israel and the church).[45] Victorinus, for example, says she represents "the ancient Church of fathers, and prophets, and saints, and apostles" (that is, Israel) awaiting the coming of the Messiah as a man.[46] They are symbolized or represented by Mary the mother of the Messiah.[47]

As Thomas comments, "It is as though in the emerging image of the woman clothed with the sun that the promises regarding the messianic seed given to Eve, Israel,

---

39. Cf. Aune, *Revelation 6–16*, 689–90.

40. Cf. Pataki, "Non-combat Myth," 269. Moloney argues that the child is forcefully taken away *from* the woman, who then "falls" from heaven (Moloney, *Apocalypse of John*, 177–178), but this is not the emphasis of the text which sees the child's removal as a positive event and does not explain why the woman then flees into the desert.

41. This confirms that these events are happening on the earth, as opposed to what comes next (Thomas, *Apocalypse*, 360). Beale sees cultic overtones in the idea of a "place prepared for her by God" which he interprets as "God's invisible spiritual sanctuary" (Beale, *Book of Revelation*, 648).

42. For a critique of Futurist interpretations of this passage, see Leithart, *Revelation 12–22*, 14–15.

43. Cf. Koester, *Revelation*, 56; Papandrea, *Wedding of the Lamb*, 110–12.

44. For a historical summary of interpretations, see Koester, *Revelation*, 525–27. For the main alternative views today, see Koester, *Revelation*, 542–43; Mayo, *Those Who Call Themselves Jews*, 152–58; and Aune, *Revelation 6–16*, 680–81, 691. See also Beale, *Book of Revelation*, 628–32. The image of the woman may be a parody of an ancient goddess such as Artemis worshiped in Ephesus (A. Collins, "Feminine Symbolism," 21).

45. Cf. Beale, *Book of Revelation*, 625, 628–30; Mayo, *Those Who Call Themselves Jews*, 155–57. Leithart emphasizes the ongoing labor pains of Israel and the church trying to bring forth the messiah, based on Gal 4:19 (Leithart, *Revelation 12–22*, 26–28).

46. Victorinus, *Commentary*, ANF 7:355.

47. Cf. Mayo, *Those Who Call Themselves Jews*, 153–55.

and Mary converge in this one image."[48] The text also recalls Israel's original experience after leaving Egypt,[49] inviting the audience to think of some kind of "second exodus."

But there is also a clear reference to a very ancient international myth here, the "combat myth," found in varying forms in many ancient and Near Eastern cultures. This myth tells of a threat to order in the world, a threat of chaos, posed by a rebellious god and its defeat by a special man or god.[50] The version that most of John's readers/hearers would probably have known was the one about Leto and Apollo. As Koester explains,

> Greco-Roman sources tell of a woman named Leto,
>
> who was pregnant by Zeus [the chief god of the Greeks].
>
> Her antagonist was Python the dragon, who tried to kill her
>
> in order to prevent her from giving birth. She was rescued by
>
> the north wind, which carried her away to the island of Delos . . .
>
> There she gave birth to Apollo and Artemis, who received
>
> arrows as gifts. Four days later, Apollo pursued the dragon,
>
> soon slaying the monster to avenge his mother.[51]

This myth was used in the first century to justify Roman rule over its empire: Caesar was seen as the savior figure who defeated the chaos monster and restored peace and harmony. Augustus Caesar was the paradigmatic example, but an emperor like Vespasian could similarly claim to be the ultimate peacemaker after a period of chaos in AD 68–69. The Old Testament contains references to this myth, and sometimes interprets creation or Israel's history in such terms, usually with Yahweh himself playing the role of Savior (Exod 15 referring to the Red Sea deliverance; Pss 74:13–14; 89:9–10; Isa 27:1; 51:9–10; Ezek 29:3–5; 32:2–8).[52] In this case, as Beale argues, "John paints pictures in such as manner as to ring bells in the minds of his readers, many of whom were formerly pagan and would have been familiar with some of these myths."[53] This perhaps is to assure them that Jesus fulfills the yearnings of all cultures for salvation.[54]

---

48. Cf. Thomas, *Apocalypse*, 360; Aune, *Revelation 6–16*, 712; Leithart, *Revelation 12–22*, 19–23.

49. Cf. Thomas, *Apocalypse*, 361–63. Thomas claims that "the woman . . . has morphed into the church at this point" (ibid., 363). Egypt was the archetype behind such imagery in the OT as in Ezek 29:3, especially the Septuagint where Pharaoh is called "the great dragon" (cf. Beale, *Book of Revelation*, 632–33).

50. The classic work on this is A. Collins, *Combat Myth in the Book of Revelation*. See extended discussion in Aune, *Revelation 6–16*, 667–74.

51. Koester, *Revelation*, 555; cf. Aune, *Revelation 6–16*, 670–71, 712–13; Edwards, "Rider," 529–33; Paul, *Revelation*, 214; Beasley-Murray, *Revelation*, 192–94; A. Collins, "Feminine Symbolism," 22–23.

52. For a fuller analysis of mythology associated with Revelation 12, see Koester, *Revelation*, 527–30, 555–60; Bauckham, *Climax of Prophecy*, 186–98.

53. Beale, *Book of Revelation*, 634. For discussion of a Dead Sea Scrolls parallel, see ibid., 637–39. Cf. Leithart, *Revelation 12–22*, 16–18; Fekkes, *Isaiah and Prophetic Traditions*, 178–79; Pataki, "Non-combat Myth," 270–72.

54. Cf. Beasley-Murray, *Revelation*, 196; Friesen, *Imperial Cults*, 171–72.

But John apparently goes back to what may be a much more ancient form of this story, found in Genesis 3. In the aftermath of Adam and Eve's disobedience to God at the instigation of the serpent, Yahweh says to the serpent, "And I will put enmity between you and the woman, and between your offspring and hers; he will crush your head, and you will strike his heel" (Gen 3:15). Here we have the same protagonists as in Revelation 12: a woman, a serpent (equivalent to the dragon in Rev 12:9), and a male offspring who will crush the head of his enemy.[55] Thus, no matter what their background, all listeners in the seven churches will "get" the point, *viz.*, the promised deliverer is not Caesar but the Messiah promised in Psalm 2 and other places in Hebrew prophecy, that is, Jesus.[56]

> **And war erupted in heaven, Michael and his angels warring against the dragon. And the dragon fought back with his angels, and he was not strong enough nor was a place found for them any longer in heaven. (Rev 12:7–8)**

The audience's focus is now dragged from Genesis to Daniel. There are heavenly struggles going on behind the earthly ones the audience is facing, and indeed behind the events of verses 1–6.[57] This may be a fresh perspective for the hearers, as up to now, heaven has been seen exclusively as the place of God's throne and worship of God.[58] There is a clear allusion to Daniel 10–11 through the mention of Michael. In that passage, Daniel had been praying and struggling about the future of Israel since the set time for the end of its exile was drawing to a close (Dan 9:2–3). A glorious human (or human-like) figure appeared to him (Dan 10:4–9). This figure was involved in a struggle: "Soon I will return to fight against the prince of Persia, and when I go, the prince of Greece will come" (Dan 10:20). However, "No one supports me against them except Michael, your prince" (Dan 10:21). The Gentile empires that dominate the Jews (Persian and Greek) have their heavenly representatives or "princes," and their opponent is Israel's prince, Michael.[59] He is apparently fighting for the restoration of Israel.

After a period of great persecution, "Michael, the great prince who protects your people, will arise," and "There will be a time of distress such as has not happened from the beginning of nations until then" (Dan 12:1). It seems that John is describing (and interpreting) these developments. Since Michael seems to initiate this war, something must have happened to empower or encourage him to do so.[60] A great struggle in heaven is occurring, which must somehow relate to the future of Israel,

---

55. Cf. Fekkes, *Isaiah and Prophetic Traditions*, 60–61, n. 5. Malina sees all this as referring to primeval events, but this seems to be negated by v. 11, at least (cf. Malina, *Genre and Message*, 55–56).

56. Cf. Beale, *Book of Revelation*, 624–25. Aune argues that the NT contains a Christian combat myth which perhaps gave rise to "the classic idea of the atonement," the view that emphasizes the atonement as a victory over Satan bringing liberation to believers (Aune, *Revelation 6–16*, 669).

57. Cf. Beale, *Book of Revelation*, 650–51.

58. Cf. Thomas, *Apocalypse*, 364; Aune, *Revelation 6–16*, 691–92.

59. Cf. Koester, *Revelation*, 548; Aune, *Revelation 6–16*, 693–94; Leithart, *Revelation 12–22*, 30–31.

60. Hendriksen, *More Than Conquerors*, 141.

represented probably by the woman with her twelve stars. However, the stakes might be even higher, as John regularly applies prophecies related to Israel in a much wider way.[61] But if John is claiming that Daniel 12 is being fulfilled here,[62] the heavenly war must lead to a great time of distress on earth.

> **And the great dragon was thrown down, the ancient serpent, who is called the devil and Satan, who deceives the whole world, he was thrown down onto the earth, and his angels were thrown down with him. (Rev 12:9)**

The dragon is clearly identified with three other names known to John's audience: the ancient serpent, the devil, and Satan.[63] All three names carry significant intertextual and intratextual baggage. The ancient serpent takes the hearers back to the Garden and Genesis 3 (as we saw already).[64] The devil (Greek *diabolos*) would recall 2:10 (where the devil is said to cast believers into prison), the temptations of Jesus (Matt 4:1–11; Luke 4:1–13), and perhaps John 8:44, if the audience was familiar with those texts. And the word Satan reminds them of opposition to the seven churches (2:9, 13, 24; 3:9) and several Old Testament stories, although in the Septuagint translation he is called "the devil" (Greek *ho diabolis*) in these passages.[65] These include David's fateful census as told by the author of 1 Chronicles 21:1, the instigation of Job's testing (Job 1–2), and the accusation against Joshua the high priest in Zechariah 3:1–2.

As well as this, the dragon is identified by his work: he "deceives the whole world" (v. 9), recalling the work of Jezebel in 2:20.[66] So we have here a complete picture of this adversary in all his glory and power, in all his wickedness as well as his limitations.[67] And his personal nature is also stressed; as Leithart says, "Satan is not a power but a conscious, willing, reasoning being" who yet works "through the institutions and structures of social life."[68]

The dragon has suffered a major defeat. He has been thwarted in his plot to devour the messiah, defeated in the heavenly struggle against Michael's forces, and "thrown down to the earth" (v. 9).[69] This does not appear to be a reference to a primeval fall of the devil due to his ambition or pride, sometimes deduced from Isaiah 14 or Ezekiel 28, two passages about the downfall of Babylon and Tyre respectively. Whenever the devil "fell" morally or spiritually, this fall from heaven to earth is attributed by

---

61. See also Beale, *Book of Revelation*, 650–54.
62. And perhaps Dan 2:35; cf. Beale, *Book of Revelation*, 655.
63. Cf. Aune, *Revelation 6–16*, 668; Beale, *Book of Revelation*, 656.
64. Beale also argues that "John appears . . . to have chosen the image of a snake because it was the most pervasive picture of pagan divinity in Asia Minor" (Beale, *Book of Revelation*, 565).
65. Cf. Aune, *Revelation 6–16*, 697.
66. Cf. Grabiner, *Revelation's Hymns*, 64–65.
67. Cf. Thomas, *Apocalypse*, 367–69; Koester, *Revelation*, 549–50; Aune, *Revelation 6–16*, 696–98.
68. Leithart, *Revelation 12–22*, 25.
69. Cf. Thomas, *Apocalypse*, 366–67; Aune, *Revelation 6–16*, 698–99.

Revelation to the ascension of Christ (v. 5), the victory of Michael and his angels in heaven (vv. 7–8), and the witness of followers of Jesus based on his blood (v. 10–11).[70]

> **And I heard a loud voice in heaven that said, "Now the salvation and the power and the kingdom of our God, and the authority of his Messiah, has arrived. For the accuser of our brothers (and sisters), who accuses them before our God day and night, has been thrown down." (Rev 12:10)**

This gives a heavenly interpretation of the events. First, the victory has messianic significance. This repeats the claims made in 11:15 about the kingdom and confirms the messianic identity of the "male child" in verse 5.

Second, the victory has great implications for the hearers/readers. This statement explains the reasons for the previous claim, as is evident in the word "for" (Greek *hoti*).[71] The hearers would again be reminded of Old Testament passages where Satan accuses God's people. In particular, they would think of Job 1:9–11 and 2:4–5 where Satan accuses Job of only serving God because of God's protection, the basis of all Job's troubles when God allows Satan to test him. Then they would think of Zechariah 3:1 where Satan accuses the high priest Joshua before the angel of the LORD and is rebuked by the LORD. This is followed by a scene where Joshua's filthy clothes are replaced with fine and clean garments, which may be one of the references from Revelation 7:14, where the great multitude wash their robes in the Lamb's blood.

In both of these passages, Satan has access to the presence of God to make his accusations, but now he has apparently lost this access.[72] However, if that is true, why does John report that Satan "accuses them before our God day and night" (present active participle)? Is this just to emphasize what Satan has done up to this point, though he can no longer do so, or does Satan continue his accusations even after being hurled down from heaven, only this time from an earthly location? John would be implying that his accusations continue, but have no force, perhaps like Paul in Romans 8:33–34. This second possibility has merit in that the hearers would be familiar with many accusations against them from their neighbors, from unbelieving Jews (2:9 and 3:9), and from various civil and Roman authorities (2:10, 13).[73]

The third possibility, that these accusations are caused by Satan whispering into the consciences of believers, an idea frequently brought up by evangelical and Pentecostal preachers in the past, is less likely. However, this may be a legitimate secondary application of the text. This explanation of the fall of Satan may also shed light on the war in heaven. We are meant to envisage not a military struggle but a legal one where

---

70. Cf. Mayo, *Those Who Call Themselves Jews*, 160.
71. Cf. Thomas, *Apocalypse*, 370–71.
72. Cf. Koester, *Revelation*, 551–52.
73. Cf. Thomas, *Apocalypse*, 371; Aune, *Revelation 6–16*, 655, 700–701 (Aune argues that the phrase should be translated in the past tense).

Satan brings accusations against God's people (as he did with Job in Job 1–2) and seeks a condemning verdict from God as Judge.[74]

> **And they conquered[75] him on account of the blood of the Lamb and on account of the word of their testimony, and they did not love their lives even till death. (Rev 12:11)**

The means by which the "brothers and sisters" gained this victory is now spelled out. The victory is theirs, in spite of the reference to Michael and his angels winning the war in verse 7. Whatever Michael's army did was only possible because of what the believers here did. Thus, the idea that what happens in heaven is reflected on earth is turned on its head. The centrality of human action is emphasized; these indeed are the conquerors to whom special promises have been made in Revelation 2–3. As Pablo Richard comments, "history-making is not restricted to God. Martyrs, prophets, and those who resist adoring the Dragon, its image and its mark are also makers of history: they defeat Satan, they destroy the powers of evil . . . and they rule over the earth."[76]

However, their victory is also predicated on the work of another, on "the blood of the Lamb." Jesus' sacrificial death "freed us from our sins" (1:5), triumphed so as to open the sealed scroll (5:5–6, 9), "purchased for God persons from every tribe and language and people and nation" (5:9), and washed white the robes of the multitude (7:14). Now John claims that it has defeated every accusation of the devil against God's people.[77] The hearers are reminded again that "Not a cosmic super-hero but a slain Lamb is the key player" in this victory.[78] But once again the attention is shifted back to the believers: their victory depended on the blood of the Lamb but also required "the word of their testimony," and that in a situation where death was threatened.

The audience would imagine a hostile setting such as might be represented by a synagogue, or more likely a local or Roman court. In such a setting, Christians would indeed be accused of various offences: atheism (refusing to honor the Greco-Roman deities), disloyalty or treason (refusing to offer incense to Caesar), or even hatred of mankind (as related by the Roman historian Tacitus).[79] They might indeed be imprisoned, exiled, or executed on such charges, as 1:9, 2:9–10, and 2:13 make clear.[80] In such threatening situations, they would only triumph, that is maintain their testimony to Christ, if indeed they did not hold their lives (literally souls) dear. As Jesus stresses in Matthew 10:39, "Whoever finds their life will lose it, and whoever loses their life for my

---

74. Cf. Beale, *Book of Revelation*, 661–63. Aune discusses an interesting passage from 3 Enoch that has a similar idea (Aune, *Revelation 6–16*, 701).

75. The Greek is ἐνίκησαν [*enikēsan*], from the Greek νικαω [*nikaō*]. This word appears repeatedly in the seven prophetic messages of Revelation 2–3.

76. Richard, "Resistance, Hope, and Liberation in Central America," 150.

77. Cf. Beale, *Book of Revelation*, 658–61.

78. Pattemore, *People of God*, 95; cf. Grabiner, *Revelation's Hymns*, 106–10.

79. Tacitus, *Annales* 15.14, as quoted in Koester, *Revelation*, 586.

80. Cf. Koester, *Revelation*, 564–65.

sake will find it," in a context promising heavy opposition and persecution.[81] But if the Christians faithfully maintained their testimony, they would defeat the dragon and cause him to lose his place in heaven, just as 4 Maccabees 4:11 asserts that the faithful Jews persecuted by Antiochus Epiphanes "by their endurance . . . conquered the tyrant."[82]

Thus, Revelation might be subtitled "the Triumph of the Martyrs." The onus is on human beings loyal to Jesus, who does not directly intervene in this struggle,[83] to overcome the dragon. However, this does not mean that only literal martyrs are envisaged as victorious here. Rather, it refers to all victorious believers who are willing to maintain their testimony to Christ, even at the cost of martyrdom.[84] As Bauckham argues, "The martyrs conquer not by their suffering and death as such, but by their faithful *witness* to the point of death."[85] In this way, "the church which John portrays is a martyr church."[86]

This reading of Revelation 12:8–11 thus negates two other possible readings. Revelation 12 uses language from primeval stories in the Bible such as Genesis 3.[87] But the fall of the devil here is not a primeval event, where the devil leads an angelic rebellion against God and is then evicted from heaven, a reading sometimes supported from passages like Isaiah 14:12–15, a denouncement of Babylon.[88] Nor is Revelation predicting a future triumph over the devil at the end of the age here, though he may be doing so in Revelation 20. Rather, the triumph is both past (at the Cross) and ongoing (through the witness of the martyrs).[89]

> **Because of this rejoice, heavens[90] and those who dwell in them. Woe to the earth and the sea, for the devil has gone down to you, having great wrath, knowing that he has (only) a little time. (Rev 12:12)**

John's loud voice now declares the outcome of all this. Heaven is glad to be rid of the devil and his angels, but on earth things will get worse, not better! The devil knows his time is limited.[91] He is furious because of his defeat, and he will mount a fresh campaign against God and God's people. This may be the time of the third woe, signaled

---

81. Thomas, *Apocalypse*, 372–73; Aune, *Revelation 6–16*, 703.

82. Cf. Aune, *Revelation 1–5*, 76; Aune, *Revelation 6–16*, 702; Bauckham, *Climax of Prophecy*, 236–37.

83. Leithart, *Revelation 12–22*, 32–33, 36; cf. Bauckham, *Climax of Prophecy*, 235.

84. Cf. Beale, *Book of Revelation*, 665–66.

85. Bauckham, *Climax of Prophecy*, 237.

86. Pattemore, *People of God*, 114.

87. Cf. Leithart, *Revelation 12–22*, 33–34; contra Aune, *Revelation 6–16*, 695–96. Clearly, Jewish myths relate various versions of such a primeval fall as seen in some of the apocalyptic literature.

88. Contra Malina, *Genre and Message*, 166–73.

89. Cf. Koester, *Revelation*, 550–51.

90. Cf. Aune, *Revelation 6–16*, 655–56, for discussion of the plural here.

91. Cf. Thomas, *Apocalypse*, 375, on the use of time (Greek καιρος [*kairos*]) here. See also Aune, *Revelation 6–16*, 704.

in 11:14 but never announced.[92] It is probably to be equated with the "little longer" of 6:11 and the various phrases equivalent to three-and-a-half years, perhaps even the "short time" of 20:3.[93]

> **And when the dragon saw that he'd been thrown to the earth, he pursued the woman who'd given birth to the male (child). And the woman was given the two wings of the great eagle, so that she might fly into the desert to her place, where she is nourished for a time and times and half a time (away) from the presence of the serpent. (Rev 12:13–14)**

John now tells the readers exactly what the freshly earth-bound devil will do in his various guises such as dragon or serpent. John uses these names interchangeably: it is the dragon in verses 3, 4, 7, 9, 13, 16, and 17; the devil in verses 9 and 12, and the serpent in verses 9, 14, and 15. His first strategy is to pursue the woman, the mother of the messiah (v. 13). She is vulnerable since she is also on the earth, but she is miraculously removed and protected. The language here is reminiscent of Exodus 19:4, where God at Sinai, referring to the Exodus event, declares that He "carried you on eagles' wings and brought you to myself" (see also Deut 32:11–12).[94] Possibly the language here in Revelation 12 alludes to a literal evacuation of some kind, maybe even the withdrawal of the Christians from Jerusalem when the Roman armies approached (see Mark 13:14–20). This was the "flight to Pella,"[95] or to Asia, the province to which John is prophesying.[96]

The text emphasizes both the place of safety and care for the woman (parallel with Israel's wilderness experience) and the time involved: "a time, times and half a time," a phrase drawn from Daniel 7:25, 9:27, and 12:7. In Daniel, this is a period of oppression of the saints. John identifies it with 1,260 days in verse 6 of this chapter, referring back to the period of the two prophetic witnesses in 11:3, and thus seems to reinterpret the period as a time of partial or spiritual protection for the witnesses (11:5–6) and the woman.[97]

---

92. But cf. Thomas, *Apocalypse*, 374; Beale, *Book of Revelation*, 667.

93. Cf. Beale, *Book of Revelation*, 667–68.

94. Cf. Koester, *Revelation*, 553. Note "the wings of *the* great eagle" (v. 14). Aune comments "John may be referring here to 'the great eagle' in a story well known to his audience but unfortunately unknown to us" (Aune, *Revelation 6–16*, 657). He also points out that the woman is not rescued by the eagle but given eagle's wings so she herself can escape, a probable reference to Greek mythology or perhaps Isa 40:31 (Aune, *Revelation 6–16*, 704–6). Another possible allusion is to David's prayer in Ps 55:6–7 (cf. Beale, *Book of Revelation*, 669–70). See also Leithart, *Revelation 12–22*, 40–42.

95. Cf. Aune, *Revelation 6–16*, 706; Beale, *Book of Revelation*, 642, 647, 648–49; Taushev, *Ancient Christianity*, 180. R. H. Charles even suggested it was the Pharisees fleeing Jerusalem that lies behind this (Charles, *Critical and Exegetical Commentary* 1:310). He gave no source for this, however.

96. Cf. Leithart, *Revelation 12–22*, 39.

97. Cf. Thomas, *Apocalypse*, 377; Beale, *Book of Revelation*, 646–47; Waddell, *Spirit of the Book*, 169.

Koester argues that "this period can signify protection . . . and affliction . . . both characterize the situation of the faithful during the time between Jesus' exaltation and return . . . "[98] Beale sees this as fulfilling the promise of a new exodus (especially prominent in Isaiah) in which Israel would be restored and protected in the wilderness.[99] However, it may be significant that the image of a woman in the desert recurs in the picture of the great prostitute in chapter 17.[100] Is there some link between these two women, maybe an adversarial relationship?

> **And the serpent threw out from his mouth waters like a river after the woman, so that she might be swept away by it. (Rev 12:15)**

Maybe attempting to do to Israel what was done to the army of Egypt in Exodus 14,[101] the serpent tries to kill the woman with a flood of water. Sea and waters are often seen as enemies of God in the Old Testament (Pss 77:16; 93:3–4; Nah 1:4; Hab 3:8–10).[102] This passage may also recall the imagery of invasion in passages like Isaiah 8:7–8 and Daniel 9:26, 11:10, 40.[103] Perhaps the devil tries to use an army to crush the woman; maybe there is a reference to some aspect of the Roman-Jewish conflict of AD 66–70.[104] Or the devil's river is a reference to a flood of temptation and evil, or persecution or false doctrine, aimed at overwhelming the church (see Pss 18:4, 15, 16; 32:6; 69:1, 14, 15; 124:1–5).[105]

> **And the earth helped the woman, and the earth opened its mouth and drank the river that the dragon threw out from his mouth. (Rev 12:16)**

This agency of the earth is in a sense ironic if Genesis 3 is part of the intertextual background to this story since there the earth was cursed (Gen 3:17). Perhaps John is signaling the lifting of this curse with the earth fighting for the woman. However, the first mention in Scripture of the earth opening its mouth is to receive Abel's blood (Gen 4:10–11). Later the earth had been an agent of God's judgement in the story of the rebellion of some Israelite leaders in the wilderness when it swallowed the rebels and their families (Num 16:28–33; 26:10; Deut 11:6). The earth as a protector and ally of the church is no doubt symbolic here. Certainly, the theological point is God's protection of his people against the devil's attacks.

---

98. Koester, *Revelation*, 553; cf. Hendriksen, *More Than Conquerors*, 143–44.

99. Beale, *Book of Revelation*, 643–45.

100. Cf. Corsini, *Apocalypse*, 220, 393.

101. Cf. Thomas, *Apocalypse*, 378; Leithart, *Revelation 12–22*, 38–39; Mayo, *Those Who Call Themselves Jews*, 150.

102. On other non-Hebrew allusions here, see Aune, *Revelation 6–16*, 706–7.

103. Cf. Koester, *Revelation*, 553.

104. Josephus reported that in 68, a flood of the Jordan prevented Jews from escaping Roman soldiers, and hence they were killed (Josephus, "War of the Jews" 4:433–436; cf. Beale, *Book of Revelation*, 671).

105. Cf. Koester, *Revelation*, 566; Beale, *Book of Revelation*, 672–74.

However, this part of the story may have extra resonance for us in a freshly earth-conscious time. There are several potential applications to twenty-first century ecological issues here. The fact that there are several allusions to the Exodus, and wilderness narratives of the Old Testament, in this passage is also important. The story of Israel's exodus, march to the promised land, and capture of Jericho has been a significant intertextual theological reference point for Revelation from the beginning. This theme remains prominent to the end of the book, making Revelation a kind of corporate "pilgrims' progress."[106] There is also a kind of "mouth-to-mouth combat" here: the dragon throws a river out of his mouth, but the earth opens its mouth and swallows that river. This may signify a verbal struggle, a propoaganda war such as will be described in the next chapter.

> **And the dragon was enraged at the woman and went off to make war against the rest of her seed, those who keep the commandments of God and have the testimony of Jesus. (Rev 12:17)**

The war continues on the earth after the eviction of the dragon from heaven.[107] The dragon was unable to devour the woman's male child (the messiah) or the woman herself, but he can reach her other children,[108] the brothers and sisters of the messiah (an allusion to Mic 5:3), defined by their obedience to God's commands and their testimony about Jesus. This is another fulfilment of Genesis 3:15, which predicts conflict between two groups of "offspring" when it says "And I will put enmity between you and the woman, and between your offspring and hers . . ."[109] We need not limit "those who keep God's commands" to only Jewish believers. All Christians are meant to obey the commands of God; more likely, their obedience to God's commands is a reference to their rejection of idolatry.[110]

In both Daniel and Acts, Christ is identified with his followers. In Daniel 7, for example, the victory of the son of man is interpreted as the time coming when "the holy people of the Most High . . . possessed the kingdom" (Dan 7:22). In Acts 9, Saul,

---

106. Cf. Koester, *Revelation*, 566; Beale, *Book of Revelation*, 675–76.

107. Thomas points out the developing uses of the phrase "make war": the beast makes war on the two witnesses (11:7), there was war in heaven (12:7), and now the dragon will "wage war" against the other children of the woman (12:17); this will occur in 13:7 (Thomas, *Apocalypse*, 380).

108. Cf. Thomas, *Apocalypse*, 380. This makes the woman the "mother" of the believers in Christ. However, if the woman represents the church as God's people, the distinction between her and her children is confusing. Cf. Beale, *Book of Revelation*, 676–78. One possible way of reading this is that the woman represents faithful Israel as seen in the early Jewish church and the rest of her children represents the church at large across the Roman world. This would imply a reference to the war of AD 66–70 in verses 7–16. The Jewish church in Judea successfully escaped the war, but believers elsewhere were still prey to persecution.

109. The Greek for "seed" in v. 17 is σπέρματος [*spermatos*]. Here, as in Gen 3:15, the woman has seed, normally attributed only to males; cf. Aune, *Revelation 6–16*, 708.

110. Cf. Beale, *Book of Revelation*, 679. But see Thomas, *Apocalypse*, 381. Thomas interprets this in the light of John's gospel as referring to love for each other including laying down their lives.

the arch persecutor of Christians, is asked by the ascended Christ, "Why do you persecute me?" (Acts 9:4). Saul's story is another potential historical event behind this part of John's narrative. Satan cannot directly touch the ascended Christ, but he can persecute his followers, the believers. Their victory over him (v. 11) is not the end; he will come back with new strategies.

For the hearers in the seven churches, this passage will remind them that their struggles are part of a larger "cosmic struggle"[111] between the forces of God and Satan. Their choices about eating food sacrificed to idols, and other cultural pressures, have a bigger context, just as the local struggles of today's church have. And the persecutions they face are not evidence of a losing struggle against the overwhelming power of a hostile society or government, but rather a sign that the devil has been defeated and is summoning up violent action as he knows his time is short.[112]

Before we leave chapter 12, I want to discuss a minority Pentecostal interpretation of this story. Against the background of a dispensationalist reading of Revelation, though it may go back to the very early days of Pentecostalism, this interpretation modifies the "pretribulation rapture" and tries to differentiate between two kinds of Christians. There are variations on this line, but basically it involves a Futurist reading in which the woman and the "male child" represent different "levels" of Christian commitment. The Christians who successfully "overcome" (KJV language), as urged by the seven messages in Revelation 2–3, are symbolized by the "male child." Revelation 12:5 foretells their rapture; they are rewarded by being caught up to heaven and escaping at least the worst of the three-and-a-half year tribulation.[113]

Less victorious Christians remain but are protected: they are the "woman." In some versions, there is a third group, the "rest of her offspring" (v. 17) who must endure horrific persecution in order to be saved at the end. The difference between these groups may be attributed to the baptism with the Holy Spirit. The parable of the ten virgins, some of whom were left behind because they ran out of oil, is used to support this view (see Matt 25:1–13).[114] This interpretation has some coherence, but it depends on a Futurist reading (itself problematic), is open to a sectarian misreading (an "us" versus "them" division among Christians), and ignores the fact that the martyrs are the heroes of Revelation, as this very chapter affirms.

And he stood on the sea shore. (Rev 12:18)[115]

This leads into chapter 13.

111. Cf. Koester, *Revelation*, 555.

112. Cf. Koester, *Revelation*, 555.

113. This aspect is not unique to Pentecostal interpreters (Beale, *Book of Revelation*, 641).

114. For a peculiar variation on this, see Conner, *Book of Revelation*, 380–99. Conner sees the manchild as a sinless company born from the marriage of Christ and the church (the woman of Revelation 12).

115. An alternative manuscript source has John standing on the sea's shore watching the beast coming up from the sea; cf. Aune, *Revelation 6–16*, 725; Beale, *Book of Revelation*, 681.

Revelation Chapter 13

This is perhaps the most famous passage in Revelation, certainly the most controversial and memorable with its gruesome beasts and the famous "mark of the beast" and "number of the beast," 666.

There have been multiple interpretations of the beast and the mark and especially the number 666. The most prevalent have been:

1. A Historicist interpretation: The beast is the papacy or the Roman Catholic church. This is based on one of the pope's titles adding up to 666 in Latin, the clear references to Rome (here and in 17:9 and 18), the political power exercised by the papacy after the fall of the Western Roman Empire, and the violent suppression of Christian dissidents (especially Protestants) by Catholics in the sixteenth and seventeenth centuries. The papacy is an easy target, and this interpretation dominated Protestant exegesis for a few hundred years. However, it is at least dated and skewed towards western European history, ignoring the east, where Revelation was written. John's original hearers would have no way of understanding the passage this way, although Revelation chapters 2 and 3 do warn of churches departing from the faith.

2. A Futurist interpretation: The beast is a future world ruler, maybe arising out of the UN, the EU, the USA, or a "revived Roman empire"[1] of some kind. You can let your imagination go here, and new technology sometimes suggests new possibilities such as computer chips under people's skin (the mark on the forehead or hand). This reading throws up lots of prospective bad guys and conspiracy theories. Once again, it's very unlikely that John (or the Holy Spirit) would intend such an interpretation for a first-century vision. It would also imply that John's original hearers would have no way of understanding the passage. It seems more like a case of importing current trends or anxieties into the text.

3. A Preterist or ancient history interpretation: The beast represents the Roman Empire, or a particular emperor. The cry, "Who is like the beast? Who can wage

---

1. Walvoord, *Revelation*, 197–98.

war against it?" (v. 4) would certainly fit the Roman Empire in John's day. Nero is the favorite individual emperor candidate since a Hebraized version of his name fits both 666 and the alternative text, which has 616 as the beast's number. He was also the first emperor to actively persecute Christians, and there were persistent myths about a renascent Nero returning with an army from the Parthian Empire to the east of the Roman one and reclaiming his throne, even though he had committed suicide "on the run."[2] More broadly, the increasing cult of Caesar in the later first century, particularly popular in the cities of Revelation, demanding a form of allegiance that amounted to worship, makes this interpretation plausible.[3] Also the fatal wound that was healed could apply to two periods in the Roman Empire where the whole Empire seemed like it might implode in vicious civil war. In both cases, Augustus and Vespasian respectively managed to reunite the empire and restore Roman dominance.

This third interpretation makes a lot of sense and would certainly have been a likely way John's original audience could have understood the passage, but the danger with it is that it can relegate Revelation to purely historical interest. As Moloney puts it, "they limit the scope of this book's perennial message."[4]

4. A Modified Idealist reading suggests that the beasts are always a threat as fresh challenges arise to the Christian church when a losing Satan attempts to use coercive political power to hold his kingdom together. So Roman Emperors may fit, but more recent figures like Hitler, Stalin, and Mao also function as the beast. The contemporary issues that Futurist interpreters worry about may be better addressed from this reading, which invites Christian readers to interpret their world from the apocalyptic perspective of the text. Let's see if this works.

13:1–10 The Beast from the Sea

> **And I saw a wild beast[5] rise up from the sea, which had ten horns and seven heads, and on his horns ten diadems, and on his heads blasphemous names. And the wild beast which I saw was like a leopard, and his feet like a bear's, and his mouth was like a lion's mouth. And the dragon gave him his power and his throne and great authority. (Rev 13:1–2)**

---

2. Cf. Aune, *Revelation 6–16*, 737–40. See below on verse 3.

3. Cf. Friesen, "Myth and Symbolic Resistance," 303. The classic analysis of this cult as it operated in the province of Asia is Price, *Rituals and Power*. Michael Naylor summarizes the literature on the cult and its links to Revelation up to 2010 in "The Roman Imperial Cult and Revelation." See also Boring, *Revelation*, 18–21.

4. Moloney, *Apocalypse of John*, 192.

5. The Greek word θηριον [*thērion*] is the ordinary word for an untamed or wild animal, though it could also be translated "monster." In this case, it is a kind of hybrid animal, an idea common in all ancient cultures, e.g., sphinx, mermaid, centaur.

There was previously a reference to "the beast that comes up from the abyss" (11:7), who put the two witnesses to death. The hearers may wonder if this is the same beast as that one, though it seems that coming from the sea is equivalent to emerging from the abyss.[6] Certainly, these beasts are both on the same side, and both persecute God's people, as we will see. Moreover, the hearers will hear of the beast coming up from the abyss in 17:8, and he (or it) is simply "the beast" in 19:19–20 and 20:4, 10, so presumably, these are all the same beast.[7] Any doubt over the allegiance of the beast would be removed by the reference to the blasphemous names on each of its seven heads, possibly recalling the "slander" (Greek *blasphēmian*) of the false Jews in 2:9 and perhaps "closely connected to the identity of God and his people."[8]

He is said to come up out of the sea perhaps because that is how Asians experienced the Roman Empire's representatives coming across from Italy.[9] Leithart suggests that the sea represents the Gentile world,[10] and some Jewish literature views the Romans as invaders from the sea.[11] Also, as I will discuss below, this is partly an allusion to Daniel 7, where four beasts come out of the sea. But there are broader allusions that many of John's hearers would pick up on.

The sea itself has connotations of evil, or at least chaos, in the Old Testament. In Genesis 1, it simply represents the unformed state of the original creation prior to God's creative speaking, held in check perhaps by the hovering of the Spirit or wind of God (Gen 1:2). In the exodus narrative (one of the key narratives lying behind Revelation), the sea represents a threat of destruction to Israel and Egypt. Only by means of a great miracle of God's wind are the Israelites able to cross safely, whereas Pharaoh's army is drowned (Exod 14–15). It is a force for death and destruction for Jonah, though he is saved by a great sea creature (Jonah 1:11—2:6).

The sea is also the home of one of the great mythical creatures, Leviathan (Job 41; Ps 104:26), which has features of a dragon (Job 41:19–21) and is a powerful foe: "Nothing on earth is its equal" (Job 41:33).[12] In Job and Psalm 104, Leviathan is God's creature. But in Psalm 74, Leviathan is the multiple-headed monster in the Red Sea, whose heads were crushed by God in the exodus event (Ps 74:13–14). It is also a force for evil for Isaiah, which predicts that in a time of judgement and resurrection, after God's wrath "has passed by" (Isa 26:20),

---

6. Aune, *Revelation 6–16*, 755. See also Beale, *Book of Revelation*, 684.

7. Cf. Thomas, *Apocalypse*, 382.

8. Thomas, *Apocalypse*, 383. Aune suggests these names may refer to titles assumed by Roman emperors that belong to God or Christ alone, e.g., "savior" or "son of God" (Aune, *Revelation 6–16*, 734).

9. Cf. Paul, *Revelation*, 230.

10. Leithart, *Revelation 12–22*, 51.

11. E.g., 4 Ezra 11:1; cf. Koester, *Revelation*, 569; Aune, *Revelation 6–16*, 732–33.

12. Job (Job 40:15–41:34) and later Jewish literature, such as apocalypses, mention both Leviathan (a sea monster) and Behemoth (a land monster); cf. Aune, *Revelation 6–16*, 728–29, 732, 755–56; Beale, *Book of Revelation*, 682; Bauckham, *Climax of Prophecy*, 187–96; Friesen, "Myth and Symbolic Resistance," 304–7.

> ... in that day
> the LORD will punish with his sword—
> his fierce, great and powerful sword—
> Leviathan the gliding serpent,
> Leviathan the coiling serpent;
> he will slay the monster of the sea. (Isa 27:1)[13]

Similar myths are found in other cultures that might have influenced John's audience, such as the Babylonian creation story, the Enuma Elish.[14] All these would give them the clear idea that a beast from the sea (or from the abyss, as in 11:7 and 17:8) represents chaos and trouble.

The beast from the sea is sponsored by the dragon, the devil.[15] It's important to note here that the dragon is not acting from a position of strength, in spite of his apparent dominance in this episode, represented by his "throne" and "great authority."[16] If John's listeners were facing increasing persecution and even violence, their faith might just waver in view of the apparent invincibility of their opponents and their own apparent helplessness, as vocalized in verse 7. But John's apocalyptic strategy is to "go behind the scenes" and provide a spiritual reinterpretation of what was happening.

The dragon is making a strong political attack on God's people, and trying to reinforce his control of the nations, but this is because he has suffered a series of defeats in chapter 12. He has failed to destroy the messiah (12:4–5); he has lost the war in heaven (12:7–8); he has been cast out of heaven with his angels (12:8–9, 13); he has been defeated by the followers of the Lamb (12:10–11); and he has failed to destroy the woman, the messiah's mother (12:13–16). Revelation 12:17 has told us, "And the dragon was enraged at the woman and went off to make war against the rest of her seed, those who keep the commandments of God and have the testimony of Jesus." At least if he can't destroy the woman or her male child, he can make life very difficult for "the rest of her seed," that is Christians, maybe Jewish Christians in particular if we understand the phrase "keep the commandments of God" as a reference to the Torah, though it could have a broader meaning.

Thomas notes the strong language used here ("power, throne, authority"). Previously in Revelation, "power" is ascribed only to God (4:11; 7:12; 11;17; 12:10), Jesus (1:16; 5:12), or believers (3:8); something similar applies to "throne," though Satan has a "throne" in Pergamum (2:13), and "authority." All this confirms that the dragon is mounting a serious challenge to God's kingdom.[17] The language of verses 2 and

---

13. Cf. Howard-Brook and Gwyther, *Unveiling Empire*, 214.
14. Cf. Dumbrell, *End of the Beginning*, 172–73; Goldingay, *Daniel*, 151, 153.
15. Cf. Leithart, *Revelation 12–22*, 56.
16. Cf. Grabiner, *Revelation's Hymns*, 39–41.
17. Thomas, *Apocalypse*, 384–85; cf. Beale, *Book of Revelation*, 699. Aune, however, sees these references to the dragon as added by a later redactor (Aune, *Revelation 6–16*, 725–26, 735).

4 recalls the investiture of the Lamb in 5:8–13. Jesus was given a place of worship alongside God; now the dragon does the same for his false messiah.

The wild beast coming out of the sea (v. 1) is clearly the dragon's agent, representative, or puppet: people "worshiped the dragon, which had given authority to the wild beast" (v. 4). This suggests a spiritual or religious basis for the beast's empire, which was a common feature of nearly all ancient empires. The Romans believed their dominance and victories were built on their piety in the form of sacrifices and other acts of worship to their gods.[18] The imagery here confirms this origin of the beast: the dragon has "seven heads and ten horns" (12:3), and the beast has "ten horns and seven heads" (v. 1).[19] The only difference is that the dragon has seven diadems on its heads (12:3) whereas the beast has ten diadems on its horns (v. 1).

Seven is a number usually associated in Revelation with completion or fullness (usually in a positive spiritual sense; as in seven churches), whereas ten is associated with political power and alliances (17:12; 2:10). However, there is one major exception: the beast carrying the whore of Revelation 17 also has "seven heads and ten horns" (17:7), and the seven heads are interpreted as "seven hills on which the woman sits" (17:9) and "seven kings" (17:10). If we put all these hints together, perhaps John is originally showing us the spiritual-religious basis of the empire in the city of Rome. The picture includes the empire's divine kings (the seven crowned heads of the dragon) and the outworking of the empire's rule in the political realm (the ten crowned horns of the beast).[20]

John's sketch of what the beast looks like (v. 2) makes a clear allusion to Daniel 7.[21] Daniel sees "the four winds of heaven churning up the great sea" and "four great beasts, each different from the others, came up out of the sea" (Dan 7:2–3). The first beast "was like a lion, and it had the wings of an eagle" (Dan 7:4). The second beast "looked like a bear" (Dan 7:5). The third beast "looked like a leopard" but "on its back it had four wings" and "four heads" (Dan 7:6). The fourth beast is not compared to a specific animal but is described as "terrifying and frightening and very powerful. It had large iron teeth; it crushed and devoured its victims and trampled underfoot whatever was left. It was different from all the former beasts, and it had ten horns" (Dan 7:7).

Out of it emerged another little horn that uprooted three of the other horns (Dan 7:8), spoke boastfully (Dan 7:8, 11, 20), and defeated God's holy people for a set time (Dan 7:21, 25) before the kingdom of God triumphed (Dan 7:22, 27). Daniel is told that "the fourth beast is a fourth kingdom that will appear on earth. It will be different from all other kingdoms and will devour the whole earth, trampling it down and crushing it" (Dan 7:23).

---

18. Cf. Koester, *Revelation*, 570, 580–81, 585–86.

19. The four beasts of Daniel 7 have a total of seven heads and ten horns (Koester, *Revelation*, 569; Beale, *Book of Revelation*, 683). Beale says that "the number of *seven* heads and *ten* horns emphasizes the completeness of oppressive power and its worldwide effect" (Beale, *Book of Revelation*, 684).

20. Cf. Aune, *Revelation 6–16*, 733.

21. Cf. Beale, *Book of Revelation*, 683, 728–29; Moyise, *Old Testament in the Book of Revelation*, 52–53.

John's beast from the sea is then meant to be read either as Daniel's fourth beast or a composite of all four.[22] Certainly, it has features of the first three of Daniel's beasts, implying perhaps that there is an ongoing continuity in these empires, which in John's worldview is represented by the dragon. In other words, the devil is the spiritual force behind the Gentile empires of history, beginning perhaps with Babel (Genesis 11) and continuing on through Egypt, Assyria, Babylon, Media-Persia, Greece, and Rome.

Daniel may have seen Antiochus Epiphanes (the oppressive Greek ruler of the Seleucid Empire) as the apex of evil,[23] but John probably sees it as Rome, if not a specific Caesar. In other words, the Roman Empire is clearly interpreted as an agent of the devil, an enemy of God's kingdom and God's people. This is a powerful rhetorical move by John to paint the empire in negative, threatening terms, in contrast with its own propaganda.[24]

> **And one of his heads was as slaughtered to death, and the plague of his death was healed. And all the earth was amazed at the wild beast and worshiped the dragon which had given authority to the wild beast, and they worshiped the wild beast, saying, "Who is like the wild beast and who is able to make war against it?" (Rev 13:3–4)**

The healing and survival of this beast stands out and is mentioned again in verses 12 and 14, which adds the detail that the beast "was wounded by the sword and yet lived" (NIV). It is one of the apparent reasons behind the amazement and worship accorded to the beast.[25] This probably does not refer to a physical wound and healing, but a political or military reality. This fits very neatly with events in the Roman Empire in the memory (or experience) of John's audience. The Roman Empire had been devastated by civil strife in the "year of the four emperors" after the literal wound of the suicide of Nero (AD 68–69), but its wound had been healed by Vespasian.[26] One historian comments that "the Empire's darkest year was in fact proof of its stability."[27]

---

22. Cf. Thomas, *Apocalypse*, 383–84; Koester, *Revelation*, 569–70; Beale, *Book of Revelation*, 685; Corsini, *Apocalypse*, 235; Leithart, *Revelation 12–22*, 51–53. Leithart argues that these beast-empires were originally meant to be guardians of Israel but betrayed this trust.

23. Cf. Goldingay, *Daniel*, 174, 179–81, 186–88.

24. Cf. Friesen, "Myth and Symbolic Resistance," 309. This was a form of parody according to Koester (Koester, *Revelation*, 578–579; cf. Aune, *Revelation 6–16*, 735). Beale adds that such a portrayal applies to future world empires as well (Beale, *Book of Revelation*, 685–86).

25. Cf. Beale, *Book of Revelation*, 693–94.

26. Cf. Beale, *Book of Revelation*, 689–91; Bauckham, *Climax of Prophecy*, 442–44. In earlier days, a Greek orator Cineas was "said to have reported that the Roman people were like a many-headed monster whose numbers would keep on being replenished" (Fox, *Classical World*, 305; see also 317). The Roman world experienced many civil wars and the rule of Augustus Caesar (and his successors) had emerged out of the civil wars which followed the assassination of Julius Caesar (cf. ibid., 402, 449). Walvoord, however, sees this as evidence of a future revived Roman Empire (Walvoord, *Revelation*, 199).

27. Fox, *Classical World*, 544.

Or more specifically, since the fatal wound was in only "one of the heads of the beast" (v. 3), John is referring just to Nero's suicide, which sent the empire into a period of chaos.[28] Alternatively, this detail refers to the Jewish rebellion against Rome in AD 66, which threatened Rome's dominance in just one province of the empire. After an extended struggle (at least three-and-a-half years), this was put down with massive loss of life and physical destruction, including the destruction of the second temple in Jerusalem. Truly, for the Jews, "Who is able [successfully] to make war against it?" Leithart argues, based partly on his early dating of Revelation, that John has the assassination of Julius Caesar and the resulting civil wars ended by the great emperor Augustus in mind.[29]

Perhaps more importantly, since Genesis 3 is a primary intertextual source in Revelation 12, this healing is a direct spiritual challenge to God's judgment that the male child or seed of the woman will crush the head of the serpent (Gen 3:15).[30] The "ancient serpent" (i.e., dragon) has been defeated and hurled down (12:9), defeating the dragon's plans to devour the child (12:4–5). But the fatal wound of the dragon's surrogate was healed, so the battle is not over yet! The devil's side is making a defiant counter-attack.[31] This is what happens throughout history, as 20:3, 7 also reminds us. The devil keeps making "comebacks" until the final judgment. Therefore, as Beale says, "the chief opponent of Christ cannot be limited to one historical person or epoch."[32]

The "resurrection" of the beast, its recovery from its fatal wound, is also a parody of the death and resurrection of Christ the Lamb,[33] literally it is "as slaughtered to death," the same language used of the Lamb's death in 5:6. This suggests "competing salvific claims."[34]

The beast and his sponsor, the dragon, are worshiped (v. 4), just as the believers of the seven churches have experienced in the Caesar cult and the general idolatry of

---

28. Cf. Koester, *Revelation*, 581. Koester argues that John wants his readers "to see that in Nero the empire shows its true face" (ibid., 581). Many scholars see an allusion to a myth that Nero had not died but would return with a Parthian army to reclaim his throne. Cf. Aune, *Revelation 6–16*, 736–40; Bauckham, *Climax of Prophecy*, 407–31; Koester, *Revelation*, 570–71; Keener, *Revelation*, 337–39. There were several pretenders who claimed to be Nero and managed to convince people for a time, including Parthian leaders (MacMullen, *Enemies of the Roman Order*, 143–46; Bauckham, *Climax of Prophecy*, 412–14). Bauckham argues that John uses and adapts this myth for his own purposes rather than being controlled by it (Bauckham, *Climax of Prophecy*, 438–39, 449–51).

29. Leithart, *Revelation 12–22*, 58. There were repercussions in the political life of the Jews in all this and the Herods and Sadducees were allied with, or dependent on, Rome (cf. ibid., 58–59).

30. Cf. Beale, *Book of Revelation*, 688.

31. Cf. Koester, *Revelation*, 570; Beale, *Book of Revelation*, 688–89.

32. Beale, *Book of Revelation*, 691.

33. Cf. Beale, *Book of Revelation*, 691–92; Bauckham, *Climax of Prophecy*, 431–32; Whitaker, *Ekphrasis*, 196.

34. Thomas, *Apocalypse*, 385. Thomas suggests that this wound was inflicted by the witnesses in Rev 11 (ibid., 385, 386).

their cities, including temples to Roma (Rome's goddess) and other historical figures, especially Augustus.[35] This is seen as a deliberate strategy of the beast.[36]

Something else is also reflected in the phrase, "Who is like the beast and who is able to make war against it?" (v. 4). This is a parody of the praise offered to God after the exodus-Red Sea miracle where we read, "Who among the gods is like you, LORD? Who is like you—majestic in holiness, awesome in glory, working wonders?" (Exod 15:11).[37] The implication here would not be lost on many of John's hearers: the beast is contesting God's claims and exalting itself as a victorious Leviathan. Psalm 74:13–14 said, "you broke the heads of the monster in the waters . . . you crushed the heads of Leviathan." But this latter-day Leviathan claims he has won after all: his head wound is healed.

> **And he was given a mouth to speak great (things) and blasphemies, and authority was given to him to act for forty-two months. And he opened his mouth in blasphemies to God, to blaspheme his name and his dwelling, those who dwell in heaven. (Rev 13:5–6)[38]**

Once again, the audience would likely be reminded of Daniel 7, and particularly the activities of the little horn on Daniel's fourth beast (Dan 7:8, 11, 20, 25).[39] John's audience might recognize several acts of blasphemy or slander here. They would include Roman verbal attacks on the claims of the Jewish God, worship of the gods of Rome and of the Caesars,[40] and the silencing of the prayers and sacrifices associated with the second temple in AD 70. The AD 70 disaster led to the looting of the temple and carrying off of some of its sacred vessels. Titus' triumphal arch in Rome is still there reminding us of this tragedy. The tax subsequently imposed on the Jews, replacing the temple tax with one dedicated to the temple of Jupiter in Rome,[41] would also be seen as blasphemous.

The beast blasphemes or slanders not only God but also "his dwelling, those who dwell in heaven." Maybe this is because the dragon and his forces have been expelled from heaven, so the beast can only shout at the heavenly beings from his place on earth. This also emphasizes the ultimate weakness of his position: he can say "great

---

35. Cf. Koester, *Revelation*, 574, 582; Leithart, *Revelation 12–22*, 55–56; Bauckham, *Climax of Prophecy*, 447–48; Aune, *Revelation 6–16*, 741. The Greek προσκυνηω [*proskuneō*], "to prostrate oneself in worship," reflects a practice demanded by some Roman emperors such as Caligula, Nero, and Domitian (Aune, *Revelation 6–16*, 741–42).

36. Cf. Thomas, *Apocalypse*, 387.

37. Cf. Thomas, *Apocalypse*, 387–88. Similar phrases occur in the Psalms and other Jewish literature (Aune, *Revelation 6–16*, 741; Beale, *Book of Revelation*, 694).

38. Cf. Thomas, *Apocalypse*, 390–91; Aune, *Revelation 6–16*, 742, 744; Beale, *Book of Revelation*, 696–97.

39. Cf. Beale, *Book of Revelation*, 698.

40. Cf. Koester, *Revelation*, 569, 582–83.

41. Cf. Aune, *Revelation 1–5*, 171. This tax was vigorously enforced under Domitian.

things," but ultimately they are empty words. Note he was given "a mouth" to say great things; this suggests a propaganda campaign. I am reminded of the Nazi dictum, "Tell a lie, make it big, repeat it often, and people will believe you."[42] Hearers might remember the battle of mouths in 12:15–16. The beast has a limited time to mount his blasphemies and other evils: forty-two months, equivalent to 1,260 days or "time, times and half a time."

> **And he was permitted[43] to make war against the saints and conquer them, and he was given authority over every tribe and people and language and nation. And all those who dwell on the earth will worship him, (those) whose names have not been written in the book of life of the Lamb, who was slaughtered from the foundation of the world. If anyone has ears, let them hear. (Rev 13:7–9)**

Rome's claim to be invincible is confirmed by its ability to "conquer" God's people and its "authority over every tribe and people and language and nation" (v. 7).[44] The believers seem defenseless before him (v. 7). They conquered the devil in 12:11, but now they are conquered by him,[45] and everyone will worship the beast (v. 8).[46] Later authoritarian regimes have also oppressed the church, seemingly with impunity. Truly, the devil thinks he has won.

Some in the audience would have heard the story of the devil tempting Jesus by "showing him all the kingdoms of the world," and offering them all to him, on condition of Jesus worshiping him (Matt 4:8–9; Luke 4:5–7).[47] Jesus rejected the offer, but now it looks like the devil has achieved his goal of being worshiped after all, through a pseudo-Christ (Rev 13:4, 8). John may be drawing on the antichrist tradition found in 1 John 2:18, 22; 4:3, 2 John 7; and perhaps 2 Thessalonians 2:1–12. Futurist readings of Revelation assume that John's beast is the eschatological antichrist or man of lawlessness. But there are significant differences; e.g., the beast does not occupy God's temple (unlike 2 Thess 2:4), and the miracles are performed by the second beast (unlike 2 Thess 2:9). Moreover, the antichrists of 1 and 2 John seem to be apostate Christians, similar to the enemies portrayed in Revelation 2–3.[48]

---

42. This quote has been attributed to Hitler's propaganda chief, Goebbels.

43. One could more literally render this "it was given to him" (Greek ἐδόθη αὐτῷ [*edothē autō*]), another example of a divine passive.

44. This is a common phrase describing other empires (Dan 3:4; 5:19; 6:25), and it also appears with this function in Roman propaganda (Koester, *Revelation*, 587).

45. This reflects Dan 7:21. See also Aune, *Revelation 6–16*, 746.

46. The addition of "all" and the change of verb tense from aorist (past) to future in verse 8 may imply that this aspect of the beast's rule is still future (to John), perhaps meaning that the final emperor is still coming. Cf. Aune, *Revelation 6–16*, 746. Beale, *Book of Revelation*, 687.

47. In effect, Satan offered to make Jesus the Roman emperor (cf. Aune, *Revelation 6–16*, 736).

48. On "the eschatological antagonist," see Aune, *Revelation 6–16*, 751–55; Beale, *Book of Revelation*, 691.

So much of the language here is threatening. The beast emerges, survives a fatal attack, garners worldwide worship, blasphemes God with impunity, claims divine victory, defeats all opposition, conquers God's holy people, and kills many of them. This language parodies Roman propaganda of the first century, which portrayed Roman rule as beneficial, popular, and irresistible (vv. 3–4). But John subtly undermines this propaganda and reminds the hearers of several limitations to the beast's power. First, the use of the divine passive ("was given") three times in verses 5 and 7 reminds the hearers that the beast operates only within God's sovereign permission.[49] Even the healing of the fatal wound can only come about by God's permission, even though it seems to happen by the work of the dragon. Second, the beast's triumph is short-lived; it lasts only for "forty-two months" (v. 5).[50]

Third, while "all those who dwell on the earth" will worship the beast, this is immediately qualified—"(those) whose names have not been written in the book of life of the Lamb" (v. 8). In other words, no matter how successful the beast appears to be, no matter how much he conquers the saints, no matter how many of them he kills, there will always be some who resist and refuse to bow down. They may go into captivity, or perhaps exile, like John himself; they may be killed with the sword (as Paul apparently was) (v. 10). But God always has a "remnant," just like the seven thousand who did not bow to Baal in 1 Kings 19:18 or the three servants who refused the worship the golden statue (Dan 3). Modern examples include the faithful believers who outlived communism in the Soviet Union and its "satellites," and those currently suffering in China, North Korea, Saudi Arabia, Iran, and many other places.

Here the remnant is those whose names are written in the Lamb's book of life, reminding the hearers of what was said to the church in Sardis (3:5), that the victorious believers, the ones who were awake and not asleep, would not have their names blotted out from the book of life.[51] No wonder that here we read, "If anyone has ears, let them hear" (v. 9), a further echo of the repeated exhortation in Revelation 2–3, "Those who have ears, let them hear what the Spirit is saying to the churches."[52]

Finally, John draws the hearers' attention again to what Jesus has accomplished: "the Lamb who was slaughtered from the foundation of the world" (v. 8). The Greek allows for two valid translations here, indicating either that the Lamb was slain "from the creation of the world" (so NIV, KJV, NKJV, REB) or that the names were written in his book of life from the creation of the world (so RSV, NRSV, JB, NEB, ESV). The decision has to be made on theological grounds, though the parallel with Revelation

---

49. Cf. Thomas, *Apocalypse*, 386, 388–89, 392; Aune, *Revelation 6–16*, 743; Beale, *Book of Revelation*, 730. The passive seems at first to refer to the dragon as the source of the beast's healing and power, but the hearers know that all this is subject to God's sovereignty. For the opposite view, see Grabiner, *Revelation's Hymns*, 45–46.

50. See below. Cf. Thomas, *Apocalypse*, 389; Koester, *Revelation*, 572–73, 585.

51. Cf. Thomas, *Apocalypse*, 394–95; Koester, *Revelation*, 575; Beale, *Book of Revelation*, 701–2.

52. Cf. Beale, *Book of Revelation*, 704–5.

17:8 probably supports the second interpretation.[53] Either translation raises theological or philosophical issues.

But whichever translation is followed, this phrase underlines God's sovereignty, emphasizing that God has an eternal plan of salvation, which (by implication) will not be defeated or thwarted. It also speaks back to the apparent victory of the devil and beast in the healing of the head wound, reminding hearers again of Genesis 3:15. It reminds the hearers of what the text said earlier about the Lamb, that his slaughter "purchased for God . . . (people) from every tribe and language and people and nation" (5:9) who will "reign on the earth" (5:10; see also 1:5–6; 7:14–17). Despite his propaganda, the devil and the beast will be resoundingly defeated—but not yet.

> **If anyone is (destined) for captivity, to captivity they will go. If anyone is to be killed[54] by the sword, by the sword they will be killed. Here is the perseverance and the faith[55] of the saints. (Rev 13:10)[56]**

First more suffering and persecution must be endured.[57] This passage speaks to Christians in all ages, including many Pentecostals today. Indeed, it speaks to all who face overwhelming opposition and persecution by rulers who make blasphemous claims and seem invincible. It encourages believers to resist and endure with patience and faith (or faithfulness), rather than deny their testimony to Jesus Christ. Thus, they will conquer the beast, even while apparently being conquered by him, as foreshadowed by their conquest of the devil in 12:11 and as proven in real history.[58]

Before we move on, let's look again at the period of time allocated to the beast's rule: forty-two months (v. 5). This period of three-and-a-half years is based on two OT traditions. Daniel 7:25 says that the bad king (the little horn) will "speak against the Most High and oppress his holy people" who "will be delivered into his hands for a time, times and half a time." This period is repeated in Daniel 12:7 and implied by the "broken week" of Daniel 9:27. Approximately similar lengths are given for the

---

53. Koester contends that the NIV rendering is "incongruous" (Koester, *Revelation*, 575; cf. Aune, *Revelation 6–16*, 746–47). The second reading easily gives rise to a Calvinist predestinarian interpretation, as Beale proposes (Beale, *Book of Revelation*, 700–3). For a long defence of the first reading and its theological implications, see Moloney, *Apocalypse of John*, 198–204.

54. Nearly all ancient manuscripts read "if anyone kills with the sword, by the sword they will be killed," reflecting Matt 26:52. The NRSV follows these manuscripts even though NA28 and UBS4 do not. In this case, John would be warning his hearers against armed resistance to the beast. But as Pattemore argues, "for Asian Christians in the late first century, violent reaction to the authorities was not an option" (Pattemore, *People of God*, 172). Cf. Beale, *Book of Revelation*, 706–7; Aune, *Revelation 6–16*, 719, 731, 750.

55. The Greek πίστις [*pistis*] can also be translated as either "faith" or "faithfulness."

56. Verse 10 draws on Jer 15:2 and 43:11, but they speak of punishments from God whereas Rev 13:10 applies it to the sufferings of the saints. This is another example of the irony in this chapter, where God's promises are seemingly overturned. Cf. Aune, *Revelation 6–16*, 730–31, 749–50; Beale, *Book of Revelation*, 704–6; cf. Leithart, *Revelation 12–22*, 61.

57. Cf. Thomas, *Apocalypse*, 396–97.

58. Cf. Pattemore, *People of God*, 195.

abolition of the daily sacrifice and the "abomination that causes desolation" (Dan 12:11–12).[59]

Meanwhile, Elijah's drought (1 Kgs 17:1; 18:1) in some texts was three-and-a-half years long (Jas 5:17; Luke 4:25). In Revelation, the Gentiles "trample on the holy city for forty-two months" (11:2), the two witnesses "prophesy for 1,260 days" (11:3), the woman is protected in the wilderness for 1,260 days (12:6) or "for a time, times and half a time" (12:14), and the beast's authority lasts "for forty-two months" (13:5). If these periods all refer to the same time (a courageous supposition),[60] they seem to envisage a time of intense persecution of the saints, in which some, however, are supernaturally protected and two prophets operate with power, perhaps protesting at what is happening and inflicting damage on the enemies of the saints.

While the three-and-a-half years is probably not a literal time period, there are roughly similar periods that Revelation's audience might recall. These could include the original fulfillment of Daniel's prophecy in the period of Antiochus Epiphanes (167–164 BC),[61] the earthly ministry of Jesus, the early days of the infant church in Jerusalem (Acts 1–7), the Neronic persecution in Rome, and perhaps most likely, the Roman-Jewish war of AD 66–70 until the destruction of the Second Temple. All of these were periods of intense struggle, which is the common element in Daniel, the Elijah narrative, and Revelation.

Many Christians saw this as a future period of trial instigated by Satan through the antichrist. This idea is central to Futurist readings of Revelation, whereas Historicists read this as a period of 1,260 *years* of papal oppression (probably now past). John seems to envisage imminent events (1:1, 3; 22:6).[62] But as Koester comments, "Time does not unfold at the same pace in the visionary world and the readers' world" and this time probably presents the "the period between Christ's first and second comings."[63]

13:11–18 The Beast from the Earth

And I saw another wild beast coming out from the earth, and he had two horns like a lamb,[64] and spoke like a dragon. (Rev 13:11)

---

59. Cf. Goldingay, *Daniel*, 181. Goldingay argues that in Daniel such phrases are more indefinite, implying simply a period that was somehow cut off.

60. Cf. Aune, *Revelation 6–16*, 743.

61. An important source here is the books of Maccabees, which are not included in Protestant Bibles, especially 1 Macc 1:10, 41–63; 4:54; 2 Macc 6:1–11.

62. Cf. Koester, *Revelation*, 572–73.

63. Koester, *Revelation*, 585; see also Beale, *Book of Revelation*, 695.

64. As lambs do not have horns, Aune concludes this should be understood as a ram (Aune, *Revelation 6–16*, 719).

The original Lamb had seven horns (5:6), so perhaps this beast is like a smaller version of the Lamb, a copy of the real. The two horns might remind listeners of the two witnesses of Revelation 11 (this beast produces anti-prophets)[65] or the two-horned ram of Daniel 8:3–7, representing the Medo-Persian Empire.[66] It arises from the land, perhaps emphasizing its human origin as opposed to the first beast,[67] or more likely its "indigenous" origin in that emperor worship came out of Asian Greek culture, going back to Persian influence in the time of Alexander the Great's conquest of the Persian Empire.[68]

Since the earth was on the side of the woman in 12:16, something has changed if the earth now produces a beast at enmity with God.[69] Or perhaps John sees the land beast as somehow operating in the church, sowing deception and encouraging believers to submit to the sea beast, in line with his earlier criticism of the Nicolaitans and Jezebel (2:14–15, 20–24). This might cohere with the idea found in 1 John that the antichrist is a false prophetic influence within the church (1 John 2:18–22; 4:1–6).[70]

> **And he acted with all the authority of the first wild beast in his presence,[71] and he made the earth, and those who dwell in it, to worship the first wild beast, whose deadly wound was healed . . . (Rev 13:12)**

This beast is clearly not on the same side as the Lamb of God. It speaks like a dragon (the devil) and acts as a support to the wild beast from the sea, implying a delegation of power from the dragon to the sea beast and now to the land beast. Clearly, this new beast, whatever it represented in John's day,[72] serves the beast from the sea faithful-

---

65. There are significant parallels between this beast and the two witnesses (cf. Koester, *Revelation*, 600; Beale, *Book of Revelation*, 707).

66. Cf. Thomas, *Apocalypse*, 398; Beale, *Book of Revelation*, 707, 708. If this is what John intends, perhaps he is interpreting Daniel 8 in way that undermines the idea of the Persian Empire being more sympathetic to the Jews than either Babylon or the Greeks. Cyrus released the Jews from captivity and sponsored the rebuilding of the temple (Ezra 1); Darius re-authorized this after a temporary hiatus (Ezra 6), and Artaxerxes authorized and financed the rebuilding of the walls of Jerusalem (Neh 2:1–9). However, the Persian rulers were susceptible to manipulation by anti-Jewish elements (Ezra 4; Dan 6; Esth 3), and one of these nearly led to genocide. So Daniel would see all four empires as equally evil. Maybe John is hinting that the more tolerant side of Rome is only a mask; the empire is an enemy!

67. But in Dan 7:17, the four beasts who came up from the sea (Dan 7:3) are said to be "four kings that will arise from the earth." This beast would remind the hearers of the mythical monster Behemoth, parallel to Leviathan (Job 40:15–19; 41:1–34; 1 Enoch 60:7–8; 4 Ezra 6:49–52). Cf. Koester, *Revelation*, 601. Another suggestion is that this beast represents a revival of traditional Roman religion (Papandrea, *Wedding of the Lamb*, 49–50).

68. Cf. Paul, *Revelation*, 230, 235.

69. Cf. Corsini, *Apocalypse*, 227.

70. Cf. Pattemore, *People of God*, 167; Beale, *Book of Revelation*, 707–8.

71. Literally "in his presence" but clearly on his authority (Aune, *Revelation 6–16*, 757–58). The Greek here is present tense, "perhaps suggesting that the activity of this beast is an ongoing reality for John and his church" (Thomas, *Apocalypse*, 399).

72. See discussion of alternative identities in Koester, *Revelation*, 589–90; Aune, *Revelation 6–16*, 756, 773–75.

ly.⁷³ Many interpreters see a kind of false Trinity here: dragon/sea beast/land beast.⁷⁴ But John does not seem to emphasize this. However, he does draw attention to these three, and the later whore, by a kind of chiastic structure: he introduces them in one order (dragon, devil/sea beast/land beast/whore) and narrates their destruction in the reverse order.⁷⁵ The primary aim of the second beast is to make people worship the first beast (vv. 12, 15), and it has a clever strategy to that end.⁷⁶

The identity of this second beast is much contested. Many scholars see it as representing local authorities in Asia implementing the imperial cult.⁷⁷ Others who focus more on events in Judea read it as representing the Herods, or the temple authorities who are allied to Rome.⁷⁸ Beale sees it as a force also operating within the church.⁷⁹

> ... and he did great signs, so that he even made fire come out of heaven on to the earth before people, and he deceived those who dwell on the earth by the signs which were given to him to perform before the wild beast ... (Rev 13:13–14a)

For the hearers this is just as shocking as the healing of the beast's fatal wound, for the only person in Scripture capable of regularly calling down fire from heaven was Elijah, and this is what proved that God alone was a true god, for Baal's prophets could not do this (1 Kgs 18:22–39).⁸⁰ Signs and wonders are attributed in the Old Testament to Pharaoh's magicians (Exod 7:11–12, 22; 8:7) and their "secret arts" (Exod 8:7),

---

73. However, Moloney suggests this second beast "works for its own ends" and is actually manipulating the political power of the first beast (Moloney, *Apocalypse of John*, 207).

74. E.g., Thomas, *Apocalypse*, 399–400. Koester rather sees the beasts as a "demonic incarnation" (Koester, *Revelation*, 579). Both readings seek to show how the devil is imitating the work of God.

75. Cf. Koester, *Revelation*, 576.

76. While there is not a perfect parallel, the strategy undertaken by these two beasts resembles the way totalitarian regimes in the twentieth century established total control over their people through a combination of propaganda, economic pressure, violent suppression of dissent (and especially the church), and cultural activities focused on "worship" of the dictator. Cf. Richard, "Resistance, Hope, and Liberation in Central America," 160.

77. Aune seems inclined to identify the land beast with the provincial league of Asia whose "central function ... was the oversight of the imperial cult" (Aune, *Revelation 6–16*, 775) or with the "high priest" of Asia attached to the imperial cult temple (ibid., 774, 779, 780; cf. Beasley-Murray, *Revelation*, 216; Beale, *Book of Revelation*, 717; Friesen, "Myth and Symbolic Resistance," 300–302; Friesen, *Imperial Cults*, 30–31, 41–43). Another possibility is that the reference is to the "land" of Israel, suggesting that the land beast represents false prophets among the Jews (cf. Smolarz, *Covenant*, 348–49).

78. Leithart argues that the land beast represents unbelieving Judaism in alliance with Rome (the sea beast), parallel to the image of the whore riding the beast in 17:3, 7, suggesting that the land beast may be specifically the Herods (Roman client kings of Edomite origin) or the Jewish high priests, both allied to Rome and opposed to Jesus and the church, and that the corrupted Herodian temple, their power base, is, in effect, a Roman idol (Leithart, *Revelation 12–22*, 65–72).

79. This would be like the false apostles of 2:2 or Jezebel (2:20, 24) (Beale, *Book of Revelation*, 708–9, 726).

80. Fire also came down in response to prayers by David (1 Chr 21:26) and Solomon (2 Chr 7:1), but these are isolated instances. Cf. 2 Kgs 1:10–14, which suggests that calling down fire was a distinctive feature of Elijah's ministry. See also Rev 11:5. Cf. Koester, *Revelation*, 602–3; Leithart, *Revelation 12–22*, 70–71. Leithart also sees a parody of Moses here (Leithart, *Revelation 12–22*, 63).

but only within very limited boundaries (Exod 8:18–19; 9:11). Israelites are warned against false prophets doing miracles in Deuteronomy 13:1–3, and the land beast is later referred to as the "false prophet" (16:13; 19:20; 20:10).

Limited powers are also attributed to non-Christian agents in Acts 8:9–11; 16:16–18, and 19:13, but in each case, these are subjected to the name of Jesus. Paul warns his Thessalonian readers of the coming "lawless one" who will "use all sorts of displays of power through signs and wonders that serve the lie" (2 Thess 2:9; see also Mark 13:22; Matt 24:24). Now the false prophet seemed to have the power to do all that God's men could do.[81] Deception is a major theme in Revelation, beginning with Jezebel's deceptive teaching in the church of Thyatira (2:29), and a central characteristic of the dragon (12:9).[82] This is a major challenge to Pentecostals with their strong focus on "signs and wonders," calling them to exercise discernment when such claims are made.[83]

> **. . . saying to those who dwell on the earth to make a statue of the wild beast which had the wound of the sword and (yet) lived. (Rev 13:14b)**

This statue or image[84] would focus their allegiance to the beast in a public and visible way, as many religious and political leaders have proved. Hearers in John's day would remember the statue erected by Nebuchadnezzar in Daniel 3.[85] Similarly, the emperor Caligula ordered a statue of himself to be erected in the Jerusalem temple; this plan was only aborted by his death.[86] Similar statues or icons played a large part in the imperial cult, and this was one of tests later used by Pliny to test Christians.[87]

The people of the province of Asia hardly needed encouraging: they were already enthusiastically making images, setting up statues, and building temples in honor of Caesar and associated figures.[88] A colossal statue of Domitian (or perhaps Titus) erected in Ephesus may be the specific event that John has in mind here, and festivals in honor of the emperor frequently put strong pressure on everyone to make acts of worship.[89]

---

81. Cf. Thomas, *Apocalypse*, 400. In Greco-Roman religion, Jupiter/Zeus was the god of thunder and lightning who could send down fire and was often seen as the source of imperial authority (Koester, *Revelation*, 592). In Rev 20:9, "fire came down from heaven and devoured" the armies of Gog and Magog.

82. See the contrast with the two witnesses as discussed in Thomas, *Apocalypse*, 401. Whitaker points out that the plural "signs" (Greek σημεια [*sēmeia*]) is always deceptive in Revelation (Whitaker, *Ekphrasis*, 183–84).

83. Cf. Johnson, *Pneumatic Discernment*, 359–61.

84. The Greek behind "image" is εἰκόνα [*eikona*].

85. Cf. Beale, *Book of Revelation*, 711–12.

86. Beale, *Book of Revelation*, 710.

87. Cf. Aune, *Revelation 6–16*, 761, 765.

88. Cf. Koester, *Revelation*, 590–93; Aune, *Revelation 6–16*, 777–79; Bauckham, *Climax of Prophecy*, 445–47; Howard-Brook and Gwyther, *Unveiling Empire*, 95; Veyne, *Bread and Circuses*, 309, 313–14. "By the end of the first century A.D., all the cities addressed in the Apocalypse's letters had temples dedicated to the deity of Caesar" (Beale, *Book of Revelation*, 710).

89. Cf. Beale, *Book of Revelation*, 712–14.

> **And it was given to him to impart spirit to the statue of the wild beast, so that the statue of the wild beast might speak, and make whoever did not worship the statue of the wild beast to be put to death. (Rev 13:15)**

This is another astonishing sign, also blasphemous in that only God can give life to a physical or dead object (Rev 11:11; Gen 2:7; Ezek 37:4–10). The risen Christ claimed "the keys of death and Hades" (Rev 1:18; see also 2:10), and John has previously stated that "idols . . . cannot see or hear or walk" (9:20). We know that there were certain ways of making a statue seem alive and even seemingly talk in the ancient world, but whether John has this in mind, or a supernatural set of signs, is not clear.[90] Certainly, the divine passive ("it was given") is in operation (vv. 4, 15), unless the passive refers rather to the pseudo-divine dragon.

The second beast's next strategic move was more ominous: to kill all those who refused to worhip that image. The language suggests that the living image could itself put people to death, but more likely this would be done by enforcement authorities. The audience would likely think of Daniel 3, where Daniel's three friends surrendered their lives to a blazing furnace rather than worship the golden statue erected by Nebuchadnezzar. Perhaps at the stage Revelation was written, no one was being killed for not bowing down to statues or images of Caesar, but such consequences were coming, as evidence from the early second century shows.[91] As Whitaker notes, images (Greek *eikōn*) are always associated with beast worship in Revelation (13:14, 15, 16; 14:9, 11; 15:2; 16:2; 19:20; 20:4).[92]

> **And he made everyone, the small and the great, and the rich and the poor, and the free people and the slaves, that they might give them a mark on their right hand or on their forehead, and that no one was able to buy or sell, without having the mark of the name of the wild beast, or the number of his name. (Rev 13:16–17)**

This move put economic pressure on top of the threat of violence and added to the focus in the strategy of "beast religion." Dissenters would be easily exposed by the visible image in a public place and the visible sign of allegiance.[93] But what exactly was this mark of the beast? Some commentators have suggested that a literal mark is now possible, as seen with identification chips used on pets. However, there is no need to insist on a physical mark, any more than the seal on the foreheads of God's slaves (7:3, see also 14:1) or the names written on the victorious Philadelphian believers (3:12) would denote a visible, physical mark.

---

90. Cf. Scherrer, "Signs and Wonders in the Imperial Cult," 600–604; Thomas, *Apocalypse*, 403–4; Koester, *Revelation*, 593–594, 603; Aune, *Revelation 6–16*, 762–765; Beale, *Book of Revelation*, 711; Whitaker, *Ekphrasis*, 185–87; Court, *Revelation*, 60–61; Fiorenza, *Vision of a Just World*, 85–86. Price points out that, "miraculous behavior is often associated with statues at this date by sources both pagan and Christian" (Price, *Rituals and Power*, 198).

91. Cf. Koester, *Revelation*, 594, 604.

92. Whitaker, *Ekphrasis*, 188, 208–9.

93. Thomas, *Apocalypse*, 405–6; Koester, *Revelation*, 95; Walvoord, *Revelation*, 209.

Rather, I think John's readers would envisage a sign that clearly identified someone as either loyal to the gods and Caesar or not, one that was publicly seen and that had consequences, economically and legally.[94] They might think of the tattooing of fugitive slaves or soldiers, or a religious symbol.[95] They might think of trade guilds: in order to perform certain trades, it was necessary to belong to a guild and take part in activities that included feasts in honor of their patron gods. Those who did not take part could be expelled and unable to "buy or sell."[96] They would understand that the temples acted as banks so it was difficult to conduct business without being entangled with them.[97] They might envisage responses to the Caesar cult.

Refusing to participate in ceremonies and honor statues of the emperor could result in discrimination, loss of trade or employment, and even prison or execution (see 2:10, 13). By the early second century, people accused of being Christians were tested by being required to offer sacrifices or burn incense before images of the gods or Caesar, and those found guilty because they refused to do these things could be executed, often in public stadiums.[98] Later people had to prove they'd performed the required sacrifices by producing a certificate called a *libellus*.[99]

To this day, there are certain visible signs that show whether a person is a loyal follower of Jesus or prepared to compromise. They vary from place to place and from century to century, and the consequences are more or less severe, but we should apply this passage according to the context we find ourselves in.[100] As Koester comments, "Revelation assumes that the conflict between God and evil takes tangible political, religious, and economic forms."[101] As Thomas says, "the lines of demarcation between God and the dragon have been drawn absolutely and definitively . . . there is absolutely no middle ground."[102]

---

94. Cf. Beale, *Book of Revelation*, 716.

95. Cf. Thomas, *Apocalypse*, 406; Aune, *Revelation 6–16*, 767–68. Jews in Alexandria were forced to have a tattoo of the sign of Dionysus on their bodies in the third century BC (Koester, *Revelation*, 595). Similar humiliating identification of Jews was part of the Nazi oppression in 1933–1945.

96. Cf. Koester, *Revelation*, 595–96; Aune, *Revelation 6–16*, 768. As I noted earlier, Aune contends that no such "guilds" with "regulatory or protective functions" existed then; the *collegia* were more like associations (Aune, *Revelation 1–5*, 186). Membership of such associations was voluntary but involved cultic participation. In this situation, there would be pressure to join with the implied threat of boycott for dissidents.

97. Howard-Brook and Gwyther, *Unveiling Empire*, 103–4.

98. Pliny the Younger, *Letters* 10:96–97.

99. Papandrea, *Wedding of the Lamb*, 50, 68, 157

100. Some early Pentecostals applied this passage to the conscription and other enforced measures during World War I (Johnson, *Pneumatic Discernment*, 123–24, 139–41, 185–86). Others took a more futurist position (ibid., 183–85).

101. Koester, *Revelation*, 601.

102. Thomas, *Apocalypse*, 406, 407; Koester, *Revelation*, 604.

Here is wisdom. Let the one who has a mind figure out the number of the wild beast, for it is a human number, and his number is six hundred and sixty-six. (Rev 13:18)

Clearly, the second beast's strategy is very successful. John, on the other hand, wants to expose and defeat it, at least for his hearers/readers.[103] This passage concludes with a final sign that the fatal mark is at work, using John's frequent recourse to numbers. A little earlier, he has called on the hearer to hear well (v. 9). Now he urges them to think well also and to calculate (Greek *psēphisatō*, "figure out, count") "the number of the wild beast."

This may well be an appeal to an ancient practice called *gematria*, where a name was coded in numbers, using the fact that most ancient cultures used letters for numbers; Roman numerals are still used today.[104] It's not an exact procedure because there could be many names that add up in numbers to the same total; it would only work if you already knew the likely names you needed to choose from.[105] So it is likely that John assumed such knowledge on the part of his readers, implying that the beast was alive in his day.[106]

But this is why there have been so many false attempts to decode this number from the first century until now. In fact, some commentators have tried a simpler solution and worked out John's meaning as three digits of six rather than the number 666. That way we can say it's six, the number of man, three times, or three sixes representing incompletion.[107] In Australia, a new credit card was devised in 1974 by the leading banks, called Bankcard. The cards had a logo of a stylized b in three colors that could be interpreted as 666, which made many Bible-believing people very anxious. But the Greek text suggests we are looking at the number 666.

The only possible OT allusion here would be to the weight of gold brought to Solomon annually (1 Kgs 10:14). This might imply something about the corruption of wealth. Leithart sees the land beast as a corrupted and apostate Jewish order based in the temple which is doomed to destruction, with strong parallels to Solomon in his later days. He suggests that the mark of the beast is Jewish phylacteries that become corrupt when those wearing them oppose Jesus.[108]

---

103. One way to do this would be by portraying the elites of Roman Asia as beastly figures like Behemoth (Friesen, "Myth and Symbolic Resistance," 310).

104. Cf. Thomas, *Apocalypse*, 411–13; Koester, *Revelation*, 596–99, 605–6; Beale, *Book of Revelation*, 718–20). The challenge resembles traditional riddles (Koester, *Revelation*, 605; Aune, *Revelation 6–16*, 772).

105. Beale, *Book of Revelation*, 720–21.

106. Aune, *Revelation 6–16*, 769.

107. Cf. Beale, *Book of Revelation*, 722–27.

108. Leithart, *Revelation 12–22*, 74–81; cf. Thomas, *Apocalypse*, 410; Beale, *Book of Revelation*, 727; Johnson, *Pneumatic Discernment*, 286–87.

However, bearing in mind the numerous allusions to the Roman Empire in this chapter, the most likely candidates for 666 are the emperor Nero, the emperor Domitian, and Irenaeus' suggestion of Lateinos.[109]

Nero is a likely candidate, not just because a Hebraized spelling of Nero Caesar adds up to 666 in Hebrew,[110] but because he was the first emperor to legally and physically persecute Christians, executing the apostles Peter and Paul (and many others) in a short but bloody pogrom in Rome itself.[111] He also began the war against the Jews in AD 66. However, if Revelation was written in the late-90s of the first century, Nero would only be a representative candidate, a kind of generic emperor. If Domitian, the likely emperor when Revelation was written, was also systematically harassing Christians and demanding to be worshiped as "Lord and God," perhaps John and others saw him as a kind of reincarnation of Nero.[112] Domitian's abbreviated title and name that might have appeared on coins and translated into Greek could also add up to 666.[113] The ambiguity of the reference is probably deliberate then; Christians would get the meaning, but others would not.

As Thomas and Bauckham both point out, 666 is also a distinctive number anyway, a "doubly triangular number," a "king amongst numbers" appropriate for a beast claiming divine honors and powers.[114] All this suggests that we should refrain from calculating contemporary people's numbers in ancient languages today. As Beale suggests, "the exhortation in Rev 13:18 concerns discernment of truth in the midst of falsehood and not a calculation pinpointing one specific evil individual."[115]

This does not mean that the beast only has significance for ancient historians or futurologists. The main thrust of this chapter is incredibly relevant for most believers at any time. Often those who hold political or economic power are inclined to demand

---

109. Irenaeus, *Haer.* 5.30.3, ANF 1:559. Cf. Aune, *Revelation 6–16*, 770. Irenaeus also suggests Teitan, alluding to another ancient myth of giants who challenged the gods. Cf. Corsini, *Apocalypse*, 238–39.

110. It also works with the alternative manuscript that has 616 as the number, and in both variations the Hebrew translation of the word "beast" yields the same two possible numbers. See Aune, *Revelation 6–16*, 770–71; Bauckham, *Climax of Prophecy*, 384–90; Paul, *Revelation*, 239–42.

111. Cf. Thomas, *Apocalypse*, 413–14; Koester, *Revelation*, 597–98, 606. At least one Roman writer called Nero a beast with multiple heads (Koester, *Revelation*, 568–69; Bauckham, *Climax of Prophecy*, 409–10; cf. Beale, *Book of Revelation*, 719–20). Stramara suggests the underlying person whose name originally added to 666 was Nimrod (Gen 10:8–10), believed to be the founder of Babylon (Stramara, *God's Timetable*, 107–110), and that 666 was originally a good number, the numerical value of the twelve tribes of Israel, alluded to in the very next verse (14:1; ibid., 121–25).

112. Portraying Domitian this way is no longer seen as viable by many commentators (Koester, *Revelation*, 578). Alternatively, John is making use of the myth that Nero would return from the East as an antichrist figure with a large Parthian army (cf. Bauckham, *Climax of Prophecy*, 396, 407–31).

113. Papandrea, *Wedding of the Lamb*, 133; Mounce, *Revelation*, 264.

114. Thomas, *Apocalypse*, 414–16; Bauckham, *Climax of Prophecy*, 390–94. As Aune points out, however, this doesn't help the reader identify the individual concerned (Aune, *Revelation 6–16*, 772). For a different take on this, cf. Malina, *Genre and Message*, 184–87.

115. Beale, *Book of Revelation*, 726.

excessive loyalty and compliance from their subjects, even to the point of absolute submission. They then harass, discriminate against, persecute, and even murder those who resist, especially if they do so on the grounds of Christian faith. This is happening in many countries as I write, and Pentecostal Christians are particularly suffering, partly because they are more open and aggressive in their faith. God seems to allow this in order to "separate the sheep from the goats," to expose false or nominal believers and bring the ancient struggle between God and the devil into the open. As Thomas puts it, "the calculation to which they [the hearers] are called is no mere parlor game" but "must take place in the Spirit."[116] The stakes here are enormous!

---

116. Thomas, *Apocalypse*, 409; cf. Beale, *Book of Revelation*, 723, 725.

Revelation Chapter 14

We have been reading through several chapters of intense struggle between God, the Lamb, and the disciples of the Lamb on one side, and a range of anti-God forces on the other. In chapter 12, this has been very carefully focused, exposing the nature of the struggle more clearly. Readers now know not only that the struggle is fundamentally between God and Satan, but also that Satan attacks God largely by attacking his messiah (Jesus) and the messianic community of his followers (the church, Christians).

And in chapter 13, Satan, having lost a war in heaven and having been thrown down to earth, uses his political clout to maintain control of the Roman Empire (and other similar empires) through his agent, the wild beast, and the beast's agent, the second beast (false prophet). This is very successful, at least in the short term. All the people now worship the beast and the devil, except for a seemingly small minority of those whose names are written in the Lamb's book of life, and subject to God's sovereign permission.

But now God is ready to launch a counterattack.[1] The beast and the little horn of Daniel 7 were defeated when "one like a son of man" came and received international dominion from God (Dan 7:13–14), delegated also to "the holy people of the Most High" (Dan 7:27). Revelation 1:7 has already promised such a coming, and it will be reimagined by John in Revelation 14.[2]

14:1–5 The Messianic Army

> **And I saw, and behold the Lamb standing on mount Zion, and with him one hundred and forty-four thousand who had his name and his Father's name written on their foreheads. (Rev 14:1)**

---

1. Beale reads this more as "another prophetic narration of the actual, future final judgment and reward" (Beale, *Book of Revelation*, 731). This depends on reading chs. 6–19 as recapitulating the same basic events, which I discussed and rejected above (at the start of ch. 12). I think John is talking about real events or forces in his era, and throughout the age, not just final judgment.

2. Cf. Pattemore, *People of God*, 174–78.

John often signals a new section with "and I saw" (Greek *kai eidon*); similar introductions are found in verse 6 and verse 14.[3] What he sees now is significant. First, it is the Lamb who appears, whom the hearers have learned "was slaughtered from the foundation of the world" (13:8), and previously, that he "purchased for God by your blood (people) from every tribe and language and people and nation . . . and they will reign on the earth" (5:9–10). In other words, the mention of the Lamb reminds the hearers that God's cause is based on the Lamb's death and will be successful in redeeming a huge international multitude (7:9, 14).

Second, the Lamb is standing[4] on Mount Zion. As Koester suggests, this is a "militant posture"[5] and it probably alludes specifically to Psalm 2:6, a psalm which John frequently refers to or echoes. Therefore, it emphasizes the messianic rule of the Lamb, not just in the future, but now (compare Acts 4:25–30).[6] Rather than just a geographic location, Mount Zion is the place of authority and worship, as well as David's capital, and hence the messiah's headquarters, anticipating the New Jerusalem.[7] It is also the focus of the "new exodus" in Isaiah, the place to which the Israelites will return (Isa 2:3; 35:10; 40:9; 49:14; 51:3, 11, 16; 52:1, 2, 7; 59:20; 60:14; 61:3; 62:1, 11). It also represents salvation in the era of the ourpoured Spirit and cosmic shakings (Joel 2:28–32), that is, the era of the church. Here the Lamb is in a strategic position to defeat the beast and his allies, who cannot overthrow his rule no matter how hard they try (see Ps 2:1–6).[8]

Third, the Lamb is accompanied by 144,000. This group was mentioned in Revelation 7, where it is said to be made up of 12,000 from every tribe of Israel in a census with military overtones.[9] Here they "stand with the Lamb in opposition to the triumvirate of evil, ready to do battle."[10] In chapter 7, they were sealed on their foreheads; now the hearers learn that the name of the Lamb and his Father[11] are writ-

---

3. For a sophisticated structural analysis of this chapter and its reuse of phrases from other parts of Revelation, see Aune, *Revelation 6–16*, 794–800; cf. Leithart, *Revelation 12–22*, 81–85.

4. The fact that he is standing at all is significant given the question "who is able to stand?" in 6:17. There may also be an echo of Acts 7:55–56 where the martyr Stephen sees "the Son of Man standing at the right hand of God."

5. Koester, *Revelation*, 607.

6. Cf. Leithart, *Revelation 12–22*, 85; Bauckham, *Climax of Prophecy*, 230.

7. See Ps 132, especially vv. 11–18, and Heb 12:22–24. Cf. Thomas, *Apocalypse*, 418; Koester, *Revelation*, 616–17; Leithart, *Revelation 12–22*, 86, 88.

8. Cf. Beale, *Book of Revelation*, 733; Pattemore, *People of God*, 179–81; Aune, *Revelation 6–16*, 803–4. Aune argues for an earthly Mount Zion.

9. See above on 7:4–8. For more analysis of the 144,000, see Thomas, *Apocalypse*, 418–19; Koester, *Revelation*, 617. As there is no "the" before 144,000, some suggest this is a different group than that in Rev 7 (e.g., Aune, *Revelation 6–16*, 784, 804), but I find it unlikely that the audience would draw such a conclusion.

10. Thomas, *Apocalypse*, 419.

11. Cf. Thomas, *Apocalypse*, 419–20; Koester, *Revelation*, 608. Koester points out that Zeus and Caesar were both portrayed as fathers of humankind in Roman thinking. There are just five references

ten on their foreheads, as promised to the conquerors of Philadelphia (3:12) and the final "slaves" of the Lamb (22:4), and in contrast to the mark of the beast referred to in chapter 13.

These forehead markings are not to be taken as literal physical tattoos, but rather indicate the ultimate allegiance of those so marked, either the beast or the Lamb, and the protection afforded by such allegiance.[12] They are covenant marks, and in drawing attention to them, John is sharpening the division between two categories of humanity. He is also identifying these people (the 144,000) as the "conquerors" mentioned in every prophetic message of Revelation 2–3, and implied by the names in the book back in 13:8.[13] Thus, he hopes to motivate his audience to be like them, "to make their decision for salvation and for the word of God."[14]

> And I heard a sound from heaven like a sound of many waters, and like the sound of a loud thunder, and the sound[15] which I heard was like harpists playing their harps. And they sang a new song before the throne, and before the four living beings and the elders, and no one was able to learn the song except the 144,000, those purchased from the earth. (Rev 14:2–3)

This description is hard to really imagine: harps sounding like thunder?[16] It's a loud sound, a bit like a rock concert perhaps (compare 19:6). Harps have been mentioned previously in 5:8, with the singing in honor of the Lamb, but this time three words from the same Greek root *kithar-* are employed, emphasizing the harping here.[17] All this reminds the hearers of the role that praise and worship of God play in the narrative, celebrating and even pushing events forward and contesting the praise of other gods and Caesar.[18] This praise is, of course, in heaven, but it provides a model for the church on earth. As Leithart comments, "God is a God of music, and he has made us in his image," and "worship is warfare. Liturgy is conquest."[19]

On this occasion, the song is specifically to be learned and sung by the 144,000: no one else is permitted to learn it.[20] It is a "new song," a phrase used in Psalms to describe

---

to God as Father in Revelation, all of them speaking of God as Jesus' Father (1:6; 2:28; 3:5, 21; 14:1).

12. Cf. Beale, *Book of Revelation*, 734; Leithart, *Revelation 12–22*, 87. Leithart sees these as Jewish martyrs who "are not marked to avoid death; they are marked to rise again from the grave" (ibid.).

13. Cf. Koester, *Revelation*, 607–8; Pattemore, *People of God*, 182–83.

14. Fiorenza, "Followers of the Lamb," 132, 134.

15. I have translated the Greek φωνὴν [*phōnēn*] as "sound" in four places, although it sounds rather wooden, so as to show you that it is the same Greek word each time. It can be translated as sound, noise, or voice.

16. Voices like "the sound of rushing waters" (Rev 1:15) or thunder (6:1; 10:3–4) have been heard before, but this choir, or something like an orchestra accompanying the 144,000, must have been amazingly loud. Cf. Aune, *Revelation 6–16*, 807–8; Leithart, *Revelation 12–22*, 87–88.

17. Thomas, *Apocalypse*, 421. For more on Greek harps [*kithara*], see Koester, *Revelation*, 608.

18. Cf. Koester, *Revelation*, 617–18.

19. Leithart, *Revelation 12–22*, 86, 89.

20. Koester, on the other hand, reads the passage as saying that angels were singing the song (based

celebrations of God's great acts in history (Pss 96:1; 98:1;[21] 144:9–10; 40:3; 149:1; Isa 42:10), often with a reference to salvation or revelation to the nations (Pss 96:3, 7, 10; 98:2–3), and to the future "coming" of God to judge the world (Pss 96:13; 98:9). This phrase is also found in Revelation 5:9 about the "new song" to the Lamb, with similar reference to the salvation of the nations.[22] New acts of God demand new songs!

> **These are those who have not defiled (themselves) with women, for they are virgins, those following the Lamb wherever he goes. They have been purchased from people as firstfruits to God and to the Lamb, and in their mouths no lie was found. They are unblemished. (Rev 14:4–5)**

The 144,000 have been "purchased from the earth" (v. 3) or "from people" (v. 4), presumably as a result of the slaughter of the Lamb (using the same Greek verb, *exagorazō*). They are among those "purchased for God" by his blood (5:9), in an ironic contrast to the beast economy (13:17). John doesn't unpack this in detail or develop a consistent doctrine of atonement, but he clearly believes that people are redeemed or purchased for God by Jesus' death. As he puts it in 1:5, Jesus is "the one who loves us and released us from our sins by his blood."

They are offered as firstfruits to God and the Lamb (v. 4), which links to their purity (v. 5), as only pure animals could be offered to God.[23] This suggests that they are in some sense the first believers in Christ[24] or especially devoted to him,[25] which is consistent with the idea that they are believing Israelites or Jews (as in Jer 2:3) since the first Christians were Jews and is therefore consistent also with the census of chapter 7. But they could equally represent all "conquering" believers, as 22:4 suggests.[26]

Language of "firstfruits" also signals a great harvest to come (perhaps as early as verse 15); that is, there will be many others converted to Christ through their ministry, just as the original mention of the 144,000 in Revelation 7 leads straight into the uncountable international multitude of converts.[27] John may have in mind a concept similar to Paul

---

on 5:9–10), but the 144,000 had the exclusive understanding of what it meant (Koester, *Revelation*, 609; cf. Aune, *Revelation 6–16*, 784, 806, 808–9). I find this supposition unnecessary; even if the 144,000 are on earth, they can still sing along with heaven. See Beale, *Book of Revelation*, 737; Pattemore, *People of God*, 184.

21. This psalm also refers to harps in verse 5.

22. Cf. Thomas, *Apocalypse*, 422–24.

23. Cf. Koester, *Revelation*, 611–12; Aune, *Revelation 6–16*, 823. For a detailed study of "first fruits," see Aune, *Revelation 6–16*, 814–18. This also implies martyrdom (Leithart, *Revelation 12–22*, 87), though perhaps not literally in every case, more like total surrender.

24. Cf. Rom 16:5; 1 Cor 16:15; 2 Thess 2:13.

25. See Jer 2:2–3, which also compares God's people's holy love as a bride to being firstfruits of his harvest (Koester, *Revelation*, 619).

26. Cf. Beale, *Book of Revelation*, 733–34.

27. Thomas, *Apocalypse*, 427–28. James 1:18 has a similar thought, though maybe speaking of Christians in general as a foreshadowing of redemption of all creation, similar to Rom 8:22–23. Cf. Beale, *Book of Revelation*, 742–44.

in Romans 11, where Gentile believers in Christ are grafted into Israel (the concept of "firstfruits" is mentioned in Rom 11:16). Perhaps this is pointing forward to 20:3, where Satan is unable to deceive the nations any longer as a result of the victory won in chapters 14–19. In other words, the 144,000 open the way for world evangelization.

The hearers learn some other significant facts about this group, which suggests they are meant to be seen as a kind of military force, though not literally.[28] They "have not defiled themselves with women, for they are virgins" (v. 4). This difficult verse has been criticized heavily by some feminist commentators as it seems misogynistic on a number of levels,[29] and males are rarely called virgins in the ancient world,[30] but it probably relates to rules for soldiers in ancient Israel: no sex before battle (Deut 23:9–10; 1 Sam 21:4–5)![31]

There may be an allusion to what Jesus said to the Pergamum church (2:14) about Balaam, who came up with the idea of seducing the Israelite army as a military strategy (Num 31:16). John is probably not advocating some kind of monastic celibacy, though in later centuries this was an effective way of raising up evangelistic forces to preach the gospel in new fields. More likely, he is just commending sexual self-control, that is, avoidance of immorality, as in the Pergamum message. Or better still, such purity is metaphorical for spiritual purity and uncompromising loyalty to God or discipleship to Jesus (see Luke 14:26; 1 Cor 7:1; 2 Cor 11:2–3), as God's people are sometimes referred to as virgins (Isa 37:22; Jer 18:13; 31:4; Matt 25:1–13).[32] This is part of the romantic thread in the narrative, which will becaome more blatant in 19:7–9 and 21:2, 9.[33]

These people are "following the Lamb wherever he goes" (v. 4): they are devoted disciples of Jesus, which implies a willingness to die for him.[34] And "in their mouths no lie was found. They are unblemished" (v. 5), unlike the lies coming from the beasts' side and from some Jews (2:9; 3:9), but *like* the Servant of Isaiah 53:9 (compare 1 Pet 2:21–23) and the remnant of Zephaniah 3:13.[35]

---

28. Cf. Aune, *Revelation 6–16*, 814.

29. If the hearers were familiar with John's Gospel, they would be unlikely to see a misogynistic attitude here, according to Thomas, since there is no negativity towards women there (Thomas, *Apocalypse*, 424–25). Koester links this to the romantic themes in Revelation: the 144,000 are part of the bride of Christ (cf. Koester, *Revelation*, 609–10, 618–19).

30. Cf. Aune, *Revelation 6–16*, 811–12.

31. Cf. Bauckham, *Climax of Prophecy*, 230–31. Or it could relate to priesthood (cf. 5:9–10) or even prophecy. See also Aune, *Revelation 6–16*, 810, 812, 819–22; Leithart, *Revelation 12–22*, 90.

32. Cf. Fiorenza, "Followers of the Lamb," 133.

33. Cf. Bauckham, *Climax of Prophecy*, 231–32; Beale, *Book of Revelation*, 738–41; Koester, *Revelation*, 610–11; Aune, *Revelation 6–16*, 811–12, 820–22; Pattemore, *People of God*, 185–87. Another possible intertext is Exod 19:14–15, where sexual abstinence is required at the giving of the Law at Sinai (cf. Stramara, *God's Timetable*, 70–71).

34. Cf. Thomas, *Apocalypse*, 426–27; Aune, *Revelation 6–16*, 813–14; Beale, *Book of Revelation*, 741; Pattemore, *People of God*, 187–89.

35. Cf. Beale, *Book of Revelation*, 745–47; Fekkes, *Isaiah and Prophetic Traditions*, 191–92.

It seems then that we are hearing the description of God's army about to counterattack, not with physical weapons but with truth, holiness, praise, devotion to Christ, and evangelism. As Bauckham claims, "in the eschatological destruction of evil in Revelation there is no place for real armed violence, but there is ample space for the imagery of armed violence."[36]

14:6–13 The Warnings of Three Angels

> **And I saw another angel flying in mid-heaven, having an eternal gospel to preach good news to those sitting on the earth, and to every nation and tribe and language and people . . . (Rev 14:6)**

John now sees three angels in succession. The first is described as "another angel flying in mid-heaven" (v. 6; compare the eagle of 8:13 with three woes),[37] described as "another," perhaps as an acknowledgment of the numerous angels so far in the narrative. This angel is doing something normally assigned to human witnesses:[38] proclaiming the gospel (v. 6, maybe echoing Matt 24:14).[39] The phrases about the nations here are repeated in several key places in the text. We read, "all people on earth" mourn because of Jesus when he comes on the clouds (1:7); to the victorious believers, Jesus will "give authority over the nations" (2:26); the Lamb's blood purchases "persons from every tribe and language and people and nation" (5:9); and a great uncountable multitude stands in heaven "from every nation, tribe, people and language" (7:9). Later John is freshly commissioned to "prophesy again about many peoples, nations, languages and kings" (10:11), but the sea beast "was given authority over every tribe and people and language and nation" (13:7). This shows that in John's view, the gathering of all these people would be done by the preaching of the Christian gospel, but that God's intention to have a great multitude from all peoples will be contested by the devil.

This is almost the only place where gospel language is directly used in Revelation (see also 10:7), but here this language is repeated to emphasize the point.[40] Literally the text says that the angel "has an eternal gospel to evangelize . . . " John is probably drawing particularly from Isaiah 40:9 and 52:7, which are part of the promise of restoration for Zion.[41]

---

36. Bauckham, *Climax of Prophecy*, 233; see full discussion, 232–37.

37. Both the three woes and the three angelic messages in this chapter have structural significance (Leithart, *Revelation 12–22*, 92–93).

38. However, there is some NT precedent for an angel bringing good news (Luke 1:19; 2:10; perhaps Gal 1:8).

39. Cf. Aune, *Revelation 6–16*, 827.

40. On the OT and Greco-Roman background, see Koester, *Revelation*, 612. On NT comparisons, see Leithart, *Revelation 12–22*, 94–95.

41. Aune, *Revelation 6–16*, 825–26. He is building on the work of A. P. van Schaik.

Bauckham sees Psalm 96 as the main source due to the use of the phrase "the eternal gospel" (Greek *aiōnion euangelion*) which reflects the Septuagint (Greek) of Psalm 96:2 ("proclaim his salvation day after day," using *euangelizesthe* for "proclaim"). The context shows the target audience is "all the earth" (Ps 96:1), "the nations," and "all peoples" (Ps 96:3), as here in Rev 14:6.[42] This phrase "eternal gospel" is unique to this verse in the whole New Testament; it may serve to emphasize the ancient origins of the gospel, as 10:7 implies, or its permanent validity,[43] or a contrast to the "gospel" of Caesar,[44] or the eternal consequences of accepting or rejecting it, which will soon be underlined.[45] Its occurrence here is important since the audience has recently heard that "all those who dwell on the earth will worship" the beast (13:8).

> . . . saying in a loud voice, "Fear God and give him glory, for the hour of his judgment has come, and worship the one who made the heaven and the earth and sea and springs of water." (Rev 14:7)[46]

It seems that the door to salvation is still open[47] to those who respond to the call to fear God, give him glory, and worship him as Creator. God is to be feared and worshiped because of his role as Creator and imminent Judge,[48] not as Savior (compare Acts 14:15; 17:24–31; 1 Thess 1:9–10), not that John is uninterested in redemption, as verse 3 implies. Fearing and giving glory to God seems to be equivalent to repentance in John's mind (compare 11:13, 18).[49] The timing here ("the hour of his judgment has come") reflects earlier announcements in 6:17 and 11:18 and anticipates 18:10, underlying the imminence of the day of judgment and the urgency of repentance. The aorist tense of "come" has a future (proleptic) meaning (or prophetic perfect), but anticipates the language of the two harvests later in this chapter.[50]

> And another, second, angel followed, saying, "Fallen, fallen is Babylon the Great, who from the wine of the fury of her immorality made all the nations drink." (Rev 14:8)

---

42. Bauckham, *Climax of Prophecy*, 286–89.
43. Cf. Aune, *Revelation 6–16*, 826.
44. Cf. Beale, *Book of Revelation*, 750.
45. Cf. Beale, *Book of Revelation*, 748–50.
46. Cf. Thomas, *Apocalypse*, 430–31; Koester, *Revelation*, 612–13.
47. Cf. Thomas, *Apocalypse*, 432; Koester, *Revelation*, 620. Beale, however, argues that there is no expectation that anyone will respond to this gospel; it is simply a witness against resistant unbelievers and "good news" only to believers, "because it means the downfall of the ungodly system" (Beale, *Book of Revelation*, 750, see also 751–54).
48. Cf. Ps 96, whose "new song" includes the same message. Cf. Bauckham, *Climax of Prophecy*, 286–89.
49. Cf. Thomas, *Apocalypse*, 458; contra Beale, *Book of Revelation*, 751–53.
50. Cf. Aune, *Revelation 6–16*, 828; Leithart, *Revelation 12–22*, 95–96.

This is the first mention of Babylon, though "the great city" was mentioned (under the names of Sodom and Egypt) in 11:8 as the place where the two witnesses were killed. The phrase "great Babylon" is derived probably from Daniel 4:30, where Nebuchnezzar boasts of his capital on the eve of his period of insanity. Babylon will occupy the central focus of Revelation 17–18, and, as Leithart comments, mention of Babylon implies a "second exodus" described in Isaiah.[51]

The fall of Babylon is a key part of the "good news" announced in Isaiah, since it means freedom from exile and oppression, freedom to return to Zion. At this point, John's hearers have only a general idea of the identity of this "Babylon," though the word would already have connotations of immorality, idolatry, sorcery, exile, and the oppression of God's people, especially for those familiar with Daniel 1–5 or Jeremiah 50–51.[52] The original fall of Babylon is announced in Isaiah 21:9. The announcement here in Revelation 14, in the context of the previous chapter, would imply an association with the beast. Perhaps Babylon is his capital![53]

The emphasis here is on Babylon's "immorality," its violence (Greek *thumos*, "fury, passion"), and its international influence and power (Babylon "made all the nations drink").[54] As Koester explains, the image being conjured up is one of a "bawdy banquet where a prostitute makes clients drunk while luring them into sexual liaisons."[55] John frequently uses sexual immorality as a kind of symbol for idolatry (2:14, 20), commercial relationships (18:3),[56] and political alliances (17:2; 18:9).[57] However, this announcement is intended to undermine any confidence people (especially professing Christians) might have in Babylon, and therefore help them see their need to turn to the Creator and Judge, especially after the catastrophic events of the seven trumpets.

> **Another, third, angel followed them, saying in a loud voice, "If anyone worships the wild beast and its statue, and receives a mark on their forehead or on their hand, they also will drink the wine of the fury of God that is mixed undiluted[58] in the cup of his wrath, and they will be tormented with fire and sulfur before (the) holy angels and before the Lamb. And the smoke of their torment goes up forever and ever, and they have no rest day and night, those who worship the wild beast and its statue, and if anyone receives the mark of his name." (Rev 14:9–11)**

---

51. Leithart, *Revelation 12–22*, 96.

52. Cf. Beale, *Book of Revelation*, 755.

53. On the reasons for equating Babylon with Rome, see Aune, *Revelation 6–16*, 829–31. This will be discussed more when we consider Revelation 17.

54. Cf. Thomas, *Apocalypse*, 434; Leithart, *Revelation 12–22*, 97.

55. Koester, *Revelation*, 620.

56. Cf. Beale, *Book of Revelation*, 756–58.

57. Cf. Koester, *Revelation*, 621. Even today we speak of people "getting into bed with" people they are allied to in some way.

58. Cf. Aune, *Revelation 6–16*, 833.

Before the audience has any time to digest news of Babylon's fall, they hear of a "third angel." He speaks with "a loud voice," a common event in Revelation. And what he says is perhaps the most serious and lengthy warning in the whole book. This angel is drawing a line in the sand, showing John's hearers what is at stake here.

They must choose between God and the devil, between the Lamb and the beast, between taking the mark of the beast and receiving the holy names on their foreheads. This is a choice between Babylon and Zion, between drinking the fury of Babylon and that of God (the same Greek construction is used for both in verses 8 and 10).[59] The consequences of refusing the mark of the beast have already been spelled out: economic deprivation and even death (13:15–17). But the consequences of taking that mark, that is of giving one's allegiance to the beast, are even more serious: eternal torment. This is an essential element of the gospel proclaimed in this passage.

Here we find the most explicit statement of the traditional doctrine of hell in the New Testament: it is unending, uninterrupted, conscious torture.[60] Torture or torment (Greek *basanismos*) has previously been used in Revelation to describe the effects of the locusts (9:5) and the effects of the ministry of the two prophets (11:10). But this is a new level![61]

The imagery here draws on several Old Testament passages: the destruction of Sodom and Gomorrah (Gen 19:24–28; Deut 29:23), the prophesied destruction of Assyria (Isa 30:33) and Edom (Isa 34:9–10),[62] and the ambush of the city of Ai (Josh 8:19–21). Perhaps the eruption of Mount Vesuvius and the destruction of Pompeii and Herculaneum with literal fire and sulfur[63] would also feed into this picture.

The hearers must be warned and so must every hearer and reader since, because the same choice faces every generation, whether to give their allegiance ultimately to God or the devil. Only the outward form of the choice is different.[64] The fact that this torture occurs "before the holy angels and before the Lamb" (v. 10) should not be taken as implying they take some kind of sadistic pleasure in the suffering of their enemies; perhaps the idea is more that they act as witnesses of God's justice.[65]

---

59. Cf. Thomas, *Apocalypse*, 435–36; Beale, *Book of Revelation*, 759; Aune, *Revelation 6–16*, 834. Aune lays out parallel phrases (nearly all using *thumos*) from 14:8, 10, 19; 15:7; 16:1, 19; 18:3; 19:15. The imagery of drinking for God's judgments is derived from several OT passages, most explicitly Jer 25:15–17, Ps 75:8, and Isa 51:17. Cf. Fekkes, *Isaiah and Prophetic Traditions*, 205–6.

60. Cf. Rev 20:10. Cf. Koester, *Revelation*, 613–14, 621; Beale, *Book of Revelation*, 761–65; Leithart, *Revelation 12–22*, 98–99. Many commentators argue that only the smoke is seen as never ending; the people have eventually been destroyed (e.g., Paul, *Revelation*, 250). But it's specifically "the smoke of their *torment*" that rises forever and ever. The language here seems uncompromising.

61. Cf. Thomas, *Apocalypse*, 436–37; Beale, *Book of Revelation*, 760.

62. Cf. Fekkes, *Isaiah and Prophetic Traditions*, 206–8.

63. This phrase is used elsewhere in Revelation to describe the plague from the horses in 9:17–18 and the fate of the wicked in the lake of fire (19:20; 20:10; 21:8).

64. Cf. Beale, *Book of Revelation*, 761.

65. Cf. Aune, *Revelation 6–16*, 835.

> **Here is the perseverance of the saints, those who keep the commands of God and the faith of Jesus. (Rev 14:12)**

These are the same people whom the dragon has been targeting since 12:17. They are exhorted, in view of the permanent and costly nature of their decision, not to give in to the pressure of the beast, but to patiently endure whatever is thrown at them in words almost the same as in the previous chapter (13:10; see also 1:9; 2:2–3, 19; 3:10). Perseverance, or "patient endurance" (NIV), is a key message of Revelation.[66] This endurance would be shown in keeping God's commands, and keeping the faith of Jesus or remaining faithful to Jesus (Greek *pistin Iēsou*), as in 12:17. No doubt this consciousness of eternity was a major motivation for the martyrs of the first centuries. (There is evidence of this in the early Christian literature.)[67] Indeed, the same motivation has spurred on every believer since who has faced torture and death for their witness to Jesus.

> **And I heard a voice from heaven that said, "Write: 'Blessed (are) the dead who die in the Lord[68] from now on.'" "Yes," says the Spirit, "so that they may rest from their hard work, for their works follow after them." (Rev 14:13)**

There is now an encouraging promise to the believers who have to risk their lives in this struggle. This strong word is emphasized by it being written down.[69] It also uses the format of beatitude, the third of seven beatitudes in Revelation (see 1:3 which has two; 14:13; 19:9; 20:6; 22:7, 14). It is confirmed by the voice of the Spirit, a rare event apart from the seven prophetic proclamations of Revelation 2–3.[70] This is designed to further strengthen the believers in their fight, their resistance to the beast. Death for them (though inevitable) will be a blessing, introducing them to rest (in contrast to the "no rest" for those who give in to the beasts in verse 11) and a reward for what they have done (compare Dan 12:13).[71] The text uses eternal factors in its rhetoric: the rewards and punishments to be received from God the Judge far outweigh the temporal rewards and punishments which the beasts can inflict.[72] In this, one can detect shades of Pascal's wager![73]

---

66. Cf. Thomas, *Apocalypse*, 438; Beale, *Book of Revelation*, 765–67.
67. E.g., "Epistle Concerning the Martyrdom of Polycarp," ANF 1:39.
68. On dying "in the Lord," see Leithart, *Revelation 12–22*, 100–101.
69. This is a common feature of Revelation; see 1:11, 19; 2:1, 8, 12, 18; 3:1, 7, 14; 10:4; 14:13; 19:9; 21:5. Cf. Thomas, *Apocalypse*, 439.
70. Cf. Leithart, *Revelation 12–22*, 103, especially on the Trinitarian implications of the Spirit speaking here.
71. Cf. Thomas, *Apocalypse*, 439–41; Koester, *Revelation*, 614–15; Beale, *Book of Revelation*, 767–69.
72. Cf. Koester, *Revelation*, 616, 622.
73. Pascal, a French Christian philosopher of the 17th century, urged people to "bet" on the existence of God rather than the opposite since the consequences of rejecting God (if God exists) are much worse than the consequences of believing if God does not exist after all. See Pascal, *Pensées*, sect. III.

14:14–20 Two Harvests

> **And I saw, and behold a white cloud, and on the cloud sitting (one) like a son of man, having on his head a golden crown and in his hand a sharp sickle. (Rev 14:14)**

Clouds and "(one) like a son of man" would arouse several memories in the audience's mind. In Revelation itself, they have heard of Jesus "coming in the clouds" (1:7) and "one like a son of man" standing in the midst of the seven golden lampstands (1:13). Both of these have already reminded them of the vision in Daniel 7, in which "with the clouds of heaven there came one like a son of man" (Dan 7:13), who then received dominion from God. They might also have heard accounts of Jesus ascending to heaven in a cloud (Acts 1:9), there to remain until the time of restoration (Acts 3:21). So they are likely to interpret this image as referring to Jesus "seated" in his glorified ruling state and possibly coming again.[74]

The "crown of gold on his head" would confirm this.[75] The sharp sickle in his hand is a new image, though it may be compared with the "sharp sword" coming out of Jesus' mouth (1:16; 2:12), and it clearly evokes the idea of a harvest.[76]

> **And another angel came out from the temple [in heaven] and cried out in a loud voice to the one sitting on the cloud, "Send your sickle and reap, for the hour to reap has come, for the harvest of the earth is ripe." And the one sitting on the cloud threw his sickle into the earth and the earth was reaped. (Rev 14:15–16)**

The idea of an angel telling Christ what to do may seem odd, but in the narrative, it simply signifies timing, not some kind of authority.[77] The idea of timing is often mentioned in Revelation; for example, "the time for the dead to be judged" (11:18) or "no more delay" (10:6). And timing is central to the imagery of harvest: harvest only occurs when the crops are ripe. But what kind of harvest is in view here? The hearers might think of Joel 3:13, where a reaping action is part of the eschatological war, though this matches more the language of the grape harvest coming up later in Revelation 14.[78] Otherwise, they would have to choose between a positive and a negative understanding of the harvest.

It might refer to a great response to the gospel, as in John 4:35–38; Luke 10:2; Matthew 9:37–38; and probably Mark 4:26–29. Or it might refer to a final ingathering

---

74. Cf. Koester, *Revelation*, 623, 627–28; Beale, *Book of Revelation*, 770–71. Other possibilities are summarized in Aune, *Revelation 6–16*, 841. In several places, NT authors combine references to Dan 7:13 with Ps 110:1 (about sitting at God's right hand).

75. Cf. Koester, *Revelation*, 624. However, Aune points out that there is no mention of such a crown in 1:13, as part of his lengthy argument that the "one like a son of man" here is an angel, not Christ (Aune, *Revelation 6–16*, 800–801, 841–43).

76. Cf. Thomas, *Apocalypse*, 442.

77. Cf. Beale, *Book of Revelation*, 772.

78. Cf. Aune, *Revelation 6–16*, 844.

of souls to God's kingdom, consequent to the *Parousia* (as in Matt 24:30–31; Mark 13:26–27), or a harvest of martyrs,[79] or even a final judgement (as in Matt 13:39–42).[80] However, two facts slightly tip the balance towards the more positive reading of an evangelistic harvest in response to the gospel (v. 6). First, this harvest is reaped by the son of man (v. 16), whereas the parallel passages in the gospels have angels as reapers; second, generally speaking, the sickle connotes "an instrument of peace" (Isa 2:4; Mic 4:3).[81] This fits the language of angelic evangelism in verse 6. Also, in this case the son of man remains sitting on the cloud rather than coming in it, as the reaping-at-*Parousia* passages would suggest. This harvest of souls is what the early Pentecostals were expecting as an outcome of the "latter rain" prior to the second coming of Christ. This passage perhaps supports that idea.

> **And another angel came out from the temple that is in heaven, who also had a sharp sickle. And another angel [came out] from the altar having authority over the fire, and he spoke with a loud voice to the one who had the sharp sickle, saying, "Send your sharp sickle, and gather the grapes of the earth's vines, for the grapes are ripe." And the angel threw his sickle into the earth and gathered the vineyard of the earth and threw (it) into the great winepress of the fury of God. (Rev 14:17–19)**

The reference to fire is already unsettling, reminding the audience of 8:5, 7 and other trumpet disasters.[82] Moreover, whereas the first harvest may be seen as a harvest of grain (though the text does not explicitly say this), this one is clearly a harvest of grapes, meaning that the whole process of wine-making is being envisaged, as verse 19 describes. The harvest has a negative connotation since we read of "the great winepress of the fury of God," using the same Greek word *thumos*. The same word was previously used of the passion and fury of Babylon (v. 8) and God (v. 10), with links to wine and drunkenness (see also Isa 63:3, where God tramples the winepress alone in anger).[83] Timing is again implied by the statement that "the grapes are ripe": perhaps vengeance for those who killed the martyrs is no longer postponed (see 6:10–11).[84]

---

79. Leithart understands both of these harvests as the martyrdom of the 144,000 (Leithart, *Revelation 12–22*, 106–10, 115).

80. Cf. Thomas, *Apocalypse*, 442–44; Fekkes, *Isaiah and Prophetic Traditions*, 192–96; Koester, *Revelation*, 628–29; Bauckham, *Climax of Prophecy*, 290–96. Koester and Bauckham both mount a strong case for a positive reading of this harvest. Aune summarizes arguments both ways but leans towards the negative reading, i.e., both harvests speak of judgement (Aune, *Revelation 6–16*, 801–3, 843–44). Beale takes the same view pointing to the uniform use of ὥρα (*hora*, literally "hour") for the judgment of the unfaithful or the trials of believers (Beale, *Book of Revelation*, 774). At least one of these cases is debatable (Rev 11:13) because, although it refers to judgment, the judgment arguably leads to repentance.

81. Koester, *Revelation*, 624.

82. Cf. Beale, *Book of Revelation*, 775.

83. Cf. Bauckham, *Climax of Prophecy*, 290–293; Fekkes, *Isaiah and Prophetic Traditions*, 196.

84. Cf. Koester, *Revelation*, 629.

> **And the winepress was trampled outside the city and blood came out from the winepress up to the horses' bridles for one thousand six hundred stadia. (Rev 14:20)**[85]

This is a very graphic and horrifying scene for the audience to imagine, a veritable river of blood, which normally could only come about by the deaths of a huge multitude of people (compare Isa 34:3; Ezek 32:6; 1 Enoch 100:1–3; 4 Ezra 15:35). Keener argues that "the image of blood flowing in terrible streams became standard in ancient descriptions of wars."[86] Informed hearers would certainly recall Joel 3:13, where it is the evil of the nations that causes the grapes to be ripe and brings eschatological judgement to pass.[87] But they might also remember the wars they had experienced or heard of, where bloodshed was enormous, such as the civil wars in the Empire (AD 68–69) or the horrible ill-fated rebellion of the Jews against Rome (AD 66–70).[88]

The phrase "outside the city" would perhaps send their thoughts in this direction as they contemplated the destruction of Jerusalem in AD 70 and other prophecies about Jerusalem (e.g., Zech 14:1–4). Certainly, there was huge bloodshed in this period. Possibly this phrase implies protection for those *inside* the city, in a parallel with 11:1–2, where the outer court of the temple is trampled and the inner court spared, thus implying the destruction of the wicked and protection of the true church.[89] Beale suggests that the phrase "outside the city" anticipates 22:15 and 20:9, making this a scene of judgment of the unbelievers outside the new Jerusalem.[90]

However, the same phrase may also evoke the crucifixion of Jesus "outside the city" (see Mark 15:20–22; Heb 13:12), in which case the blood may signify the scope of his redemptive sacrifice for sin, as the Italian commentator Eugenio Corsini has argued.[91] Other possibilities are that it is a punishment for Jesus' execution[92] or the

---

85. On the significance of 1,600 stadia, see Koester, *Revelation*, 626; Beale, *Book of Revelation*, 782.

86. Keener, *Revelation*, 377. And Beale agrees that this is "figurative battle language," that is, hyperbole (Beale, *Book of Revelation*, 781). But it is still a gruesome picture.

87. Cf. Thomas, *Apocalypse*, 444–47; Beale, *Book of Revelation*, 775–76; Koester, *Revelation*, 630. Koester points out that "a victorious army was said to trample its foes" much like people trampling grapes to make wine (Koester, *Revelation*, 625).

88. This resembles the report of the Jewish historian Josephus in "War of the Jews" 6:8.5 (cf. Aune, *Revelation 6–16*, 848; Papandrea, *Wedding of the Lamb*, 125). Similar images are found in an old Jewish description of the Jews' defeat by Hadrian in AD 135 (Beale, *Book of Revelation*, 783; Bauckham, *Climax of Prophecy*, 41, 46; Keener, *Revelation*, 378). Perhaps a case could be made that John was predicting this later slaughter, but the details are similar rather than identical. More likely John is using a traditional Jewish phrase also employed by contemporary and later texts (Bauckham, *Climax of Prophecy*, 40–48).

89. Cf. Koester, *Revelation*, 630.

90. Beale, *Book of Revelation*, 780–81.

91. Corsini, *Apocalypse*, 269–72.

92. In Aune's language, this would be "poetic justice" (Aune, *Revelation 6–16*, 847), though he is not advocating this reading.

blood of the martyrs for Jesus.[93] Ian Paul suggests that the river of blood is figurative only,[94] but if so, figurative of what? In any event, this is a climactic scene.

Summing up, these two harvests may be understood as two outcomes of the second coming (gathering the saints and judging the unrighteous, as in Matt 13:37–43; 24:30–31; 25:31–46). Another option is to see the harvests as a single outcome of judgment, or they might stand for two "end-time" events (an evangelistic harvest and a severe disaster for the unrepentant, either in the first century or the future). Alternatively, the harvests might be two aspects of Jesus' earthly ministry (gathering disciples and shedding his blood to satisfy God's wrath at sin). The sheer size of the flow of blood in verse 20 inclines me to think of Jesus' blood as the referent ("spreading over all the earth"),[95] but it's hard to be dogmatic here. However, if that is the correct understanding, John would be implying that the shed blood of Jesus is the key factor underlying the great evangelistic harvest of souls from the nations described metaphorically in the first harvest scene (vv. 14–16), anticipated in the "first fruits" of the 144,000 (vv. 3–4), responding to the gospel proclaimed to all nations (v. 6), and confirming the promise of 5:9. Thinking of the goal of the narrative supports this way of reading this chapter.[96]

---

93. Cf. Beale, *Book of Revelation*, 782; Caird, *Revelation*, 192–94; Leithart, *Revelation 12–22*, 108–9, 116.

94. Paul, *Revelation*, 255–56.

95. Corsini, *Apocalypse*, 271. See also Moloney, *Apocalypse of John*, 225–27. Moloney suggests, in view of the evil horses narrated in Revelation 6 and 9, that "the blood of the crucified Jesus flows to the height of the bridles of these demonic powers and stops them in their tracks" (ibid., 227).

96. Cf. Sweet, *Revelation*, 230–32.

Revelation Chapter 15

A massive struggle between Good and Evil has been raging throughout the last few chapters, and this struggle has taken various forms. For instance, the dragon fought the representatives of God (the woman, the male child, Michael, and the children of the woman). Likewise, the two beasts opposed the people of God. This overarching struggle has not yet ended, but God is about to inflict a crushing defeat on his opponents as he moves towards his final goals for creation.

15:1–8 Preparing the Stage for the Seven Last Plagues

> **And I saw[1] another great and amazing sign in heaven, seven angels having the seven last plagues, because with these the fury of God is completed. (Rev 15:1)**

This language of a sign matches the first two great signs from Revelation 12—the woman clothed with the sun and the great red dragon (12:1, 3). These signs in heaven clearly foreshadow new and serious developments in the plot, raising "the hearers' level of expectancy" to a great height,[2] but also connecting this new development with what began in chapter 12.

However, it isn't as novel as the previous signs, since Revelation has had a cast full of angels. Indeed, the trumpets sequence was also inaugurated by seven angels blowing those trumpets (8:2, 6). Clearly, this new stage has previous parallels, as will become clearer as the narrative progresses. Plagues are also not new.[3]

The word "plagues" has been used just four times before in Revelation. First, there are "the three plagues" coming from the mouths of the horses under the sixth trumpet (9:18). Then at the end of the six trumpet disasters, the reader is told that "the

---

1. He introduces this section with "And I saw" twice (vv. 1–2; and again, in v. 5) and "another . . . sign" (v. 1). These phrases show the hearers/readers that a new stage in the narrative/vision is beginning. Cf. Aune, *Revelation 6–16*, 863.

2. Thomas, *Apocalypse*, 448.

3. Cf. Beale, *Book of Revelation*, 803; Leithart, *Revelation 12–22*, 115. Leithart says that these plagues are aimed specifically at Jerusalem.

rest of mankind who were not killed by these plagues" failed to repent in response (9:20). Next, it comes up in the narrative of the two witnesses who had power "to strike the earth with every kind of plague" (11:6). Fourth, it is used with reference to the fatal wound suffered by the wild beast (13:3, 12, 14). Otherwise, the mention of coming plagues would perhaps call the audience's attention to the plagues on Egypt in Exodus, and the threatened punishments for Israel if they broke God's covenant (Deut 28:59), which are to be "seven times" worse than before in Leviticus 26:21–26.

But what stands out this time is that these plagues are "last" (Greek *eschatas*), because with them "the fury of God is completed." The Greek verb is the aorist passive of *teleō*, meaning finish, complete, come to an end, or fulfill.[4] The same word was used in 10:7 for the accomplishment of the mystery of God. The wrath of God has been emphasized in 14:9–11 and 14:19, but now the narrative seems to be entering a literally eschatological stage.[5] And this is not a positive development, but one marked by plagues and wrath from God.

> **And I saw (something) like a glassy sea mixed with fire, and those who had triumphed over the wild beast and over his statue and over the number of his name, standing on the glassy sea, having harps of God. (Rev 15:2)**

This scene recalls the heavenly throne room scene of 4:6 with its "sea of glass like crystal," with the change that it is now "mixed with fire," hinting perhaps at the imminent judgment of the plagues since fire has been an agent of judgment in 8:7, 8, 10, and 11:5. It may also remind the hearers of the warfare that has been prominent in chapters 12–14 or the revelation of Christ with his eyes "like blazing fire" (1:14; 2:18).[6]

But more promisingly, John sees "those who had triumphed [literally "conquered"] over[7] the beast and over its statue and over the number of its name." In Revelation 13, John told his audience that the beast "was permitted to make war against the saints and conquer them" (13:7), using the same verb as here, two forms of *nikaō* (conquer, overcome). In chapter 13, only those whose names are written in the book of the Lamb would refuse to worship the beast. But it seems that in the very act of being conquered and probably killed (13:10, 15), these faithful believers are said to conquer the beast.

As in 12:11, which uses the same language of defeating the dragon, it is the martyrs who ultimately win. Not only do they enter into rest (14:13) but they conquer.

---

4. Cf. Leithart, *Revelation 12–22*, 115. Aune translates this as "spent" emphasizing the ending aspect of the verb (Aune, *Revelation 6–16*, 852). See the somewhat convoluted discussion of the time language in Beale, *Book of Revelation*, 785–88.

5. Cf. Thomas, *Apocalypse*, 449–50.

6. As Thomas points out, fire is associated with Christ, the Spirit (4:5), the altar on which prayers are placed (8:3–5) as well as judgments (*Apocalypse*, 450–51). The connections of fire and water/sea are also explored in Leithart, *Revelation 12–22*, 119.

7. The Greek ἐκ [*ek*] is usually translated "from" or "out of." "Conquered over" is not proper English, so I translated "triumphed over."

They very definitely triumph over the beast, its statue, and the number of its name.[8] The fact that these conquerors are "standing" beside the sea would recall the question back in 6:17, "who is able to stand?" The question refers to the day of wrath. Now, the day of wrath has arrived, and they are standing![9]

This is a very strong rhetorical point: the audience may themselves be facing the beast in some way, and they need to have this firm promise of victory, provided so that they don't flinch. As Leithart explains, the church constantly faces "the beast and its image and . . . the number of its name" in the form of power, propaganda, and the pack (the beast's mob).[10]

And they sang the song of Moses the slave of God and of the Lamb, saying: (Rev 15:3a)

As often happens in Revelation (parallel with 14:2–3), the heroes break into song, accompanied by harps (vv. 2–3). This implies that this very act of praise is part of their secret; in fact, these harps are from God (v. 2).[11] Here, they sing "the song of Moses the slave of God and of the Lamb," a phrase that recalls the exodus narrative at the Red Sea, to which the "glassy sea" might also allude.[12] The exodus event also flows from the Passover Lamb deliverance earlier in Exodus.[13] Exodus 15:1 tells us that "Moses and the Israelites sang this song to the LORD" after the miraculous deliverance through the Red Sea, a mighty triumph of God and his people over Pharaoh and his army.[14] The joining of Moses and the Lamb also recalls the song sung to the Lamb in 5:9–10, after the vision of the Lamb reinterprets the messianic hope.

The combination of Moses and the Lamb also recalls the phrase describing the children of the woman and the targets of the dragon in 12:17, i.e., "those who keep the commandments of God and have the testimony of Jesus." It further brings to mind the two divine companies in Revelation 7—one from Israel's tribes and the other from all nations (7:4–9). So these victors are heirs to both old and new covenants, and may originally have represented the early Jewish believers in Christ; at the very least, they are well educated in the Old Testament narrative.

---

8. Cf. Koester, *Revelation*, 634; Thomas, *Apocalypse*, 451.

9. See Thomas, *Apocalypse*, 452. This might confirm Leithart's view that they are the 144,000 martyred in chapter 14 (Leithart, *Revelation 12–22*, 118–19).

10. Leithart, *Revelation 12–22*, 120.

11. Possibly this means they are sacred harps used exclusively for worship. Cf. Aune, *Revelation 6–16*, 852; Leithart, *Revelation 12–22*, 121.

12. Cf. Beale, *Book of Revelation*, 789–93.

13. Cf. Gause, *Revelation*, 203.

14. Cf. Thomas, *Apocalypse*, 453; Koester, *Revelation*, 633. Other songs are attributed to Moses in the OT (Deut 31:30—32:43; Ps 90) and the Greek may indicate a song *about* Moses and the Lamb as opposed to a song *by* them; however, Exod 15 is the most likely reference (cf. Aune, *Revelation 6–16*, 872; Beale, *Book of Revelation*, 785; Leithart, *Revelation 12–22*, 122).

But the song they sing is not totally like that sung in Exodus 15, as it expresses a much bigger vision than Moses and his generation could have visualized.[15]

> **Great and amazing (are) your works,**
> **Lord God the Almighty.**
> **Just and true (are) your ways,**
> **King of the nations.**[16]
> **Who would not fear you, Lord,**
> **and glorify your name?**
> **For (you) alone (are) pure,**
> **for all the nations will come**
> **and worship before you,**
> **for your just deeds have been made apparent. (Rev 15:3b–4)**

In a highly structured hymn,[17] God is acclaimed for his deeds and ways, as in the other song of Moses (Deut 32:4), for his justice, his sovereignty ("King of the nations"; compare Jer 10:7; Pss 22:28; 47:8; 96:10; 99:2; Rev 11:15), and his holiness and righteousness, using two related Greek words to describe God as just and righteous.[18] He is said to be worthy of fear, glory, and worship from all humanity (14:7). In articulating this, the song employs a rhetorical question reminiscent of OT passages (such as Exod 15:11; Isa 40:18, 25; Jer 10:7; Mic 7:18). The question also responds to the angel's call in 14:7 and directly contradicts the rhetorical question about the beast in 13:4.[19]

And the choir adds, "all nations (Greek *panta ta ethnē*)[20] will come and worship before you" (v. 4). This is a great note of hope! The martyrs can sing of their triumph, and it consists in the conversion of the nations into worshipers of God. Importantly, these are the very nations that worshiped the beast and the dragon.[21] This is where the

---

15. As Thomas points out, it has a "biblical feel" in its language and structure and is full of OT content drawn not just from Exod 15 but Deut 32, Psalms, and other places (Thomas, *Apocalypse*, 454; cf. Koester, *Revelation*, 634–35; Beale, *Book of Revelation*, 794; Archer, *Worship in the Apocalypse*, 242). Beale argues that these allusions are not random but governed by the exodus theme (Beale, *Book of Revelation*, 799).

16. Some manuscripts have "king of the ages" but this is unlikely to be the original wording (cf. Koester, *Revelation*, 632; Beale, *Book of Revelation*, 795–96).

17. Cf. Archer, *Worship in the Apocalypse*, 241.

18. Cf. Leithart, *Revelation 12–22*, 123–24; Beale, *Book of Revelation*, 795. Some of this reflects the martyrs' prayer in Rev 6:10.

19. Cf. Thomas, *Apocalypse*, 458; Beale, *Book of Revelation*, 796.

20. The phrase πάντα τὰ ἔθνη [*panta ta ethnē*] occurs five times in Revelation: 12:5 (where John is referring to Ps 2 and the destiny of the messiah to "rule all the nations"); 14:8 and 18:3 (where Babylon makes all the nations drink her wine); 15:4 ("all nations will come and worship before you"); and 18:23 (where the nations are led astray by Babylon's sorcery). There is a mixture of condemnation and hope here, reflecting other NT uses of this phrase. It is negative in Matt 24:9 but has a hopeful context in relation to the Christian gospel in Matt 24:14; 28:19; Luke 24:47; Acts 15:17; Rom 1:5; 15:11; Gal 3:8; 2 Tim 4:17; and possibly Acts 14:16; it is related to final judgment in Matt 25:32, the purpose of the temple in Mark 11:17, and the exile of Jews after AD70 in Luke 21:24. Cf. Aune, *Revelation 6–16*, 688–89.

21. Cf. Thomas, *Apocalypse*, 459–60; Bauckham, *Climax of Prophecy*, 296–307.

story is going, though there will be many "twists and turns" before we arrive there in Revelation 21. As Gause observes, referring to Malachi 1:11 and Philippians 2:8–11, "The universal worship of God is the end toward which all history moves."[22] However, there is no promise that the *individuals* who worshiped the beast will be converted and turn to worship God. Keep in mind that 14:9–11 has pronounced their doom. As Beale points out, the universalist note here does not imply "the salvation of all without exception but of all without distinction."[23] In other words, people *from* "every nation, tribe, people, and language" (7:9) will worship but not neccessarily *all* people.

However, this caveat must not diminish the sheer size of what God has planned, "a great multitude that no one could count." Somehow the nations that those individuals belonged to (or many within those nations) will repent and worship the one true holy God, as has been proclaimed repeatedly in the Old Testament (see Pss 22:27; 86:9;[24] Isa 2:2–4; 45:14; 60:3; 66:23; Jer 16:19; Zech 8:22; Mal 1:11).[25] Beale speaks of people being forced to acknowledge God in the end, but Revelation's vision is bigger than that. As Bauckham argues, in Revelation the nations respond to God's judgments either by repentance or resistance, never by forced submission.[26] All this will happen because "your just deeds have been made apparent" (v. 4; compare Ps 98:2),[27] referring either to God's acts of judgement, God's righteous ordinances, or more broadly to include Jesus' life, death, and resurrection considered as the actions of God.[28]

> **And after these (things) I saw, and the temple of the tent of witness in heaven was opened, and the seven angels came out from the temple, [those] having the seven plagues, dressed in clean bright linen,[29] and girded about the chest (with) golden belts. (Rev 15:5–6)**

The language recalls both the original wilderness tent[30] of meeting and the more elaborate temples (Greek *naos*) that followed it. Both of these were related to testimony,[31] as in Numbers 1:50. The older version of the NIV actually translated this as "tabernacle

---

22. Gause, *Revelation*, 205.
23. Beale, *Book of Revelation*, 798, 799.
24. Cf. Beale, *Book of Revelation*, 797.
25. Cf. Koester, *Revelation*, 636.
26. Bauckham, *Climax of Prophecy*, 307–8. Herms contends that "the communicative intent in 15.2–4" is "to be vindication—both of God and his faithful people" (Herms, *Apocalypse for the Church*, 182). This is undoubtedly true, but limited.
27. As Beale points out this psalm has several points of contact with Rev 15:3–4 (Beale, *Book of Revelation*, 798–99).
28. Cf. Aune, *Revelation 6–16*, 876; Beale, *Book of Revelation*, 797–99; Leithart, *Revelation 12–22*, 124.
29. This was clothing of priests (Aune, *Revelation 6–16*, 878) or devotees of a god in solemn procession (Koester, *Revelation*, 652). Some manuscripts have "stone" (Greek λιθον [*lithon*]) instead of "linen" (Greek λινον [*linon*]) (cf. Beale, *Book of Revelation*, 804–5).
30. The Greek for "tabernacle" is σκηνης [*skēnēs*], that is tent or dwelling place more generally.
31. This is a key theme in Revelation, of course, suggesting a Christological emphasis since Jesus himself is "the faithful witness" (Rev 1:5). Cf. Gause, *Revelation*, 206.

of the Testimony."[32] In other words, this was God's dwelling place among the people of Israel, which was closed off to the ordinary person. But now it, or rather its heavenly template, is opened (as in 11:19).[33] However, it has not been opened for John to enter (unlike Rev 4), but for seven angels to emerge from it. The clothing of the angels (v. 6) recalls the appearance of the "son of man" in 1:13. The phrase "seven plagues," introduced in verse 1, recalls the previous pattern of sevens: seven seals and seven trumpets.

> **And one of the four living beings gave the seven angels seven golden bowls filled with the fury of God, who lives forever and ever." (Rev 15:7)**

The four living beings were introduced in 4:6–8, as worship leaders in God's throne room (see also 5:6, 8, 11, 14; 7:11; 14:3), and so far, they have played a limited role in the narrative, calling out the four horses and riders (6:1, 3, 5, 7) at the opening of the first four seals. Now again they are releasing the disasters prepared by God, in a way that is vaguely liturgical since the plagues are found in seven bowls (Greek *phialis*, a bowl that might contain incense as in 5:8).[34] This suggests that the prayers of the saints are pushing the narrative forward. This resembles 8:3–6 where the prayers anticipate the seven trumpets, though *these* bowls are filled with wrath, not prayer.[35]

> **And the temple was filled up with smoke from the glory of God and from his powers, and no one was able to enter the temple, until the seven plagues of the seven angels were completed. (Rev 15:8)**

John's audience would have been reminded of several Old Testament stories here. When the tent of meeting was completed, there was the cloud covering it, and the glory of God filled it so that "Moses could not enter the tent of meeting" (Exod 40:34–35). Something similar happened when the Solomonic temple was completed. "When the priests withdrew from the Holy Place, the cloud filled the temple of the LORD. And the priests could not perform their service because of the cloud, for the glory of the LORD filled his temple" (1 Kgs 8:10–11). In 2 Chronicles 5:13–14, this phenomenon is precipitated by musical praise.[36]

---

32. Cf. Koester, *Revelation*, 644; Beale, *Book of Revelation*, 801–2.

33. As Aune argues, a temple door opening of itself would be considered a prodigy, but not necessarily a good one, as in Josephus (Aune, *Revelation 6–16*, 876; see Josephus, "War of the Jews" 6:293–296, where this is one of a number of signs of the impending doom of the second temple).

34. Cf. Koester, *Revelation*, 645, 653; Aune, *Revelation 6–16*, 879. However, bowls could also refer to the planets or comets and thus be a kind of portent of disaster (Leithart, *Revelation 12–22*, 113). On the liturgical and covenantal implications of bowls, see Leithart, *Revelation 12–22*, 131–32.

35. Cf. Koester, *Revelation*, 652; Beale, *Book of Revelation*, 806. Aune points out that if God's wrath is directed at all the nations, it "presupposes a universal divine law or standard, repeated violations of which are now thought to have caused a final eschatological manifestation of the wrath of God" (Aune, *Revelation 6–16*, 870). This seems to be implied by the indictment of 9:20–21 and the more precise language of 14:7 and 9, but 16:5–6 points to the murder of God's representatives as the main charge. Leithart sees the bowls as filled with the blood of the martyrs, for which the nations are held accountable (Leithart, *Revelation 12–22*, 129, 131).

36. Cf. Aune, *Revelation 6–16*, 881–82.

Then there was the annual ceremony of Yom Kippur, the Day of Atonement, where the high priest entered the Most Holy Place, taking incense so that "the smoke of the incense will conceal the atonement cover . . . so that he will not die" (Lev 16:13).[37] More ominously, however, in Isaiah's vision, when he sees the Lord "high and exalted, seated on a throne" and being worshiped by six-singed seraphim (Isa 6:1–3), "at the sound of their voices the doorposts and thresholds shook and the temple was filled with smoke" (Isa 6:4).[38] This introduces words of impending disaster for the people of Judah (Isa 6:8–13). This story seems closer to John's vision here, and another intertext seems to be Ezekiel 10:2–5, part of the withdrawal of God's glory from the doomed temple prior to its capture by Babylon; here too "the cloud filled the temple" (v. 4).[39]

In Revelation itself, the previous seven disasters were preceded by "silence in heaven for about half an hour" (8:1) and the release of smoky incense (8:4). More ominously, the opening of the abyss in 9:2 produced smoke "like the smoke of a great furnace" that darkened the sun and sky. Theophanies can have a positive or negative significance. Clearly, the whole episode of chapter 15 underlines the nature of what is about to happen: a powerful expression of God's wrath with the ultimate goal of the nations coming to worship him.

---

37. Cf. Leithart, *Revelation 12–22*, 132–33.

38. Cf. Fekkes, *Isaiah and Prophetic Traditions*, 200.

39. Cf. Beale, *Book of Revelation*, 806–7.

Revelation Chapter 16

16:1–7 The First Three Plagues

And I heard a loud voice from the temple saying to the seven angels, "Go and pour out the seven bowls of the fury of God onto the earth." (Rev 16:1)

The action is initiated by "a loud voice from the temple" (compare 14:7, 9, 13, 15, 18). These seven disasters recall events of the plagues on Egypt in Exodus,[1] they function as possible answers to ancient prayers (such as Ps 79, especially vv. 6, 10–12), they are targeted at the beast's empire, and guided by strict justice (vv. 5–7). Nevertheless, like the Exodus plagues, they do not evoke any repentance.[2] Rather, this series is more like an all-out attack on the enemy camp inflicting a crushing defeat on the enemies in the end.

The resemblance to the Exodus plagues also suggests that one of the aims of this attack is to release God's people from bondage to empire so that they can fulfill their destiny. In Exodus, the hardening of Pharaoh's heart (and that of Moses too)[3] serves to prevent any compromise being reached that would leave Israel still in Egypt. It was God's purpose to get them out of there, and into their promised land (Exod 3:8). This

---

1. God's anger is "poured out" on other occasions too; for example, Jer 7:20; 14:16; Lam 2:4; Ezek 9:8 (directed to Judah); Ezek 14:19. There is also a possible allusion to Lev 26, where God threatens an unfaithful Israel, "I will punish you for your sins seven times over" (vv. 18, 21, 24, 28). Cf. Thomas, *Apocalypse*, 466; Smolarz, *Covenant*, 350–57. The terminology is liturgical (cf. Aune, *Revelation 6–16*, 883).

2. Cf. Leithart, *Revelation 12–22*, 137–38. Thomas suggests that the cultic nature of the angels' actions implies that repentance is still possible (Thomas, *Apocalypse*, 467, 468). However, if so, no such repentance is forthcoming (16:9, 11, 21). Beale insists that "the bowl plagues are better viewed as judgments instead of mere warnings . . . as punishments that further harden people" (Beale, *Book of Revelation*, 811), that is, they are not intended to provoke repentance. This, however, is in tension with the promise of 15:4. Richard Woods argues that this section of Revelation can be seen as a warning against human greed and oppression, and a call to repentance in order to avoid such ecological catastrophes (Woods, "Seven Bowls").

3. Moses had to be stubborn and unwilling to compromise in order for God's plan to be accomplished (e.g., Exod 10:8–9, 24–26).

series also amounts to "de-creation" as God attacks all aspects of his earthly creation, with parallels to the seven days of creation in Genesis 1–2, preparing for the revealing of his new creation in chapter 21.[4]

> **And the first angel went out and poured out his bowl onto the earth, and bad and evil boils broke out on the people who had the mark of the wild beast and those who worshiped his statue. (Rev 16:2)**

This is like the plague of boils inflicted on humans and animals in Egypt (Exod 9:8–11; compare Deut 28:27, 35). As in 9:4, God's people seem to be spared; only those already doomed to eternal torment (14:9–11) are affected. As Thomas points out, in their case, the mark of the beast is replaced by God's sore.[5] As Gause observes, this shows that the beast's mark failed to protect them from harm.[6] Thus, the two groups are dualistically contrasted as Revelation consistently argues.

> **And the second (angel) poured out his bowl into the sea, and it became[7] blood as of a dead (person), and every living soul that (was) in the sea died. (Rev 16:3)[8]**

This recalls the second trumpet plague in which "a third of the sea became blood and a third of the living creatures that were in the sea died and a third of the ships were destroyed" (8:8–9). Only this time it is more devastating as one-third becomes "every living soul." This plague and the next also remind the audience of the first plague on Egypt in which the Nile and other water sources were turned to blood (Exod 7:17–24), though again this plague is much more far reaching.[9]

If the blood here is to be taken literally, these disasters imply a massive "bloodbath," probably the result of massive violence or warfare, reminding the audience of the imagery in 14:20. However, it is more likely that the sea turns into something *like* blood which then causes death.[10] Koester observes that "the creation joins with the Creator in the service of divine justice."[11] Alternatively, as Beale suggests, the sea is

---

4. Cf. Leithart, *Revelation 12–22*, 134.

5. Thomas, *Apocalypse*, 467. Koester points out that to the Romans, "outbreaks of illness and skin disease were signs of divine wrath that made people seek out the divine will," but not here (Koester, *Revelation*, 646).

6. Gause, *Revelation*, 209.

7. The Greek here is ἐγένετο [egeneto] from *ginomai* meaning "become." Leithart points out that uses of *ginomai* are concentrated in this chapter, in an apparent recall of 1:1, "what must soon happen." In other words, chapter 16 answers the question, *what* must take place? Cf. Leithart, *Revelation 12–22*, 136.

8. Possibly we see here a parody of common Greco-Roman rites of pouring offering bowls into the sea before embarking on a ship (Koester, *Revelation*, 647).

9. Cf. Thomas, *Apocalypse*, 468–69. But see Beale, *Book of Revelation*, 808–12. Beale emphasizes the similarity between the trumpet and bowl disasters and sees the bowls as recapitulating the trumpets "in greater detail" (ibid., 810).

10. Cf. Aune, *Revelation 6–16*, 884. Such events would be seen by ancient Greeks and Romans as "a sign of divine wrath and impending disaster" (Koester, *Revelation*, 647).

11. Koester, *Revelation*, 654.

"figurative for ungodly humanity," and thus, this plague is "figurative, at least in part, for the demise of the ungodly world's economic life-support system."[12]

> **And the third (angel) poured out his bowl into the rivers and the springs of water, and they became blood. (Rev 16:4)**

This also sounds like a heightened version of the third trumpet plague (8:10–11) in which the blazing star causes a third of the waters to become bitter and "many people died" (8:11). This would likely have severe economic effects.[13]

> **And I heard the angel of the waters saying, "You are just, the one who is and who was, the pure one, for you have judged these (things), for they poured out the blood of saints and prophets, and you gave them blood to drink. They deserve it."[14] And I heard the altar saying, "Yes, Lord God Almighty, true and just are your judgments." (Rev 16:5–7)**

There is a distinct rationale for these plagues given by "the angel of the waters" (v. 5). This title implies that angelic beings have delegated authority over aspects of creation. Greco-Roman peoples had specific gods for these tasks and the similarities between Greco-Roman and Jewish worldviews are interesting.[15] As Bruce Malina suggests, the powerful stars of Greco-Roman thinking are demoted in John's Judeo-Christian cosmology to servants of the one true God.[16]

The text is making a contentious point: the beast and its followers deserve punishment because they have killed God's people and prophets. The punishment given is strictly measured to the crime,[17] though not totally since the perpetrators are still alive.[18] God's judgment is affirmed and justified (as in 15:3),[19] as against the worldview of the Greeks and Romans who attributed natural disasters to the anger of the gods provoked by the neglect of sacrifices to them.

This statement also stands against the postmodern western worldview, which is reluctant to attribute anything to God's justice. God's right to judge and the justice of his judgment are both contended for here.[20] And it is significant that the altar[21] joins

---

12. Beale, *Book of Revelation*, 815 (see Rev 17:1, 15); cf. Leithart, *Revelation 12–22*, 138–39. Leithart views the sea as symbolic of the Gentile world, and it is defiled by blood since the Romans killed the saints.

13. Cf. Beale, *Book of Revelation*, 816.

14. Or "they are worthy."

15. Cf. Aune, *Revelation 6–16*, 865–66, 884–85; Beale, *Book of Revelation*, 818. This language is more common in the Jewish apocalypses such as 1–2 Enoch which have a more elaborate cosmology than Revelation; but see Rev 7:1–2.

16. Malina, *Genre and Message*, 261.

17. Cf. Thomas, *Apocalypse*, 473; Beale, *Book of Revelation*, 818–20; Koester, *Revelation*, 648.

18. Koester, *Revelation*, 655.

19. Cf. Thomas, *Apocalypse*, 470–71.

20. See also Neh 9:33; Ps 7:11; Dan 9:14.

21. Cf. Leithart, *Revelation 12–22*, 142. Probably it is not the altar as such but the souls of the

in here because this act of judgment is a clear answer to the cry of the souls under the altar in 6:9. These ones had been "slaughtered on account of the word of God and on account of the testimony which they had." They are the ones who had asked, "Until when, holy and true master, will you not judge and avenge our blood from those who dwell on the earth?" (6:10).²² Justice demands that the persecutors are judged; now it is happening, and the martyrs affirm the justice here. As Leithart puts it, "Heaven gives voice to the voiceless, and God avenges."²³

16:8–21 Building to a Climax

> **And the fourth (angel) poured out his bowl on the sun, and it was allowed²⁴ to burn the people with fire. And the people were scorched with severe burns, and blasphemed the name of God who had the control over these plagues, and they did not repent (so as) to give him glory. (Rev 16:8–9)**

This plague contrasts with the fourth trumpet disaster (8:12) and the parallel plague on Egypt (Exod 10:21–23), which struck the sun and brought darkness. This time the sun's effects are magnified, in contrast with the promise to the believers in 7:16. This scorching weather is ultimately attributed to God, as implied by the passive "the sun . . . was allowed . . . " (v. 8), and the statement that God "had the control over these plagues" (v. 9). "Control" translates the Greek *exousian*: "authority."

Those who suffer seem to understand that their suffering²⁵ has derived from the fact that "they blasphemed the name of God" (v. 9). Nonetheless, they were unresponsive, and "they did not repent" (v. 9).²⁶ Disasters generally do not produce repentance in Revelation, as 9:20–21 has reminded the listeners. The only exception is in 11:13, where the survivors of a severe earthquake "became afraid and gave glory to the God of heaven," the very thing the sufferers in Revelation 16 refuse to do, because of the witness and resurrection of the two prophets.

The rationale behind such a blasphemous reaction in the Roman world could be that they blamed the Christians for these disasters since the Christians were refusing

---

martyrs or an angel (cf. Koester, *Revelation*, 648).

22. Cf. Thomas, *Apocalypse*, 474–475; Beale, *Book of Revelation*, 820.
23. Leithart, *Revelation 12–22*, 142.
24. The Greek ἐδόθη [*edothē*] can literally be translated "given."
25. Cf. Koester, *Revelation*, 648.
26. Cf. Thomas, *Apocalypse*, 476–78; Beale, *Book of Revelation*, 823.

to offer sacrifices to the traditional gods.²⁷ Today, it's more likely due to the idea that God, if God exists, should always be nice to people no matter what.²⁸

> **And the fifth (angel) poured out his bowl on the throne of the wild beast, and his kingdom became darkened, and they gnawed their tongues in agony, and blasphemed the God of heaven in their agony and their boils, and they did not repent from their works. (Rev 16:10–11)**

This plague recalls the three days of total darkness inflicted on Pharaoh and Egypt, but from which the Israelites did not suffer. This penultimate plague actually caused Pharaoh to try to compromise with Moses (Exod 10:21–24). However, ultimately "the LORD hardened Pharaoh's heart, and he was not willing to let them go" (Exod 10:27).²⁹ Again, however, this event is worse. These people are already doomed because they accepted the mark of the beast (14:9–11), but their suffering starts even in this life.

Beale explains this as "times of anguish and horror when they realize that . . . they are separated from God and that eternal darkness awaits them."³⁰ The beast they trusted in cannot help them; even his own throne (that is, his power, the gift of the dragon; 13:2) is vulnerable to God's attack.³¹ Nevertheless, like Pharaoh, "they did not repent from their works" (v. 11).³² The time for repentance has passed; people have made their choice between the beast and the Lamb and must accept the consequences.³³ This outcome faces every generation in history.

> **And the sixth (angel) poured out his bowl onto the great river Euphrates, and its water was dried up so that the way may be prepared for the kings from the East. (Rev 16:12)**

As usual in these disaster sequences, things really move in the sixth event, though the parallels are not precise. The sixth seal leads to a cosmic upheaval, people hiding in the caves and rocks of the mountains afraid of the wrath of God and the Lamb (6:12–17). The sixth trumpet leads to a massive military invasion from the Euphrates region

---

27. This is exemplified by Tertullian's complaint (in the 2nd cent.) about the widespread perception that Christians were the source of all disasters brought against the human race by the gods. "They think the Christians the cause of every public disaster, of every affliction with which the people are visited. If the Tiber rises as high as the city walls, if the Nile does not send its waters up over the fields, if the heavens give no rain, if there is an earthquake, if there is famine or pestilence, straightway the cry is, 'Away with the Christians to the lion!'" (Tertullian, "Apology," *ANF* 3:47).

28. Cf. Gause, *Revelation*, 212.

29. There may also be a reference to the darkness associated with Jesus' crucifixion (Mark 15:33), but in any case, darkness is indicative of judgment in the OT. See Aune, *Revelation 6–16*, 890.

30. Beale, *Book of Revelation*, 824.

31. Cf. Thomas, *Apocalypse*, 479; Leithart, *Revelation 12–22*, 147–48.

32. Their own Greco-Roman culture taught them that such events indicated divine wrath, but they would interpret this as the gods (plural) being angry with them (Koester, *Revelation*, 649).

33. Cf. Beale, *Book of Revelation*, 825. However, the passage functions as a warning to John's hearers so that *they* might repent before they get to this stage (ibid., 826); cf. Koester, *Revelation*, 649, 664.

(9:13–19). Something very similar happens now. This might almost be the same event described in different ways. Drying up the Euphrates would be unprecedented, although it was diverted by Cyrus as part of his strategy to defeat Babylon (as alluded to in Jer 50:38).[34] It might ironically recall the drying up of the Red Sea and the Jordan for Israel to pass through (Exod 14:21–22; Josh 3:15–17; see also Isa 51:10). It might also recall the second exodus promise of Isaiah 11:15, which includes breaking up the Euphrates into seven easily fordable streams.[35] In all these cases, the drying up of a waterway was for Israel's salvation. Is this what John is implying here, the fulfilment of Isaiah 11:15? Perhaps, but it seems like we are looking at some kind of judgment,[36] which make these ironic references.

For John's audience, "kings from the east" might rather evoke thoughts of the Parthian Empire, a continual threat to the Roman Empire on its eastern border,[37] or earlier invasions of Israel by the Assyrians and Babylonians.[38] However, Beale argues that "the drying up of the Euphrates again marks the prelude to the destruction of Latter-day Babylon" and cannot be taken as a "literal geographical reference." Rather it is "a picture of how the multitudes of Babylon's religious adherents throughout the world become disloyal to Babylon."[39]

> **And I saw (coming out) of the mouth of the dragon, and out of the mouth of the wild beast, and out of the mouth of the false prophet, three unclean spirits like frogs . . . (Rev 16:13)**

It seems that the evil empire is about to strike back against the overwhelming forces of God so far unleashed against it in the first five bowl disasters. These spirits are not from God; rather, they are "unclean."[40] They originate from, or are channeled through, the three anti-God characters described since chapter 12: the dragon (i.e., the devil or Satan; 12:3–12), the sea beast (13:1–8), and the land beast. This land beast is now named "the false prophet," probably because of his role in deceiving people[41] and caus-

---

34. Beale, *Book of Revelation*, 827.

35. Cf. Fekkes, *Isaiah and Prophetic Traditions*, 201–2; Thomas, *Apocalypse*, 480; Aune, *Revelation 6–16*, 890–91; Koester, *Revelation*, 665.

36. But see Leithart, *Revelation 12–22*, 149–50.

37. See 1 Enoch 56:5–8 and the discussion in Aune, *Revelation 6–16*, 866–67. The Parthians did successfully invade Judea in 40 BC, and temporarily installed their own puppet high priest, before being driven out again by the Romans (Bruce, *Israel and the Nations*, 189–90). On the longer history of Roman-Parthian relations, see Aune, *Revelation 6–16*, 891–94; Koester, *Revelation*, 657. The Euphrates was the normal border between the two empires. There may be a reference to rumors of Nero returning to reclaim the Roman throne with a Parthian army (Koester, *Revelation*, 657–58, 665).

38. Koester, *Revelation*, 657.

39. Beale, *Book of Revelation*, 828.

40. The Greek word *akatharta* [ακαθαρτα] stands behind "unclean." It is an adjective frequently used in the gospels to describe demons that Jesus casts out of people; e.g., Mark 1:23.

41. Perhaps this happens even in the churches, as in the case of "Jezebel" in Thyatira. Beale points out that the language of false prophets in the NT always describes someone who "speaks falsehood

ing them to worship the sea beast (13:11–15). Specifically, these spirits come out of the mouths of the unholy trio (compare 12:15; 13:5–6), suggesting that they are activated by speech, perhaps a form of propaganda,[42] or expressive of their evil nature (compare Mark 7:14–23).

> ... for they are demonic spirits doing signs, which go out to the kings of the whole world, to gather them for the war of the great day of God Almighty. (Rev 16:14)

The specific role of these demons (Greek *pneumata daimoniōn*, "spirits of demons") is to gather forces for a major battle. Probably the beasts are calling on their allies and subordinate powers (the kings of the whole world or the kings of the East) to support them in this war, as the Roman emperors often did. But this has spiritual significance since it is spirits who are involved and they are reinforcing their message with signs (Greek *sēmeia*, implying miraculous or supernatural events), as the land beast had done in 13:13–15.

The audience might remember the plague of frogs in Exodus (Exod 8:1–15), which was duplicated by Pharaoh's magicians with their "secret arts" (Exod 8:7).[43] John's audience was used to spiritual and miraculous powers associated with the gods of the Greco-Roman world and the magical arena generally. Everyone in the ancient world believed in such signs and powers, and the Ephesians might remember the power encounters caused by the clash between demonic and godly forces during Paul's outreach in the city (Acts 19:11–20). The audience would also be familiar with the practice of seeking favorable portents before going to war, and probably this is what the text is referring to here. A favorable portent might take the form of a word from the oracles of Delphi (or the like), a sign discerned in entrails of an animal sacrifice, or a heavenly sight.[44]

The analysis so far is based on the assumption that the two armies here—that of the "kings from the east" (v. 12) and the army of "the kings of the whole world" (v. 14)—are the same army, or at least allied forces opposed to God and his saints. No saints' army is specifically described here (though see 17:14; 19:14). However, some commentators see them as opposing armies and interpret the "kings from the east" as a good army executing God's justice against Babylon and led in some way by the returning Christ making a surprise attack (v. 15). Thus, Leithart argues, "The kings from the sunrising . . . cross to engage the kings of the *oikoumene* as a new army of conquest, led by Jesus/Joshua, who comes like a thief to fight at Har-Megiddo."[45] How-

---

within the covenant community of Israel or the church" (Beale, *Book of Revelation*, 831, emphasis in the original). Cf. Koester, *Revelation*, 658–59.

42. Contrast the two-edged sword coming out of Jesus' mouth (1:16; 2:12, 16; 19:15, 21), the fire from the mouths of the two witnesses (11:5), and the statement about the 144,000 that "no lie was found in their mouths" (14:5). Cf. Koester, *Revelation*, 666.

43. Cf. Beale, *Book of Revelation*, 832–34.

44. Cf. Fox, *Classical World*, 299.

45. Leithart, *Revelation 12–22*, 150. For the full argument, see ibid., 149–58.

ever, this is not a literal attack but represents "a battle of suffering and martyrdom"[46] and "the end of the old mountaintop religion of Sinai and Zion."[47] This interpretation is suggestive in view of the eschatological language of verses 14–15, but ultimately seems too subtle.

But this is not just any battle: there is a distinctly eschatological (or climactic) edge when the audience hears that this battle is associated with "the great day of God Almighty" (v. 14).[48] Gathering the world's nations to fight against God's people anticipates 19:19 and 20:8, suggesting that this is the same eschatological battle.[49] This phrase would also remind the audience of similar language in the Old Testament, such as Zechariah 14:2 where God gathers the nations against Jerusalem, but perhaps especially Joel 2–3, a passage already in their focus through the language of Revelation 9 and 14:17–20.

Joel speaks of a mighty army in the "day of the Lord" (Joel 2:11; see also Zeph 1:14–16) followed by a decisive battle for which God "will gather all nations" (Joel 3:2, 11) and which functions as God's judgment on them (Joel 3:12). The language used has already been referred to in the vision of John. For example, it is seen in the trampling of grapes in a winepress (Joel 3:13; Rev 14:17–20), the darkening of heavenly bodies (Joel 3:15; 2:10; Rev 6:12; 8:12; 16:10), and vengeance for innocent blood (Joel 3:21; Rev 16:6). Joel announces, "the day of the Lord is near in the valley of decision" (Joel 3:14), a phrase used of the massive locust plague earlier in the book (Joel 1:15; 2:1, 11). By these allusions, John shows that this battle of Revelation 16 is not just engineered by the demonic spirits but is planned by God as part of his plan to vindicate his people.[50]

A similar passage in Isaiah 34 might also be recalled by John's listeners. Here Isaiah describes "a day of vengeance" of the Lord (Isa 34:8), during which God brings destruction of the armies of all nations (Isa 34:2), and the heavens are disturbed, using language similar to Revelation 6 (compare Isa 34:4; Rev 6:12–14). Edom in particular is destroyed (Isa 34:5–17), using language similar to Revelation 14:10–11.

The audience might also recall Isaiah 13, which speaks of "the day of the Lord" as being near (Isa 13:6) using the language of warfare (Isa 13:4–5), terror (Isa 13:7–8), and cosmic upheaval and darkness (Isa 13:10, 13) to describe the destruction of Babylon by the Medes (Isa 13:1, 17–22). Each of these passages describes God's judgment on the Gentile nations who have oppressed Israel. The passages also describe his vindication of his people, often after he has disciplined Israel by those same Gentile nations. Hence John's informed hearers might see something similar going on, as verses 5–6 have also suggested. They (the faithful Christians) will be vindicated through this

---

46. Leithart, *Revelation 12–22*, 156; cf. Papandrea, *Wedding of the Lamb*, 104–6.
47. Leithart, *Revelation 12–22*, 158.
48. Cf. Aune, *Revelation 6–16*, 896.
49. Cf. Beale, *Book of Revelation*, 835; Koester, *Revelation*, 665–66.
50. Cf. Thomas, *Apocalypse*, 482.

battle, restored to victory, and rewarded. All of this is in keeping with the promises to the victorious believers in the seven messages of Revelation 2–3.

> **Behold I am coming like a thief. Blessed (are) those who stay alert, and keep their clothes, so that they do not walk about naked and (people) see their shame. (Rev 16:15)**

The narrative about the gathering of the nations for battle is interrupted by the voice of Jesus. It seems that preparations for the eschatological battle may somehow be associated with the possibility of the second coming, or a similar event, anticipating Revelation 19. The outcome of the impending great battle is not to be the only focus of the believers. The language used here would recall several previous places in the text. In 1:7, John declares, "Behold he is coming with the clouds, and every eye will see him and those who pierced him and all the tribes of the earth will mourn over him." One of the intertexts there was Zechariah 12:10, and the context in Zechariah includes a reference to Megiddo (Zech 12:11).

Several places in the seven prophetic messages to the churches refer to Jesus "coming" in some kind of disciplinary action or relief to those congregations (2:5, 16, 25; 3:3, 11). The closest language to 16:15 is found in the message to Sardis, which focuses on the need to stay awake since the church is apparently asleep (3:2–3). The message to Sardis also uses clothing as a metaphor for victorious living (3:4–5), and it contains the only other reference in Revelation to Jesus coming "like a thief" (3:3), that is, unexpectedly. However, the warning about being naked recalls the message to Laodicea, whose members are so described (3:17–18). So the words of 16:15 function as both an encouragement and a warning. Jesus will come unexpectedly, without warning, and a wise disciple will make every effort to be found alert and "clothed" when he comes.

Such disciples will be "blessed" (v. 15). This is the third beatitude in Revelation (see also 1:3 and, more relevantly, 14:13, where those who "die in the Lord" are blessed). If the message to Sardis is meant to be recalled here, the consequences are serious. Those who maintain alertness and a state of being clothed by living a life of purity are saved. Their names remain in the book of life and are confessed by Jesus before God and the angels (3:5). But those who do not stay alert and clothed will suffer shameful exposure because of their laziness and compromise, when Jesus comes like a thief.[51]

> **And they gathered them to the place called in Hebrew Harmagedon. (Rev 16:16)**

It is significant that a Hebrew name is given here, reinforcing the Old Testament flavor of this passage. However, the word "Harmagedon" is ambiguous. It literally refers to

---

51. Cf. Thomas, *Apocalypse*, 483–84; Beale, *Book of Revelation*, 837–38; Koester, *Revelation*, 660. On the relationship between nakedness and shame in Judaism and Greco-Roman culture, see Aune, *Revelation 6–16*, 897–98.

Megiddo or "hill of Megiddo," which does not exist.[52] The battles associated with that area include both Deborah and Barak's victory over the Canaanites (Judg 5:19) and the disastrous campaign by one of Judah's most godly kings, Josiah, against an Egyptian Pharaoh (2 Kgs 23:29–30) at the Euphrates.

This would be an ominous allusion since not only are God's people defeated by a Gentile nation in the case of Josiah, but the author of Second Kings apparently attributes this to their sins under the previous king Manasseh. He quotes the LORD as saying, "I will remove Judah also from my presence as I removed Israel, and I will reject Jerusalem, the city I chose, and this temple, about which I said, 'My Name shall be there'" (2 Kgs 23:27).[53] So the expectations created in John's audience by the language of verses 12–16 would be mixed.[54]

> **And the seventh (angel) poured out his bowl into the air,[55] and a loud voice came out of the temple from the throne which said, "It is done." (Rev 16:17)**

The seventh item in each of the three numbered series in Revelation stands in different relationships to the series as a whole. With the seals, there is a significant delay between the sixth and seventh seal, which then unveils half an hour's silence and segues into the seven trumpets (8:1–2). The seventh trumpet also follows a delay (or at least, the events under the sixth trumpet are extended) but sounds a note of climactic triumph (11:15). The seventh bowl follows immediately after the sixth and also has a sense of climax, but the language is less positive than the seventh trumpet. The lack of delay before the seventh event may indicate that the time for repentance has passed.[56]

The loud announcement comes from the temple and the throne of God, recalling the temple language at the start of this sequence (15:5–8) and the throne language at the start of the vision (4:2). It probably suggests that God's work of judgement is now finished, which was indicated in 15:1. The phrase, "it is done," translates the Greek *gegonen*, from *ginomai*, "become" or "happen." Forms of this verb occur five times in verses 18–19, and this form occurs again in 21:6.[57] It suggests completion of God's program and may remind some listeners of Jesus' last words from the cross in John 19:30.[58] God has won the victory and his enemies are completely defeated.

> **And there was lightning and noise and thunder and there was a great earthquake, which had not happened from when people came on the earth, so great**

---

52. Cf. Koester, *Revelation*, 660–61, 667–68; Fekkes, *Isaiah and Prophetic Traditions*, 202–4.

53. Cf. Leithart, *Revelation 12–22*, 156.

54. Cf. Thomas, *Apocalypse*, 485–86; Aune, *Revelation 6–16*, 898–99; Beale, *Book of Revelation*, 838–41. Beale argues convincingly that Armageddon is not meant to be understood as a literal place.

55. Cf. Beale, *Book of Revelation*, 841.

56. Cf. Koester, *Revelation*, 664.

57. Cf. Leithart, *Revelation 12–22*, 159.

58. Moloney uses this reference among others to argue that this is a reference to Jesus' victory on the Cross (Moloney, *Apocalypse of John*, 249). However, John there uses a different Greek verb.

was that earthquake.[59] **And the great city was broken**[60] **into three parts, and the cities of the nations fell. (Rev 16:18–19a)**

Such theophanic manifestations have been seen before in Revelation (see 4:5; 6:12–14; 8:5; 11:13, 19), but as usual in this series, this event is bigger than its predecessors. A huge earthquake is predicted in Zechariah 14 in the midst of an international attack on Jerusalem:

> The LORD will go out and fight against those nations, as he fights on a day of battle. On that day his feet will stand on the Mount of Olives, east of Jerusalem, and the Mount of Olives will be split in two from east to west, forming a great valley, with half of the mountain moving north and half moving south. (Zech 14:3–4)

This allowed God's people to flee. But again, the earthquake in Revelation 16 is bigger, the biggest ever in human history, not only in its physical results but also its political ones.

And Babylon the Great was remembered before God to give her the cup of the wine of the fury of his wrath. (Rev 16:19b)

Reference to God's memory shows the historical roots of this event, though it means God is about to take action, rather than that his memory has been jogged. Possibly God is about to answer prayers about Babylon.[61] Babylon was the most significant enemy of Judah in the Old Testament and was used by God to inflict punishment on a disobedient nation, taking the Jews into exile in 587 BC. Even then, the prophets predicted that Babylon itself would not be spared, but ultimately would suffer a worse fate as God turned to restore his people.

Beale rightly points out that a literal Babylon, or even just Rome, is not in view, but rather "all the world's cultural, political, economic, and sociological centers."[62] The language of a cup of wine as a metaphor for God's wrath and consequent disaster recalls 14:10, the judgment on those who take the beast's mark. It also recalls Isaiah 51:17 (referring to judgement on Jerusalem), Jeremiah 25:15–17 (judgments on multiple nations, beginning with Judah), and Jeremiah 51:7 (where Babylon makes other nations drink her wine).[63] The idea was that such a punishment made the people like drunkards, unable to stand firm or make sober decisions, and hence vulnerable to attack.[64]

---

59. Beale sees here a reference to Dan 12:1 about unprecedented tribulation which is also associated with the final resurrection (Beale, *Book of Revelation*, 842; cf. Koester, *Revelation*, 662; Bauckham, *Climax of Prophecy*, 199–209).

60. The Greek word ἐγένετο [*egeneto*] is in the aorist tense and can be literally rendered "became."

61. Cf. Aune, *Revelation 6–16*, 859.

62. Beale, *Book of Revelation*, 843; cf. Koester, *Revelation*, 662–63. As Koester points out, there are numerous oracles in the OT against nations of the ancient Near East (ibid., 663).

63. Cf. Thomas, *Apocalypse*, 488.

64. Cf. Beale, *Book of Revelation*, 843.

> And every island fled and no mountain was found.⁶⁵ And large hail as a talent (in weight) fell from heaven on the people, and the people blasphemed God for the plague of hail, for this plague was exceedingly great. (Rev 16:20–21)

This also recalls one of the Exodus plagues (Exod 9:18–26), the Joshua narrative (Josh 10:11), and the defeat of Gog (Ezek 38:19–22). Hail has been mentioned previously in Revelation (8:7; 11:19), but once again, this is hail like never before. In fact, it's difficult to take this literally. It's the most dramatic language until 20:11.⁶⁶ But it certainly is meant to give the hearers the idea of a complete collapse of the world as they knew it. The sense of a massive crushing victory by God over the forces of the dragon and the beast is inescapable. However, there are still people resisting God, and armies are being prepared for the last great battle.⁶⁷ So the vision will now turn to give more of a "back story" to this judgement on Babylon.

---

65. Similar language is found in 6:14 and 20:11. Leithart takes it as referring to the AD late-60s situation in the Roman Empire and Judea (Leithart, *Revelation 12–22*, 160–61).

66. There may be an allusion to the rocks used by the Romans in their assault on Jerusalem in AD 70 (Josephus, "War of the Jews" 5:270–271). Otherwise severe hail was often seen as a prodigy, a warning from the gods (Aune, *Revelation 6–16*, 902).

67. Cf. Koester, *Revelation*, 651, who contends that "The plagues do not take the lives of God's opponents." But see Beale, *Book of Revelation*, 845. Beale sees this as part of the last judgment.

Revelation Chapter 17

John's audience in the seven churches have been taken on an exciting but terrifying journey via his graphic visions. In the past few chapters, they have listened in awe as John told them of a red dragon, war in heaven, war also on earth, the reign of the beast, and God's massive counter-attack. They have been warned severely of the consequences of compromise or sleepiness in their service of Jesus Christ, but encouraged by the promises of eternal rest and rejoicing in heaven after he comes again.

From time to time, they have heard of "the great city" (11:8; 14:20, perhaps; 16:19) and "Babylon the Great" (14:8; 16:19). These cities (or this city, if they are one and the same) are enemies of God and his people and labelled as such, for every name in Revelation has some kind of intertextual significance. In fact, the "great city" in 11:8 is also named "Sodom and Egypt." But what does it all mean? The listeners are about to find out.

This section (17:1—19:3) has been interpreted many ways over the centuries.

- Many early Christians saw the whore as referring to Rome (the city and empire).
- Later Protestants, including many Pentecostals, saw it as referring to the papacy or Roman Catholic church.[1]
- Some Pentecostals saw it as an unfaithful church, maybe traditional, maybe ecumenical (as in World Council of Churches), maybe liberal or modernist, maybe even a mega-religion unifying all existing religions, not just Christians; certainly a "church" to which Pentecostals must not belong.[2]
- Some Fundamentalist interpreters have pointed to the "treaty of Rome" as the basis for the European Union.
- Recent scholars have tended to go back to ancient Rome or to see modern manifestations of "Empire" such as global capitalism as being contemporary applications.

---

1. Cf. Johnson, *Pneumatic Discernment*, 126.
2. Most Pentecostal movements are not affiliated with the World Council of Churches.

- Some Preterist scholars see the whore as a reference to unfaithful Israel (in Jesus' day) and the beast she sits on as Rome, seeing that the beast turns on the whore and destroys her, perhaps referring to the events of AD 66–70.[3] Leithart, for example, contends, "Babylon is Jerusalem rather than Rome or a generic 'city of man'"[4] though he later says, "Babylon is an institutional force in or of Judaism that lures the rulers of Israel and the land-dwellers to her immorality."[5]

I will discuss this again at the end of chapter 18.

17:1–11 The Seductive Prostitute and Her Beast

> **And one of the seven angels who had the seven bowls came and spoke with me, saying, "Come here, I will show you the judgment of the great prostitute sitting upon many waters..." (Rev 17:1)**

Perhaps this angel is the last angel in the bowl series since the seventh bowl was associated with the judgment on "the great city" and "Babylon the Great."[6] The previous passage is not forgotten, and there is also a connection with 21:9, where perhaps the same angel appears again. The reference to "sitting on many waters" would also recall Jeremiah 51:13, part of Jeremiah's prophetic polemic against ancient Babylon.[7] But the tone of the text changes from one of "step-by-step" narrative to something more descriptive, artistic, and also mysterious, in the sense of crying out for explanation.

The use of "judgment" (Greek *krima*) foreshadows to the hearers that this will not end well, recalling also the cry of the martyrs (6:10) and other proclamations of impending judgment (11:18; 14:7).[8] The description of the prostitute as "great" (Greek *megalēs*, "big," a version of one of John's favorite words) shows that what follows is of great significance. The fact that she *sits* implies sovereignty, or at least security (see vv. 1, 3, 9, 15; see also 18:7);[9] she also "rides" the beast (v. 7) and "rules over the kings of the earth" (v. 18).[10]

> **...with whom the kings of the earth committed sexual immorality and those who dwell on the earth became drunk from the wine of her immorality." (Rev 17:2)**

---

3. Cf. Koester, *Revelation*, 675; Leithart, *Revelation 12–22*, 168–86. Parallels with Ezekiel (Leithart, *Revelation 12–22*, 168, 172) are a persuasive factor in favor of this reading.

4. Leithart, *Revelation 12–22*, 170; cf. Smolarz, *Covenant*, 238–42, 271–82.

5. Leithart, *Revelation 12–22*, 177; cf. Moloney, *Apocalypse of John*, 264–270.

6. Cf. Thomas, *Apocalypse*, 491.

7. Cf. Aune, *Revelation 17–22*, 929.

8. Cf. Thomas, *Apocalypse*, 492.

9. Cf. Leithart, *Revelation 12–22*, 180.

10. Cf. Beale, *Book of Revelation*, 848.

The picture of the whore portrays the seductive side of evil and empire, in contrast to the oppressive nature of the beast.[11] This seductive aspect of the Roman empire was very real to many in Asia, at least the elites, who voluntarily engaged in the imperial cult. The language of immorality would remind the audience of the Nicolaitans (2:14) and Jezebel (2:20–22); in other words, even the churches can be seduced.[12] However, note the Greek *porneias*—which means "immorality," possibly sex with prostitutes—is not the specific word for adultery.[13]

There were several kinds of prostitutes in the Greco-Roman world of John's day. There were common prostitutes, usually slaves, who made a profit for their masters.[14] And there were "high class" prostitutes or courtesans whose clients were wealthy men and who lived in relative luxury. The most famous of these was actually Messalina, the wife of the emperor Claudius, who was reputed to indulge in night-time sexual immorality as a prostitute with Roman men.[15] Most likely, the courtesans are the model for this portrait since the great prostitute's clients were kings,[16] although John uses the Greek word for common prostitutes, not the specific terms for courtesans.[17] There could be a particular woman in mind as a model for John's portrait, however, such as Messalina, or Claudius' next wife, Agrippina (the mother of Nero),[18] or maybe Berenice, the Jewish queen who was the lover of Agrippa II and later of the emperor Titus.[19]

The imagery of wine and intoxication is used here to evoke the attractiveness, pleasure, addictiveness, and physical effects of such immoral activity. However, it is unlikely that this vision is meant to be taken very literally, as describing actual kings committing physical immorality with specific historical persons. John has already

---

11. Cf. Beale, *Book of Revelation*, 848. Roman authors observed how conquered tribes were "softened" and made compliant by exposure to the pleasures and luxuries of Rome (Fox, *Classical World*, 526).

12. Cf. Thomas, *Apocalypse*, 492.

13. Forms of this word are found in 17:2, 4; 18:3, 9; 19:2. However, Leithart argues that in Scripture, it refers to "the disloyal treachery of a bride, specifically of God's people to their divine husband" and hence can only apply to Jerusalem (Leithart, *Revelation 12–22*, 175, 172). Cf. Smolarz, *Covenant*, 272–82.

14. It was commonly believed that there were also temple prostitutes, usually slaves dedicated to female gods; the original idea was increased fertility through sexual activity and possibly income for the temple. However, the evidence for such a phenomenon in the first-century Greco-Roman world is very weak. Cf. Baugh, "Cult Prostitution in New Testament Ephesus." More broadly, Budin in *The Myth of Sacred Prostitution in Antiquity*, denies such a phenomenon ever existed in the ancient world.

15. Cf. Aune, *Revelation 17–22*, 929. Roman critics often used prostitution language as a tool to criticize various emperors. Cf. Glancy and Moore, "How Typical."

16. Cf. Aune, *Revelation 17–22*, 935. But see Koester, *Revelation*, 671, 688. Ian Paul suggests John deliberately evokes both courtesans and common prostitutes to debase this woman in his audience's mind (Paul, *Revelation*, 281).

17. Glancy and Moore, "How Typical," 551.

18. Cf. Stramara, *God's Timetable*, 93–96, 111–15. She is another possible 666.

19. Lupieri, *Commentary*, viii. Another suggestion is the Egyptian queen Cleopatra (Valentine, "Cleopatra").

used sexual language of false teaching, wrong association and idols, as in the case of "Jezebel" in 2:20–22, though in this case some elements of literal immorality may be included.[20]

The original Jezebel foreshadowed aspects of the wild beast and the prostitute, as she persecuted the prophets and everyone loyal to God and seduced Israel to the worship of Baal and Asherah (1 Kgs 16:31–33; 18:13, 19; 19:1–2). Her doom was similar to that of Babylon (2 Kgs 9:30–37; Rev 17:16). The Jezebel of Thyatira seemed at least to advocate compromise with Greco-Roman religion.[21]

Similar metaphorical uses of sexual language are found in the Old Testament, such as Deuteronomy 31:16—"these people will soon prostitute themselves to the foreign gods of the land . . . "[22] This use is especially evident in Ezekiel. Ezekiel has two chapters describing Jerusalem's unfaithfulness to God in graphic sexual language (Ezek 16; 23), referring to idolatry and alliances with Gentile empires, respectively. In both cases, it doesn't end well as the women are stripped and violently killed (Ezek 16:35–40; 23:22–30).[23]

Here too, the immorality and prostitution is most likely referring to a political, religious, or economic relationship, perhaps like Tyre's trading network (Isa 23:15–17)[24] or Nineveh's imperial oppression of nations (Nah 3:4).[25] Fekkes comments, "At the very least John wishes to expose what he perceives as the nations' sycophantic relationship with Rome . . . and their partnership in the inevitable corollaries of vast and irresponsible power and wealth: violence, social injustice, and immorality."[26]

And he carried me away "in the Spirit" into a desert. (Rev 17:3a)

This is structurally significant, the third time John reports being "in the Spirit" (the earlier occasions are in 1:10 and 4:2, also associated with a visionary journey; see also 21:10).[27] On this occasion, he is taken[28] into a desert,[29] a setting with associations of need, danger, and loneliness, but also of protection (12:14) and spiritual significance,

---

20. Sexual relations between prominent leaders was a well-known feature of the Greco-Roman world. Cleopatra's relationships with Julius Caesar, and later Mark Antony, were perhaps the most famous. Marriage alliances have always been a feature of monarchical systems.

21. Cf. Smolarz, *Covenant*, 278, 282–83

22. Cf. Aune, *Revelation 17–22*, 907.

23. Cf. Leithart, *Revelation 12–22*, 168.

24. Cf. Aune, *Revelation 17–22*, 930–31; Beale, *Book of Revelation*, 848–50. Beale argues that the harlot metaphor of Tyre "is the closest verbally to Rev 17:2" (ibid., 850).

25. Cf. Beale, *Book of Revelation*, 850; Leithart, *Revelation 12–22*, 173.

26. Fekkes, *Isaiah and Prophetic Traditions*, 212.

27. Cf. Thomas, *Apocalypse*, 490, 493–94. The language of showing is also associated with each of these (1:1; 4:1; 17:1; 21:9). Cf. Leithart, *Revelation 12–22*, 164–65.

28. Perhaps he is in a trance (Koester, *Revelation*, 673; Aune, *Revelation 17–22*, 933). The idea of the Spirit carrying a prophet to a new location is also found in Ezek 3:14; 8:3; 11:1, 24; 43:5; 1 Kgs 18:12; 2 Kgs 2:16; Acts 8:39.

29. The Greek here is ἔρημον [*erēmon*] meaning "desert, wilderness, uninhabited place."

as is seen in the wilderness experience of Israel.[30] John's listeners may well have been familiar with the story of Jesus' temptations by the devil in the wilderness (Matt 4:1–11; Mark 1:12–13; Luke 4:1–13), especially as this was initiated by the Spirit. It might be a strange place for a prostitute, however, as prostitution is more associated with urban environments. Nonetheless, the desert might have importance as a sign of her fate.[31] The good woman of chapter 12 also fled into the wilderness (12:6, 14), where she was threatened by the dragon, but protected. The wilderness is thus a place of conflict; it doesn't mean that the good woman is now a prostitute.[32]

> **And I saw a woman sitting on a scarlet wild beast, covered with blasphemous names, having seven heads and ten horns. (Rev 17:3b)**

John first notes the beast on which the woman sits. It is scarlet, like the red dragon in 12:3, covered with blasphemous names,[33] like the sea beast in 13:1, and has "seven heads and ten horns," like the dragon (12:3) and the sea beast (13:1). So somehow this woman is reliant on the beast, probably the same beast as in Revelation 13.[34] This could be alluding to the dependence of the Jerusalem elite on Rome (as portrayed graphically in the Gospel accounts of the trial of Jesus)[35] or the dependence of the city of Rome on its empire and its military. It could also validly be applied to portray a state-sanctioned church seeking security in such a relationship and persecuting dissident congregations of believers.[36]

> **And the woman was clothed with purple and scarlet, and covered with gold and precious stones and pearls, having a golden cup in her hand filled with detestable and unclean (elements) of her immorality . . . (Rev 17:4)**

This confirms the courtesan image and emphasizes the luxury associated with her; there is also an implied contrast with the "woman clothed with the sun" in 12:1.[37] John is stressing the sheer excess and immorality of her luxurious lifestyle, providing his hearers with a thoroughly negative picture. It also suggests idolatry and demonic

---

30. Cf. Thomas, *Apocalypse*, 494–95.

31. Cf. Koester, *Revelation*, 673. In Isa 21:1–10, an invader comes from the desert and the fall of Babylon is announced (cf. Beale, *Book of Revelation*, 851–52).

32. For a defense of this point of view, see Thompson, *Book of Revelation*, 82.

33. Possibly this is a reference to the pretentious titles given to emperors that were only appropriate for God (Koester, *Revelation*, 673).

34. Cf. Beale, *Book of Revelation*, 853. Aune argues against this on the basis that John sees "*a* scarlet beast," not "*the* scarlet beast" (Aune, *Revelation 17–22*, 908). But while there are differences in details, it is hard not to see some connection with the beast(s) of Revelation 13.

35. See John 11:48. Cf. Leithart, *Revelation 12–22*, 179.

36. Cf. Leithart, *Revelation 12–22*, 181–82.

37. Cf. Thomas, *Apocalypse*, 496.

influence as suggested by "unclean" (Greek *akatharta*), recalling the "unclean spirits," that is "demonic spirits," of 16:13–14.[38]

> ... and on her forehead a secret name (was) written: "Babylon the Great the Mother of prostitutes[39] and detestable (things) of the earth." (Rev 17:5)

Her identity is revealed in "the name written on her forehead," possibly a custom for prostitutes in Rome[40] and a commonplace of identity in Revelation (see 7:3; 9:4; 13:16; 14:1, 9; 22:4), which is a secret (Greek *mustērion*). Perhaps there is a reference to the "mystery religions" of the ancient world here.[41] Her secret name is not entirely revealing, but John's hearers would at least learn two things from it. This is a picture of "Babylon the Great," previously mentioned in 14:8 and 16:19 (and originally in Dan 4:30), and she is an originator ("mother")[42] of prostitution or sexual immorality and what is "detestable" (Greek *bdelugmatōn*, possibly also meaning sacrilegious), referring generally to idolatry, or particularly to desecrating a sacred space, as in Daniel 9:27; 11:31; and 12:11.[43] This implies that she represents a very ancient and even "transtemporal" reality.[44] Leithart claims "she is the final expression of the Babel project" from Genesis 11.[45]

> And I saw the woman drunk with the blood of the saints and with the blood of the witnesses of Jesus. (Rev 17:6a)

This picture of the woman "drunk with the blood"[46] of the martyrs makes her an ally of the dragon (12:17) and the beast (13:7–10; 16:6).[47] It is a revolting picture for John's audience in the seven churches and may well confirm their experience of the upper classes of the Roman Empire with their luxury, immorality, and hostility to God and the churches.[48] Many Pentecostals have had similar experiences with upper class elites. According to Leithart, this drinking of human holy blood *is* the abomination

---

38. Cf. Beale, *Book of Revelation*, 856–57; Thomas, *Apocalypse*, 497.

39. The Greek is πορνῶν [*pornōn*]—the plural noun for female prostitutes.

40. Only very common prostitutes would have such a name tattooed on their foreheads, like wayward or runaway slaves. Cf. Koester, *Revelation*, 674; Beale, *Book of Revelation*, 858; Whitaker, *Ekphrasis*, 199.

41. According to Beale, "mystery" has "end-time associations" (Beale, *Book of Revelation*, 858).

42. Jezebel was also a mother (2:23) as was the woman of Revelation 12 (12:2–5, 17). John is setting up a strong dualistic contrast here (cf. Thomas, *Apocalypse*, 499), though Leithart suggests that the woman of Revelation 12 morphs into the whore of Revelation 17. That is, Israel turns into God's adversary (*Revelation 12–22*, 184–86; cf. Thompson, *Book of Revelation*, 82).

43. Cf. Beasley-Murray, *Revelation*, 252–53, n. 2. This could support the idea of a reference to AD 70 in view of Matt 24:15 and Luke 21:20.

44. Beale, *Book of Revelation*, 859; Thomas, *Apocalypse*, 498–99.

45. Leithart, *Revelation 12–22*, 181.

46. This uses the present active participle, that is, "being drunk . . ."

47. For other connections here, see Thomas, *Apocalypse*, 500–501.

48. This would be true whether or not there was extensive official persecution at that time. For a discussion of the contrasting female figures in Revelation, see Koester, *Revelation*, 682–83; Beale, *Book of Revelation*, 889–90.

that causes her to be made desolate, fulfilling Daniel's and Jesus' prophecies of the "abomination that makes desolate."[49]

And I was greatly amazed when I saw her. (Rev 17:6b)

The Greek reads literally, "I was amazed with great amazement" using *thauma* (wonder, amazement), the kind of reaction one might have to a miracle. It raises the question, why amazement and not, say, disgust? Is it the sight of such a brightly dressed courtesan that amazes him or the fact that she is sitting on the beast? The reaction suggests an element of surprise, as if John is seeing the reality of something for the first time. Perhaps John is even tempted to bow down before this sight, or he is just "perplexed."[50] His reaction parallels that of "those who dwell on the earth" (v. 8), suggesting that John is tempted or allured by this image.

And the angel said to me, "Why are you amazed? I will tell you the secret of the woman and of the wild beast that carries her, which has the seven heads and the ten horns." (Rev 17:7)

The angel reacts with surprise at John, and then goes on to "de-mystify" the image. In Revelation, some previous secrets or mysteries have been explained: the mystery of the seven stars and seven lampstands in the first vision (1:20), the identity of the huge international multitude (7:13–14), and the identity of the dragon (12:9). Other secrets have not been decoded so that the audience must work it out for themselves, such as when they are challenged to "figure out the number of the beast" (13:18). In this case, the explanation is extensive,[51] but has caused more debate and confusion than clarification. However, we must assume that it made sense to those original hearers, at least those who could see "the world as the author does."[52]

"The wild beast which you see was and is not and is about to come up out of the abyss and go to destruction,[53] and those who dwell on the earth will be amazed,

---

49. Leithart, *Revelation 12–22*, 183. This could be true even if the woman does not represent Jerusalem as Leithart thinks. See 16:5–6; 18:22–24; 19:2.

50. Aune, *Revelation 17–22*, 910; cf. Beale, *Book of Revelation*, 861–63; Thomas, *Apocalypse*, 502. Is John outdoing himself in that his description of the whore is such an attention-getting image, using the ancient art of *ekphrasis*? (Cf. Whitaker, *Ekphrasis*, 176, 203–7). Another possibility is that the harlot's dress and jewels recall the vestments of the Jewish high priest. This would indeed be a shocking revelation to John (cf. Beale, *Book of Revelation*, 886; Leithart, *Revelation 12–22*, 178–79, 186).

51. Aune comments, "it is the only vision paired with a detailed interpretation, a feature common in Jewish apocalyptic literature" (Aune, *Revelation 17–22*, 915; see also 919). It was also found in other ancient literature such as *ekphrasis* which often involved the description and interpretation of a work of art (ibid., 924).

52. Koester, *Revelation*, 690.

53. Possibly this is a parody of the name of God as "the one who is, and who was, and who is coming" (1:4) or of the resurrection of Jesus or a funeral formula or a reference to the myth of a Nero come-back (cf. Koester, *Revelation*, 676–77, 689; Aune, *Revelation 17–22*, 939–41; Beale, *Book of Revelation*, 864; Thomas, *Apocalypse*, 505–6; Leithart, *Revelation 12–22*, 189–90). As Beale points out, the end of the beast's career is "destruction" in a parallel to Satan in Rev 20:1–11 (Beale, *Book of Revelation*, 864–65).

> (those) whose names are not written in the book of life from the foundation of the world, when they see the wild beast that was and is not and will be present." (Rev 17:8)

This sounds like the sea beast in chapter 13 in many ways[54] because it caused people to wonder (13:3) and was worshiped by those whose names have not been written in the Lamb's book of life, reminding the audience of 13:8.[55] But the current absence of the beast at the time of John's vision is a puzzle, especially if the beast represents the Roman Empire in some way; this point is repeated here and in verse 11. Perhaps the earlier reference to the beast's fatal wound would help the audience to make sense of this. If the vision was seen (or communicated) at a time when the empire was in danger or somehow inoperative or at a time between two emperors, this might have made sense to them.

This leads some to suggest that the vision may have occurred during the "year of four emperors" (AD 68–69), the period between Nero and Vespasian when three short-lived claimants to the throne (Galba, Otho, and Vitellius) rose and fell.[56] In this short period, the future of the empire was uncertain, so it "was and is not," perhaps. Certainly, the seven heads of the beast did exist (vv. 7, 9) and one king "is" (v. 10).[57] The amazement of unbelievers uses similar language to John's amazement in verse 6, stressing the allure of this figure.

> "Here (is) the mind that has wisdom. The seven heads are seven mountains, which the woman sits on." (Rev 17:9)

The angel calls for mental effort or "wisdom" (Greek *sophian*) here,[58] reflecting the task enjoined on the audience in connection with the number of the wild beast in 13:18. However, what is stated next suggests the listeners would have understood John without much effort to mean the city of Rome with its famous seven hills.[59] In fact, a coin from Vespasian's time portrays the goddess Roma (personifying the city of Rome) reclining on seven hills. Cults to Roma were common in the province of Asia,[60] and three of the

---

54. But see Leithart, *Revelation 12–22*, 187–89.

55. On application to the imperial cult, see Koester, *Revelation*, 687, 689. Beale grounds this in a Calvinistic view of predestination (*Book of Revelation*, 866), but the text does not state why some people's names "are not written in the book of life from the foundation of the world" (17:8). Cf. Thomas, *Apocalypse*, 506.

56. It might also refer to the earlier crisis caused by the assassination of Julius Caesar, which led to prolonged civil war until Octavian (Augustus) triumphed (Leithart, *Revelation 12–22*, 191).

57. Cf. Koester, *Revelation*, 691. Koester seems to be arguing that there was a lull in persecution that might cause the believers to become complacent.

58. This is what Thomas calls "pneumatic discernment" (Thomas, *Apocalypse*, 506).

59. Koester, *Revelation*, 677, 685, 690; Aune, *Revelation 17–22*, 944–45; Caird, *Revelation*, 216; Victorinus, *Commentary*, ANF 7:357–58. Beale suggests a more figurative interpretation, as mountains usually refer to kingdoms, though he does not discount a reference to Rome altogether (Beale, *Book of Revelation*, 868–70). For some reasons why John would describe Rome as Babylon, see Friesen, *Imperial Cults*, 138–40.

60. Aune, *Revelation 17–22*, 920–23; A. Collins, "Feminine Symbolism," 27.

cities Revelation is sent to had temples to the goddess Roma, which would suggest an immediate association in the minds of the audience.[61] Portraying her instead as a prostitute makes a very strong political comment, though it may have Roman roots.[62] Note that the woman is described as sitting on "many waters" (v. 1), "a scarlet wild beast" (v. 3), and "seven mountains" (v. 9). It suggests that these represent related, if not identical, realities. Thomas argues that "it is not likely that the imagery of the seven mountains would be exhausted by the identification of Rome with the beast," but "would be taken to convey the idea of universal power."[63] This would allow it to be applied to later situations.

> "And they are seven kings. Five have fallen, one (now) is, the other has not yet come, and when he comes, it is necessary for him to remain a little (time). And the wild beast which was and is not, is also an eighth, and is from the seven, and goes to destruction." (Rev 17:10-11)

So the seven heads are in one sense a simultaneous reality (seven mountains) and a consecutive reality (seven kings, one after the other).[64] This series of kings has puzzled commentators. Are they successive Roman emperors? If so, where do we start to count them and who do we include?[65] The statements about the eighth king complicates it further: Adapting the table given by Aune,[66] if we start from Julius Caesar and count all Caesars,[67] we get this list:

1. Julius Caesar
2. Augustus
3. Tiberius
4. Gaius (Caligula)
5. Claudius
6. Nero (the last of the Julio-Claudian line)
7. Galba
8. Otho

---

61. Caird, *Revelation*, 211–12.
62. Cf. Aune, *Revelation 17-22*, 926–27.
63. Thomas, *Apocalypse*, 507.
64. While the seven mountains and kings may "represent the oppressive power of world government throughout the ages" rather than "seven particular kings or kingdoms" (Beale, *Book of Revelation*, 869), the interpreter must give due attention to the succession language here: "five have fallen, one (now) is, the other has not yet come . . . "
65. Cf. Koester, *Revelation*, 73, 75–76; Aune, *Revelation 17-22*, 946–49; Beale, *Book of Revelation*, 871–75.
66. Aune, *Revelation 17-22*, 947; cf. Beale, *Book of Revelation*, 874.
67. Consistent with the Roman historian Suetonius' *The Twelve Caesars*, which starts with Julius Caesar and finishes with Domitian. Another Roman historian, Tacitus, starts with Augustus in his *Annals*. Cf. Aune, *Revelation 17-22*, 946.

This would mean the vision was seen in Nero's time and then Galba came for a short time only (as happened), but this would make Otho the eighth, which seems unlikely.

If instead we start with Augustus, the first true prince, and count all Caesars, Vitellius is the eighth with Otho as the short-lived king.

If we leave out the three short-lived claimants and start with Augustus Caesar, we get this list:

1. Augustus
2. Tiberius
3. Gaius (Caligula)
4. Claudius
5. Nero (the last of the Julio-Claudian line)
6. Vespasian (the first of the Flavian dynasty)
7. Titus
8. Domitian

Titus might make a good seventh king, in view of his short reign and his role in the defeat of the Jewish uprising and destruction of the temple and city of Jerusalem. Domitian fits the eighth king if he is seen as a "second Nero" and incarnation of the beast. This would make the vision itself happen during Vespasian's reign.

If we include only those who died violently ("fallen"), we might get:[68]

1. Julius Caesar (stabbed to death)
2. Gaius (Caligula; also stabbed)
3. Claudius (poisoned)
4. Nero (suicide)
5. Galba (stabbed)
6. Otho (suicide)
7. Vitellius (beaten to death)
8. Domitian (stabbed)

Or we could start with Caligula, the first emperor after the crucifixion of Christ and an instigator of the imperial cult in Jerusalem, making Domitian the sixth and reigning emperor when John wrote, if we omit the three brief emperors in AD 68–69.[69] David May has suggested that the evidence of coins circulating around AD 80 points to a different list based on the emperor Titus' selection of "good" emperors: Augustus,

---

68. Cf. Koester, *Revelation*, 678, but he doesn't support this interpretation. See also Aune, *Revelation 17–22*, 949.

69. Cf. Beale, *Book of Revelation*, 874.

Tiberius, Claudius, Galba, and his father, Vespasian. This would make Titus himself (who ruled AD 79–81) the emperor when Revelation was written and Domitian the seventh emperor about to come.[70]

Or following the ancient commentator Victorinus, we might count backwards from Domitian so that the five fallen emperors are Titus, Vespasian, Otho, Vitellius, and Galba; he then has Nerva as the seventh but the resurrected Nero as the eighth, the antichrist.[71] Another possibility is that the seven hills and kings denote seven successive empires, an option favored by many futurist interpreters, with the empire of the antichrist still to come.[72]

It's unlikely that working out any such correspondence would be expected of the hearers.[73] Perhaps the main point is that there is an eighth king, identified as the beast who "goes to destruction" (v. 11), speaking perhaps of the final futile and brief stand of Satanic power, futile because the beast has already been defeated at the cross,[74] brief since it is "a little time" (v. 10; compare 12:12), even just "one hour" (v. 12).[75]

This all sounds very complicated. Let's see if we can simplify. The whore seems clear enough: it is superficially a city, most likely Rome (though possibly Jerusalem), and more deeply represents an abiding force opposed to God and persecuting his saints (many recent expressions can be seen). The beast is probably the same beast as the sea beast of Revelation 13, representing the Roman Empire in John's day, but applicable to "empires" of all ages.

But when we drill down farther, we run into John's time language: something about this empire "was and is not and will be present" (v. 8),[76] but at the same time, seven kings of whom "five have fallen, one (now) is, the other has not yet come" (v. 10) and there are ten kings "who have not received a kingdom" (v. 12). The prophecy is apparently being given in a hiatus or transition period in the Roman world, leading up to a brief and violent struggle with the saints. This involves the future seventh king who must remain for "a little" time (v. 10), and the ten kings receive authority for "one hour" (v. 12). They "make war against the Lamb" (v. 14), but he and his

---

70. May, "Counting Kings." Papandrea begins with Nero (the first emperor to persecute Christians) and finishes with Nerva (Papandrea, *Wedding of the Lamb*, 168–69). Stramara starts with Claudius (as the adoptive father of Nero) and has Vespasian as the sixth, Titus as the seventh, and Domitian as the eighth who is "from" the seven (Stramara, *God's Timetable*, 105; see also 91–96, for his reasons for starting with Claudius). There were supposed to be exactly seven kings in the pre-republic early history of Rome (Aune, *Revelation 17–22*, 948, 961), but none of these could be described as existing when John wrote (v. 10).

71. Victorinus, *Commentary*, ANF 7:358.

72. Cf. Beale, *Book of Revelation*, 874–75; Smolarz, *Covenant*, 276–78.

73. Cf. Koester, *Revelation*, 678–79; Thomas, *Apocalypse*, 509.

74. Cf. Beale, *Book of Revelation*, 876–77.

75. Cf. Thomas, *Apocalypse*, 511–12.

76. This represents a kind of paraody of the name of God in Revelation as "him who is, and who was, and who is coming" and a parallel to the eschatological coming of Christ (1:4). Cf. Bauckham, *Climax of Prophecy*, 435–37.

followers defeat them. So the most plausible immediate reference is to the shaking of the empire with the events late in Nero's reign that led to his suicide and the end of the Julio-Claudian dynasty, and the coming resurgence of the empire under the Flavians (Vespasian, Titus and Domitian). These Roman events are parallel to the first systematic persecution of the church by Rome (AD 64–68) and the Jewish revolt against the empire (AD 66–70), both about three-and-a-half years long.

17:12–18 The Prostitute's Downfall

> "And the ten horns which you see are ten kings, who have not received a kingdom, but will receive authority as kings for one hour with the wild beast. These will have one purpose and will give their power and authority to the wild beast." (Rev 17:12–13)[77]

Of course, the beast has ten horns (vv. 3, 7; see also 13:1; Dan 7:7, 20, 24). The future-focused language here ("have not received . . . will receive") reflects the beast who "is not" (vv. 8, 11) or "has not yet come" (v. 10). A new development is impending for the audience. The Roman Empire often used client kings as surrogate rulers; the Herod family is a famous example.[78] This language may reflect a time during the civil wars of AD 68–69 when such kings allied themselves to a contender for the throne, perhaps Vespasian himself. This language also implies a situation when these client kings had to choose whom to follow. However, we do not have enough information to make a strong hypothesis about the exact historical situation, if there is one.

Beale may be right in arguing that "the horns are earthly agents through whom the spiritual forces of Satan and the beast work, both throughout the age and at the end of the age"; he sees this as especially a future development.[79] Revelation is more concerned about the loyalty of its hearers than their capacity to work it all out intellectually. As Koester puts it, "the issue is not whether readers can identify the kings, but whether they identify *with* them."[80]

> "These will make war with the Lamb, and the Lamb will conquer them, for he is lord of lords and king of kings, and those with him (are) called and chosen and faithful." (Rev 17:14)

What we can see in John's text is the two events that follow from this alliance in a short space of time ("one hour"): first, a persecution of Christians; next, a plundering or destruction of Rome itself. These kings can only attack the Lamb through his people,

---

77. On the significance of ten here, see Thomas, *Apocalypse*, 511.
78. Cf. Koester, *Revelation*, 679; Aune, *Revelation 17–22*, 951.
79. Beale, *Book of Revelation*, 879. For an alternative interpretation which sees the ten horns as successive Roman emperors, see Leithart, *Revelation 12–22*, 202. Papandrea sees them as the ten persecuting emperors from Nero to Galerius (Papandrea, *Wedding of the Lamb*, 47–48).
80. Koester, *Revelation*, 692.

as the audience knows from 12:17. Some would see a connection with Jesus's words to Saul outside Damascus, if they had heard that story (Acts 9:4–5). However, in contrast to the situation in 13:7, where the beast "was permitted to make war against the saints and conquer them" (compare Dan 7:21), this time the Lamb and his followers "conquer" (Greek *nikēsei*) the beast-led alliance. This anticipates 19:11–21 and answers back to 13:4 ("Who is like the wild beast and who is able to make war against it?").[81]

Whatever form the persecution of Christians took, it was unsuccessful; as 12:11 reminds us, the martyrs win![82] Here this victory is attributed to the supreme authority of the Lamb as "Lord of lords and King of kings,"[83] recalling 1:5 ("the ruler of the kings of the earth") and Psalm 2, but not without mention of his followers, "those with him" who are "called and chosen and faithful" (see also 12:11; 14:1–5; 19:14).[84] Hendriksen interprets it this way: "Throughout history, especially throughout this entire dispensation, the Lamb constantly defeats and shall defeat every form of antichristian dominion."[85]

> **And he said to me, "The waters which you see where the prostitute sits, they are peoples and crowds and nations and languages. And the ten horns which you see and the wild beast, these will hate the prostitute and make her desolate and naked, and devour her flesh and burn her down with fire . . ." (Rev 17:15–16)**[86]

The setback for the beast-led alliance is followed by an attack on the city, which the hearers already identify with Rome itself (v. 9), an identification supported by the interpretation of another detail in the vision. Recalling similar phrases in 5:9; 7:9; 10:11; 13:7; and 14:6, the "peoples and crowds and nations and languages" are the people currently under satanic rule but many of whom will turn to Christ.

Roman rulers often had a love/hate relationship with the city of Rome itself and its population. Nero was widely believed to have started the fire that destroyed much of the city. He did so in order to clear the way for the erection of grander buildings. Other armies plundered the city and destroyed parts of it during civil wars; the temple of Jupiter was set on fire in one such incident during the year of four emperors.[87] Most emperors now owed their position to their own armies, rather than the support of the Roman senate or populace or family relationships with their predecessors. Such

---

81. Cf. Beale, *Book of Revelation*, 880. This also reflects Dan.7:22.

82. Their victory is legal, not military, as 12:11 has implied (see also 6:9–10). As Leithart explains, "The more martyr blood they [the beast and his allies] shed, the more the land quakes with the cries of Abel, clamoring for justice, clamoring for the Divine Avenger to arise, a clamor that refuses to be silent until justice is done. God turns the tide so his enemies make his case, his case *against them*" (Leithart, *Revelation 12–22*, 201; emphasis in original).

83. On this phrase, see Aune, *Revelation 17–22*, 953–55; Thomas, *Apocalypse*, 513; Leithart, *Revelation 12–22*, 199.

84. Cf. Aune, *Revelation 17–22*, 956; Thomas, *Apocalypse*, 514.

85. Hendriksen, *More Than Conquerors*, 172.

86. Cf. Aune, *Revelation 17–22*, 957. Beale reverses the order of events, claiming that the attack on the harlot *precedes* the war against the Lamb (Beale, *Book of Revelation*, 883).

87. Suetonius, *Twelve Caesars* 9.15; Tacitus, *Histories* 3.71–73. Cf. Stramara, *God's Timetable*, 112.

armies had no great loyalty to the city of Rome itself and saw its wealth more as an opportunity for plunder.[88]

The language of verse 16 is gruesome and, to twenty-first century ears, even misogynistic in its portrayal of such violence in neo-sexual terms.[89] However, this was a common way of portraying conquest in those days, and it has Old Testament resonances (Ezek 16:37–41; 23:22–27; Nah 2:10; 3:5). Even in the twentieth century, we spoke of such events as the "rape of Nanking"[90] as a metaphor for conquest and destruction, including the literal rape of defenseless women. Some imperial art "depicts Roman emperors overpowering foreign nations pictured as partially unclothed women."[91] There is also a likely allusion to the judgment promised to Jezebel and her followers (2:22; see also 2 Kgs 9:30–37),[92] and to the warning of 16:15, both directed at Christians.[93] The difference is that this time the target is Rome itself. This language is meant to shock the reader, but John clearly sees it as justice, strict justice, especially if the gruesome torture of Christians by Nero is considered, as verse 16 is similar to that.[94]

> "... for God has given into their hearts to do his purpose, and to carry out one purpose, and to give their kingdom to the wild beast until the words of God are fulfilled." (Rev 17:17)

These developments are part of God's judgment on the beast's rule (as seen in Revelation 16); only here it is God using the beast and its allies to punish the dominant city itself.[95] No doubt, John's hearers would derive encouragement from this language, at a time when they seemed defenseless themselves against the Romans. The prophecy reminds them that God is sovereign over the emperor and over the whole empire, including the city of Rome itself, and that he has a plan to fulfill his prophetic words.[96]

---

88. Cf. Aune, *Revelation 17–22*, 961.

89. Cf. Carson, "Harlot, the Beast and the Sex Trafficker"; A. Collins, "Feminine Symbolism," 32–33.

90. This refers to Japanese atrocities in this Chinese city in 1937.

91. Koester, *Revelation*, 680, 693–95. See also Friesen, "Myth and Symbolic Resistance," 293–94, 302; Huber, *Like a Bride Adorned*, 91–92; Dyer, "Four Horsemen," 141.

92. Cf. Smolarz, *Covenant*, 278.

93. Cf. Thomas, *Apocalypse*, 516; Beale, *Book of Revelation*, 884; Leithart, *Revelation 12–22*, 206.

94. Tacitus alleged that under Nero's orders, Christians "were additionally made into sports: they were killed by dogs by having the hides of beasts attached to them, or they were nailed to crosses or set aflame, and, when the daylight passed away, they were used as nighttime lamps" (Tactius, *Histories* 15.44). Cf. Leithart, *Revelation 12–22*, 205.

95. A key word here is "authority" (see verses 12, 13, and 17) which ultimately derives from God (see John 19:10–11) as we see in the divine passives in Revelation (e.g., 13:7, 14, 15). This remains the case even when the direct conferring of authority comes from the dragon or beast (e.g., 13:2, 5, 12). Cf. Leithart, *Revelation 12–22*, 203.

96. Fulfilment of God's plans, as in OT prophecy, is a major theme in Revelation (see also 10:7; 15:1; 16:17). Cf. Beale, *Book of Revelation*, 887–88.

> "And the woman which you see is the great city which has dominion over the kings of the earth." (Rev 17:18)

The chapter closes with a further reminder of what the prostitute represents. Some Preterist writers argue that the whore was actually meant to depict Jerusalem, which was literally destroyed in a way like John's description after the war between Rome and the Jews (AD 66–70). This makes some sense because the Jews began as allies of Rome under the Hasmonean dynasty; in fact, the Romans helped them gain independence from the Seleucid Greek Empire[97] and they became dependent on Rome just as the woman depended on the beast until the Romans eventually took their kingdom over in 63 BC.[98] John would be following in the steps of the prophets who condemned Judah for depending on great power alliances for protection, which they equated with depending on the gods of those powers. The most convincing arguments are those of Leithart.[99] However, verse 18 seems to point to Rome, as does verse 9 and other details of the chapter.[100]

John accurately portrays aspects of the Roman Empire here. The city rules, at least nominally, but it depends on the beast, perhaps standing for the military power exercised in the name of the city, but not under its control, which periodically turns on the city itself with rapacious violence. Behind all this are the spiritual realities represented by the throne and the victorious Lamb. The statement about God's sovereign control over events here reflects the throne of God (Rev 4) and the victory of the Lamb (see Rev 5). These cause him to triumph over the beast's forces. John thus shows his audience how to interpret the situation they face "apocalyptically," in such a way that they are motivated to stand firm against the propaganda and intimidation of the empire and maintain their confession that Jesus is Lord.[101] This is also a great encouragement to many Pentecostals today who are politically powerless and vulnerable to persecution by powerful political and economic forces that represent Babylon to them.[102]

---

97. See Bruce, *Israel and the Nations*, 140–42, 152, 159, 166–67.

98. See Bruce, *Israel and the Nations*, 181–83.

99. Leithart, *Revelation 12–22*, 170–86, 203–4.

100. Cf. Aune, *Revelation 17–22*, 931; Beale, *Book of Revelation*, 887. Other futurist interpreters see a reference to a "harlot church" at the end of the age in parallel to unfaithful Israel depicted in Ezekiel 16 and 23. Beale partly agrees (Beale, *Book of Revelation*, 884–85), but concludes that "she includes the entire evil economic-religious system of the world throughout history" (ibid., 888).

101. Cf. Koester, *Revelation*, 682. Not all Christians would have seen Rome as negatively as John did, so he had to use imagery and even satire to make his point (ibid., 684–88).

102. Cf. Koester, *Revelation*, 683–84.

Revelation Chapter 18

Chapter 17 has shown the hearers in a graphic way the true nature of Roman rule and its effects. This portrait confirms aspects of their experience but also takes them "behind the scenes" (as John regularly does) to provide an authoritative apocalyptic interpretation of the situation. This "behind the scenes" perspective encourages the audience to remain true to Jesus. In chapter 18, the revelation of the fall of Babylon is portrayed just as graphically in a different combination of genres: prophetic lawsuit, lament, taunt song, and even funeral dirge.[1] Additionally, Old Testament passages such as Isaiah 13–14, Jeremiah 50–52, and Ezekiel 27–28 are drawn on to help portray the downfall of Babylon here.[2]

18:1–8 Announcing the Fall of Babylon

> **After these (things) I saw another angel coming down from heaven, having great authority,[3] and the earth was lit up from his glory. (Rev 18:1)**

John emphasizes the chronology of his vision. *After* seeing the prostitute and beast and hearing the interpretation from one of the seven bowl angels (in ch. 17), he sees "another angel." This is the most impressive angel since the super-angel of chapter 10, so the audience will be expecting a significant development.

> **And he cried out in a strong voice, saying, "Fallen, fallen (is) Babylon the Great, and it has become a dwelling place of demons, and a prison for every unclean spirit, and a prison for every unclean and hateful bird [and a prison for every unclean wild beast]." (Rev 18:2)**

---

1. Cf. Beale, *Book of Revelation*, 891.
2. Cf. Bauckham, *Climax of Prophecy*, 342–46; Fekkes, *Isaiah and Prophetic Traditions*, 88–91. For a more sophisticated literary analysis of this chapter, see Aune, *Revelation 17–22*, 975–83. Aune argues that only verses 20 and 24 are explicitly Christian, in that the rest of the chapter could be written by a Jewish prophet or even (in places) a Roman critic.
3. Cf. Leithart, *Revelation 12–22*, 216–17.

The angel is shouting like the one in 10:3; as we have seen, Revelation is a book of loud voices.[4] This is the third time that John's audience has heard of the fall of Babylon (see 14:8; 16:19), and the opening words would also recall Isaiah 21:9, originally about the neo-Babylonian empire. This empire had destroyed Judah and the first Jerusalem temple. So to Jewish ears, this is good news. But also this will be a scene of devastation, of a city reduced to ruins, uninhabited, and open to wild animals, a similar idea to the sexual violence imagery just before (17:16). However, this is worse because demons and unclean spirits will also dwell there, recalling the spirits like frogs in 16:13–14, and in keeping with her abominations (17:4). In fact, she is literally a prison (Greek *phulakē*) for spirits and unclean creatures.[5]

In the minds of some of the audience, the prophetic words of Isaiah 13–14 and Jeremiah 50–51[6] might be remembered as they hear this chapter. Specifically, here they might be reminded of Isaiah 13:21–22 and Jeremiah 50:39 and 51:37, which speak of wild animals and birds inhabiting a ruined Babylon.[7]

> "For from the wine of the fury of her immorality (she made) all the nations to drink,[8] and the kings of the earth committed immorality[9] with her and the merchants of the earth were made rich from the powers of her arrogant luxury." (Rev 18:3)

John is never content just to narrate events; he wants to interpret them. So now the audience hears why this has happened. This is almost an exact repetition of 14:8 and 17:2. The language of luxurious indulgence and orgies is again to the fore, alongside the focus on trade and profit, recalling the message to Laodicea (3:17), and the trading restrictions of the beast (13:17).[10] The Greek words which I have translated as "immorality" are variations on the basic words for sexual immorality from the *porn-*root. We need not think that John is referring to unfaithfulness in marriage, as similar condemnation of Israel might suggest, though the language does not *exclude* such an

---

4. In fact, the phrase φωνη μεγαλη (*phōnē megalē*, loud voice or noise) occurs eighteen times in Revelation, though in this case the best reading is ἰσχυρᾶ φωνὴ (*ischura phōnē*, strong voice). See Aune, *Revelation 17–22*, 965.

5. Thomas, *Apocalypse*, 521. But see Koester, *Revelation*, 697–98, where it is translated "lair." Aune translates "preserve" (Aune, *Revelation 17–22*, 965). See also Beale, *Book of Revelation*, 894–95.

6. Aune analyses the influence of Jeremiah on this chapter with a table (Aune, *Revelation 17–22*, 983).

7. Cf. Fekkes, *Isaiah and Prophetic Traditions*, 214–16; cf. Zeph 2:14 (about Nineveh); Isa 34:11–14 and Mal 1:3 (about Edom); Jer 9:11 (about Jerusalem). See also Beale, *Book of Revelation*, 894; Leithart, *Revelation 12–22*, 217–19.

8. In some manuscripts "all the nations *have fallen* because of the wine . . ." Cf. Koester, *Revelation*, 698; Aune, *Revelation 17–22*, 965–66; Beale, *Book of Revelation*, 897.

9. Cf. Is 51:17. Cf. Aune, *Revelation 17–22*, 987.

10. Cf. Thomas, *Apocalypse*, 523–24.

interpretation.[11] However, the language suggests seduction, immorality, promiscuity, drunkenness, and running wild.[12]

It is probably metaphorical language for political and economic alliances involving nations, kings, and merchants with idolatrous connections.[13] As Bauckham comments, whereas the beast of Revelation 13 represented Rome's military might, the harlot portrays "the city of Rome as a *corrupting influence* on the peoples of the empire."[14] The original audience would almost certainly continue to think "Rome" as they heard this and the rest of this chapter.

> **And I heard another voice from heaven that said, "Come out from her, my people, so that you may not partner with her sins, and from her plagues, so that you will not receive (them) . . ." (Rev 18:4)**

This seems to be God's voice,[15] a rare event in Revelation. It is probably meant to jolt the listeners. They are also in danger of the judgment about to be visited on Babylon. They would perhaps recall Jeremiah 51:6, where the Jews are called to "Flee from Babylon! Run for your lives! Do not be destroyed because of her sins," or Jeremiah 51:45, where, as the prophet predicts the fall of Babylon, he urgently cries, "Come out of her, my people! Run for your lives! Run from the fierce anger of the LORD." And Isaiah 48:20 says, "Leave Babylon, flee from the Babylonians!" The situation envisaged in these cases is the downfall of the Neo-Babylonian Empire. The Jews should get out before they are caught up in a siege or battle where they too might be killed, even though this might mean they become homeless refugees. In such a situation, the temptation is to stay in a place of apparent safety with one's belongings, but one must get out before it is too late.

This is also a kind of "second exodus" as proclaimed frequently by Isaiah, only now from Babylon rather than Egypt.[16] The fate of Lot's wife is perhaps another intertextual idea here (Gen 19:26), recalling the language of Revelation 11:8, where the "great city . . . is figuratively called Sodom and Egypt." And Luke reports Jesus as saying, "When you see Jerusalem being surrounded by armies, you will know that its desolation is near. Then let those who are in Judea flee to the mountains, let those in the city get out, and let those in the country not enter the city" (Luke 21:20–21). This has caused some interpreters to read this passage in Revelation as a reference to

---

11. I emphasize this because authors who identify "Babylon" as first-century Jerusalem often argue that the woman could only be a harlot if she had had a covenant relationship with God (e.g., Smolarz, *Covenant*, 238–39, 272). This argument, however, is not conclusive, as OT prophecy uses harlotry language of nations other than Israel (e.g., Isa 23:15–17; Nah 3:4).

12. Cf. Koester, *Revelation*, 699. However, the increasing sexual dissoluteness of Rome in the first century is probably coloring the picture. Cf. Fox, *Classical World*, 505–7.

13. Cf. Koester, *Revelation*, 715; Aune, *Revelation 17–22*, 988; Beale, *Book of Revelation*, 895–96.

14. Bauckham, *Climax of Prophecy*, 343.

15. It is also possible that the voice belongs to Christ (Aune, *Revelation 17–22*, 990–91).

16. Cf. Leithart, *Revelation 12–22*, 209, 222.

the destruction of Jerusalem by the Romans in AD 70, and the exhortation in verse 4 would be a very literal warning to the Christians to get out of Jerusalem, echoing Luke 21:21.[17] This could be a valid application, but there is enough evidence in both Revelation 17 and 18 that John is primarily talking about Rome.

But if the call to "come out of her my people" (v. 4) does not mean a literal flight from war, what is it asking the listeners to do? Many earlier Pentecostals, who interpreted the prostitute as the mainstream churches which had rejected the Azusa Street Revival and subsequent moves of the Spirit, saw this as a clear call to every Spirit-baptized Christian to "come out" of these decadent churches (represented by the prostitute) and join the Pentecostal groups.[18] This is not advocated often these days, though some Fundamentalists and Pentecostals still see the prostitute as a coming ecumenical or interfaith religious entity, probably headed up by the papacy, with which faithful believers should have no truck.

John's audience literally could not have thought this, however, but neither could they envisage physically fleeing from the Roman Empire itself (where would they go?).[19] More likely, then, the call to "come out of her" would be a further exhortation not to take part in the religious activities of the Greco-Roman world, a point already emphasized in the prophetic messages to the seven churches (see especially 2:6, 14–16, 20–23). It is a call to take a stand, to make a judgment on the surrounding society and to disassociate oneself from their unjust, idolatrous, and immoral behavior, lest you become complicit with them,[20] though this would also mean disassociating themselves from other believers who became so complicit (such as Jezebel or the Nicolaitans, referring back to 2:6, 14–15, 20–24). Paul also makes similar demands of his readers (2 Cor 6:14–18).[21] In both cases, the current and imminent crises for the church are bound up with this doomed society.[22] Christians would not thereby escape the events associated with the physical downfall of Rome, but they would escape God's judgment on her, and the unbelieving world in general, and be qualified to enter the holy city.[23]

And today we are called to "come out" from the ungodly world system, its immorality, injustice, indulgence, idolatry, and violence. This might include coming out from churches that engaged with that ungodly world system. Other earlier Pentecostals "came out" by refusing to take part in wars like World War I. Every reader will need to discern their particular context and take the action God is calling for.

17. Cf. Leithart, *Revelation 12–22*, 218–19.

18. Cf. Johnson, *Pneumatic Discernment*, 153.

19. As Thomas points out, the two witnesses do not flee from the great city but confront it and die in it (11:3–8) (Thomas, *Apocalypse*, 525).

20. Cf. Pattemore, *People of God*, 104; A. Collins, "Persecution and Vengeance," 741.

21. Cf. Koester, *Revelation*, 715–16; Aune, *Revelation 17–22*, 991; Leithart, *Revelation 12–22*, 213; Bauckham, *Climax of Prophecy*, 376–77.

22. Cf. Herms, *Apocalypse for the Church*, 162.

23. Cf. Beale, *Book of Revelation*, 898–99.

> "... for her sins have piled up to heaven and God has remembered her unjust deeds." (Rev 18:5)

This suggests that the time for judgment has arrived and cannot be postponed further. God has always been aware of the "unjust deeds" (Greek *adikēmata*, "crimes, wrongs") committed by Babylon, but he has apparently not taken action until now. The language of sins "piled up to heaven"[24] might remind listeners of Jeremiah 51:9, which says of Babylon, "her judgment reaches to the skies, it rises as high as the heavens" (compare Ezra 9:6).[25] The idea that God has now "remembered" Babylon's crimes also suggests that he is about to take action as justice demands.[26] God postpones acting in judgment, waiting for repentance, as Revelation itself implies (2:21–22; 9:20–21). Some listeners might also think of Genesis 15:16, where God tells Abram that his descendants will not return to the land until the "fourth generation" because "the sin of the Amorites has not yet reached its full measure."

> "Give back to her as she also gave and give her double, according to her works, in the cup which she mixed, mix double."[27] (Rev 18:6)

Her devastation will be proportional and consistent with her crimes, as in Psalm 137:8 and Jeremiah 50:15, 29.[28] Every human empire is built on violence, injustice, and oppression,[29] and every empire eventually falls with similar effects. John sees this as God's justice at work, a perspective very much in line with that of the Old Testament prophets, who predicted the devastation of Israel or Judah at the hands of Near Eastern empires (Egypt, Assyria, and Babylon), followed by the violent downfall of each of those oppressive regimes.

The command to "give back" and "give double" is in the second person plural, which may suggest that it is addressed to a foreign army, perhaps the ten kings (17:16), or even perhaps the Christians ("my people" of verse 4) or destroying angels.[30] In this case, the punishment will be "double." This may remind listeners of Isaiah 40:2, which

---

24. Or their sins are clinging to heaven (Leithart, *Revelation 12–22*, 220), which has a similar effect of demanding punishment.

25. Sometimes this is seen as a threat to God's sovereignty, perhaps with reference to Babel (Gen 11:4–6). I read it more as a call for heaven's attention. Cf. Aune, *Revelation 17–22*, 992.

26. Cf. Koester, *Revelation*, 716.

27. This is difficult to translate partly due to three occurrences of words built on the root διπλ- (dipl-), "double."

28. Cf. Thomas, *Apocalypse*, 527; Aune, *Revelation 17–22*, 993.

29. As Koester argues, "Babylon's influence on the earth is destructive ... a city where relationships are degraded into matters of pleasure and profit" (Koester, *Revelation*, 714).

30. Cf. Koester, *Revelation*, 700; Beale, *Book of Revelation*, 900–901; Aune, *Revelation 17–22*, 993–94. Aune argues that it is the Christians, which makes sense grammatically but perhaps not theologically as Christians suffer violence rather than exercise it in Revelation (except perhaps in 11:5). Moreover, it is hard to see how the believers in John's seven churches could feasibly have imposed such sufferings on Babylon as are described in verses 6–8. Verse 8 identifies God as the source of these sufferings, which makes more sense if applied to the whole paragraph in spite of the grammatical problem.

promises Jerusalem "her sin has been paid for, that she has received from the LORD's hand double for all her sins." More likely they would recall Jeremiah 16:18, where God threatens the people of Jerusalem that he will "repay them double for their wickedness . . . because they have defiled my land . . . with their detestable idols."[31] The idea of a cup of wine as an image of judgment has already been used in 14:10 and 16:19 and again carries the idea of reciprocity: Babylon made others drunk from her cup (17:2; 18:3), so now she has to drink that same brew with double strength.

> "As she glorified herself and lived in luxury,[32] give her such torment and mourning. For in her heart she says, 'I sit as queen and am not a widow and will never see mourning.'[33] For this reason, in one day her plagues will come, death and mourning and hunger, and she will be burned with fire, for strong is the Lord God who judges her." (Rev 18:7–8)

Her punishment is contrasted with her current state of "glory and luxury," and perhaps, by implication, the "torment and mourning" she caused to others. Her proud boast, a bit like that of the Laodicean church (3:17), will be defeated.[34] Her expectation of permanence (possibly a reference to Rome as the "eternal city")[35] is contrasted with the suddenness of her downfall: "in one day her plagues will come" (v. 8). Later we even read "one hour," (vv. 10 and 17).[36]

The usual features of military destruction, especially sieges, are here: death, mourning, famine, and fire.[37] The city will be devastated. Feminine language is used again: she is a "queen" and not a "widow." However, this has a different thrust than the imagery of Revelation 17; now Babylon is not a prostitute but a married woman, a queen, though John's listeners may remember the wife of the emperor Claudius who played both roles. The hearers may recall similar language in Isaiah 47:7–9a, which John comes close to quoting:

> You said, "I am forever—
>
> the eternal queen!"
>
> But you did not consider these things

---

31. Cf. Beale, *Book of Revelation*, 901–2.

32. Luxury was a controversial topic among Romans and periodic attempts were made to restrain excessive indulgence by the wealthy. Nero's downfall was attributed to his indulgence (Fox, *Classical World*, 507–8).

33. Aune calls this a "hybris soliloquy," similar to Ezek 28:2; Jer 5:12; Rev 3:17 (Aune, *Revelation 17–22*, 995). In each case, the claim of the speaker is then negated. In this case, the claim reflects Roman propaganda (ibid., 996). Cf. Beale, *Book of Revelation*, 903.

34. Cf. Mathews, "Imputed Speech," 335–37.

35. Cf. Howard-Brook and Gyther, *Unveiling Empire*, 233–35. The Flavian emperors (Vespasian, Titus, and Domitian) adopted *Aeternitas* as their motto on coins and inscriptions (Caird, *Revelation*, 231).

36. This may recall the destruction of Pompeii by volcanic eruption, a warning to Rome and its empire.

37. Cf. Aune, *Revelation 17–22*, 996.

> or reflect on what might happen.
> Now then, listen, you lover of pleasure,
> lounging in your security
> and saying to yourself,
> "I am, and there is none besides me.
> I will never be a widow
> or suffer the loss of children."
> Both of these will overtake you
> in a moment, on a single day:
> loss of children and widowhood.[38]

The voice from heaven concludes with a strong affirmation that it is God himself who is inflicting this fate on Babylon (v. 8). God judges and punishes the empires for their injustice.

18:9–20 Lamenting the Fall of Babylon

Perhaps the "voice from heaven" (v. 4) continues to speak of Babylon's downfall, or maybe John himself is speaking under inspiration of the Spirit. It makes little difference. In this section, the response of the kings (vv. 9–10), merchants (vv. 11–17a), sailors (vv. 17b–19),[39] and God's people (v. 20) to the devastation of Babylon is imagined (or predicted). The text uses the genre of lament, which can be used of a loved city or of a city that is seen to deserve its fate, in which case it can be a taunt song (compare Lam 1 and Ezek 27, for example).[40]

> **And the kings of the earth who committed immorality with her, living luxuriously, will cry and mourn over her, when they see the smoke of her burning, standing afar off for fear of her torment, saying,**
> **"Woe, woe, the great city,**
> **Babylon the strong city,**
> **for in one hour her judgment has come." (Rev 18:9–10)**

These kings were closely allied to Babylon and benefited from being part of her empire. The audience would think of rulers like Herod the Great who owed their position, power, and wealth to the Romans. While John depicts ten kings taking part in the assault on Rome (17:12–13, 16), they had much to lose if the Roman Empire collapsed. The "smoke of her burning" might remind the audience of the doom pronounced on the beast's followers (14:11), the fall of Sodom (Gen 19:28), and the judgment on

---

38. Cf. Leithart, *Revelation 12–22*, 221; Fekkes, *Isaiah and Prophetic Traditions*, 218–21.

39. Cf. Bauckham, *Climax of Prophecy*, 371–76. They represented a "sociopolitical world" (Leithart, *Revelation 12–22*, 225).

40. Cf. Koester, *Revelation*, 712–13; Aune, *Revelation 17–22*, 978–79.

Edom (Isa 34:10), which will be an intertextual feature in chapter 19. The two "woes" recall the woes pronounced in the trumpet plagues (8:13; 9:12; 11:13; 12:12), and perhaps Ezekiel 16:23, concerning Jerusalem.

The language here has some similarities to Ezek 26:16–18, where "princes of the coast" lament at the fall of the trading empire of Tyre. The suddenness of it all is underlined again with the phrase "in one hour" (see also 17:12). The kings are said to stand "afar off" (v. 10) in fear, even as they mourn the loss of Babylon: fear of God or fear of being swept up in the events of the fall of the city. The same thing is said of the merchants (v. 15) and sailors (v. 17).[41]

> **And the merchants of the earth will cry and mourn over her, for no one buys their merchandise any longer . . . (Rev 18:11)**

Here again John's language borrows from Ezekiel's prophecy against the trading empire of Tyre (Ezek 27).[42] The merchants too have been beneficiaries of the economic and trading system associated with the Roman Empire, the flow of wealth to Rome, the increase in trade due to the suppression of piracy in the Mediterranean Sea, the Roman roads, and the general *Pax Romana*.[43] Here John's negative comments about merchants ironically reflect the attitude of Roman nobles, who saw merchants as devious and dishonest.[44] In these days of worldwide trade and resultant profits, Christians can also be sucked in by the capitalist system, especially by "get rich quick" schemes, and forget how fragile all this is, as the periodic recessions and financial crises remind us.

> **. . . merchandise of gold and silver and precious stones and pearls and fine linen, and purple (cloth) and silk and scarlet (cloth), and every citrus wood[45] and every ivory vessel, and every vessel (made) from precious wood and bronze and iron and marble, and cinnamon and spice and incense and myrrh and frankincense and wine and olive oil and fine flour and grain, and cattle and sheep, and horses and carriages and bodies, and human souls. (Rev 18:12–13)**

The goods traded in this system are now listed: first, precious items, then fine clothing, craft items, spices, quality food ingredients, animals for food and transport, and finally slaves. There is a similar list in Ezekiel 27 when he is lamenting the fall of Tyre (see especially Ezek 27:5–7, 12–24). This list shows the extent of the trading networks emanating out of Rome and reaching into Asia and Africa; Ezekiel's list actually gives

---

41. Cf. Thomas, *Apocalypse*, 531–32, 537–38; Koester, *Revelation*, 717; Beale, *Book of Revelation*, 906–7.

42. Cf. Bauckham, *Climax of Prophecy*, 342, 345.

43. Cf. Koester, *Revelation*, 702. Roman traders brought goods from India, Arabia, and Africa. Goods from China, such as silk, came via India or the Parthian Empire (Aune, *Revelation 17–22*, 999). One estimation says that 6,000 ships would have to arrive at Rome's port every year just to feed the city with grain (Howard-Brook and Gwyther, *Unveiling Empire*, 99).

44. Cf. Veyne, *Bread and Circuses*, 52–54.

45. "Tables made of citrus wood were exorbitantly expensive, but fashionable Romans considered them essential" (Koester, *Revelation*, 718); cf. Aune, *Revelation 17–22*, 999–1000.

the origins of the goods Tyre traded.[46] It also shows the oppressive nature of the system; as with most imperial trade, it was the capital city that mainly benefited and many other nations were plundered in effect.[47]

As Thomas notes, "the majority of items in this list are luxury items" far away from most people's lives;[48] they were signs of status.[49] There are also twenty-eight items (4 x 7), maybe signifying the involvement of all the earth (4) and the comprehensiveness of the trade (7).[50]

The most shocking aspect to us is the final item, the huge slave trade. This was built on warfare (many slaves were prisoners of war), piracy (many slaves were victims of kidnapping), abandonment of unwanted children, and economic oppression or dislocation (some slaves were formerly landless peasants or debtors).[51] John's audience would not have been shocked as they knew about the slave trade and probably accepted it as "part of life." Ephesus was a major center for slave trading[52] and the biggest regional slave market was on a nearby island. However, the way John phrases this underlines the injustice involved—these are people with "souls."[53] Clarice Martin also points out that, unlike the list in Ezekiel 27, John puts slaves last in a list in order of descending value, exposing the values of Rome and the merchants involved in its economic system.[54] We are finding out now that slavery is anything but dead, with human trafficking and debt slavery flourishing in many lands. This calls for fresh judgment from God.

> "And the fruit of the strong desire of your soul has gone from you and every dainty and shiny (thing) has been lost from you and they may no longer be found (in you)." (Rev 18:14)

---

46. Similar accounts are given by Roman authors such as Aelius Aristides and Pliny (see Aune, *Revelation 17–22*, 980–81). Leithart points out that Ezekiel's list builds on the list of materials plundered from Egypt for use in the tabernacle (Exod 25:1–7; Leithart, *Revelation 12–22*, 228–29). Cf. Moyise, *Old Testament in the Book of Revelation*, 73–74.

47. Cf. Bauckham, *Climax of Prophecy*, 363; Fekkes, *Isaiah and Prophetic Traditions*, 90–91, especially n. 62.

48. Thomas, *Apocalypse*, 534; Aune, *Revelation 17–22*, 998. For a detailed analysis of each item, cf. Koester, *Revelation*, 702–6, 718–20; Bauckham, *Climax of Prophecy*, 350–68. Roman and Greek writers themselves were critical of the pursuit of luxury goods and materialistic values of the day (Koester, *Revelation*, 713; Bauckham, *Climax of Prophecy*, 367–68; cf. Aune, *Revelation 17–22*, 998–1003).

49. Cf. Koester, *Revelation*, 718–20; Fox, *Classical World*, 392–93.

50. Cf. Thomas, *Apocalypse*, 534; Leithart, *Revelation 12–22*, 227. This section is thus carefully structured. Leithart also points out the alliteration in the Greek (Leithart, *Revelation 12–22*, 224).

51. Cf. Bauckham, *Climax of Prophecy*, 365–66.

52. Koester, *Revelation*, 706.

53. Cf. Thomas, *Apocalypse*, 535; Koester, *Revelation*, 720–22; Leithart, *Revelation 12–22*, 229–30; Bauckham, *Climax of Prophecy*, 370–71.

54. Martin, "Polishing the Unclouded Mirror," 99. Martin as a "womanist" interpreter is reading the text in the light of American slavery (see ibid., 82–107).

This may be the speech of the merchants as the NIV implies. Babylon's hope for permanency has gone permanently. Her luxuries have vanished, or perhaps more literally "been destroyed" (Greek *apōleto*, from *apollumi*, "lose, destroy").[55]

> **These merchants who were made rich by her will stand afar,**
> **for fear of her torment, crying and mourning, saying,**
> **"Woe, woe the great city,**
> **who was clothed in fine linen and purple and scarlet,**
> **and overlaid with gold and precious stones and pearls,**
> **for in one hour such wealth has been made desolate." (Rev 18:15–17a)**

The description of Babylon recalls the prostitute of 17:4, "clothed with purple and scarlet and covered with gold and precious stones and pearls" and Ezekiel 28:13 (about Tyre's king). But it may also recall the OT high priest's attire (Exod 28:17–20) and the adornment of Jerusalem in Ezekiel's prophecy (Ezek 16:13).[56] The merchants exhibit sadness for their own loss, fear of what is happening (and perhaps its implications for their own future), and shock. Perhaps their fear and mourning (vv. 15, 9–10) even leads to repentance, as in 11:11–13 and 14:7, where God's current and future judgments rightly cause fear.[57]

> **And every ship's pilot and all who sail in any place and sailors and those who work at sea will stand afar off and cry out, seeing the smoke of her burning, saying, "Who is like the great city?" And they throw dirt on their heads and cry out, crying and mourning, saying,**
> **"Woe, woe, the great city,**
> **by which all those who had ships on the sea were made rich from her precious (goods), for in one hour she has been made desolate." (Rev 18:17b–19)**

Ships' crews had also profited from Rome-centered trade. They too bewail their loss, even throwing dust on their heads as a mark of grieving, using language similar to Ezekiel 27:30–32.[58] The parallels between Rome and Tyre obviously impress John, even though they were quite different kinds of empires. Perhaps he understands that empires often grow out of the desire for favorable trade and access to valuable resources; this was certainly true of the modern European empires.

---

55. Cf. Thomas, *Apocalypse*, 537.

56. Beale, *Book of Revelation*, 912–13. According to Beale, this implies John is attacking not only paganism but also compromising Christians and Jews. Leithart writes of the extensive corruption, extortion, and profiteering associated with the first-century temple and its authorities, backed by Roman power, as condemned in Malachi and later Jewish sources as well as by Jesus (Leithart, *Revelation 12–22*, 230–33).

57. Cf. Leithart, *Revelation 12–22*, 236–39. It is an intriguing thought and supportive of my overall argument in this commentary but weakened by verse 11: "The merchants of the earth will weep and mourn over her because no one buys their cargoes anymore." A good parallel would be the reaction of some Egyptians to the plagues and their admiration of Moses (Exod 10:7; 11:2–3).

58. Cf. Beale, *Book of Revelation*, 914.

All three mourning groups stand afar off, cry out "Woe, woe," call Babylon a "great city," and emphasize the suddenness of her fall ("in one hour").[59] But now the text suggests a different response from God's side.

> "Rejoice over her, heaven and the saints and the apostles and the prophets,
> for God has given judgment for you on her." (Rev 18:20)

Perhaps some of the believers in the audience had themselves been beneficiaries of the economic system, but, as Christians, they had distanced themselves from the idolatry and immorality and injustice of the system, and had even become victims of it. Certainly, here, the people of God are called on to rejoice (as in Jer 51:48–49).[60] So are the leaders, "the apostles and the prophets," the most visible of the early Christians who would have suffered the most for their service to Christ. It is implied that judgment had been given against these servants of God by Roman tribunals, but now such judgment is reversed.[61]

This is the only use of the phrase "apostles and prophets" in Revelation.[62] John rarely mentions apostles, and certainly never claims to be one, though related "sent" language occurs in 1:1 and 22:6 (of angels) and 5:6 (of the "seven spirits").[63] He seems to see himself as a prophet and does not limit the term prophets to the Old Testament era. But this verse suggests there were both apostles and prophets who had suffered under the Roman Empire. And it emphasizes one of the major reasons for the devastation of Babylon: her persecution of the church and its leaders. This has been a major theme throughout Revelation; her judgment of them is now reversed.[64]

This call to rejoice over the violent devastation of a city may not resonate with our (post) modern ears. Yarbro Collins, for example, sees it as "tainted by vengefulness."[65] And many of those in John's audience would have had something to lose themselves if the Roman Empire fell, as they would be producing, consuming, or selling some of the goods listed in verses 12–13.[66] Then there was the prospect of relatives, friends, and trading partners who might be killed.

However, in John's view of things, God's judgment is just and must prevail. Even today, there are forces that treat Christians with terrible violence; Islamic terrorist

---

59. Cf. Aune, *Revelation 17–22*, 997.

60. Cf. Beale, *Book of Revelation*, 915–16.

61. Cf. A. Collins, "Persecution and Vengeance," 738.

62. But see Eph 2:20; 3:5; 4:11; 2 Pet 3:2. Aune contends that each case refers to the twelve apostles, which is more likely in Revelation (21:14) than in Paul (Aune, *Revelation 17–22*, 1007).

63. See comments in Thomas, *Apocalypse*, 543.

64. An alternative translation of verse 20b is "God has judged your judgment on her." Cf. Caird, *Revelation*, 229–30; Beale, *Book of Revelation*, 916–18; Leithart, *Revelation 12–22*, 241–42.

65. A. Collins, "Persecution and Vengeance," 738.

66. Cf. Koester, *Revelation*, 717–18; Beale, *Book of Revelation*, 910. Many of the main products of Asia Minor, for example, were exported through Ephesus (Aune, *Revelation 17–22*, 980).

groups, the regime in North Korea and others spring to mind as I write. Justice demands that they are held accountable for these crimes, both in this life and after death.

18:21–24 Dramatizing the Fall of Babylon

> **And one strong angel lifted up a stone like a great millstone**
> **and threw (it) into the sea, saying,**
> **"Even so will Babylon the great city be thrown down**
> **(like a stone whizzing through the air)**
> **and will not be found any more..." (Rev 18:21)**

Many of the hearers would remember that Jeremiah performed a very similar action in relation to the Neo-Babylonian Empire. He deputized a staff officer called Seraiah to read aloud in Babylon a scroll containing a list of disasters to come on Babylon. Then:

> When you finish reading this scroll, tie a stone to it and throw it into the Euphrates. Then say, "So will Babylon sink to rise no more because of the disaster I will bring on her. And her people will fall." (Jer 51:63–64)

But in Revelation, the action is done by a "strong angel," and he throws a much larger object into the sea, which may be equivalent in meaning to the Euphrates for Babylon itself. The meaning is similar.

> **"... and the sounds of harpists and musicians and flautists and trumpeters,**
> **will be heard in you no more,**
> **and every craftsman of every craft will not be found in you anymore,**[67]
> **and the sound of a millstone**
> **will not be heard in you anymore,**
> **and (the) light of a lamp**
> **will not appear in you anymore,**
> **and the sound of a bridegroom and bride**
> **will not be heard in you anymore..." (Rev 18:22–23a)**

This further speech declaring the permanent destruction of Babylon and its justification begins with a list of actions that will never be found in Babylon again. The repetition is rhetorically powerful. It reinforces the impression given in verse 2 that the city would be deserted, destroyed, and devastated with no future (compare Jer 25:10).[68] All the usual activities of a society would disappear permanently as the city becomes a kind of "ghost town."[69] Moreover, as Thomas points out, the silencing of music in the

---

67. Possibly this is an allusion to the trade guilds from which Christians were ostracized for their unwillingness to worship their patron gods (Beale, *Book of Revelation*, 919).

68. A prophecy prior to the Jewish revolt of AD 66–70 included the phrase, "a voice against the bridegrooms and the brides" (Josephus, "War of the Jews" 6:301). Cf. Aune, *Revelation 17-22*, 1009.

69. Cf. Leithart, *Revelation 12-22*, 243–44. As I write, the coronavirus pandemic is giving us a kind

destroyed city contrasts with the loud music of harps and trumpets in heaven: there is good and evil music.[70]

> ". . . for your merchants were the great ones of the earth,
> for by your sorcery you deceived all the nations,
> and in her (the) blood of prophets and saints was found
> and of all those slaughtered on the earth." (Rev 18:23b–24)

The statement about merchants may just be factual, or it may imply that the economic system of Rome was inherently unjust and inequitable, and an underlying cause of the other crimes.[71] It may even be a somewhat satirical or sarcastic remark, since in John's world "merchants were considered dishonest and vulgar."[72] But most likely it reflects Isaiah 23:8, where speaking of Tyre, the prophet says, "whose merchants are princes, whose traders are renowned in the earth," implying self-glorification.[73]

Certainly, the charge of deceiving the nations (from the Greek *planaō*, "deceive, mislead, lead astray") is significant, and connects with the idea of the prostitute seducing "those who dwell on the earth" with "the wine of her immorality" (17:2). She is said here to have done this by sorcery; the Greek here is *pharmakeia*, "sorcery, witchcraft" (also used in 9:21). Sorcery, magic, and witchcraft were ubiquitous in the Greco-Roman world, and Ephesus especially was famous for it, as Acts 19:19 confirms. This had its origins in ancient Babylon, as Isaiah 47 also claims, after speaking of Babylon's downfall, when it says that the disasters "will come upon you in full measure in spite of your many sorceries and all your potent spells" (Isa 47:9; see also verses 12–13).

John seems to be accusing Rome of using sorcery, which was seen as a threat to society by the Romans,[74] to gain power over the nations. This would be quite an insult as the Romans attributed their imperial power to their piety towards the gods. Finally, the charge of murdering God's prophets and saints is repeated against Babylon, as was mentioned in 17:6 and 18:20.[75] However, here John changes from the second person ("you") to the third ("her"); he is not addressing Babylon but speaking about her. Moreover, the text adds, "and of all those slaughtered on the earth" (v. 24). If the "and" is meant to identify a broader group of people slaughtered, then Rome/Babylon is being blamed for a much bigger number of unjustified deaths, not just those of Christians. This charge may partly reflect the massive death toll in the Roman-Jewish war

---

of foretaste of what this would be like.

70. Thomas, *Apocalypse*, 546; cf. Archer, *Worship in the Apocalypse*, 257; Koester, *Revelation*, 723; Leithart, *Revelation 12–22*, 245.

71. According to Aune, "Rome is condemned for her economic domination of the Mediterranean world, which is viewed from the perspective of exploitation" (Aune, *Revelation 17–22*, 1010).

72. Koester, *Revelation*, 710; cf. Aune, *Revelation 17–22*, 988–89.

73. Cf. Beale, *Book of Revelation*, 921–22; Fekkes, *Isaiah and Prophetic Traditions*, 221–23.

74. Koester, *Revelation*, 724.

75. This may support the idea that "Babylon" is actually Jerusalem, based on the parallel with this accusation and Jesus's words in Matt 23:34–35 (cf. Leithart, *Revelation 12–22*, 211–12).

of AD 66–73.⁷⁶ While persecuting the believers is a huge issue, it is not the only form of injustice of which the empire is guilty.⁷⁷

Babylon for Today?

Before moving on, it's worth taking a little time to think about how these chapters (Rev 17–18) apply to our lives today in the twenty-first century. I've been discussing this from the perspective of the people in the seven churches to which Revelation was explicitly addressed (1:11). John portrays Rome and its empire as characterized by opulent wealth and indulgence, rapacious commerce, oppressive power which is vulnerable to civil war, deception (especially idolatry and the imperial cult), and violence, especially to believers. What similar powers exist today?

Clearly, the first base in any interpretation is to ask, what could this have meant to its original audience? Gordon Fee even says that it cannot mean today what it didn't mean then.⁷⁸ I'm not sure I totally agree: I think there can be a fuller meaning in a prophecy which the first audience couldn't grasp; but nor can I totally agree with Historicists who argue that the true meaning of a prophecy only becomes clearer as we reach the time of its fulfillment. The meaning to the original audience still has to be our starting point.

This is important for this passage because it has a real history of multiple interpretations and applications. Even those who believe the original audience is the first touchstone for interpretation disagree about what they would have made of it. Is it mainly referring to Rome, as most current scholars think, or the fall of Jerusalem, as David Chilton, Peter Leithart, and others argue? Or is it a prediction of another Rome in the future to John, papal Rome, perhaps, as many Historicist Protestants thought, or something related to the very end of our era, such as a decadent and unbelieving church, as many Fundamentalists and Pentecostals have thought?

A purely Preterist reading of Revelation can be a very dry academic exercise. Revelation was recognized by the early church as Scripture, and hence capable of bringing a word from God, beyond the seven original churches of Asia, to the whole church in any century. So perhaps the Protestants were right to see papal Rome as a new manifestation of the same reality John was seeing. Maybe there will be a fresh manifestation of that reality today or in our future.

Several writers, for example, see here a condemnation of the modern capitalist economic order with its luxury items, its focus on self-indulgence, its exploitation of

---

76. Cf. Aune, *Revelation 17–22*, 1011. Roman armies had killed millions of people around their world; for example, Juluius Caesar alone was responsible for a million deaths in Gaul (Fox, *Classical World*, 379).

77. Cf. Thomas, *Apocalypse*, 550–51.

78. Cf. Fee and Stuart, *How to Read the Bible*, 26.

the "majority world," its injustice to the poor,[79] its destruction of the natural environment, its seduction of the nations, and its increasing hostility to Christians. What they are trying to do is use Revelation as a set of prophetic "glasses" to interpret the world today.[80]

This raises another issue. Was John predicting the downfall and destruction of ancient Rome, as he seems to be doing? If so, was he a false prophet, since that didn't happen, at least not to the degree his language suggests? The Western Roman empire did fall in the sixth century, but Rome as a city, while it was sacked[81] and became much less significant, survived and started to grow again in the modern era. Moreover, the Eastern Empire, where John lived, continued on to the fifteenth century until the fall of Constantinople in 1453.

Some Preterists thus believe John was talking about Jerusalem under the guise of "Babylon" because it was decisively destroyed in AD 70 and then again in AD 135.[82] But even Jerusalem was reborn and is now a modern city, so its destruction wasn't permanent either. Historicists, of course, take John to be predicting the downfall of the papacy, or at least its political power, which could be dated to 1799 or maybe 1870. And Futurists read the language as predicting a Rome still to be revealed, though maybe derived from the "Treaty of Rome" which was the basis for the original European Union in 1957. There is no easy answer to all this. The city of Rome was devastated several times in the imperial period, beginning with the fire under Nero in AD 64 and ending in the last days of the western Empire with the barbarian "sackings" of the city. There was no exact, literal fulfilment of Revelation 17–18, but I think we can be satisfied with the conclusion that the eventual downfall of Rome and its empire is what John (and the Spirit) had in mind.

But the real message here is that every empire falls, each in its own way. Babylon itself survived as a city well beyond the downfall of the Neo-Babylonian Empire and even became a prominent center of Judaism.[83] The Roman Empire fell, but Rome survived. The Holy Roman Empire sputtered out by the early nineteenth century. The Ottoman Empire finally fell in 1918, but Turkey (and Islam) survived. The British Empire, on which the sun never set when I was growing up, is no more, but London is still a financial capital and many former colonies (like Australia) still swear allegiance to the British Crown. The American world order under which we now live seems to be losing its way and China may become the next big empire (not for the first time).

---

79. The global economy even depends on slave labor in some cases such as the production of chocolate in parts of Africa, the prison factories of China, and the "sweat shops" of Bangladesh.

80. Cf. Howard-Brook and Gwyther, *Unveiling Empire*.

81. The first such sacking occurred in 410 by the Goths (Aune, *Revelation 17–22*, 985).

82. Cf. Leithart, *Revelation 12–22*, 211–12, 246. Beale rightly criticizes such interpretations because they do not make sense of the language of Revelation 18 (Beale, *Book of Revelation*, 925).

83. However, it was largely deserted in c. AD 115 when Trajan visited it (Aune, *Revelation 17–22*, 987).

As a beneficiary of the British and American Empires, I tend to look at them with a certain fondness, but history demonstrates that they also have been violent, exploitative, and oppressive to much of the world. So as a Pentecostal believer, I need to keep a prophetic distance even from my own government, praying for our rulers as 1 Timothy 2 exhorts, but seeing the system through apocalyptic eyes. Even our empires will fall. As Beale says, "the Apocalypse's Babylon is not just one Satanic nation but a corporate, depraved worldwide system spanning the ages . . . "[84]

Revelation passes judgment on all human civilizations, both the most cruel (Assyria, for instance, or the Soviet Empire) and the most benevolent (western civilization, perhaps). All are flawed, infected with sin, oppression, and injustice. All are humanistic and over-ambitious like the original Babel. As Leithart writes, "Babylon the great/the great city is the highest achievement of humanity, but it must fall as the city of God descends."[85]

And that's good news for many Pentecostal and other Christians who live under extreme oppression and attack under communist, corrupt, neo-colonial, military, or Islamic regimes. Whether we are being oppressed, intimidated, or seduced by the deceptive prostitute, we are called to "come out of her" by standing firm for the truth of Christ. But it's also a call for us to "distance ourselves" from deceptive voices in the church and nation who try to lead us to violence in the name of patriotism, nationalism, racism, and religious hatred, in a word, "Babylonishness."[86]

---

84. Beale, *Book of Revelation*, 924.
85. Leithart, *Revelation 12–22*, 215.
86. Cf. Leithart, *Revelation 12–22*, 246.

Revelation Chapter 19

Chapter 19 transitions from the fall of Babylon to the huge battle which was foreshadowed in 16:14, 16, and acts as a climax to the story. The struggle between the beast and the false prophet and God comes to a head and is resolved. The way into the millennial reign of Christ is opened.

19:1–10 Heavenly Celebrations

The setting of Revelation 17–18 has been very earth-bound: a wilderness (17:3), seven hills (17:9), the world-ruling city (17:18), destruction and plagues (17:16; 18:4–8), and a ruined city (18:2, 9–23). But even then, the heavens are called on to rejoice at Babylon's downfall (18:20). Now it is time for heaven's voices to be heard again for the first time since 15:1–4, in a kind of conclusion to Revelation 18.

> **After these (things) I heard (something) like the loud noise of a large crowd in heaven, saying,**
> **"Hallelujah!**
> **The salvation and the glory and the power (belong to) our God, for his judgments are true and just . . ." (Rev 19:1–2a)**

The choir of heaven has been a regular participant in the narrative, singing the praises of God, the eternal and almighty Creator (4:8–11), loudly acclaiming the slaughtered Lamb (5:8–12), declaring God's praise in the context of the great multitude of the redeemed (7:9–12), announcing the kingdom of God, again with "loud voices" (11:15–18), and singing the song of Moses and the Lamb (15:2–4).

A close reading, of course, shows that this choir is not uniform in membership: sometimes purely angelic, sometimes including the redeemed humans (as here),[1] sometimes including the whole creation. But their loud worship not only provides a commentary on the narrative; it also helps to advance the story to its next phase. It

---

1. Leithart points out that the Greek ὄχλος [*ochlos*] always indicates a human crowd in Revelation (Leithart, *Revelation 12–22*, 252).

also contrasts with the silence coming over Babylon (18:22).² Significantly, for Pentecostals, the choir invites us to join in and encourages us to make a similar loud noise with a new song.

Hallelujah is, of course, a Hebrew word roughly translatable as "praise the LORD" (that is, YHWH) and very frequently found in the Psalms (e.g., Pss 106, 111–113, 117, 135, 146–150),³ but only here in the New Testament (four times in this chapter).⁴ As with everything else in Revelation, its praise language is firmly rooted in the Hebrew Scriptures, which is an encouragement to all believers to use the Psalms and other Old Testament praise and prayer passages to articulate their conversation with God.⁵

The hymn here also makes theological statements, it has real content. "The salvation⁶ and the glory and the power belong to our God" would perhaps remind John's listeners of 7:10 ("*Salvation* belongs to our God") and 7:12 ("Blessing and *glory* and wisdom and thanks and honor and *power* and strength be to our God for ever and ever"). These words were uttered by the great multitude from every nation and the angels in heaven, and perhaps they together make up the huge choir here, in contrast with those who refuse to worship God and instead worship idols or the beast.⁷ As Beale suggests, "the focus . . . is on the entire assembly of saints as they praise God at the consummation of history."⁸ They emphasize the unique role of God in saving his people.

Next the choir shouts, "for his judgments are true and just," a very important confession in view of the graphic judgment language in the past several chapters (Rev 16–18) and indeed reiterating what was affirmed there (16:5–7; 18:5–6, 20). The two statements are connected by "for" (Greek *hoti*), reminding the listeners that the divine salvation and glory and power *consist in* the truth and justice of his judgments.⁹

> "... for he has judged the great prostitute,
> who corrupted¹⁰ the earth with her immorality,
> and avenged the blood of his slaves from her hand."¹¹ (Rev 19:2b)

2. Cf. Thomas, *Apocalypse*, 552.

3. Leithart, *Revelation 12–22*, 253–54. Hallelujah is a phrase only found in the Psalms and associated with David's monarchy and the temple's praise. Some Pentecostals associate this with the "restoration of David's tabernacle" (Acts 15:16 KJV).

4. See discussion in Aune, *Revelation 17–22*, 1024.

5. Cf. Koester, *Revelation*, 733. Koester suggests that "these hymns may reflect elements of Christian worship at the time Revelation was composed." Aune, however, argues that 19:1–10 "was expressly composed to fit its present literary context" (Aune, *Revelation 17–22*, 1022).

6. Aune translates this as "victory" as in 7:10 (cf. Aune, *Revelation 6–16*, 429).

7. Cf. Thomas, *Apocalypse*, 553.

8. Beale, *Book of Revelation*, 926.

9. Cf. Thomas, *Apocalypse*, 554.

10. This is the Greek word ἔφθειρεν [*phtheiren*] "corrupted" or "destroyed," and it is related to the verbs in Rev 11:18 (cf. Beale, *Book of Revelation*, 927). Koester has "ruined" (Koester, *Revelation*, 727; see also 734).

11. Or we might translate it: "he brought justice for the blood of his servants, which was shed by her own hand," emphasizing the reason why she was judged (Koester, *Revelation*, 725, 727; cf. Aune,

This makes explicit what was implied in 18:24—the punishment of the great prostitute is related to the killing of Christian martyrs as well as her general corruption. The audience would remember the cry of the martyrs under the altar in 6:10, "Until when, holy and true master, will you not judge and avenge our blood from those who dwell on the earth?" Finally, this prayer has been fully answered.[12] Justice has been done, which is the key thought behind the Greek word translated "avenge" (Greek *ekdikeō*). In John's mind, God's justice demands such "vengeance," which is not some kind of petulant outburst, but justice itself.[13] The persecutors will have to face the bar of God's court, but only after being given opportunity to repent, which is the reason for the delay.[14]

> **And a second time they said,**
> **"Hallelujah!**
> **And her smoke goes up forever and ever." (Rev 19:3)**

This phrase takes the hearer's mind back not to just to the language of chapter 18 (such as 18:8–9 with its reference to fire and smoke and Isa 34:9–10), but more specifically to 14:11, which said, "the smoke of their torment will rise for ever and ever." In other words, the punishment being contemplated is not just the destruction of the city, but the eternal punishment of its inhabitants because they followed the beast and received its mark (14:9), as part of the intimate relationship between the prostitute and the beast (17:3).[15]

> **And the twenty-four elders fell down with the four living beings and worshiped**
> **God who sits on the throne, saying,**
> **"Amen.[16] Hallelujah!" (Rev 19:4)**

The hearers would recall the first mention of these heavenly beings round God's throne in chapter 4. Periodically they have re-appeared in the narrative. One or more elders are seen in 5:5; 7:13; and 11:16; the four living creatures are active in 6:1, 3, 5, 7; 15:7, and both groups are mentioned in 5:8, 11; 7:11; 14:3; and here in 19:4. To the extent that they have distinctive roles in the narrative beyond that of worship, it appears that the elders sometimes act as guides and interpreters of the vision (5:5; 7:13), and the

---

Revelation 17–22, 1015; Leithart, *Revelation 12–22*, 256).

12. Thomas points out that the Greek word ἐκδικέω [*ekdikeō*], "avenge, vindicate," is used only in 6:10 and 19:2 (Thomas, *Apocalypse*, 555–56). Cf. Beale, *Book of Revelation*, 928; Pattemore, *People of God*, 100–106. Beale and Thomas also see an allusion to OT Jezebel (2 Kgs 9:7). Koester notes that "the Apocalypse shows that the same event—the fall of Babylon—can be seen in two different ways" depending on whether the speaker profited or suffered from her (Koester, *Revelation*, 734).

13. See comments on "imprecatory" elements here and in the Psalms, in Leithart, *Revelation 12–22*, 265–67.

14. Koester, *Revelation*, 735.

15. Contra Koester, *Revelation*, 735; Aune, *Revelation 17–22*, 1026. Aune see this just as an indication that the devastation of Babylon is permanent. On the theme of smoke throughout Revelation, see Leithart, *Revelation 12–22*, 258.

16. On "Amen," see Koester, *Revelation*, 727–28; Leithart, *Revelation 12–22*, 259.

four living beings sometimes play a role in releasing events, specifically judgments (6:1, 3, 5, 7; 15:7). Here, in their last appearance in the narrative, they echo what has been said by the "great multitude" and Psalms 146–148.[17]

> **And a voice[18] came out from the throne that said,**
> **"Praise our God**
> **all his slaves**
> **[and] those who fear him,**
> **the small and the great." (Rev 19:5)**

Here the audience is explicitly called on to join in the praises.[19] Some of the audience would perhaps recall Psalm 134, which begins, "Praise the LORD, all you servants of the LORD." A special emphasis here is on two features of these slaves (Greek *douloi*). They fear God (Greek *phoboumenoi*), unlike the unbelieving inhabitants of the world, but *like* those who respond to the severe earthquake in 11:13, who are said to be terrified (Greek *emphoboi*, "full of fear") and to give glory to God.[20]

Second, they are all equal, "the small and the great" (Greek *hoi mikroi kai hoi megaloi*). This may be intended as a criticism of the Roman world with its intense hierarchies and social classes, recently perhaps satirized in 18:23 ("your merchants were the great ones of the earth"). Such class distinctions are not recognized in God's kingdom, as reflected in many Pentecostal churches especially in the majority world.

> **And I heard (something) like (the) noise of a great crowd and as (the) noise of**
> **many waters and as (the) noise of strong thunder, saying,**
> **"Hallelujah!**
> **For the Lord [our] God Almighty has reigned." (Rev 19:6)**

Is this the same multitude as in verse 1? They are certainly making a huge noise,[21] which John describes using a combination of previous similes for loud praises,[22] and which in part reminds hearers of Psalm 29:3 (the voice of the LORD). It also recalls the voice of the son of man in 1:15, whose "voice was like the sound of rushing waters," and the "sound from heaven like the roar of rushing waters and like a loud peal of thunder" (14:2) introducing the new song learned by the 144,000.

This is the fourth and final "Hallelujah." It leads into an affirmation of God's sovereignty. In the Greek, it is an aorist verb which is best translated as "reigned."

---

17. Beale, *Book of Revelation*, 930; Leithart, *Revelation 12–22*, 258–59. Leithart interprets this final appearance as indicating a handover from angelic beings to human worshipers and kings (see Rev 5:10).

18. On the theme of voice in Revelation, see Leithart, *Revelation 12–22*, 261–62.

19. Thomas, *Apocalypse*, 559; Aune, *Revelation 17–22*, 1027. The word for praise (Greek αἰνεῖτε [*ainete*], in the second person plural) only occurs here in Revelation (ibid., 1028).

20. Leithart, *Revelation 12–22*, 260.

21. Leithart comments, "Christian praise should be *loud*" (Leithart, *Revelation 12–22*, 261).

22. Thomas, *Apocalypse*, 560.

In other words, it is not so much speaking of an eternal truth about God as about a specific action God has taken, recalling perhaps 11:17, which said, "you have taken your great power and reigned."[23] To put it another way, this is announcing the coming of God's kingdom in greater fullness than ever before, as a result of God's destruction of Babylon. This seems to lead better into what follows.

> "Let us rejoice and celebrate and give the glory to him,
> for the marriage of the Lamb has come, and his bride has made herself ready
> and it was given to her that she might be clothed with bright clean linen."
> For the linen is the righteous deeds of the saints. (Rev 19:7–8)

A great note of celebration comes in here, because of what God is about to do as he has begun to reign (v. 6). And it is a wedding![24] The audience hearing this may have been very surprised at this development because there has been no mention of this before in the text.[25] The dominant theme so far has been one of struggle or war. However, they may recall Jesus' rebuke of the church in Ephesus because "you have left your first love" (2:4) and of the church in Laodicea "because you are lukewarm" (3:16). That message has some allusions to the Song of Solomon with its erotic language (3:20; Song 5:2–6).

The work of the Lamb in redeeming an international company of people (5:9) and shepherding them (7:17) may take on new significance, in view of this announcement, as may the words about the 144,000 that they "did not defile themselves with women," but "follow the Lamb wherever he goes" (14:4). In retrospect, therefore, the audience would recognize that there has been a subtle "romantic" theme in the narrative, though only now is it becoming explicit.[26]

This is obviously a very special wedding, the wedding of the Lamb, a royal and messianic figure who will soon be portrayed riding out to battle. Only in Psalm 45 do we have this combination of bridegroom-as-warrior and bride. To the king, it says "In your majesty ride forth victoriously in the cause of truth, humility, and justice" (v. 4) before addressing his bride in verses 10–17. But who is the bride and why is the wedding impending only at this stage of the story?

The only hint at the identity of the bride comes in verse 8, where it is apparently equated with "the saints" (Greek *tōn hagiōn*). The only apparent reason for the timing is in verse 7: "his bride has made herself ready" (Greek *hētoimasen*, from *hētoimazō*,

---

23. Cf. Thomas, *Apocalypse*, 561; Beale, *Book of Revelation*, 931–32; Aune, *Revelation 17–22*, 1016; contra Koester, *Revelation*, 736.

24. Miller suggests that "the wedding is to be taken as the manifestation of God's reign" (Miller, "Nuptial Eschatology," 302).

25. On the OT and NT background, including the tradition of a final messianic feast, as in Isa 25:6–8, see Aune, *Revelation 17–22*, 1029–30, 1032–34.

26. For a full treatment of this theme in Revelation and other places in the Bible, cf. Smolarz, *Divine Marriage*. For discussion of this in Revelation, see McIlraith, *Reciprocal Love* and "Works and Wife"; Newton, "Reading Revelation Romantically"; Miller, "Nuptial Eschatology."

prepare or make ready). Leithart comments here, "only after the Bride has been built from the wound in Jesus' side is the Last Adam prepared to have dominion,"[27] alluding to John 19:34 and Genesis 2:21–23.

This would be interpreted by the audience in the light of marriage customs of their world; for example, the Greek word translated "bride" is *gunē* (literally "wife"), pointing to the stages of marriage in ancient Jewish and Greco-Roman custom.[28] As McIlraith explains, "A Jewish woman was legally married, was a wife, before she became a bride."[29] But whatever they would understand by a bride making herself ready for her wedding, the text adds that "it was given to her that she might be clothed with bright clean linen" (v. 8). Some of the preparation comes from outside (that is, *given* by God) with the provision of bridal wear.[30] And yet this is immediately interpreted as referring to "the righteous deeds of the saints" (v. 8).[31] So perhaps it is the doing of these deeds that constitutes "making herself ready" for the wedding.[32] Or, as Miller argues, "nuptial union . . . begins in this age . . . in battle."[33]

A similar combination of thoughts is found in Isaiah 61:10, in the context of the restoration of Israel, which says:

> I delight greatly in the LORD;
>
> my soul rejoices in my God.
>
> For he has clothed me with garments of salvation
>
> and arrayed me in a robe of his righteousness,
>
> as a bridegroom adorns his head like a priest,
>
> and as a bride adorns herself with her jewels.[34]

This restoration of Israel theme supports Smolarz's view that "the restoration of the marriage of God (through the Messiah) and his people has in view the inauguration of the new covenant."[35] This idea finds support especially in Jeremiah 31:31–32 where

27. Leithart, *Revelation 12–22*, 262.

28. Cf. McIlraith, "For the Fine Linen," 524–25; Koester, *Revelation*, 728–30, 737; Thomas, *Apocalypse*, 564; Smolarz, *Covenant*, 57–58.

29. McIlraith, "For the Fine Linen," 525.

30. Cf. Thomas, *Apocalypse*, 564–65. The fact that it was linen probably alludes to the priests' garments in the OT (Exod 28:5–8, 39, 42; Ezek 44:17–18). Cf. Beale, *Book of Revelation*, 938.

31. This is a definite contrast with the unrighteous deeds of Babylon, just as the fine linen of both women are in contrast (Thomas, *Apocalypse*, 565–66). These deeds are perhaps those spelled out in 2:19 (McIlraith, "For the Fine Linen," 526–27).

32. Cf. Thomas, *Apocalypse*, 566–67. Beale suggests this refers to "holding to the testimony of Jesus" and resisting the attractions of Babylon (Beale, *Book of Revelation*, 934) or "*purity resulting from a test of persevering faith*" (ibid., 936; emphasis in the original). It could also refer to acts of God's judgment vindicating the saints (ibid., 936–43). Cf. Koester, *Revelation*, 730–31, 738.

33. Miller, "Nuptial Eschatology," 305.

34. See also Isa 62:4–5 and Hos 2:20. Cf. Beale, *Book of Revelation*, 938–41; Fekkes, *Isaiah and Prophetic Traditions*, 232–38.

35. Smolarz, *Divine Marriage*, 252.

the old covenant is explicitly related to God being a "husband" to Israel (see also Jer 2:1; Hos 2:18–20).

There is therefore a note of excitement in the narrative; we are approaching the climax of the story. Some Pentecostals, with their restorationist view, see the final preparations of the bride as reflecting the final glory of the true church as spelled out in Ephesians 5:27, where Paul writes that Jesus will present the church as his bride "to himself as a radiant church, without stain or wrinkle or any other blemish, but holy and blameless" (NIV).

And the reference to the bride's clothing climaxes a theme that has been present throughout Revelation, whereby clothing reveals the status of a person. Think back to 1:13 (Christ in a long robe), 3:4–5 (Sardian Christians dressed in white or soiled clothes), 3:17–18 (Laodicea, naked and needing white clothes), 4:4 (24 elders dressed in white), 6:11 (the martyrs under the altar given white robes), and 7:9, 13–14 (the great multitude wearing white robes because of the blood of the Lamb). Consider 10:1 (the super-angel robed in a cloud), 11:3 (the two witnesses clothed in sackcloth), 12:1 (the woman clothed with the sun), 15:6 (seven angels "dressed in clean, shining linen"), and 16:15 (the need to be clothed, not naked). These positive uses of clothing imagery stand in sharp contrast to the negative ones. For instance, recall 17:4 (the prostitute dressed in purple and scarlet), 17:16 (the prostitute stripped naked), and 18:10 (the "great city dressed in fine linen, purple and scarlet"). Then in this chapter we read of the bride given fine linen, bright and clean, to wear (v. 8), the rider "dressed in a robe dipped in blood" (v. 13), and the armies of heaven "dressed in fine linen, white and clean" (v. 14). Finally, we look forward to 21:2 (the Holy City "beautifully dressed for her husband") and 22:14 ("blessed are those who wash their robes").

> **And he[36] said to me, "Write: blessed are those who are invited to the marriage feast of the Lamb." And he said to me, "These are the true words of God." (Rev 19:9)**

So not only is the audience having to visualize a bride and groom; there are also wedding guests invited to this glorious occasion. Interpreting this might be confusing: If the bride is made up of the saints, the people of God, who are the guests?[37] Maybe the audience would not worry about being exact here. Maybe they would also have known of a famous parable Jesus told about a wedding that the original guests refused to attend so that the host's slaves had to gather in a most unlikely crowd for the celebratory feast (Matt 22:1–14; Luke 14:16–24; based on Isa 25:6–7). A feature of Matthew's version of this story is that one of the new guests was not properly dressed and therefore thrown out (Matt 22:11–14).

---

36. Probably the speaker is the angel, though this is not explicit in the Greek text. Cf. Aune, *Revelation 17–22*, 1019.

37. Beale suggests that the bride is "the corporate church" and the guests are "individual Christians" (Beale, *Book of Revelation*, 945).

In Revelation, this is the fourth "blessing" pronounced, the center of the series of seven,[38] and the recipients are perhaps identified as one with those previously blessed. These were: the readers and hearers of the prophetic text (1:3), "the dead who die in the Lord from now on" (14:13), and the alert and "clothed" believers (16:15). This implies that "those who are invited to the marriage feast" are, like the others, those who are described as conquerors in Revelation 2–3.[39] John is building a picture of these victorious Christians to inspire and challenge the hearers of the prophecy. The angel underlines the importance of his message by commanding John to write and calling them "the true words of God" (v. 9).

> **And I fell down before his feet to worship him. And he said to me, "Don't do that! I am a fellow slave with you and of your brothers who have the testimony of Jesus. Worship God. For the testimony of Jesus is the spirit of prophecy." (Rev 19:10)**

This is another surprising, even shocking, twist in the story. John does something totally unexpected and seemingly out of character. The hearers are given no clue as to why John does such a seemingly stupid thing as attempt to worship an angel.[40] His action is provoked by the solemn words "These are the true words of God" (v. 9) or perhaps by the blessing announcement as well. But neither of these statements really prepares the listeners for John's response.[41] It is particularly shocking, given that the message of the prophecy has emphasized the importance of worshiping God alone, repeatedly and as a central theme—not idols (9:20), not the beast (13:8, 15; 14:7, 9–11)—and has held out the hope that all nations will eventually worship God (15:4). In fact, in chapter 19 we are in the midst of a great moment of powerful worship and praise to God. John's action thus makes for a discordant note.

But the message that emerges is clear: John's attempt to worship the angel is totally and curtly rejected.[42] The angel makes it clear that he is not *above* the believers but "a fellow slave," a point that perhaps people in the audience need to hear clearly in view of the glory that has attended some of the angels in the narrative. Angels are "brought down to size," so to speak,[43] perhaps as part of the introduction of the new

---

38. Cf. Aune, *Revelation 17–22*, 1031.

39. See also 14:4 and 17:14; Thomas, *Apocalypse*, 568. Dining is a significant image in Revelation (2:7, 17; 3:20).

40. I am assuming this was an angel; verse 9 doesn't specifically call him one. But clearly this person is not divine! Thomas speculates that he might be one of the martyrs under the altar based on the common language of "fellow slaves" (6:9–11; Thomas, *Apocalypse*, 570–71). This might make John's action a little less surprising and a little more prophetic since veneration of martyrs became a problem later in the church.

41. On the possible literary background to this, see Aune, *Revelation 17–22*, 1035–37. This may be "a traditional apocalyptic motif" (Bauckham) or parallel to the frequent Greco-Roman literary motif of "mistaking a human being for a deity" (reflected in Acts 10:25 and 14:11–15). However, in my opinion, neither of these parallels help us understand what is happening here.

42. Cf. Beale, *Book of Revelation*, 946–48.

43. This does not imply that there was a practice of angel worship in the seven churches, as some

covenant.⁴⁴ Also, as Koester points out, "John's account of his mistake reinforces his credibility as a witness" by honestly reporting his error.⁴⁵

The "testimony of Jesus" is emphasized as the key thing: this is what God's servants (including angels) hold on to and which the Spirit inspires.⁴⁶ The NIV renders this differently: "For it is the Spirit of prophecy who bears witness to Jesus" (v. 10b). This suggests that witness to Jesus is inspired and enabled by the Holy Spirit (Spirit with a capital S), a thought consistent with Acts 1:8 ("But you will receive power when the Holy Spirit comes on you; and you will be my witnesses . . . "), a key verse for Pentecostals. Pentecostals have always emphasized that a key purpose of the Holy Spirit, especially when he "comes on" believers, is to enable them to be witnesses to Jesus. And this is a prophetic act because Pentecost has made all believers capable of prophesying (Acts 2:17–18).⁴⁷ The NIV translation thus supports a Pentecostal reading. As Beale phrases this interpretation, "those giving the testimony to [and from] Jesus are a prophetic people."⁴⁸

But it is not the translation I have adopted; my translation is actually like the earlier NIV: "for the testimony of Jesus is the spirit of prophecy." It is a tricky statement to interpret. However, in view of the role of testimony in Revelation, "the testimony of Jesus" is probably not Jesus' own testimony, but testimony to (or about) Jesus (translating the genitive form "of Jesus" as an objective genitive).⁴⁹ The word *pneuma* probably refers to the (Holy) Spirit rather than the human spirit (as the one inspiring the testimony). "Prophecy" probably refers to such Spirit-inspired testimony by believers,⁵⁰ as in the case of the text we are reading, as opposed to fulfilment of Old Testament prophecy.⁵¹ So the two translations are not very different.

It isn't clear how that constitutes an answer to John's error in attempting to worship the angel. Possibly the emphasis on the Spirit is also meant to relativize the role played by angels which has been so prominent in Revelation up to this point.

---

commentators have suggested. However, there is evidence of angel worship in Judaism and in Anatolia, near to the seven cities of Revelation. Cf. Koester, *Revelation*, 732; Aune, *Revelation 17–22*, 1036.

44. Cf. Leithart, *Revelation 12–22*, 264; Corsini, *Apocalypse*, 346; Stuckenbruck, *Angel Veneration*, 93.

45. Koester, *Revelation*, 739.

46. Cf. Koester, *Revelation*, 731–32; Thomas, *Apocalypse*, 572–73.

47. Cf. Waddell, *Spirit of the Book*, 189–91.

48. Beale, *Book of Revelation*, 947.

49. Contra Bauckham, *Climax of Prophecy*, 161. It could be *both* testimony about/to Jesus *and* Jesus' own testimony (Thomas, *Apocalypse*, 571–72; cf. Leithart, *Revelation 12–22*, 265).

50. Cf. Mark 13:11; Matt 10:20; Luke 12:11.

51. Cf. Aune, *Revelation 17–22*, 1039; Koester, *Revelation*, 732.

19:11–21 The Big Battle

And I saw heaven opened, and behold a white horse and the one sitting on it [called] Faithful and True. (Rev 19:11a)

There is another sudden shift here. The audience has been hearing celebration at the downfall of Babylon the Great, followed by the announcement of the forthcoming wedding of the Lamb and his bride, and then the strange confrontation between John and the angel. Now they hear of an opened heaven and a white horse. The hearers are familiar with the idea of an opened heaven. John's vision, after the prophetic messages to the seven churches, had begun with "a door opened in heaven" followed by the call to "Come up here" (4:1). Later, after the seventh trumpet blast, "the temple of God in heaven was opened and the ark of his covenant was visible in his temple" (11:19). Revelation 15:5 employs similar language: "And after these (things) I saw, and the temple of the tent of witness in heaven was opened." Following this the seven bowl angels emerged. An opened heaven is a big event in Revelation, suggesting something very important is happening.[52]

But the listeners also have to process the image of "a white horse," not normally associated with heaven. The last time a white horse was mentioned, it came with the opening of the first seal: "And I saw and behold a white horse, and the one who (was) sitting on it had a bow and a crown was given to him and he went out conquering and so that he might conquer" (6:2). This image was ambiguous (was the horse and rider in 6:2 a good or evil entity?) though white is usually an indicator of good in Revelation.[53] Here in chapter 19, however, there is no ambiguity since "the rider is called Faithful and True" (v. 11), recalling the description of Jesus as "the faithful witness" (1:5) and "the faithful and true witness" (3:14).[54] So John is starting to show this rider to his audience as Jesus Christ himself.

And in justice he judges and fights.[55] (Rev 19:11b)

This is clearly a military situation, resuming the theme of war that has dominated much of the narrative, though not necessarily involving literal violence. The rider has divine qualities of justice, which were mentioned back in verse 2, and reflect Pss 9:8; 96:13; and 98:9. The waging of war takes the audience back to 17:14, where the ten kings "will make war with the Lamb and the Lamb will conquer them." So the audience is prepared to see this rider as a messianic figure, probably the Lamb, riding

---

52. Cf. Thomas, *Apocalypse*, 573–74; Leithart, *Revelation 12–22*, 278–79; Malina, *Genre and Message*, 50.

53. Cf. Beale, *Book of Revelation*, 950; Thomas, *Apocalypse*, 574.

54. Possibly there is also a reference to 3 Macc 2:11, where the context is the hope of vindication of God's people from their persecutor Antiochus Epiphanes in the 2nd cent. BC. Cf. Beale, *Book of Revelation*, 950.

55. We can also translate the Greek πολεμεῖ [*polemei*] as "makes war."

out to save his people, as portrayed in Zechariah 9:9, though there he rides a donkey rather than a war horse. Or they would recall Psalm 45:3–5, as mentioned above.

But the listeners would also recall Jesus' threat to the less faithful believers in Pergamum, "I am coming to you quickly and will fight against them with the sword of my mouth" (2:16). Jesus is a militant ruler. The justice referred to here may remind the audience of Isaiah 11:4, which tells us that the "shoot" from the "stump of Jesse" (Isa 11:1) will act as a judge. "With righteousness he will judge the needy, with justice he will give decisions for the poor of the earth" (Isa 11:4). So the justice here is not just some kind of vengeance but a kind of social justice, justice *for* the poor (see also Pss 45:4; 72:2–4).[56] This suggests that Jesus is coming to give justice *for* his people, and perhaps for others who have suffered injustice, as well as *against* their persecutors.[57]

> **And his eyes (were) [as] flames of fire, and on his head (were) many diadems and he had a name written that no one knew except himself. (Rev 19:12)**

These blazing eyes would recall the son of man in 1:14,[58] a further hint of who this is, and the opening words of the prophetic word to the church in Thyatira (2:18), as well as Daniel 10:6. This picture is overwhelming, in line with the experience of both Daniel (Dan 10:7–9) and John (Rev 1:17). The many crowns or diadems (as opposed to wreaths)[59] contrast with the seven crowns of the dragon (12:3), and with the ten crowns of the beast (13:1), showing the messiah's superior authority.[60]

Special names, sometimes secret, are a feature of Revelation. The victorious Christians of Pergamum are promised "a white stone and on the stone a new name written which no one knows except the one who receives it" (2:17). To those from Philadelphia, Jesus promises, "I will write on them the name of my God and the name of the city of my God ... and my new name" (3:12). Such language recalls the promises to Zion in Isaiah 62:1–5, which include vindication, a new name, and becoming a crown and royal diadem in God's hand, as well as marriage to God. Possibly the audience would also recall Exodus 6:2–3, where God tells Moses how he did not reveal his name YHWH to the patriarchs.[61] The point is not so much cognitive knowledge of the word as understanding the person and their character, or having control over him, as magicians attempted to do with their gods. The fact that his name is secret may suggest that "the full significance of Christ's identity as King and Lord has been

---

56. See extended discussion in Leithart, *Revelation 12–22*, 285–286.

57. Cf. Fekkes, *Isaiah and Prophetic Traditions*, 223–25.

58. Cf. Leithart, *Revelation 12–22*, 277–78, on parallels with John's initial vision of Jesus.

59. The crowns of the rider in Rev 6:1, the woman in Rev 12:1, and the one like a son of man in Rev 14:14 are "wreaths" (Greek στεφανος [*stephanos*]) which has the connotation of a prize for victory as opposed to a mark of royalty. Diadems signify authority over a given territory. But neither word describes what modern people think of as a crown. Cf. Thomas, *Apocalypse*, 576; Koester, *Revelation*, 754.

60. Cf. Aune, *Revelation 17–22*, 1054.

61. Cf. Beale, *Book of Revelation*, 954–57; Koester, *Revelation*, 755; Aune, *Revelation 17–22*, 1055–57.

hidden" and "not even Christ's followers know the full extent of his lordship until he discloses it."[62]

And he was clothed in a robe dipped in blood, and his name was called the word of God. (Rev 19:13)

So they do learn something of his name if not everything: "the word (Greek *logos*) of God." If they were familiar with John's Gospel, there would be a connection here that would shed more light on the identity of this rider (see John 1:1–14),[63] but they would also remember this phrase from 1:2 and 9, where it sums up what John has seen and the cause of his exile, and is linked to the testimony of Jesus (see also 6:9).[64] The plural "words of God" was also used in verse 9 to affirm the blessing on those invited to the wedding supper of the Lamb.

The rider's robe is "dipped in blood" (Greek *bebammenon*, a perfect passive participle of *baptō*, "dip"; so literally "having been dipped" or perhaps "dyed"[65] in blood). How would the audience have interpreted this? Why is his robe bloody like this, and whose blood has it been dipped in? It could be a reference back to 14:20, where the great winepress of God's wrath is trodden, leading to a massive river of blood "up to the horses' bridles."[66] So a rider riding through that river would get covered with blood.

Both passages would also likely recall Isaiah 63, which begins,

> Who is this coming from Edom,
>
> from Bozrah, with his garments stained crimson?
>
> Who is this, robed in splendor,
>
> striding forth in the greatness of his strength?
>
> "It is I, proclaiming victory,
>
> mighty to save."
>
> Why are your garments red,
>
> like those of one treading the winepress?
>
> "I have trodden the winepress alone;
>
> from the nations no one was with me.

---

62. Koester, *Revelation*, 765; cf. Thomas, *Apocalypse*, 577–578. As Aune points out, secret names in the OT were attributed to a divine being (Gen 32:29) or an angel (Judg 13:17–18); however, the angel in Judges 13 is a very high angel, "the angel of YHWH" (Judg 13:3), possibly Christ (Aune, *Revelation 17–22*, 1055).

63. Cf. Koester, *Revelation*, 756–757; Thomas, *Apocalypse*, 578–579; Leithart, *Revelation 12–22*, 281–82.

64. Thus, it usually refers to the gospel (Aune, *Revelation 17–22*, 1058).

65. Koester, *Revelation*, 755. Some manuscripts have variable words meaning "sprinkle" instead of "dip" (Aune, *Revelation 17–22*, 1043).

66. Leithart argues for this identification, contending that in both cases the blood is that of martyrs for Christ (Leithart, *Revelation 12–22*, 280–81).

> I trampled them in my anger
>
> and trod them down in my wrath;
>
> their blood spattered my garments,
>
> and I stained all my clothing . . .
>
> I trampled the nations in my anger;
>
> in my wrath I made them drunk
>
> and poured their blood on the ground." (Is 63:1–3, 6)

In both passages, the image is that of a military leader figuratively wading through the blood of his enemies as he wins a violent victory over them. In the Old Testament, Edom is the archetypical enemy of Israel[67] and God is pictured in Isaiah 63 as defeating them and bringing salvation to his people.

However, there is a significant difference here in Revelation 19, and it comes back to the word "dipped." This word suggests, not so much a robe splashed with the blood through which the rider passes, but some kind of formal ceremony in which his robe is dipped in a pool of blood. Therefore, the audience might possibly recall, not just the river of blood in Revelation 14, but also the references to the redeeming blood of Jesus as the Lamb (1:5; 5:9; 7:14; 12:11). The redeemed have indeed "washed their robes" (7:14) in this blood. As Koester notes, his robe is dipped in blood before the battle starts.[68] The imagery remains somewhat ambiguous,[69] but I think it is indeed a reference to the blood of the Lamb.[70]

And the soldiers [that] (are) in heaven followed him on white horses, clothed in white clean linen. (Rev 19:14)

So we have a whole cavalry force of riders on white horses dressed in a similar way to the bride of the Lamb earlier in this chapter ("clothed with bright clean linen" v. 8a). This implies that the rider's followers are to be identified with the Lamb's bride, and they are together going out to war. They are not therefore angels, even though they are "the soldiers that are in heaven," but most likely the Lamb's "called and chosen and faithful" followers (17:14), who triumph over the beast and the ten kings. They

---

67. Edom was later a code word for Rome among Jewish rabbis and this association may have been present when John wrote Revelation (Aune, *Revelation 17–22*, 1050; Fekkes, *Isaiah and Prophetic Traditions*, 209–10).

68. Koester, *Revelation*, 756; cf. Thomas, *Apocalypse*, 578; Taushev, *Ancient Christianity*, 245. Similar details (such as in v. 19) show that this passage is not the same as a Roman triumph, which would happen after a victory (Koester, *Revelation*, 763), although Aune suggests there might be a reference to "the phenomenon of the posthumous triumph" sometimes marking the deification of a recently deceased emperor (Aune, *Revelation 17–22*, 1051). Leithart also argues for viewing this as a triumph in Leithart, *Revelation 12–22*, 291–94.

69. Cf. Beale, *Book of Revelation*, 958–60. Fekkes argues strongly that the influence of Isa 63 demands a reading in which the blood is that of God's enemies (Fekkes, *Prophetic Traditions*, 197–98).

70. Cf. Pataki, "Non-combat Myth," 264–65; Boring, *Revelation*, 196; Caird, *Revelation*, 242–44.

are the 144,000 who follow the Lamb "wherever he goes" (14:4).[71] They are strikingly contrasted with the huge army of 9:16.

> **And from his mouth went out a sharp sword, so that with it he might strike the nations, and he will shepherd them with a rod of iron, and he tramples the wine press of the fury of the wrath of God the Almighty. (Rev 19:15)**

Here there are three striking statements about the rider's intentions. This sharp sword from the mouth of Christ has been mentioned before in 1:16 as part of the initial vision of the risen Christ and then again in 2:12, 16 as part of the warning to the church in Pergamum. It is a deliberate contrast with what comes out of the mouths of the dragon (12:15) and the evil threesome (16:13), implying a contest of words.[72]

But the listeners also hear that the purpose of this sword is "to strike [from the Greek *patassō*, "strike, strike down"] the nations." This brings to mind Isaiah 11:4, where the messiah "will strike the earth with the rod of his mouth," as part of his saving work to Israel and the nations. The audience would also recall Isaiah 49:2, from one of the "servant songs" of Isaiah. Here the servant testifies, "He made my mouth like a sharpened sword," in preparation for his ministry to restore Israel and bring salvation to the Gentiles (Isa 49:6).[73] Among other things, this means that those who testified to Jesus in the "spirit of prophecy" (v. 10) are vindicated and their testimony is proved true.[74]

The second statement is a direct quote from Psalm 2:9. This too is messianic language from one of Revelation's favorite psalms,[75] saying, "He will shepherd [from the Greek *poimainō*, "tend like a shepherd"] them with a rod of iron." Having struck down the nations, the messiah will rule over them; the "rod of iron" suggests a firm, stern rule.[76] But the OT context of the references suggests that the ultimate purpose of the judgment, striking down and wrath, is the salvation of Israel and the nations.

The third statement reflects Revelation 14:19–20 and Isaiah 63:3, 6: "he tramples the wine press of the fury of the wrath of God the Almighty." This cavalry force has come out to display and carry out God's wrath. The "trampling of the winepress" refers back to the robe dipped in blood (v. 13) as well as the imagery of 14:18–20. I suggest that the winepress and blood actually refer to Jesus' blood shed on the cross, which is the ultimate force that claims the nations and defeats the dragon and his allies (5:9; 7:14; 12:11), but there is clearly also a note of judgment here.

---

71. Cf. Thomas, *Apocalypse*, 579–80; Beale, *Book of Revelation*, 960–61; Koester, *Revelation*, 757; Aune, *Revelation 17–22*, 1059; Miller, "Nuptial Eschatology," 308. Koester argues that this army consists of both saints and angels. Leithart says they are martyrs who have been in heaven since being killed (Leithart, *Revelation 12–22*, 277, 279).

72. Cf. Koester, *Revelation*, 766; Leithart, *Revelation 12–22*, 287.

73. Cf. Thomas, *Apocalypse*, 581; Beale, *Book of Revelation*, 961–63.

74. Cf. Beale, *Book of Revelation*, 949.

75. Cf. Aune, *Revelation 17–22*, 1061.

76. Cf. Koester, *Revelation*, 758.

> And he has, on his robe and on his thigh,[77] a name written: King of kings and Lord of lords. (Rev 19:16)

The audience has now had four statements about his identity: "Faithful and True" (v. 11), an unknown name (v. 12), "the word of God" (v. 13), and now "King of kings and lord of lords" (v. 16), which clearly recalls the description of the Lamb in 17:14 as "lord of lords and king of kings."[78] So clearly, the Rider is Jesus Christ. To put it another way, the Messiah is coming to put down the nations or Gentiles and rule over them as a shepherd, as declared in Psalm 2:8–9. But as Psalm 2 also implies, this will not be without resistance from those nations. Sure enough, the resistance now emerges.

> And I saw one angel standing in the sun, and he cried out [in] a loud voice, saying to all the birds flying in mid-heaven, "Come gather for the great dinner of God so that you may devour the flesh of kings and the flesh of commanders and the flesh of (the) strong and the flesh of horses and of those sitting on them and the flesh of all free and slaves and small and great." (Rev 19:17–18)

The happy "wedding supper" of verse 9 is now contrasted with a much more ghoulish idea; namely, that of birds of prey feasting on the dead bodies (accentuated with the repetition of *sarx*, flesh) of a slain army.[79] This army has been utterly devastated and humiliated.[80] The language would remind the audience of Ezekiel 39:4, 17–20, which is part of the description of the destruction of "Gog, chief prince of Meshek and Tubal" (Ezek 39:1). In the description, Gog attacks Israel after Israel's restoration (Ezek 37) and prior to its final glory (Ezek 40–48). The purpose of all this is to "make known my holy name" to both Israel and the nations (Ezek 39:7), which is what occurs in Revelation 19:16.[81] For John's audience, this language serves as a warning against compromising with pagan culture and religion.[82]

> And I saw the wild beast and the kings of the earth and their armies gathered to make war against the one sitting on the horse and against his army. (Rev 19:19)

This recalls 16:14 and 16, where the demonic spirits sent from the dragon, the beast, and the false prophet gather the kings of the earth for battle at Armageddon. It also

---

77. This refers probably to his role as bridegroom (Leithart, *Revelation 12–22*, 282) or to the Apollo myth as represented in ancient statuary (Edwards, "Rider").

78. Cf. Thomas, *Apocalypse*, 583. For the polemical implications of this title, see Koester, *Revelation*, 759.

79. This would remind the hearers of the consuming of the prostitute's flesh by the beast and the ten horns in 17:16. Cf. Thomas, *Apocalypse*, 586.

80. Cf. Leithart, *Revelation 12–22*, 288–89.

81. Cf. Beale, *Book of Revelation*, 966.

82. Cf. Thomas, *Apocalypse*, 586–87. Leithart suggests that, since this is a spiritual battle and Jesus' sword "is the sword of the Word, not a sword of steel," it is possible that what happens is the destruction of the enemies' flesh in order to bring them to salvation (Leithart, *Revelation 12–22*, 289–90). This is tempting but perhaps too optimistic.

brings to mind 17:14 where the ten kings and the beast "make war against the Lamb."[83] These repeated references back to 16:14, 16, and 17:14 suggest that this is all the same conflict, long anticipated and now released.[84]

The move of the beast and the kings reads like conventional warfare, but this is metaphorical language, as the Lamb has no conventional army and is coming from heaven. The language more likely reminds the audience of OT passages where God is said to wage war for Israel (such as Exod 15:3–4; Deut 33:26–27; Ps 18:6–19; Isa 59:16–18; Hab 3:8). However, this conflict does involve an army of Christ, which suggests that persecution of believers is part of the "making war" here.

> **And the wild beast was seized and with him the false prophet who made the signs before him, and who had deceived those who received the mark of the wild beast, and those who had worshiped his statue; the two were thrown alive into the lake that burns with fire and sulfur. (Rev 19:20)**[85]

There is no real battle because the leaders of the resistance to the messiah are immediately seized (from the Greek *piazō*, "seize, arrest, take hold of").[86] The text focuses on the "false prophet," telling the audience that he had deceived the unbelieving world, recalling the passage about the second beast in 13:11–17. This is the first mention of the "lake" of fire, but torture by "burning sulfur" recalls Ezekiel 38:22, which says, "I will pour down torrents of rain, hailstones and burning sulfur" on Gog and his army. Other passages that the audience might recall are Genesis 19:24 (the destruction of Sodom and Gomorrah) and Daniel 7:10–11 (the destruction of the beast by fire).

They would also recall earlier events in Revelation itself: 9:17–18 (the plagues coming out of the mouths of the horses in the huge army) and 14:10–11, where torment by fire and sulfur is the fate of all those who "worship the wild beast and its statue" and those who receive "the mark of his name" (repeated in 20:10). The imagery here would perhaps draw on people's experience of volcanic eruptions.[87] Both the beasts (seen as real people as well as representing forces such as the Roman Empire)[88] and their followers suffer the same punishment.

> **And the rest were killed by the sword coming out of the mouth of the one sitting on the horse, and all the birds were filled with their flesh. (Rev 19:21)**

The picture of the scavenging birds is very real, and all members of the audience who had experienced warfare would immediately visualize it and be reminded of similar

---

83. It also anticipates Rev 20:8, as we will see. The OT also has many prophecies of such a final battle; e.g., Joel 3:1–16; Zeph 3:8; Zech 12–14. See Aune, *Revelation 17–22*, 1064.

84. Cf. Leithart, *Revelation 12–22*, 282–84.

85. Cf. Beale, *Book of Revelation*, 969; Thomas, *Apocalypse*, 589–90.

86. Cf. Thomas, *Apocalypse*, 588.

87. On other possible origins, see Aune, *Revelation 17–22*, 1066–67.

88. Cf. Leithart, *Revelation 12–22*, 290–91.

threats in the Old Testament (such as Deut 28:26; 1 Kgs 14:11; 16:4; 21:24).[89] But is this a description of a real historical battle? Is it perhaps a description of the second coming of Christ? Or is something else going on here? Apocalyptic language is not easy to translate. Certainly, the imagery of the bodies of a slain army being picked over by birds is very graphic and realistic, as well as recalling us to Ezekiel 39. The seizure of the beast and the false prophet is also easy to imagine. But the description of the rider is very metaphorical in nature, even though the audience can understand this is the messiah, and he is winning a major victory over his enemies here. In particular, the "sword coming out of the mouth" (v. 21) makes no sense taken literally, and its previous use in 2:16 hardly suggests physical violence. Moreover, the lack of description of an actual battle may suggest that the language of mass destruction is not meant literally.[90]

Many commentators take this to be an apocalyptic description of the second coming of Christ. The Rider is clearly meant to be Jesus Christ, as we have just seen. He is coming to take over and rule the nations; he defeats all his enemies, and this leads to the passage about his thousand-year reign (20:4) including the "first resurrection" (20:5–6).[91] However, some of the details don't entirely fit.[92] The tradition of Jesus being accompanied by holy angels (Matt 16:27; 25:31) is perhaps reflected in verse 14. But there is no suggestion here of Jesus coming "like a thief" as in 16:15. There is no description of him actually coming down to the earth. Much of the language seems to be imagery, and there is a delay of a thousand years before the final judgment, which in other prophecies of the second coming seems to follow immediately (Matt 25:31–46; 2 Thess 1:6–10).

None of this proves that John has another idea in mind, but a Pentecostal reading may instead focus on spiritual warfare. There is a spiritual struggle going on behind all the events in Revelation. In fact, this is partly what the text is about, taking its readers/hearers "behind the scenes" to the real struggle behind the earthly events, the conflict between God and the devil (the dragon, invisible to earthly eyes, but very real nonetheless).[93] On earth, this struggle is played out as a conflict between the church and the forces opposed to the church and its mission. These opponents use a strategy of intimidation (threats of persecution and death, represented by the sea beast), deception (propaganda and signs, represented by the land beast, the false prophet), and

---

89. It would remind the audience of the denial of burial to the two witnesses of 11:9, and would provoke a deep-seated fear in most listeners (Thomas, *Apocalypse*, 591; Aune, *Revelation 17–22*, 1067–68).

90. Cf. Koester, *Revelation*, 764.

91. Cf. Koester, *Revelation*, 753–54.

92. Cf. Aune, *Revelation 17–22*, 1046, 1053, 1069.

93. Cf. Papandrea, *Wedding of the Lamb*, 162. Malina argues that Revelation "unveils the cosmic forces behind particular social events observable by earth-bound persons and their historians" (Malina, *Genre and Message*, 47). I would qualify that by specifying that the observable events would be those related to the church's mission, as in Acts.

seduction (represented by the prostitute). Their goal is to defeat the church and its messianic mission.

How can the church win this war? Ultimately, only if the messiah himself comes to her aid (as represented by the rider on the white horse).[94] But her weapons and strategies of spiritual warfare can still be effective, and Revelation contains at least eight of these, confirming Paul's contention in 2 Corinthians 10:4 that "the weapons we fight with are not the weapons of the world. On the contrary, they have divine power to demolish strongholds."

Revelation 19 itself alludes to several important "weapons" of spiritual warfare mentioned elsewhere in the Bible. These include, notably, loud praise (vv. 1–6; compare Pss 149–150), testimony to Jesus as stimulated by the Spirit (v. 10; compare 12:11; Acts 1:8), the name of Jesus (vv. 13, 16; compare John 14:13–14; Acts 3:6), the blood of Jesus (v. 13; compare 12:11), and the word of God as the sword of the Spirit (vv. 3, 15, 21; compare Eph 6:17). To these may be added righteous actions (v. 8; compare Eph 6:14), martyrdom (v. 2; compare 12:11), and following Jesus faithfully (v. 14; compare 14:4). To this list, we might add prayer (8:3–4; compare Eph 6:18). So Revelation 19 (and indeed the whole book of Revelation) can perhaps be read as a textbook case of spiritual warfare that climaxes in the intervention of Christ; he rides to the aid of his people as God does in Psalm 68 (see especially Ps 68:4—"sing to God, sing in praise of his name, extol him who rides on the clouds"). Or to put it another way, this is the climax of the church's long struggle against the forces of darkness, with Christ bringing the victory.[95]

Koester points out that "human agents do not play a military role in the battle."[96] It is true that the beast and false prophets are simply "seized" and "thrown alive" into the "lake of fire" (v. 20), and the others are "killed by the sword coming out of the mouth of the one sitting on the horse" (v. 21). However, this does not necessarily mean that "the soldiers in heaven" (v. 14) are only passive spectators, given that they are targets of the enemy forces (v. 19), and considering the role attributed to the witnesses/martyrs elsewhere (12:11; 20:4). Leithart puts it well:

> The Lamb's warfare . . . is a liturgical warfare, conducted not by sword and spears, rocket launchers and helicopters, but by the Word-Bread, the Word

---

94. A key example of this is the appearance of Jesus to the arch-persecutor Saul (Acts 9:1–9; 22:4–11; 26:9–18) which saved the infant Jewish church from obliteration and launched Saul/Paul as one of Jesus' chief apostles. Note that Jesus identifies himself with the church when he asks Saul, "why do you persecute me?" (Acts 9:4).

95. This might be a literal postmillennial reading but not including many ideas often associated with postmillennialism (cf. Koester, *Revelation*, 747). However, as Koester warns, "Revelation portrays God's final victory over evil without giving readers a way to translate it directly into the world of time and space" (ibid., 751).

96. *Revelation*, 763; cf. Aune, *Revelation 17–22*, 1065. However, one possibility is that John is predicting Constantine's legendary victory at Milvan Bridge using the sign "Chi Rho" representing Christ (cf. Papandrea, *Wedding of the Lamb*, 195).

and Sacrament of the Lamb and his companions. It is a war of witness, the overcomers being the people of Word and Wine who overcome by self-giving.[97]

Or to put it another way, this is a missional war, conducted by the church in preaching the gospel in the power of the Spirit with boldness and with praise, even against opposition and in the face of suffering and death.[98]

---

97. Leithart, *Revelation 12–22*, 287.

98. Cf. Leithart, *Revelation 12–22*, 294–27. Here Leithart argues that Rev 19:11–21 represents "a final surge of first-century mission as a triumphal procession of the heavenly hosts led by the conquering King" (ibid., 295).

Revelation Chapter 20

The members of the audience in the seven churches of Asia have been engaged with the narrative of Revelation as it has been read aloud to them in each city. Since the recommissioning of John in chapter 10, they have heard about a colossal struggle between God and the devil, especially between the Lamb on one side and the beasts and the prostitute Babylon on the other. This struggle came to a head in chapter 19, after the description of the fall of Babylon (chs. 17–18), and now the beast and the false prophet have been removed to the "the lake that burns with fire and sulfur" (19:20). Their followers have been destroyed, and the listeners are excitedly waiting for more news about the marriage of the Lamb (19:7–9). God's cause seems to be triumphant in the earth.

20:1–6 The Thousand Years

> **And I saw an angel coming down from heaven, having the key of the abyss and a great chain in his hand. (Rev 19:1)**

There have been many angels in this story and there is nothing in particular to distinguish this one from the others, except that he is holding both "the key of the abyss and a great chain." This is the first mention of the abyss for a while. It had previously been seen as like a giant furnace, from which strange locusts emerged, when it was opened by a fallen star that was given the key to its shaft (9:1–3).[1] These locusts functioned like an army under the leadership of "the angel of the abyss" named Abaddon and Apollyon (Destroyer) (9:11). Later the audience heard of "the beast that comes up from the abyss" to kill the two witnesses of God (11:7), and of the beast carrying the prostitute who "is about to come up out of the abyss" (17:8). It seems like a horrible place, out

---

1. Keys have been an occasional feature of the text: "I have the keys of death and Hades" (1:18); Jesus "has the key of David" (3:7); a fallen star "was given the key of the pit of the abyss" (9:1). Keys stand for authority or control. Keys and binding are linked together in Jesus' promise to Peter and the church about which we read in Matt 16:19. Cf. Koester, *Revelation*, 769–70; Leithart, *Revelation 12–22*, 302–4.

of which come evil forces, but control over this place, including its entrance and the activity of its denizens, seems ambiguous.

But now things have changed: the key is clearly held by one of God's angels (parallel to Jesus' claim to "have the keys of death and Hades" in 1:18),[2] and this angel also has a great chain in his hand. The abyss was opened in 9:1–3, unleashing all manner of evil, and is now to be locked up again. The devil's forces were released for a season but are now confined.[3]

> **And he took the dragon, the ancient snake, who is (the) devil and Satan, into custody and bound him (for) a thousand years and threw him into the abyss, and locked and sealed (it) over him so that he might no longer deceive the nations until the thousand years were completed. After these (things) he must be released (for) a short time. (Rev 19:2–3)**

So the abyss is to function as a jail for the ultimate enemy of God for an extended period of time. He will be chained up and locked into the abyss for a thousand years, a period of time that dwarfs the periods he can oppress the saints.[4] John may be referring partly to Isaiah 24:21–22, which says:

> In that day the LORD will punish
> the powers in the heavens above
> and the kings on the earth below.
> They will be herded together
> like prisoners bound in a dungeon;
> they will be shut up in a prison
> and be punished after many days.[5]

The listeners already know about this prisoner, who has been mentioned many times in his various names: as a synagogue controller (2:9; 3:9), a prison master and persecutor of believers (2:10), enthroned in his capital at Pergamum (2:13), guardian of certain "secrets" (2:24), and above all as the great red dragon, enemy of the messiah (12:3–4). He has been seen as the leader of an army of angels (12:7–9), the deceiver of the world (12:9), the accuser of the saints (12:10), the pursuer of the mother of the

---

2. Hence, Beale asserts that the abyss "is probably a synonym for 'death and Hades'" (Beale, *Book of Revelation*, 984). The alternative reading, that this angel is the same as the fallen star in 9:1, makes little sense. This angel is coming down from heaven whereas that star was on the earth after falling; this angel is going to lock up the devil whereas that star had released demonic forces onto the earth.

3. Leithart, *Revelation 12–22*, 302.

4. Cf. Thomas, *Apocalypse*, 594–97. See the chart and discussion in Koester, *Revelation*, 782–83. Koester and others see the three-and-a-half years of Revelation as the period between the first and second comings of Christ (Koester, *Revelation*, 783); this seems theologically appropriate, but I question whether the initial audience would understand it this way

5. Cf. Aune, *Revelation 17–22*, 1078. See also 2 Pet 2:4. Aune also points to similarities in two passages in 1 Enoch 10. See also Aune, *Revelation 17–22*, 1081–83; Beale, *Book of Revelation*, 989–91.

messiah and her other children (12:13–17), and the evil force behind the wild beast (13:1–4). The hearers would also think back to Genesis 3 with the mention of "the ancient snake."[6] So the capture and imprisonment of the dragon continues the great victory won over the enemies of God in the previous chapters.[7] Other books in the NT suggest that this binding began with Jesus' earthly ministry (e.g., Luke 10:17–19; 11:19–22) and his death and resurrection (e.g., Col 2:15) and continues with the expanding mission of the church.[8]

The purpose of the incarceration of the dragon is "so that he might no longer deceive the nations." Deception is a big theme in Revelation. Satan was earlier said to "deceive the whole world" (12:9), and here he is accused of deceiving the nations, using different forms of the Greek *planaō* ("lead stray, mislead, deceive"). His agent, the second (land) beast, or false prophet, also "deceived those who dwell on the earth" (13:14) by miraculous signs, as part of his propaganda campaign on behalf of the first (sea) beast. Such deception has kept the nations away from God and apparently prevented them from repenting in response to God's judgments (9:20–21). Hence, the incarceration of the devil in the abyss will make the nations open to God and the gospel, it would seem.[9] Other works of the devil are not mentioned, but since the beast and false prophet are also out of action, and Babylon is a ruin, his other strategies of intimidation and seduction are also perhaps removed. Some kind of gospel "golden age" seems to be imminent.

However, while this situation is apparently lengthy, after the thousand years, "he must be released for a short time." The text gives no reason for this; it simply insists that it must happen, using the Greek *dei*, which implies a necessary or proper event.[10] The audience may recall similar language at the beginning of the text, which says that God shows his servants "what *must* soon happen" (1:1). In any event, his future "short time" (similar to 12:12) is contrasted with his lengthy imprisonment of "a thousand years." I will return to this later.

> **And I saw thrones and (people) sat on them and judgment was given to them, and the souls of those who had been beheaded on account of the testimony of Jesus and on account of the word of God, and who had not worshiped the wild**

---

6. Cf. Thomas, *Apocalypse*, 593–94.

7. Cf. Koester, *Revelation*, 783–84.

8. Cf. Hendriksen, *More Than Conquerors*, 187–89.

9. Cf. Thomas, *Apocalypse*, 598. Beale argues that the devil's "restraint" begins with Christ's resurrection and mainly destroys his prior "authority over the realm of the dead," his ability to prevent "'all people' throughout the earth being drawn to Jesus (John 12:31–32)" (Beale, *Book of Revelation*, 985), his capacity to "delude" and attack God's people and his ability to "stop the spread of the preaching of the gospel" (ibid., 988–89). It is "not a complete curtailment of all the devil's activities but only a restraint on his deceiving activities" (ibid., 986). I think he is right about the nature of the "binding," but the narrative of Revelation implies that the work of Christ has to be enforced first by the struggle of the martyrs. Cf. Leithart, *Revelation 12–22*, 301, 305, 308.

10. Cf. Corsini, *Apocalypse*, 368.

beast nor its statue and had not received its mark on their foreheads and on their hands. They lived and reigned with the Messiah (for) a thousand years. (Rev 19:4)

The text does not specify who the people sitting on thrones are.[11] Their role is also ambiguous; the NIV speaks of them being given "authority to judge," but the more literal translation here may imply not so much that they become judges as that a verdict has been given in their favor (as in Dan 7:22). However, the implication that people sit on thrones tends to support the NIV translation and may remind the audience of the thrones of the twenty-four elders (4:4), as well as the promise to the conquerors of a seat with Jesus on his throne (3:21).[12] The language of their living uses the Greek *ezēsan*, aorist indicative of *zaō*: "live, be alive, come back to life." Beale concludes, "the saints are pictured as beginning to reign and to execute the judicial function that they will carry out consummately at the end of the age..."[13]

The word "souls" (Greek *psuchas*) may recall the souls under the altar in Revelation 6, crying out for vengeance for their blood after being "slaughtered on account of the word of God and on account of the testimony which they had" (6:9).[14] This statement in verse 4 may then indicate that these martyrs have now been vindicated, a point made already in 19:2 ("avenged the blood of his slaves from her hand").[15]

John mentions a specific detail here: these martyrs were "beheaded," the only time this kind of execution has been mentioned.[16] Crucifixion is mentioned in 11:8 in relation to Jesus and execution by the sword in 13:10, but generally the manner of people being killed as martyrs is not specified. Beheading seems to have been a form of execution reserved for people of higher status such as Roman citizens.[17]

This verse also recalls the enforced marking of all kinds of people in 13:16–17 and the killing of all who did not worship the first beast (13:15). These martyrs are those who did not worship the beast, implying that their names were written in "the book of life of the Lamb" (13:8), though this should probably not be restricted to literal martyrs.[18] The tables have been turned; those beheaded by the beast are now

---

11. See alternative possibilities in Koester, *Revelation*, 771; Aune, *Revelation 17–22*, 1084–85; Beale, *Book of Revelation*, 996.

12. Cf. Thomas, *Apocalypse*, 600; Koester, *Revelation*, 771–72; Beale, *Book of Revelation*, 995–97; Leithart, *Revelation 12–22*, 311–15.

13. Beale, *Book of Revelation*, 997.

14. Cf. Aune, *Revelation 17–22*, 1087–88; Beale, *Book of Revelation*, 997.

15. Cf. Pattemore, *People of God*, 108–9.

16. It was, however, the way John the Baptist was executed (Matt 14:10–11), and possibly James the brother of John (Acts 12:2). Thomas points to the contrast with the head wound of the beast (Thomas, *Apocalypse*, 601–2).

17. Koester, *Revelation*, 772. See more detailed discussion in Aune, *Revelation 17–22*, 1086–87.

18. Cf. Koester, *Revelation*, 773, 786; Beale, *Book of Revelation*, 999–1000.

alive and reigning with Christ,[19] and apparently have been in some way resurrected for this purpose.

> **The rest of the dead[20] did not live until the thousand years were completed. This is the first resurrection. Blessed and holy are those who have a share in the first resurrection. Over these the second death has no authority, but they will be priests to God and to the Messiah and will reign with him for [the] thousand years. (Rev 19:5–6)**

This verse may suggest that a physical resurrection is in view here,[21] though it is less clear as we read on. This is also the fifth blessing in Revelation; like the others, this is aimed at faithful Christians, the conquerors (compare 1:3; 14:13; 16:15; 19:9; 22:7, 14), and here it fulfills the earlier promise of them both reigning and acting as priests of God (see 1:6; 5:10).[22] John seemingly envisages two deaths and two resurrections here: perhaps ordinary physical death followed by something worse ("the second death"), and a physical resurrection followed by something worse (vv. 5, 12), a "second resurrection" to judgment. Perhaps the two resurrections are both physical then, but spaced apart and involving different people. Those involved in the first resurrection are exempt from the second death (see also 2:11). Those involved in the second resurrection (a phrase John doesn't use) are vulnerable to the second death. But everyone undergoes the first death.[23]

Many commentators find this confusing. The mention of "souls" and the language of "first" resurrection, coupled with other places in the New Testament that envisage everyone rising again at once (John 5:25–29; Acts 24:15), suggest that the "first" resurrection may be spiritual in nature (as in Eph 2:4–6), and so prior to physical death. It amounts to a participation in Christ's resurrection which may most accurately be

---

19. The text does not say whom they reign over (cf. Koester, *Revelation*, 773) or where (cf. ibid., 787–88). Maybe John's thinking is similar to Paul's in Rom 5:17b where he says, "how much more will those who receive God's abundant provision of grace and the gift of righteousness reign in life through the one man, Jesus Christ!"

20. Koester argues that "the rest of the dead" refers to the ungodly, who are in Hades awaiting resurrection and final judgment after the battle of Revelation 19, as opposed to the non-martyred believers (Koester, *Revelation*, 774–75). But presumably other people are born during the thousand-year period. If everyone is either wiped out or resurrected to reign with Christ, then the resurrected ones would reign over an empty earth, which is what Seventh-day Adentists think. Their official statement of beliefs says, "The millennium is the thousand-year reign of Christ with His saints in heaven between the first and second resurrections. During this time the wicked dead will be judged; the earth will be utterly desolate, without living human inhabitants, but occupied by Satan and his angels" (General Conference of Seventh-day Adventists, *28 Fundamental Beliefs*, 2015. Available at: https://szu.adventist.org/wp-content/uploads/2016/04/28_Beliefs.pdf).

21. As argued by Thomas, *Apocalypse*, 602–5. But see Beale, *Book of Revelation*, 1103–5.

22. Cf. Thomas, *Apocalypse*, 607; Koester, *Revelation*, 787.

23. As Aune points out, only a first resurrection and a second death are specifically spoken of here (*Revelation 17–22*, 1090; see also 1104, 1091–93, on parallel Greek and Egyptian ideas). Cf. Koester, *Revelation*, 775–76, 786–87. As Koester says, "Revelation is unusual in dividing the future resurrection into two phases" (Koester, *Revelation*, 786). Cf. Beale, *Book of Revelation*, 1005–7.

seen as the *first* resurrection (see Eph 2:4–6; Rom 6:4–13; 1 Cor 15:20).[24] However, it is hermeneutically dangerous to try to import other New Testament teaching into Revelation.

Alternatively, these resurrected souls are reigning with Christ in heaven immediately after death.[25] Certainly, these resurrected saints are priests and kings with God and Christ, recalling Exodus 19:6; Revelation 1:6 (" . . . made us a kingdom, priests to his God and Father"); and 5:10 ("made them a kingdom and priests to our God, and they will reign on the earth"). Another intriguing possibility is that the "first resurrection" is actually a reference to Ezekiel 37, the passage that promises a national resurrection of dead Israel, whether that means a spiritual, "political," or physical resurrection (see Ezek 37:11–14).[26] This makes a lot of sense given that the thousand years is followed by what Ezekiel prophesies in Ezekiel 38–39 (God and Magog), but raises other hermeneutical questions.

The imagination runs into difficulties if the hearer or reader takes all this too literally. The unbelieving world seems to have been destroyed in 19:21. So who are the nations that are no longer deceived (v. 3)? Who do the resurrected martyrs reign over (v. 6)? We can only infer that the destruction of 19:21 was not a total annihilation of unbelievers.[27] And what about believers who have not been beheaded (v. 4)? Are they the subjects of the resurrected martyrs? And are those resurrected martyrs still subject to physical death? The fact that they reign with Christ for a thousand years suggests not. At the very least, they would have to live very long lives (compare Isa 65:20; the genealogies in Genesis 5).[28] But would John's hearers have entertained the idea of resurrected and un-resurrected people living together?

And what about the "thousand years" itself? What would John's original audience have made of that?[29] It may be a mathematical symbol of completeness and symmetry (10 x 10 x 10): John uses numbers and multiplication elsewhere to make a

---

24. For example, "The mention of the saints' resurrection in 20:4–5 probably is a reference to their share in Christ's own resurrection, which gives them power to rule spiritually over the devil" (Beale, *Book of Revelation*, 993; see also 1004–5, 1014–15). However, Beale argues that this actually refers to postmortem ascension of the disembodied souls (cf. Beale, *Book of Revelation*, 1011–12. Cf. Beale, *John's Use of the Old Testament*, 376–82.

25. Cf. Beale, *Book of Revelation*, 998–99, 1008–11; Hendriksen, *More Than Conquerors*, 191–93.

26. Cf. Leithart, *Revelation 12–22*, 326.

27. Cf. Leithart, *Revelation 12–22*, 327.

28. Another ancient Jewish writing called *Jubilees* speaks of a day when people will live for a thousand years, unlike the ancients whose long lives were cut short before then (Beale, *Book of Revelation*, 1019).

29. Cf. Koester, *Revelation*, 773–74, 787. While some Jewish apocalyptic writings speak of a messianic period before the final end, the length of this age is not given as a thousand years (cf. Aune, *Revelation 17–22*, 1104–8; Beale, *Book of Revelation*, 1016–21). Koester rightly points out that this messianic reign has already begun (3:21; 12:5) since Christ is "*already* the ruler of the kings of the earth." The millennium does not start his reign, it only means the saints share in it more fully (Koester, *Revelation*, 787; emphasis in the original). But according to 1:5–6, they already share in it.

theological point; 144,000 = 12 x 12 x 10 x 10 x 10, for example, in 7:4.[30] There are also ancient texts that predict that world history lasts six-thousand years plus a "sabbath" of one-thousand years.[31] The phrase "a thousand years" only occurs here in the New Testament, except for 2 Peter 3, which draws on Psalm 90 as part of its explanation of the delay in the promised return of Jesus (2 Pet 3:3, 4, 8, 9).

We can't be sure that John's hearers would have known of 2 Peter, but they may have recalled its intertext in Psalm 90:4, which says, "a thousand years in your sight are a like a day that has just gone by, or like a watch in the night." The psalmist's point is based on the misery and brevity of human life compared to God; he cries out, "How long?" (Ps 90:13), looking for a divine intervention bringing a new life of gladness. The thousand years in the psalm functions as a metaphor for the present age or life spent waiting for God to intervene, a long time to us but very brief to God. Now if they did allow that idea into their minds as they heard the reading, the audience of Revelation might have interpreted the thousand years as referring to the present age in which believers experience spiritual resurrection already, but wait for the second coming to bring their physical resurrection and eternal life. Or if they followed 2 Peter, they might understand the thousand years as referring to the long delay in the second coming.[32]

What John does tell us is that this thousand years represents an age in which the devil is powerless to deceive the nations. Hence, unlike the pre-Christ era, the knowledge of God is released freely into all the world (see Hab 2:14), including the "nations" or Gentiles (Greek *ethnē*), a prominent theme in the New Testament as a whole.[33] Some commentators have argued for this reading based also on the "binding of Satan" as something done at the cross, as perhaps in Colossians 2:15 ("And having disarmed the powers and authorities, he made a public spectacle of them, triumphing over them by the cross").[34] This, however, ignores the role of the martyrs in making this happen (as Col 1:24 may suggest), and trying to harmonize Revelation with the rest of the New Testament may destroy its unique message.

Some other commentators, wanting to take the language as literally as possible, scoff at the idea that we are living in an age where Satan is bound in the abyss given the rampant evil and wickedness, even deception, around us. Certainly, the most simple,

---

30. Cf. Beale, *Book of Revelation*, 995. Leithart argues, "It is best to view the number as symbolic" (Leithart, *Revelation 12–22*, 307).

31. Cf. Beale, *Book of Revelation*, 1020.

32. But see Beale, *Book of Revelation*, 1018.

33. E.g., Matt 24:14; 28:18–20; Mark 16:15; Luke 24:47; Acts 1:8; 11:18; 13:46–48; 15:14–19; Rom 1:16; 11:11–13; 15:9–18. Moloney, however, sees the thousand years as representing the pre-Christ history of Israel, virtually ignoring the phrase about the nations not being deceived (Moloney, *Apocalypse of John*, 305–306).

34. This view is advocated by Beale, as summed up in his two lengthy headings (Beale, *Book of Revelation*, 972). For a different amillennial reading from an ancient commentator, see Victorinus, *Commentary*, ANF 7:358–59.

straightforward reading of this passage as part of John's narrative would include the idea of the "thousand years" as something future to the *original* audience, even if not to modern readers—that is, something for the original hearers to look forward to after the eventual defeat of the pagan Roman Empire.[35]

But none of the traditional interpretations of the "millennium" are without problems. The premillennial view (which says that the millennium flows from the second coming), embraced by nearly all Pentecostals, makes sense of the narrative flow,[36] if we assume that 19:11–21 is referring to the *Parousia*. But it has a hard time dealing with the details we are wrestling with here and the discrepancies with other New Testament eschatology.[37] Many premillennialists also import detail from selected Old Testament prophecies into Revelation 20, in violation of their probable original meaning. Moreover, some embrace a dispensational reading that doesn't help interpret Revelation as a whole, especially John's focus on the martyrs as heroes. Dispensationalism is really an enemy of Pentecostalism with its rejection of contemporary miracles and its pessimism about the church and its mission.

The amillennial view (which says that the millennium is more of a metaphor for the current gospel age) makes Revelation 20 compatible with the rest of the New Testament, but at the expense of avoiding some of the details of the passage and the narrative flow of Revelation. It seems to require a recapitulation reading, which minimizes the sense of climax in Revelation 19 and 20.[38] For instance, the binding of the devil makes no sense if he was already bound before chapter 19, the resurrection of the martyrs likewise implies that they had been killed previously, and the seizing of the devil in 20:1 makes more sense if he was not already in the abyss, but on earth, as a result of the events of Revelation 12.

The postmillennial view (which expects a future great era brought in by the church or the Spirit) maintains a sense of narrative flow, and mostly enables an interpretation compatible with the rest of the New Testament, but depends on 19:11–21

---

35. Cf. Koester, *Revelation*, 784–85.

36. Thomas, for example, writes, "it is difficult to imagine the Johannine hearers would not take these words [Rev 20:1] in continuity with what preceded and in some sense of chronological development" (Thomas, *Apocalypse*, 592).

37. Cf. Beale, *Book of Revelation*, 1014; Merkle and Krug, "Hermeneutical Challenges."

38. See Beale's arguments for such a reading in Beale, *Book of Revelation*, 974–76, 980–83; Beale, *John's Use of the Old Testament*, 359–71. Beale sees Rev 20 as recapitulating both Rev 19 and Rev 12 (Beale, *Book of Revelation*, 992–95). Beale's argument that it makes no sense to say that the devil could not deceive the nations for a thousand years (20:3) if they had been destroyed at the second coming in chapter 19 (Beale, *Book of Revelation*, 980–81) depends on two assumptions. First, it assumes that 19:11–21 is about the second coming and second, it assumes that "the rest" who "were killed" in 19:21 refers to everyone on earth as opposed to the armies of the beast. This second assumption may be supported by 19:18, which had a broader wording ("the flesh of all") but how broad is that "all"? The rest of Revelation makes little sense if every person on earth is literally destroyed in Rev 19. The strongest point in favor of recapitulation is the repetition of language from Ezekiel 38–39 in both 19:17–21 and 20:8–9. For further arguments in favor of Beale's amillennial interpretation, see Beale, *Book of Revelation*, 987. Cf. Hendriksen, *More Than Conquerors*, 184–85.

not being about the *Parousia*. It is also somewhat vague or conflicted about what this future breakthrough might look like. As a result, it has also led to false expectations, especially in the nineteenth century.

Whereas premillennialism tends to excessive pessimism, postmillennialism tends to excessive optimism; amillennialism is maybe more realistic but tends to sideline the passage completely.[39] What all interpretations struggle to explain is the next event in John's narrative.

20:7–10 The Final Rebellion

And when the thousand years are completed, Satan will be released from his prison . . . (Rev 20:7)

This development has been flagged already in verse 3, but again no reason for the release of Satan is given to the reader/hearer.[40] Can we think of why this might happen, indeed why it "must" happen (v. 3)? One possibility is that Satan has repented, but this is clearly not the case as he behaves the same as before his release (v. 8). A second possibility is that his crimes only deserve a one-thousand-year term in jail; this is a possibility but unlikely since his subordinates were cast into "the fiery lake of burning sulfur," presumably forever (19:20), as will later happen to the devil too (20:10).

I can only think of two rational bases for his release. The first is that the church has lost its martyr spirit. Satan is sent to prison because the faithful believers gave up their lives for Christ and won the right to rule for a thousand years (vv. 1–6); what about after that? If more martyrs continue to defiantly suffer death rather than compromise their faith, Satan's term in jail may be extended and the church's rule may continue, but if not, or if the church goes to sleep due to an absence of persecution, he must be released.[41]

The second possible, and related, reason for Satan's release may relate to the reason why the devil was allowed to exist in the first place, and may represent a basic law of God's universe that everything must be tested. As seen in the original story of the ancient serpent (Gen 3), the devil is God's agent in testing people (he was permitted to test Jesus himself according to the synoptic Gospels).[42] So again the saints are to be

---

39. For a historical survey of Christian beliefs about the millennium, see Koester, *Revelation*, 741–50. Leithart's view that the millennium is introduced with the fall of Jerusalem in AD 70 and the triumph of the first-century martyrs makes a lot of sense, but he sees the limitations in the light of subsequent events. I think he believes more in a potential millennium in the current age, which makes him slightly postmillennialist. Cf. Leithart, *Revelation 12–22*, 308–25.

40. See discussion of possibilities in Koester, *Revelation*, 788; Leithart, *Revelation 12–22*, 328–29.

41. Leithart argues that Satan "remains there [in the abyss] as long as martyrs rule. He remains there *because* martyrs rule (Leithart, *Revelation 12–22*, 311; emphasis in the original). Thus, one might argue that the post-Constantinian alliance of church and empire released the devil again.

42. Cf. Thomas, *Apocalypse*, 599.

tested as the devil goes out to "deceive the nations" (v. 8) and threaten God's people (v. 9). Will they fall prey to such deception or intimidation?

> . . . and will go out to deceive the nations that are in the four corners of the earth, Gog and Magog, to gather them together for war, and their number (is) as the sand on the seashore. (Rev 20:8)

Certainly, Satan has not been reformed by his long prison sentence. Rather, the main difference John identifies between the thousand years and the post-millennial period is the removal and reintroduction of Satanic deception into the nations.[43] Deception seems to be Satan's "main game." And his deceptive work is particularly directed at the nations or Gentiles.[44] In fact, the passage emphasizes the global reach of his efforts, "the four corners of the earth."[45]

John then introduces a reference to Ezekiel 38–39 with the mention of "Gog and Magog" as equivalent to "the nations that are in the four corners of the earth."[46] Ezekiel had been describing the restoration of Israel with the vision of the restoration of the dry bones (Ezek 37:1–14) and making a direct prophecy of a reunited Israel in their own land under one king, a new David. They are released from all idolatry and living in "an everlasting covenant" with God, including his permanent presence, increasing numbers, and a great reputation among the nations (Ezek 37:14–28), a classic messianic vision that would be compatible with all major interpretations of Revelation's thousand years.[47]

But Ezekiel then foresees this great era being challenged by a Gentile force, led by "Gog, of the land of Magog, the chief prince of Meshek and Tubal" (Ezek 38:3), and including armies from many nations (Ezek 38:5–6, 13, 15). This grand army will invade Israel, which has become "a land of unwalled villages . . . a peaceful and unsuspecting people—all of them living without walls and without gates and bars" (Ezek 38:11). But God is in this development (Ezek 38:3, 4, 16, 17; 39:2, 3) and will be "proved holy" before the nations (Ezek 38:16; see also 39:21–29) when he annihilates the invading force through a great earthquake, infighting among the participating nations, plague, rain, hailstones, and "burning sulfur" (Ezek 38:18–23). The immense invading army will fall "on the mountains of Israel" and serve "as food to all kinds of carrion birds and to the wild animals" (Ezek 39:4). This will all serve to reveal God's holiness in

---

43. Cf. Thomas, *Apocalypse*, 608–9; Aune, *Revelation 17–22*, 1079–80

44. In all three eschatological war scenes in Revelation, Satanic deception is involved (16:13–14; 19:20; 20:8), but it is more explicit in 20:8. Cf. Beale, *Book of Revelation*, 980.

45. See discussion of the identity of these nations in Koester, *Revelation*, 776–77; Aune, *Revelation 17–22*, 1095.

46. Cf. Koester, *Revelation*, 777–78; Beale, *Book of Revelation*, 1024–25.

47. Cf. Beale, *Book of Revelation*, 1012–13, 1022–23; Leithart, *Revelation 12–22*, 326. Beale rightly draws attention to the parallels between Ezek 37–48 and Rev 20–22, arguing that John has spiritualized the resurrection vision of Ezek 37 and "universalized" it to apply to the church. Cf. Moyise, *Old Testament in the Book of Revelation*, 67–68, 81–82.

punishing, and then restoring, Israel (Ezek 39:23–28). This long passage finishes by saying, "I will no longer hide my face from them, for I will put out my Spirit on the people of Israel, declares the Sovereign LORD" (Ezek 39:29).

Some of the details of this passage have appeared in Revelation before, and the feast of the carrion birds was a feature of the great battle in 19:17–21. But the story of Gog and his great international army is more explicitly referred to here, in Revelation 20.[48] As in Ezekiel 38, the vision speaks of a great international army[49] gathered for battle: "their number is as the sand on the sea shore" (v. 8). The number recalls the uncountable multitude of the redeemed in 7:9, OT descriptions of Israel (Gen 22:17; 1 Kgs 3:8), and OT descriptions of their enemies (Josh 11:4; Judg 7:12; 1 Sam 13:5).

And they climbed up[50] onto the breadth of the earth, and encircled the camp of the saints and the beloved city, and fire came down out of heaven and devoured them. (Rev 20:9)

The text conjures up the image of an invading army attacking Israel and Jerusalem, as in Ezekiel 38, even though "the saints" by this time include people from all the nations. Jerusalem is described in mixed terms in Revelation, as "the holy city" (11:2) and "the great city which is spiritually called Sodom and Egypt" (11:8), but now as "the beloved city," a phrase that could evoke language of the psalms about Zion (Pss 87:1–3; 132:13–16; see also Jer 12:7). However, as Koester argues, this language probably does not refer to a literal city but is "a metaphor for the Christian community";[51] if so, then the warfare here is probably also metaphorical. Alternatively, the reference is to the new Jerusalem already present on earth.[52]

Such a massive end-time invasion is prophesied in several places in the Old Testament prophets (Joel 3:1–16; Zech 14:1–19; compare Zeph 3:8). Jesus also speaks of such an invasion, but in his prophecy it ends in disaster, not a great divine intervention (Mark 13:1–31; Matt 24:1–35; Luke 21:5–33), reflecting what happened in AD 66–70. John returns to the prophets here by forecasting such a divine intervention, reflecting Ezekiel 38:22; 39:6; Zechariah 14:3–4; and the earlier downfall of Sodom and Gomorrah in Genesis 19:24. Fire plays a starring role again here.[53]

---

48. Cf. Koester, *Revelation*, 789; Aune, *Revelation 17–22*, 1093–95; Leithart, *Revelation 12–22*, 326. Beale argues that 20:8–10 in fact recapitulates 19:17–21, both drawing on and fulfilling Ezekiel 38–39 so that both describe a war *after* the millennium (Beale, *Book of Revelation*, 976–81, 1022–23).

49. Possibly these are resurrected unbelievers as predicted in v. 5, but more likely the descendants of those not killed in ch. 19 (cf. Beale, *Book of Revelation*, 1023–24).

50. We could also translate the Greek word ἀνέβησαν [*anebēsan*] as "they ascended." (As Aune points out, "In Israelite and early Jewish idiom, people always went *up* (never *down*) to Jerusalem" (Aune, *Revelation 17–22*, 1096; emphasis in the original); e.g., Ps 122:4; Isa 2:3. But this is normally in the sense of pilgrimage, whereas here the nations are coming up to besiege the city.

51. Koester, *Revelation*, 779, 789–90; cf. Aune, *Revelation 17–22*, 1097–99; Beale, *Book of Revelation*, 1026–27.

52. Cf. Leithart, *Revelation 12–22*, 327.

53. Cf. Aune, *Revelation 17–22*, 1099. Fire has been used by both sides in the struggle narrated

The fire coming down and devouring the hordes of Satan may indicate that this is the time of the *Parousia, after* the thousand years. Jesus' second coming is associated with fires of judgment and leads into the final judgment in Matthew 25:31–46; 2 Peter 3:4–10; and 2 Thessalonians 1:7–10.[54]

> **And the devil who deceived them was thrown into the lake of fire and sulfur, where also the wild beast and the false prophet (were), and they will be tormented day and night forever and ever. (Rev 20:10)**

There is a general chiastic structure here in that the enemies appear in the order Satan/Dragon, Beast and False Prophet, and finally Babylon. They are removed in reverse order: Babylon, Beast and False Prophet, and lastly Satan/Dragon.[55] At last, the devil is permanently off the scene, having begun in heaven, been thrown down to earth, imprisoned in the abyss, released again onto the earth, and now thrown into the "lake of fire and sulfur." This is the end of the main plot.[56] No more devilish deception can occur, which implies that no one can hide from God's truth. The language of everlasting torment recalls the punishment for all who followed the beast in 14:10–11.[57] If this punishment seems excessive, remember that the devil had been imprisoned for a thousand years without repenting, and was responsible for huge amounts of suffering in his vain attempt to overthrow God's kingdom. Remember also Hitler, Stalin, and other dictators of the twentieth century who also never repented of the evil things they did and the huge death toll they caused.

20:11–15 The Final Judgment

The major enemies of God have been defeated and destroyed or thrown into the "lake of fire and sulfur." There remains one more step to close the age and prepare the way for the new world order.

> **And I saw a great white throne and the one sitting on it, from whose presence the earth and heaven fled, and no place was found for them. (Rev 20:11)**

---

in Revelation. Fire is hurled onto the earth in the trumpet series (8:5, 7, 8, 10); it comes out of the mouths of the two prophetic witnesses and "devours their enemies" (11:5); the second beast causes fire to come down from heaven like Elijah (13:13); "fire and sulfur" is the source of the torment of those who follow the beast (14:9; cf. 19:20; 20:10, 15); the beast and ten horns burn the prostitute Babylon with fire (17:16; 18:8).

54. Moloney sees this rather as the time of Jesus' death and resurrection, his final victory over Satan, perhaps influenced by John 12:31 (Moloney, *Apocalypse of John*, 311–314).

55. Cf. Koester, *Revelation*, 750.

56. Some commentators suggest that the ongoing existence of the devil and the beasts, albeit in the lake of fire, implies that evil is still a possibility (e.g., Moloney, *Apocalypse of John*, 322–323). But the language of final judgment and new creation militates agsinst this view.

57. Cf. Thomas, *Apocalypse*, 611–13; Koester, *Revelation*, 790; Beale, *Book of Revelation*, 1028–31. As Beale points out, this is not a physical place and not a physical torment since Satan and Death and Hades are not physical beings (ibid., 1036).

Hearers in the seven churches already understand that God is known by his throne. This was the first thing John saw when he journeyed to heaven "in the Spirit" (4:2), and God is often described as "the one sitting on the throne" (4:9, 10; 5:13; 6:16). God's throne is the place of Jesus' glorification (3:21), of endless worship in heaven (4:6–11), of celebration for the redeemed (7:9–12; 14:3), of final comfort for the sufferers (7:15–17), and of altar prayer (8:3). But this throne seems different, partly because of what it now signifies as a throne of judgment, though its color shows that such judgment will be holy and righteous.[58]

The statement about the earth and heavens fleeing from God's presence conveys a sense of awe, even literal fear. Nothing can stand before God, though this does not literally mean earth and heaven cease to exist.[59] For the audience, it might recall the scene at the sixth seal, when people called on mountains and rocks to fall on them and hide them "from the face the one sitting on the throne" (6:16). Or they may think of the climax of the ascending judgments in Amos 4, with its regular refrain "yet you have not returned to me" (Amos 4:6, 8, 9, 10, 11), and finally the ominous warning, "prepare to meet your God" (Amos 4:12).

> **And I saw the dead, the great and the small, standing before the throne. And books were opened, and another book was opened, which is (the book) of life, and the dead were judged out of what was written in the books according to their works. (Rev 20:12)**

This is the general resurrection predicted in verse 5: the living are not mentioned,[60] and it involves all kinds of people, as implied by the phrase "the great and the small."[61] This is a somber scene which was no doubt meant to instill fear, or at least serious reflection, in the hearers. The opening of the books, recalling Daniel 7:10,[62] adds to a sense of suspense. Books or scrolls are very significant in Revelation. The whole book is a written text commissioned for the seven churches (1:11, 19), and the larger narrative begins with the sealed scroll being opened by the Lamb (Rev 5–6). Moreover, the second commissioning of John includes the eating of a little scroll (10:2, 8–11), and "the book of life" serves to divide people into two categories with enormous consequences (3:5; 13:8; 17:8; 21:27; compare Dan 12:1).[63]

As Koester notes, "the context suggests that both the righteous and the unrighteous now stand before God,"[64] which is in tension with a physical "first resurrection"

---

58. Cf. Thomas, *Apocalypse*, 613; Koester, *Revelation*, 779; Aune, *Revelation 17–22*, 1100.

59. The audience might also recall Dan 2:35, which states that the world's empires will be swept away without trace when God's kingdom comes. Cf. Moyise, *Old Testament in the Book of Revelation*, 48.

60. Aune, *Revelation 17–22*, 1101.

61. Cf. Thomas, *Apocalypse*, 615; Leithart, *Revelation 12–22*, 331.

62. And possibly it also recalls other Jewish apocalypses (Aune, *Revelation 17–22*, 1102).

63. Cf. Koester, *Revelation*, 780.

64. Koester, *Revelation*, 791.

earlier. In this case, the books record the deeds ("works") of every person. The judgment is not based on opinion but on recorded evidence.[65] Koester helpfully identifies "two complementary dimensions of justice" in this passage: first, "a just God will not allow evil to continue afflicting the vulnerable"; and second, "human accountability."[66]

> **And the sea gave up the dead that (were) in it, and Death and Hades gave up the dead that (were) in them, and each (person) was judged according to their works. (Rev 20:13)**

No one is left out, even those whose bodies were in irretrievable locations.[67] As Thomas writes, "standing before the throne is inevitable, a fate from which nothing or no one is able to deliver."[68] The basis of judgment "according to their works" is repeated for emphasis.

> **And Death and Hades were thrown into the lake of fire. This is the second death, the lake of fire. And if any were not found written in the book of life, they were thrown into the lake of fire. (Rev 20:14–15)**

These two terms (Death and Hades) serve to sum up the location or state of the dead and Jesus says, "I have the keys of death and Hades" (1:18). They work together to kill a fourth of the earth in the fourth seal (6:7–8). Here they are personified in a way Greeks would relate to, since they saw them as gods, Thanatos and Hades.[69] Now they are destroyed, a very significant moment in the story.[70]

But instead there is "the lake of fire" which is "the second death," referred to earlier in relation to the first resurrection (v. 6). Moreover, "if any were not found written in the book of life, they were thrown into the lake of fire" (v. 15),[71] joining the beasts (19:20), the devil (v. 10), and "Death and Hades" (v. 14). Judgment has a twofold basis

---

65. Cf. Thomas, *Apocalypse*, 616; Koester, *Revelation*, 780, 791. Beale, however, claims that "the record books are metaphorical for God's unfailing memory" (Beale, *Book of Revelation*, 1033).

66. Koester, *Revelation*, 782.

67. Bauckham shows that such ideas related to final resurrection, including the giving back of the dead by the locations of their bodies, were common in first-century Judaism (Bauckham, *Climax of Prophecy*, 56–70). Aune refers to popular ideas among Greeks, Romans, and others "that the souls of those who die at sea did not enter Hades but remained where they died in the water" (Aune, *Revelation 17–22*, 1103). Cf. Beale, *Book of Revelation*, 1034.

68. Thomas, *Apocalypse*, 615.

69. Perhaps they are viewed as "actual Satanic forces" governing the region of the dead (Beale, *Book of Revelation*, 1035). Or simply "'Death and Hades' here stand for all the unrighteous dead" (Aune, *Revelation 17–22*, 1103).

70. Cf. Koester, *Revelation*, 781, 792.

71. Cf. Koester, *Revelation*, 781; Leithart, *Revelation 12–22*, 332–35. Other Jewish texts (Targums on Isa 65:5–6 and Jer 51:40, 57, respectively) "identify the second death with the fires of Gehenna," and it "deprives a person of life in the age to come" (Koester, *Revelation*, 781). See also Isa 66:24, a verse referred to several times by Jesus in the Gospels (e.g., Mark 9:48). Papandrea suggests that people may possibly be purified in the lake of fire and then released, which makes it function more as a kind of purgatory (Papandrea, *Wedding of the Lamb*, 59, n. 9). But the text gives us no hint of this.

then: the record of a person's life and deeds, and whether or not their name is in the book of life. While the evidence in the books of people's deeds may show relative goodness or evil, the book of life gives a clear cut "black or white" verdict.[72] The text of Revelation displays a rigid binary approach to salvation as symbolized by this book.

No doubt this has a clear rhetorical purpose to challenge the hearers to ask themselves, "Is my name in the book of life?" Clearly, not all church members are in the book; in fact, according to Revelation, it is possible to have your name erased from it (3:5). Clearly, there is no room for compromise because only those whose names are there will resist the beast (13:8; 17:8). This adds an element of predestination.[73] So Christians listening to this text read aloud are invited to self-examination and challenged to total commitment without compromise with the surrounding culture, one of the key purposes of the whole book. The consequences of not having one's name in that book are unthinkable. No doubt the oral reader in each church emphasized such statements and perhaps paused to let the warning sink in. On the other hand, these words would offer strong comfort to those who were staying faithful at the risk of death.[74]

---

72. Leithart suggests that "The two books perhaps signify the relation of grace and works" (Leithart, *Revelation 12–22*, 332).

73. Cf. Koester, *Revelation*, 791.

74. Cf. Thomas, *Apocalypse*, 618; Koester, *Revelation*, 791–93.

Revelation Chapter 21

God has been dealing decisively with his enemies in Revelation 17–20. Babylon is no more. The beasts and allied kings have been destroyed. The devil has finally been thrown into the lake of fire, and so have all those throughout human history whose names were not found written in the Lamb's book of life. Human civilization as we have known it (or as the original audience had known it) has been overthrown, it seems. Death and Hades have also been removed. As Fekkes argues, "the elimination of everything which threatens the messianic community and stands in opposition to the divine Creator is a necessary prerequisite to the uniting of the heavenly and earthly communities and the universal establishment of God's kingdom."[1] So what will that kingdom look like?

21:1–8 A New World Order

> **And I saw a new heaven and new earth. For the first heaven and the first earth went away, and the sea is no longer. (Rev 21:1)**

This statement stands in contrast to Genesis 1:1–2, where "God created the heavens and the earth" and water was a prime element of the original creation, albeit one that had to be restrained and limited (Gen 1:6–10; see also Pss 104:6–9; 33:7; Jer 5:22). Water was then part of God's first major cataclysmic judgment in the flood, after which he promised there would be no such sea event again (Gen 9:11–16). The crossing of the Red Sea by Israel was a parallel divine event (Exod 14–15), an exodus prefiguring a future salvation in Isaiah (Isa 43:2), even amounting to a "new creation."[2] In Revelation, the sea has become associated with evil, as it is the place from which the wild beast emerges (13:1) and represents the pagan nations ruled by the prostitute (17:15),[3] as well as "the range of afflictions that formerly threatened God's people in the old world."[4]

---

1. Fekkes, *Prophetic Traditions*, 227.
2. Cf. Dumbrell, *End of the Beginning*, 170.
3. Cf. Koester, *Revelation*, 795–96, 803; Beale, *Book of Revelation*, 1042–43.
4. Beale, *Book of Revelation*, 1043; see also 1050–51.

John is also quoting Isaiah 65:17, in which God says, "See, I will create new heavens and a new earth" and then, "The former things will not be remembered." So there is a strong emphasis on the newness of this (Greek *kainos*), though it doesn't necessarily mean that existing realities are destroyed. In the same way, when believers get their new names and identities, their existing nature is not destroyed (2:17; 3:12). Yes, "the first heaven and the first earth went away," but this is probably a way of emphasizing that a radical change is happening. It does not indicate that an absolute cosmological replacement has taken place. It is a renovation as opposed to a replacement—transformation not destruction.[5]

In Isaiah 65 this new world order involves a new Jerusalem (vv. 18–19), increased longevity (v. 20), permanent security, blessing for God's people (vv. 21–24), and an end to the struggle and violence. Indeed "'the wolf and the lamb will feed together, and the lion will eat straw like the ox, and dust will be the serpent's food. They will neither harm nor destroy on all my holy mountain,' says the LORD" (Isa 65:25; compare Isa 11:6–9). And this is a permanent change, according to Isaiah 66:22.[6]

And I saw the holy city, new Jerusalem, coming down out of heaven from God, prepared a bride adorned for her husband. (Rev 21:2)

Isaiah often speaks of a renewed Jerusalem after its destruction:

> Burst into songs of joy together,
> you ruins of Jerusalem,
> for the LORD has comforted his people,
> he has redeemed Jerusalem. (Isa 52:9)

> For Zion's sake I will not keep silent,
> for Jerusalem's sake I will not remain quiet,
> till her vindication shines out like the dawn . . .
> and give him no rest till he establishes Jerusalem
> and makes her the praise of the earth. (Isa 62:1, 7)

> I will create Jerusalem to be a delight
> and its people a joy.

---

5. Cf. Koester, *Revelation*, 794–95, 803; Beale, *Book of Revelation*, 1040–41; Faber, "Revelation 21:1–8," 297; Fekkes, *Isaiah and Prophetic Traditions*, 229; contra Dumbrell, *End of the Beginning*, 167. See Rom 8:19–21; Isa 13:9–13; 51:6; 66:15–16; Jer 4:23–28; Zeph 1:2–3, 18; Matt 19:28; Mark 13:31; Luke 21:25–26; 2 Pet 3:7–13. Thomas suggests that this is a radical new order, based partly on 20:11, implying *more* discontinuity than I am suggesting (Thomas, *Apocalypse*, 619–20). Some continuity seems to be implied with the continued existence of nations and kings (Rev 21:24, 26), and indeed people (21:3). However, it is difficult to be certain here as we cannot fully grasp the vision that John received. See the lengthy discussion of ancient texts in Aune, *Revelation 17-22*, 1117–20.

6. Similar wording is found in 1 Enoch 91:16 (cf. Aune, *Revelation 17-22*, 1116).

> I will rejoice over Jerusalem
>
> and take delight in my people;
>
> the sound of weeping and of crying
>
> will be heard in it no more. (Isa 65:18b–19)

John's audience might also recall the extended prophecy of Isaiah 54 about "the barren woman" (v. 1) and "afflicted city" (v. 11) that would be restored and rebuilt. Much of Revelation 21 draws its imagery from this chapter in Isaiah, especially the ideas of romance (vv. 1, 4–8) and jewels (vv. 11–12). Similar ideas are found in Isaiah 49:14–21. The difference in Revelation 21 is that the new Jerusalem is not the restored city of Nehemiah, also called "the holy city" (Neh 11:1), but comes down "out of heaven."[7] If Revelation was written well after the year AD 70, when the city was destroyed by the Romans, there would be a comforting sense of replacement here. Earthly Jerusalem has been destroyed, but a new Jerusalem is coming down from heaven![8]

The "coming" is a present active participle, suggesting that it was already in process as John wrote. As Rudolph Faber puts it, "The assurance in Revelation is that *more* than something *has* been done; it is *being* done and it *will* be done."[9] Isaiah was looking for a second exodus and a restored Israel and Jerusalem; his prophecy is far surpassed in John's vision.[10]

This new Jerusalem also recalls the romance ideas of 19:7–9, which spoke of the forthcoming "wedding of the Lamb." Hence, the bride of the Lamb is equated with the city "adorned for her husband" (v. 2).[11] And thus, she is "prepared" (Greek *hētoimasmenēn*, perfect passive participle of *hetoimazō*, "prepare, make ready") and "adorned" (Greek (*kekosmēmenēn*).[12] There is a preparation process implied here: the trials and sufferings of the church have helped prepare her for this day, especially if she has responded with "righteous deeds" (19:8). Beale proposes that "the purpose of this last major segment is to highlight the contrast between the church imperfect (chs. 1–3) and the church perfected . . . to exhort believers in the present to persevere through temptations to compromise, so that they might participate in the consummated glory of the church."[13]

---

7. Cf. Koester, *Revelation*, 804; Thomas, *Apocalypse*, 621–22. As Leithart maintains, God's goal is to bring heaven to earth, not to bring saints to heaven (Leithart, *Revelation 12–22*, 279).

8. Judea is portrayed as a captive woman in coins minted under the Roman emperor after AD 70, emphasizing the shame and defeat the Jews had suffered (Aune, *Revelation 17–22*, 1122).

9. Faber, "Revelation 21:1–8," 297; emphasis in the original.

10. Cf. Leithart, *Revelation 12–22*, 342.

11. Cf. Koester, *Revelation*, 804; Leithart, *Revelation 12–22*, 383–85.

12. Note in the Greek word the origin of the English "cosmetic." There is also an etymological link with *kosmos* [world order, universe]. Maybe this signifies that the new city is prepared and adorned, not only for her husband, but also for life on the new earth.

13. Beale, *Book of Revelation*, 1039, 1045; cf. Eph 5:25–27, where Paul speaks of Christ having "loved the church" and given himself up for her "to make her holy and to present her to himself as a radiant church without stain or wrinkle or any other blemish . . . "

> **And I heard a loud voice from the throne,[14] saying, "Behold the dwelling place of God (is) with humanity, and he will dwell with them, and they will be his peoples, and God himself will be with them [(and be) their God] ... " (Rev 21:3)**

There are two different Greek words for "people" in this verse: first, *tōn anthrōpōn,* a general reference to humanity; and later, *laoi autou,* which means literally "his peoples," using the word more often used for Israel in the singular. Together these words make the claim that humans in general may now be considered as God's peoples.[15] "This is the covenant at its very relational heart," says Mazzaferi,[16] but God's covenant is no longer restricted to Israel; he is willing to dwell with all peoples and be their God (see Zech 2:11; Gen 12:3).[17] Of course, as Faber reminds us, this is through "the adventing Bride-Church" as verse 2 implies.[18]

Many in the audience would be reminded of similar promises to Israel in the Old Testament, such as Leviticus 26:11–12 ("I will put my dwelling place among you, and I will not abhor you. I will walk among you and be your God, and you will be my people"), Jeremiah 32:38, and Ezekiel 37:27; 43:7. This is not just about God's presence: for God to be "with" people and "be their God" suggests enjoyment of God's favor and protection. He will answer their prayers and give them victory (see Gen 21:22; 31:5; Deut 7:21; Josh 1:5; 1 Sam 16:18; 1 Chr 22:18).[19] The dwelling language (Greek *skēnē,* "tent"; and *skēnōsei,* the plural of pitching a tent) also echoes John 1:14 ("the Word became flesh and made his dwelling among us"), though not all of the original audience would have made this connection. Nevertheless, the bold statement of this verse represents a major breakthrough in the narrative,[20] with implications of unity between God and humanity and romantic overtones.[21]

> **" ... and he will wipe away every tear from their eyes, and there will be no more death nor sorrow nor crying nor pain any longer, [for] the first (things) have gone away." (Rev 21:4)**

This statement echoes 7:17, where the Lamb acts as shepherd of the redeemed and "God will wipe away every tear from their eyes." God's people have suffered sorrow and pain, sometimes as punishment for their sins (though this has not been the primary emphasis in Revelation), but those days are now gone, and they are comforted

---

14. Cf. Koester, *Revelation,* 797; Thomas, *Apocalypse,* 622–23.

15. As Mayo puts it, "John changes the singular 'people' (λαός; Ezek 37.27; cf. Jer 11.4; 31.33) of the OT prophetic tradition to "peoples" (λαοί), reflecting his own universal perception of the people of God" (Mayo, *Those Who Call Themselves Jews,* 171).

16. Mazzaferi, *Genre of the Book of Revelation,* 367.

17. Cf. Koester, *Revelation,* 798, 805; Thomas, *Apocalypse,* 623–24; Beale, *Book of Revelation,* 1046–48; Bauckham, *Climax of Prophecy,* 310–13; Pattemore, *People of God,* 201.

18. Faber, "Revelation 21:1–8," 299.

19. Cf. Aune, *Revelation 17–22,* 1123–24.

20. Cf. Bauckham, *Climax of Prophecy,* 310–13; Koester, *Revelation,* 805–6.

21. Cf. Leithart, *Revelation 12–22,* 350–351.

by God himself. But bigger transformations are in view with the end of death and sorrow and the passing of "the old order of things."[22] Once again the listeners' minds are sent back to Isaiah, this time to Isaiah 25:8, which declares:

> he will swallow up death forever.
> The sovereign LORD will wipe away the tears
> from all faces.

Significantly in Isaiah 25, God will do this "in this mountain" (vv. 6, 7), and it is promised for "all peoples" (vv. 6, 7). The hearers might also think of Isaiah 43:18–19, where God is said to be doing "a new thing" and the people are urged to "forget the former things." Isaiah 35:10 and 51:11 both speak of the Israelites enjoying such gladness that "sorrow and sighing will flee away."[23] No wonder that John says "the first things [Greek *prōta*, "first, foremost, former"] have gone away," alluding to Isaiah 65:17, which says, "the former things will not be remembered."[24]

A wonderful new age is dawning, without all the causes of human suffering or misery.[25] The new order far surpasses the old order of creation and the old covenant. As Dumbrell suggests, John is describing a new Jerusalem, a new temple, a new covenant, a new Israel, and a new creation in these verses.[26] Thus, God's program for restoration of Israel and reconciliation of the world is coming to its fulfillment. The age of glory is in the future,[27] especially with the elimination of death, the enemy that entered with sin (Gen 2:17; 3:19; see also Rom 5:12–14; 1 Cor 15:26).[28] However, some of it can be experienced now.

And the one sitting on the throne said, "Behold I am making everything new," and he said, "Write, for these words (are) faithful and true." (Rev 21:5)[29]

This is the first clear time God himself has spoken directly since 1:8, this time from his throne. It is thus underlined as an emphatic and unambiguous declaration, almost amounting to an oath.[30] The Creator himself (see 4:11) is even now (the verb is present

---

22. Thomas observes that "these words describe the intimate relationship with God in the New Creation by what is missing," just as he said the sea is gone (Thomas, *Apocalypse*, 624–25).

23. As Beale explains, this is all part of Isaiah's "new exodus" theme, a major idea for Revelation (Beale, *Book of Revelation*, 1049).

24. Cf. Fekkes, *Isaiah and Prophetic Traditions*, 256–58.

25. Cf. Aune, *Revelation 17–22*, 1124–25.

26. Dumbrell, *End of the Beginning*.

27. Cf. Leithart, *Revelation 12–22*, 343–44.

28. See discussion about the original creation and the future new creation in Leithart, *Revelation 12–22*, 348–50.

29. There is a chiastic arrangement in verses 1–5 which occurs when elements are stated in one order then in the reverse order, to highlight the central point: "new" (vv. 1, 5); "first . . . passed away" (vv. 1, 4); "no longer/more" (vv. 1, 4); so the central point is verses 2–3 (Aune, *Revelation 17–22*, 1113–14).

30. Cf. Beale, *Book of Revelation*, 1053.

tense)³¹ recreating or renewing his whole creation, and ensuring that this promise is recorded!³² This is also the final time John is commanded to write what he sees or hears (compare 1:11, 19; 2:1; 14:13; 19:9, etc.).³³ Clearly, the narrative is nearly completed.

And he said to me, "They are done. I (am) the Alpha and the Omega, the Beginning and the End." (Rev 21:6a)

The finality of his action is shown in the Greek *gegonan*—the perfect active indicative of *ginomai*, "become"—in the third person plural,³⁴ suggesting that all of God's plans have now been completed.³⁵ A loud voice had made a similar declaration in 16:17 when the seventh bowl was poured out. Only God can make such an emphatic statement. And it is followed by names that apply to God alone, also recalling similar phrasing in 1:8³⁶ and underlining the sovereignty of God over all history so that his promises will certainly be fulfilled.³⁷

"To the one who is thirsty I will give from the spring of the water of life (as a) free gift." (Rev 21:6b)

Careful listeners would note that the timing has changed from the future (vv. 3–4) to the present (vv. 5–6). This does not annul the future eschatological orientation of the passage, emphasized by the strong declarations of verses 1 and 4 in particular, but it does modify it. The possibility is opened that the "thirsty" may be able to drink that "water of life" even now.³⁸ Certainly, many hearers would be reminded of another passage in Isaiah 55, which begins,

> Come, all you who are thirsty,
>
> come to the waters; and you who have no money,
>
> come buy and eat!
>
> Come, buy wine and milk
>
> without money and without cost. (Isa 55:1)³⁹

---

31. Contra Beale, *Book of Revelation*, 1052–54, who views this as a "prophetic present" speaking of a future reality. However, Beale concedes elsewhere that this renewal has already begun, as taught by Paul (ibid., 1052).

32. Cf. Koester, *Revelation*, 807; Thomas, *Apocalypse*, 626.

33. Cf. Paul, *Revelation*, 343–44. Paul sees this as implying equality with Scripture.

34. So Koester translates "All is done" (Koester, *Revelation*, 799) and Thomas translates "They are completed" (Thomas, *Apocalypse*, 627).

35. Cf. Beale, *Book of Revelation*, 1054–55; Fekkes, *Isaiah and Prophetic Traditions*, 93–94.

36. Cf. Koester, *Revelation*, 799; Thomas, *Apocalypse*, 628.

37. Beale, *Book of Revelation*, 1055; see also Leithart, *Revelation 12–22*, 352–53.

38. Cf. Fekkes, *Isaiah and Prophetic Traditions*, 262–64. Fekkes sees this as a future promise only made to "conquerors," but that of 22:17 as available now to interested unbelievers. I see both promises as available now both to new converts seeking eternal life (cf. Rom 6:23) and to believers seeking more of God's Spirit.

39. Cf. Fekkes, *Isaiah and Prophetic Traditions*, 260–261.

In this Isaianic passage, this transaction is explained largely in terms of listening to God's word (vv. 2–3, 10–11), and embracing the messianic covenant (vv. 3–4). But other passages in Isaiah suggest a link with the Holy Spirit, for example Isaiah 44:3.

> For I will pour water on the thirsty land,
>
> and streams on the dry ground;
>
> I will pour out my Spirit on your offspring,
>
> and my blessing on your descendants. (See also Isa 41:17–18; 43:20; 49:10.)

Any hearers in the seven churches who were acquainted with the Fourth Gospel would also think of John 4:14 and 7:37–39, where living water refers both to eternal life and the gift of the Spirit.[40] If they were acquainted with Paul's letters, they might recall that he saw the coming of the Spirit as a foretaste of heaven (2 Cor 1:22; 5:5; Eph 1:13–14).

"Those who conquer will inherit these (things), and (I) will be God to them and they will be sons[41] to me." (Rev 21:7)

The phrase "those who conquer" would remind the hearers of the repeated promises to the churches in Revelation 2–3, where the victorious believers ("overcomers" or "conquerors") are singled out for eschatological rewards. These rewards include privileges such as the right "to eat from the tree of life" (2:7), exemption from the second death (2:11), portions of hidden manna, a secret new name (2:17), "authority over the nations," and the possession of the "morning star" (2:26, 28). Others were promised white robes, acknowledgment before the Father (3:5), permanently being present in God's temple, eschatological names (3:12), and a share in Christ's throne (3:21).

While some of these promises are special in nature, most of them simply relate to eschatological salvation: inclusion in the final blessings of the new order.[42] This is underlined by the rest of verse 7, where God promises that they will inherit all this and be his sons. This is covenantal language similar to verse 3, but using inheritance language as opposed to marital imagery.[43]

---

40. Cf. Aune, *Revelation 17–22*, 1127–29.

41. These words are singular in the Greek; I have used the plural for gender inclusive purposes but refrained from adding "or daughters" or translating "children" because this would obscure the inheritance language status implied here in the context of patrilineal inheritance.

42. Cf. Koester, *Revelation*, 808; Leithart, *Revelation 12–22*, 365–66.

43. Cf. Aune, *Revelation 17–22*, 1129–30; Koester, *Revelation*, 808; Thomas, *Apocalypse*, 629; Beale, *Book of Revelation*, 1057; Leithart, *Revelation 12–22*, 353–54. These scholars all see an echo of God's promise to David about his descendants (2 Sam 7:14). This is also the first time Revelation has envisaged God as the Father of believers as opposed to Jesus, using the Greek term υἱός [*huios*], "son"; Thomas points out that such language is absent in all the other Johannine literature (Thomas, *Apocalypse*, 629), though I think it is implied in John 1:12. It implies a very intimate relationship and standing with God in Christ as the unique son of God.

> "But to the cowardly and unbelieving and detestable and murderers and sexually immoral and sorcerers and idolaters and all liars, their part (is) in the lake that burns with fire and sulfur, which is the second death." (Rev 21:8)

The binary oppositions are stark: in the end, there are only two kinds of people and two destinies. It is a case of the name of Jesus or the name of the beast, Christian or idolater, life or death, salvation or damnation, inheriting God's new order or being consigned to the lake of fire.[44] Thus, John forces the hearer or reader to choose. He emphatically denies any possibility of compromise or a middle way or third alternative. He consistently opposes any Christianity that is less than fervent or white hot or that tolerates the ways of the surrounding Greco-Roman culture (or any worldly culture).

The list of sinners here recalls 9:20–21, which lists the sins that the recalcitrant survivors of the trumpet plagues had committed. Some of the items describe common Greco-Roman practices such as idolatry, sorcery/magic, and sexual immorality.[45] Others might describe specific dangers for Christians, such as cowardice.[46] There are also parallels with the Ten Commandments, though they are not complete.[47] The use of nouns describing the persons, rather than their practices, suggest that these people are defined by their dominating sins. The description of their fate—"the lake that burns with fire and sulfur" also known as "the second death"—reiterates the language of 2:11; 14:10–11; 19:20; 20:6, 10, 14, 15.

21:9–27 The Holy City New Jerusalem

> And one of the seven angels who had the seven bowls filled with the seven last plagues came and spoke with me, saying, "Come, I will show you the bride, the wife of the Lamb." (Rev 21:9)

After God's speech finishes, the angelic guidance resumes. There is a strong emphasis on "seven" here which is repeated twice. This angel had come out of the temple (15:6), received a bowl from one of the four living creatures (15:7), and poured out his bowl onto the earth with disastrous consequences for the recalcitrant sinners (Rev 16). This must have been difficult work; now he has the privilege of guiding John around the glorious new Jerusalem, contrasting the plagues inflicted in Revelation 16 with "the city that offers healing."[48] The romance language is resumed (from 21:2 and 19:7–9);

---

44. Cf. Thomas, *Apocalypse*, 633; Leithart, *Revelation 12–22*, 354–55.

45. Cf. Beale, *Book of Revelation*, 1059–60. However, some pagan groups had similar moral standards to Revelation as seen in an inscription in ancient Philadelphia (Aune, *Revelation 17–22*, 1132).

46. Cf. Thomas, *Apocalypse*, 630–33; Beale, *Book of Revelation*, 1059–60. Koester points out that cowardice was mainly a sin for soldiers, which is very relevant here since John constantly envisages believers in a spiritual war where a lack of commitment would be fatal (Koester, *Revelation*, 800–801, 809).

47. Cf. Aune, *Revelation 17–22*, 1131.

48. Koester, *Revelation*, 811.

John is about to see "the bride [*numphēn*], the wife [*gunaika*] of the Lamb" (see Isa 54:5; Hos 2:19–20). This is a key image for the rest of this chapter[49] and represents the theological climax of Revelation.[50]

> **And he carried me away "in the Spirit" to a great and high mountain, and showed me the holy city Jerusalem coming down out of heaven from God . . . (Rev 21:10)**[51]

John had had a similar experience in chapter 17. The parallels between the two passages are very close:[52]

Revelation 17–19	Revelation 21–22
One of the seven angels who had the seven bowls came and spoke with me (17:1)	*one of the seven angels who had the seven bowls filled with the seven last plagues came and spoke with me* (21:9)
"Come here, I will show you the judgment of the great prostitute sitting upon many waters, with whom the kings of the earth committed sexual immorality" (17:1, 2)	*"Come, I will show you* the bride, the wife of the Lamb" (21:9)
And he carried me away "in the Spirit" into a desert" (17:3)	*And he carried me "in the Spirit"* to a great and high mountain (21:10)
And I saw a woman sitting on a scarlet wild beast, covered with blasphemous names (17:3)	and showed me the holy city Jerusalem coming down out of heaven from God (21:10)
Lamentation and celebration of her destruction (18:1—19:3)	Celebration of her construction (21:10–27)
And I fell down before his feet to worship him. And he said to me, "Don't do that! I am a fellow slave of you and of your brothers who have the testimony of Jesus. Worship God." (19:10).	*I fell down to worship before the feet of the angel who was showing them to me. And he said to me, "Don't do that! I am a fellow slave with you and your brothers the prophets and those keep the words of this book. Worship God."* (22:8–9)

---

49. Cf. Koester, *Revelation*, 811–12; Thomas, *Apocalypse*, 635–36.

50. Cf. Leithart, *Revelation 12–22*, 365.

51. Beale points out the parallel of hearing and seeing, where the second interprets the first, here (bride-city) and in Rev 5:5–6 (lion-lamb) (Beale, *Book of Revelation*, 1063). However, perhaps the first image interprets the second, too. Leithart asks why there are *two* descents of the new Jerusalem (vv. 2 and 10) and concludes that John is actually describing two stages in its history; the new vision in verses 9–26 takes the reader back to the millennium (i.e., now) because of its reference to nations outside the city (Leithart, *Revelation 12–22*, 338–40, 357–62).

52. For more extended parallels between 17:1—19:10 and 21:9—22:9, see the chart in Aune, *Revelation 17–22*, 1144–45. Aune explains this in terms of a process of editing by the final redactor (ibid., 1146). Cf. Beale, *Book of Revelation*, 1117–19; Mayo, *Those Who Call Themselves Jews*, 172. Leithart explains the parallel as a feature of Revelation's plot: both cities are Jerusalem—unfaithful Jerusalem doomed to destruction versus new Jerusalem during the millennium (Leithart, *Revelation 12–22*, 363–65). Cf. Filho, "Apocalypse of John," 226–29. Some other interpreters see the woman figure in Revelation 12 continuing and changing: she is first Israel (or original humanity), then the prostitute (having allied herself with Empire) and finally the bride of the Lamb. Cf. Moloney, *Apocalypse of John*, 268–270, 319, 327–328.

Both scenes begin with one of the bowl angels who says he will show John a specified woman, and then carries him away "in the Spirit" (Greek *en pneumati*), recalling the previous instances where John is "in the Spirit" and sees important things (1:10; 4:2).[53] The parallels between the two scenes serve to highlight the contrast between them.[54] The location of the visions is different: a wilderness versus a high mountain. The high mountain would remind many listeners of Ezekiel's final vision, which is an important background throughout this section of Revelation. "In visions of God he took me to the land of Israel and set me on a very high mountain" (Ezek 40:2; see also Exod 24:12–18).[55]

But more importantly, the women are direct opposites: a prostitute as against a bride-wife. Sexual language is in the forefront. Clearly, John is showing the illegitimacy of the relationship in the first case as opposed to the holiness of the second. Moreover, both women represent cities: "the woman which you see is the great city which has dominion over the kingdoms of the earth" (17:18), and the bride is "the holy city Jerusalem" (21:10). Rome is contrasted with Jerusalem, but not just the historic cities. It is Rome as the imperial city, the archetype Babylon, the anti-God culture or force contrasted with the new, heavenly Jerusalem (as opposed to the Jerusalem of Rev 11), the holy city, the city of God, and the bride of the Lamb.[56]

Beale argues that neither image should be taken literally: there was no literal prostitute in Revelation 17, and there is no literal city here.[57] This is partly true, but there *was* a literal city in Revelation 17, even though it had a bigger significance, and there may be a literal new Jerusalem even though some of the language is imagery, not literal description. Whereas in 19:7–9 the focus was on the people, "the saints" and those invited to the wedding, now the focus is on the city represented as a bride.

But both the opposing symbols would gather up the citizens of both cities as well as the force or culture they stand for.[58] As Koester puts it, "Cities have been a major motif in Revelation," beginning with the seven cities whose churches are the primary audience and continuing with the impact of "the great city" (11:8; 17:1—18:24) as opposed to "the holy city" (11:2), "the beloved city" (20:9), and now climaxing in the ultimate holy city and bride (21:2, 10).[59] The holy city is described as "coming down out of heaven from God" (v. 10), which suggests its divine origin, its pre-existence in heaven (compare Gal 4:26), and its process of "coming down." This may even imply

---

53. Cf. Beale, *Book of Revelation*, 1065. See Thomas, *Apocalypse*, 636, for a discussion of what the audience might expect when they heard the Greek *en pneumati* [ἐν πνεύματι].

54. Cf. Beale, *Book of Revelation*, 1064.

55. Cf. Beale, *Book of Revelation*, 1061, 1065; Thomas, *Apocalypse*, 636–37; Mayo, *Those Who Call Themselves Jews*, 177–78. Listeners familiar with the traditions behind Matthew and Luke might also recall Jesus' transfiguration on a mountain (Matt 17:1–2; Mark 9:2–3; Luke 9:28–29) and his temptation on a high mountain (Matt 4:8; Luke 4:5). Cf. Aune, *Revelation 17–22*, 1152.

56. Cf. Koester, *Revelation*, 827–28.

57. Beale, *Book of Revelation*, 1064–65.

58. See discussion in Koester, *Revelation*, 683.

59. Cf. Koester, *Revelation*, 826.

that the city is already coming down spiritually, as the author of Hebrews perhaps thought (Heb 12:22).[60]

> ... which had the glory of God, her radiance like a precious stone, like jasper and crystal. (Rev 21:11)[61]

This imagery might recall aspects of the throne room of God in 4:3 and 6. In particular, it causes us to remember that God was "in appearance like jasper stone and carnelian" (4:3). Now the city has God's glory and is like jasper. There is also an allusion to Ezekiel 43:2, which introduces the post-exilic return of God's glory to the new land and temple so that "the land was radiant with his glory."[62] God and his throne have come down to earth as verse 3 suggested: "the dwelling place of God is with humanity" or "the peoples."

> It had a great and high wall, (which) had twelve gates and at the gates twelve angels, and names written, which are [the names of] the twelve tribes of Israel's sons; on the east three gates, and on the north three gates and on the south three gates and on the west three gates. And the wall of the city had twelve foundation (stones) and on them twelve names of the apostles of the Lamb. (Rev 21:12-14)

Every ancient city would have a high wall with foundations and gates; it was shameful for a city's walls to be broken down, as Nehemiah declared (Neh 1:3; 2:3, 17).[63] Similarly, Isaiah prophesied that people would one day sing, "we have a strong city; God makes salvation its walls and ramparts" (Isa 26:1),[64] and predicted, "you will call your walls Salvation and your gates Praise" (Isa 60:18), reflecting the call to "enter his gates with thanksgiving and his courts with praise" (Ps 100:4). This vision therefore contains by implication a call for pilgrims to praise God as they go through the gates of this new Jerusalem.[65]

But this city specifically has twelve gates and twelve angels[66] *and* twelve foundations.[67] Twelve is a highly intertextual number:[68] the zodiac (not mentioned but certainly available to the minds of the audience),[69] the tribes of Israel (based on the sons of Jacob, recalling 7:4–8), and the original apostles of Jesus. The second and third of

---

60. Cf. Aune, *Revelation 17–22*, 1153. On Platonic and Stoic concepts of the "ideal" city, see ibid.

61. Cf. Thomas, *Apocalypse*, 638–639. The NIV has "clear as crystal." But Beale translates "shining like crystal" (Beale, *Book of Revelation*, 1068).

62. Cf. Beale, *Book of Revelation*, 1066–1067; Leithart, *Revelation 12–22*, 370–371.

63. Cf. Koester, *Revelation*, 814.

64. Cf. Beale, *Book of Revelation*, 1068.

65. Cf. Dumbrell, *End of the Beginning*, 3.

66. On guardian angels here, see Aune, *Revelation 17–22*, 1154–1155. There may be a reference to the "watchmen" on the walls of Jerusalem in Isa 62:6 (cf. Fekkes, *Isaiah and Prophetic Traditions*, 264–65).

67. Cf. Thomas, *Apocalypse*, 639.

68. On the relationship between 7 (4 + 3) and 12 (4 x 3), see Leithart, *Revelation 12–22*, 376.

69. Cf. Beale, *Book of Revelation*, 1082; Leithart, *Revelation 12–22*, 374–75.

these are mentioned specifically here. The original good woman in 12:1, the mother of the messiah, had "a crown of twelve stars on her head." The city therefore combines the heritage of Israel, reflected in the name Jerusalem and the twelve tribes, the promises of a reunited twelve-tribed kingdom under the messiah (as in Ezek 37:16–25; Isa 49:6; Hos 1:11; Rev 7:4–8), and the new covenant people, headed by twelve apostles.

This is the first time the twelve apostles have been mentioned in Revelation.[70] However, perhaps the audience would be aware of the Lukan literature, with its accounts of the apostles on thrones "judging the twelve tribes of Israel" (Luke 22:30; see also Matt 19:28) and the replacement of Judas to make up the twelve in Acts 1:12–26.[71]

Beale notes that having the apostles as the foundation and the tribes of Israel as the gates is surprising, given that Israel is chronologically earlier, and suggests "Specific reference to historical Israel in the OT is not in mind here. Rather, the apostles are portrayed as the foundation of the *new* Israel, which is the church."[72] He is right to draw attention to this feature of the vision (compare Eph 2:20); however, I think he draws too strong a contrast with the Old Testament. The phrase "twelve tribes of Israel's sons" (v. 12) is meaningless apart from historical Israel, although its meaning isn't limited to historical Israel.

The arrangement of the gates would also cause many listeners to think of the arrangement of the camp of the Israelites in Numbers 2 in four directions, with three tribes in each and the Levites in the middle, the twelve oxen under the sea in Solomon's temple (1 Kgs 7:25),[73] and also of the gates of Ezekiel's restored city (Ezek 48:30–34).[74] Summing up, the description speaks of restoration and newness in the people of God in both old covenant and new covenant language.[75]

> **And the one speaking with me had a gold measuring rod[76] so that he might measure the city and its gates and its wall. (Rev 21:15)**

The listeners would recall that John himself was earlier given "a measuring rod like a staff" and told to measure "the temple of God and the altar and those who are worshiping in it" excluding the outer court (11:1–2). This measurement was restricted and related probably to either the literal second temple in Jerusalem or the church as

---

70. Cf. Thomas, *Apocalypse*, 642–44. The combination of twelve tribes and twelve apostles may recall the twenty-four elders of Rev 4:4. Cf. Beale, *Book of Revelation*, 1069–1070.

71. Cf. Aune, *Revelation 17–22*, 1157–58.

72. Beale, *Book of Revelation*, 1070; cf. Mayo, *Those Who Call Themselves Jews*, 181; Leithart, *Revelation 12–22*, 380.

73. Cf. Leithart, *Revelation 12–22*, 377–80.

74. Cf. Thomas, *Apocalypse*, 640–42; Aune, *Revelation 17–22*, 1155–56; Beale, *Book of Revelation*, 1068–69.

75. Cf. Koester, *Revelation*, 815.

76. This detail suggests the precious nature of what the angel is measuring perhaps (cf. Thomas, *Apocalypse*, 644).

God's temple. But now the angel is measuring a whole city, which is "coming down out of heaven" (v. 10), signifying that this is sacred space belonging to God (see v. 3).[77]

There is a similar measuring of the new city and temple in Ezekiel 40–42; these visions include at the outset "a man whose appearance was like bronze" with "a measuring rod in his hand" (Ezek 40:3), and proceed to a very detailed description and measurement of the temple area and the temple itself. Also in Zechariah 2, the prophet sees "a man with a measuring line in his hand" (Zech 2:1), who is going "to measure Jerusalem, to find out how wide and how long it is" (Zech 2:2) because it will be a very large and populous city "without walls" (Zech 2:3). But the city of Revelation 21 is even bigger than either Ezekiel or Zechariah imagined.

Beale argues that this measuring "pictures the security of its inhabitants" in contrast to the walls of old Jerusalem and "representing a decree to guarantee his [God's] presence with his people" grounded in an eternal decree of election.[78] Certainly, walls speak of protection (v. 15). However, this is not what the immediate context emphasizes, at least until v. 27; rather, the measuring serves to emphasize the vast size of the city and its glory, though this also includes God's presence (v. 22). If election is in view, the thrust here is the huge number of the elect.

> **And the city was laid out foursquare, and its length was as great as its width. And he measured the city with the rod at twelve thousand stadia, length and width, and its height is equal. And he measured the wall 144 cubits in human measurement, which is angelic. (Rev 21:16–17)**[79]

An ideal city to the ancient Greek world would be square in shape, like many modern planned cities. Babylon was supposedly such a city, and so was Ezekiel's new Jerusalem (Ezek 48:16).[80] John's city is 144,000 square stadia in the area of its base (recalling the 144,000 Israelites in 7:4–8), but it is a cube[81] of unimaginable size, literally 2,200 kilometers or 1,400 miles wide, long, and high.[82] The implied contrast to the earthly Jerusalem, and even to Ezekiel's vision, is stark: the circumference of Ezekiel's city is 18,000 cubits, roughly 9.5 kilometers; John's city's circumference is over 900 times that size.[83]

---

77. Leithart, *Revelation 12–22*, 380–81.
78. Beale, *Book of Revelation*, 1072; see also 1079.
79. Cf. Thomas, *Apocalypse*, 646–48; Aune, *Revelation 17–22*, 1162–63.
80. Cf. Howard-Brook and Gwyther, *Unveiling Empire*, 187; Koester, *Revelation*, 815–16, 829–30; Aune, *Revelation 17–22*, 1160–61; Beale, *Book of Revelation*, 1074–76. The city may be more like a pyramid, thus showing a contrast with Babylon (and perhaps Egypt), which is clearly part of John's purpose in this chapter.
81. The cube reminds hearers of the Most Holy Place of the Jerusalem temple, but this is much bigger (cf. Koester, *Revelation*, 816).
82. Cf. Thompson, *Book of Revelation*, 89.
83. Cf. Thomas, *Apocalypse*, 645–46; Leithart, *Revelation 12–22*, 382. See other ideas about the future Jerusalem in Koester, *Revelation*, 816; Aune, *Revelation 17–22*, 1161–62.

The audience cannot fail to notice the ongoing prominence of twelve (144 = 12×12) in the wall measurements.[84] But the dimensions make a similar point to the contrast between 144,000 Israelites and the uncountable multitude in Revelation 7:4–9. The new order of things outshines the old order of Israel, even in its restored condition, as implied perhaps by Isaiah 54:2–3.[85] Beale calculates that "the size of the city is apparently the approximate size of the then known Hellenic world";[86] thus, it would include all the Gentile world, not just Israel. The multiples of twelve are again prominent, anchoring the imagery in the Old Testament and focusing on the reality of God's people.

> **And the wall was constructed**[87] **in jasper, and the city (with) pure gold like pure glass. The foundation (stones) of the walls of the city were adorned with every (kind of) precious stone. The first foundation (stone was) jasper, the second sapphire, the third chalcedony, the fourth emerald, the fifth onyx, the sixth sardus, the seventh chrysolite, the eight beryl, the ninth topaz, the tenth chrysoprase, the eleventh jacinth, the twelfth amethyst . . .**[88] (Rev 21:18–20)

The vision is of incredible splendor and monetary value, far outshining any Roman or other palace or temple. The listeners might be reminded of the promise in Isaiah 54:

> Afflicted city, lashed by storms and not comforted,
> I will rebuild you with stones of turquoise,
> your foundations with lapis lazuli.
> I will make your battlements of rubies,
> your gates of sparkling jewels,
> and all your walls of previous stones. (Isa 54:11–12; see also Isa 61:10; Tob 13:17)[89]

Once again, we see here both a note of restoration and a totally new order of things. This might be supported by a possible reference to Ezekiel 28:13,[90] about the king of Tyre. If this was John's intention, he might be making a statement about restoration, since the king of Tyre was stated as having been in "Eden, the garden of God," and adorned with "every precious stone" (Ezek 28:13), before "wickedness was found in you" (Ezek 29:15). Many Pentecostals read Ezekiel 28 as referring to the origins and fall of the devil. Maybe John is reading it more as the fall of humanity, now reversed.

---

84. Cf. Beale, *Book of Revelation*, 1076–78.
85. Cf. Beale, *Book of Revelation*, 1078–79.
86. Beale, *Book of Revelation*, 1074; cf. Paul, *Revelation*, 350. See also Dan 2:35.
87. This is a difficult phrase to translate. Probably a literal translation would be "the construction material of its wall (was) jasper." The Greek ἐνδώμησις [*endōmēsis*] could also mean "the structure of the wall." Cf. Fekkes, *Isaiah and Prophetic Traditions*, 240; Mathewson, *Handbook*, 294.
88. The exact identies of the stones in English is problematic.
89. Cf. Beale, *Book of Revelation*, 1083–86.
90. Cf. Fekkes, *Isaiah and Prophetic Traditions*, 241.

The hearers are invited to count off the precious stones, leading again to twelve, which might refer partly to the zodiac[91] or recall the twelve stones on the high priest's breastplate symbolizing the twelve tribes (Exod 28.17–21; 39:10–14),[92] but now applied to the apostles whose names are on these foundations (vv. 14, 19).[93] This adornment also continues the romance theme, first explicitly introduced in 19:7–8 and picked up in 21:2.[94] Comparing a bride to a city possibly recalls Song of Solomon 6:4, where the bride is "lovely as Jerusalem" (see also Rev 4:4; 7:4; 8:10).

> . . . and the twelve gates (were) twelve pearls, each one of the gates being a single pearl.[95] And the great street of the city (was) pure gold like transparent glass. (Rev 21:21)

This refers back to the tribes whose names were written on these gates (v. 12). It is probably meant to contrast with 11:8 where the word translated here as "great street" (Greek *plateia*) is used of the place where the bodies of dead witnesses lie in the "public square of the great city."[96] The earthly Jerusalem or world city was defiled by the dead bodies of the witnesses it rejected.[97] The new heavenly Jerusalem is undefiled and precious, indeed "pure" (Greek *katharon*), a word with ritual connotations. But there is also an implied contrast with the gold-covered floor of the original Jerusalem temple (1 Kgs 6:30); now the entire city's streets are gold![98]

> And I did not see a temple in it, for the Lord God Almighty is its temple and the Lamb. (Rev 21:22)

If the description so far has been of a much bigger and grander Jerusalem than before, with strong notes of heritage and restoration, now it takes an unexpected direction to those familiar with Isaiah and Ezekiel, the main intertextual references in this passage. For the city, unlike *any* city known to the hearers, has no temple. This is consistent with verse 3, which stated, "the dwelling place of God is with humanity (the people)," but unlike ancient cities, including Jerusalem. Second temple Judaism was focused on the

---

91. John reverses the order of stones normally associated with the zodiac, implying that the new order of God turns things upside down (Leithart, *Revelation 12–22*, 374; Caird, *Revelation*, 277), as the protestors against Paul in Thessalonica argued (Acts 17:6).

92. Cf. Koester, *Revelation*, 817–18. Koester suggests that these precious stones have significance as bridal, priestly, and creation imagery. For other implications of this list, see Thomas, *Apocalypse*, 648–50; Aune, *Revelation 17–22*, 1165, 1187; Beale, *Book of Revelation*, 1080–88; Leithart, *Revelation 12–22*, 372–75; Mayo, *Those Who Call Themselves Jews*, 182–86.

93. Cf. Beale, *Book of Revelation*, 1080–81.

94. Cf. Fekkes, *Isaiah and Prophetic Traditions*, 247–53.

95. As Thomas observes, pearls have previously been mentioned only in relation to Babylon (Rev 17:4; 18:12, 16). But this city outshines Babylon in wealth almost infinitely (Thomas, *Apocalypse*, 651).

96. Cf. Koester, *Revelation*, 820; Aune, *Revelation 17–22*, 1166.

97. Cf. Beale, *Book of Revelation*, 1089.

98. Cf. Thomas, *Apocalypse*, 651; Beale, *Book of Revelation*, 1079. This imagery was probably derived from Isa 54:11 via Tob 13:16–17 (Fekkes, *Isaiah and Prophetic Traditions*, 245–47).

magnificent restored Herodian temple in Jerusalem, now in ruins (or about to be).[99] One reason, apparently, for the lynching of Stephen was his criticism of the Jerusalem temple (Acts 6:13–14; 7:44–50),[100] though he had Jeremiah on his side (Jer 3:16–18; 7:1–14).[101] Jewish hearers of Revelation might have been greatly disappointed that the temple in Jerusalem would not be rebuilt. Some Dispensationalists are still expecting this to happen, though earlier in the story than here.

Temple rituals and temple structures were required to enable God to dwell among the Israelites due to sin, keeping a measure of separation between God and the people. Even in Ezekiel's vision, this idea is retained (Ezek 40–44), with mention of guardian priests (Ezek 40:45–46; 44:14, 16), an inner sanctuary with restricted access (Ezek 41:15–17; 44:13, 16), and a "Most Holy Place" (Ezek 41:21–24). There are also an altar (Ezek 43:13–17), offerings for sin (Ezek 42:13; 43:18–27), and rules for ritual purity (Ezek 42:14; 44:17–27; 46:19–20). Into this temple the glory of God returns after previously departing from the first temple (Ezek 43:1–9; 44:4).[102] While there is a hint of God being a "holy place" in Isaiah 8:14, and Jesus speaks of his body as the temple in John 2:19–21,[103] John is much more blatant.

If such a temple system is no longer necessary, there must have been an extraordinary change. John does not explain the change, but the fact that God and the Lamb are now the temple implies that the work of the Lamb in redemption is a key to the revolution. And as a consequence of it, the citizens of the city have, therefore, nothing to fear in this divine presence since the second temple order is now obsolete.[104]

To put it another way, the heavenly temple, which has been the focus in the narrative so far (3:12; 6:9; 7:15; 8:3; 11:19; 14:15, 17; 15:5–8; 16:1, 17), and is synonymous with God's throne room (4–5; 7:15; 8:3), has now come down to earth in the presence of God and the Lamb. According to Leithart, John "is announcing the end of the post-lapsarian world, the end of exclusion from Eden,"[105] which has already arrived in the church and in which God himself *is* the temple and believers dwell *in God*, completely overturning every ancient culture's ideas.[106]

---

99. Cf. Koester, *Revelation*, 831–32.

100. Cf. Aune, *Revelation 17–22*, 1166–68, 1191.

101. Cf. Dumbrell, *End of the Beginning*, 53–54.

102. Cf. Mayo, *Those Who Call Themselves Jews*, 178, 193; Dumbrell, *End of the Beginning*, 35–38. Dumbrell points out that there is no promise of a rebuilt temple in Isaiah or Jeremiah, but it is dominant in Ezekiel (ibid., 54–55). However, "Ezek 40–48 makes no provision for Davidic kingship" (ibid., 59).

103. See also Matt 21:42; Mark 12:10; Luke 20:17; Acts 4:11; Eph 2:20 (all referring to Ps 118:22), speaking of Christ as the chief cornerstone of the temple.

104. Cf. Koester, *Revelation*, 820–21. This is expressed elsewhere in the NT in terms of the church being a temple of the Spirit (1 Cor 3:16; Eph 2:21–22), an idea which may be derived, or at least anticipated, to some extent from the Qumran community (cf. Beale, *Book of Revelation*, 1071; see also 1091–92).

105. Leithart, *Revelation 12–22*, 388.

106. Leithart, *Revelation 12–22*, 387–89.

> **And the city has no need of the sun, nor of the moon, that they might shine on it, for the glory of God gives it light, and its lamp (is) the Lamb. (Rev 21:23)**

This recalls Isaiah 60:19, where we read,

> The sun will no more be your light by day,
> nor will the brightness of the moon shine on you,
> for the LORD will be your everlasting light,
> and your God will be your glory.[107]

It also brings to mind the primeval situation before Genesis 1:14, when God is said to have created the sun, moon, and stars. But John does not assert that the sun and moon are abolished, simply that the city does not rely on them for light, for it is enlightened by the glory of God and the Lamb. They shine on the city and dispel the darkness of deception and sin.[108] This may also recall Psalm 132:17, which says, "I will . . . set up a lamp for my anointed one," only here the lamp *is* the anointed one and it is set up *for* the city.[109]

> **And the nations will walk by its light and the kings of the earth will bring their glory into it . . . (Rev 21:24)**[110]

The nations will look for guidance to the light of God and Christ, shining in and through the new Jerusalem.[111] But the nations (or at least Gentiles) still exist. The new Jerusalem acts as a kind of world capital from which light goes out to all the world and to which all human glory is brought in dedication to God. The audience here would remember the promise of Isaiah 60:

> Arise, shine, for your light has come,
> and the glory of the LORD rises upon you.
> See, darkness covers the earth
> and thick darkness is over the peoples,
> but the LORD rises upon you
> and his glory appears over you.
> Nations will come to your light,
> and kings to the brightness of your dawn. (Isa 60:1–3)[112]

---

107. Cf. Fekkes, *Isaiah and Prophetic Traditions*, 266–67.

108. Cf. Thomas, *Apocalypse*, 653; Fekkes, *Isaiah and Prophetic Traditions*, 268.

109. Cf. Aune, *Revelation 17-22*, 1170.

110. Leithart attempts to read this as "kings of the land," i.e., Jews who come to submit to Christ, but this reading is undermined by the reference to the "nations" in verses 24 and 26 (Leithart, *Revelation 12-22*, 396).

111. Cf. Leithart, *Revelation 12-22*, 389–93; Bauckham, *Climax of Prophecy*, 313–16.

112. Cf. Fekkes, *Isaiah and Prophetic Traditions*, 269–71.

> *... and its gates are never shut by day, for there will be no night there,*[113]
> **and they will bring the glory and the honor of the nations into it. (Rev 21:25–26)**

This paraphrases Isaiah 60:11, "Your gates will always stand open, they will never be shut, day or night, so that people may bring you the wealth of the nations." The whole of Isaiah 60 is full of this note, and forms the background to verses 22–26 of Revelation 21.[114] Again this portrays Jerusalem as a world capital, open and accessible to all the nations, which come in pilgrimage to bring their glories there, as prophesied in Isaiah 2:2–5, Micah 4:1–5, and Zechariah 14:16, which envisage the nations coming to Zion for instruction and judgments in a peaceful world.[115] Beale rightly explains, "they are bringing not literal riches but themselves as worshipers before God's end-time presence,"[116] though I think that it includes their good cultural achievements (music, architecture, art, literature, etc.).[117] Herms also sees a reference to the language of Solomon's rule in 1 Kings 10:24–25 and 2 Chronicles 9:23; in both passages people from other nations seek to hear Solomon's wisdom and bring him tribute.[118]

The implications of all this for the conversion of the hostile nations and kings and their salvation are staggering.[119] In particular, this is in stark contrast to their atittudes in 17:14 (where they make war on the Lamb), 18:3 (where they commit sexual immorality with the prostitute), 18:9 (where they mourn the fate of Babylon), and 19:19 (where they gather for war against the rider on the white horse). Now they are resourcing the new Jerusalem, not as an act of subservience (as in Isa 60:10–12) but one of willing worship based on conversion, as suggested by v. 27.[120]

This would reflect passages such as Isaiah 45, where we find God saying,

> Turn to me and be saved
> all you ends of the earth;

---

113. Cf. Beale, *Book of Revelation*, 1096.

114. Cf. Leithart, *Revelation 12–22*, 397–98; Fekkes, *Isaiah and Prophetic Traditions*, 99, 265; Herms, *Apocalypse for the Church*, 245–51.

115. Contrast Roman ideas about Rome's dominance as world capital (Koester, *Revelation*, 832).

116. Beale, *Book of Revelation*, 1095; see also 1096; cf. Fekkes, *Isaiah and Prophetic Traditions*, 272.

117. Cf. Leithart, *Revelation 12–22*, 346–48.

118. Herms, *Apocalypse for the Church*, 216, 252–53.

119. Cf. Thomas, *Apocalypse*, 654–56; Beale, *Book of Revelation*, 1097. There is obviously a tension between this statement and the destruction of hostile nations and people in 19:21 and 20:8–9 and the passing away of the "first heaven and the first earth" in 21:1. Either God has created a new batch of nations or these cataclysmic events are not as exhaustive as they may appear. Cf. Aune, *Revelation 17–22*, 1171–73; Caird, *Revelation*, 251; Leithart, *Revelation 12–22*, 376–77, 384. Leithart seems to see here a kind of idealized post-Constantinian Christendom, where the Gentile kings submit to Christ and support the church, as indeed many did historically, especially in the Medieval age (ibid., 398–400). This is appealing but Pentecostals would be wary of visualizing a godly order that does not require individual conversion, as indeed v. 27 emphasizes.

120. Cf. Mayo, *Those Who Call Themselves Jews*, 194. Herms explains this as a contrast between the New Jerusalem and Babylon the prostitute city of Revelation 17–18 (Herms, *Apocalypse for the Church*, 244).

for I am God, and there is no other . . .

Before me every knee will bow;

by me every tongue will swear. (Isa 54:22, 23; see also Zech 2:11; Phil 2:10–11.)

And there will not go into it everything common and [those] who practice detestable (things) and lies, but only those written in the book of life of the Lamb. (Rev 21:27)

The universal openness and accessibility of the city are severely qualified here. The recorded citizens[121] of the city, and of the nations that come in pilgrimage, are only those whose names are in the book by God's grace and who have persevered as disciples of Christ under pressure. This reminds the hearers that all mentions of people in the Lamb's book of life are in the context of pressure to compromise (compare 3:5; 13:8; 17:8; 20:12, 15).[122] John's severe binary thinking comes to the fore again.

There is diversity and even a kind of multi-cultural society extending a liberal welcome in this new world order, unlike the rules for Ezekiel's restored temple, which stated, "No foreigner uncircumcised in heart and flesh is to enter my sanctuary, not even the foreigners who live among the Israelites" (Ezek 44:9; see also Isa 52:1).[123] But it has strict boundaries; it is an exclusively *Christian* new world order. The purity of the city cannot be compromised; otherwise the world would return to its older chaos and violence. Thus, while Revelation speaks of the "conversion of the nations," not just their destruction, it does not promise complete universalism, but rather offers the nations an alternative future to destructive judgement.[124] Aune also points out that the language is metaphorical here and in 22:14, speaking of "entering" the eschatological kingdom of God, language frequently used by Jesus in the Gospels.[125]

Summing up, the vision of the new Jerusalem reflects the prophetic promises of a restored city and Israel, especially found in Isaiah, Jeremiah, Ezekiel and Zechariah,[126] and symbolized by the number twelve. But it goes beyond these promises in its size and scope, reflecting the new covenant order introduced by the blood of the Lamb. It is open to people of all nations, but on condition of having their names written in the Lamb's book of life, that is, on condition that they become Christians.

---

121. Cf. Koester, *Revelation*, 822–23.

122. Cf. Beale, *Book of Revelation*, 1102.

123. Cf. Fekkes, *Isaiah and Prophetic Traditions*, 273–74.

124. Cf. Koester, *Revelation*, 832–33; Thomas, *Apocalypse*, 658; Beale, *Book of Revelation*, 1097–1103; Leithart, *Revelation 12–22*, 398. Beale also contends that "the focus is on those who made profession of faith but contradicted it by their sinful lifestyle" (Beale, *Book of Revelation*, 1101).

125. Cf. Aune, *Revelation 17–22*, 1174; Beale, *Book of Revelation*, 1098–1100. Beale interprets the spatial language of these verses nonspatially.

126. See fuller description of the allusions in Koester, *Revelation*, 812.

Revelation Chapter 22

22:1–5 The Final Order

John has been receiving a vision of the Holy City, the new Jerusalem, throughout Revelation 21. This section gives the hearers the final details of the city and the new world order. It begins with a river.

> **And he showed me a river of living water,[1] clear as crystal, flowing out from the throne of God and of the Lamb. (Rev 22:1)**

The listeners' minds would probably go back mainly to two Old Testament passages at this point: the original river flowing out of Eden (Gen 2:10), and the river flowing out of the restored temple in Ezekiel's final vision (Ezek 47:1–12), which became increasingly deep as its depth was measured at specific points (Ezek 47:3–6). This river brought life wherever it flowed freely (Ezek 47:8–10) and nourished fruit trees on the banks: "their fruit will serve for food and their leaves for healing" (Ezek 47:12).

They might also recall similar language in Zechariah 14:8, which says, "On that day living water will flow out from Jerusalem, half of it east to the Dead Sea and half of it west to the Mediterranean Sea . . . " Two other relevant passages would be Joel 3:18 ("A fountain will flow out of the LORD's house") and Psalm 46:4 ("There is a river whose streams make glad the city of God, the holy place where the Most High dwells"). The Eden imagery might also recall Isaiah 51:3, where Isaiah prophesies, "The LORD will surely comfort Zion . . . he will makes her deserts like Eden, her wastelands like the garden of the LORD."[2] All these passages function as promises of restoration, their imagery signifying a return to Zion and even a return to Eden.

In Revelation 22, the river flows "from the throne of God and of the Lamb," speaking of a divine and messianic kingly origin. Some hearers might connect this to Psalm 110:1, a commonly used New Testament intertext about Jesus sharing the

---

1. The Greek phrase ὕδατος ζωῆς [*hudatos zōēs*] can simply mean "running water" or "water of life" (as in NIV), i.e., eternal life (Aune, *Revelation 17–22*, 1139).

2. Koester also compares this to the Greco-Roman city (Koester, *Revelation*, 834–35).

divine throne, as in 3:21.³ Or they might recall the words of Jesus in John 4:13–14 about "the water I give them" becoming "a spring of water welling up to eternal life" and John 7:37–38 where Jesus claims to be the source of "rivers of living water" that will "flow from within" the believers, which John (the author of the Fourth Gospel) interprets as the promise of the Spirit (John 7:39).⁴

It also resembles what Peter proclaimed about the gift of the Spirit in Acts 2:33—"Exalted to the right hand of God, he has received from the Father the promised Holy Spirit and has poured out what you now see and hear." This promise is extended far and wide to "all who are far off" (Acts 2:39), parallel to the "healing of the nations" (Rev 22:2). Pentecostals have built on these passages a rich set of teachings about embracing the "flow" of the Holy Spirit. Koester suggests the implication of the imagery relates to spiritual thirst and cleansing.⁵ Thomas goes broader when he writes, "this river is God's river; it is the Lamb's river. It is their salvific gift to all those who believe in and offer faithful witness to them; a complete gift that provides abundantly for all soteriological needs."⁶ Such an understanding sees the river as a present, not just a future, reality.

> **In the midst of its street, and of the river, on both sides (was) a tree of life bearing twelve (kinds) of fruit, and each month yielding its fruit, and the leaves of the tree (are) for healing of the nations." (Rev 22:2)**

Ezekiel's vision spoke of "fruit trees of all kinds" growing on "both banks of the river" that bear fruit every month, "because the water from the sanctuary flows to them" (Ezek 47:12). But John is more specific; it is the "tree of life" that bears the fruit, referring the hearers back to Genesis 2:9 and 3:24, the narrative of the original tree of life, access to which was lost through the disobedience of the first pair of humans. Clearly, John intends the audience to understand that this access has been regained in the new order.⁷ But it is not just a restoration of Eden, because this is a city, not a garden; rather, as Howard-Brook and Gwyther put it, John describes the "greening" of the city.⁸

John also modifies the Ezekiel passage in another significant detail. Whereas in Ezekiel 47:12 the leaves of the various trees are "for healing," reflecting the medicinal use of leaves in the ancient world,⁹ in Revelation 21:2, "the leaves of the tree [singular, the tree of life] are for the healing of the nations." Coming to the tree of life brings healing for the nations or Gentiles (Greek *ethnōn*). Whether this means healing of

---

3. Cf. Aune, *Revelation 17–22*, 1177.
4. Cf. Beale, *Book of Revelation*, 1104–5.
5. Koester, *Revelation*, 823, 835.
6. Thomas, *Apocalypse*, 659.
7. Cf. Mayo, *Those Who Call Themselves Jews*, 195–96.
8. Howard-Brook and Gwyther, *Unveiling Empire*, 190–91.
9. Cf. Koester, *Revelation*, 824.

individual Gentiles (physical or spiritual)[10] or healing of national "diseases" is not spelled out.[11] Either way, this adds to the completeness of the saving work God has been engaged in throughout history and throughout the narrative of Revelation.[12]

> **And every curse will no longer exist. And the throne of God and of the Lamb will be in it, and his slaves will serve him, and they will see his face, and his name (will be) on their foreheads. (Rev 22:3–4)**

The audience would remember the original curse pronounced on the ground in Genesis 3:17.[13] That was part of the beginning of the Big Story of Scripture, which lies behind Revelation. The Story is nearly finished. The work of God is completed, as 21:6 has implied. All that was lost in the bad old days of Genesis 3 and thereafter has been restored. Some of the details are spelled out in this passage: access to the tree of life is restored (v. 2; compare Gen 3:24), though of course this applies only to the redeemed, as others are suffering the ultimate curse of the second death/lake of fire (21:8).[14]

But this final state is better than Eden.[15] To see God's face is the ultimate blessing, not granted to Moses because it was too dangerous (Exod 33:18–23), even though God spoke with him "face to face" and he was said to see "the form of the LORD" (Num 12:8). Jacob claimed that he had seen God "face to face" when he wrestled with a "man" (Gen 32:30, 24). Isaiah testified that "I saw the Lord, high and exalted" (Isa 6:1), but that probably didn't include "seeing his face,"[16] and this language is probably metaphorical.[17] David was confident he would see God's face probably after death (Ps 17:15). Jesus' generation did see the face of God in the flesh according to John's Gospel (John 1:14, 18), but he is now in heaven.[18]

Mayo spells out what John is claiming here:

---

10. Cf. Thomas, *Apocalypse*, 661.

11. Aune asserts that "the allusion is simply mechanical . . . since there is no real place in the eschatological scheme of Revelation for 'the healing of the nations' construed as their conversion" (Aune, *Revelation 17–22*, 1178). He does not give reasons but presumably this comment is based on the "apparently striking inconsistency in the eschatological scenario of Revelation" whereby the nations still exist after being previously destroyed (ibid., 1171). However, as John mentions the nations three times in his description of the holy city (21:24, 26; 22:2), this cannot be "simply mechanical" and readers must adjust their interpretation of the destruction passages accordingly.

12. Cf. Beale, *Book of Revelation*, 1106–8.

13. Cf. Thomas, *Apocalypse*, 662; Beale, *Book of Revelation*, 1109–13. Beale sees fulfillment of Gen 1–3 in Rev 22 in the light of priestly-temple themes. Aune argues from similar language in Zech 14:11 that it is specifically the curse of war that is in view (*Revelation 17–22*, 1178–79; cf. Beale, *Book of Revelation*, 1112; Bauckham, *Climax of Prophecy*, 316–17).

14. Cf. Beale, *Book of Revelation*, 1112.

15. Cf. Leithart, *Revelation 12–22*, 400–401

16. Cf. Koester, *Revelation*, 824.

17. Cf. Aune, *Revelation 17–22*, 1179–80.

18. On seeing God's face, see also Whitaker, *Ekphrasis*, 118–25.

This unadulterated presence has never before been experienced by any person or people group on earth. There are no more veils, no more holy of holies, and no more priestly intercessors. God's redeemed sanctified people now eternally serve him in his presence and look without fear upon his face.[19]

If they see his face, they will certainly want to serve him, or worship him. The Greek word here is *latreuein*, meaning "to serve in prayer, obedience, and devotion," the same word as in 7:15, where the uncountable multitude coming out of the great tribulation will "serve him day and night in his temple."[20] This seems to allude to Isaiah 61:6 ("and you will be called priests of the Lord, you will be named ministers of our God").[21]

Having his name on their foreheads underlines the fact that they belong to him, not to the wild beast, recalling the promise to the conquerors in Philadelphia (3:12), a promise which also comes to fulfilment in the new Jerusalem, and as seen in the virginal army of 14:1. It also confirms their priestly role, with access to God previously only possible for the high priests who also had God's name on their foreheads.[22] The conquerors have served Jesus faithfully, resisting the allurements of the great prostitute, the city and culture of Rome, and not being intimidated by the wild beast and the Empire's military might and oppressive power. The ultimate reward is to be with him forever.

And there will be no more night, and they will have no need (of the) light of a lamp, and (the) light of the sun, for the Lord God will shine on them, and they will reign forever and ever. (Rev 22:5)[23]

This recapitulates 21:23, which provides a metaphor for security and transparency, and perhaps reminds the audience of the priestly blessing in Number 6:25, that is, "the Lord will make his face shine upon you."[24] The mention of reigning fulfills promises made to the churches (2:26–27; 3:21) and restores the dominion originally given to humans in Genesis 1:26–28. This is the dominion promised to the saints in Daniel 7:18, 22. Thus, this verse closes off the plot begun in chapter 5, where heaven sang,

---

19. Mayo, *Those Who Call Themselves Jews*, 171.

20. Or as Archer puts it, "Seeing God is the goal of worship!" (Archer, *Worship in the Apocalypse*, 282). Thomas points out the deliberate ambiguity here: whose face do the faithful believers see, God's or the Lamb's? It raises all kinds of theological questions about "the unique relationship and solidarity between God and the Lamb" (Thomas, *Apocalypse*, 663). The language also opens up all sorts of possibilities for the believers since "Absolutely nothing stands in the way of such incredible intimacy that awaits in New Jerusalem" (ibid.). Cf. Beale, *Book of Revelation*, 1113–14.

21. Cf. Beale, *Book of Revelation*, 1113.

22. Cf. Beale, *Book of Revelation*, 1114.

23. Such a length of "reign" dwarfs not only the beast's forty-two months (13:5) and the one hour of the ten kings (17:12) but even the thousand years of 20:4 (Thomas, *Apocalypse*, 665).

24. See also Pss 4:6; 31:16; 67:1; 80:3, 7, 19; 118:27. Cf. Aune, *Revelation 17–22*, 1181; Beale, *Book of Revelation*, 1116; Fekkes, *Isaiah and Prophetic Traditions*, 275.

"You have made them to be a kingdom and priests to serve our God, and they will reign on the earth" (5:10), and the larger plot of the whole Bible. As Dumbrell argues, "for biblical readers the city is pre-eminently a symbol of world government" and "asserts the fact of final Kingdom of God rule."[25]

However, this reign probably does not imply domination of others, but more likely governing the earth as the original humans were assigned to do (Gen 1:26–28).[26] Beale suggests, "The saints are so identified with the throne of the Messiah that they are identified with both his priestly and kingly roles,"[27] as implied also by Daniel 7:27. God's program, announced in the seven sealed scroll on the basis of Jesus' painful death, and advanced in the thick of great resistance and suffering, is now completed. As Aune says, "the final goal of salvation is now realized."[28]

Interpreting the New Jerusalem

How should this section of Revelation be understood by today's reader, some 2000 years removed from the world and concerns of the original audience?

First, it can be justly read as a more or less literal expectation of the future. John teaches today's reader to expect a "new heaven and new earth" (21:1), with a much better experience of God's presence and favor (21:3). It also teaches us to expect a release from all the afflictions that currently beset humanity. He prophesies, "there will be no more death nor sorrow nor crying nor pain any longer, [for] the first (things) have gone away" (21:4). He promises there will be no more curses (22:3). In particular, the victorious Christians, and they alone, would enjoy this new order of things (21:7), for they alone would gain admittance to the new Jerusalem, since their names are in "the book of life of the Lamb" (21:27). But Revelation 21 implies there will be a huge number of them.

They will see the face of Jesus, bear his name on their foreheads, and "reign forever and ever" (22:5), whereas the unrighteous would be consigned to the lake of fire (21:8). The new city embraces the faithful of Israel, as symbolized by the tribal names on the city gates (21:12). However, it also embraces the new Christian believers, as symbolized by the apostolic names on its foundations (21:14). This setup reflects the portrayal of the faithful people of God throughout the book, such as the 144,000 Israelites as contrasted with the infinite number of Christians from all nations in Revelation 7. It is also consistent with New Testament eschatological expectations in general and would strengthen the hearers' hope in a context of stress. Today it would have

---

25. Dumbrell, *End of the Beginning*, 31.
26. Cf. Beale, *Book of Revelation*, 1116.
27. Beale, *Book of Revelation*, 1116.
28. Aune, *Revelation 17–22*, 1188. Or as Beale says, this passage "affirms the future fulfillment of the main prophetic themes of the OT and NT, which all find their ultimate climax in the new creation" (Beale, *Book of Revelation*, 1119).

a similar effect on most readers. However, the details of the vision cannot be taken completely literally without descending into farce, such as trying to visualize pearls as big as gates (21:21).[29]

Second, John's portrayal of the ideal city, the one that comes down from heaven and therefore has divine design, stands in contrast to the Greco-Roman philosophy and practice regarding cities. The new Jerusalem is similar in many ways to ancient Babylon, including the "river flowing through it with a series of trees on either side,"[30] and it reminds the audience in part of the ideal Greek polis. For the ancient Greeks, "the city was the ultimate famework of social life, even when the Empire had become the ultimate framework of political life."[31] As Koester points out, "For ancient theorists, the city was a divinely ordained form of political life."[32] However, he notes that "physical aspects of the cities in the empire reflected the Roman power structure,"[33] with honor given to emperors, their families, Roman deities, and the provincial elites who donated special buildings and other features.

But "the New Jerusalem reflects a different power structure" focused on God and the Lamb, rivers of life for all, including every nation, and its size alone overwhelms all human cities. Hence, "New Jerusalem critiques the power structures of this world from a perspective that is not captive to this world."[34] As we saw earlier, the new Jerusalem is visualized explicitly in contrast with the earthly city of Babylon.[35] This critique is as relevant today as it was then, and reflects the stance and rhetoric of Revelation as a whole text, challenging its readers to re-examine their values and commitments.[36]

Third, the new Jerusalem is ultimately not a physical city but a people who constitute the bride of the Lamb (21:2, 3, 9–10).[37] Thus, Aune states that "the description of the New Jerusalem is a combined image of the adorned bride and a description of a utopian city"[38] and "the city is a transparent symbol for the people of God, the

---

29. Cf. Beale, *Book of Revelation*, 1089; see also 1076, 1077, 1079, 1093.

30. Beale, *Book of Revelation*, 1074.

31. Veyne, *Bread and Circuses*, 39.

32. Koester, *Revelation*, 826. Dumbrell claims that "the legendary foundation of the city was invariably understood to be a religious act" in the ancient world generally and in the OT (Dumbrell, *End of the Beginning*, 2).

33. Koester, *Revelation*, 826, 829. However, Greeks and Romans also entertained views of a utopia that was often more rural and occasionally more egalitarian (Aune, *Revelation 17–22*, 1192–94).

34. Koester, *Revelation*, 827.

35. Cf. Beale, *Book of Revelation*, 1117–21. There is also some reference to the original Babel whose builders were "looking for the governmental unity by which men might be perfectly regulated" (Dumbrell, *End of the Beginning*, 19; see also 130).

36. Cf. Howard-Brook and Gwyther, *Unveiling Empire*, 192–95.

37. Koester, *Revelation*, 828–29; Thomas, *Apocalypse*, 621; Beale, *Book of Revelation*, 1062; Dumbrell, *End of the Beginning*, 6; Mayo, *Those Who Call Themselves Jews*, 173–79. But see Aune, *Revelation 17–22*, 1122.

38. Aune, *Revelation 17–22*, 1164.

Church."³⁹ All the hallmarks of this glorious new Jerusalem represent the glorious state of the faithful victors who have conquered with their uncompromising lifestyle and witness grounded in the atoning work of the Lamb.

So the city is unimaginably huge (21:16) because its population is infinitely large (7:9). This is consistent with a literal city of this size, but the dimensions seem too huge (especially in height) to be taken literally. It's better to see them as symbolic of the extraordinary number of saved people in the end, in keeping with God's eternal purpose.⁴⁰ The purpose of this is to motivate hearers of the prophecy to become such conquerors and thus citizens of this city.⁴¹

But fourth, this picture is also capable of being understood spiritually in the "here and now."⁴² Some of the promises seem to be available to believers in this age; for example, "To the one who is thirsty I will give from the spring of the water of life (as a) free gift" (21:6; see also 22:17). The picture of the river and tree of life seem to stand for the present experience of salvation in the Spirit, as much as for its future consummation. Certainly hearers familiar with the Fourth Gospel might well take John's language that way (John 4:13–14; 5:24; 6:35, 40; 7:37–39). As the city is already "coming down out of heaven from God" (21:10), it may be said to be affecting the present age of grace. This is what makes Leithart's argument that this is referring to the present (millennial) age plausible.⁴³ The geography of John's description also fits the present age: the city has walls (real boundaries, moral as much as physical) and sinners are clearly "outside" (22:15), but its gates are always open to those whose names are in the Lamb's book of life and who "wash their robes" (22:14), that is, those who come to Christ and trust in his blood (7:14). In this way the nations or Gentiles are healed through Christ (22:2).⁴⁴

Moreover, the thought of the nations bringing their "glory and the honor" (cultural achievements) into the holy city (21:26) is suggestive for a Christian theology of culture that claims all good culture for Christ. A Pentecostal reading of this passage would certainly want to allow for this way of applying it to today's Spirit-filled believer and Spirit-filled church. Many Pentecostal preachers have spiritualized the "river of

39. Beale, *Book of Revelation*, 1187; see also 1222.

40. Cf. Mayo, *Those Who Call Themselves Jews*, 186–87; Osborne, *Revelation*, 752–54.

41. Cf. Beale, *Book of Revelation*, 1119–20.

42. Cf. Hendriksen, *More Than Conquerors*, 198; Moloney, *Apocalypse of John*, 325–344. Moloney equates the new Jerusalem with the church.

43. Cf. Leithart, *Revelation 12–22*, 357–62, 401–9. Leithart insists that there have been times in history, for example, when the church has played a significant part in bringing peace and grace to a broken world. And even when the church has failed to live up to its holy calling, this vision of John "stands as a mission statement and measure of faithfulness" (ibid., 407) calling the church back to its full potential.

44. Cf. Beale, *Book of Revelation*, 1108. Beale wants to resist the idea that the leaves "continue to heal throughout eternity," probably in order to avoid the conclusion that unsaved people can still be saved after the last judgement (cf. ibid., 1098), but he does not entertain the possibility that this healing may take place during the current age.

the water of life," based especially on Ezekiel 47, as a metaphor for the reviving flow of the Holy Spirit, which believers can now enjoy and even swim in! There may be a danger here of trivializing the immense vision of John. However, it can also provide a powerful vision. This river flows out of the Spirit-filled church, beginning at Pentecost when it was "poured out" (Acts 2:33); it renews the whole world, sweeping away all the tawdry obstacles in its path as a mighty flood, and brings healing wherever it flows through willing missionaries.

As Isaiah once prophesied,

> From the west, people will fear the name of the LORD,
> and from the rising of the sun they will revere his glory.
> For he will come like a pent-up flood
> that the breath of the LORD drives along. (Isa 59:19)

22:6–17 Closing Exhortations

Revelation 22:5 is arguably the end of the story. The "goodies" have won. The "baddies" have been eliminated, and the heroes will live "happily ever after," or in John's language, "they will reign forever and ever" (v. 5). So the rest of Revelation 22 acts as a postscript and application.[45]

> **And he said to me, "These (are) the faithful and true words, and the Lord God of the spirits of the prophets has sent his angel, to show his slaves what must soon happen." (Rev 22:6)**

Affirming the trustworthiness of the prophecy repeats 21:5, which also added the imperative of writing it down because of its divine source via an angel to God's servants, recalling 1:1. Is this a claim to authority on par with the canonical prophets? Probably Christian church prophets are in view, although there is some ambiguity.[46] But certainly this phrase does make a claim to divine origin and authority. It also shows how active prophets were in the churches, especially those John was related to, and implies that John was one of a number of "prophets" and "slaves" who received this revelation, though perhaps the others received it through John.

This claim apparently ignores the testing that good churches subjected prophecy to (2:2, 20) and the "pneumatic discernment" they needed to exercise.[47] It also repeats the idea of the imminence of the coming events found in 1:1 when it says "what must soon [Greek *en tachei*, "speedily, quickly, without delay"] happen," in contrast with

---

45. On the parallels between 22:6–21 and the opening verses (1:1–3), cf. Aune, *Revelation 17–22*, 1148–49, 1205–6. Both passages are "metatextual" since they both comment on "the text of Revelation" as a whole (ibid., 1201). Cf. Beale, *Book of Revelation*, 1122–23; Leithart, *Revelation 12–22*, 411–14.

46. Cf. Aune, *Revelation 17–22*, 1182; Beale, *Book of Revelation*, 1124–26.

47. Cf. Thomas, *Apocalypse*, 667.

the delay language in Daniel (Dan 2:45; 12:4, 9, 13).[48] But it also reminds the hearers of the similar themes in Daniel and Revelation; that is, "that Revelation, like Daniel 2, is primarily about the establishment of God's kingdom throughout the earth and the judgment of evil world kingdoms."[49] And it reaffirms the necessity of these events: they "must . . . happen" (Greek *dei genesthai*), as stated previously in 1:1 and 4:1.[50]

> "And behold I am coming quickly. Blessed are those who keep the words of the prophecy of this book." (Rev 22:7)

This promise of an imminent coming recalls 1:7 (though the time indicator does not occur there), 2:16, and 3:11 (where it seems to indicate a spiritual and local coming).[51] All interpretations that seek to take this word literally as referring to the *Parousia* struggle at this point. How soon is soon? When does the "clock" start, so to speak?[52] As Koester argues, "the internal dynamics of the book caution against trying to determine what 'soon' means chronologically"[53] since the plot extends for over a thousand years. Moreover, in Revelation Jesus comes spiritually and locally (as in 2:5, 16; 3:3, 20), as well as physically and finally.[54] But John's emphasis is on what this coming means for the believers.

This is the second to last beatitude in Revelation (see 1:3; 14:13; 16:15; 19:9; 20:6; 22:14) and reminds the listeners especially of the first beatitude, which relates to reading, hearing and taking to heart "the words of the prophecy" (1:3). Several of the beatitudes are connected to the nearness or coming language of Revelation: "for the time draws near" (1:3); "Behold, I am coming like a thief" (16:15); and this verse. As the text nears its end, there is a strong emphasis on keeping the prophecy (22:7, 9, 10, 18, 19). The Greek *tēreō* can mean "observe, obey or pay attention to," "keep under guard," or "maintain." John's emphasis is on hearing and obeying, "maintaining one's faithful witness to God and the Lamb through a Spirit empowered prophetic life . . . with a view toward the conversion of the nations,"[55] *and* on preserving the scroll inviolate.[56]

> And I, John, (am the one) who was hearing and seeing these (things). And when I had heard and seen them, I fell down to worship before the feet of the angel who was showing them to me. (Rev 22:8)

48. See the interesting discussion in Caird, *Revelation*, 235–36.
49. Beale, *Book of Revelation*, 1124.
50. Cf. Aune, *Revelation 17–22*, 1184.
51. Cf. Thomas, *Apocalypse*, 668.
52. Cf. Koester, *Revelation*, 838–39, 850–51; Leithart, *Revelation 12–22*, 418–20. Leithart emphasizes the time language here above the interpretation of "coming" as Jesus' *Parousia*. For him, what is imminently coming is the end of the old order and the beginning of the new order with the unveiling of the bride of Christ.
53. Koester, *Revelation*, 850; see also Beale, *Book of Revelation*, 1134–36.
54. Koester, *Revelation*, 851; see also Beale, *Book of Revelation*, 1127.
55. Thomas, *Apocalypse*, 669.
56. On parallels between the opening and closing of Revelation, see Koester, *Revelation*, 847.

This emphasizes the human authorship of the book for the first time since chapter 1 (1:1, 4, 9), and positions John again as a witness, one who hears and sees "in the Spirit." This again recalls both the opening sequence (1:2, 19) and the constant language of seeing and hearing throughout the narrative.[57] Such declarations were a common part of prophetic oracles (Num 24:15) and apocalypses (Dan 12:5; 1 Enoch 1:2), but signified mainly an act of witness.[58]

But then the audience is shocked to hear again that John falls down to worship the guiding angel. John was rebuked for a similar action in 19:10; why is he doing this again? It may not be possible to answer this question.[59] We may speculate that he was overwhelmed by the glory of the angelic interpreter, but he doesn't say. However, the rhetorical effect is to present John as a humble witness, prone to error, thus highlighting by contrast the divine inspiration of the text,[60] as verse 6 had implied. It may also be told as a rebuke to any Christians prone to angel worship, though there has so far been no hint of this anywhere in the narrative.[61] Alternatively, as Whitaker suggests, the text is using these accounts to show that the word is more reliable as a revelation of God than a visual sight, part of John's attack on idols.[62]

> **And he said to me, "Don't do that! I am a fellow slave with you and your brothers the prophets, and those keep the words of this book. Worship God." (Rev 22:9)**

Angels are thus not to be exalted: they are no more than equals to John and the other Christian prophets and indeed all faithful believers who "keep the words of this book." As Koester puts it, "Although angels are heavenly beings and people are mortal, they are alike in that both receive messages from God and offer worship to God."[63] The text is very jealous about worship; this is a key emphasis throughout Revelation. Only God, not angels nor human rulers nor Satan nor especially the beast may legitimately receive worship,[64] which makes the worship given to the Lamb in Revelation 5:8–14 all the more striking.[65]

---

57. Cf. Aune, *Revelation 17–22*, 1185.

58. Cf. Koester, *Revelation*, 839.

59. Aune attributes this repetition to the work of an author-editor as part of "the final redactional stage of composition," in keeping with his source-critical approach (Aune, *Revelation 17–22*, 1186). This neatly solves the problem of how John could make the same mistake twice, but at the expense of his veracity as a reporter or witness, or the competence of later copyists or editors. Cf. Stuckenbruck, *Angel Veneration*, 245–61.

60. Cf. Bauckham, *Climax of Prophecy*, 134.

61. Corsini, however, argues that "the relationship between the angels and Jesus Christ is . . . fundamental to the Apocalypse" as well as being a serious issue in early Christianity (Corsini, *Apocalypse*, 49).

62. Whitaker, *Ekphrasis*, 209–13; cf. Stuckenbruck, *Angel Veneration*, 260.

63. Koester, *Revelation*, 852. Thomas also suggests that angels have a role to play in interpreting God's words (Thomas, *Apocalypse*, 671). See also Leithart, *Revelation 12–22*, 416–18.

64. Cf. Thomas, *Apocalypse*, 671; Beale, *Book of Revelation*, 1128; Leithart, *Revelation 12–22*, 418.

65. Cf. Bauckham, *Climax of Prophecy*, 136–39.

Revelation Chapter 22

> And he[66] said to me, "Do not seal up the words of the prophecy of this book, for the time is near." (Rev 22:10)

There is a striking contrast here with Daniel 8:26 ("seal up the vision, for it concerns the distant future"), Daniel 12:4 ("roll up and seal the words of the scroll until the time of the end"), and Daniel 12:9 ("the words are rolled up and sealed until the time of the end"). Daniel's scroll had to be sealed up "until the time of the end" in "the distant future."[67] Revelation implies that that time had now arrived, "the time is near."[68] The sealed scroll in heaven had been unsealed by the Lamb (5:1—6:17; 8:1). As Koester says, "Revelation was designed to be an open book that addressed issues facing its earliest readers,"[69] an important interpretive consideration. However, some words were not yet released: "Seal up what the seven thunders have said, and do not write it down" (10:4).

> "Let those who do unjustly keep doing unjustly, and the ones who are filthy, let them stay filthy, and let the just do what is just and the holy keep being holy." (Rev 22:11)

Since the end is imminent, John gives the audience a kind of proverb.[70] It is too late to change, even though change has been called for throughout the book and probably John is trying to shock the hearers/readers to change.[71] Again the audience may think of Daniel 12:10 ("but the wicked will continue to be wicked") and Ezekiel 3:27 ("whoever will listen let them listen, and whoever will refuse let them refuse"). There is a note of hardening in Revelation, a pessimism about the likelihood of people repenting, in many sections (Rev 9:20–21;13:8; 16:9, 11, 21; see Isa 6:9–10; Acts 28:26–27).[72]

> "Behold, I am coming quickly, and my reward (is) with me to repay each one according to their works." (Rev 22:12)

---

66. As Aune and others have pointed out, it is often difficult to say who is speaking in this section of the book (cf. Aune, *Revelation 17–22*, 1204, 1236). Some have tried to solve this problem and make the section more coherent using a liturgical structure (ibid., 1206–8).

67. Cf. Koester, *Revelation*, 840. Aune explains this differently, on the assumption that Daniel was not the real author and the book under his name was written 400 years later (Aune, *Revelation 17–22*, 1216). This implies that the author of Daniel expected the prophecies to be fulfilled in his time. Whatever may be the case then, John is not working with any kind of "*ex eventu*" prophecy, nor is he placing his prophecy in the mouth of Daniel or any other ancient hero.

68. Cf. Beale, *Book of Revelation*, 1129–30.

69. Koester, *Revelation*, 852. Moloney claims instead that "this book" refers to the Old Testament, unveiled, fulfilled, and explained in Jesus Christ, as seen in Revelation (Moloney, *Apocalypse of John*, 350–354, 358–360).

70. Cf. Thomas, *Apocalypse*, 672–73.

71. Cf. Koester, *Revelation*, 840–41. Koester suggests that this exhortation is ironic (ibid., 853). Cf. Thomas, *Apocalypse*, 674; Beale, *Book of Revelation*, 1131–33; Leithart, *Revelation 12–22*, 421.

72. This may support the view that the imminent event in view here is the destruction of Jerusalem and its temple in AD 70. Beale takes it more as a reference to a "spiritually lethargic" church and to a process of predestination (Beale, *Book of Revelation*, 1133).

Jesus is now speaking, it appears. The previous "coming" announcement was related to keeping the words of the prophecy (v. 7). This one encourages the hearers to vigilance in their personal lives with a promise of reward (Greek *misthos*, "pay, wages, reward, recompense, retribution"). This reflects the language of the last judgment as stated in 11:18—"and the time for the dead to be judged and to give reward to your slaves the prophets and to the saints and those who fear your name" (see also Rev 20:13; Isa 40:10; 62:11;[73] Prov 24:12).[74] Taken with the previous verse, this promise encourages the righteous and holy listeners to persevere in their good lifestyle.

> "I am the Alpha and the Omega, the First and the Last, the Beginning and the End." (Rev 22:13)

This not only emphasizes the claim of Jesus to be eternal, but recalls the words of God in 1:8 ("I am the Alpha and the Omega . . . who is, and who was, and who is coming, the Almighty") and 21:6 ("I am the Alpha and the Omega, the Beginning and the End."), and also Jesus' own words in 1:17 ("I am the First and the Last"). There seems to be a clear implication in these titles and his role as judge (v. 12) that Jesus is God.[75]

> "Blessed are those who wash their robes so that they will have the right to the tree of life and enter through the gates into the city." (Rev 22:14)

This final beatitude is a kind of summary of John's message to his hearers. "Those who wash their robes"[76] takes the hearers back to Revelation 7, where John sees a great international multitude "standing before the throne and before the Lamb . . . clothed in white robes" (7:9) and hears they "have washed their robes and made them white in the blood of the Lamb" (7:14). This multitude is experiencing similar blessing to what the new Jerusalem represents; for example, "God will wipe away every tear from their eyes" (7:17).

So clearly, this final blessing is addressed to those who trust in the Lamb and are redeemed by his blood since only the Lamb is worthy and therefore able to redeem sinners (see also 5:3–5, 9).[77] On this basis, they are authorized to eat of the tree of life (see also 22:2; 2:7) and enter the city (see 21:27) through its open gates (see Isa 60:11; 62:10;

---

73. Cf. Fekkes, *Isaiah and Prophetic Traditions*, 276–78.

74. See also Matt 16:27 and 25:31–46. Leithart comments, "Judgment according to works is the consistent teaching of Jesus, Paul, and John" (Leithart, *Revelation 12–22*, 423).

75. Cf. Koester, *Revelation*, 854; Thomas, *Apocalypse*, 675–76; Aune, *Revelation 17–22*, 1237; Beale, *Book of Revelation*, 1138.

76. Many ancient manuscripts have "do his commandments" instead of "wash their robes." For discussion of this, see Aune, *Revelation 17–22*, 1197–98.

77. Koester points out the verb is present active, suggesting that the believers must continually wash with "ongoing repentance and faith" (Koester, *Revelation*, 842). Cf. Beale, *Book of Revelation*, 1138–39; Leithart, *Revelation 12–22*, 424–25; Thomas, *Apocalypse*, 677–78. Thomas also sees a possible allusion to foot washing here. For other possibilities, see Aune, *Revelation 17–22*, 1220–21.

Rev 21:25).[78] Thus, as Aune concludes, "the ban that barred people from access to the tree of life [see Gen 3:22–24] and the immortality that it symbolizes has been lifted."[79]

> **"Outside (are) the dogs[80] and the sorcerers [see Deut 18:9–14] and the sexually immoral and the murderers and the idolaters and all who love and do falsely." (Rev 22:15; see also Rev 2:2; 14:5)**

Again John's ethical and soteriological dualism and exclusivism comes into play.[81] And this statement somewhat saddens the modern reader because the redemption narrative hasn't claimed everyone. The story is finished, the tree of life is again within reach, but thousands are still excluded. Does this also mean that things can still go wrong? Tina Pippin claims, "the order is tenuous at best, with evil lurking outside the walls."[82] But people must live with the choices they have made, and John offers no hope of ultimate reconciliation for all. In the end, there are only two classes of people, as 21:7–8, 27 has already made clear.[83] The list of sinners is similar to 21:8 as seen in this comparative chart.

Rev 21:8	Rev 22:15	Greek terms
Cowardly		*deilois*, "cowardly, afraid"
Unbelieving		*apistois*, "unfaithful, unbelieving"
Vile		*ebdelugmenois*, "detestable, vile, corrupt"
Murderers	Murderers	*phoneusin/phoneis*, "murderers"
Sexually immoral	Sexually immoral	*pornois*, "one who practices sexual immorality"
Those who practice magic arts	Those who practice magic arts	*pharmakois*, "one who practices sorcery, witchcraft, or magic"
Idolaters	Idolaters	*eidōlolatrais*, "an idolater"
Liars	Everyone who loves and practices falsehood	*pseudesin/pseudos*, "liar/lie, untruth"
	Dogs	*kunes*, "dogs"[84]

---

78. Cf. Beale, *Book of Revelation*, 1139–40.

79. Aune, *Revelation 17–22*, 1221; cf. Leithart, *Revelation 12–22*, 425.

80. Sometimes this is seen as a reference to homosexuals, but many other possibilities are credible (cf. Aune, *Revelation 17–22*, 1222–23). Beale sees it as referring to false Christians, based on Phil 3:2–3 and 2 Pet 2:20–22 (Beale, *Book of Revelation*, 1141–42). Rick Strelan argues that it refers to pagan rites to do with purification, protection, and entrances, especially associated with the goddess Hecate and especially at the time of death, which makes sense in the context of v. 14 (R. Strelan, "Outside Are the Dogs," 148–56).

81. Cf. Leithart, *Revelation 12–22*, 425–27.

82. Pippin, "Peering into the Abyss," 253.

83. John locates these people "outside" the city, in fact outside the new heavens and earth. The geography of the new order is complex; the "lake of fire," if it is a real place, must be "inside" the universe. All this implies that the language should not be taken literally. Cf. Beale, *Book of Revelation*, 1061.

84. Cf. Thomas, *Apocalypse*, 678–79.

While the two lists are similar, the first list probably contains more words that could apply to Christians who fall away under pressure.[85]

> "I, Jesus, have sent my angel to testify to you these (things) for the churches. I am the root and the offspring of David, the bright Morning Star." (Rev 22:16)

This is the first time Jesus has been specifically revealed as the source of the text since chapter 1 (1:1, 2) and the messages to the seven churches (Rev 2–3). In fact, this is the first mention of Jesus by name since chapter 1.[86] So clearly, the audience is being reminded of the beginning of the prophecy as it now draws towards its close. Its source is Jesus (as in 1:1, 2). Its mediator is an angel (singular, as in 1:1, though there have been numerous angels taking part in the revelation), specifically "my angel" (as in 1:1 which speaks of "his angel"). Its messenger is "you" (plural), so not just John, as in 1:1–2, 11; it may be a circle of Christian prophets or those who would read Revelation aloud or carry the text to various destinations, perhaps the "slaves" of 1:1.[87] Finally, it functions as a testimony (as in 1:2), and its audience is the churches of Asia (as in 1:4, 11, 20).

When Jesus continues, "I am the root and the offspring of David, the bright Morning Star" (v. 16b), this would take the hearers back to the seven messages in Revelation 2–3, all of which begin with a self-description of Jesus. However, the content is different. The "root of David" was one of the messianic titles used in 5:5 of the one worthy to open the seven-sealed scroll, and also recalls 3:7 (Jesus holding "the key of David").

The "morning star" was referred to in 2:28, but as something given by Jesus to the victorious believers in Thyatira. However, the two titles together point to Jesus' human descent from David and his messianic status (see Isa 11:1; Num 24:17), and the inaugurated fulfilment of these prophecies.[88] The image of the "bright morning Star" suggests that Jesus inaugurates a new day, a day of salvation and blessing (compare 2 Cor 6:2; Isa 60:1–3; 2 Pet 1:19).[89] It also connects with the Lamb as the lamp of the new Jerusalem (21:23).[90] Such claims were the issue between the Jews and Christians, which perhaps lay behind John's description of local synagogues as "synagogues of Satan" (2:9; 3:9).

> And the Spirit and the bride say, "Come." And let those who hear say, "Come." (Rev 22:17a)

Now an authoritative liturgical response is set out, presumably a prompt to the audience in the churches. They say "Come," because Jesus has now twice said he is coming

---

85. Cf. Koester, *Revelation*, 855. Thomas argues that, "most, if not all, the terms in this list have special meaning derived from the Apocalypse itself" (Thomas, *Apocalypse*, 678, 678–81).

86. Cf. Koester, *Revelation*, 855–56; Thomas, *Apocalypse*, 681.

87. Cf. Aune, *Revelation 17-22*, 1225–26, 1237; Beale, *Book of Revelation*, 1143–46; Bauckham, *Climax of Prophecy*, 85–87; Koester, *Revelation*, 843, 856; Thomas, *Apocalypse*, 681.

88. Cf. Thomas, *Apocalypse*, 682; Aune, *Revelation 17-22*, 1226–27; Beale, *Book of Revelation*, 1146–48.

89. Cf. Bauckham, *Climax of Prophecy*, 324–25.

90. Cf. Koester, *Revelation*, 856.

soon (vv. 7, 12). The Spirit has not spoken much since Revelation 2–3 where seven times the audience heard, "let them hear what the Spirit is saying to the churches." There the Spirit was a kind of spokesperson or facilitator for the words of Jesus. He also is quoted as saying of the martyrs, "Yes . . . they may rest from their hard work, for their works follow after them" (14:13), in response to one of the beatitudes. But in this verse, the Spirit joins with the churches in inspiring a cry of longing for Jesus.[91] The bride could be expected to long for her bridegroom, using the romantic language that has peppered the last few chapters (19:7–9; 21:2, 9), and the Spirit leads her to speak such a one-word cry.[92] The hearers are also called on to join in.[93]

> **And (let) those who are thirsty come, (let) those who want (it) take the water of life as a free gift. (Rev 22:17b)**

The onus is now on the hearers to "come." Are they thirsty? Are they longing for the "water of life"? If so, they can come and take the free gift (Greek *dōrean*), the "water of life," recalling the river of 22:1 and "the springs of the water of life" in 21:6, as well as Isaiah 55:1. In both 21:6 and 22:17, it is emphasized that this water of life is available as a free gift for those who are thirsty (from the Greek verb *dipsaō*, "be thirsty, long for"), recalling also John 7:37. This seems like another reference to the Spirit as a "gift," and it is clearly meant to stir up the listeners to respond by coming and taking that gift as they listen, not just as a hope for the future.[94] This sounds somewhat like a Pentecostal "altar call" for the baptism in the Holy Spirit.

22:18–21 The Final Word

As he brings his text to a close, John seems anxious about how it will be received and preserved, even after he dies.[95] He appends two solemn warnings like curses.[96]

> **I testify to all who hear the words of the prophecy of this book: if anyone adds to them, God will add to them the plagues written in this book, and if anyone takes away from the words of the book of this prophecy, God will take away**

---

91. Cf. Thomas, *Apocalypse*, 683; Beale, *Book of Revelation*, 1148.

92. Koester views the bride as exclusively the future city breaking into the present here and "awakening the desire to meet the bridegroom at his coming" (Koester, *Revelation*, 856–57). But surely this awakening is to take place in the hearts of John's present readers/hearers in the seven churches, as 2:4–5; 3:1–3, and 3:19–20 would imply. Coulter shows how such themes were found in the early Pentecostal literature in the USA and UK (Coulter, "Spirit and Bride," 304–13).

93. Thomas sees this cry as not addressed so much *to* Jesus as *from* Jesus to "the kings and nations of the earth" (Thomas, *Apocalypse*, 684), a kind of "altar call" like Pentecostal churches frequently have, and which definitely informs the second part of verse 17. Cf. Aune, *Revelation 17–22*, 1228.

94. Cf. Beale, *Book of Revelation*, 1149–50; contra Koester, *Revelation*, 857; cf. Aune, *Revelation 17–22*, 1228–29.

95. Cf. Aune, *Revelation 17–22*, 1232, on why John might have valid concerns.

96. Though Koester and Thomas argue that Jesus is still speaking here (Koester, *Revelation*, 844; Thomas, *Apocalypse*, 684–85). Cf. Aune, *Revelation 17–22*, 1229.

their part from the tree of life and from the holy city, which is written in this book. (Rev 22:18–19)

These warnings share a common "If . . . then . . . " structure; a human sin leads to a corresponding response from God using the same verb ("add" or "take away"). They do not necessarily amount to a claim to be writing Scripture in spite of the parallels with Deuteronomy 4:2, in which Moses says, "Do not add to what I command you and do not subtract from it, but keep the commands of the Lord your God that I give you" (see also Deut 12:32; Josh 1:7). However, they do imply a claim to inspiration, as verses 6, 7, and 16 have implied; John insists that he is not writing his own opinions or teaching, but a prophecy based on divine revelation from Jesus, and hence his manuscript needs to be preserved intact without any change, and read and received in full without modification.[97] As Thomas puts it, "they must embrace it in its entirety, not giving in to the temptation of compromising it by addition or diluting its message by deletion."[98]

The exact consequences that John warns of are themselves theologically and hermeneutically significant. The first threat, that "God will add to them the plagues written in this book," implies that these plagues or disasters are not just predictions of one-off historical events, but rather consequences that anyone can experience at any time.[99] This supports an Idealist or spiritual reading of Revelation. The second threat, that "God will take away their part from the tree of life and from the holy city," is a warning of loss of salvation.[100] Both warnings presumably apply primarily to professing Christians, who have an interest (or stake) in the prophecy. Whether one argues that such professing Christians who take away from the text are, or are not, true believers, their potential share in the eschatological blessings would be forfeited.[101]

However, there is no suggestion that these warnings are generalizable to a canonical "New Testament." While John appears to believe he is writing the "end" of the Big Story of God's salvation, this does not mean he is writing the "last" book of the Bible. The warnings apply to his manuscript alone, and there is no sign he has such a "canon" in his thinking, except perhaps in the mention of just "twelve apostles" (21:14).

Nor is there anything here that prohibits the future exercise of the gift of prophecy in the church. John is in favor of prophets, as verse 6 ("the spirits of the prophets") and verse 9 ("I am a fellow slave with you and your brothers the prophets") have made clear. He is only critical of false prophets, like the second beast (13:11–17; 16:13;

---

97. Cf. Koester, *Revelation*, 858; Beale, *Book of Revelation*, 1154. Aune calls this an "integrity formula" and gives many examples of how these functioned in the ancient world, combined with "conditional curse formulas" (Aune, *Revelation 17–22*, 1208–15, 1229–32, 1237–38). Leithart reads it as more of an exhortation to obedience to the prophecy than to its preservation (Leithart, *Revelation 12–22*, 428–29).

98. Thomas, *Apocalypse*, 685.

99. Aune compares them to "land mines awaiting detonation" (Aune, *Revelation 17–22*, 1238).

100. Cf. Thomas, *Apocalypse*, 686; Aune, *Revelation 17–22*, 1232.

101. Cf. Beale, *Book of Revelation*, 1153.

19:20) or Jezebel, who "calls herself a prophet" (2:20), both of which are faulted because they encourage compromise with the Greco-Roman idolatrous religions and the imperial cult. He himself prophesies, and he envisages others doing so, such as the two witnesses (11:3–6). John's concern in these warnings is simply the preservation and proper use of the text he has nearly finished writing.

> **The one who testifies these (things) says, "Yes, I am coming quickly." Amen,[102] come Lord Jesus." (Rev 22:20)[103]**

The predictions of Jesus' second advent are more prominent in this last chapter than anywhere else (see vv. 7, 12, and 17). This is one of the last thoughts John wants to leave with his audience. While John's concept of the timing and nature of the second coming is not always clear, the importance of it is central to his outlook.[104] Once again, he models a response to that for the churches. This longing cry sums up the fervent disciples' attitude to their master which John's text has tried to stir up throughout the narrative, often using romantic language to do so. It resembles Paul's Aramaic *Maranatha* in 1 Corinthians 16:22. The two books have common features in their endings: the author identifies himself (1 Cor 16:21; Rev 22:8, 16), pronounces a curse (1 Cor 16:22; Rev 22:18–19), calls out "Come, Lord" (1 Cor 16:22; Rev 22:20), and pronounces a grace blessing (1 Cor 16:23; Rev 22:21). Possibly these common endings reflect the fact that both texts would be read aloud in a congregational setting, inviting a congregational response.[105]

> **The grace of the Lord Jesus (be) with all. (Rev 22:21)[106]**

John finishes in his epistolary framework, recalling the second beginning to the text in 1:4 ("John, To the seven churches in the province of Asia"). Some Greek manuscripts of Revelation have a final "Amen," which seems appropriate as John has been calling for specific liturgical responses in this last chapter. This last verse reminds us that Revelation is a specific letter written to a specific group of churches at a specific point in history. While it can be, and should be, applied to us today, being part of the canonical New Testament, we must not forget the original hearers. Rather, I think John would have us join *with them* in crying "Come, Lord Jesus," and responding with our "Amen" to the prophecy, not just nominally but with a wholehearted commitment to "keep," that is observe and obey, its words.

---

102. On "Amen," see comments in Thomas, *Apocalypse*, 687.

103. There is an implied contrast with Greco-Roman magicians trying to command a deity to come. Cf. Aune, *Revelation 17–22*, 1233–34, 1238.

104. Cf. Thomas, *Apocalypse*, 686–87; Aune, *Revelation 17–22*, 1233–34; Beale, *Book of Revelation*, 1155; Leithart, *Revelation 12–22*, 431.

105. Cf. Koester, *Revelation*, 848; Aune, *Revelation 17–22*, 1234–36; Beale, *Book of Revelation*, 1155. The ancient Christian document, the Didache, may support this in relation to the Lord's Supper.

106. For parallels with the endings of Paul's letters, see Koester, *Revelation*, 846; Aune, *Revelation 17–22*, 1239–40. For some implications of the epistolary structure, see Beale, *Book of Revelation*, 1156.

CONCLUSIONS

We have journeyed together with John and his original first-century audience through his visionary experience and his interpretation of that experience. I have argued that Revelation must be read first as a message to them, the believers in those seven Asian churches and other early Christians. This is the best anchor for good interpretation and helps exclude some of the more fanciful readings that have proliferated over the centuries since Revelation was published.

I have also argued that Revelation as a narrative prophecy has two main themes which build hope in the mixed Jewish and Gentile audience. John sees the atoning work of Jesus (his blood), his resurrection, and the subsequent outpouring of the Holy Spirit at Pentecost, leading to worldwide witness (Acts 1:8), as doing two key things. On the one hand, God is fulfilling the prophetic promises of the Old Testament of the restoration of Israel and Jerusalem through a new exodus, a point emphasized by John's repeated allusions to these prophecies and to the original exodus story. On the other hand, God is simultaneously fulfilling much earlier and wider promises (such as that of Gen 3:15) and recapturing the whole world—the nations (Gentiles)—for his kingdom. This makes Revelation good news in spite of the sometimes violent struggles it takes to get to that outcome.

How might all this apply to us, reading Revelation in the twenty-first century? My colleague U-Wen Low has coined three "W's" which may make a good starting point: Worship, Witness, and Wait.[107] Expanding on those and building on this commentary, I want to suggest seven (there had to be seven!) key messages that Revelation brings to readers of all ages:

1. Repentance
2. Faith
3. Discipleship
4. Worship
5. Witness
6. Welcome
7. Wait

1. Repentance. Revelation is a call to repentance both to the world and to the Christian church. Five out of seven of the churches were explicitly called to repent.

107. Low, "Out of the Great Ordeal."

Local churches everywhere need to be aware that Jesus will visit them with reward or judgment (3:3, 11). The overall narrative challenges readers to consider their lives, align with the heroes of the story (such as the 144,000 of Rev 14), disassociate themselves from "Babylon" (18:4), avoid the common sins of the world (as in 22:15), and qualify for entry into the holy city (22:14).

2. Faith. Revelation keeps bringing the redemptive work of Jesus (his "blood") to the reader's attention. Not only does this purchase people for God from every people group on earth (5:9), but it also makes the believer clean and able to stand before God (7:14) with confidence. Revelation rarely speaks of faith as such, but everything it encourages readers to do demands such absolute faith in Jesus.

3. Discipleship. The romantic thread in Revelation reminds the reader that Jesus loves us (1:5) and is looking for love in return. In fact, that is more important than hard work, perseverance, and correct doctrine (2:2–5). Jesus wants a bride (19:7), and this bride is made up of those who are totally dedicated to him as his disciples (14:4).

4. Worship. Worship is a key issue in Revelation. People are called on to only worship the one true God and the Lamb (Rev 4–5), especially excluding idols and human leaders (9:20; 13:8). The text also teaches its readers how to worship, and what to say, by giving a number of models, almost a complete liturgy. Such worship is demonstrative, loud, and full of truth, and dangerous in a world opposed to God.

5. Witness. The true disciples of the Lamb boldly testify to him, in spite of the opposition and threats they encounter. They lay down their lives rather than compromise. Thus, they become literal or figurative martyrs, the heroes of the book, who prevail against the opposition (12:11). As Stephen Pattemore concludes, "the church which John portrays is a martyr church . . . modelled on Christ in every dimension of its existence," and "John's audience are consistently challenged to identify with the martyr church."[108]

6. Welcome. This might sound like an odd feature since Revelation has a strong binary emphasis, dividing all humanity into two exclusive and opposing groups. But in fact, Revelation destroys the "normal" divisions that existed in the first-century world (ethnic, religious, economic, and social), and the new Jerusalem welcomes people from all nations provided they follow the Lamb (21:24–25). It reminds readers that the Christian church is an international egalitarian fellowship.

7. Wait. Revelation brings hope to the believing reader or listener. The existing, threatening, unjust, violent, painful world will be replaced by a new heaven and new earth (21:1–5). This hope prevents readers from engaging three false or

---

108. Pattemore, *People of God*, 114–15.

extreme responses: a despairing resignation and submission to the demands of "empire" (whatever shape it takes), a violent reaction that seeks to force the pace and create a Christian empire with believers in power, or an escapist sectarianism leading to passivity, waiting for the "rapture" that vindicates us and destroys everyone else. The hope engendered by Revelation encourages readers to witness bravely, knowing that they will be rewarded (20:4) and that their witness will be used by God to draw all nations to himself (15:4).

This all calls for discernment. Christians living under authoritarian and persecuting rulers must be ready to suffer for the essentials of the faith. Christians living in supposedly tolerant and affluent regimes are more prone to the Laodicean sickness of complacent lukewarmness, which may include uncritical patriotic loyalty to their nation or tribe[109] and indifference to the sufferings of the martyrs. Pentecostal readers should come out of a dispensationalist passivity and expect the Spirit to do mighty works through their witness to the kingdom of God, anticipating a huge worldwide harvest of souls before the story is over.

To some extent, the reading of Revelation in this commentary validates the Pentecostal expectation of the "latter rain" ingathering at the end of the ages, although my idea of what that looks like is influenced by the tremendous growth of Pentecostalism since 1906 and the shape it has taken worldwide. But just here is a major spiritual danger, that of "triumphalism." Revelation does not support a sectarian interpretation that shows any particular form of Christianity to be right or favored by God.

Pentecostals should be grateful for what God has done in and through this movement. They should realize that it has all been as a result of God's grace alone. And they should hear the voice of the Spirit in Revelation unveiling their weaknesses, errors, failings, even heresies, and calling them to a faith that is pure, holy, courageous, committed, and in the best sense ecumenical, respecting what the Spirit is saying and doing through other branches of the Christian church.

But they should be encouraged with great hope and confidence, knowing that the Father's kingdom will come and his will shall be done on earth as in heaven (Matt 6:10), not just suddenly by the return of Christ, but steadily by the work of the Spirit in and through the church. May this commentary stir up such faith and courage in believers everywhere.

---

109. Pentecostals in the West have tended to become more vulnerable to this in recent years. For example, the earlier pacifism that marked Pentecostals has largely been abandoned. Cf. Alexander, *Pentecostals and Nonviolence*.

Bibliography

Alexander, Kimberly Ervin. "Under the Authority of the Word and in Response to the Spirit: The Written Work and Worship of R. Hollis Gause." In *Passover, Pentecost & Parousia: Studies in Celebration of the Life and Ministry of R. Hollis Gause*, edited by Steven Jack Land, Rickie D. Moore, and John Christopher Thomas, 1–32. Blandford Forum: Deo, 2010.

Alexander, Paul N., ed. *Pentecostals and Nonviolence: Reclaiming a Heritage*. Eugene: Pickwick, 2012.

Althouse, Peter. *Spirit of the Last Days: Pentecostal Eschatology in Conversation with Jürgen Moltmann*. Sheffield: Sheffield Academic, 2003.

Anderson, Allan. *An Introduction to Pentecostalism*. Cambridge: Cambridge University Press, 2004.

Archer, Melissa L. *'I Was in the Spirit on the Lord's Day': A Pentecostal Engagement with Worship in the Apocalypse*. Cleveland: CPT, 2015.

Aune, David E. "The Apocalypse of John and the Problem of Genre." *Semeia* 36 (1986) 65–96.

———. *The New Testament in its Literary Environment*. Philadelphia: Westminster, 1987.

———. *Prophecy in Early Christianity and the Ancient Mediterranean World*. Grand Rapids: Eerdmans, 1983.

———. *Revelation 1–5*. WBC 52A. Dallas: Word, 1997.

———. *Revelation 6–16*. WBC 52B. Nashville: Thomas Nelson, 1998.

———. *Revelation 17–22*. WBC 52C. Nashville: Thomas Nelson, 1998.

Baldwin, Joyce G. *Daniel*. TOTC. Leicester: IVP, 1978.

Bandy, Alan S. "The Layers of the Apocalypse: An Integrative Approach to Revelation's Macrostructure." *JSNT* 31, no. 4 (2009) 469–99.

Barr, David L. "The Apocalypse of John as Oral Enactment." *Int* 40 (1986) 243–256.

———, ed. *Reading the Book of Revelation*. Atlanta: SBL, 2003.

———. "The Story John Told: Reading Revelation for Its Plot." In *Reading the Book of Revelation*, edited by David L. Barr, 11–23. Atlanta: SBL, 2003.

———. *Tales of the End: A Narrative Commentary on the Book of Revelation*. Salem, OR: Polebridge, 2012.

Bauckham, Richard. *Bible and Mission: Christian Witness in a Postmodern World*. Milton Keynes: Paternoster, 2003.

———. *The Climax of Prophecy: Studies on the Book of Revelation*. Edinburgh: T. & T. Clark, 1993.

———. *The Theology of the Book of Revelation*. Cambridge: Cambridge University Press, 1993.

Baugh, S. M. "Cult Prostitution in New Testament Ephesus: A Reappraisal." *JETS* 42, no. 3 (1999) 443–60.

Baxter, Irvin. "Chernobyl—Third Trumpet of Revelation?" *Endtimes Magazine*, March 20, 2011. https://www.endtime.com/articles-endtime-magazine/chernobyl-third-trumpet-revelation/.

Beale, G. K. *The Book of Revelation*. NIGTC. Grand Rapids: Eerdmans, 1999.

———. *John's Use of the Old Testament in Revelation*. JSNT Sup. Sheffield: Sheffield Academic, 1998.

———. *The Use of Daniel in Jewish Apocalyptic Literature and in the Revelation of St. John*. Lanham: University of America, 1984.

Beasley-Murray, G.R. *The Book of Revelation*. New Century Bible. London: Oliphants, 1974.

Biguzzi, Giancarlo. "Ephesus, Its Artemision, Its Temple to the Flavian Emperors, and Idolatry in Revelation." *NovT* 40 (1998) 276–90.

Blackwell, Ben C., John K. Goodrich, and Jason Maston, eds. *Reading Revelation in Context: John's Apocalypse and Second Temple Judaism*. Grand Rapids: Zondervan Academic, 2019.

Blandino, Stephen. *Creating Your Church's Culture: How to Uproot Mediocrity and Create a Healthy Organizational Culture*. Self-published, Amazon Digital Services, 2013. Kindle.

Blount, Brian K. "The Witness of Active Resistance: The Ethics of Revelation in African American Perspective." In *From Every People and Nation*, edited by David Rhoads, 28–46. Minneapolis: Fortress, 2005.

Boring, M. Eugene. "The Apocalypse as Christian Prophecy: A Discussion of the Issues Raised by the Book of Revelation for the Study of Early Christian Prophecy." In *The SBL 1974 Seminar Papers*, vol. 2., edited by George MacRae, 43–62. Cambridge: SBL, 1974.

Bowman, John Wick. *The Drama of the Book of Revelation*. Philadelphia: Westminster, 1955.

———. *Revelation*. Interpreter's Dictionary of the Bible. Louisville: John Knox, 1989.

———. "The Revelation to John: Its Dramatic Structure and Message." *Int* 9 (1955) 436–53.

Boyd, Gregory A. *God At War: The Bible and Spiritual Conflict*. Downers Grove: IVP, 1997.

Bredin, Mark R. J. "The Synagogue of Satan Accusation in Revelation 2:9." *BTB* 28 (1999) 160–164.

Brown, Raymond E. *The Community of the Beloved Disciple*. New York: Paulist, 1979.

Bruce, F. F. *The Book of the Acts*. NICNT. Grand Rapids: Eerdmans, 1987.

———. *Israel and the Nations*. Exeter: Paternoster, 1983.

Bucur, Bogdan G. "Hierarchy, Prophecy, and the Angelomorphic Spirit: A Contribution to the Study of the Book of Revelation's *Wirkungsgeschichte*." *JBL* 127, no. 1 (2008) 173–94.

Budin, Stephanie Lynn. *The Myth of Sacred Prostitution in Antiquity*. Cambridge: Cambridge University Press, 2008.

Butler, Charles White Robby. "John Wesley's Church Planting Movement: Discipleship That Transformed a Nation and Changed the World." *Mission Frontiers*, September 1, 2011. https://www.missionfrontiers.org/issue/article/john-wesleys-church-planting-movement.

Caird, G. B. *The Revelation of St. John the Divine*. London: A. & C. Black, 1984.

Campbell, Gordon. "Findings, Seals, Trumpets, and Bowls: Variations Upon the Theme of Covenant Rupture and Restoration in the Book of Revelation." *WTJ* 66 (2004) 71–96.

Carey, Greg. "The Apocalypse and Its Ambiguous Ethos." In *Studies in the Book of Revelation*, edited by Steve Moyise, 163–80. Edinburgh: T. & T. Clark, 2001.

Carr, G. Lloyd. *The Song of Solomon*. TOTC. Leicester: IVP, 1984.

Carrell, Peter R. *Jesus and the Angels: Angelology and the Christology of the Apocalypse of John*. Cambridge: Cambridge University Press, 1997.

Carson, Marion. "The Harlot, the Beast and the Sex Trafficker: Reflections on some Recent Feminist Interpretations of Revelation 17–18." *ExpTim* 122, no. 5 (2011) 218–27.

Cartledge, David. *The Apostolic Revolution: The Restoration of Apostles and Prophets in the Assemblies of God in Australia*. Chester Hill: Paraclete Institute, 2000.

Cettolin, Angelo Ulisse. *Spirit Freedom and Power: Changes in Pentecostal Spirituality*. Eugene: Wipf and Stock, 2016.

Chand, Samuel R. *Cracking Your Church's Culture Code: Seven Keys to Unleashing Vision and Inspiration*. San Francisco: Jossey-Bass, 2011.

Charles, R. H. *A Critical and Exegetical Commentary on the Revelation of St. John*. 2 vols. Edinburgh: T. & T. Clark, 1920.

Charlesworth, James H., ed. *The Old Testament Pseudepigrapha*. 2 vols. Peabody: Henrickson, 1983.

Chevalier, Jacques M. *A Postmodern Revelation: Signs of Astrology and the Apocalypse*. Toronto: University of Toronto Press, 1997.

Chilton, David. *The Days of Vengeance: An Exposition of the Book of Revelation*. Tyler: Dominion, 1987.

Collins, Adela Yarbro. *The Combat Myth in the Book of Revelation*. Missoula: Scholars, 1976.

———. *Crisis and Catharsis*. Philadelphia: Westminster, 1984.

———. "Feminine Symbolism in the Book of Revelation." *BibInt* 1 (1993) 20–33.

———. "Persecution and Vengeance in the Book of Revelation." In *Apocalypticism in the Mediterranean World and the Near East*, edited by David Hellholm, 729–49. Tübingen: J. C. B. Mohr, 1983.

Collins, John J. *The Apocalyptic Imagination*. New York: Crossroad, 1984.

———. *Between Athens and Jerusalem*. New York: Crossroad, 1983.

———. "Pseudonymity, Historical Reviews and the Genre of the Revelation of John." *CBQ* 39 (1997) 329–43.

———. "Towards the Morphology of a Genre." *Semeia* 14 (1979) 1–20.

Collins, John J., and James H. Charlesworth, eds. *Mysteries and Revelations: Apocalyptic Studies Since the Uppsala Colloquium*. Sheffield: JSOT, 1991.

Conner, Kevin J. *The Book of Revelation (An Exposition)*. Vermont: KJC, 2001.

Corsini, Eugenio. *The Apocalypse: The Perennial Revelation of Jesus Christ*. Translated by Francis J. Moloney. Wilmington: Michael Glazier, 1983.

Coulter, Dale M. "The Spirit and the Bride Revisited: Pentecostalism, Renewal, and the Sense of History." *JPT* 21, no. 2 (2012) 298–319.

Court, John M. *Revelation*. New Testament Guides. Sheffield: Sheffield Academic, 1994.

Cox, Harvey. *Fire from Heaven: The Rise of Pentecostal Spirituality and the Reshaping of Religion in the Twenty-First Century*. Reading: Addison-Wesley, 1995.

Craffert, Pieter F. "Altered States of Consciousness." In *Understanding the Social World of the New Testament*, edited by Dietmar Naufeld and Richard E. De Maris, 126–46. Oxford: Routledge, 2010.

Cukrowski, Kenneth. "The Influence of the Emperor Cult on the Book of Revelation." *Restoration Quarterly* 45 (2003) 51–64.

deSilva, David A. "Final Topics: The Rhetorical Functions of Intertexture in Revelation 14:14—16:21." In *The Intertexture of Apocalyptic Discourse in the New Testament*, edited by Duane Watson, 215–41. Atlanta: SBL, 2002.

———. "Honor Discourse and the Rhetorical Strategy of the Apocalypse of John." *JSNT* 71 (1998) 79–110.

———. *Seeing Things John's Way*. Louisville: Westminster John Knox, 2009.

de Smidt, Kobus. "Hermeneutical Perspectives on the Spirit in the Book of Revelation." *JPT* 14 (1999) 27–47.

de Waal, Kayle B. *An Aural-Performance Analysis of Revelation 1 and 11*. Studies in Biblical Literature 163. New York: Peter Lang, 2015.

Den Dulk, Matthijs. "Measuring the Temple of God: Revelation 11.1–2 and the Destruction of Jerusalem." *NTS* 54 (2008) 436–49.

Desrosiers, Gilbert. *An Introduction to Revelation: A Pathway to Interpretation*. London: Continuum, 2000.

Duff, Paul. *Who Rides the Beast?: Prophetic Rivalry and the Rhetoric of Crisis in the Churches of the Apocalypse*. New York: Oxford University Press, 2001.

Dumbrell, William J. *The End of the Beginning: Revelation 21–22 and the Old Testament*. Homebush West: Lancer, 1985.

Dunham, Scott A. "The Ecological Violence of Apocalyptic Eschatology." *SR* 32, no. 1–2 (2003) 101–12.

Dyer, Keith. "The Four Horsemen of the Apocalypse and the Consequences of War (Revelation 6.1–11)." In *Ecological Aspects of War: Engagements with Biblical Texts*, edited by Anne Elvey and Deborah Guess, 133–48. London: T. & T. Clark, 2017.

Edwards, James R. "The Rider on the White Horse, the Thigh Inscription, and Apollo: Revelation 19:16." *JBL* 137, no. 2 (2018) 519–36.

Elliott, J. K. "The Greek Manuscript Heritage of the Book of Revelation." In *1900th Anniversary of St. John's Apocalypse: Proceedings of the International and Interdisciplinary Symposium*, 217–26. Athens: Holy Monastery of St. John the Theologian in Patmos, 1999.

"Epistle Concerning the Martyrdom of Polycarp." In Vol. 1, *Ante-Nicene Fathers*, edited by Alexander Roberts and James Donaldson, 37–44. Peabody: Hendrickson, 2004.

Evans, Craig A., and Stanley E. Porter, eds. *Dictionary of New Testament Background*. Downers Grove: IVP, 2000.

Faber, Rudolph. "Revelation 21:1–8." *Int* (1986) 296–301.

Farrer, Austin. *The Revelation of St. John the Divine*. Oxford: Clarendon, 1964.

Faupel, D. William. *The Everlasting Gospel: The Significance of Eschatology in the Development of Pentecostal Thought*. Blandford Forum: Deo, 2009.

Fee, Gordon D. *Revelation*. New Covenant Commentary Series. Eugene, OR: Cascade, 2011.

Fee, Gordon D., and Douglas Stuart. *How to Read the Bible for All Its Worth*. 2nd ed. Grand Rapids: Zondervan, 1993.

Fekkes, Jan. *Isaiah and Prophetic Traditions in the Book of Revelation: Visionary Antecedents and Their Development*. Sheffield: Sheffield Academic, 1994.

Filho, Jose Adriano. "The Apocalypse of John as an Account of a Visionary Experience: Notes on the Book's Structure." *JSNT* 25, no. 2 (2002) 213–34.

Fiorenza, Elisabeth Schüssler. *The Book of Revelation: Justice and Judgment*. Minneapolis: Fortress, 1998.

———. "Composition and Structure of the Book of Revelation." *CBQ* 39 (1977) 344–66.

———. "The Followers of the Lamb: Visionary Rhetoric and Social-Political Situation." *Semeia* 36 (1986) 123–46.
———. *Revelation: Vision of a Just World*. Minneapolis: Fortress, 1991.
———. "The Words of Prophecy: Reading the Apocalypse Theologically." In *Studies in the Book of Revelation*, edited by Steve Moyise, 1–20. Edinburgh: T. & T. Clark, 2001.
Foster, Thomas. *Amazing Book of Revelation Explained!*. Richmond: Crusade Centre, 1983.
Fox, Robin Lane. *The Classical World: An Epic History from Homer to Hadrian*. London: Penguin, 2006.
Friedrich, Nestor Paulo. "Adapt or Resist?" *JSNT* 25, no. 2 (2002) 185–211.
Friesen, Steven J. *Imperial Cults and the Apocalypse of John*. Oxford: Oxford University Press, 2005.
———. "Myth and Symbolic Resistance in Revelation 13." *JBL* 123 (2004) 281–313.
———. "Satan's Throne, Imperial Cults and the Social Settings of Revelation." *JSNT* 27, no. 3 (2005) 351–373.
Frilingos, Christopher A. *Spectacles of Empire: Monsters, Martyrs, and the Book of Revelation*. Philadelphia: University of Pennsylvania Press, 2004.
Garrow, A. J. P. *Revelation*. New Testament Readings. London: Routledge, 1997.
Gause, R. Hollis. *Revelation: God's Stamp of Sovereignty on History*. Cleveland: Pathway, 1998.
Gentry, Kenneth L., Jr. "A Preterist View of Revelation." In *Four Views of the Book of Revelation*, edited by C. Marvin Pate, 37–92. Grand Rapids: Zondervan, 1998.
Giblin, Charles Homer. "Recapitulation and the Literary Coherence of John's Apocalypse." *CBQ* 56 (1994) 81–95.
Gilbertson, Michael. *God and History in the Book of Revelation*. Cambridge: Cambridge University Press, 2003.
Glancy, Jennifer A. "Torture: Flesh, Truth, and the Fourth Gospel." *BibInt* 13, no. 2 (2005) 107–36.
Glancy, Jennifer A., and Stephen D. Moore. "How Typical a Roman Prostitute Is Revelation's 'Great Whore'?" *JBL* 130, no. 3 (2011) 551–69.
Glasson, T. Francis. "What Is Apocalyptic?" *NTS* 27 (1980) 98–105.
Goldingay, John E. *Daniel*. WBC 30. Dallas: Word, 1987.
Gonzalez, Justo L. "Revelation: Clarity and Ambivalence, a Hispanic/Cuban American Perspective." In *From Every People and Nation*, edited by David Rhoads, 47–61. Minneapolis: Fortress, 2005.
Grabiner, Steven. *Revelation's Hymns: Commentary on the Cosmic Conflict*. Library of New Testament Studies 511. London: T. & T. Clark, 2015.
Green, Chris. "The Spirit that Makes Us (Number) One." *Pneuma* 41, no. 3–4 (2019) 397–420.
Gregg, Steve, ed. *Revelation: Four Views*. Nashville: Thomas Nelson, 1997.
Hamstra, Sam, Jr. "An Idealist View of Revelation." In *Four Views of the Book of Revelation*, edited by C. Marvin Pate, 95–131. Grand Rapids: Zondervan, 1998.
Hanson, Paul D., ed. *Visionaries and Their Apocalypses*. Philadelphia: Fortress, 1983.
Hatina, Thomas R. "Intertextuality and Historical Criticism in New Testament Studies: Is there a Relationship?" *BibInt* 7 (1999) 28–43.
Heil, John Paul. "The Fifth Seal (Rev 6, 9–11) as the Key to the Book of Revelation." *Bib* 74 (1993) 220–243.
Hellholm, David, ed. *Apocalypticism in the Mediterranean World and the Near East*. Tübingen: J. C. B. Mohr, 1983.

———. "The Problem of Apocalyptic Genre and the Apocalypse of John." *Semeia* 36 (1986) 13–64.
Helms, Charles Robert. "The Apocalypse in the Early Church." PhD diss., Oxford University, 1991.
Hemer, Colin J. *The Letters to the Seven Churches of Asia in Their Local Settings.* Grand Rapids: Eerdmans, 2000.
Hendriksen, William. *More Than Conquerors: An Interpretation of the Book of Revelation.* Grand Rapids: Baker, 1982.
Herms, Ronald. *An Apocalypse for the Church and for the World: The Narrative Function of Universal Language in the Book of Revelation.* Berlin: Walter de Gruyter, 2006.
Heschel, Abraham J. *The Prophets: An Introduction.* 2 vols. New York: Harper and Row, 1962.
Hill, David. "Prophecy and Prophets in the Revelation of St John." *NTS* 18 (1972) 401–18.
Horton, Stanley M. *The Ultimate Victory: An Exposition of the Book of Revelation.* Springfield: GPH, 1991.
Howard-Brook, Wes. *"Come Out, My People!": God's Call Out of Empire in the Bible and Beyond.* Maryknoll, NY: Orbis, 2012.
Howard-Brook, Wes, and Anthony Gwyther. *Unveiling Empire: Reading Revelation Then and Now.* Maryknoll, NY: Orbis, 1999.
Huber, Lynn R. *Like a Bride Adorned: Reading Metaphor in John's Apocalypse.* New York: T. & T. Clark, 2007.
Humphrey, Edith M. "The Sweet and the Sour: Epics of Wrath and Return in the Apocalypse." In *SBL 1991 Seminar Papers,* edited by Eugene H. Lovering, 451–60. Atlanta: Scholars, 1991.
Hurtgen, John E. *Anti-Language in the Apocalypse of John.* Lewiston, NY: Mellen Biblical, 1993.
Isgrigg, Daniel D. "The Latter Rain Revisited." *Pneuma* 41, no. 3–4 (2019) 439–57.
Jack, Alison M. "Out of the Wilderness: Feminist Perspectives on the Book of Revelation." In *Studies in the Book of Revelation,* edited by Steve Moyise, 149–62. Edinburgh: T. & T. Clark, 2001.
———. *Texts Reading Texts: Sacred and Secular.* JSNT 179. Sheffield: Sheffield Academic, 1999.
Jang, Young. "Narrative Function of the Apocalypse." *Scriptura* 80 (2002) 186–96.
Johnson, David R. *Pneumatic Discernment in the Apocalypse: An Intertextual and Pentecostal Exploration.* Cleveland: Centre for Pentecostal Theology, 2018.
Josephus, "The Antiquities of the Jews." In *The Works of Josephus,* translated by William Whiston, pages 27–542. Peabody: Hendrickson, 1987.
Josephus, "The Wars of the Jews." In *The Works of Josephus,* translated by William Whiston, pages 543–772. Peabody: Hendrickson, 1987.
Kallas, James. "The Apocalypse—An Apocalyptic Book?" *JBL* 86 (1967) 69–80.
Keener, Craig S. *Revelation.* NIV Application Commentary. Grand Rapids: Zondervan, 2000.
———. *Spirit Hermeneutics: Reading Scripture in Light of Pentecost.* Grand Rapids: Eerdmans, 2016.
Koch, Klaus. *The Rediscovery of Apocalyptic.* Translated by Margaret Kohl. London: Student Christian Movement, 1972.
Koester, Craig R. "The Message to Laodicea and the Problem of Its Local Context: A Study of the Imagery in Rev. 3:14–22." *NTS* 49 (2003) 407–24.
———. *Revelation.* Anchor Yale Bible. New Haven: Yale University Press, 2014.

———. *Revelation and the End of All Things*. Grand Rapids: Eerdmans, 2001.
Kovacs, Judith, and Christopher Rowland. *Revelation*. Blackwell Bible Commentaries. Oxford: Blackwell, 2004.
Kraybill, J. Nelson. *Apocalypse and Allegiance: Worship, Politics, and Devotion in the Book of Revelation*. Grand Rapids: Brazos, 2010.
Krodel, Gerhard A. *Revelation*. ACNT. Minneapolis: Augsburg, 1989.
Ladd, George Eldon. *A Commentary on the Revelation of John*. Grand Rapids: Eerdmans, 1972.
LaHaye, Tim. *Revelation Unveiled*. Grand Rapids: Zondervan, 1999.
Land, Steven J. *Pentecostal Spirituality: A Passion for the Kingdom*. Sheffield: Sheffield Academic, 1993.
Lawrence, D. H. *Apocalypse*. London: Heinemann, 1960.
Lee, Michelle V. "A Call to Martyrdom: Function as Method and Message in Revelation." *NovT* 40, no. 2 (1998) 164–94.
Leithart, Peter J. *Revelation 1–11*. ITC. London: T. & T. Clark, 2018.
———. *Revelation 12–22*. ITC. London: T. & T. Clark, 2018.
Lichtenwalter, Larry L. "Creation and Apocalypse." *Journal of the Adventist Theological Society* 16, no. 1 (2004) 125–37.
Linton, Gregory Leroy. "Intertextuality in the Revelation of John." PhD diss., Duke University, 1993.
———. "Reading the Apocalypse as an Apocalypse." In *SBL 1991 Seminar Papers*, edited by Eugene H. Lovering, 161–86. Atlanta: Scholars, 1991.
Long, Tim. "A Real Reader Reading Revelation." *Semeia* 73 (1996) 79–107.
Longman, Tremper, III, and Daniel G. Reid. *God Is A Warrior*. Carlisle: Paternoster, 1995.
Lord, Andy. "Good News for All?: Reflections on the Pentecostal Full Gospel." *Transformation* 30, no. 1 (2013) 17–30.
Low, U-Wen. "'Out of the Great Ordeal': Reading Revelation in a Global Pandemic." *Stimulus* 27, no. 1 (May 2020) 26–30.
———. "'What have the Romans ever done for us?' Postcolonialism, Mimicry and Hidden Transcripts in the Book of Revelation." *Pacifica* 27, no. 3 (2014) 253–70.
Lowell, Lawrence A. "The Judicial Use of Torture." *Harvard Law Review* 11, no. 4 (1897) 220–33.
Lupieri, Edmondo F. *A Commentary on the Apocalypse of John*. Translated by Maria Poggi Johnson and Adam Kamesar. Grand Rapids: Eerdmans, 2006.
Ma, Wonsuk. "Biblical Studies in the Pentecostal Tradition." In *The Globalization of Pentecostalism: A Religion Made To Travel*, edited by Murray W. Dempster et al., 52–69. Oxford: Regnum, 1999.
———. "David Yonggi Cho's Theology of Blessing: Basis, Legitimacy, and Limitations." *ERT* 35, no. 2 (2011) 140–159.
MacMullen, Ramsay. *Enemies of the Roman Order: Treason, Unrest, and Alienation in the Empire*. Cambridge: Harvard University Press, 1966.
Maier, Harry O. *Apocalypse Recalled: The Book of Revelation after Christendom*. Minneapolis: Fortress, 2002.
Malina, Bruce J. "How A Cosmic Lamb Marries: The Image of the Wedding of the Lamb (Rev. 19:7ff.)." *BTB* 28 (1998) 75–82.
———. *The New Testament World*. Louisville: Westminster John Knox, 2001.

Bibliography

———. *On the Genre and Message of Revelation: Star Visions and Sky Journeys.* Peabody: Hendrickson, 1995.

Martin, Clarice. "Polishing the Unclouded Mirror: A Womanist Reading of Revelation 18:13." In *From Every People and Nation*, edited by David Rhoads, 82–109. Minneapolis: Fortress, 2005.

Mathews, Mark D. "The Function of Implied Speech in the Apocalypse of John." *CBQ* 74 (2012) 319–38.

Mathewson, David. "Assessing Old Testament Allusions in the Book of Revelation." *EvQ* 75 (2003) 311–25.

———. *Revelation: A Handbook on the Greek Text.* Waco: Baylor University Press, 2016.

May, David M. "Counting Kings (Revelation 17:10): A Novel Approach from Roman Imperial Coinage." *Review & Expositor* 114, no. 2 (2017) 239–46.

———. "Interpreting Revelation with Roman Coins: A Test Case, Revelation 6:9–11." *Review & Expositor* 106 (2009) 445–65.

Mayo, Philip L. *"Those Who Call Themselves Jews": The Church and Judaism in the Apocalypse of John.* Eugene, OR: Pickwick, 2006.

Mazzaferi, F. D. *The Genre of the Book of Revelation from a Source-Critical Perspective.* Berlin: Walter de Gruyter, 1989.

McGavran, Donald A., and C. Peter Wagner. *Understanding Church Growth.* 3rd ed. Grand Rapids: Eerdmans, 1990.

McIlraith, Donal. "'For the Fine Linen Is the Righteous Deeds of the Saints': Works and Wife in Revelation 19:8." *CBQ* 61 (1999) 512–29.

———. *The Reciprocal Love between Christ and the Church in the Apocalypse.* Rome: Columban Fathers, 1989.

McKnight, Edgar V. *Post-Modern Use of the Bible: The Emergence of Reader-Oriented Criticism.* Nashville: Abingdon, 1988.

McQueen, Larry R. *Toward a Pentecostal Eschatology.* Blandford Forum: Deo, 2012.

Mendels, Doron. *The Rise and Fall of Jewish Nationalism.* Grand Rapids: Eerdmans, 1997.

Merkel, Benjamin L., and Krug, W. Tyler. "Hermeneutical Challenges for a Premillennial Interpretation of Revelation 20." *EvQ* 86, no. 3 (2014) 210–226.

Metzger, Bruce M. *Breaking the Code: Understanding the Book of Revelation.* Nashville: Abingdon, 1993.

Michaels, J. Ramsey. *Interpreting the Book of Revelation.* Grand Rapids: Baker, 1992.

Miguez, Nestor. "Apocalyptic and the Economy: A Reading of Revelation 18 from the Experience of Economic Exclusion." In *Reading from This Place*, vol. 2, edited by Fernando F. Segovia and Mary Ann Tolbert, 250–262. Minneapolis: Fortress, 1995.

Miller, Kevin E. "The Nuptial Eschatology of Revelation 19–22." *CBQ* 60, no. 2 (1998) 301–18.

Minear, Paul S. "The Cosmology of the Apocalypse." In *Current Issues in New Testament Int*, edited by William Klassen and Graydon F. Snyder, 223–37. London: SCM, 1962.

———. *New Testament Apocalyptic.* Nashville: Abingdon, 1981.

———. "Ontology and Ecclesiology in the Apocalypse." *NTS* 12 (1965) 89–105.

Moberly, R. W. L. *Prophecy and Discernment.* Cambridge: Cambridge University Press, 2006.

Moloney, Francis J. *The Apocalypse of John: A Commentary.* Grand Rapids: Baker Academic, 2020.

Moore, Stephen D. "The Beatific Vision as a Posing Exhibition: Revelation's Hypermasculine Deity." *JSNT* 60 (1995) 27–55.

Morales, Jon. *Christ, Shepherd of the Nations: The Nations as Narrative Character and Audience in John's Apocalypse*. London: T. & T. Clark, 2018.
Morris, Leon. *Apocalyptic*. Grand Rapids: Eerdmans, 1972.
———. *Revelation*. TNTC. 2nd ed. Leicester: IVP, 1987.
Motyer, Alec. *The Prophecy of Isaiah*. Leicester: IVP, 1993.
Mounce, Robert H. *The Book of Revelation*. NICNT. Grand Rapids: Eerdmans, 1977.
Moyise, Steve. "Does the Lion Lie down with the Lamb?" In *Studies in the Book of Revelation*, edited by Steve Moyise, 181–94. Edinburgh: T. & T. Clark, 2001.
———. "Intertextuality and the Study of the Old Testament in the New." In *The Old Testament in the New: Essays in Honour of J. L. North*, edited by Steve Moyise, 14–52. JSNT 189. Sheffield: Sheffield Academic, 2000.
———. *The Old Testament in the Book of Revelation*. JSNT 115. Sheffield: Sheffield Academic, 1995.
———. "The Psalms in the Book of Revelation." In *The Psalms in the New Testament*, edited by Steve Moyise and Maarten J. J. Menken, 231–46. London: T. & T. Clark, 2004.
———, ed. *Studies in the Book of Revelation*. Edinburgh: T. & T. Clark, 2001.
Murphy, Frederick J. *Fallen Is Babylon: The Revelation to John*. NT in Context Commentaries. Harrisburg: Trinity, 1998.
Naylor, Michael. "The Roman Imperial Cult and Revelation." *CBR* 8, no. 2 (2010) 207–39.
Newton, Jon K. "The Epistemology of the Book of Revelation." *HeyJ* 59, no. 4 (2018) 733–46.
———. "The Full Gospel and the Apocalypse." *JPT* 26, no. 1 (2017) 86–109.
———. "Holding Prophets Accountable." *JEPTA* 30, no. 1 (2010) 63–79.
———. "Not Who They Seem: Community and Identity in the Seven Churches of Revelation." *Colloquium* 50, no. 2 (2018) 71–88.
———. "Patmos and Southland: Australasian Pentecostal Readings of the Book of Revelation." *APS* 17 (May 2015). https://aps-journal.com/index.php/APS/article/view/9473.
———. "Reading Revelation Romantically." *JPT* 18, no. 2 (2009) 194–215.
———. *Revelation Reclaimed: The Use and Misuse of the Apocalypse*. Milton Keynes: Paternoster, 2009.
———. *The Revelation Worldview*. Eugene: Wipf and Stock, 2015.
———. "The Scope of Christian Prophecy." *APS* 13 (2010) 59–86.
———. "Story-lines in the Book of Revelation." *ABR* 61 (2013) 61–78.
———. "Time Language and the Purpose of the Millennium." *Colloquium* 43, no. 2 (2011) 147–68.
Nogueira, Paulo Augusto de Souza. "Celestial Worship." *JSNT* 25, no. 2 (2002) 165–84.
O'Donovan, Oliver. "History and Politics in the Book of Revelation." In *Bonds of Imperfection: Christian Politics, Past and Present*, edited by Oliver O'Donovan and Joan Lockwood O'Donovan, 24–47. Grand Rapids: Eerdmans, 2004.
Osborne, Grant R. *Revelation*. Grand Rapids: Baker, 2002.
Papandrea, James L. *The Wedding of the Lamb: A Historical Approach to the Book of Revelation*. Eugene: Pickwick, 2011.
Parker, F. O., Jr. "'Our Lord and God' in Rev. 4,11: Evidence for the Late Date of Revelation?" *Bib* 82 (2001) 207–31.
Pascal, Blaise. *Pensées*. New York: E. P. Dutton & Co., 1958.
Pataki, Andras David. "A Non-combat Myth in Revelation 12." *NTS* 57 (2011) 258–72.
Pate, C. Marvin. *Communities of the Last Days: The Dead Sea Scrolls, the New Testament and the Story of Israel*. Leicester: Apollos, 2000.

———, ed. *Four Views on the Book of Revelation*. Grand Rapids: Zondervan, 1998.

Pattemore, Stephen. *The People of God in the Apocalypse*. Cambridge: Cambridge University Press, 2004.

Paul, Ian. *Revelation: An Introduction and Commentary*. TNTC. Downers Grove: IVP Academic, 2018.

Perry, Aaron. "On Enduring Political Authority: Comparing Oliver O'Donovan and the Book of Revelation." *Journal for Christian Theological Research* 12 (2007) 37–64.

Peters, Olutola K. "Politics of Violence in the Apocalypse of John: Moral Dilemma and Justification." In *SBL Seminar Papers 2004*, 1–18. https://ntweblog.blogspot.com/2004/09/sbl-seminar-papers-on-line.html.

Pippin, Tina. *Death and Desire: The Rhetoric of Gender in the Apocalypse of John*. Louisville: Westminster John Knox, 1992.

———. "Eros and the End: Reading for Gender in the Apocalypse of John." *Semeia* 59 (1992) 193–210.

———. "The Heroine and the Whore: The Apocalypse of John in Feminist Perspective." In *From Every People and Nation*, edited by David Rhoads, 127–45. Minneapolis: Fortress, 2005.

———. "Peering into the Abyss: A Postmodern Reading of the Biblical Bottomless Pit." In *The New Literary Criticism and the New Testament*, edited by Elizabeth Struthers Malbon and Edgar V. McKnight, 251–67. JSNT 109. Sheffield: Sheffield Academic, 1994.

Pliny the Younger. "Letters." Translated by J. B. Firth. *Bibliotheca Augustana*. http://www.attalus.org/info/pliny.html.

Poloma, Margaret M. *The Assemblies of God at the Crossroads*. Knoxville: University of Tennessee Press, 1989.

Portier-Young, Anthea E. *Apocalypse against Empire: Theologies of Resistance in Early Judaism*. Grand Rapids: Eerdmans, 2011.

Poythress, Vern Sheridan. "Genre and Hermeneutics in Rev. 20:1–6." *JETS* 36, no. 1 (1993) 41–54.

Price, S. R. F. *Rituals and Power: The Roman Imperial Cult in Asia Minor*. Cambridge: Cambridge University Press, 1984.

Raber, Rudolph W. "Revelation 21:1–8." *Int* 40, no. 3 (1986) 296–301.

Ramsay, W. M. *The Letters to the Seven Churches of Asia: And Their Place in the Plan of the Apocalypse*. London: Hodder and Stoughton, 1904.

Resseguie, James L. *The Revelation of John: A Narrative Commentary*. Grand Rapids: Baker Academic, 2009.

Rhoads, David, ed. *From Every People and Nation: The Book of Revelation in Intercultural Perspective*. Minneapolis: Fortress, 2005.

Richard, Pablo. *Apocalypse: A People's Commentary*. Maryknoll: Orbis, 1995.

———. "Reading the Apocalypse: Resistance, Hope, and Liberation in Central America." In *From Every People and Nation*, edited by David Rhoads, 146–64. Minneapolis: Fortress, 2005.

Ricoeur, Paul. *Essays on Biblical Interpretation*. Edited by Lewis S. Mudge. Philadelphia: Fortress, 1980.

Rienecker, Fritz, and Cleon Rogers. *Linguistic Key to the Greek New Testament*. Regency Reference Library. Grand Rapids: Zondervan, 1980.

Rissi, Mathias. *Time and History: A Study on the Revelation*. Translated by Gordon C. Winsor. Richmond: John Knox, 1965.

Roberts, Alexander, and James Donaldson, eds. *ANF*. 10 vols. Peabody: Hendrickson, 2004.

Rojas-Flores, Gonzalo. "The Book of Revelation and the First Years of Nero's Reign." *Bib* 85 (2004) 375–92.

Rowe, C. Kavin. *World Upside Down: Reading Acts in the Graeco-Roman Age*. Oxford: Oxford University Press, 2009.

Rowland, Christopher. *The Open Heaven: A Study of Apocalyptic in Judaism and Early Christianity*. London: SPCK, 1982.

———. *Revelation*. London: Epworth, 1993.

Royalty, Robert M. Jr. *The Streets of Heaven: The Ideology of Wealth in the Apocalypse of John*. Macon: Mercer University Press, 1998.

Ruiz, Jean-Pierre. "Betwixt and Between on the Lord's Day: Liturgy and the Apocalypse." In *SBL 1992 Seminar Papers*, edited by Eugene H. Lovering Jr., 654–72. Atlanta: Scholars, 1992.

———. "Praise and Politics in Revelation 19:1–10." In *Studies in the Book of Revelation*, edited by Steve Moyise, 69–84. Edinburgh: T. & T. Clark, 2001.

Russell, D. S. *The Method and Message of Jewish Apocalyptic*. London: SCM, 1964.

Satterthwaite, Philip E., Richard S. Hess, and Gordon J. Wenham, eds. *The Lord's Anointed: Interpretation of Old Testament Messianic Texts*. Carlisle: Paternoster, 1995.

Scherrer, Steven J. "Signs and Wonders in the Imperial Cult: A New Look at a Roman Religious Institution in the Light of Rev.13:13–15." *JBL* 103, no. 4 (1984) 599–610.

Seal, David. "Emotions, Empathy, and Engagement with God in Revelation 6:9–11." *ExpTim* 128 (2017) 1–9.

Setel, T. Drorah. "Feminist Insights and the Question of Method." In *Feminist Perspectives on Biblical Scholarship*, edited by Adela Yarbro Collins, 35–42. Atlanta: Scholars, 1985.

Sims, James H. *A Comparative Literary Study of Daniel and Revelation*. Lewiston, NY: Mellen Biblical, 1995.

Skaggs, Rebecca, and Priscilla C. Benham. *Revelation*. Pentecostal Commentary Series. Blandford Forum: Deo, 2009.

Skaggs, Rebecca, and Thomas Doyle. "Lion/Lamb in Revelation." *CBR* 7, no. 3 (2009) 362–75.

Smalley, Stephen S. *The Revelation to John: A Commentary on the Greek Text of the Apocalypse*. Downers Grove: IVP Academic, 2005.

———. *Thunder and Love: John's Revelation and John's Community*. Milton Keynes: Nelson Word, 1994.

Smith, James K. A. *The Fall of Interpretation: Philosophical Foundations for a Creational Hermeneutic*. Downers Grove: IVP, 2000.

———. *Thinking in Tongues: Pentecostal Contributions to Christian Philosophy*. Grand Rapids: Eerdmans, 2010.

Smolarz, Sebastian R. *Covenant and the Metaphor of Divine Marriage in Biblical Thought*. Eugene, OR: Wipf and Stock, 2011.

Snyder, Barbara Wootten. "Triple-Form and Space/Time Transitions: Literary Structuring Devices in the Apocalypse." In *SBL 1991 Seminar Papers*, edited by Eugene H. Lovering, 440–460. Atlanta: Scholars, 1991.

Spilsbury, Paul. "Flavius Josephus on the Rise and Fall of the Roman Empire." *JTS* 54 (2003) 1–24.

Staniforth, Maxwell, ed. and trans. *Early Christian Writings: The Apostolic Fathers*. Harmondsworth: Penguin, 1968.

Stefanovic, Ranko. "The Meaning and Significance of the ἐπὶ τὴν δεξιάν for the Location of the Sealed Scroll (Revelation 5:1) and Understanding the Scene of Revelation 5." *Zeitschrift: Biblical Research* 46 (2001) 42–54.

Stone, Michael E. "Lists of Revealed Things in the Apocalyptic Literature." In *Magnalia Dei*, edited by F. M. Cross, W. E. Lemke, and P. D. Miller, 414–52. New York: Doubleday, 1976.

Stramara, Daniel F., Jr. *God's Timetable: The Book of Revelation and the Feast of Seven Weeks*. Eugene: Pickwick, 2011.

Strelan, John G. *Where Earth Meets Heaven: A Commentary on Revelation*. Adelaide: Openbook, 1994.

Strelan, Rick. "'Outside Are the Dogs and the Sorcerers . . .' (Revelation 22:15)." *BTB* 33 (2003) 148–57.

Stuckenbruck, Loren T. *Angel Veneration and Christology: A Study in Early Judaism and in the Christology of the Apocalypse of John*. Tübingen: J. C. B. Mohr, 1995.

Suetonius. *The Twelve Caesars*. Translated by Robert Graves. Harmondsworth: Penguin, 1979.

Sweet, John. *Revelation*. TPINTC. London: SCM, 1990.

Tacitus. *Histories and Annals*. Translated by J. Jackson. London: Heinemann, 1962.

Taushev, Archbishop Averky. *The Apocalypse in the Teachings of Ancient Christianity*. Translated and edited by Fr. Seraphim Rose. Platina: St. Herman of Alaska Brotherhood, 1995.

Taylor, Charles. *Revelation as World History*. Gosford: Good Book Company, 1994.

Tertullian. "Apology." In Vol. 3, *Ante-Nicene Fathers*, edited by Alexander Roberts and James Donaldson, 16–70. Peabody: Hendrickson, 2004.

Thayer, Joseph Henry. *The New Thayer's Greek-English Lexicon of the New Testament*. Peabody: Hendrickson, 1981.

Thimmes, Pamela. "Women Reading Women in the Apocalypse: Reading Scenario 1, the Letter to Thyatira (Rev.2.18–29)." *CBR* 2, no. 1 (2003) 128–44.

Thiselton, Anthony C. *The Two Horizons: New Testament Hermeneutics and Philosophical Description*. Carlisle: Paternoster, 1980.

Thomas, John Christopher. *The Apocalypse: A Literary and Theological Commentary*. Cleveland: CPT, 2012.

Thomas, John Christopher, and Frank D. Macchia. *Revelation. The Two Horizons New Testament Commentary*. Grand Rapids: Eerdmans, 2016.

Thomas, Robert L. *Revelation 1–7: An Exegetical Commentary*. Chicago: Moody, 1992.

Thompson, Leonard L. *The Book of Revelation: Apocalypse and Empire*. Oxford: Oxford University Press, 1990.

———. "Ordinary Lives: John and His First Readers." In *Reading the Book of Revelation*, edited by David L. Barr, 25–47. Atlanta: SBL, 2003.

———. "Spirit Possession: Revelation in Religious Studies." In *Reading the Book of Revelation*, edited by David L. Barr, 137–50. Atlanta: SBL, 2003.

Travis, Stephen H. *Christian Hope and the Future*. Downers Grove: IVP, 1980.

Trites, Allison A. *The New Testament Concept of Witness*. Cambridge: Cambridge University Press, 1977.

Valentine, Kendra Haloviak. "Cleopatra: New Insights for the Interpretation of Revelation 17." *EvQ* 87, no. 4 (2015) 310–330.

Van Iersel, Bas. "The Sun, Moon, and Stars of Mark 13, 24–25 in a Greco-Roman Reading." *Bib* 77 (1996) 84–92.

Vermes, Geza. *Jesus and the World of Judaism.* London: SCM, 1983.

Veyne, Paul. *Bread and Circuses.* Translated by Brian Pearce. London: Allen Lane, 1990.

Victorinus. *Commentary on the Apocalypse of the Blessed John.* In *ANF*, vol. 7, edited by A. Cleveland Coxe, 244–360. 1886. Repr. Peabody: Hendrickson, 2004.

Vorster, W. S. "'Genre' and the Revelation of John: A Study in text, context and intertext." *Neot* (1988) 103–23.

Waddell, Robby. *The Spirit of the Book of Revelation.* Blandford Forum: Deo, 2006.

Wainwright, Arthur W. *Mysterious Apocalypse.* Nashville: Abingdon, 1993.

Wall, Robert W. *Revelation.* New International Biblical Commentary. Peabody: Hendrickson Publishers, 1991.

Walvoord, John F. *The Revelation of Jesus Christ.* Chicago: Moody, 1966.

Watson, Duane F., ed. *The Intertexture of Apocalyptic Discourse in the New Testament.* Atlanta: SBL, 2002.

Webber, Randall C. "The Apocalypse as Utopia: Ancient and Modern Subjectivity." In *SBL 1993 Seminar Papers*, edited by Eugene Lovering Jr., 104–18. Atlanta: Scholar, 1993.

Whitaker, Robyn J. *Ekphrasis, Vision, and Persuasion in the Book of Revelation.* Tübingen: Mohr Siebeck, 2015.

White, Adam. "Pentecostal Preaching as a Modern Epistle: A Comparison of Pentecostal Preaching with Paul's Practice of Letter Writing." *JPT* 25 (2016) 123–49.

Wilken, Robert L. *The Christians as the Romans Saw Them.* New Haven: Yale University Press, 1984.

Wilkens, Ulrich. "The Understanding of Revelation within the History of Primitive Christianity." Translated by David Granskou. In *Revelation As History*, edited by Wolfhart Pannenberg et al., 72–15. London: Collier-Macmillan, 1968.

Wink, Walter. *Unmasking the Powers: The Invisible Forces That Determine Human Existence.* Philadelphia: Fortress, 1986.

Witherington, Ben, III. *Revelation.* New Cambridge Bible Commentary. Cambridge: Cambridge University Press, 2003.

Wong, David K. K. "The Beast from the Sea in Revelation 13." *BSac* 160 (2003) 337–48.

Woods, Richard. "Seven Bowls of Wrath: The Ecological Relevance of Revelation." *BTB* 38 (2008) 64–75.

Wright, N. T. *The New Testament and the People of God.* Minneapolis: Fortress, 1992.

Yhearm, Brian. "The Sitz im Leben of Revelation: An Examination of the Literary and Social Environment of the Apocalypse of John." PhD diss., University of Newcastle upon Tyne, 1995.

Yong, Amos. "The Science, Sighs, and Signs of Interpretation: An Asian American Post-Pentecost-al Hermeneutics in a Multi-, Inter-, and Trans-cultural World." In *Constructive Pneumatological Hermeneutics in Pentecostal Christianity*, edited by L. William Oliverio Jr., and Kenneth J. Archer, 177–95. New York: Palgrave Macmillan, 2016.